EXPLORATIONS IN ENVIRONMENTAL HISTORY

A John D. S. and Aida C. Truxall Book

EXPLORATIONS

IN *Essays by Samuel P. Hays*

ENVIRONMENTAL

HISTORY

UNIVERSITY OF PITTSBURGH PRESS

Published by the University of Pittsburgh Press, Pittsburgh, Pa. 15261
Copyright © 1998, University of Pittsburgh Press
Manufactured in the United States of America
Printed on acid-free paper
10 9 8 7 6 5 4 3 2 1

Library of Congress Cataloging-in-Publication Data
Hays, Samuel P.
     Explorations in environmental history : essays by Samuel P. Hays /
by Samuel P. Hays ; with a foreword by Joel Tarr.
          p.   cm.
     Includes bibliographical references.
     ISBN 0-8229-3996-7 (alk. paper). — ISBN 0-8229-5643-8 (pbk. :
alk. paper)
     1. Environmental policy—United States—History.
2. Environmentalism—United States—History. 3. Air—Pollution—
Government policy—United States—History. 4. Forest ecology—
Government policy—United States—History. I. Tarr, Joel A. (Joel
Arthur), 1934–   . II. Title.
GE180.H39   1998
363.7'00973—dc21   97-23775

A CIP catalog record for this book is available from the British Library.

CONTENTS

FOREWORD

Samuel P. Hays has been called one of the leading American historians of the second half of the twentieth century. As Michael Ebner observed at a 1992 symposium in his honor, "The scholarly interests of Sam Hays defy convention."[1] Trained in American history, he has exercised scholarly influence over four of its subfields: environmental history, political history, social history, and urban history. Yet Hays himself would insist that there is a continuity in his work that bridges the subfield boundaries and provides a unity in his writing. This continuity involves a focus on the link between power and values and their relation to organizations and institutions, and on the social forces (especially centralization and decentralization) that bring about evolution and change.

This volume deals specifically with environmental history. As Hays notes in his introduction, it is "a distinctive journey in the field." The journey follows various pathways, exploring Hays's fluctuating involvement in environmental themes and his growing interest of and publication in environmental history after 1970. These essays, written by Hays between 1976 and 1994, reflect an astonishing range, covering the role of values, environment and urbanization, environmental regulation, forest issues, matters of air quality, and considerations of environmental politics since World War II. They bear both similarities and differences with his earlier work. While some essays are directly related to his best known environmental history publication, *Beauty, Health, and Permanence: Environmental Politics in the United States, 1955–1985* (published in 1987 in collaboration with his wife Barbara), others go considerably beyond this collection.[2] A special benefit is the inclusion of four in-depth essays that have not previously been published.

Hays's introduction reveals his deep personal commitment to environmental issues and to his belief in the importance of history for understanding the environmental impulse, environmental policy, and environmental controversy. Hays's own environmental interests and commitments actually began during his southern Indiana boyhood and were reinforced in the years from 1943 to 1946 when he worked with the Oregon and California Revested Lands Administration on public forests in western Oregon.[3] This interest continued in his graduate work at Harvard where his dissertation dealt with the theme of the Progressive movement and conservation; Harvard University Press published the revised dissertation in 1958 as *Conservation and the Gospel of Efficiency,* and it has since been reprinted and is continually cited.[4]

The approximately twelve- to fifteen-year interregnum between the publication of this book and Hays's refocus on environmental issues was marked by his concern with urban political and social history and the conceptual implications of social research. These years were very productive for Hays, as he published a group of seminal articles in political and social analysis, especially in an urban context; built a major research-oriented Department of History at the University of Pittsburgh; and trained a number of talented historians. Interaction with graduate students was especially important for his intellectual development. In a 1975 interview for the *Journal of Urban History,* Hays noted that "there is hardly a seminar paper or dissertation which has not shaped my thinking in some way." In addition, he recruited a faculty for his new department that was oriented toward "different types of human activities and social processes over time" rather than traditional approaches, and many stimulating discussions were held between colleagues around those topics. The most important articles from this period were republished in 1980 under the title *American Political History as Social Analysis: Essays by Samuel P. Hays,* an essential work for understanding urban political history.[5]

It is important to note that there is a significant difference between the methodological process involved in the writing of the articles collected in *American Political History as Social Analysis* and the process that led to Hays's environmental work. Unlike his social/political articles, Hays's environmental history research and writing was produced largely without graduate student involvement and did not benefit from ongoing faculty discussions at the University of Pittsburgh.[6] In fact, Hays never taught a graduate seminar nor a graduate course concerned with the environment. His only environmental course was one in environmental politics for advanced undergraduates, and his single environmental graduate student was Richard H. K. Vietor, now the Senator John Heinz Professor of the Environment at the Harvard Business School.[7]

Hays's return to work on the environment after 1970 marked an important intellectual as well as methodological shift of direction on his part. This was a period of great environmental enthusiasm—the celebration of Earth Day, the passage of NEPA, and the founding of the Environmental Protection Agency. For Hays it was a return to an earlier set of interests, but driven by new events: by the imperatives of the exploding environmental movement, by a trip West that rekindled his interest in environmental and conservation issues, and by several personal factors such as the opportunity to share scholarly interests with his wife Barbara ("Bobby"), a biologist.[8] Intellectual stimulus for his environmental work came largely from outside his own department, including conversations with his wife, with colleagues at the Wilson Center during a visiting year as a fellow (1978– 1979), from participants in aspects of the environmental movement, and from his own activities as a participant and observer of current environmental affairs.[9] By 1987, Hays had served as a commentator on environmental policy on more than fifty occasions, gathering research sources wherever he went.[10]

Because environmental history is, as Hays notes, "contemporary history," it involves a somewhat different set of issues than does more traditional history. In his introduction to *American Political History as Social Analysis,* Hays remarks that he was rather "indifferent to the direct role which my historical writing plays in current political issues."[11] The same can not be said about his environmental writings, and Hays's experience in the environmental domain was qualitatively different from his experience in writing political history. First of all, his environmental concerns had direct links to his upbringing and to major experiences during his young manhood. In addition, as the environmental movement became increasingly active, he became directly involved, speaking and acting on contemporary environmental affairs, serving on the board of the National Parks and Conservation Association, as an organizer and leader of the Pennsylvania chapter of the Sierra Club, and as an adviser to a variety of environmental organizations and leaders. Sam Hays is definitely a leader in environmental affairs, as well as an environmental historian.

The historian involved in contemporary affairs in such a manner, Hays notes, is faced by a great temptation to become an advocate of one side or the other. Hays argues that he has resisted the temptation, believing that historians would play their most valuable role by providing historical perspective for current debates. These essays, therefore, bring history to bear on such important contemporary issues as the limits-to-growth question, clean air policy, values in lead analysis, and environmental politics. They make their contribution to environmental history by clarifying the forces of change and especially the role of values rather than by taking positions in ongoing debates.

And yet, anyone who knows Sam Hays also knows of his deep commitment to environmental values and environmental improvement. Witness, for example, his continued involvement in contemporary environmental affairs and his attempts to elucidate and clarify environmental issues through letters to editors, comments, and publication of "Forest Briefs," an occasional bulletin and commentary on forest issues issued over e-mail. Witness his involvement with the Sierra Club on a variety of "wilderness" issues, including the eastern wilderness movement. Witness his founding of the Hayswood Nature Reserve and Indian Creeks Woods Nature Reserve in Harrison County, Indiana, consisting of his father's former 360-acre Guernsey dairy farm. And witness his establishment of an endowment through the Community Endowment for Southern Indiana to provide funds for the upkeep of Indian Creek Woods. These actions are those of a person with a committed set of environmental values, even though as a professional historian he has attempted to prevent these values from unduly influencing his work.

As can be expected, Hays has had a profound effect upon the emerging field of environmental history. As author of two of the preeminent books in the field, as the writer of a number of important articles (most reprinted in this volume), and as a frequent paper presenter and participant on panels dealing with environmental history, he has continually stressed the importance of core values and of value change in understanding the environmental movement. He has also insisted on the importance of urban and industrial issues within environmental history, emphasizing that the field goes beyond considerations of nature, wilderness, and the West, or the acknowledged "saints" of the environmental movement—Henry Thoreau, John Muir, and Aldo Leopold. And he has conveyed his message with integrity and with rigor.

Hays's message has occasionally provoked conflict among fellow historians. For him, the "environmental interest was an expression of deeply rooted aspirations for a better life" rather than a yearning for a return to a simpler, more "natural" way of life.[12] He links environmental values to quality of life goals associated with home, family, leisure, and recreation. Skeptical of fringe interpretations or those resting too much on cultural factors, he has persistently argued that American society has been marked by forces that produce evolutionary and incremental change—hence the title of his early book, "The *Response* to Industrialism" [italics added]. Hays views environmental history as part of American history, embedded in its larger processes, and as an idealist he is optimistic that the problems of the society, environmental and otherwise, can be solved. From his perspective, it is the role of the historian to analyze and clarify the forces and values at work in American society and to convey them to the public.

Environmental historian William Cronon recently noted that "no one has done more to shape our understanding of environmental politics in the twentieth century" than Samuel P. Hays.[13] It is for this reason that in 1997 the American Society of Environmental History awarded him their first Career Achievement Award for Lifetime Contributions to Environmental History, to be added to his previously won honors of the Theodore C. Blegan Award of the Forest History Society (1982), the Pennsylvania Governor's Award for Excellence in the Humanities (1991), and the Historical Society of Western Pennsylvania History Makers Award (1993). They all stand, with his writings and his environmental involvement, as testimony to his outstanding career as citizen and as historian.

Joel A. Tarr

INTRODUCTION

An Environmental Historian Amid the
Thickets of Environmental Politics

This collection of articles reflects a distinctive journey in the field of environmental history and hence this semibiographical approach to the introduction. My own involvement in environmental history has come in two stages, the first, beginning with graduate work and publication of *Conservation and the Gospel of Efficiency* and, after a lapse of over a decade, beginning in 1970 with a renewed interest in the subject, now called environmental history, which led to a more sustained level of teaching and writing on the subject. The two stages have their own distinctive origins and their distinctive biographical role.

My first interest in conservation history began with two and a half years of experience in Civilian Public Service during World War II with the Oregon and California Revested Lands Administration in the forests of western Oregon. Before that time, some relevant earlier predispositions were from personal experience with the U. S. Soil Conservation Service on our farm in southern Indiana, personal experience with the work of a CCC camp on a state forest near where we lived, and a two-month involvement with an American Friends Service Committee work camp on a demonstration farm in eastern Tennessee that was part of the program of the Tennessee Valley Authority. From these experiences I had some knowledge of conservation affairs.

The Oregon experience between 1943 and 1946 sharpened this knowledge into an intellectual interest in the subject. The stint with the government agency, the so-called O&C, involved woods work ranging from planting trees and fighting forest fires to being a cook and truck mechanic to sharpening jackhammer bits. Along the way I became interested in the agency itself and was made "project education" leader with the task of informing members of the camp about the O&C, its history, and its program. Based on a bit of research I conducted into the agency, I issued a regular newsletter about it and the forest work in which we were engaged.

When in 1948 I began work at Harvard for a Ph.D. in American history with Frederick Merk, the western historian, as my advisor, my first seminar paper was on the origins of the Taylor Grazing Act of 1934. I took an "outside field" in American politics, one course of which was in resource problems taught by Arthur Maass, who had come to Harvard from the Little Hoover Commission where he worked on issues arising from the peculiar role of the O&C lands. Knowing of my evolving interest, Professor Merk suggested that I might apply for a doctoral fellowship offered to anyone working on the life of Theodore Roosevelt and that a fit subject would be the conservation history of that time. I took up the proposal, and it ended up with a dissertation and the book, *Conservation and the Gospel of Efficiency: the Progressive Conservation Movement, 1890–1920,* published in 1958.[1]

At first I had ambitions of teaching "conservation history," but after I found no takers from about twenty-five letters to the state agricultural colleges, that idea went by the board. During my teaching career first at the University of Illinois, then at the State University of Iowa, and then at the University of Pittsburgh, my interest in conservation history gave way first to political history, initially with an interest in farm policy of the thirties, forties, and fifties, then voting behavior, and finally social history in an urban context. This led to a series of articles on society and politics, many of which were published by the University of Tennessee Press in *American Political History as Social Analysis.*[2] This phase of my historical development emphasized both specific areas of social and urban history and the more general theory that the ongoing innovations in that field implied. Hence by the time I came back to my original interest in the late 1960s, now called environmental history, it involved a quite different perspective from that of the earlier work.

The difference was greatly influenced by the newly developed public interest in environmental affairs and elicited a full-fledged effort both to track those affairs as they appeared and at the same time to think about them from a historical perspective. My strategy in developing this approach was to gather a wide range of current documents, material produced by the environmental movement, documents pertaining to legislation and administration, magazines pertaining to environmental science, technology, and law, and to keep track of what was happening. At the same time, I contacted individuals to follow the events as they saw them. Much of my perspective is implicit in this search for evidence. The range of subjects in the articles in this volume follows the same range as the evidence I acquired; my perspective was there at the start in deciding what materials to collect, a perspective that was deeply rooted in my training and work as an historian.

My focus on the political groups impinging on policy and the administrative context of politics simply continued the approach laid out in my earlier book and was extended to the fields involved in administrative politics such as science and law. But new twists also emerged. One was the focus on values and value change as fundamental to understanding the environmental movement. This was a direct result of my initial exposure to the importance of religious and cultural values in voting behavior[3] and an interest in placing the history of human meaning in the context of transitions from more traditional to more modern values, which I thought could inform much of twentieth-century environmental engagement.[4] Another was the integrative focus I had developed in social and political history. The range and complexities of environmental history gave rise to a similar integrative challenge.

These approaches appeared in two forms. One was a series of articles, many of which now appear in this volume. The other was the book *Beauty, Health and Permanence: Environmental Politics in the United States, 1955–1985,* which appeared in 1987.[5] That book was an attempt to integrate the vast array of elements in environmental affairs. The project was greatly strengthened by continuous conversations with Barbara Darrow Hays, an ecologist who not only introduced me to subjects such as ecology and evolution, but also took up special inquiries into acid rain and population and kept me in touch with a host of new documentary sources in those fields. Our continuous conversations about what we read and saw as we hiked and traveled around the United States and Europe and attended conferences, helped me to work out the way in which all this seemed to fit together.

But it also gave rise to a new twist, as I inevitably was asked to speak and write in forums involving contemporary environmental affairs as well as history, and it gave rise to a number of "close encounters" between the two. At the same time, I served for a number of years on the board of the National Parks and Conservation Association and at various times took up issues on behalf of several groups such as the Sierra Club in Pennsylvania. I benefited especially from my work with the Sierra Club. Here I wrote and submitted testimony on a wide range of legislative and administrative issues, all of which greatly enhanced my understanding of processes in both branches of government and helped me to translate general ideas into concrete applications, which was essential to effective argument. This role also gave me an inside understanding of the way in which environmental organizations function, of both their strengths and their weaknesses. I also brought to these activities my role as a teacher in which I sought to enhance the knowledge and understanding of those engaged in citizen environmental activity about the larger meaning of what they did, a task that continually sharpened my own thinking. As an observer as well as a participant in these activities, I was able to learn from those experiences without continually passing judgment on them.[6]

Experience with these encounters is the theme that I take up in this introduction: how does an environmental historian fare amid the rough-and-tumble of contemporary environmental politics? I have developed the outrageous belief that historians can be more independent in their thinking and bring a useful perspective to contemporary environmental affairs in a way that those involved in the thickets of current political debate cannot. This belief has continually inspired an effort to define a clear historical perspective while trying to infuse that perspective into contemporary affairs.

I have been more than intrigued by the clash in perspectives reflected in these encounters. On the one hand, those involved in contemporary debate organize evidence and ideas to win their battles, and this is the case whether they are environmental advocates, members of the environmental opposition, or those who occupy the "middle ground." In each case, actors are intensely committed to hammering out the tools to win in the immediate fray. And all, therefore, seek to use the past in some fashion to bolster their case, to create a host of historical interpretations depending upon what part of the present debate they occupy.

But I have also been much intrigued by the temptations presented by these political pressures to professional historians. Many, in diverse ways, have chosen to align themselves with contemporary advocates of environmental objectives by extolling the historical roots of contemporary issues.[7] Others have been critical of environmental advocates by exposing the errors of their thought or by taking up one side or the other of the continuing debates within various sectors of the "movement," such as serving as advocates of the environmental justice movement.[8] And still others have avoided matters which the contemporary debate seeks to avoid, such as the political role of scientists and administrators or the evolution of the environmental opposition.[9] These are vital subjects for historical analysis even though they inject one immediately into the uncomfortable world of environmental controversy and hence are often shunned.

Into this fray steps the historian with considerable caution. No matter what is said, the historical view will be suspect and subject to severe criticism as each side seeks to use history to its own advantage. The environmental community does not like the twist I put on the role of environmental values in modern society, they seek to root their efforts in more universal truths rather than to analyze the behavior of people in their own environmental context, and they seek to greatly expand the historical significance of "major writers" such as Thoreau or Muir rather than to limit their significance in terms of the breadth of their audience rather than the inherent meaning of their ideas. The environmental scientists and administrators do not like their claim to represent universal truth to be scrutinized and their distinctive values to be examined; the administrators do not like the spotlight to be focused on their political choices, and the professionals who occupy the lofty "middle ground" do not accept the argument that in their search for the "middle" they have their own distinctive axe to grind.[10] And the environmental opposition denies that it exists as an opposition and tends to dismiss analysis of it as simply a part of the contemporary political debate and unworthy as a topic of professional examination. Yet that opposition is as significant and serious a topic of contemporary environmental history as is the environmental impulse itself.

I write this essay both to outline the points at which these different perspectives are engaged and to affirm what the historian has to offer to the world of contemporary public affairs. A number of my writings have involved real live experiences within the thickets of environmental politics.[11] Yet amid those experiences I have continued to believe that historians can shift perspective from the demands of current debate and make a historical framework relevant to that debate. It is not always the safest route to take. I have had several articles accepted and then rejected because they seemed to clash with the particular nonhistorical perspective of the journal in which they were to be published; some of these essays are published here.[12] In one case, I was confronted with what I considered to be a threat of a lawsuit over a footnote reference by an author deeply involved in the scientific debate over the health hazards of lead.[13] In still another, I was widely condemned by a public administrator because my writing constituted an undesirable influence in debate over forest policy.

A HISTORICAL PERSPECTIVE

What is a historical perspective? To most people and to some historians it means that one recounts events from the past that pertain to an issue that one wishes to understand today. One observes the present "in the light of the past." Therefore, merely to recount what a community did about air pollution in the 1890s or to reissue the writings of Henry David Thoreau provides the requisite "history." But history is not just about the past; it is a distinctive way of looking at affairs both past and present. Many who confine themselves to uprooting facts about the past, in fact, fail to contribute to a historical perspective about the subject on which they write.

Historians can make two contributions to the analysis of society and politics, past or present. One is the search for context, the constant tendency to want to place events, ideas, and people in a larger whole. Of course, historians, like all specialists, often take events and people out of context and examine them largely in abstract fashion. But such historians often face the fire of fellow historians who have done the same thing for their special piece of historical turf and claim that their piece of the picture should be taken into account. In all fields of specialized knowledge there is the temptation to abstract from context. In some fields, such as the natural sciences, this can be done without much sense of guilt because scientists feel more comfortable with examining specialized knowledge separate from context. Historians do not enjoy such freedom, for within the profession there is an atmosphere of legitimacy for those who continually demand that their fellow historians look at the larger whole.

The contemporary environmental scene reflects a narrowing of vision generated by the same tendency to take a small piece of the picture and deal with it divorced from context. Environmental subjects are so diverse that it is quite easy to adopt this approach. There is, of course, the rather vague assumption, even more so than in science, that each specialist is really part of a larger subject encompassing the human impact on the environment. Hence there is some room in the environmental business for those with a larger perspective to try to fit it all together. And that is where the historian, who finds such a perspective more congenial, can play a constructive role. But to play this role one must self-consciously seek to broaden one's vision about the wide-ranging complexity of environmental affairs, the connections between values and institutions, the variations in how they work out in different circumstances.

The historian has a second perspective to bring to environmental affairs, the context of evolution and change. The temptation is always there to define what one examines in history in the same immediate, present-minded way that shapes the contemporary debate. But if one imposes on that debate a larger sense of historical evolution and places the current idea, event, personality, in the midst of long-term change, then the historian brings to the debate a quite different context and perspective. In contemporary analyses of debates over the meaning of science, for example, one frequently encounters the argument that some have the conclusions right and others have them wrong. "Meaning" is boiled down to reason versus emotion and intelligence versus ignorance. A more evolutionary perspective would view each step in science as a part of a long-term process that never ends, the interactive sequence of newly defined problems and newly developed techniques for analyzing those problems, the transition from initial stages of knowing to more widely accepted conclusions. The meaning comes not from just who is right and who is wrong, fostered by how meaning is disciplined by the need to make a decision, but from a broader understanding of the interaction of thought and action on the part of people who shape the process of discovery.

A historical perspective emphasizes the integrative incrementalism of American society and politics. This involves two major elements. First are the various integrative forces that make up the political context of public issues that must be brought together in some degree if we are to understand what goes on. Closely connected with those interactive forces is the second factor, evolutionary and incremental change, the way in which the new evolves out of the old. Many wish to understand these processes through the drama of big decisions and hence to shape analysis in terms of dramatic conflicts between ideas and people. But the historian has a more sensitive nose for varied values and institutions that grow and evolve into distinctive patterns of society and politics in relatively small and incremental ways over the years. At the same time, the historian has a feel for those patterns of change that mark the distinctions between more rapid and slower changes in values and institutions.

A historical perspective such as this is not welcomed by those engaged in the rough-and-tumble of contemporary political encounter. The environmental citizens' organizations want to place their values in a sharper historical focus so as to give them firmer roots and political justification;[14] environmental opponents seek historical support for their contention that environmental measures threaten the future economic well-being of the society; scientists and technologists avoid analysis of their own world of decision making because it challenges their notion that they reflect only a search for universal truth. And the media are so focused on what is "newsworthy," the search for drama to excite the public, that a more detached view is dismissed as irrelevant.[15]

There is a sense among all actors that everyone is much too narrow and specialized and too present-minded and that doses of "perspective" are needed to broaden the field of vision. And this occasionally calls for the historian's approach. But when push comes to shove, that broader perspective is cast aside in favor of shaping more advantageously the battle of the moment.

Hence the historian continues to wander in the political thickets, capable of surviving primarily in academic institutions where teaching and research enable one to read widely, think independently, and occasionally spread wisdom amid the occasional openings in the world of competitive information.

Among historians today there is a relatively new venture called *public history,* which in some fashion conveys the notion that it is concerned with current history. But I distinguish sharply between public history and contemporary history. Public history is concerned primarily with training historians who can take jobs in fields other than traditional teaching positions, such as with museums or government agencies. Its field of interest locates the historian in a more "public" field than teaching in an academic institution. There is, at the same time, a hope that public history will be able to carve out an intellectual domain that in some fashion can bring the past and the present together through a new breed of historians.

Yet this has not occurred, and the intellectual basis of public history, if there is one, has yet to be identified. There is, on the other hand, a relatively clear meaning to contemporary history, an approach which looks at present events within a broader range of social, economic, and political circumstances and as a point of time within long-term evolutionary developments. It shapes the questions that the historian asks of the present, how a distinctive view of the present defines problems for analysis and how conclusions are drawn. While public history often leads simply to the creation of history in the service of contemporary institutions that seek a positive aura from the past to fulfill their role in the present, contemporary history seeks to bring the insight of the historian to bear on how the present is understood.

THE HISTORIAN AND THE MEDIA

For the historian, the most challenging competitor in the attempt to shape an understanding of the contemporary environmental world is the mass media. Both historians and the mass media focus on the events unfolding around them and both are in a position to help shape how those events are understood by others. But their modes of understanding differ markedly. Among all the observers with whom the historian comes into competition, members of the news media are the most intensely preoccupied with the immediate event, unlike the historian, who is preoccupied with the larger context of meaning and understanding.

The media searches out the excitement and drama of the Santa Barbara oil spill, Earth Day 1970, Three Mile Island, Bhopal, Chernobyl, and Earth Day 1990. The more extensive the event in terms of human impact and the more dramatic that event, the more appealing it is to the news media. Reporting of such events fashions meaning into broad statements that often take the form of ideologies and symbols, with a heavy reliance on buzzwords, and it tends to organize these symbolic and ideological meanings into opposites so as to simplify the issues for a mass audience.

In contrast, the historian seeks to go beyond the surface to observe more wide-ranging and deeper implications and the meaning of an event in terms of what went before and what might predictably come after it. As one observes the excitement of Earth Day 1990, how can one sort out what is a result of a vast media event, promoted by the environmental community (but made possible by its "newsworthiness" and predictably short-lived) and what is more long-lasting because it is more deeply rooted in persistent and cumulative social, economic, and political changes?

There is a major difference in strategy here. The media specialist tends to become excited by "unearthing the truth" through detective work about a specific event, whether by using the freedom of information process to ferret out documents or by interviewing participants. Reporters are honored for the intensity of their search and its results. Historians work in a quieter way, thinking less of "unearthing" hidden materials and reading more widely in documentary evidence, with some associated interviewing, to bring into view the larger context of a problem and its evolutionary twists and turns over the years. The difference in approach is closely connected with the difference in the kinds of understanding and meaning which the research conveys .

Historians differ from news reporters in another way. The news media tend to create understanding through very general ideologies that abound with symbols and myths. Understanding moves rather directly from reporting dramatic events to constructing symbolic and mythological meaning. The historian, on the other hand, is interested in observing those symbols and myths through the lens of other evidence and of action. Does the meaning conveyed in symbol and myth add up when exposed to a wide range of knowledge about the subject, and is there a difference between what people say about themselves and what they do? Symbols and myths are difficult to penetrate; their repetitive and cumulative effects become powerful as presumptive "truth" and are difficult to question.

The role of media-created symbols and myths abounds in environmental affairs, and as the historian examines the evidence, these come into view as quite at odds with the world of action and practice. A host of issues that have been the subject of major media stories in recent years have been etched in the minds of the public in terms of myths and symbols rather than their world of action: emissions trading under the Clean Air Act of 1990;[16] the "jobs versus owls" debate in the Pacific Northwest; the "Alar case," which obscured the real thrust of the Natural Resources Defense Council report, entitled *Intolerable Risk;*[17] the role of the EPA in eliminating lead in gasoline. In these cases the historian, seeking to reconstruct the issue even as it is currently active, develops a vastly different context of understanding from the media. The evidence used by the historian is usually easier to acquire than that ferreted out by the media reporter. But because the questions reporters ask are quite different, the results appear to the historian to be limited and superficial.

The media process of creating symbols and myths creates a perspective to which the media have such an intense commitment that it resists questioning or revision. In the face of this commitment, the historian is challenged to raise a counter and corrective voice that can set the record straight by placing the meaning of symbols in a larger context of institutions and values.

In tracing the larger contours of the role of environmental history within the various realms of environmental debate, I will organize the analysis around three major segments of the political forces implicit in environmental affairs: (1) the impulse to bring environmental objectives to the public arena and to focus on these public values in continuous and progressive fashion; (2) the opposition to those impulses, which seeks to retard their role in public affairs; and (3) the middle ground of professionals and administrators, legislators and courts, who, with a focus on implementing policy, seek to mediate between the first two and establish lines of adjustment and compromise. The environmental historian has contributions to make to each element of the environmental political equation.

THE ENVIRONMENTAL IMPULSE

The environmental impulse involves two major drives: to expand environmental knowledge, and to implement emerging environmental values. These two impulses interact to shape public policy. There may well be some controversy over which is more leading than the other. Does science develop new environmental frontiers of knowledge that the public then takes up, or do new public values arise which then lead to new scientific explorations?

The Environmentalist and the Historian

The most immediate confrontation faced by the environmental historian is with the environmental activist. Environmental advocates usually seek to use history to bolster their current case. As with most "social movements" generally, they select out of the past those writers, leaders, or events that give historical meaning to their distinctive current venture, with little examination of context. The historian must ask: just how significant was this little piece of the past amid the larger context of society and politics at that time? The activist ignores that question in favor of how that piece of the past will bolster the present strategy.

To understand the central feature of environmental circumstance—the relation between human-caused pressures and a finite environment—is fundamental to the perspective that environmental knowledge and insight can bring to human affairs. Yet this understanding seems too far distant from the current environmental scene when political action requires that people be aroused rather than informed. Historical heroes that enhance contemporary action win out over historical understanding. Thus, John Muir is a historical hero to many contemporary environmental advocates largely because the "movement" extends and enhances his image. A historian might be more inclined to bring forward Muir's contemporary, J. Horace McFarland, as a far more important builder of environmental institutions whose fate it was in historical memory to have no later advocates.[18]

Three popular arguments often play this role of attachment between historians and the contemporary environmental movement: (1) natural processes leading to an ecological climax are an appropriate guide for human action; (2) Native Americans "lived in harmony with their environment"; and (3) environmental values are "gender" organized, that is, an expression of feminine rather than masculine values and therefore significant in the struggle of women against men, who are environmental exploiters. These three arguments have become major themes of heated debate in environmental history. None stands very close scrutiny, and my arguments to that effect run into much resistance from those who bring a more forceful advocacy view into their environmental history.[19]

In contrast, the environmental movement neglects important features of the central historical environmental circumstance, stages in the historical process of environmental degradation stemming from the evolution of the pressures of population, consumption, and technology on the finite environment of land, air, and water. That subject, while accepted at the most general level, hardly suffices to arouse and inspire action and hence is far less acceptable. More popular is the argument that associates environmental degradation with private "capitalism," an argument that would be more convincing if it extended to large-scale environmental impacts arising from either private or public large-scale investments.

Some environmental historians who are closely attached in their own values with the environmental community are reluctant to examine the distinctive social roots of environmental values that lie at the heart of modern public environmental interests. These changes in values are what make writers and events popular; hence we must first understand why those changes take place. Environmental advocates are tempted to think of the imperative to preserve the environment as universal, implicit in the nature of things. As with many social movements, their history is written largely in terms of historical values derived from sources outside human history which are thwarted from realization only by human opposition.

Analysts of environmental affairs often are misled by these tendencies to focus on environmental ideologies rather than human environmental circumstance. This is a particular problem in environmental sociology. Sociologists tend to become interested in "social movements" and to develop a particular way of analyzing them that runs in a sequence of thought from changing social circumstances that drive protest to the developing political ideologies that shape and formulate directions for those protests. Sociologists interested in environmental affairs write of "paradigms" that constitute massive social divides; in doing so, they give special prominence to those groups, usually on the fringes of public affairs, whom they see as forerunners of the future. But such an approach usually distances the sociologist from human circumstance and precludes careful analysis of variations in attitudes and values that are peculiar to various historical circumstances.[20]

The tendency to think in terms of simple and often universal general ideologies is a convenient way of thinking not only for environmental advocates but also for their opponents. Just as some are tempted to focus on the more expansive ideologies to describe and explain environmental affairs in a positive way, others are tempted to do the same when subjecting environmental defense activities to criticism. Hence antienvironmental sectors in the contemporary debate select general environmental writings to attack and avoid the circumstantial context of human experience and action.[21] The entire subject of environmental affairs is attributed to the writings and ideas of some widely read author such as Rachel Carson or Paul Ehrlich, when, in fact, the source of those affairs is found far more in the immediate human circumstances that people experience.[22] Despite their limited recognition of complex human environmental circumstances, these writings are well received by other antienvironmentalists, who cast their arguments equally in general terms.

In recent years, a genre of writing has emerged that attempts to critique the "environmental movement" from within and to do so against a backdrop of ideology that is equally divorced from circumstance. Thus, many writers take up the theme of "deep ecology" as a beginning statement of what environmental affairs are all about and then proceed to outline its shortcomings. Even environmental historians who are tempted to play the role of environmental critic often establish the same beginning point in their arguments. But the approach is highly divorced from the real world of human environmental affairs because its beginning point, deep ecology, represents only a small fringe of environmental writers and actors rather than the vast number of people involved in environmental activity.[23] Human environmental engagement is derived not from such ideologies but primarily from what people value in their environmental circumstances and the desire to improve their quality of life within those circumstances.

Human experience at a given place and time is the starting point in effective environmental analysis. Examination of the timing of the rise and spread, the distinctive geographical location, and the distinctive social roots of environmental values is necessary for a closer and more adequate environmental history. Hence as I began to analyze the variations in environmental activities across the nation, comparing this region with that, or within regions, comparing one area with another, I sought to determine why some places had higher levels of environmental interest than others.[24] I could not attribute that variation to differences in general ideas, such as the books that people read, but to variations in values as to what was important to them and the role of their environmental circumstances in working out those values. Areas of high environmental quality, such as mountains or rivers or bays, or cleaner air or cleaner water generate far higher levels of environmental values than do areas which lack such features or are burdened with previous environmental degradation.

Science and the Historian

Science plays a distinctive role in the environmental debate. Many analysts divide the subject into contention between "good science" and "bad science." Yet, from a larger perspective, the role of environmental science is quite different.

Environmental science has been one of the most rapidly developing scientific fields in the last half of the twentieth century. The result has been an outpouring of scientific work and activity: research, scientific meetings, publications, new organizations. The process seems to be unending. Each new discovery opens up more of the frontier of the unknown, leading to the conclusion that the unknown expands faster than the known. The continuous exploration of the frontiers of environmental science defines its direction and the ensuing excitement.[25]

Yet little of that sense of frontier exploration pervades the discussion of environmental science. Instead, it is cast almost entirely in terms of whether or not each new piece of science fosters truth or falsehood. The question lurking in the minds of most people is what the science means for public policy, rather than for the scientific venture itself. How rarely does one observe work in environmental science with the same sense of exploration into the unknown world that one feels in space science? Or how rarely does one capture the sense of marching into the unknown that the "New World" explorers created for those who lived in Europe 500 years ago? Environmental science, in contrast, is organized around a far more limited focus on decisions in which each piece of science is significant not for the cumulative process but for whether or not it provides sufficient proof for immediate political action.

Scientists seeking to explore the environmental world and citizens' organizations seeking to extend environmental benefits have jointly fostered new research and brought new discoveries into public view. But their efforts have been caught up in pressures to shape the decision of the moment rather than to foster a larger historical understanding. Hence they have not been able to convey the historical significance of what they do.

Those in the regulated community, on the other hand, seek to limit the application of this new scientific knowledge to public policy. They seek to undermine the credibility of the emerging environmental science as "bad science" in the face of their own "good science." And they deplore the expansion of scientific knowledge on the grounds that it reveals more fully the problems that might be subject to public action. Thus, the chemical industry has complained about the dangers of measuring chemicals at smaller and smaller levels of concentration because this will lead to demands for new restrictions based on an expansion of the definition of environmental problems. In land issues, on the other hand, scientific knowledge about wetlands, endangered species, and biodiversity, has given rise to warnings that it is not more knowledge but changes in policy that are needed. And in Utah the governor abolished the entire nongame species scientific program because economic interest groups felt the resulting science to be a threat.[26]

There are two quite different perspectives here, the debate over "proof" and the task of tracing the evolution of science as a process of human discovery. The first is organized by decision making for which science is fundamental and which requires each side to make a case for the science that supports its position. In this realm the focal point is "proof," and the issue continually revolves around what is sufficient proof for action. "Good" and "bad" science, and the need for "better science" and "conclusive proof," commonly used terms, reflect the organization of ideas about science in terms of absolutes, proof and error, which in many ways removes the issue from the real world of science and keeps it firmly embedded in decision-focused disputes.

To track the evolution of environmental science is quite a different venture and provides an evolutionary perspective in which to place each piece of new science. The key element is the ongoing process of scientific discovery as exploration of a relatively uncharted environmental world. Sometimes new methods, such as the gas chromatograph or the mass spectrometer in chemical analysis of the "radio collar" in wildlife research, open up vast new worlds for discovery. At other times, breakthroughs involve new ways of thinking— for example, the current spate of research on the biological effects of clearcutting forests arising from ecological disturbance and recovery theory, a viewpoint that has long been obscured by the silvicultural penchant for wood production and forest regulation.

It is far too much to presume that the various combatants in environmental affairs will change their strategies toward scientific knowledge and scientific proof. The pressures of the moment are far too great. However, a historical and evolutionary view of environmental science would provide a more meaningful context in which to understand the debate.

THE ENVIRONMENTAL OPPOSITION

The environmental opposition is far more complex than the environmental impulse. Its components are far more diffuse; it uses more varied strategies to express opposition; it develops and evolves over time to establish a coherent, persistent force for countering environmental initiatives. It is observed in pieces but not as a continuing whole. Contemporary observers identify the environmental impulse as a coherent force in modern society, but they rarely speak of the environmental opposition in similar fashion as a movement having like features of distinctive social, economic and political roots. The subject remains an untapped exploration for environmental historians.[27]

While the environmental impulse is considered to be somewhat extraneous to political affairs, to be even an illegitimate historical force and hence subject to scrutiny as to just why, when, and how it is expressed, the environmental opposition is considered to be central, almost inherent, and sufficiently legitimate to hardly require examination. But the historian will see both as continuous historical forces evolving in modern society in tandem and is especially interested in the interplay between them.[28]

The environmental opposition appears at every turn. Each environmental legislative proposal, each administrative action, each realm of environmental activity—from environmental education, to media reports, to environmental science and environmental analysis—sustains and reinvigorates the environmental opposition. Media reporters assume that for every issue there is both an environmental side and another side comprised of the opposition; to be "fair," the media must search out both opinions. Yet there is little attempt to identify that opposition as a persistent and systematic counterforce to the environmental protection impulse. The opposition in specific cases, in other words, is disengaged from the persistent environmental opposition as a historical force.

Analysis of the environmental opposition is an intricate undertaking that requires varied analysis and careful gathering of evidence. How does it arise at first rather piecemeal from various sectors of the economy and society and then come together as a larger political movement? How does it spurt ahead, then after a time spurt ahead again, almost in tandem with the apparent success of the environmental impulse itself? What differences are there between the opposition that looks upon environmental values as illegitimate and outside the pale of acceptability in American society versus those see themselves engaged in pragmatic contests for the allocation of public and private resources? Further, what are the strategies and techniques of environmental opponents as they seek to influence the institutions of government, federal, state, and local, to shape science in their behalf and engage in the battle to influence public opinion?

Seen from a historical perspective, the debate over environmental affairs involves continuing conflicts between economic development values and objectives, on the one hand, and environmental protection values and objectives, on the other, that are deeply rooted in personal, community, and social objectives. Conflicts arise at every stage of the game, from initial definitions of the legitimate public objectives at stake, to definition of problems that inhibit realization of those objectives and how they should be dealt with. Neither ends up with "solutions" because they both represent continuing aspirations that never come to a fixed end. Developmental objectives are widely shared among the community at large, but so also are environmental objectives; each represents human desire for a better life. Both drive personal and social aspirations; they reflect competing values and require continual trade-offs in personal life and public policy at the community, state, and national level. There is no reason to believe that either the environmental impulse or the environmental opposition will go away.

The Economy and the Historian

Several types of historical analyses pinpoint the circumstances. One is the chestnut of the allegedly hostile relationship between the environment and the economy, involving arguments in which much of the environmental opposition is rooted. The problem is formulated usually in terms of the sound-bite phrase, the "environment versus the economy," and that focus has been shaped largely by the regulated industries who protest that environmental protection requirements restrict their ability to produce. At the same time, a battery of economists who think about the economy in much the same way join in approval. Environmental considerations, so the argument goes, lie outside the central context of economic affairs and hence only hurt rather than benefit fundamental economic processes.

Historians view economic development as a dynamic interplay between new and old, focusing on the new that arises out of the old and reshapes economic life. Newer technologies succeed older ones; newer markets arise to replace older ones; newer consumption patterns emerge out of older ones; older skills and occupations give way to new; newer forms and scales of entrepreneurial organization replace previous ones. The resulting tensions between old and new have been continuous over the decades in every economic field: agriculture, commerce, banking, communications, money and exchange.

From this point of view, environmental affairs are part of a "new economy" consisting of a wide range of new types of goods and services that gradually take on increasing importance in relationship to the old—the economies of health, leisure, learning, and recreation, for example. Among these new sectors of consumption and production is the environmental economy, a new world of demand and supply that was not a significant part of the economy several decades ago. Some of this new environmental economy involves consumer "purchases" of nature and the natural world, such as outdoor recreation, watching television wildlife programs, or observing wildlife in natural settings.[29] Other sectors of the environmental economy involve expenditures for cleaner surroundings in a community or region. Each of these has its own sector of demand and supply in the total economic picture.[30]

The history of consumption is a key to understanding the contemporary economy, alongside the more traditional focus on production. New consumer wants and desires, enormous in their range, have arisen in recent years. An earlier sharp focus on the elementary features of necessities—food, clothing, and shelter—has been superseded by a growing proportion of personal and social income devoted to conveniences and amenities and to satisfying basic necessities with products of higher quality. A new breed of economic observers, marketing specialists with their penchant for studying human values, follow these changes. They provide more insight about the environmental economy than economists still caught up in older production analysis.

The historian views the economy as continually in motion and hence looks upon the current scene as another case of the interplay between the old and the new. The old extractive and primary processing industries, for example, decline relatively and the newer service industries grow relatively; this change in balance has been going on for over a century. Much of the controlling factor in economic change in recent decades has been more clearly observable on the consumption and market side, in which changes in values lead to new consumption desires and these, in turn, give rise to new types of goods and services to fill them.

So while the pressures of contemporary issues bias the debate toward the impact of environmental affairs on the "older economy," historical analysis would shift the context of discussion to the larger field of economic change. The environmental economy emerges as an element in the larger "new economy," with a special emphasis on enhancing environmental quality as a service that people desire in order to realize their personal and social values.[31]

Land Development

The historical role of the environmental opposition can also be examined in land development and technology. Both involve ongoing alternatives around which the environmental impulse and the environmental opposition have organized and hence provide clear and striking contexts within which the environmental opposition can be identified.

An enduring and widespread objective of the environmental movement is to increase the area of natural environment within the urbanized society in which most Americans now live. The areas covered by this impulse vary from urban backyards and parks, to the rural countryside of relatively undeveloped land, to the wildlands of forests and free-roaming wildlife.

Proposals have energized opposition from land developers. To them undeveloped land is a waste of private and public resources. While some are quite willing to assist in removing some land from the private market for permanent protection, the main direction of the opposition is to counter the drive to protect natural areas, since it interferes with their own projects for land development. The most intensely fought cases involve the public regulation of private lands for public objectives, but there are equally intense battles over the use of public lands.[32]

To a historian, this opposition to public objectives in the use of land has deep roots in the past; the adverse effects of private land use has long been a subject of controversy. Those controversies were fought out in the courts, which sought to draw lines between the proper and improper uses of private lands. But as common law disputes developed into statutes to promote public environmental objectives, the arguments, though similar in substance, shifted to battles over public policy. While history reveals periods of time in which assertions of the rights of private property waxed and then waned, those involved in contemporary disputes will hardly remember such fluctuations in attitude. Historians have an opportunity to place such matters in an evolutionary context and to define them as ways in which the ownership of private property involves a legal right and, at the same time, affects the wider society and hence generates adverse reactions.

Technological Innovation

A second large issue in environmental affairs around which the environmental opposition gathers is technological innovation. The environmental community seeks to improve community standards of living by fostering a cleaner environment, and hence cleaner technologies become the focal point of attention. The environmental impulse of recent decades has fostered a spate of new production technologies collectively referred to as "green technologies."[33]

Opposition to these technological innovations has been rather persistent, on the grounds that they are fanciful or too costly. Resistance to innovation has often taken the form of attempting to denigrate the environmental impulse as "antitechnology," but its main direction has been to resist the introduction of environmentally more acceptable technologies. Debate has erupted over technologies in a host of "environmental protection" issues, from waste treatment to source reduction of pollutants in industrial processes. It has involved attempts by environmental organizations to monitor production technologies for their relative effects on the environment and attempts by the environmental opposition to prevent such scrutiny.[34]

The results of these efforts on both sides are so technical and mundane as not to attract the time and energy of analysts who play to more dramatic issues. Yet they have several important implications. One is that the world of industrial production is filled with both technologies that are advanced, efficient, and often less environmentally damaging, as well as those that are less advanced, more polluting, and far more environmentally damaging than older technologies. While the environmental impulse seeks continually to advance the former, a significant segment of the production economy resists and defends the latter. Economic transition from the old to the new comes slowly, and the important feature for the historian is to identify the circumstances in which that transition proceeds more slowly or more rapidly.[35]

The size and scale of production in any given enterprise often solidifies resistance to technological innovation. Large investments in one set of technologies creates a built-in resistance to new technologies that require new investments. The persistent pursuit of financial profit sets the direction of many decisions about environmental technologies. On this score, the support by environmentalists on behalf of more advanced technologies, such as waste treatment or waste prevention, chlorine-free paper production, or, even more, the advance of kenaf as a paper fiber, meets roadblocks that are only slowly overcome. Frequently they depend on the location of niches in the production process that can be filled by small-scale ventures that are sufficiently profitable to compete with the economies of scale possible in large-scale ventures.

Analyzing the Environmental Opposition

The environmental opposition takes many forms and many directions; its adherents are often intensely "ideological" and reject environmental values outright. The general questions raised here are only a part, even though a significant part, of the scope of appropriate analysis required to understand their position. Preoccupation with the intense battles of the moment makes it difficult to back off and examine the evolution of that opposition as the product of a coherent historical process. While the contemporary combatants do not seem capable of that perspective, the historian is. The environmental opposition does not relish the resulting exposure, but a historical perspective could well enhance markedly the quality of the contemporary environmental debate.

Analyzing the environmental opposition is a challenging task primarily because of the difficulty of securing evidence. In contrast to the environmental movement, the opposition's activities are more concealed from view. The range of exposure varies. The more exposed actions, such as in the realm of legislative politics, are far easier to assess than are actions given less scrutiny such as technological performance within a firm.

The most readily available evidence about the activities of the environmental opposition comes from national legislative activity. Here, while the opposition prefers secrecy, such as protection via executive privilege, activists are often forced to make their views and tactics known through legislative hearings, investigations, and oversight.[36] News reporters, moreover, are often tempted to probe into the legislative opposition on their own, so that, for example, in the heady days of the Republican control of the 104th Congress, the intensity of environmental opposition from regulated industries came through rather clearly.

From such evidence one concludes that the direction and intensity of the opposition has not changed much over the past several decades. While they have come to accept some innovations, in such matters as air and water quality standards, or nature protection, this acceptance often seems to be only a temporary response that gives way to more fundamental opposition when opportunities arise to reverse policy. Such was the case in the Reagan administration and in the 104th Congress in which regulated industries sought to make extensive changes in legislation, either by tacking smaller measures onto more general bills or through major changes in statutory authority.[37]

Legislative opposition is mirrored in attempts to weaken legislation through regulatory rule making. Since the regulatory process is required to be relatively open, this realm of decision making is somewhat visible to the investigator. But regulatory proposals are quite technical in detail and require time and effort to follow. Hence most observers, whether media reporters, academic analysts, or historians, usually find these opportunities too burdensome to take up.[38]

When rule making is succeeded by implementation, activities of the environmental opposition are almost impossible to follow. Most environmental implementation involves direct and face-to-face relationships between the regulators and the regulated. This can be followed through the permitting process if one wishes to work one's way through hundreds and thousands of permits. But on the whole observers forgo this opportunity because of the time and effort it takes. Writing about the relationship between the regulators and the regulated seems to veer persistently toward ideologies, the general wisdom of "government" versus "market forces." This may well sort out ideological positions, but it hardly examines the continuing interface between regulators and the regulated. Hence this opportunity to examine environmental opposition falls by the wayside in favor of the temptation to substitute vague references to "command and control" and "market forces," which convey little about behavior.

The role of the regulated industries in environmental science is also fairly easy to follow because the choices made by both the regulators and the regulated are presented in the documentary evidence. In this case, one can go behind the general ideologies of science, such as "good science" and "bad science," to the substantive differences. For many years, for example, one issue regarding the health effect of carcinogens has revolved around how one counts up tumors in the resulting tissues in animal studies, and this, in turn, depends upon how one distinguishes between tumors that are malignant and tumors that are not. If one wishes to pursue these matters of scientific dispute, the evidence is usually there, but most observers outside the scientific fields in dispute shun the task because they think it too complex and of little relevance.[39]

In two major fields of environmental opposition, the evidence is far less available because it is more fully controlled by the opposition: public relations and performance. The public relations activities are rather widely publicized, but while they indicate what the opposition wants the public to know, they provide little opportunity to check statements against performance. Hence most public relations statements are impossible to use as evidence in environmental analysis. Their usefulness is limited to revealing how the opposition formulates issues, in contrast to alternative statements from other sources such as environmental organizations or administrative agencies.

Environmental performance is even harder to verify. Attempts to require independent monitoring of environmental protection measures by measuring points along the line of industrial processing are few and only weakly established, so that such factors as how far industries have succeeded in source reduction cannot be stated with confidence.[40] The regulated industries are quite aware that their own statements of performance are suspect. Until some system is developed to provide independently verifiable performance information, this crucial realm of the environmental opposition will go uncharted.[41]

The most popularly attractive form the environmental opposition has taken is the "wise use" movement. Because it has some popular base and because of the large role of the extractive industries in the opposition movement, it provides grist for the media mill. At the same time, because of its highly ideological flavor and its strategies for manipulating the media through ideologies, the "wise use" movement is relatively easy to monitor through its own documents and statements.[42]

Analysis of the environmental opposition is perhaps the most crucial element in an environmental historian's attempt to bring a broader perspective to bear on contemporary environmental affairs. The persistent political presence of that opposition tends to turn observers away from the subject because of its political implications. As it stands currently, historians are far more inclined to engage in close examination of the environmental movement itself and to ignore the equally vast subject of the environmental opposition.[43]

PROBLEM SOLVERS IN THE MIDDLE GROUND

One might find it easy enough to understand the historian's difficulties with those who are active parties to the world of environmental engagement and politics. But more strange are the differences between the historian and those engaged in the equally contemporary task of solving environmental problems. This includes those who analyze political affairs through what is known as legislative history, those engaged in the task of environmental administrations, and policy analysts who seek to develop "objective" analyses of the public world around them.

These actors apply their knowledge to a world of "environmental problems" that have been identified through legislation and which then require extensive analysis of environmental circumstances. The problem solver and the historian have quite different perspectives. For while the first takes problems as given and then seeks action to solve them, the second seeks to understand the human values and institutional commitments that gave rise to the definition of problems in the first place. While the environmental historian seeks to root environmental affairs in the broader public and private context, the environmental problem solver shuns such implications in favor of narrowing the context of analysis and action.

Legislative History

A certain style of history arises from those engaged in the legislative process, a style that is called legislative history. Studies in this vein are written for decision makers so as to establish the statutory and legal context within which new legislation is considered. One traces a proposed statute back through previous statutes and their legal interpretation to determine how each successive government action has modified or sustained a previous one. Legislative history, however, rarely establishes the real-world context of political give-and-take within which decisions are made; it does not lay out the options that were debated and represented by the contending forces at work.[44]

To the historian, meaning lies more in that context than in the resulting event; events come and go, but the underlying context continues. In legislative history, one's historical vision is narrowed, a quite understandable process in terms of the purposes of legislative history—to prevent decision makers from being misinformed about the statutory and legal context in which they work. But that narrowing provides little basis for grasping the complex of forces and circumstances inherent in the event or the pattern of continuity or change from event to event, usually incremental and often so subtle as to be hardly observable.

The historian might want to understand, in the light of known active political forces, what the legislation did not deal with, as well as what it did. Or one might want to relate the scientific assessments supporting the legislation to the give-and-take among scientists as discoveries were made and some degree of workable agreement emerged among them. The legislation might take on meaning amid the possibilities of technical innovation. Further, one might wish to understand the legislation in terms of the choices made to establish authority and power at local, state, or federal levels; for their incremental contribution to the balance of power within executive, legislative or judicial branches of government.[45]

One realm of environmental analysis that has the potential of drawing together the contemporary and the historical is environmental law. Law journals are invaluable resources for environmental analysis because they investigate a wide range of subjects rather intensively. In teaching I found that students could get engaged in environmental public issues more quickly through law journals than almost any other source. At the same time, law journals have limitations in that they tend to adopt the "legislative history" approach that removes subjects from historical context. My own experience on this score has been mixed. Five of my articles have appeared in five different law journals; in each case, the editor's general attitude was a desire for the broader perspective I could bring to the subject in contrast to the more narrowly conceived approach of the standard law journal format. A sixth, an article on the Clean Air Act of 1990, printed here for the first time, was prepared at the request of the editor of a prominent law journal but met with objections from the new staff on the grounds that it was not in conventional legal style. I did not wish to write in such a style and hence did not pursue the matter further.

Administration

The world of administration is a world of "problem solving" and depends on the close association of technical experts—scientists, economists, policy analysts and engineers—to solve problems. The dynamics of the administrative task require that environmental affairs be separated from the broader context of the present and of change over time so that energies can be sharply focused on a problem. For the most part, administrative history brings legislative history as a style of observation to bear on the government agency—its legislative origin and mandate and its activities in carrying out that mandate. As the time dimension of administrative history grows, however, the role of history increases to such an extent that the agency develops its own historical rationales but confines those rationales to those that enhance the image of the agency.[46]

Administrators are preoccupied with their own self-image and focus primarily on agency accomplishments. Moreover, they seek to convey the image that they do not make significant decisions themselves, but, as a neutral body, only implement decisions made in the legislature. The historian will want to scrutinize this self-image through the lens of the opposite assumption, that agencies make significant, even massive, choices that are often more significant than those made by the legislature. To the historian, this fact of administrative choice is not unusual, subject to the taint of impropriety or scandal as the media might define it, but as a normal part of administrative history.[47]

Administrative self-images are often divorced from an evolutionary context simply because agency administrators have such short memories, know only a small piece of their own history, and are incapable of formulating a truly evolutionary focus. Those who provide agency leadership come and go; one administrative generation knows little of the previous one.[48] Agencies are pushed and pulled amid the competing pressures of ideology and opportunism from the contending political forces who seek to place decisions in the context of past failures and future promises if only the agency would adopt their solutions. Historians have a firmer sense of the incremental and evolutionary character of administration over the long run as a wide range of factors come together to shape both continuity and change in persistent but not revolutionary ways.[49]

Policy Studies

Policy analysts also focus sharply on the event and the sequence of events rather than on context, either in the range of factors to be analyzed or their evolutionary development. They concentrate more on the tip of the iceberg rather than its massive and formative underbelly, and they usually confine their historical thinking to legislative-outcome history rather than full-fledged contextual history. Because historians can provide a perspective of greater depth and evolutionary development, they can contribute quite a different type of understanding.

The sequence in policy analysis by specialists in the field usually begins with the statement of a problem to be solved, followed by debate over proposed solutions and an account of the resulting legislative and administrative decision. This "problem-policy" format organizes the selection of what is written about, the evidence selected, and the resulting analysis. It is heavily normative in tone, with judgment about the wisdom (or lack thereof) of a given proposal and a considerable emphasis on administrative and legislative process as the main element in relative success in the achievement of policy results.[50]

In contrast, the historian is less interested in policy analysis and judgment and more interested in relating the event under scrutiny to a larger underlying set of circumstances. The historian will focus on the struggle to define the problem as a political choice; will search for scientific context in terms of the process by which scientists define problems, explore the world of the environmental unknown, and assess the results; and will use planning, cost-benefit and risk-benefit analyses not as decision-making tools but as political strategies and as major contributors to symbol and myth in environmental political ideologies.[51] The historian will look for the cumulative effect of both evolving science and evolving administration in terms of how one step in each leads to another, rather than whether or not they contributed to the "right" solution.[52]

The limited context of most environmental policy analysis, however, is reflected in a limited range of evidence. That evidence is heavily oriented toward the policy process and the legislative and administrative event rather than the context of political forces at work. Evidence is drawn heavily from secondary sources and especially from "beltway" sources such as the *Congressional Quarterly* or the *National Journal* on the one hand, or the reading world of beltway "thought leaders" such as the *New York Times,* the *Washington Post,* the *Wall Street Journal,* and the news magazines that define the world of those leaders. Political analyses rarely include a range of evidence that might be used to establish a broader perspective: legislative and administrative newsletters, law journals, background information in proposed regulations published in the *Federal Register,* publications by interested parties ranging from the environmental community to the regulated industries, science publications such as *Environmental Science and Technology,* documents of state agencies, or regional and local news media beyond the beltway. Because of their broader perspective, historians are more receptive to such evidence.

These differences in source material are a convenient way to chart differences in perspective. Consider, for example, an issue in science, where for the decision maker and the policy analyst the main question is how to assess existing scientific data; does it justify this action or that—meaning, in practical terms, can the decision withstand political opposition? For the historian, an understanding in depth would focus on the scientific enterprise and how it generates one particular stage of research and then the next, or how that process as it evolves in the scientific community is shaped by legislative and administrative decisions to foster this or that research, or how the demand for this or that research becomes an instrument of strategy in the policy debate. Rarely does an account of policy written by a policy analyst go very deep into this substructure of science, despite the fact that it has a profound effect on the decision.

THE MEANING OF IT ALL

This accumulated writing about environmental affairs, much of which is included in this volume of essays, reflects a wide range of subjects. The choices of scholarly interest represented are not always understandable. My interest in forestry and air quality is clear enough. But almost all of the essays were written at the request of a journal or an author, and hence the range of topics reflects the varied directions of interest within the profession at large as much as my own. In attempting to understand why I was asked to write this or that, I found that the request came from something I had already written; in accepting such a request I often found an opportunity to work out a problem which, at the beginning, I had only sensed rather than fully defining it in my own mind. In each case, this provided an opportunity to develop directions of thought that had been only half formed.

At the same time, beyond the specific choice of subjects, these essays reveal a sense of direction and perspective that has accumulated over the years and which I summarize briefly to close this semiautobiographical foray. First are a set of unfolding ideas as to how one thinks about history in general, which then are applied to how one thinks specifically about environmental history—concepts about historical context and historical change. Second is an interest in broadening the range of inquiry rather than narrowing it. This appears in the continual tendency to look into a wider variety of environmental subjects and to find ways of integrating them into a whole. While I worked from the particular to the general and back again, I was continually attempting to extend the range of meaning in environmental history. Third was a life of searching for evidence, weighing, and evaluating it. I was continually using the mails and telephone to acquire documents, and my habit was to read widely, file material, and then use my document library as a basis for building the evidence for the writing. This meant that I was continually mulling over the meaning of the evidence as I read it, day by day. It also meant developing an acute awareness that the evidence I was acquiring was becoming a unique archive which, because it contains material collected and preserved when it was produced, will be invaluable to environmental historians in years to come.[53]

Fourth, I was also continually thinking about how all this applied to contemporary affairs. Here I was attempting to play a complex role, becoming knowledgeable about the details of current affairs, for example, the ins and outs of the often arcane subject of administrative politics, but not becoming so deeply involved in those events as to lose the broader perspective which I sought to maintain. In the process, I was also continually attempting to entice the environmental audience, at times citizen-activists, at times academic specialists, at times administrators, and at times the environmental opposition, into adopting a broader perspective about the environmental circumstances in which they were involved.

Finally, I sought to define and maintain a clear historical perspective so as to sustain the contextual, evolutionary, and integrative concepts laid out at the beginning of this essay. I sought to enable the subject of environmental history to stand by itself rather than become simply an adjunct to contemporary political and policy debates. To the reader who might find this autobiographical foray intriguing, I would offer this as the major challenge of environmental history.

I *The Big Issues*

THE LIMITS-TO-GROWTH ISSUE

A Historical Perspective

ENVIRONMENTAL CONSERVATION PROBLEMS are persistently moving toward a context of the limits to growth. The writings of Forrester and the Meadows have given an overall formulation to a set of predispositions and hunches that have been rather widespread in a variety of more disparate and piecemeal issues.[1] The impact has seemed rather astounding. The Meadows' writings especially took us off guard, so much so that at the start they were considered in an atmosphere of transient sensationalism. Yet there is a persistence to the insights in all this that has remained and will remain for a long time to come. As the sensationalism of the initial impact wears off, the relevance of the idea becomes more concretely pervasive. A frame of mind is developing in which environmental conservation problems are defined in terms of the tension between a finite physical environment and increasing human pressure upon it.

What sense can a historian make of all this? These moods of thought and

Originally published in Chester L. Cooper, ed., *Growth in America* (Westport, Conn.: Greenwood Press, 115–42. Copyright © 1979 by the Woodrow Wilson International Center for Scholars. Reprinted with permission.

outlook, of course, are relatively new, and it would be a major temptation simply to look back and contrast the old and the new. In the nineteenth and early twentieth centuries a sense of optimism pervaded American society that the nation's physical environment had no limits, that resources were infinitely exploitable, and that America was technologically capable of transforming at will the physical world around it. There was little thought of limits, for although some of that physical world was destroyed there was more of it to be had "out there." Even in the days of revulsion against the massive timber cutting in the late nineteenth and early twentieth centuries the sense of having reached limits was only temporary. In fact, the conservation movement of the early twentieth century carried with it far more a sense of optimism about the vast and unlimited potential of technology, applied science, and large-scale system than about environmental limits. It was only a pause toward a new variant of continued physical development.

But to contrast the human perception of limitlessness in the past with that of limits in the present would not help much to understand where we are today. It is far more important to focus on the process by which the change came about. Let us assume that the task of history is to understand the processes of long-run social change, the transformations in societies as they change over long periods of time. In the current instance the problem is to understand the present perception of limits in terms of the evolution of a frame of reference, to identify the process by which a sense of limits grew and developed out of a past when a different frame of mind prevailed. The task in this essay, therefore, will be more modest than a sweeping panorama of historical wisdom. It will be confined to some observations about social change in twentieth-century America, which may provide some insight into the changing perceptions of the nature of our environment.

Let me make one other point by way of introduction. The context of what follows will be political. We are speaking here of human choices and the values and perceptions that lie behind those choices. It is true that the relevant conditions of life can be described variously as economic or social or cultural, that the substance of the issues concern how we make a living, what we produce in goods and services, what we prefer to consume with personal and social resources. Yet all this still involves choices, which, in turn, reflect preference and values. The shift from a concern with food and clothing to a concern for material goods to a concern for nonmaterial services to a concern for environmental quality involves values and choices that can be understood fully only as political phenomena. What values, perceptions, and preferences are operative, and how is the interplay of the variety of conflicting preferences worked out in the form of social decision and social action? We are dealing here with emerging preferences and emerging choices, and all this requires a form of social understanding at that fundamental level.

I I

As an initial backdrop let me contrast the earlier twentieth-century conservation movement with the more recent environmental concerns. There are continuities that I shall dwell on later, but it is important that we first understand the differences.

Prior to the 1960s the conservation movement was dominated by the perspective of "efficient production."[2] The term "conservation" arose initially to describe new approaches to resource management that involved the application of science, technology, and planning to the development and use of those resources. In its origin the movement was closely related to the practice of scientific management, not only in its concepts but also in its leaders. There was some emphasis on the limits of resources and the need to save resources to live within those limits, but that emphasis was minor and ephemeral. The major focus was on the way in which science and technology could eliminate waste and increase the material base of human life. The movement affirmed, and did not seriously question, the perspective of an abundant and unlimited future if the methods of science and technology were used to manage resources "wisely."

Three different focal points of activity illustrate this approach. First was multiple-purpose river development. Unharnessed rivers flowing to the ocean without being used by man were deplored as wasteful; they could be made far more productive if brought under control by large-scale public works such as dams and reservoirs. Moreover, if located and constructed with multiple uses in mind, entire rivers could be harnessed for multiple benefits of navigation, flood control, irrigation, and hydroelectric power production. Engineers extolled the seemingly unlimited possibilities if the manifold uses of a single resource, water, could be dovetailed according to concepts of efficiency and under centralized planning and direction by experts. Glimmerings of this approach began in the first decade of the twentieth century, by the 1920s it had begun to jell and by the 1930s projects were in full swing. The Tennessee Valley Authority was the most dramatic consequence.

Sustained-yield forest management reflected a similar focus. Wasteful lumbering practices could be prevented and future supplies of timber could be assured if timberlands were managed according to the scientific principles of sustained yield, that is, the annual cut should be balanced with annual growth. This was the spirit of "scientific forestry" that Gifford Pinchot popularized and instilled into the minds of young foresters whom he attracted into the new profession. Pinchot was committed to the forests as commodity resources that should be developed for commercial purposes, and he vigorously opposed efforts to allocate lands in the national forests for parks and other noncommercial purposes. Hostile to what he called "preservationists" he played a major role in establishing the dominant mood of conservation as efficient, scientific, economic development.[3]

The new contribution of the 1930s—the soil conservation movement—continued this approach. The immediate problem it tackled was soil erosion and in doing so it generated the new movement of scientific soil management. Erosion was easily construed as an economic problem; it depleted the capital base of agriculture. A new science and a new technology could reverse that trend and both stabilize and restore that capital. Focusing on the intricate relationships of soil and water, the movement, of which Hugh Hammond Bennett was the symbolic and de facto leader, continued to inject into the conservation impulse its traditional theme of efficient production. Forest, soil, and water became a complex of perspectives and interests that readily dovetailed in the "conservation movement."

Throughout all these years a quite different perspective persisted, but in a subordinate and often obscured role. This was the park and outdoor recreation movement. Its major focus was the "preservation" of lands from commercial development or production in order that they might be enjoyed for their natural beauty. The development of national parks and the growth of the National Park Service, established in 1916, represented this focus.[4] At the state level programs for fish and wildlife "conservation" constituted a different but related focus.[5] And the outdoor recreation movement, represented by hiking clubs, trail riding organizations, and camping groups, was another.[6] All of these came into sharp conflict, at one time or another, with the efficient development perspective and played a subordinate role to it through the 1950s.

In the 1960s all this came to be modified or often superseded by the "environmental movement," with a strong connotation of "quality" or "amenity" rather than efficient economic development.[7] New concepts arose that went beyond production to the enjoyment of life and concern for the quality of the environment necessary for that enjoyment. Air, water, and land each came to be conceived of not as a commodity to be molded into a material product or as a public facility for the disposal of waste, but as the environment in which people work, live, and play. The "environment" was not a thing to be used for material purposes, but the context of life and the enjoyment of life required that the context be of one kind rather than another. The phrase "environmental quality" arose, embedded in such public action as the "Council on Environmental Quality," and soon began to compete with the older word "conservation."

This amenity focus is increasingly at odds with the earlier production focus of conservation, and many heroes of the conservation past have become villains of the environmental present. As opposition to river "impoundments," dams, and reservoirs has grown, not only the U.S. Army Corps of Engineers and the Bureau of Reclamation, but also the Tennessee Valley Authority, have come in for sharp attack.[8] TVA, the conservation hero of the 1930s, is rapidly becoming a major target of environmental criticism, not only for its dam building proclivities but also for its role as a major purchaser of strip-mined coal. The Soil Conservation Service, changed from a protector of soil from erosion to a developer of undeveloped land through wetland drainage and stream channelization, has become equally a villain in the current scene. The U. S. Forest Service, with its dominant focus on commodity timber production and its close, "incestuous" relationship with the timber industry, has come under more than usual attack. The issue of clear-cutting, offensive to aesthetic sensibilities among environmental conservationalists, has presented the Forest Service with one of the major crises of its history.[9] Even the National Park Service, because of its increasing involvement in mass, developed recreation, has been severely criticized.[10] But it, more than the other agencies mentioned, has begun to make sharp adjustments in its thinking under the stark realization that increasing human pressure is threatening its scarce resources with destruction. On the whole, it has been painful for the old "conservationists" to adjust to the new "environmentalism" because the two emphases are, more often than not, incompatible. Quality or amenity is a direct challenge to efficient production.

Echoes of the distinction in perspectives between production and amenity persist within the environmental quality movement itself. For many, environmental quality means primarily "clean production" with the emphasis, as much as in the old conservation movement, on production, including an acceptance of the ideology of material growth. They would simply add the word "clean" to "efficient" production. For others, however, environmental quality means a sharper, more direct, and more thorough emphasis on "quality" as a goal coordinate with and not derivative of production. Amenity or quality should not merely guide the manner in which production goals are carried out but should become a fundamental goal itself, coordinate with production goals.[11] This difference in approach is an important, but as yet not widely manifest, aspect of the controversy over the "environmental impact" or "102" statements now required of all federal construction agencies. Production-oriented agencies such as the U.S. Forest Service, the U.S. Army Corps of Engineers, the Department of Transportation, or the Energy Research and Development Administration view these as merely examining environmental consequences of their primary production mission. Most controversy over the statements has focused on the adequacy of that examination. But much of the environmental quality movement demands that "quality" enter in decision making in the initial planning not as consequences but as goals. Clean production is not enough; basic production goals must be restricted to make way for "quality-of-life" goals.

The concern for the limits of growth emerges from this "amenity" sector of the environmental conservation movement. Clearly it is vastly at odds with the older emphasis upon large-scale, efficient production. But it also rarely finds much support among those more modern environmentalists who are primarily occupied with clean air and clean water or even with environmental health. All these assume that what technology has created in the form of waste, technology can clean up, and if completely closed-loop recycling systems are possible in the treatment of technological waste, there is no need to be concerned with the scale of resource throughput.[12] A concern for a wide range of amenities on the other hand has the possibility of raising the question of limits as a forceful element of human perspective. If quality of life is a major goal, then it pervades a wide range of decisions—from the number of children one has to the personal enjoyment of a clean, quiet, and natural environment. As we shall see later on, the role of space in environmental quality values, and especially the problem of land use, raises questions of limits of growth far more forcefully than do problems of technological waste.

III

Basic to the new concerns for environmental quality and the limits to growth are changes in human values and preferences that have come over the American people since World War II. And basic to these changes in values is the enormous productivity of the American economy, which has permitted a significant proportion of the population to think in terms of and choose amenities. Rapid economic growth after World War II led to sharply rising incomes, rapid vertical mobility, and increased levels of education. Fully half of Americans by 1970 were white-collar workers and more than that had completed a high school education; median family income by 1972 had reached well over $10,000; and 25 percent of Americans were upper-middle-class individuals with some years of college education. While income and economic conditions remained unequally distributed, an increasing proportion of American families in the upper half of the income scale could and did think beyond the material comforts of life to amenities. Education was an especially important factor in changing the values of Americans and developing an interest in matters termed "quality of life." Individuals began to allocate their personal resources differently because they had more to allocate and the American economy as a whole could allocate an increasing share of its resources to those amenities.

It is relatively tempting to think of all this in terms of economic aggregates, of changes in overall allocation of resources in response to changing wants. Yet to understand it fully we must focus on the human situation and human circumstance. It is the way in which individuals think, prefer, and choose that add up to the total sum of actions. Consider one major aspect of value change involving amenities—family size. Family size has undergone a long-run decline over many decades since long before World War II. That change reflects new ideas about quality of life. This has gone through several stages. Urbanized people in the nineteenth century most probably had relatively small families, while rural family size remained much higher, and immigrants, mainly from rural origins, persistently injected large families into the urban social order and kept the overall family size quite large.[13] However, with each generation modern values had a major impact on newcomers and by the mid-twentieth century there were few influences left toward large family size. By this time the family size of eastern European migrants of the late nineteenth and early twentieth centuries had declined markedly, and that of Mexicans and blacks, recently rural with rural preferences for larger families, were equally and markedly affected. Current data indicate that almost no ethnocultural group is free from the inverse correlation between educational level and family size.[14]

This indicates changing value preferences within the family, which add up to marked social changes. The desire to have fewer children is a decision about the allocation of family resources and a reorientation from quantity to quality. Wants and aspirations by children and parents for themselves go far beyond keeping body and soul together. They escalate, and a decision is made to allocate more and more real income among fewer and fewer people.

Modern birth-control methods are significant within this context of changing wants. There are two phases. In the past the main thrust of birth control has been to bring the actual number of births into line with the desired number of children.[15] The gap between the two had been quite large and, due to birth control, it has been narrowed. The wider use of abortion permits closure of the gap even more completely. But a second process also seems underway, involving changing views as to the appropriate family size. There has been a marked decline from the post–World War II level of three or four children to approximately two. Very few today believe that one child is desirable but the number who prefer no children at all is increasing very slightly. If the latter were to continue it would indicate even more strikingly the persistence of a historical tendency toward quality-of-life emphases. Adults would increasingly prefer to spend their income on themselves and not on children at all or to limit their own income to levels that reduce time spent at earning a living and increase time spent in consuming goods and services with quality-of-living objectives.

Change in family size is only one of the more readily identifiable indexes of change in value preferences that reflect a concern for quality of life and experience rather than quantity of goods and services. As the emphasis on consumption beyond necessities increased, Americans first began to consume more material goods to make life in the home more pleasant and to reduce physical labor—thus, the expansion of the durable-goods sector of the economy in the 1920s and beyond. After this came an emphasis on services and especially so as leisure time activities began to loom larger and larger. These changes were accompanied by an emphasis on the quality of external surroundings. Moves to the suburbs constituted a search for more space within the home and more open area outside it to making living more comfortable.

The values behind this are reflected in studies indicating that far more people today wish to live in less congested areas than can do so; the desire can be fulfilled only partially.[16] The move to the suburbs has been with us for over a century and a quarter, from the first stages of rapid urban growth in the mid-nineteenth century. Formerly only a fraction of urban dwellers could participate in it; more recently a larger proportion can and does. The large-scale suburbanization of the 1920s and beyond is one of the first major expressions of the search for environmental amenities, for less congested surroundings, clean air, and less noise. It was but a small step from this to the desire to bring those features of environmental quality to the city itself. Thus the values implicit in the search for quality of surroundings in suburbanization were brought back into the city. Even beyond that, the outward thrust from the city, as we shall see in more detail, led to the use of the wider countryside and remaining wildlands, the enjoyment of the environmental quality of even less congested and less environmentally degraded area.[17] This use was usually confined to nonoccupational times of one's life, either vacations or in retirement years, but it gave even more extensive expression to the search for clean, quiet, less developed, and more natural surroundings.

These changes in values that lie behind the focus on amenities can safely be predicted to grow, for the conditions that lead to them are increasing. Only a very small segment of society had these values and could realize them in the nineteenth century; only a few then, for example, moved to the suburbs to live or used the open countryside for vacations. The data are imprecise and not yet developed, but we might well speculate roughly that in mid-nineteenth century America less than 3 percent of families expressed these values while today far more than 50 percent do.[18] Incomes rose, levels of education rose, mobility and the possibility of escaping environmental degradation increased, and with all this came a more intensive interest in the quality of the surrounding environment as an aspect of a higher standard of living. The search for environmental quality has been transformed from an elitist to a broad mass movement.[19]

There are, of course, conflicts between the continuing interest in a higher material standard of living and the search for greater environmental quality. Automobiles are one example. People wish the mobility advantages of the car and will not give it up as readily as they have reduced the size of their families. Many changes in style of life that seem socially desirable to enhance environmental quality do not come easily and, if they come, will probably involve efforts to persuade people to change preferences. Those responsible for environmental degradation and who attack the drive for environmental quality love to focus on these paradoxes and to belittle thereby the search for environmental quality as temporary and transient. Yet the paradox will not be resolved that quickly. The search for environmental quality is as fundamental as the search for a higher material standard of living: in fact the former is an outgrowth of a further development of the latter. We can look forward to a politics of conflict and paradox between the two.

I V

A second long-run secular development has provided a setting that closely relates to the search for environmental quality. This is the new capacity for environmental transformation or environmental degradation. We have learned ways and means of effecting environmental change far more powerful and far more extensive than ever before. Some of these are technological, involving new earth-moving and resource-moving capacities or new physical and chemical processes producing waste products in far greater diversity and extent than before. Others are organizational—the vastly increased scale in the capacity to organize and direct a technology from a central source of decision making, the increased size and scale of both private corporate enterprise and public governmental administrative systems. In both technology and organization larger scale has replaced smaller, and with it the capacity to destroy the human environment has been greatly enhanced. Just as people have become consciously concerned about enhancing the quality of their environment, we have also been engaged in the practice of destroying it more fully and completely. The two tendencies are closely related.

Let us sketch briefly the rise of three of these: resource-moving and -transforming equipment, production of waste, and generation of electric power. Three issues that have become important in the current environmental conservation movement are strip mining, clear-cutting, and highway construction.[20] All involve land use and all involve modern capabilities to modify the land surface extensively. Behind each is a technology that has developed in its present form since World War II. The giant drag lines and shovels used in strip mining, with their multiton loads, seem like massive vultures moving over the countryside, defacing and destroying, representing in fact and in symbol man's arrogant capacity to transform his physical environment at will. Clear-cutting is a practice that seems more justified by forest technology than by silviculture, by the cost of removing and regenerating trees than by multiple-purpose management of wildlands; it is peculiarly adapted to the large-scale machinery of modern logging, machinery that is incapable of selecting trees for cutting and requires that all growth be consumed in one giant, sweeping operation. And the ribbons of interstate, multilane highways cutting across the countryside are more massive, leaving larger scars, and disrupting wider areas than any highway construction did ever before. The reaction against all three of these is in the degree to which they themselves represent the capability of massive land transformation.

Our waste-producing capacities have also escalated beyond anything known in previous years.[21] The traditional practice of using air, water, and land for disposing of waste seems no longer feasible because of our enormously increased capacity for producing waste. It is one of those questions of finite environmental limits and exponentially increasing human pressure. There is only so much air, land, and water in which to dump waste, but the amount of waste produced by modern technology has escalated. New chemical processes have developed in industrial technology (for example, textile production) in such a way as to expand waste output and alter dramatically its character. Solid waste, in new forms of packaging, has grown apace without much attention to what is to be done with it. Larger and larger technical processes have produced greater outputs of pollution into the air as well. All this comes from the size and scale of modern technology and production, their capability of throwing a load of material into the environment that we have not before experienced. In the face of an increasing concern for environmental quality, the capability is, to say the least, not appreciated.

Finally, the generation of electric power seems to have focused many aspects of the impact of large-scale technology into one major enterprise.[22] The scale of electric power plants has increased enormously and the scale of distribution systems has grown similarly. The capacity for air pollution is well known, as the large plants in the Plains and mountain West testify; the capacity for thermal pollution is equally great; the occupation of land for production and distribution is more extensive than ever before. Nuclear energy is an even greater example of the problem, for it involves a massive scale of production with massive uses of water and resulting thermal pollution and massive production of a new and, to many people, fearful kind of waste. The environmentally transforming capacities of modern electric generation are undoubtedly the source of much of the attack upon it by environmental conservationists.

Note two aspects of this accelerating capacity for environmental transformation. One is that the very forces that constituted the conservation movement of the early twentieth century now have come to be the source of environmental damage. That early twentieth-century movement asserted the possibilities of a glowing resource future through large-scale, efficient management. In doing so it was only one factor among many preparing the way for large-scale, efficient, resource transformation and degradation. It is no wonder that the logical extensions of the early twentieth-century movement —large-scale, multiple-purpose river development and large-scale timber technology—should have been transformed from earlier conservation triumphs to later environmental disasters. The resource processes involved in

this have continued to develop in the same direction; it is the human preferences and values that have changed course. Those preferences have displayed
considerable flexibility and modification; but technology has remained rigid,
moving ahead in the same direction as before toward larger and more massive
environmental modification and somewhat removed from changing human
wants and values. What is especially striking is the failure to develop decentralized technology and decentralized autonomous management that might
well be more responsive to growing preferences for environmental quality.

A second implication is more significant. These capabilities represent two
quite different developments. Massive waste production can, for the most
part, be dealt with effectively by massive amounts of technology. That is what
the new clean water, clean air, and solid disposal drives are all about. There are
major issues over recycling versus diffusion of air and water waste and over
recycling versus reduction in waste production at the source. But much of the
modern environmental movement is an attempt to apply technology and
scale to the redirection of waste products away from our finite land, air, and
water, which have been used in the past as waste receptacles. It is thus possible to deal with the problem of finite resources and growing human pressure
on them in the field of waste by redirecting waste with technology.

But there are other uses of finite air, land, and water that are not so easily
solved. These resources are used directly as space for human activities, both
permanent habitation and temporary enjoyment, activities for which there
are no possibilities whereby a redirected technology can reduce their impact.
It would be possible to change human values and persuade people to want to
live in more congested areas. But the desire for open space seems not so easily
changed; so long as it is a major element of the drive for a "better" standard of
living, it constitutes an exponentially increasing pressure upon finite air, land,
and water resources.[23] It is for this reason that the land transforming processes
implicit in highway construction, strip mining, clear-cutting, and second-
home development become so crucial. It is for this reason that the word "conservation" which traditionally has been associated with land problems,
remains with us, not wholly replaced by the word "environment" and leading
to a more appropriate phrase, "environmental conservation."[24] It is for this
reason that the new interest in land use will raise issues far more intense than
issues of pollution and waste. For while there is a way out of the conflict between resource limits and exponential increases in waste, there is no way out
of the conflict between resource limits and exponential increases in direct
human occupation of land and its surrounding air and water. Finite resources
will not expand, and if the value placed upon open space continues, the only

solution is to reduce the pressure upon the land. As we shall argue later, this version of the experience of finite resources and increasing human pressure is one of the most significant sources of the concern about the limits to growth.

V

There are very different thrusts within the environmental conservation movement, and the concern for the limits to growth has deeper and stronger roots in some of them than in others.[25] Consider, for example, the dynamics of the recent wave of concern for air pollution. For the most part this is an urban-based political drive. People living in and around cities have reacted against the increasing use of urban air as a dumping ground for urban wastes, and urban-based organizations have raised an outcry for cleaner air. This impulse seems relatively divorced from concerns about limits of growth. The experience is one of an undesirable manmade urban environment; values and political strategies are worked out in terms of cleaning up that immediate environment. There is little in the primary urban experience to turn one's thoughts to relationships to the wider world, such as the environmental load that the city places upon the countryside. Matters of air pollution are experienced and worked out within a more confined urban experience, an environment that can be manipulated for improvement as well as for degradation.

Waste water problems develop within a slightly different context of experience. Water pollution concerns stem from a wider range of people, beyond cities, as well as from those within, for streams flow through wider reaches of territory, cutting across both rural and urban areas. Historically it has been those who use streams in this larger fashion, such as fishermen, who have been the major force behind clean water. But in recent years they have been joined by urban people who want to clean up the Cuyahoga, the Ohio, Lake Erie, the Savannah, and a host of other rivers and lakes. Out of this has come a movement to dispose of waste before it reaches streams and lakes, control at the source rather than diffusion, an affirmation that the traditional use of rivers as a waste receptacle is no longer acceptable. We are now in the midst of a new mode of thought, of divorcing liquid-waste disposal from rivers by means of closed-loop systems or land recycling. It is symbolized by the goal of "zero discharge." The possibilities of these innovations have divorced the movement to reduce water pollution from problems of limits.

Solid-waste disposal displays similar political perspectives. For the most part cities, which produce the vast share of solid waste, seek only to transfer the wastes elsewhere, and their interest lies primarily in the cost of transfer. "Out there," in the surrounding countryside, land is to be had—current waste land, abandoned strip mines—which could just as easily be a source of land for solid waste disposal. The problem is the cost of getting the waste to it.[26] Where such possibilities do not exist, such as in the more congested East, there is more serious thought about a large-scale system involving more genuine recycling—thus the inauguration of a statewide waste recovery program recently in Connecticut. For the most part a consciousness of limits to growth does not arise naturally from the experience of urbanites coping with the mountains of solid waste they produce.

In all these aspects of the rapid growth of technological waste there is always the temptation to feel that space is available elsewhere for waste disposal; there is little inclination on the part of most urbanites to view the problem from the vantage point of the wider countryside, which is a potential dumping ground for waste. From this point of view, for example, the crucial question in air pollution is "air degradation," the process whereby cleaner air in the open countryside is permitted to become dirtier.[27] Those who would permit air degradation argue that urban air can be cleaned up only if urban pollution sources move to areas where air is cleaner. The Four Corners energy generation projects, for example, simply transferred pollution from electric power production from Los Angeles to the less settled Southwest. This is another version of a "diffusion solution" rather than control at the source. It is significant that the drive to apply and enforce effectively the nondegradation clause of the Clean Air Act of 1970 has come not from the urban-based air pollution citizen groups but from the Sierra Club, concerned primarily with natural beauty and the environmental quality of the wider countryside as well as the city.[28] True, some cities and many urban states joined in the effort as friends of the court, but they had to be drawn into it and did not jump spontaneously to the enforcement. In similar fashion this is one section of the act that the Environmental Protection Administration has tried and continues to try to wriggle out of and around; its perspective, too, is dominated by the problems of the city, and it looks to the transfer of pollution to the countryside as a major answer to the urban problem.

The transfer of water-quality standards from the city to the countryside is a different matter. In this case the fishermen users constitute a political force within the countryside itself. Moreover, polluted water in the countryside can have serious consequences for down-river cities, and in this fashion the cities become more interested in their wider environment. It is significant, therefore, that the same principle involved in the hotly debated air nondegradation concept—that areas cleaner than acceptable standards not be allowed to get dirtier—has long been taken as a working principle in matters of water quality. In a number of states rivers are classified in terms of degrees of water quality, and differential standards are adopted in which rivers of a higher quality level are not permitted to be reduced to a lower quality level. This is a simple nondegradation policy applied to water, a response to a force within the countryside that demands that the waste-producing influences of economic growth, arising largely from urbanization, not degrade this aspect of their environment.[29]

With solid waste disposal the political setting is more complex. New standards of disposal, especially the establishment of sanitary landfills, are being brought rapidly to the countryside. However, this comes not from forces indigenous to the countryside or from the cities directly, but from public health concepts that are urban based in their origins and that have broad political support, that are generalized outward through the state from state public health administrations. Yet even here the relative cheapness of land for solid waste disposal renders this approach far more readily acceptable to the rural community than does a secondary treatment sewage system, which is a more costly proposition. As of yet there is relatively less thought that there are limits to the growth of solid waste because there is still land "out there" for its ready disposal.

Two aspects of this brief overview of the politics of technological waste disposal should be stressed. First, the political movement involved does not readily produce a concern for the limits of growth; we must look for the roots of that concern elsewhere. For the most part those who generate waste feel that there are abundant opportunities for disposal, and those who are concerned with cleaning up have similar views. Few thrusts in the environmental movement assume that we must stop producing waste because there are finite limits to our waste receptacles of land, air, and water. That lurks in the background, and such cases as the reuse of bottles are exceptions,[30] but the more widespread experience is that there are alternatives far short of such limits and that technology can clean up waste with pollution controls and recycling.

Second, the city and the urban experience are, for the most part, self-contained and do not give rise readily to a more extensive vision concerning the impact of the city on the wider world. The city is the source of the increasing pressure on the environment, a "growth machine" as one economist has called it.[31] Here the forces making for increasing human loads on our finite resources are generated in the first place, the bulk of the increasing waste is produced, and the demand for more resources, including use of space, is created. Yet urban people do not experience directly the impact of their pressures. They live within the manmade environment of the city and their most active political impulses are confined to modifying that environment as a living and working space. Their secondary environment, that beyond the city which they use in greater intensity as time passes, is one they use occasionally, temporarily, or at remote distances and which is, therefore, beyond their immediate and sustained political interest. Consequently, urban people who are confined within the primary urban experience do not for the most part spontaneously develop a concern for the limits of growth. Their main concern in the environmental movement is air pollution and waste disposal, a set of problems that generate only limited perspectives and experiences restricted for the most part to the manmade walls and corridors of the city.

V I

There are other forces in the environmental conservation movement, rooted in different experiences, generating different definitions of environmental quality, that do give rise, far more readily, to a concern for the limits to growth. They are concerned with air, water, and land as living space rather than as receptacles for waste or as commodities for throughput. Let us examine these forces in more detail, distinguish them from other forces, and relate them to the past.

One of these focuses on metropolitan open space and arises out of the relatively open atmosphere of the metropolitan suburb. Its main experience is that of an expanding metropolitan system—people, highways, buildings, stores, "development"— closing in on a previously more open environment, on limited air, land, and water.[32] The choice to live away from the congested center of the city constitutes a search for more physical openness, more open space, less congested air, land, and water, less noise, in short for "amenities." When it is discovered that environmentally degrading influences are being transplanted to the new community, a severe shock ensues and gives rise to the drive to protect these amenities, to exercise some "control" over development. This generates the formation of a host of groups, often dispersed and local, frequently focused on the residential community, geared to controlling the pace and shape of development in their neighborhoods. The examples, especially dramatic on the East and West coasts, are legion. These groups are by no means uninterested in pollution problems; in fact they are extremely active in attempts to cope with them. But they have a larger perspective—the entire physical environment of their communities, and especially open space. Their experience leads them directly to a basic concern for land-use planning, a phase of environmental conservation rather remote from the activities of clean air and clean water organizations. They are concerned primarily with the use, present and future, of the land and streams of their immediate environment. To them the concept of open space is crucial; their basic concern is to retain and increase that open space. Is land more valuable in open space than in more traditional types of development? Such a question is frequently raised. Far more typical of the expertise closely allied with their views is the landscape architect. And rather than relying on Barry Commoner's *The Closing Circle* for inspiration, they prefer Ian McHarg's *Design with Nature.*[33]

Because of the concern for quality of space, the metropolitan open-space perspective is drawn steadily into the whole realm of amenity questions. This tendency stands in sharp contrast with a technological waste vantage point, which is often at odds with larger amenity issues. The two perspectives differ strikingly. While the concern for pollution focuses on environmental repair, the open-space perspective seeks to prevent environmental damage in the first place. It finds common ground, therefore, with many other groups that seek preventive rather than ameliorative action, that are concerned with wilderness and natural space, with air and water nondegradation, with pastoral landscapes, and with population and consumption problems.[34] Its concerns are more versatile, more extensive, and run deeper into the entire environmental conservation movement than are those whose primary interests focus on technological waste.

Dovetailing with metropolitan open space impulses are the drives to maintain the natural quality of an even larger space, the wilder and less developed rural and forested areas. Here a climatic historical process has been taking place since World War II. Up to that time rural and forested areas had experienced a persistent decline in population and occupancy for many decades, roughly from the 1880s onward. Post–World War II economic growth reversed this trend and gave rise to a vigorous increase in the number of urban people seeking to use the countryside for second homes, for recreation at reservoirs and ski areas, for tourism, for highways, for fishing and hiking and backpacking, for off-road vehicle recreation, for a wide variety of purposes geared to the needs of urban inhabitants. Because of the material advantage these activities bring—such as higher land values—many rural areas were and are vulnerable to participation in this process of urban-induced change. But many others fear such an impact and have moved to protect their amenities against urban-generated environmental degradation. At the same time, some urban users of the countryside seek to protect the amenities they already enjoy from prospective overuse by others. All this might well be considered a phase of the metropolitan open-space movement writ larger.

Reaction against urban penetration of the countryside has been expressed in a number of ways. States have established preferential tax programs intended to reduce the turnover of open rural land to other uses, which is often brought about by taxing land at its potential value rather than its actual use.[35] The pressure of urban-based activities upon hunting land generates among sportsmen a concern for the preservation of wild life habitat.[36] Hiking trail clubs, accustomed to enjoying the solitude of a natural setting for hiking, have faced encroachment on the disruption of their right-of-way by residential and economic development.[37] And those who have been in the vanguard of establishing permanent or temporary homes in a wildland setting because of its amenities resist the onrush of newcomers whose desire to do the same thing destroys the environmental quality of open space. From many sources come the concrete and adverse experience of population pressure upon areas less developed. Such experience gives form and substance to the view that levels of population and consumption have gone too far.

All this has several major implications. First, interest in the problem of the limits of growth arises most readily from a concern about space, the space of air, land, and water, and the search for space in more natural surroundings, which are uncongested and free from urban noise. One does not read about matters of population and limitation of consumption in magazines devoted to problems of technological waste. The best source of information about the limits-of-growth movement, in fact, consists of publications from Zero Population Growth.[38] Even more suggestive is the organizational base of some state activities. The first state group to focus sharply on population growth was the Michigan Population Council.[39] It was inaugurated by the Michigan branch of the American Association of University Women, which was joined by the Michigan umbrella organization of ZPG, the Mackinac Chapter of the Sierra Club, and the Michigan organization of sportsmen, the Michigan United Conservation Clubs. This range of interests leans more heavily toward the perspective of amenities as goals than the more limited view of a clean environment.

Second, it may be that the primary urban environment cannot readily give rise to a concern for the pressure of population growth and consumption upon the larger region and the nation. Urban people confine their definition of reality to the city and not far beyond. Extraurban and extratechnological experience of some sort seems essential to generate a basic concern for the limits of development. Many urban people seek out these experiences, using the countryside for their recreational activities, and it is from some of these that a concern for the limits of growth seems most likely to arise. Such a wider view is currently most rooted in people who in their own experience and activities face directly the adverse effect of the urban load and urban-rooted growth on the larger world.

VII

Several types of primary experience generate and sustain the view that there are limits to the growth of our population, our level of living, and our economy. Some of these involve a scarcity of commodities that we consider essential for a satisfactory material level of living. The shortage of petroleum for heating and fuel is the most dramatic current example. Usually material shortages do not translate themselves directly into perceived restrictions on human activities; they are more often than not obscured by their indirect effects. But heating and fuel shortages bear directly upon the daily lives of individuals and generate a sharp consciousness of limitation. The connection between the larger limits of resources and the limits of personal daily activities is close and well understood.

The impact of the energy shortage on popular thinking, however, is not at all clear yet. The public is not yet convinced that an energy shortage is really upon us and is inclined to believe that it is contrived, if not wholly at least in part, and that the limitations upon human activities it imposes are not permanent. Establishment experts argue that the shortage is only temporary and that several decades of intensive research and development will resolve it. In very few quarters is there held the view that the problem presents a permanent crisis of consumption and that we must scale down the pressure of our energy demands upon finite resources. Only a few environmental organizations seem to be willing to argue that serious attention should be given to the task of reducing energy demands. And few have been willing to give special attention to those facets of the economy that constitute highly intensive energy consumption such as air, automobile, and truck passenger travel and freight, so as to guide research and development into far less intensive modes of transport. This generates the notion that our level of energy consumption can keep on growing, or that there is some fat in consumption patterns that can make possible the necessary adjustments without many sacrifices and provide for selective energy growth.

Another type of experience that gives rise to notions about the limits to growth comes from the adverse environmental consequences of technology. This problem is the main thrust of the "environmental impact" statements. Although it is often easy to justify environmental degradation in these analyses on the grounds that the economic benefits outweigh the environmental costs, there are an increasing number of cases in which this is clearly not the case. Land and water manipulation in Florida has endangered the fresh water aquifer and thereby the water supplies of east coast Florida cities; engineering works to control sand dunes and offshore islands along the south Atlantic coast have become so expensive that the National Park Service has decided to let nature take its course and to adjust human activities to the limits of geological forces; flood plain occupancy, it is now realized, produces social costs far greater than the social benefits and, from a simple cost vantage point, must be restricted.

All these involve human occupancy and settlement and their impact on resources in such a way that the consequences, both immediate and more remote, are detrimental to society. In many cases these detrimental consequences are experienced solely in terms of general, unfocused, and indirect social costs, that is, general adverse consequences that render an environment undesirable. But in other cases a specific and focused social cost results, such as in the cases previously mentioned, in which one can balance direct costs with direct benefits. Thus, one can determine the relative cost over benefit of flood plain occupancy when the taxpayer is called upon to provide funds for flood victims for relief and reconstruction. When this is the case the issue becomes sharp and the environmental limits to human activities become clear. Most analyses of the environmental consequences of development, however, are not so striking and do not generate a sense of environmental limits.

At this point the most significant experience that generates a sense of the limits to growth comes from the development of new amenity values rather than from a desire for more material production and is closely connected with quality of space. The experience is rooted peculiarly among those individuals who prize quality of space. This can be observed historically as the concern for efficient development gave way to an interest in environmental amenities. The change is due partly to the desire to enjoy experiences beyond material goods, a change fostered particularly by the wider range of perspectives implicit in more years of education and by higher incomes that enable many Americans to go beyond material wants and purchase qualitative experiences.

The process of residential suburbanization and the search for leisure and recreational experiences in more natural surroundings reflect the desire to seek a higher quality of space, where natural forces are more in evidence than in the developed and congested areas of settlement. In both cases the initial search for quality of space soon becomes threatened by others who seek the same amenities. At some point the experience of "too many" begins to take shape, and the concept of the carrying capacity of the land, air, and water begins to form. This generates the belief that overuse can destroy the resource that one wishes to enjoy and leads to a sense of limits. While technology can expand material goods by extracting material resources from all quarters of the globe and deliver them to the consumer, it cannot expand the space of air, land, or water. If space is encroached upon by development there is less space as natural environment. At this point the serious question takes shape: what shall be the balance between developed and natural environment? If acceptable levels of the latter are to be maintained, then the former must be restricted. There are limits to growth.

The tendencies that lead to a concern for the limits to growth are long run and not temporary. They have arisen out of changing values and changing technological capacities for environmental manipulation, and they arise especially from increasing pressures and claims for use of the finite space of land, air, and water, pressures that do not diminish but grow more intense with time. The predominant pollution issues of the past decade have not yet brought this into focus. The upcoming preoccupation with land and land use is likely to raise these questions of competition for space far more sharply and to bring the question of the limits to growth to our attention more dramatically.

VALUE PREMISES FOR PLANNING AND PUBLIC POLICY

The Historical Context

CONVENTIONAL WISDOM WOULD SUGGEST that certain aspects of our government are relatively neutral in their value preferences. While the main political choices, we are told in our high school civics classes for example, are worked out in the legislature, administrative and judicial bodies merely administer and interpret the laws. These are carried out, so the implication runs, in an atmosphere not of value conflict but of disinterested judgment. As the images are elaborated further, not only governmental administration but planning as well take on the connotations of being scientific, objective, and without value preferences. These functions are carried out by the experts; their only qualifications are their detailed knowledge of the subject and, therefore, their ability to bring the capabilities of disinterested experts to bear on public problems.

One knows hardly where such views come from. There are a host of possible speculations. But the fact remains that a closer look, often carried out by academic observers, but also frequently expressed by participants in these affairs, reveals a persistent set of value choices even in the most objective and

From Richard N. L. Andrews, ed.; *Land in America* (Lexington, Mass., 1979), 149–166.

expert of governmental functions. Planning is one of these. What could be more neutral than merely to forecast the future and set forth the possible options for getting there? And yet we are all fully aware that any projection of the future is analyzed in terms of what we want for the future, that there is as wide a variety of options for the future as for the present, and that the choices in values in current public affairs spill over directly into the choices in values about the future.

It is often hard to ferret all this out. In planning there is a layer of empirical data, increasingly complex and beyond the comprehension of most citizens, manipulated by computers and displayed in terms of models often powerful as much by the force of their aesthetic elegance as by their appropriate descriptions of reality, and organized and presented with sufficient expertise so as to frighten away all but the initiated. Where are the values in all this? It is not too much to say that one of the major political tasks of the present day is to cut through this weight of expertise, to lay bare the value implications of planning so that the public can understand the choices that are being suggested and make intelligent decisions about them. One of the most pervasive political impulses of the world of expertise is to drive the context of decision-making underground, beyond the purview of the general public, by imbedding it in enormous and complicated detail that makes it all but impossible to grab hold of. Those who wish a more open system of decision-making have a challenging task of bringing to the fore the choices involved in the way a problem is defined, the selection of variables to be measured, the weights to be assigned to the variables, and the treatment of the unmeasurable.

I will provide some preliminary remarks about all this in the context of regional planning, doing so by focusing on the historical development of planning. The purpose will not be just to provide a background for present activities, but to enhance a sensitivity to the value assumptions in planning itself.

FOUR BASIC ASSUMPTIONS

Let me begin with my own assumptions.[1] There are four. First, planning is an aspect of the search for social control. Planning is not simply a disinterested hobby. It would not be undertaken were it not for the fact that someone, somewhere, wants the future to turn out in a way that it might not do so otherwise. It assumes that the normal course of events, let run with individual and institutional choices apart from those who plan, has implications that one does not approve. Perhaps the problem is one of certain values not being taken into account; the environmental impact statements under the National Environmental Policy Act (NEPA) require an "interdisciplinary" analysis of the impact of major federal actions, and the courts have interpreted this broadly, arguing that a wide variety of factors must be seriously considered. Or perhaps the problem is one of the short-run versus the long-run. An action may achieve one thing next year but damage the possibility of achieving something else ten years from now. Thus, planning is injected into the picture in order to bring about a different future, to control it. The heart of planning is the search for control. If we are to understand planning correctly as a historical phenomenon, we must understand the long-run development in the search for and practice of control over broad social forces.

Second, as a result of the drive for social control, planning is deeply bound up with values and goals. Few of us desire control just for the sake of control; we desire it for a purpose. Control is linked to ends and purposes, and the choices as to which ends and purposes we prefer are the factors that clearly define the social and political relevance of our search for control through planning. A variety of choices are involved in planning. There is, for example, the outline of the "system" for which one plans, the universe that one projects into the future, from which there is output and into which there is input. Is the focus on growth or stability; on enhancement of quality or quantity of life? What are the variables that are to be taken into account? In land use, do we give as strong a focus in our variables to degrees and types of natural lands as to developed lands, with a view to defining the problem as a proper balance between the two? What are the weights to given to the variables, and especially what weights are to be given to nonquantifiable variables? Perhaps our task is to work into the planning scheme variables that are not capable of being assigned quantities, such as the aesthetic quality of clean air and the capability of long-distance visibility. The value premises in planning can be observed rather readily by focusing on these choices in each major phase of the planning process.

Third, planning is not just a public or governmental activity. In fact, the initial planning in the United States was carried out by private corporations, and I think it would not be too far off to say that despite our common association of planning with governments, still today far more planning takes place within the private corporate realm than by government. Corporations are institutional systems of long-run social control. That is their primary function. The initial planning arose when corporations, because of their huge capital investments at stake, sought to predict the future—future markets, for example, and, as time went on, an increasingly extensive range of factors impinging on corporate decisions. When governments became involved in planning, they copied the steps already taken by private corporations, and with considerable interchange and remarkable similarity between the two. The larger the corporate system, the more it developed a fit in outlook with the larger governmental system. There are, of course, differences in objectives as between private and public planning agencies and yet there are many similarities. Both desire to develop control over the future through planning; often those futures have many features that are strikingly similar.

Finally, planning is never divorced from power. The aim of planning is not merely to carry out an interesting exercise, although many model builders do often emphasize the "elegance" and aesthetic qualities of their models rather than their larger consequences. Planning, for the most part, is closely related to institutional power. Those who wish to control the future wish not merely to know about it but also to have the capability of making it turn out the way they wish. Such capability is dependent primarily upon institutional power. Today the major sources of institutional power are private corporations and governments. Those who seek long-run social control inevitably attach themselves to one or another of these sets of institutions. It should be no wonder, as a result, that one of the perennial focal points of analysis in American growth and development is the degree to which private and public corporate institutions fuse in their search for social control and planning or come into competition. Whichever happens, the process of planning remains intimately bound up with the exercise of large-scale institutional power.

THE INCREASING SCALE OF HUMAN ORGANIZATION

So much for assumptions. Planning is an integral part of the value choices we make for control of the future, and it is intimately bound up with the development of power so as to implement that desire to control. How has all this evolved in twentieth century America, as our industrial, urban, administrative society has grown? I will focus primarily on observations that pinpoint changes in the value premises in planning and will focus on the urban and regional level.

Planning at the urban and regional level is intimately bound up with changes in the scale of social organization, one of the most persistent tendencies of modern society. Historical tendencies within the city and also within the region mark the replacement of smaller-scale activities by larger-scale ones, and the absorption of smaller institutions by larger. One can trace this in a variety of phenomena.

We speak of the nineteenth-century city as a pedestrian city, one in which work, home, and leisure activities were all within walking distance of each other.[2] With time, cheaper transportation in the form of the horsecar, the mechanically powered streetcar, and the automobile, and cheap communications in the form of the telephone, changed the scale over which human relationships were established. Even more striking, however, was the way in which the smaller context of life in the early city was dominated by neighborhood and community-scale institutions that, with time, gave way increasingly to larger-scale institutions. One can trace this in the shift from the artisan-craftsman working in downstairs rooms and living in the upstairs to the large factory that needed more space and moved from one outer perimeter of the city to another with each stage of urban growth. It can also be traced in the shift from the smaller consumer-focused retail neighborhood store to the supermarket and shopping center.

The increasing scale of life reorganized public functions on a larger and larger scale. In the mid-nineteenth century, the most striking instances were the fire and police systems.[3] Formerly organized at the ward and community level, these developed into citywide systems after 1850. Frequently, the key change involved the installation of new technology that required a citywide context; the neighborhood fire company could not finance the new pump and hook-and-ladder trucks or a telegraph system for fire and police communications that required a citywide coordinated network. New citywide fire and police administrations recruited personnel through tests for skill and training rather than on a community, friends-and-neighbors basis; they established centralized system control and replaced the community organization of these services.

Similar changes took place in welfare, health, and education. Prior to the mid-nineteenth century, welfare activities took place often at the community or ward level. In Pittsburgh, for example, local aldermen, who were petty judicial officials, became involved in a wide variety of community social problems. Often they dealt in a very personal way with intrafamily or interfamily affairs, such as altercations between husband and wife or between neighbors. They became involved in problems of child neglect and the conditions of widows and orphans. Gradually, over the years, these problems were treated by institutions at a larger level of social organization as first private groups and then governmental agencies developed a variety of welfare programs.[4]

Education underwent the most dramatic change. In the mid-nineteenth century, the focus of education was the elementary ward school. By the end of the century, major steps were underway to replace this with a citywide system of administration. The initial step came with the establishment of the high school, usually one for the entire city and often called Central High School. While elementary schools remained under the control of ward elected officials, the high school was administered by the citywide board and helped to establish a citywide focus to educational administration. Gradually this expanded, invading the autonomy of the ward elementary school and bringing about an extensive abandonment of the ward school system in favor of centralization.[5]

Changes such as these brought about a similar shift in general urban government in which earlier ward systems of representation were replaced with citywide representation. Formerly, each ward had its own member on city council where councilmen spoke for the communities that had elected them. By the early twentieth century, a shift was well under way toward councils composed of representatives elected citywide to represent the entire city. Not every city went that route completely. Some retained ward representation, but with larger ward units; others combined at-large and ward representation. The city of Pittsburgh, in 1911, went completely from a ward to a citywide system.[6]

These, then, are some of the details in a long-range urban process in which large-scale activities and large-scale administration over a persistently wider geographical area replaced a smaller scale of organization. The details as to why this all came about have not been very well worked out. Yet one aspect of it seems clear. Those who sought to organize government over a large scale were people who had already been active in a similar large-scale organization of private affairs. Two such groups were businessmen and professionals. Businessmen involved had been active in efforts to increase the scale of activities over which business was organized. Professionals, such as doctors, lawyers, architects, and educators utilized large-scale perspectives rather than smaller-scale and more "parochial" points of view. A doctor concerned with the control of disease had a universal perspective; he was concerned with disease not just in a particular ward, but in the entire city. The increasing empirical bent of the professions generated a universalist system of analysis; this gave rise to a similarly universalist preference in administration—and in planning.

These same processes of social change, from small-scale to large-scale contexts of organization in economic and political affairs, took place in rural as well as urban areas. Here activities carried on at the township and community level became reorganized into larger countywide and statewide systems. Changes in the organization of schools and roads in the twentieth century are two examples. Schools, formerly operated at the township level under the jurisdiction of township trustees, went through reorganizations both in administration and in physical facilities. Roads, also formerly supervised by local officials, had been conceived of as servicing the rural community, linking farm and church and store and market, constituting a means of relating people on a small scale. In the twentieth century this gave way to a state highway system, operated under a state commission, with power of eminent domain, which constructed a state system of hard surfaced roads that linked cities over wide geographical areas. A statewide system of transportation had replaced a local one.

In both these cases, schools and roads, the historical process was one of initiative taken by cities to reorder the affairs of a larger region and of an entire state. The drive for "good roads" and for state highway administrations came from cities that wished to have more rapid transportation to other cities and for whom the more traditional jurisdictions over roads constituted a barrier to larger-scale action. The state highway commission and eminent domain constituted the instruments of political power through which they achieved their objectives. Changes in school administration were urban inspired. Advanced ideas as to what constituted improvements in teaching and curricula came from the urban areas, as did the notion that larger tax bases were essential in order to provide funds for educational innovations. They favored larger-scale administration and management and gradually, over the years, succeeded in imposing their ideas upon a more reluctant countryside.

The development of planning must be understood within this context of the shift from smaller to larger scale. Amid this process of change, planners associated themselves with those who sought to increase the scale of institutional development. Planning has almost invariably involved the assertion that better action on a wide variety of fronts required larger systems of administration and control. As the city replaced the ward as the context of action, the focus of change moved to the larger metropolitan area and a drive arose for countywide planning and later multicounty. Planning has not been associated, on the other hand, with the drive to create smaller units of human activity, to reduce the scale of human relationships, or to decentralize the patterns of human interaction. The values in planning have been associated with the politics of overcoming the resistance of smaller-scale institutions to the drive for larger-scale organization and action. Planning has supported the sociological analyses common to the proponents of larger-scale systems, which assert the wisdom of the larger system and seek to understand the "irrationalities" of opposition to it.[7] Within a mode of thought such as this, the larger-scale system is considered to be "rational" and implicitly valid, while opposition is understood in terms of nonrational or "emotional" factors.

One remaining facet of the change remains to be described. We can well consider the drive for large-scale systems as a broad, historical force in American society that is innovative or radical. Those in business, in government, and the professions who have provided the impulse toward larger-scale affairs, have wrought wholesale changes in American social, economic, and political life. They have constituted a revolutionary force in American society. Those who have resisted these changes and who have asserted the validity of past ways and past smaller-scale forms of social organization have been the conservatives, the defenders of tradition. American history is a constant series of struggles between such radicals and conservatives, and amid this planners have associated themselves with those bringing about innovations. They have played an important role in the twentieth century effort to make such radical change respectable and to discredit the conservative defense of smaller-scale life.

CHANGES IN SOCIAL VALUES

Planning today, then, must be understood in terms of the historical tension between larger-scale and smaller-scale contexts of life. It must also be understood in terms of changes in social values, and especially the emerging values of environmental quality and their tension with development values.

Planning first emerged, in both private industry and government, as part of a drive for greater efficiency in development. It constituted an effort to avoid the wastefulness of short-run decisions and to enhance efficiency in the use of resources, natural and human, for development purposes.[8] It focused on long-run processes and the need to adjust current action to long-run goals. The typical planning document has been one that predicts the future in terms of growth of some social force, such as population or employable people, and then predicts the level of activity that is needed in order to provide for such matters as employment or social services. The entire process was geared to economic development and the development of public services in such a way as to bring them about in a more orderly and efficient manner. Such an approach, it should be emphasized, did not question the values of growth in material development or in social services but was tied merely to the question of how they were to be achieved—in terms of long-run plans rather than short-run pressures.

In more recent years, however, a new set of values has emerged to challenge development values. These are embodied in the new phrase "environmental quality." The precise meaning of this is not always clear. But it does involve two ideas: first, there is a new dimension to the constant search for a better standard of living, which people describe as qualitative rather than in terms of material goods, and second, that a major element of this quality in standard of living is environmental, that is, the surroundings at home, work, or play, which can either make life more pleasant or more degraded. This drive for improvement of the quality of one's environment is symbolized by such institutions as the Council on Environmental Quality.[9]

It might be well to emphasize environmental quality values as part of larger historical tendencies with which they are associated. They did not emerge full-blown in the late 1960s to form the "environmental movement." On the contrary, they represent some historic changes in social values that have grown over the years and that have appeared in many and varied forms, including, but not limited to, environmental quality. One aspect of the drive is the constant tendency toward smaller families as material standards of living rise. This is a choice for quality instead of quantity, a choice that scarce family income will go not toward providing a minimal standard of living for more children, but a higher quality of life for fewer children. Another is the drive toward the suburbs, a process that has gone on in our cities for several centuries. That drive constitutes a search for quality of living space, for more space within the house so that individuals might have more privacy, and more space outside the house. The street life of the urban community, with its constant press of people and noise and dirt was unacceptable to many people who sought a higher degree of personal privacy, more space, and quieter conditions in more "natural" circumstances.[10]

These values have brought new considerations into the analysis of the past, present, and future of human communities, which differ markedly from those implicit in development and development planning. What is space to be used for? For intensive development alone, or for the amenities of undeveloped lands? Should air, water, and land be used for waste disposal, as a receptacle in which the wastes of our urban-industrial society are thrown, or should it be used to improve the quality of life and standard of living? These values, in turn, have come into conflict with development. It is no longer an issue of whether or not growth will be more efficient, as was the thrust of the conservation movement in the early twentieth century, but of whether or not environmental values will be maximized in balance with material development. Heretofore, the major issues have been over the efficiency of development and delivery of services. But now the issue is changed as considerations of environmental quality cannot be absorbed into new twists to development, but act so as to compromise development in the first place.

A distinction should be made in order to clarify the historical process, one between environmental effects and environmental goals. Analysis in terms of environmental effects is the framework of the environmental impact statements required by the National Environmental Policy Act of 1969 and some thirteen state environmental impact analysis programs.[11] The focus is on the conditions surrounding development. What is its environmental impact? This must be analyzed in a broad fashion, in the federal law in terms of an "interdisciplinary analysis," and alternative types of development must be set forth. Such an approach does not deal with environmental goals directly, but only tangentially, as implicit but unspecified elements in the impact analysis. This is only a halfway step toward the consideration of environmental goals. Full recognition of such goals would require that they be planned for on a coordinated basis with development goals. For the most part, this is not yet done. There is some statewide planning in terms of identifying, measuring, and establishing environmental goals. There are qualitative standards set forth as objectives in air and water laws. And in one state there is a requirement for open-space planning. Thus, we are in the midst of a historical process, a struggle for policymakers to give new values full consideration as goals and not to consider them only as derivative by-products of development.[12]

The new environmental thrust has had an extensive impact on planning as the values of environmental quality have been brought into the planning process. In the past, planning has been linked closely with development values. It is still very common to find planning and development carried out by the same commission, for example, in the area of the Appalachian Regional Commission.[13] Even if the two are separated, the major theme of planning still remains that of how best to accommodate development smoothly. Predictions of growth, of population, of economic activities, constitute the needs, the givens, the natural imperatives of the social order, and planning is tied up with the way in which it can be done more smoothly.

But clearly, the environmental quality emphasis is creating a change in mood. Almost every environmental issue is a very specific instance of a larger planning controversy between growth and quality, and these issues have not been ignored by the planning community. The historical sequence of planning documents reflects the gradual entrance of matters of environmental quality, especially in terms of open space. Land use plans financed now by federal funds are very different from earlier documents.[14] While not all county planning, or even most, has moved in this direction, a number have. Some of the most effective land use plans in terms of environmental quality goals are undertaken by private rather than public agencies.[15] And planning for air and water quality implications of land use, although fostered by recent federal air and water laws, has barely got off the ground.[16] We are in the midst of a long-run process worth watchdogging in some detail, for it involves the way in which deep-seated changes in values become institutionalized in the planning process.

One of the most significant aspects of these changes consists of the way in which problems are defined for description and analysis. Environmental quality values have given rise to many new ways of looking at the world and have opened up a wide range of new phenomena to be examined, measured, and described. The impact on planning is to create new choices in problem definition, description of variables, and weights to be attached to them when selecting goals to which to apply scarce resources. There are a number of these new perspectives; they illustrate the way in which planning may or may not respond to new values. There is, for example, the concept of the desirability of an appropriate balance between developed and undeveloped land areas. Howard and Eugene Odum have argued for this approach. In a land use model for the state of Georgia, an attempt was made to determine the percentage of acreage that should remain undeveloped in order to provide the necessary biological processes to accommodate and sustain development on the remainder.[17] Or there is the concept of irreversibility and the analysis of development in terms of the degree to which it involves reversibility—"open option" land—or irreversibility. Energy analysis has taken many new forms. There is the concept of net energy, that we must measure energy production not in gross terms but in terms of the balance between the energy output and the energy required to produce that output.[18] The implication is that one should not produce energy if the energy cost, that is, the energy required to produce it, is more than that produced. It may well take more energy to mine coal in Montana and ship it to Cleveland to burn in generating electric power than is represented by the resulting electricity. Or there is the concept of embodied energy, that every product represents a certain amount of energy required to produce it from raw material to finished product, and that products should be described in terms of embodied energy so that consumers could make choices with respect to energy consumption. Or there is the concept of energy productivity, that is, of the amount of product, of GNP, that is created by a given amount of energy. Until 1966, the energy cost of our GNP had gone down steadily, but since then it has gone up.[19]

A systems analysis of the natural water cycle is increasingly used that emphasizes the effect of upstream paving on percolation, water table replenishment, and downstream flooding, or the effect of large-scale sewage transfer of water and channelization on acquifer replenishment.[20] A new form of population analysis emphasizes that, in terms of human pressure on resources rather than mere numbers per square mile, the United States is one of the most densely populated areas of the world and India one of the least densely populated.[21] Or there is the new analysis of urban diseconomies, the added costs that come with population growth. One such approach indicates that up until about 100,000 population the per capita cost of running a city declines, and after that it rises.[22] Each of these approaches constitutes a new mode of analysis with reference to the relationship between people and their environment. Each involves a choice as how one defines a social problem. And each one leads to choices about variables, about the weight given to particular variables, and often to nonquantifiable variables. The National Environmental Policy Act of 1969 stressed the need to emphasize these variables and especially those customarily not quantified. This is a particular institutional expression of the desire to expand the range of planning to values not normally taken into account.

New environmental quality values have had considerable impact upon planning, but the full range of the impact is yet to be seen. While one can observe that in the historical tension between larger and smaller scale in human context, planning has persistently been associated with the former rather than the latter, one can also observe that planning has been receptive to emerging environmental quality values. In the future it may well stand effectively in the middle between development and quality values and mediate between them.

STATEWIDE ENVIRONMENTAL PLANNING AND MANAGEMENT

These two historical processes with which planning has been intimately associated have converged to focus on statewide environmental planning and management. This constitutes a separate phenomenon, and its development provides a third useful context through which to examine the value premises of planning.

Environmental concerns and programs have brought a new emphasis to state planning. A wide range of values connected with the use of land, air and water, growing out of federal programs in these fields, is generating new plans and management capabilities at the state level. This has developed in a particular political context in which state environmental planning has been associated with the peculiar environmental concerns of urban areas and has given rise to a planning process that often implies the manipulation of the rural community to achieve the environmental goals of the city. The state environmental planning process has become the city and metropolitan planning process writ large, representing a stage in historical development in which urban and state concerns become almost synonomous. Thus, state environmental planning does not express primarily the protection of the environmental quality of rural, less developed areas against the environmental loads of the city, but, in fact, serves as an instrument of the urban environmental thrust—often to the disadvantage of the countryside.

Statewide planning has constituted a persistent phenomenon in the twentieth century. Earlier I mentioned highway planning, which began prior to World War I; that was an important early instance. Other cases developed over the years, such as the state police and the state park systems, both of which evolved in the years prior to World War II. But here I am interested in the new phase of state administration and planning that environmental concerns have brought about. Federal air and water programs have relied upon states as the instruments of enforcement of federal standards. A major aim of these programs has been to generate state capabilities to gather data and supervise action. A federal land use program would develop a similar approach for land, and land use implications of air and water laws, yet to be developed fully, would do likewise. All this has given rise to statewide rather than merely citywide or metropolitan programs and planning and thus has enhanced a statewide context of thought, planning, and action.

This may seem obvious enough. But its larger political context requires closer attention. It relates not simply to the growth of statewide planning, but to the use of such planning by cities to transfer many of their environmental problems to the countryside. The state has become not merely an instrument by which cities develop programs to improve their own environment. It is often a means whereby cities mitigate those problems by utilizing the countryside to absorb some of the environmental degradation created by their high levels of resource pressure.

The siting of energy facilities provides a dramatic illustration. On the surface, energy facility siting involves simply the desire of energy companies to locate a power plant, onshore installations connected with offshore drilling or oil importation, or energy parks. These proposed installations have met intense opposition throughout the nation. In some cases they threaten to disrupt long-standing rural and small town communities; in others they interfere with the amenities of summer and vacation homes and recreational activities. In such instances energy companies have attempted to use states and the power of state governments to enforce siting through state programs that override local veto power. When this has been slow to achieve, demands are made that the federal government obtain the power to override state opposition to siting. And this, in turn, leads to land use planning proposals, supported by energy companies, in order to provide areas for new generating capacity, very similar to the way in which industrial promoters seek county planning in order to carve out land for industrial sites.

The political context of energy siting constitutes more than merely the initiative from utilities. It represents the city reaching out to the larger region to use it for its own purposes. Urban consumers demand great amounts of energy. Why not develop energy industries in the city or on its periphery? Cities don't want them there. They create too much air pollution, as in Los Angeles, and as a result utilities move to the Four Corners area. Or they are too risky, as in the case of nuclear power installations, which recent court decisions require be located some distance from urban centers. Or they produce other environmental results that cities don't want. So rural areas become prime "sacrifice areas" for large-scale installations to provide energy for cities. Out of this emerges a pattern of political relationships in which urban areas of the nation favor such energy development and rural areas, which are called upon to accept the brunt of environment impact, are opposed. Rural areas resist being used by the city for its own economic growth and development.

The case of energy installation is only part of a larger context of relationships between city and country involving the use of air, water, and land "out there." One such traditional issue is the use of flood storage reservoirs in which rural land is acquired, by eminent domain power, for the protection of cities against flood damage; it would be quite possible to prevent flood damage by controlling settlement patterns of the city without using rural land. Or other examples: the use of solid waste disposal sites for urban solid waste in the countryside rather then recycling; the removal of industrial plants to areas of cleaner air, permitting air deterioration there; the creation of water pollution through urban-based demands for coal mining without sufficient control of environmental effects. In all such instances, the major context of political controversy involves a more highly developed area preferring not to absorb the cost of environmental impact itself, instead seeking to export that cost elsewhere.

Where does state planning fit into all this? The use of the countryside by the city has historically been one of the major sources of increasing state functions. Cities inevitably wish to utilize land, commodity resources, air and water that are beyond its borders, and such use has given rise to resistance within the countryside. At each such step the city has called upon the state for the power to make possible the use of the countryside because it is the most accessible governmental jurisdiction through which the city can realize its objectives. In the nineteenth century, a host of right-of-way issues concerning plank roads and toll bridges and, later, railroads involved this kind of struggle. The development of twentieth century highways continued the pattern. And now the same pattern is involved in environmental controversy. Large-scale developers seek large-scale units of authority and power in order to override local units. Planning becomes a matter of alternatives within the state as a whole, and choices are made within the statewide universe of planning.

The rural community becomes the source of opposition to this planning because it is forced to modify its land use practices and programs to satisfy external demands. That community seeks to defend past ways, customary institutions, and urges that the more radical and far-reaching transformations of the wider society be checked so as to protect the values of the local community. There is opposition to becoming a "sacrifice area" and cynicism about the attempt to make large-scale development more palatable by describing them in more appealing terms such as "energy parks." Thus, there is organized reaction in Montana and Wyoming to strip mining, in New Hampshire to on-shore facilities for oil importation, and in Pennsylvania to energy parks.[23] All are protective in tone, and all seek to maintain established ways of life against disruption.

In this political stance, the rural community is reinforced in its opposition by urbanites who seek to enhance environmental quality values similar to those desired by people in the countryside. Many of these have second homes in the countryside, purchased specifically to secure the environmental values they find missing in the cities.[24] Others are vacationers there or use the countryside for its environmental qualities of cleaner air and water and more open and natural land than they find in the cities. They constitute an urban-based political force in support of those rural groups who seek to protect the same values in the less developed regions; they become a force seeking to restrain the urban-based demands upon rural areas. A considerable portion of the urban environmental movement represents this particular political thrust.

There is implicit in these issues a new form of cost analysis involving the external costs imposed by cities. We have become familiar with the argument that industries should internalize the external costs that their pollution imposes on the community. A similar argument could be made about urban-based environmental pressures. The city is a "growth machine" that imposes burdens on the wider environment beyond the city that appear in the form of costs.[25] Should not these costs be absorbed by the city? If urban dwellers are responsible for the environmental load on the country, should not they pay the cost of recycling their solid waste, locating energy facilities near cities, or fully recycle their water?

To what extent has state environmental planning been capable of expressing the values of environmental quality that these forces in the countryside are espousing? This is one of the most interesting aspects of both the politics of environmental quality and the value-role of planners. Planning to protect environmental quality values has moved forward more in specialized cases than in a comprehensive fashion. Areas of traditional special environmental values, such as the Adirondacks in New York, have been the most important vehicles for their support and expression.[26] New concerns, such as scenic rivers, as well as the interest in natural areas, have provided other vehicles. In some states, wild area and wilderness area programs do likewise. But these do not touch the broad-based problem of environmental quality in the rural countryside, and the values that cleaner air and water and more open space represent for people living there.

It seems that the "no significant deterioration" clauses of the federal clean air and clean water laws will provide one of the first opportunities for general policy formulation with respect to such matters. The land use implications of both provisions are clear and enormous. By and large, state planners have not rushed to take up the no significant deterioration aspects of either federal program; the Environmental Protection Agency has been even more reluctant. The role of planners in these programs will provide another opportunity to observe the relationship between planning and emerging social values in twentieth century America.

CONCLUSION

An analysis of the values inherent in planning focuses on a set of long-run historical circumstances. There is an emerging set of values and preferences amid the public at large, growing slowly but having the force of long-run cultural change, that is producing deep-seated changes in how problems are defined, what is observed, and what is described and analyzed. But this is taking place within an equally important historical context of increasing scale as the institutional framework of analysis and action. Planning, therefore, now faces the possibility of utilizing the instruments of large-scale manipulation in order to give expression to emerging values that inevitably are defined in terms of the quality of life in the community. Drives to maintain ecological integrity and to enhance environmental quality draw the context of action back to a smaller level of human life and scale. The open-space community in the metropolitan area and the natural environment community in the wider countryside join in giving emphasis to the quality of life in daily human living. This is the current drama in the role of values in regional planning.

PUBLIC VALUES
AND MANAGEMENT
RESPONSE

Since many of us "furriners" here are seeking to establish our western credentials, perhaps it is not inappropriate for me to add several items of my own personal history. My initial exposure to natural resource problems came during the 1940s when I worked for two and a half years for the Oregon and California Revested Lands Administration doing general forestry work. The most exciting part of that experience was a three-month stint devoted exclusively to sharpening jackhammer bits! A few years later my first research paper in graduate school was on the Taylor Grazing Act and its historical background. All this led to my later book, *Conservation and the Gospel of Efficiency,* and a long-time interest in western land matters. It also led to some notions about the kind of historical perspective which might be helpful in understanding these matters. Perhaps it would be useful at the outset to outline two elements of that perspective as I will try to apply it to the subject of this workshop.

First is the changing demography and value context of American society.

From Sally Fairfax, ed., *Developing Strategies for Rangeland Management* (Boulder, Colo., 1984), 1812–44.

Particularly important in this session are those changes which have taken place since World War II. What we generally describe as an "advanced industrial society" has marked America now for several decades and those value changes are not irrelevant to the public demands which impinge on public land management. I want to follow out some elements of inquiry about that side of the problem. The second perspective concerns management, the historical evolution of that complex of technical professionals—scientists, economists, planners, engineers and administrators—who are brought together in both private and public management. These are also to be understood as particular and distinctive influences, involving people with distinctive values and preferences. Much of the drama of use of public domain involves the interaction between these two social forces—public values on the one hand and managers on the other.

The paper by Ingram and McCool on management information systems and the BLM is cast in that context. With most of its analysis I agree. It highlights the tension between directions in management on the one hand and directions in public values on the other but within the terminology of the tension between scientific information and politics. It stresses both the possibilities of information for management and the limitations, the roadblocks which it entails for effective coping with value conflicts. My comments here will not repeat those arguments, since I don't believe that it would be of much aid to add elaboration and detail. Instead I would like to expand further on the larger context of the values implicit in that tension. For while Ingram and McCool have spelled out the more immediate context, their analysis could be made more effective, I think, by exploring the broader roots of the contending impulses arising from the two different quarters—public values and management. I think that my own contribution here can be more useful by taking this more undeveloped side of their argument and giving it more substance.

A simple scheme of analysis might be outlined at the start. Most of the papers for this workshop, and in particular the Ingram-McCool paper, focus on the immediate face-to-face relationship between management and the public, between the agency and its "clientele." Most of the existing writing on these matters is similarly focused, for example, the very recent book by Paul Culhane on the U.S. Forest Service and the Bureau of Land Management.[1] Here I would like to extend that focus out into another concentric circle beyond this immediate face-to-face setting. On the public side it extends from the direct interaction with organized groups to the larger realm of public values out of which public action arises. And on the management side it extends from management techniques to the distinctive values and perceptions of managers—their peculiar personalities, training, and professional experiences—which cause them to look at the world, including their management world, in one way instead of another. Much of the conflict, as Ingram and McCool put it, between science and politics, cannot be understood unless we go beyond the immediate face-to-face interaction to this larger realm of values, coming from very different directions and which become "engaged" in concrete cases.

My discussion will focus, then, on this larger realm of values. If one wants to end up with "advice to the agency" as we have been admonished to do, then the relevance of my comments will be to urge that BLM develop a capability to be more sensitive to the changes in larger public values surrounding it so as to reduce the adverse impact of unexpected demands which arise from those changes, and to the rigidities of thought and behavior which stem from its own professional and technical value commitments so as to be more flexible in responding to those external changes.

I

The Bureau of Land Management is confronted with many new users and uses; that is the overriding theme of post–World War II BLM history. There are two types of these, new commodity users on the one hand, involving energy and mineral companies, and environmental users on the other. The first is relatively easy to comprehend as an extension of previous user impulses; new commodity users do not behave very differently from older ones. But the new environmental users are more difficult to understand because they represent rather new types of uses and hence demands upon the public lands which differ markedly from more traditional values associated with the development of material commodities. Since they are more difficult to grasp they need to be outlined more fully. The demands they place upon managers involve far more than simply the protection of material resources to sustain their productivity into the future; they involve natural environment uses which compete with claims for more traditional material production.

Within the past few decades BLM lands have taken on new meaning to the American people as lands which are valuable in their more natural and less developed state as natural environment lands. This change can be observed in the transition from the 1964 Wilderness Act to the wilderness provisions in the 1976 Federal Land Policy and Management Act. So far as I can determine there was little if any thought in the debate over the 1964 Act that BLM lands had any wilderness potential at all.[2] Neither wilderness advocates nor public land managers nor legislators included western dry lands in their concepts about what was wilderness. And this also appears in the material produced by wilderness advocates which reflects their values. Consider, for example, articles in *The Living Wilderness*, the magazine of the Wilderness Society, or the stamps which they produced for sale and distribution; images of drylands wilderness are few and far between. By 1976, however, times had changed. There was now a mandate for study which assumed that if one looked one could find wilderness areas on BLM lands.

What this simple contrast makes clear is that the meaning of wilderness, and of natural environment resources generally, is not a fixed matter, but a changing one, evolving as values within American society change. And it is especially interesting to try to chart the evolving attitudes of the American people toward western drylands and deserts. One of the first cases of such positive attitudes is *Arizona Highways*, a publication which from the 1930s on brought the message of the beauty of the west, the drylands west, home to a small but growing number of Americans. Perhaps the major medium in the changing attitude toward western drylands was photography and especially color photography.[3] It drew an increasing number of people to travel through the drylands west and led to the communication of their experience to friends by means of color photography all of which added to the message from color television.[4] By the time that the BLM in 1976 commissioned a study of American attitudes toward the southern California desert by the Gallup Organization, over half of the sample felt that they knew enough about the western desert so that they wished to respond to questions about how it should be managed.[5] The majority of respondents preferred natural environment management to development or vehicular use. The desert had changed in the values of Americans from a place dangerous and forbidding to one of beauty, of aesthetic qualities and environmental amenities.

This change in attitudes toward the western public lands is part of a change in American attitudes toward many different types of natural environment lands, formerly thought of as relatively "useless" but now thought of as valuable in their natural condition. First were mountain tops and alpine lakes; then mountainous old-growth forested areas; then undeveloped rivers; then wetlands, pine barrens, and southern swamps. All had been bypassed in the course of American expansion because they were "lands which nobody wanted."[6] But over the course of time their meaning changed to "lands which many people wanted," and much of that new interest came from their now being valued as natural lands.[7] Hence we have a host of environmental programs geared to identifying and classifying these lands, acquiring them in public ownership, and managing them as natural environment areas. These new values attached to BLM lands came fairly late in the transformation of attitudes toward natural environments, and what came to the National Forests three decades ago is now upon us for the "public domain."

We should note several aspects of these changes in order to establish a workable perspective about them. They are, first of all, part of larger changes in American values for which there are roots prior to World War II, but which burst upon the entire society in a massive way after the War. They can be thought of as expanding the role and importance of amenities as consumer goods and services. They are part of the growth and elaboration of the American standard of living, of the increase in personal and social income to the extent that a larger share of it can be allocated to goods and services beyond necessities and conveniences. That "beyond" can be described in various ways. From the income side economists speak of "discretionary income." From the consumption side it is often described as "amenity." We can think of it as a new stage in the history of American consumption. For many years, perhaps as late as 1900, the dominant focus of American consumption was on necessities; most production was devoted to that demand. Then in the 1920s the age of conveniences came upon us, represented by the mass consumer industries, the automobile, the household appliances, which made it possible to perform "necessary" tasks with less time and effort. By 1950, for many—not all by any means—Americans these wants of necessities and conveniences had been relatively filled and they turned their consumption to new directions. There was now time for leisure and recreation; new household items such as hi-fi sets could be purchased; and many necessities and conveniences developed major aesthetic and amenity components.

Natural environments are a significant part of these new wants and desires. They constitute a new consumer item that represents part of a higher standard of living in an advanced industrial society. We should emphasize especially that they do not reflect, as so many would like to argue, a throwback to the primitive, a desire to return to a less "civilized" past. On the contrary, they reflect a desire to move ahead to a more abundant future, a new choice as to what an advanced standard of living entails, in which there is as much preference for the new material products of the advanced economy as well as its natural environments. We should also emphasize that these changes are not peculiar to the United States, but represent transformations in values and preferences in advanced industrial societies throughout the world, from central and western Europe to eastern Asia.[8] The way in which those values work out varies, nation by nation, because of their differing environmental context, but the values themselves seem to be associated with higher standards of living throughout the world.

We should also emphasize that the private economy has long recognized these changes in values and has incorporated them into their market and production strategies. Since the 1920s, when mass production industry first developed a major interest in mass consumption, it has kept a close eye on changing American values. It pioneered in "survey techniques" to study attitudes primarily because it was interested in identifying markets for its products. It watched the growth of amenity values and for those which constituted a market for salable products in the private market it set about to fill this new demand. Environmental amenities, for example, constitute a major element in buying and selling real estate, as studies of the way in which land and homes are described in real estate advertisements makes clear.[9] But many environmental amenity wants in matters of cleaner air, cleaner water, less noise, and more open landscapes are part of the "commons" and cannot be packaged for private sale. And this brings the supply and demand of environmental amenities out of the private economy into such aspects of the public economy as the public lands. What is surprising is the resistance to considering amenities as a legitimate subject for public policy action. A new "real world" which has been well recognized in the private market for over a half-century has not yet been legitimized in the public economy.

The significance of these changes became rather clear with the completion of the 1980 census. Initial analysis of population changes emphasized the shifts from the North and East to the South and West. But then a further, more disaggregate analysis was made by Professor Ronald Briggs of the University of Texas using county-level data, and a much different picture emerged.[10] There were major population shifts within the North, within the South, and within the West. Some areas grew while others declined; some grew rapidly and others slowly. These shifts within regions, examined on a county-by-county basis, cannot be understood through broad regional variations, but through more precise and more local variations. The pattern of population change seems to be most closely associated with environmental amenities. "The story of the seventies," so the authors conclude, "appears to be the amenity-rich versus the amenity-poor ... not Sunbelt versus Frostbelt."[11] As one traces these changes in the 1970s back into the past their roots can be identified in the 1950s and the 1960s. These, then, are the demographic consequences of the changes in American values which place increasing emphasis on the desirability of natural environments.

There is also a distinctive regional component to these changes which is more peculiar to the BLM setting. One can sort out different states and regions in the United States in the degree to which they participate in these value changes. Change does not take place in the same degree uniformly throughout the nation. There are leading states and there are lagging states; we can identify those which are in the forefront of innovations in valuing natural environments and those which lag behind.[12] The leading sectors include New England, New York and New Jersey, the upper Great Lakes, Florida, the Rocky Mountain States, the Pacific Coast States, and Alaska. The lagging sectors include the Gulf Deep South and the Wheat Belt from the Dakotas through Oklahoma. The "factory belt" of the North, and especially the four states from Illinois through Pennsylvania rank in the middle, distinctively low in their display of environmental values in view of their higher rank in urbanization and education. Environmental values are particularly strong in the West. Several attitude studies about natural environments sort out regional variations. They indicate that attitudes favorable to wilderness and wildlife are distinctively high in the Rocky Mountain and Pacific Coast states and Alaska.

The Rocky Mountain case is important to stress since our image of the attitudes in those eight states is often otherwise. A study by Yankelovich, Skelly, and White, sponsored by the Western Regional Council, indicates that outdoor recreation participation rates are higher in the Rocky Mountain Region than in others; people in that region are better informed about wilderness management; and their attitudes toward wilderness are more positive.[13] All this is underlined by a more localized poll conducted in 1978 by the Caspar (Wyoming) *Star-Tribune* which indicated that of those polled 75 percent used wilderness areas for recreation.[14] Another study by Stephen Kellert of Yale on attitudes toward wildlife found that in a trade-off question between wildlife and development in wilderness areas, the strongest wildlife attitudes were in Alaska, followed closely by the Pacific Coast states and the Rocky Mountain region, with areas in the East much further behind.[15] These comparatively strong environmental values in the Rocky Mountain region can be observed also through the significant amount of organized environmental activity there, often, in proportion to population, greater than in other states usually thought to be hotbeds of environmental action.[16]

The distinctive aspect of the Rocky Mountain region is not the dominance of developmental concerns, as conventional wisdom would have it, but the intensity of controversy between environmental and developmental objectives. In the past 20 years this region has witnessed the distinctive rise of both public environmental values and developmental activities, primarily in energy and extractive industries. Both have occurred at the same time, giving rise to heightened conflicts between them. Developmental institutions have been increasingly vocal, such as in the Sagebrush Rebellion, but the extent of their vocalness is a measure not so much of their strength but of their weakness. Developmentalists well know the strength of the indigenous environmental viewpoint within the Rocky Mountain West, and their "rebellion" is an attempt to overcome that strength by promoting a developmental ideology as *the* region's indigenous ideology and arguing that the environmental ideology is imported from elsewhere—the East and the Pacific Coast. We must not take their description of the Rocky Mountain area as accurate, but must reconstruct the political controversies within the region from other, more reliable evidence about values and behavior. When we do that we focus sharply on the intensity of the conflict between divergent but indigenous regional forces.

It is also well to point out that much of the environmental activity within the Rocky Mountain region takes on the character of regional defense against external developmental institutions, which differs from the developmentalist ideological effort to identify forces in contention in the opposite way. Over the past decade a considerable amount of environmental activity in the region has constituted a reaction against development that is too rapid or too monolithic, that does not distinguish between where development should take place and where it should not, and how rapidly it should proceed. Hence there has been an evolving cooperation between environmentalists and ranchers over strip mining, water supply, and the MX missile; moves to establish industrial siting laws, severance taxes, and in-stream flow regulation; and efforts to protect air quality against degradation.[17] Even more striking is the degree to which the initial response to oil and gas exploration and drilling in valuable natural environment areas has been so strong from within the area itself. The drive to prevent seismic exploration in the Bob Marshall Wilderness is being led by Representative Pat Williams from the western district of Montana,[18] and that to prevent drilling in Cache Creek in the Bridger-Teton National Forest by the Jackson Hole Alliance with support from Wyoming's congressional delegation.[19]

All this merely fleshes out the new setting of evolving values within the nation and the region which establishes the context within which the BLM makes choices. It constitutes the setting from which challenges to its decisions come to the courts as those courts give expression to new values which administrative agencies resist. This is the realm of that larger concentric circle which the agency will have to assess not just by direct communications from active clientele groups but by developing the ability to look beyond that immediate face-to-face context to the larger changes in values within the region itself. If the agency does not want to get caught up short, for example in litigation, it might be advised to go beyond the immediate issues to the larger set of political forces, assess where they are apt to go, and then seek to get out in front of them in order to enhance the continued integrity and smoothness of its agency development. But I will come back to that.

For the moment let me suggest several features of these evolving values within the Rocky Mountain West which are worth keeping in mind. One is the degree to which the organization and political expression of environmental values has become increasingly local. A host of organizations have arisen in the region within the last decade which were not there before and which emphasize state affairs—ranging from the Southwest Resource and Information Center in New Mexico to the Montana Environmental Information Center in Helena, from the Idaho Conservation League and Idaho Environmental Council to the Colorado Open Space Council.[20] Perhaps even more striking is the way in which the organization for wilderness action has become more local. First came strategies from the Wilderness Society, a Washington, D.C.–based organization; then came organization from the Pacific Coast by way of the Sierra Club in the Pacific Northwest; but more recently has come state organizations, independent of both the Wilderness Society and the Sierra Club, such as the Oregon Wilderness Coalition, the Wyoming Outdoor Council, the Nevada Outdoor Recreation Association, and the Utah Wilderness Association.[21] Increasingly these groups are coalitions of local groups in which interest in a particular wilderness area is organized locally and then, in combination with other local groups, a state-wide wilderness package is formulated. Just this past year the Colorado wilderness bill was put together that way, through a coalition of over 50 local groups in such a manner that it could not be ignored even by Senator Armstrong who is not thought of as a strong wilderness supporter.[22] Even more indicative is the way in which the Utah Wilderness Association has obtained the interest and support of Senator Jake Garn for a High Uintas Wilderness, as a result of its organizing activities within the state.[23]

This style of organization focused originally on the management of the National Forests, but one can predict, it seems to me, that it is now coming to the BLM lands in the same way. It is just that the BLM is about 20 years behind the Forest Service in facing these new circumstances. It was only in the mid-70s that BLM wilderness values began to become important to environmental groups. But they have taken them up increasingly. Perhaps the situation in Utah is not atypical where Dick Carter—a native of Utah by the way—organized the Utah Wilderness Association to take as great an interest in BLM wilderness study designations as in the USFS jurisdictions. The appeal which the Association has formulated with respect to Utah study areas is the most thorough and massive environmental action yet taken by any national or state group with respect to wilderness matters.[24] The most intensive localized interest in BLM lands in the past has come in southern California, where the Desert Protective Council has been active for several decades.[25] There it led to the most extensive application of environmental values of any instance on BLM lands, and the most intensive planning, so much so that by the 1976 Act it received separate attention.[26] I think it safe to predict that increasingly other specific BLM lands, such as the Red Desert in Wyoming, will arouse equally detailed interest.[27]

There is another feature of these changes that one should keep in mind. Although environmental interest often begins with wilderness, it extends to a much wider range of environmental values in land management. With the National Forests it has now evolved into local environmental interest in land-use planning; in a number of states environmental groups are now watch dogging national forest plans with respect to allowable cuts as fully as they are RARE II candidates.[28] For BLM lands these other concerns have been more active in the past, and especially those pertaining to the two major issues of allocations as between grazing and wildlife and the impact of stocking levels on the quality of forage. Recent changes in BLM policy reflect the ability of environmentalists to focus on those issues far more sharply. But we can expect that on this score the interest in BLM lands will not only become more localized, but also encompass a wider range of policies.[29] As urbanization increases in the region and as an increasing number of people look upon BLM lands as adjuncts to their living space—the urban regional field as some would call it—we will hear far more of specific pieces of BLM lands being the "backyards" of Billings and Casper, of Grand Junction and Logan, of Gallup and Flagstaff as well as of Missoula and Boulder.[30] The issue will be whether these lands are more valuable as sources of productive commodities or as adjuncts to one's residence and community. More and more we will be constrained to think of them as much as for one as for the other. People will be sorting out working space and living space in the Rocky Mountain region with increasing deliberateness, and it would seem the better part of wisdom for land management agencies to do so as well.

I I

These changes in social values place demands upon management and especially upon its own values. We can, of course, think of the relevant social
changes solely in terms of the new groups which have been formed to make
demands on the agencies and then examine the agency response to those
groups. But beyond that agency response arising from face-to-face encounters lies a deeper response from the particular values of the technical and
managerial personnel who speak for the agency. Here I am more interested in
the impact of social values on these technical-managerial values.

The distinction can be elaborated by reference to Paul Culhane's recent
book, *Public Lands Politics,* a comparative study of policy making in both the
Bureau of Land Management and the U.S. Forest Service.[31] These agencies, so
Culhane argues view themselves in the political middle, between developmental and environmental forces. This gives them political leverage to play
off one against the other, and especially to extract concessions from commodity groups by raising the threat of potential action from the environmental side. But it also helps to reinforce their managerial role, a point which
Culhane defines but does not explore much, as one of protecting the resource.
The agencies promote neither commodity objectives or environmental objectives, so he argues, and seek a middle ground of "resource protection."[32] The
inevitable compromises usually lead to criticism from both sides, which helps
to reinforce the agency self-image as "neutral" and "value-free" technical professionals and managers.

Yet this obscures the fact that there is more than "neutrality" and more
than resource protection. There is especially the fit between the priority of
uses as inherent in managerial thinking and the priority of uses in the changing mix of broader social values. "Protection for what?" There is always more
than protection of the resource. There is also its human use, which requires a
strategy, amid resource protection, for promoting desired kinds and levels of
human use. If one is self-consciously preoccupied with non-human resources
as a technical expert then one can be somewhat oblivious to changing human
values and thereby permit deep-seated personal managerial values to steer
use choices in a particular direction. One's personal values arising from training and experience or one's own personal psychological chemistry can become a subtle, but powerful and relatively unselfconscious factor in agency
choice. Especially one can be far less attentive to the problem of adjusting
positive agency goals beyond resource protection, in the direction of changes
in social values as they move toward environmental amenities. The rigidity of

agency values can lead to agency confrontation with social values which, in turn, lead to results which from the agency viewpoint are unanticipated and unwanted. The U.S. Forest Service has a long history of such rigidity in values which over the course of three-quarters of a century led to its loss of jurisdiction over several million acres of land to the National Park Service.[33] While it often understood the threat, it did not seem to be able to escape the iron grip of its own values. Is the BLM immune from these same constraints?

Changing values require subtle but important changes in how management thinks about the resources which it manages. A new technical apparatus is required to organize and understand the environmental characteristics of resources and of users in order to be able to think of them as natural environment resources and not just material, commodity resources. This requires new terminology and new categories for empirical description. The term "natural resources," for example, has now become ambiguous because the older custom that "natural" means "physical" and "material" now competes with a newer view that "natural" means "environmental" and "psychological" as well. Hence considerable ambiguity and controversy results when the term is used because it has dual meanings which normal conversation does not clarify. We now need two terms to distinguish between "natural commodity resources" and "natural environmental resources." Or again, the term "use" now is the focal point of considerable controversy. Amenity objectives come to be considered a "use" to compete with more commodity objectives which formerly were associated with the term. Hence, the term "use" is ambiguous and we argue vehemently over what is a "use." When confronted with this new meaning, those who attribute the older meaning to the term are prone to refer to new uses as "non-uses." But this only expresses their difficulty in adjusting to new values and new perceptions. A more effective way of shifting terminology in line with shifting values would be to use two terms, "natural environment use" and "commodity use." These innovations in terms would bring about greater clarity in discussion by avoiding the ambiguity which has arisen because old bottles are now filled with new—as well as old—wine.

There is also, however, the problem of the categories of description by which empirical data is organized so as to classify and order the world with which one works as a manager. We have long elaborated such empirical categories for material resources. In a forest, for example, there are categories which describe the different ages of a single tree, from sapling to pole to sawtimber, which have been shaped by the notion that the main characteristic of a tree is its wood content and hence its physical diameter. Or we have constructed productivity indexes in terms of a "site index" in which soil, slope, rainfall, and aspect are combined into one measurement to define the degree to which that site will produce a tree of a given height in a given number of years. Such empirical categories as these grow out of the view that the main characteristic of a forest is the volume of the merchantable wood contained in the trees. But suppose that newer values lead to the notion that the main characteristic of a forest is not its potential for wood, but its potential as an environment to make home, work, and play more aesthetically enjoyable. If this is the case, then the forest takes on new meaning and new categories of description logically result. In one such attempt new categories are based on the degree of canopy closure measured in terms of percent of area closed, and the extent of vertical vegetative layering within the forest. One could well manage a forest not to maximize wood production, but to maximize continuous canopy and vertical layering.[34] The differences in empirical descriptive categories grow out of differences in human perception as to what the resource is and hence what the objective of management should be.

I am not sure how to apply this problem of the demands which new values place upon inherited categories of empirical description to rangelands. But I suspect that is just because I know far less about what is being described—grass—than I know about forests. But there is one aspect of BLM management in which the problem does appear to be rather striking—and that is the development of wilderness categories. For many years now there has been a continuous debate over the meaning of that term, with detailed attention to the specific wording of the Wilderness Act. This is not surprising because wilderness is closely related to the continually evolving values of the American people, and one would not expect that it contain fixed meanings and definitions. The Forest Service long argued that only "virgin wilderness" could be so categorized and hence that the "restored wilderness" of the East did not qualify; because of changing values amid the public in the 1974 Eastern Wilderness Act the agency was forced to change its view.[35] It was probably to be expected that when new types of lands such as those administered by the BLM were being considered, new conditions would be brought into the older terminology. In this case the problem has focused especially on whether or not a wilderness experience must be "confined" or can remain "unconfined."[36] Hence the intense debate over the study selections in Utah. The agency wishes to distinguish between those two empirical categories and chose the former, a "confined experience," instead of the latter, and one can readily understand why. But one can also understand the wilderness advocate emphasis on an unconfined experience as an integral element of wilderness as a human experience. This underscores the point that new values require new empirical categories for description of a resource, or else management isn't well synchronized with the real world with which it deals.

These examples of interactions between technical management categories and human values, or what Ingram and McCool refer to as information and politics, involve subtle but profound changes in the orientation of managers—from one of managing resources to one of managing people. Uses are not inherent in resources, but are only what people want them to be. And hence the characteristics of resources are not just inherent in the resources themselves but in the human experience and perception of those resources. If one has a strong "commodity" or "material resource" bent then one insists that resource science involves the attempt to describe and modify a resource "out there" independent of one's particular viewpoint. But if such a view is held too firmly then one remains oblivious to those changing human values which have, in fact, changed the meaning of that resource from its "inherent" characteristics to the meaning that people find in it. This is perhaps the most difficult problem of all for traditional natural resource managers to cope with. Their personal training and professional experience have been so heavily geared toward viewing the resources they study, examine, and modify as "out there," materials divorced from people, that they find it all but impossible to make the transition to the new "real world" that those resources are what they are also because of how people value them and what they see in them. Customarily land managers have engaged in the practice of divorcing resources from people in constructing "management systems," including information systems. And they have brought people into the equation only when they become factors in either aiding or retarding implementation. Natural environment values require a shift toward the human or user side of management, not just as "public relations" strategy to enable the agency to implement its objectives more smoothly, but in redefining the meaning of a resource in the first place.

In current BLM affairs all this is focused most precisely on the issue of monitoring. What kind of technical information about changes in forage justify either reductions or increases in stocking levels? As one reads the comments submitted by occupational and citizen groups, it is quite apparent that this is one of the most critical issues in grazing policy. Grazers clearly look upon the "consultation and coordination" provisions of PRIA as providing them the opportunity to work out conclusions about forage conditions in direct day-to-day, on-site, discussions with agency personnel.[37] But environmentalists, on the other hand, distrust that relationship, fear that it will lead to agency fudging on describing the condition of the range and permit stocking levels to increase in order to maintain good working relationships between the managers and the managed.[38] They emphasize the need for an "objective" record, such as photographs which could document forage change and permit third parties to review the decisions.

There is far more to this than just the independent record. There are such questions as what is an indicator of "vigor" and "density. If a particular species is to be chosen as the indicator for a community of species, then which one? Might we not expect "standards" for forage condition to develop in terms of diversity of species not much different as has happened in forest management?[39] And particularly so as livestock operators increasingly challenge the notion of "carrying capacity" on the grounds that ideas about natural processes of recovery should be replaced by increasingly intensive management that will increase the carrying capacity?[40] Beyond all that is the expected controversy that will arise over the interpretation of the visual evidence in the photographic record. Some of the most intense controversies in environmental health have concerned the different conclusions drawn by different observers of the same visual evidence, such as of chest x-rays, slides of human chromosomes, or slides of animal tissues in toxicological experiments. Different people see different things, count up to different totals, from the same visual evidence. There is no reason to expect that photographic records of range conditions will be any less controversial.

The only way that the agency can respond to such problems intelligently, it seems to me, is to be prepared for them so that it is not overwhelmed by them and hence not prone simply to react negatively. If the agency believes that it can work out a monitoring system by itself based upon a "scientific" determination of the inherent qualities of the forage that will resolve disputes, then I think that it is sorely mistaken. For what the forage is depends upon who is looking at it, and the task before the agency is not to impose upon the decision its particular way of looking at it but to achieve some degree of agreement on what is to be measured and how it is to be measured prior to the measurement. It would seem the better part of wisdom, if one really wishes to avoid litigation, to make sure that these differences are ironed out before rather than after the fact. Otherwise one is only guaranteeing that litigation will ensue. From reading the public comment on this question I think there is no doubt that monitoring will be the tough issue, and unless the agency can obtain some agreement on this early on among the various contending parties then the courts will do it instead. If this happens there is no sense in blaming the litigants or the courts; the courts will only be fashioning "agreement" when the agency cannot.

As one observes the impact of value change on technical matters such as these, it appears that one of the critical problems involves the internal values of the agency itself in its relationship to those changes in the wider society. Choices are constrained not just by the external clienteles and pressures, as is usually the way in which agency actions are examined. They are also constrained by the internal values of the technical professionals, by the values which they bring to the choices because of their professional training, their managerial experience and, at times also, their own personality. Because of their own value background they view the world in a particular way and hence are often not free to take seriously those value changes in the wider society. It is fairly clear that this has played a major role in the response of the U.S. Forest Service to the growing public demand for new environmental uses of the forest, ranging from wilderness to the newer issues of diversity and canopy. Time and again the Forest Service found itself confronted with challenges, and time and again it lost out because it was prevented by its own internal values from shifting in line with changing public values.[41] There is a point where because of the internal value constraints in an agency its short-run strategies become detrimental to its long-run interests.

Broad changes in social values require that agencies become more knowledgeable about the larger social context in which they work, that outer perimeter of the concentric circle. It is not enough to feel that it has done a good job of "listening" or "responding" to immediate clienteles in the planning process.[42] One must go beyond that, get ahead of the game, and be able to understand what is coming down the road as a result of the value changes in the larger society. This is really not very difficult to do. Often the amenity and aesthetic values of natural environments are quickly dispensed with as factors which cannot be considered because what one person likes another one dislikes, and hence no sense can be made of them. If that is the reaction then it should be taken as a warning signal about one's personal values rather than about the values in society. For amenity values are not held willy-nilly. There is pattern and order to them which can be described and dealt with systematically.[43] They have been observed and understood and BLM agency personnel can do so as well. In fact two new empirical disciplines seem to be emerging in forestry to analyze them, "forest sociology" which emphasizes more traditional phenomena of demography and "forest psychology" which emphasizes values more directly. Both can assist the agency in being able to look beyond its immediate nose to the future.

I am struck by the way in which this is being done increasingly by the private corporate world. The analysis of social values has been carried out extensively by private corporations. They pioneered in the early attitude studies and public opinion polls because they wanted to understand their markets, both existing and potential. They associated changing consumer values with marketing possibilities. Ever since these beginnings in the 1920s some of the most extensive and sensitive analyses of public values, including systematic variations in them, have been carried out under corporate auspices. Unfortunately little of this information is available to us because it is proprietary and remains in corporate files. But the general significance can be emphasized by two extensive studies of current trends in American values. One, the Values and Lifestyles (VALS) study, is being carried out by Arnold Johnson at the Stanford Research Institute and the other, a content analysis of regional newspapers, is being conducted by John Naisbett at Yankelovich, Skelly and White in Washington, D.C.[44] Both are ten-year studies being financed by some 60 of the largest American corporations. In both cases the financial sponsors appear to be interested mainly in knowing where American society is headed. They apparently feel that in the past 20 years evolving social values got a bit beyond them and they were not prepared to respond to those changes creatively to their own advantage. From studies such as these they might get ahead of the game and thereby enhance rather than jeopardize their own objectives. Public agencies could well profit from their example.

III

It might be useful to sharpen this analysis by undertaking some comparisons of the four major federal land agencies—the U.S. Forest Service, the National Park Service, the Bureau of Land Management, and the U.S. Fish and Wildlife Service. How have each of these agencies understood the wider society in which they operate and especially as environmental values have risen? What built-in mechanisms do the agencies have in order to understand those changes, keep in touch with them, and then perhaps adjust their policies accordingly? I should emphasize once again that I am not focusing on the face-to-face interactions which have been generated by "public involvement" strategies, but on the more distant setting beyond the immediate clientele interaction which gives the agency some understanding of the larger world in which it makes decisions and at least provides it with the information about value changes "out there" which it might see fit to take into account in its management policies and programs. The four agencies, it seems to me, can be ranged on a scale in this regard, from the National Park Service, which has the most sensitive and extensive built-in "radar device," through the Fish and

Wildlife Service and the U.S. Forest Service, and then to the Bureau of Land Management which has the least.

The National Park Service displays the most effective sensitivity to the larger world of environmental value change which has occurred in recent years. This distinctive response, in fact, goes back prior to World War II; the natural environment values implicit in the drive for national parks continued as one of the major ingredients in the rapid evolution of more widespread environmental values after the war. In the conflict between developmental and environmental values the National Park Service was the continual antagonist of the U.S. Forest Service for jurisdiction over public lands of high environmental quality. That agency competition shaped both the transfer of land from the jurisdiction of the Forest Service to the Park Service and the debate over wilderness.[45] Citizens who supported the National Parks Association in behalf of the national parks also were deeply involved in the wilderness movement, leading to the formation of the Wilderness Society. They were able to use the threat of even more extensive transfers of land as a device for persuading the Forest Service to be receptive to wilderness management on the National Forests.

Within the National Park Service, moreover, there arose built-in devices which kept the agency and its personnel in close touch with public values. The most significant of these was the interpretive program, the development of a corps of naturalists, full-time and summer seasonals, who carried out extensive in-park educational activities for visitors. Some involved walks and hikes, with constant emphasis on the natural history of the park and others evening campfires with more formal presentations. These enabled park personnel to maintain a high degree of interaction with the public which they served. Personnel were chosen not just for their training and expertise in natural history but also for their skills in communication and interaction with visitors. Within the Park Service the interpretive program and the interpreters played a significant role. There were special training programs and centers which gave the entire effort considerable visibility and institutional focus. Amid the vast increase in use after World War II, the visitor centers were extended to facilitate these agency-public interactions; to construct them became a major element of "Mission '66," adopted in the mid-1950s.

These devices were significant instruments of value communication, formation, and maintenance.[46] They provided an opportunity for the public to respond to the environmental values within the parks and to communicate those values to the agency personnel, and they provided an equal opportunity for personnel who held similar values to communicate their concerns to the public. These values were expressed not only in the nature walks and camp-fire programs, but also in the slide presentations, the displays and exhibits, and the literature available in the visitor centers. It was relatively easy for a visitor who held natural environment values to feel that here were sympathetic people and a sympathetic agency simply by being exposed to these circumstances within the parks. Many a young person with environmental values came to prize the opportunity to be a summer seasonal in the Park Service. At the same time, the interpretive staff of the parks came to be a focal point of active environmental concern within the Park Service itself, a source of influence for keeping the agency on a stronger course of natural environment management amid the ever-increasing levels of human use.

These interactions between value changes in the society outside the agency and personnel within it could be observed in several tendencies in policy as the Environmental Era began with full force in the 1960s. Most striking was the modification of certain developmental tendencies which had emerged within the Park Service in the 1950s. One of these arose from Mission '66 which emphasized the need to develop more internal facilities to accommodate more users, and which was in full sway during the 1960s as environmental interest accelerated. The other came from the circumstances surrounding some of the new park units, and especially the seashores and lakeshores which had been strongly supported by local business groups which viewed them primarily as tourist attractions. The force of public environmental values modified both of these developmental tendencies. In case after case park plans which had strong developmental components came under environmental fire, were withdrawn and revised with a stronger environmental component. The classic park case involved Yosemite; the most dramatic lakeshore-seashore cases were Assateague Island and Sleeping Bear Dunes.[47] In both cases, however, the external public environmental demands found fertile ground within significant segments of the Park Service rather than facing a stone wall of opposition. These environmental concerns about the implications of overdevelopment were able to draw upon long-standing internal Park Service values and institutional arrangements which interacted positively rather than clashed with them.

During the latter part of the 1970s a new context of environmental developmental debate over the National Parks arose from the external, in contrast with the internal, threats to environmental values. A host of developmental activities outside the parks, ranging from diversion of water from the Everglades to air pollution from coal-fired power plants to parks in the southwest, to erosion and sedimentation from timber cutting on the upper watershed of creeks flowing through the Redwoods, to mining and highway building adjacent to Glacier. On these matters there was even more direct and rapid coming together of environmental values arising from the general public and from personnel within the Service. In this case there was little tension within the agency about what policies were required. The threats from outside endangered the parks, no matter what the internal environmental-developmental balance. There might be differences over strategy, but not over values. And in this case the Park Service was able to draw upon a rather easily synchronized set of interests from outside and inside the agency.

The Fish and Wildlife Service faced a much different set of circumstances arising from the Environmental Era and which gave rise to both similar and different types of agency action. But we can once again examine the agency's own efforts and capabilities with respect to its interaction with the value changes in the wider society. The significant factor in this regard was the rapid increase in public interest in wildlife as an object of observation and appreciation rather than as game to be harvested. This "non-game" or appreciative use of wildlife came on with considerable force in the years after World War II. Organizations which reflected such interests, such as the National Audubon Society, the Associate Membership of the National Wildlife Federation, and the Defenders of Wildlife, had healthy growths in membership in the 1960s and the 1970s.[48] User surveys indicated that those who used wildlands for nature observation far outnumbered hunters, even on "game lands" which had been purchased and were managed primarily for game harvest. And private business firms which catered to nature observation by selling bird feeders and bird seed, binoculars, and photographic equipment grew steadily. Clearly the public interest in wildlife was changing rapidly, and it was no wonder that an agency devoted to managing wildlife refuges would be affected by it.

The internal response of the Fish and Wildlife Service to these changes in values around it was facilitated by a common interest in habitat from both old and new wildlife users. The same habitat served as home for wildlife which one group of users wanted to view as well as for game which another wanted to harvest. There was little inherent conflict in use, save on those few days of the year when hunters were out in force and which appreciative users tended to avoid. But the rest of the year the habitat was open to this wider group of the public. To acquire wildlands as habitat for public management was a measure on which all users could agree. At the same time, the new threats to wildlife and wild life habitat from pollution also served to join rather than to divide, for water pollution, toxic chemicals, and atmospheric contamination were common threats to both game and non-game animals. There were, of course, many latent antagonisms between hunters and anti-hunters, and at times that division erupted into overt conflict. But formally organized environmental groups such as the Sierra Club and the Audubon Society were friendly to biological management as part of their ecological outlook and not at all sympathetic to the "humane" groups which expressed more a human empathetic response to wildlife rather than an ecological viewpoint. They tended to forge a middle ground.

In the face of these tendencies making for cooperation, the Fish and Wildlife Service began to respond to the new appreciative users. Many of those responses involved strategies similar to those of the National Park Service. Interpretive programs and summer seasonals came to be more common on the wildlife refuges. There were self-guiding nature trails, including automobile trails, planned nature walks and automobile trips with interpretive guides, visitor centers with slide shows, displays, and literature. The Service moved gradually toward the model of the Park Service. A measure of this public involvement in activities on the refuges was the publication in 1979 of the first *Guide to the National Wildlife Refuges* for the general public.[49] Its subtitle was: "How to Get There; What to See and Do." Its theme was public involvement with wildlife and it provided extensive information about the facilities which the Service had developed in 365 different refuges for public involvement and appreciation.

But there was another twist to the response of the Fish and Wildlife Service which went even beyond that of the National Park Service. To the Fish and Wildlife Service there was obviously something new "out there" in the public interest in wildlife matters, and the agency felt that it should both know more about it and modify its policies in response. It is not yet clear just how and when this came to a focus within the agency, but new approaches began to be publicly evident by the early to mid-1970s. One of the first was a generic Environmental Impact Statement concerning the operation of the national wildlife refuge system as a whole which appeared in final form in 1976.[50] This was not a usual kind of project-oriented analysis of environmental impacts, but a much broader programmatic analysis covering the decade from 1975 to 1985. By developing this format, however, with its provision for public response to the draft statement, the Service was able to obtain ideas about the role which the public expected it to play from an exceptionally wide range of interested groups. The Final Statement included copies of 704 pages of comments so submitted.[51] Among the four federal land agencies this venture in programmatic statement and public response was unique. It would be fair to assume that the Fish and Wildlife Service was more knowledgeable about the public interested in its affairs than any of the other four.

But the agency's effort to understand this new public setting for its activities went even further to encompass one of the most extensive studies of environmental values which has yet taken place in the United States.[52] Undertaken by Stephen Kellert of the Yale School of Forestry, under contract from the Fish and Wildlife Service, this study both developed a new categorization of human attitudes toward wildlife and at the same time investigated the social variables associated with those attitudes. The latter, the demographic analysis, was rather conventional—examination of income, occupation, education, race, and regional location associated with various attitudes toward wildlife. But the former, the categorization of the attitudes themselves, was far more novel and innovative. For it involved the assumption that the human meaning of wildlife, the relationship between the person and the object, was the key to understanding the new setting for wildlife policy. It was not enough just to categorize wildlife per se into species and habitat. One also had to realize that different people established different relationships with wildlife and that management had to be organized to respond to those different relationships. While some, for example, sought to dominate wildlife by overpowering them, others sought to establish a mutual relationship with them within a natural setting, and others sought a more empathetic relationship within a developed setting such as pets at home or animals in a zoo. These different values had become clear to many in the course of give-and-take over public policy. Kellert pinned them down in systematic terms. Combined with its programmatic environmental impact statement, the Kellert study provided the Fish and Wildlife Service with a unique body of knowledge which enabled it to understand the changing world around it and hence to adjust its policies accordingly. But like the National Park Service, it was able to do this because its own internal values were open to accepting the changes in the larger social setting rather than resisting them.

The U.S. Forest Service presents still another variant in this interactive relationship between the values of the wider public and the agency. One can readily observe that the Forest Service does not provide nearly as extensive an interpretive program or system of visitor centers as do either the Park Service or the Fish and Wildlife Service. There are some moves in this direction, especially in those parts of specific National Forests which contain special natural environment areas. In the East I think of the visitor centers at the Cranberry Bog area of the Monongahela National Forest and the Sylvania recreation area of the Ottawa National Forest in the Upper Peninsula of Michigan. Yet despite the growth of recreation management with forestry, neither the profession or the Forest Service has developed a strong emphasis on an interactive relationship with the public in terms of a common interest in environmental values. This, I think, is because the Forest Service has difficulty in sharing those values; its strong commodity orientation, with a bottom line of wood production, creates at best a mixed response to changes in values in the wider society. Often the values internal to the forestry profession and the Forest Service are more constraints than facilitators in positive responses to wider social changes and this has led the agency into stances of resistance to rather than leadership in the world of changing environmental values surrounding it.[53]

Several major tendencies within the Forest Service reflect positive responses. One of the most significant of these is the elaboration of research and management with respect to outdoor recreation. Researchers at the experiment stations and managers have adopted a scheme for classifying recreational users into a "levels of experience" spectrum, with variations in the balance between natural and developed environments which recreational users prefer. This is both an emphasis on the human factor and the natural environment component of that human experience. At the same time in its visual corridor policy the Service has recognized the public visual use of the forest and its concomitant perception of the forest as an environment. This evolved initially out of an attempt to "screen" visually unattractive logging from those who traveled along forest roads. A visual corridor policy for this purpose first worked out in the White Mountain National Forest was extended to the West, and its impact on the allowable cut has become one of the major industry objections to Forest Service policies.

But these changes constitute selective responses to the wider scene of environmental values and not an internalized acceptance of them, either within the personal values of professional foresters or the institution of the Forest Service itself. The Service has a fairly strong record of responses to environmental values which reflect the constraints of its commitment to wood production. For many years this led to a series of controversies with the National Park Service with respect to jurisdiction over National Forest land. In most of the cases the Forest Service was so constrained by its own internal value commitments to wood production that it could not provide for amenity values within its own agency and hence lost control of many lands to the Park Service. It was precisely because of such results, which came to a particular head in the 1930s, that the Service was persuaded to be more receptive to natural environment proponents in wilderness policy; this provided an opportunity to accommodate amenity values within its own jurisdiction and prevent loss of lands to the Park Service. The loss of land to the Olympic National Park was especially significant in prompting the Forest Service to bend.[54] But even in this adjustment the agency was not entirely successful. It embraced wilderness management only reluctantly and with a "rear guard" stance, rather than take up a leadership position. Hence it continued to lose jurisdiction in such cases as the North Cascades and Mineral King.

Within the U.S. Forest Service there were some sources of agency personnel which had the capacity to reach out and establish more positive relationships with changes in values in the wider society. The most visible segments were those in the experiment stations who undertook research on recreation and wilderness problems, and those within the management side who engaged in wilderness management. It is probably of some significance that the Forest Service book, *Wilderness Management* was written by leading experiment station researchers—John Hendee, George Stankey, and Robert Lucas—rather than by those involved more directly with management.[55] As the environmental issues in forest management shift from wilderness to ecological management and species diversity one observes the same problem of the constraints of a bottom line wood production set of values in finding common ground with changing public attitudes toward the forest. The perception and categorization of empirical data inherent in even-aged or uniform-area management, which constitutes a basic way in which commodity foresters look at the forest they manage, is quite at odds with the perception and organization of empirical data inherent in an ecological notion of an interactive balance among species, ages, and vertical layers.

Within the forestry profession some of these problems have been approached through a distinction between "resource management" and "people management."[56] This is more on the order of a response to the immediate clientele. On the larger score of public values, in that outer concentric circle of analysis, there is less impact on professional thinking. The general public and the professional forester have fundamentally different ways of perceiving what a forest is and what its value is in human life. While foresters still think of wilderness as a source of commodities, the public has developed the notion that it is an environment within which both human beings live, work, and play, and wildlife find a home. To the public the environmental role of the forest is far more important than its source for commodities.[57] Yet in such programs of the U.S. Forest Service as "service" forestry in which there is direct interaction with the public, that view is rarely expressed. The Service does not provide "service" forestry advice as to how to manage woodlots as natural environments, but instead heavily emphasizes management strategies to produce wood. The Service has not taken up the tack of the Fish and Wildlife Service to sponsor a study of the attitudes of the American people toward forests as a resource. And one can plausibly suspect that to do so would constitute a major strain with agency and professional values simply because it might highlight how much at variance those values are with those of the general public. The wood production values of the Service serve as a roadblock not only to agency action, but also to agency capabilities for understanding the wider world in which it functions. This, it seems to me, is a major reason for the continual controversies in which the agency is embroiled.

For the Bureau of Land Management these kinds of problems are relatively new, and hence one might not expect the agency to have developed effective radar devices, either in the form of ongoing arrangements to interact directly with the public through interpretive programs or visitor centers, or in the form of programmatic statements which might lead to identification of attitudes about its affairs in the general public or more formal attitude studies. And such is the case. Yet the impact of environmental values in the wider public is clearly upon the agency and hence as an agency-watcher one can rightfully be curious about which way it will go in response. How much will it recognize the larger environmental setting in which it works, and how much will it develop institutional devices to understand that setting and seek to accommodate to it? The BLM is a heavily commodity-oriented agency, and with the addition of oil and minerals to grass that traditional emphasis is reinforced. Yet it operates within a regional social context in the West which entails widespread public expression of environmental values. Will the course of its affairs turn out to be more like the Fish and Wildlife Service or the U.S. Forest Service with respect to its relationship with those public environmental values?

At the moment, so far as I have been able to conclude, all this is so new to the BLM that all one can do is to follow out lines of inquiry rather than draw firm conclusions. Will, for example, the obvious need to respond to recreational demands lead to more than studies and strategies just to accommodate those problems rather than to understand broader changes in public values? The public opinion studies with respect to the California Desert Plan might suggest either course. On the one hand the two California Field polls about off-road vehicles are more recreational management strategies; but the larger Gallup poll from the nationwide sample indicates that the agency was concerned about a larger social scene.[58] I do not know of the origins of these polls and whether or not they reflect a sustained interest in public values on the part of individuals within the agency or are simply one-shot affairs. And what will be the impact on the agency of the wilderness study mandate of FLPMA? For a while it appeared that the BLM was anxious to be able to demonstrate that it could do a better job on this score than did the Forest Service with RARE I and RARE II. The agency certainly drew into its wilderness study program some individuals who had the capacity of bringing environmental perspectives into its daily workings. But that all seems now to be gone and one can rightly be skeptical about the degree to which this source of interaction—comparable to the wilderness researchers in the forest experiment stations—with the wider public will play a significant role at least in the near future.

I have been intrigued with several attempts to understand the larger social context of environmental values with respect to planning on the Oregon O&C lands of the BLM. One of these, for the Jackson-Klamath unit, included in its description of "socio-economic" conditions both a more traditional type of demographic analysis and a study of attitudes toward the forest. It led to the identification of four clusters of attitudes, two associated with older commodity views and two with newer environmental views.[59] I tried to track down where this study came from and whether or not it reflected a sustained agency interest in understanding the larger context of environmental values. So far as I could determine, it seemed to be the result of initiative from the Washington, D.C., office, through a sociologist, who by the time I made the inquiry had moved to a different position and hence was no longer an influence within the agency for this kind of study.[60] At the same time it appeared that within the Oregon state office there was a desire to continue this kind of study for future planning efforts.[61] Now this of course pertains to the agency's forest lands rather than the rangelands, but perhaps it has some bearing on the development within the BLM as a whole of focal points of interest which would keep the agency abreast of the larger environmental scene so that it would not get caught up short in the future. The attitude studies concerning forest lands in Oregon could well be applied to rangelands.

This four-agency comparative analysis can achieve little at the moment for the BLM save to make it more sensitive to the problem, if it has any inclination in that direction. One can identify where the other agencies have established capabilities to understand and respond to changing social values and where they display roadblocks to that kind of strategy. But before one can learn anything from what has happened in other agencies one has to take the problem seriously and want to understand so as to act. On this score, as an observer from the outside I would conclude that there is little evidence at the moment that the BLM really wishes to go in this direction for rangeland management. There is concern about the political controversies and especially the litigation which results. But I have found little evidence which reflects a desire to go beyond the immediate crisis of events as they unfold on rangeland matters to the larger social context which would enable the agency to get ahead of the game and head off potential problems. There seems to be little of the kind of agency initiative represented, for example, by the strategies of the Fish and Wildlife Service or by the BLM for O&C lands in Oregon. Hence it is a plausible prediction, at the moment, that rangeland policy in BLM is evolving more along the Forest Service lines of commitment to commodity values which will continue to exercise constraints on agency choices, than along the lines of either the National Park Service or the Fish and Wildlife Service.

I V

What, then, of "advice to the agency" which we have been admonished to provide? First is the suggestion that while there is an overload of technical data about the resource, there is not sufficient information about the social values on the human side of the equation. This, of course, is a call for more data, but of a much different kind than a resource agency is usually prone to acquire. But if it is the larger social setting which gives rise to unexpected demands upon the agency, then it is only reasonable to suggest that one know more about what is "out there" that is creating those demands. Second, it is worth emphasizing and underlining several times that these broader environmental impulses are not hostile to scientific inquiry and, in fact, contribute significantly to advancing technical knowledge about the very resource matters with which the agency deals. Far from constituting an influence inimical to the advance of scientific and technical knowledge, the environmental movement has demanded increases in that knowledge far greater than our scientific and technical institutions can provide. The tensions arise not from the negative but from the positive attitudes of environmentalists toward science.

There is also the larger problem of the relationship between technical data on the one hand and values on the other: the setting of the Ingram-McCool paper. Technical data and scientific inquiry are shaped by values; what is investigated, the research design which forms the character of the inquiry, the monitoring system—all are heavily influenced by values. Often they are the values of the technical and managerial personnel who make the choices about lines of inquiry. Objection from the environmental public constitutes an argument that a different set of values and objectives should shape the course of technical inquiry and activity. The development of data to support one set of values can either enhance or inhibit the expression of another set of values. And if that comes to be the case, as it often does in the clash between environmental and developmental objectives, then we have an instance of technical data being used to control value choices, rather than being used in the service of values. It is often difficult to accept the notion that what appear to be technical choices are, in fact, value choices. But the larger realm of social change which has given rise to environmental values has given special focus to that phenomenon. Land management agencies should be particularly sensitive to this potential and make sure that technical data are developed and used in the service of broader public values rather than constitute a restraint upon them.

THE ROLE OF URBANIZATION IN ENVIRONMENTAL HISTORY

Environmental history, arising amid public interest in environmental affairs since World War II, has taken up as wide a range of discrete subjects as are debated in contemporary issues. The agenda is vast and diffuse. Much of it is placed within the context of an effort to attach historical meaning to current policy choices, rather than write from a context of questions defined through historical concepts of patterns of long-run change. Yet, a more clearly historical context is readily at hand for environmental historians to apply.

Environmental history encompasses two large questions. First are the long-run changes in environmental circumstance, as human activities created increasing pressures on a finite environment. Over the years population, consumption, and industrial technologies pressed ever more heavily on the finite environment of air, water, and land. Environmental history attempts to understand both the growth of these pressures and their resulting environmental effects.

Environmental history also traces changes in the way people observed, thought about, and conceived the environment around them. People placed new values on their natural and human environment, developed a new interest in observing and studying it, and made more deliberate environmental choices in their personal lives and public policy. This involves a wide range of subjects such as historical changes in personal values; science, law, and education; and public affairs.

For both of these historical problems one of the most promising conceptual vehicles is the city. The city is the focal point of increasing human congestion with its accompanying changes in urban environmental circumstance and its sharp contrast with the environmental circumstance of the less environmentally pressed countryside. Cities generated increasing loads on the wider environment which, in turn, established the tension in larger environmental conditions.

The city is also the starting point for new attitudes about the wider environment. Organized environmental action as well as favorable environmental opinion is stronger in the city than in the countryside. New views about the value of land, air, and water of the world outside the city as environments rather than as commodities arise from within the city. Resulting patterns of political controversy are organized primarily in urban-rural terms.

We first look at urbanization, therefore, in the evolution of environmental circumstance and then as the source of the new world of environmental engagement.[1]

I. THE CITY'S ROLE IN ENVIRONMENTAL TRANSFORMATION

Urbanization plays three roles in changing environmental circumstance. The first is the evolution of the environment internal to the city; second is the way in which the city reached out to influence the wider countryside; and third is the effect of this outreach on environmental transformation of that wider world. We take up each of these in turn.

The environment internal to the city went through several stages of historical development in the nineteenth and twentieth centuries. These stages should not be thought of as sequential, but cumulative, as each new stage emerged out of a previous one to continue a growing combination of newer and older environmental conditions as some changes became more extensive and others less so. We mark these changes roughly, more for convenience than for preciseness, with the first and second halves of each of the two centuries.

I.

The human/environmental setting of the emerging towns and cities of the first half of the nineteenth century (1800–1850), involved the transfer of social practices long-established in the countryside to the new places of more concentrated population. Newly arrived migrants to the city sought to continue familiar rural ways of life and found that practices quite acceptable in more spacious rural areas affected people quite differently in this more congested environment and were looked upon with revulsion and resistance. The new environmental circumstances gave rise to many town and city ordinances to restrict customary practices.

Initially, the most pervasive of these involved the role of farm animals—cows, horses, pigs, and chickens—in the towns. At first farm animals were allowed to roam the street; their smell, their waste, and the damage they did to property interfered with the lives of others. Initially they were considered to be unpleasant nuisances but soon were thought of as a health problem, giving rise to some of the first urban-inspired public health ordinances.[2] Disposal of both human and animal waste was the most compelling problem giving rise to those who either scavenged refuse or collected human and animal waste to use as fertilizer in the countryside.

Some problems were of large consequence, such as the major urban fires that came from building flammable structures close together, or the unpleasantness of city streets that, like rural roads, were carved out of dirt and remained unpaved or the smoke from wood and coal burning in home and factory that was simply tolerated. Other features of urban life are seemingly minor but instructive elements of this transition. One was the burial of the dead. In rural areas some dead were buried in formally organized church cemeteries but even more in plots on family lands. In the city places for burial were not as freely available and often the dead were not cared for and became a public health concern. Ordinances required that church sextons report deaths, but in the last half of the nineteenth century, they required that deaths be reported by a coroner. Another was the gradual removal of horse racing from urban streets to the edge of cities and then to specialized tracks removed from daily human activity as they interfered with urban transport.[3] This transfer reflected the shift of town and city street-based recreation to areas separated from urban congestion.

II.

A second phase (1850–1900) in the internal environmental history of the city arose as increasing urban density extended undesired environmental circumstance. One might describe this as the emergence of the contradictions of the city as a place to work with the city as a place to live, dilemmas that continue to the present. Some arose from the cumulating presence of urban-generated waste that gave rise to a shift from the outhouse to sewage ditches and underground lines to divert waste to nearby rivers and away from the city.[4] Others arose from the development of industrial districts, for example, for the petroleum industry, that gave rise to concentrated forms of residential degradation.[5] Still others arose from the increasing intensity of transportation that involved the loss of city streets as residentially related open space. New forms of communication such as telephones and outdoor advertising or new forms of energy such as electricity brought environmental blight along with material benefits. And still others involved attempts to control disease and improve health with safer drinking water and removal of solid waste from yards and streets. As an overall problem the increasing intensity of development preempted open space and gave rise to the city's ever increasing loss of natural features.[6]

These changes brought sharply to the city the tension between efforts to enhance benefits that came from higher density living and the accompanying liabilities in quality of life. Here was conflict between the city as a source of production and work on the one hand and the city as a place to live on the other. Greater population density gave rise to demands for new services to benefit the entire community. But they also gave rise to adverse consequences that had to be endured or ameliorated in some fashion if they were to be avoided. Urban growth and development involved both environmental improvement and environmental degradation, a tension that moved along steadily in succeeding stages of urban history.

Within the city the pressures toward more intensive development of urban land and hence to reduce open space involved a threefold set of relationships. More intensive and congested urban life led to an increasing demand for urban public services; municipal governments sought to raise revenue to pay for public services not by raising tax rates to which there was massive objection, but by raising assessed valuations and, in turn, the least painful way of raising assessed valuations was through more intensive building which raised property values. Often in future years those who sought to improve the environmental quality of the city found themselves confronted with this deeply embedded triangle of factors, a triangle that arose quite early in the history of the development of public works as public services.

III.

A third phase in the internal environmental history of the city, especially dramatic in the first half of the twentieth century (1900–1950), was generated by the attempt of many urban residents to carve out new homes and residential areas within the city that would provide more pleasant living. In earlier residential patterns, factory workers lived near their work and artisans lived in the upper floors of their shops. Increasing numbers of people became unhappy with the unpleasant impact of production on the quality of residential life; they made choices to live in places separate from work and in doing so to emphasize the desired features of new residential areas. From the earliest years of urban development this positive search for environmental quality within the city went on simultaneously with the increase in environmental degradation.

This tendency was facilitated by the courts which continually heard nuisance cases against factories brought by their neighbors, but for the most part dismissed the complaints.[7] Many plaintiffs, so the courts argued, bought their property knowing about the noise, air, and water pollution or the congestion they now faced; hence they had no case. Others who as property owners faced new factories that changed the quality of their land also had no case because the benefits from factory production outweighed the interests of residential owners. The first involved the interests of the public as a whole and the second the interests of only a few.

The desire for residential quality of life was rather widespread but the ability to fulfill it depended on sufficient income and hence was affordable to most residents only as their income increased. For those at the lower end of the occupational scale this took modest but important steps as industrial workers living in housing around mills moved upward in job skill and income and sought improved housing, often moving to new residences up the hillsides from the river-valley flats of mill housing.[8] Here they could have a more "liveable" environment both within the house—enjoying a "living room" for example—and also a more liveable environment outside the house somewhat away from the unpleasant environment of the mills.

A more visible residential pattern emerged on the part of white-collar workers, a group steadily growing in numbers over the years and by 1900 constituting a group with distinctive residential objectives with marked environmental features. Earlier these workers lived above the artisan shops of the central city while unskilled laborers lived in the back alleys. But as incomes rose these more affluent workers were attracted to new areas of the city where they could enjoy not only larger houses, but more spacious communities with front and back yards, trees along the edge of their property, vegetable and flower gardens, paved streets, piped water and sewage lines. Here one could enjoy life at some distance from the congestion and unpleasant environmental circumstances of older areas of the city.[9]

This drive to carve out more environmentally attractive areas in the city led to efforts to protect those areas from what were considered to be more environmentally undesirable influences. The private market for urban land led to frequent changes in ownership which involved the continual potential that land adjacent to residences would become commercial or industrial with its accompanying detrimental environmental effects on residential property. As a homeowner how could one control this potential danger? In some cases residential real estate developers placed stipulations in deeds that residences be set back a certain distance from the street. In other cases areas of residential property were developed with collective deed restrictions and in some, though few, cases limited access. But the most widely developed approach was zoning in which municipal zoning commissions established zones to which industrial, commercial, or residential development each would be confined.[10]

IV.

In the years after World War II (1950–2000) these varied long-evolving tendencies now came together in a more unified effort to define urban environmental conditions and to improve them as a collective set of urban circumstances called environmental. One could describe this as a relatively coherent effort to define the city as a place to live as well as a place to work. The change could be observed especially through the work of planning agencies. In its early years planning was looked upon to provide services for expansion of long-established industrial enterprise. After World War II, however, urban planning came to encompass a wide range of "quality of life" considerations such as parks, playgrounds, open spaces, hiking and biking trails, museums and recreational facilities, commercial areas with more greenery, reduction of air and water pollution, and more spacious central city areas.[11]

A wide range of activities were set in motion to carry out these objectives.

Sewage treatment works supplanted earlier established waste water pipes and channels that discharged raw sewage into streams. Air pollution was reduced through decisions by homeowners to substitute cleaner coal or natural gas for more polluting coal.[12] Cities advocated purchases of public lands by both counties and states for parks and natural areas. Changes in urban land use, such as for urban redevelopment or the decline in river-front, river-traffic-related activities, or the decision to end military uses of military bases carved out more natural environment areas accessible to urban residents.

To these new expressions of urban environmental objectives there was often much resistance. As was endemic in the history of cities, the environmental quality of the city as a place to live faced vigorous competition from pressures to define the city more as a place to work. Urban concerns for more jobs and more income continued to outweigh urban concerns for quality of life. Few urban governments sought to give environmental affairs a central place in their policies or planning for the future. While states often brought these issues together into a focused administration, few cities did so. And "futuristic" thinking was dominated by the desire to determine how urban population and income could grow rather than by how environmental quality of life could grow.[13]

The Environmental Reach of the Urbanizing Society

Cities were one of the major expansive forces in modern nineteenth- and twentieth-century America. Their history is the story of the way in which large numbers of urban people with their rising levels of consumption imposed themselves on and transformed the countryside and region. Both the imposition and the transformation are essential elements of environmental history. But this story requires a major change in the vision of urban historians who have looked upon cities as isolated from rural history and to whom rural society is only peripherally visible. An environmental perspective requires a combined urban-rural context. Environmental history, in fact, provides an opportunity for urban historians to focus more sharply on the countryside as an essential part of an integrated urban-rural context.[14]

URBAN PENETRATION INTO THE COUNTRYSIDE

Urban penetration into the countryside took place in stages as one type of outreach arose after another to blend in a cumulative development over the years. At one time the resulting urban-rural relationships were limited in scope and direction; with time the impact of cities on the countryside became more extensive and intensive. The environmental reach of the urbanizing society penetrated larger regions, nations as a whole, and the wider common environment of oceans and the atmosphere.

In its earliest outward reach people in urban areas sought the products of the earth not available within their boundaries but present in surrounding rural areas. Some were used directly for fuel, others as raw materials for more highly processed consumer products, and much was used for food. These uses were, of course, integral parts of the rural society out of which urbanization sprang, but the demands on these resources became ever-more intensive as the number of urban people and their consumer demands grew.

Forest history provides one of the more obvious and dramatic cases. Timber harvest for urban construction is one of the major themes in the history of both urbanization and forestry. Use of the vast pine forests of the Upper Lakes states for reconstructing Chicago after the Great Fire is one of the more recorded incidents in this urban-rural relationship. But many a city went through a similar experience. Demand for construction lumber was so great that the vast "virgin" forests were soon depleted and the industry moved on from region to region until the forest resources of the entire nation were extracted by urban-based demands.[15]

The most widespread urban use of the countryside, however, was for food. When people moved to cities they purchased some food, such as grain, from the markets, but also often sought to grow perishable food, such as fruit and vegetables. With time, however, and new forms of food preservation these also came to be supplied by rural growers. Urban demands on agricultural production took a new turn in the last half of the twentieth century as a host of new "farm" products began to be a major part of the consumer market: food specialties such as herbs, horticultural products such as urban flower gardening. Taken together, these more intensive urban demands from the products of farm and field constituted an increasing "load" on the limited land resources of the world beyond the city.

A distinctive phase of the urban demands on the countryside came with urban needs for water. Early towns and cities drew upon sources from rivers and wells. But as urban use increased cities reached out to obtain supplies further away. Many a growing city acquired land in watersheds above them to protect their supplies. This was especially the case in the northern states of earliest urbanization in New England and the middle Atlantic states.[16] Mid-America cities located on rivers, such as Pittsburgh, Cincinnati, or St. Louis, had nearby river supplies that were relatively accessible. Other cities, such as

Denver and Los Angeles, had to reach out to more distant supplies; here urban and rural people competed vigorously for the limited supplies.

The history of wildlife, in earlier years the history of sport fishing and hunting, played an equally significant role in the impact of cities on the countryside. Immigrants from Europe had been excluded from hunting and fishing on property of the nobility and royalty, but in America fish and game were public resources widely accessible.[17] As urban people increased their fishing and hunting activity they increased pressure on a limited resource and demanded that state agencies increase the supply by artificial propagation.[18]

Interest in wildlife for its nongame and aesthetic appeal was almost entirely a product of the cities and often led to a revulsion against hunting. Some demanded wildlife products for their ornamental value such as elk teeth prized by the fraternal society, the Elks, or bird feathers for women's hats, or furs for women's coats. In the twentieth century, urban interest in wildlife took quite a different turn with the focus on wildlife not for consumption or decoration but on its appreciation in the wild. Urban people came to be interested in forest areas as habitat for wildlife and many an urban-based organization advocated the acquisition and management of public land as habitat for a wide range of species. The term biodiversity arose to describe this new interest of urban people in a broader range of wildlife.[19]

URBAN USE OF THE COUNTRYSIDE FOR WASTE DISPOSAL

Urban people and industries produced much waste that cities did not feel they could absorb within their own boundaries. Hence they sought to use the countryside for its disposal. In some cases industries that produced particularly offensive waste were under pressure to relocate outside the city. But most urban waste was disposed of by using the countryside as a place "out there" for disposal of waste created in the city. At first that "out there" was relatively close by, but as time went on, the amount of waste increased and residential suburbs moved outward, and, in turn, the place of disposal was further and further away and often, in fact, to other countries.

Nearby rivers were one of the first places used for urban waste disposal. Water-borne wastes were dumped into drainage ditches, a process that increased dramatically with indoor plumbing. At first confined to upper income groups, indoor plumbing became extended to middle and lower income homes in the twentieth century.[20] At the same time underground sewers replaced open drainage ditches with sewer outfalls into nearby rivers. Thus, cities used public resources, rivers, to remove waste from within their borders.

At first there was little resistance from people "out there" who might find their interests in cleaner rivers to be infringed. Industries also used this public resource for their own benefit, thereby expanding the waste loads in rivers. In some cases industries argued that the highest and best use of rivers was for industrial waste disposal.

The emission and transport of airborne waste in the form of air pollution went through a similar history. Earlier one thought of air pollution as local, falling out close to the sources from which it originated. But later it was discovered that air emissions traveled long distances to be deposited hundreds and even thousands of miles away. The countryside where the airborne urban waste came to rest was extensive in its geographical scope and hence expanded the environmental reach of the city to wide-ranging areas in the region, the nation, and beyond.

A new form of airborne discharge came from the widespread use of toxic chemicals, created expressly to create materials not subject to rapid biological decay. Because they were persistent they penetrated the atmosphere far more widely than did other chemicals and were found in the environment throughout the world. In the first well-known discovery of this process, DDT was found in the fat of penguins in Antarctica. Tracking the pathways of toxic chemicals was often extremely complex, as they went through a sequence of deposition and volitalization that required far more detailed and continuous measurement. This far-reaching penetration of persistent chemicals even came to adversely affect the conduct of scientific research; dioxin in human fat, for example, was so widely distributed among human populations throughout the earth that people with no or little dioxin could not be found with which to contrast those with higher levels.

The countryside, near and far from cities, became an ultimate "sink" for chemicals generated by urban society. Treated wastewater left a residue of solids, such as sewage sludge which gave rise to urban demand for rural land disposal. Emissions of sulfur dioxide were reduced through "scrubbers" that turned airborne waste into a solid that was disposed of in landfills. For commercial and household solid waste, the rural sited landfill was the customary disposal method and the same was the case for toxic wastes from industry.

OCCUPATION OF THE COUNTRYSIDE FOR RECREATION AND LEISURE

Urban people also directly occupied the countryside and thereby extended the environmental reach of the city. Early in the development of urban areas city people sought out the countryside for diversion, relaxation, and health. If the environmental quality of cities had its drawbacks the more natural countryside had its benefits. At first this opportunity was available only to the more affluent, but over the years the urban-based use of the countryside for recreation, relaxation, health, and appreciation of nature grew in its range and intensity. This long-range process brought the city into a new and dominating influence in rural areas that linked city and country ever more tightly.

Very early in the history of American urbanization resorts grew up to cater to a small group of affluent urbanites. Warm springs for health purposes arose in the pattern of European spas. Doctors often advised patients to leave the city in the summer to improve their health through breathing cleaner air. At the same time wealthy urbanites not only established their own estates in the countryside but organized private hunting clubs, such as in the Adirondacks.

In the early twentieth century this urban-based and urban-inspired use of the more natural countryside went through a veritable revolution as a result of the automobile. As the automobile grew from a plaything of the wealthy to providing greater mobility for middle-income Americans it generated a vast increase in outdoor recreation in the countryside. Federal and state parks and recreation areas began to take shape in the 1920s, increased in the 1930s, slowed during World War II, and took off once again after the War. All this gave rise to an expansion of federal and state outdoor recreation programs, with new twists such as hiking trails, protected wild and scenic rivers, and wilderness areas.[21]

In later years urban interest in the countryside came to include the ecological context of the forest, well beyond its use for wood products, to its role as a habitat for wildlife. This was influenced heavily by the urban-based interest in "appreciative" uses of wildlife, reflected in numerous wildlife television programs and the growth of environmental education. Nongame wildlife policies arose in almost every state, leading to the purchase of natural areas to be managed for ecological purposes with "biodiversity" as the objective.[22]

Outdoor recreation came to be closely allied with tourism for which the largest number of participants came from urban areas. But it also evolved into more permanent occupation of the countryside through ownership of property there used at first for weekend recreation and relaxation and later for permanent residence. This urban-inspired demand for rural property divided forest lands into smaller properties so that most forest land in the east was owned by "non-industrial, private forest owners" rather than industrial forest corporations. These new owners valued their property far more for its natural environmental quality than as a source of wood production.[23]

Interest in less developed land in the countryside led to the growth of land conservancies, a new form of protecting land from development. These were private efforts to acquire land, manage it for its natural values, prohibit or greatly restrict development, and stress low-impact outdoor recreation, nature study, and environmental education. They often also served as centers for environmental monitoring and a base for ecological research. By the end of the twentieth century over 1,100 land conservancies had been established, most of which drew support from people interested in a particular place who sought to ensure that natural values would be "saved" for later generations.[24]

Transformation in the Countryside

Urban penetration into the larger world beyond cities transformed it in many and diverse ways. The scope and intensity of the impact increased steadily. Some changes were geological, such as soil disturbance through mining, erosion through logging and farming or wetland drainage. Some were biological as wildlife habitat was replaced with intensive agriculture, or transportation and communication corridors fractured wildlife habitat and exotic plants displaced native ones. Others involved the addition of chemicals emitted from urban-based technologies, such as fuel burning, to the natural chemical cycles that tied together much of the larger natural world. And still others were the simple process of declining open space as humans increasingly preempted that space for more permanent occupation and development.

Environmental historians have examined bits and pieces of this but usually only within the limited perspective of the urban dweller and hence somewhat oblivious to the effects of the urban-based pressures on the wider world. Here we look at it from the viewpoint of changes in the land, air, and water resources themselves. Economic history usually emphasizes penetration into the countryside in terms of the way in which it met the objectives of the developers who promoted it. Environmental historians seek to bring into this one-sided perspective the environmental transformations on their own terms.[25]

How, in the latter part of the twentieth century, does one reconstruct geological and biological changes over the past two centuries? Intrigued with the task, many researchers have tried to ferret out evidence to mark long-run environmental change. Dendrologists have long looked at tree rings to reconstruct forest history. Geologists have explored the Greenland ice cap to examine the residues of metals distributed through the atmosphere. Biologists have examined diatoms in lake sediments to examine early patterns of agricultural and forest activity and paleobiologists have examined charcoal remains to determine patterns of forest use and settlement among Native American peoples. A variety of researchers have compared levels of lead in people living in industrial cities from those in areas untouched by lead emissions or in the bones of mummies from earlier times. Most such studies, however, have been carried out by natural scientists somewhat removed from the "mainstream" of environmental history.[26]

LAND AND WATER

Extraction of minerals left many changes in the countryside, ranging from the open pits left from mining, the piles of residue coal waste, acid water that transformed the chemistry and biology of streams, or the accumulation of mining waste in sediments of lakes, rivers, and reservoirs. As people sought places to live in a more natural and pleasant environment, they found these residues from both past and present mining to be eyesores which they sought to eliminate. And as the scale of water pollution from mining increased, those who enjoyed fishing found that it threatened their recreational activity.

Forest transformation was far more extensive, involving massive biological changes over vast areas of land. The older forest at the time of European settlement was modified drastically. Native Americans had long cleared the forest through fires, but Europeans cleared it more fully and more permanently for agriculture. Forest historians have emphasized both the loss of trees through massive harvest and the regeneration of new forests. Thus the trees cut over in New England were succeeded by second-growth. But far more extensive changes took place in the forest ecosystem as a whole, well beyond the trees alone—plants of all kinds, invertebrates as well as vertebrates, lichens and butterflies, wildflowers and shrubs, frogs, salamanders and other amphibians. Recovery of the forest ecosystem was slow; some species became extinct.[27]

Land development for agriculture was the most massive transformation in the countryside. In some cases such as New England farming the hill land gave way to farming the more productive soils in the West and led many owners to abandon their land. The same pattern was repeated in the upper Great Lakes states; the hope of converting cutover pine lands to agriculture did not materialize because it was found that the soils were far too sandy. But on vast tracts of land, farming replaced forest and native wildlife, farming became increasingly intensive and a source of pollution itself.[28]

Rivers also changed. Where water was abundant and rivers flowed through terrain of only small elevations they were used for transportation, a use extended by canals. In other cases they became a water supply for industry or domestic use which led to construction of reservoirs which modified their natural flow and reduced fish populations dependent on natural habitat.[29] In areas of limited rainfall such as the West flow was diverted for agriculture and then stored in reservoirs which constituted even more massive disturbances of natural river regimes. In many cases rivers were used as the most convenient method of disposing of waste and over the years this practice went on relatively unabated. For many years these changes in rivers met with little opposition and what did occur usually only from those immediately affected. Not until after World War II did public opinion change as many people began to emphasize the value of cleaner and "free flowing" rivers.

As people penetrated the countryside to remove its raw materials, to change forestland to farmland, or to extract water from rivers, they found that some areas were not attractive and bypassed them. In some cases they were too mountainous in which to build transportation lines to make them more accessible; in other cases the soils were too thin, taking on the characteristic of what were called "barrens." Some rivers in the higher elevations were too rocky for transport of any kind, either boats or for floating logs. Some wetlands were too deep and extensive to drain for agriculture. Hence the process of human penetration was selective; the intensity of occupation varied from place to place. From the point of view of an economic history that emphasizes the extraction of resources these were merely "wastelands." But from the point of view of environmental history these were "lands that nobody wanted," left for future generations to prize as lands of great value amid the massive land and water development of the twentieth century.[30]

THE WEB OF CHEMICAL CYCLES

Changes in land and water were the most obvious environmental changes; they could readily be seen. Less visible, more subtle and perhaps more profound changes involved airborne chemicals that traveled long distances, even to other continents and around the globe. These pollutants were deposited far and wide to accumulate in the environment and affect plants, animals, and soils. Dramatic pollution episodes were fodder for media coverage, the more subtle changes were not.[31]

Chemical transport through air and water brought into environmental and ecological science the notion of chemical cycles, in which chemicals traveled long distances between their origin and their deposition, some of which were transformed during transport.[32] In the normal course of natural cycles the environment had absorbed these chemicals with little environmental disturbance. But as chemical atmospheric loads increased from human activities they constituted increasing environmental loads that were not readily absorbed. Hence one spoke of the cycles as being overloaded beyond the absorptive capacity of the underlying geological and biological environment. At the same time the idea of "critical load" arose, that is, the point at which such loads were sufficiently high to endanger the underlying ecosystem and scientists began to work out the level of deposition that could be tolerated in contrast with that which could not.[33]

This was especially the case with "persistent" or "non-biodegradable" toxic chemicals which moved through the environment to accumulate in air, water, and land and the associated plants and animals. While many chemicals degraded rapidly as they were transported through the air, others, especially metals and synthetic chemicals, were far more persistent. As environmental science persistently brought more of the environment and how it worked into the realm of knowledge, the pervasiveness of toxic chemicals became a growing part of human experience. And this included changes in biological resources beyond the cities in the countryside and the wildlands.

Concentrations of these chemicals were such that they were not readily noticeable. They required measurement at low levels of concentration in order to be tracked and understood. This was one of the major tasks of environmental science. Some studies tracked metals such as lead in areas downwind from their sources, such as from the the Pittsburgh steel industry to "sinks" some 50 miles east of the city and even at longer distances to the Greenland ice caps. Others measured accumulations in lakes or in wildlife which revealed either changes in the chemistry and biological life of lakes, or disruptive toxic chemicals in wildlife that on external observation appeared to be healthy.[34] Such studies gave rise to the view that chemical deposits were wide-ranging and all-pervasive, that waste from modern urbanized society had given rise to a comprehensive, global process of biogeochemical accumulation.

SETTLEMENT IN THE COUNTRYSIDE

Urban-inspired human settlement in the countryside generated its own forms of environmental degradation, through its impact on less highly developed areas. The countryside invited an increasing number of people who came to enjoy the higher quality environments on weekends and during vacations and then to live there. Some took up occupations more characteristic of small towns and nearby rural areas; others were retirees whose main focus was not occupation but quality of life; still others held occupations in the "footloose" industries afforded by modern communications technologies so that they could live and work in areas of considerable natural quality and carry on far-flung business ventures.[35] All this was observed even in the census of 1930 as a "rural, non-farm population." This new rural occupation grew over the years and its environmental effect was profound.

One of its most striking effects was to transform large forest land ownerships into those of much smaller scale. By the 1960s a considerable transfer of forest ownership had occurred from rural farm and commercial holdings to woodlots owned primarily by people from urban areas. Urban-based income was now used to purchase woodlands for recreation or permanent homes. A massive turnabout in rural land values resulted. Prior to World War II those values had continued to decline as farming was less and less profitable, some lands were abandoned and traditional uses declined. But after World War II rural land values rose steadily. Real estate ads reflected the process, as sellers in rural areas advertised in urban papers and described their lands for sale in highly positive environmental terms—quiet areas, cleaner air, abundant wildlife, by a sparkling stream, near a state park or forest.[36]

These new settlements greatly fractured forestlands into fragments and highlighted a condition of forest habitat known as "fragmentation." Large forest areas that constituted habitat for plants and animals requiring a distinctive type of "intact" forest declined in number and extent and small woodlots, of 100 acres or so, increased. Plants and animals living in fragmented areas were quite different from those in larger forest areas. Hence while some neotropical songbirds lived in the larger habitats others lived in the smaller ones. The decline in size of holding had a profound effect on the populations of plants and animals, producing conditions favorable to those that could coexist with humans in settled and fragmented areas and unfavorable to those that required less disturbed areas.[37]

To track these changes in the wider environment beyond the areas of high urban density but directly a result of the impact of cities on the countryside is one of the major challenges of environmental history. A convenient device for doing so is to compare areas of varied levels of urbanization, suburban areas close to cities, countryside areas further away and wildland areas, the least disturbed by humans. These impacts can be thought of as the comparative environmental effects of cities on the wider environment as urban-based human demands escalate amid the surrounding finite air, land, and water of the region, the nation, and the wider globe.

II. THE ROLE OF THE CITY IN ENVIRONMENTAL ENGAGEMENT

The city was also the origin and sustaining force of the second of our two large facets of environmental history, the self-conscious and deliberate engagement of people with their environment to improve its quality—the environmental movement.

The environmental movement was something quite new in American history. While environmental circumstance—the increasing human pressure on a finite environment—evolved continuously throughout the centuries, the self-conscious human perception and understanding of this process and resulting action appeared in significant degree only after the mid-twentieth century. There were a few such observers before that time, and their writings have been resurrected and popularized in the past half-century, and there were many instances in which people objected in specific and often limited cases to environmental degradation. But it was only after World War II that the environment was subject to much increasing deliberate thought, analysis and action.

We can trace this historical development in a rough but convincing way through popular writings, organizational activity, public affairs, law, education, and science. In all of these activities we can contrast the old and the new and environmental affairs constitute an important part of the new. By 1995, in contrast with 1950, environmental science had advanced markedly; environmental education had become popular in elementary and secondary schools as well as in many college curricula; a host of new laws had been passed both to encourage voluntary and regulatory activity; environmental organizations have arisen at all levels of society, local, state and regional, national and international; many a publishing house had specialized, in part and some in whole, on environmental subjects; magazines and journals now focused on environmental topics.

Why the change? When did the change occur and what were its social roots? Among what sectors of society did environmental values arise, along what avenues were the new values transmitted through society, and among what sectors was there resistance to change?[38] It was in the urbanizing areas that the new environmental values had their origin and their strongest support. Rural areas, on the other hand, were major sources of the environmental opposition. As areas outside the cities became urbanized in their thought and ideas, they, too, took up environmental initiatives.

This is not to argue that either cities or the rural areas influenced by urbanized culture were homogeneous in these initiatives. Within the cities there was a strong environmental opposition as urban-based interests in both development and environment clashed. And as urban values penetrated the countryside, they were met often with great hostility from those whose values were rooted in commodity-based traditions or newcomers to rural areas attracted by those traditions. As an overall observation, however, environmental culture was associated with urban people and expanded as urban culture pervaded the nation.

It may well be argued that the environmental movement is a product also of the increasing human loads on the environment that produced a wide range of visible results people found to be unacceptable. True enough. But one is also impressed with the greater intensity and range of human responses to these changes, with such force that those responses took on a major innovation in thinking, of values, perceptions, and ideas, so that the response was different in kind as well as degree. Attitudes toward the value of nature, toward human health, toward population congestion all were of quite a different order in the years after World War II than before. It is these changes in values that are rooted in the urbanization of society.

Environmental Movement or Environmental Culture

We have used the popular term "environmental movement" to introduce this subject, but the more useful term in describing its wide ramifications is "environmental culture." The roots of the "movement" lay in a complex of values, institutions, and ideas which, taken together, can best be described as an environmental culture. The term "environmental movement" denotes a set of social and political organizations which seek to use government to advance their environmental objectives; similar cases were the labor movement, the civil right movement, the peace movement. Environmental affairs, however, extend far beyond such organized efforts to pervade almost every aspect of society: science, law, education, economic enterprise, the media, homes, daily living, and leisure and recreation. We prefer, therefore, a term that reflects the way in which the environment has wormed itself into the entire society and goes far beyond an organized "movement."

But the pervasiveness of environmental values was only partial; competing cultures co-existed with environmental culture and were continually at odds within people, their communities, and wider public affairs. In engaging their environment Americans continually faced choices in which environmental quality is often, in any given circumstance, an alternative that was weighed against other alternatives. Hence in identifying and exploring the roots of environmental engagement we must place it within this larger context of competition between different directions in human values.[39]

The focus on environmental culture rather than environmental movement requires a distinction between ideologies and values. In historical analysis social movements are closely associated with ideologies. Movements generate ideas and writers which are taken up by the movement explain its place in the world, its historical roots, its future potential. Such ideas are then used to "spread the word" and attract adherents. The "environmental movement" has spawned its own share of such writers. But environmental engagement goes far beyond environmental ideologies and the writers who produce them to widely diffused attempts by people to improve their environment, not according to some ideology but according to their own values generated from personal experience and history.[40]

The stress on environmental ideologies often gives rise to the notion that the course of environmental affairs depends upon the degree to which people adhere to new "environmental paradigms."[41] Such paradigms are often based on attitude studies in which people express agreement or disagreement with ideas presented to them. One then works out the course of environmental history in terms of the coming and going of these ideas. The stress on environmental values, on the other hand, seeks to identify people in their engagement with their environment as they seek to change and improve it for what they think is the better. Such an approach recognizes not only the emergence of new values in the lives of people but also that those new values are in conflict with older values which they also hold. The course of environmental history is the course of that balance as it is worked out in personal history, community activities, and public policy.

The task of environmental history is to trace the penetration of environmental culture from its beginnings through various institutional routes to its engagement with others of contrary values who either accept those values in varying degrees or reject them. The process has been identified in several public values studies by recognizing the spectrum of environmental values as different "shades of green" and the process then by which people move from one point to another on that spectrum as environmental circumstances and environmental engagement changes. Hence the context of analysis must be far more extensive than simply the examination of a few environmental writers or broadly based environmental "paradigms." How can this be done?

I make two suggestions here. The first is to avoid concentrating on the few large and widely known national environmental organizations as the basis of one's analysis.[42] One speaks of the "big twelve" or the "big twenty" whose presence is most visible in the nation's capital. These are the organizations with the largest membership and most extensive activities. But it is not too difficult to realize that the world of environmental organization goes far beyond the "beltway." Some estimate that there are 10,000 environmental organizations in the nation at large that often go in a very different direction than do the large national ones. There are a great number of nationally organized special topic organizations; several hundred state and regional organizations; innumerable local ones. Few observers ever attempt the complex and laborious task of ferreting out what all this means, but substitute the easier task of either reading the ideas of widely available writers, or focusing on the activities of the "big twenty." Only if we broaden our attention from the most obvious pieces in the term "social movement" to the wider realm which connotes not environmental movement but environmental engagement and environmental culture will we be able to examine effectively the social context of environmental affairs.

The second suggestion is to extend analysis from the organized "movement" to the wide range of institutions into which environmental values have penetrated: science, law, education, the media, and economic entrepreneurs.[43] The relationships between these institutions and widely shared public values is more than complex, but it is certainly not simply a reflection of the environmental organizations. For the historian the challenge is to follow what happens in these fields as new values penetrate varied social institutions through their own routes. Students whose values change come to colleges and universities and take up environmental courses. Some are members of the "movement" but most are not. However, they all reflect a new environmental culture which they seek, in one way or another, to implement. To take another instance, as people seek to grapple with environmental circumstances they search out science to understand them. Hence they read about science, study it as a personal matter of self-education, reach out to scientists in academic institutions and generally become part of a new enterprise in environmental science. Such activities cannot be understood as an attempt to implement environmental ideas, but instead to come to grips with personal values that are elaborated and sustained by an environment that one wishes to engage, to either protect from degradation or restore.

In seeking to understand environmental culture a sharp difference has developed between the world of environmental ideology and the world of environmental practice, so much so that one cannot be taken for the other. People in these two worlds work in realms quite far apart, touching each other only occasionally and tangentially. The thinkers, for the most part, are composed of academics and related intellectuals in the world of writers. The practitioners are far more vast, rarely read the works of the thinkers, and tend to be preoccupied with those ideas that are directly applicable to their circumstances. The thinkers, for the most part, are not well acquainted with the values and perceptions of those engaged in the task of environmental improvement, and the practioners are not well acquainted with such streams of environmental philosophy such as ecofeminism, bioregionalism, animal rights, or decentralization. They do not even express theories of socialism or free enterprise, but willingly take up mixtures of private and public action if they seem to work. They are driven not so much by ideas as by results.

Historical analyses in terms of "environmental culture" extend the range of exploration into wider realms of human activities further than the more confined "environmental movement." When we speak of "environmental engagement" we pursue this wider world of environmental affairs. That world is not a rural world but a world of urbanization. It arises from the values of an urban society, and it penetrates a wide range of institutions associated with that society. Hence "environmental culture" whether expressed in either a rural or urban place is a product of large-scale changes in human values and perceptions rooted in the urbanized society of nineteenth- and twentieth-century America.

The Social Roots of Environmental Engagement

Who expresses environmental values and who does not? To put it differently, what were the distinctive social roots of those values that became stronger after 1950, those who held those values as different from those who did not? A variety of strategies have been used to pinpoint this problem.

One of these has been to use attitude surveys which seek responses from people of different ages, associations, residence, income, educational levels, and similar types of demographic characteristics. Another has been to use voting records in the U.S. House of Representatives to establish patterns of voting which can be associated with characteristics of legislative constituencies. Still another is to distinguish in more qualitative fashion the various states and regions in terms of their environmental cultures and environmental actions. And still another is to examine the interest groups that array themselves around environmental issues by pinpointing the constituencies which they seek to energize and activate. Each of these has some contribution to make to the overall question; each has some limitations. Taken together they provide a basis to identify the social roots of environmental engagement and contribute to the general conclusion that urban-based societies, cultures and institutions are sources in the evolution of environmental values and action.

Most environmental attitude surveys are rather crude instruments since they usually focus on generalized environmental attitudes and use only national samples that do not distinguish attitudes by geographical area.[44] Environmental engagement is usually more specific in terms of the particular topic, such as natural values, wildlife, air or water pollution, or population, and often is focused in a particular area, state, or region. Yet these surveys do point, even though vaguely, in a direction, that two factors, age and level of education, are associated distinctively with environmental values. Younger people express environmental values more strongly, and older ones more weakly; those with more education express environmental values more strongly and those with less more weakly.

A few studies dig into the demographics more deeply.[45] Some divide the nation into regions and develop samples for each region. These indicate broad regional circumstances associated with environmental values. The most significant study in this vein involved an attitude scale ranging from natural values on one end to commodity/development values on the other. One part of the study which distinguished four regions within the United States found that the highest natural values were in the northern states of the East, the Pacific Coast, and the Mountain West, and the lowest natural values were in the southern states.

Some data focuses on the urban-rural differences more precisely. One study in Minnesota examined the residence of those who allocated state income tax refunds to state wildlife programs; those in and around Minneapolis/St Paul made higher contributions than did those in less urbanized and more rural areas. Still another study identified the personnel of the U.S. Forest Service in terms of both the subject of their professional specialization and their urban-rural background.[46] Engineers and "foresters" were older and more rural in background; ecological specialists, such as in botany, wildlife biology, ecology, were younger and more urban.

A more precise examination of values involves use of voting scores in the U.S. House of Representatives over a period of years to associate levels of environmental voting with the characteristics of legislative constituencies and enables one to examine the association of values with levels of urbanization, a method that enables one to categorize 435 geographical areas in terms of levels of environmental culture.[47] Regions of higher levels were New England,

New York and New Jersey, the northern Great Lakes states of Michigan, Wisconsin, and Minnesota, the Pacific Coast states, and Florida. The lower level regions are the western Gulf states, the Plains states, and the Mountain states of the West. One can then sort out smaller areas within these regions which indicate a consistent rural-urban pattern. Within the Mountain West, for example, urban areas produce higher voting scores than do rural areas; the pattern holds within states such as California and Texas, Nebraska, Colorado, and Kansas in which members of Congress from more urbanized constituencies have higher environmental scores than do those from less urbanized ones.

Patterns of political relationships which arise from the interplay of interest groups are consistent with these patterns from the legislative voting.[48] In this case they are much sharper. Those environmental organizations that express environmental objectives directly in their political action have a distinctively urban base. The largest Sierra Club chapters and groups, for example, the organization that is most active politically, are in the cities, east and west. At the same time the most vigorous anti-environmental interest groups are those that represent agricultural and commodity activities such as lumbering, ranching, and mining.

This relatively hard evidence, expressed in quantitative terms or through interest groups, is confirmed by qualitative evidence arising from a variety of sources: media reporting, the relative strength or weakness of citizen environmental activity, the curriculum in higher education, the presence of exploratory environmental science devoted to pushing back the environmental unknowns, the relative strength or weakness of public policies in various states, or the degree to which the voting public supports environmental referenda. An accumulation of such evidence both confirms the quantitative data and rounds out its meaning. Environmental values are nurtured by modern urban society and meet resistance from an older society based on a resource commodity economy.

Several overall conclusions arise from these attempts to identify the social/demographic basis of environmental values. One concerns values expressed by individuals, that environmental values are stronger among younger people and the more highly educated. A second concerns the complex of institutions that make up environmental culture: science, law, education that intertwine with values to make up environmental culture. And third, is that both environmental values and environmental institutions are generated and nurtured in an urban context and hence become expressed more fully in a political system that organizes the expression of political views by geographical areas.

Elected representatives from more urbanized areas express these values amid the many and varied demands that arise from urban voters while those from less urbanized areas tend to oppose them.

Values in Environmental Engagement

The driving force in the new interest in shaping improved levels of environmental quality were human and social values that took on an increasing level of importance in the second half of the twentieth century. These values are the other side of the coin from demography. While demography provides some idea as to the social context of environmental engagement, we can translate that social context into the people whose values, perceptions, and ideas become the driving force behind a desire for environmental change. While the nation's growing urbanization provides the context for human values and action, we can obtain a more precise view of environmental engagement by focusing on the values, perceptions and ideas directly.

Three sets of values were involved in environmental engagement.[49] One pertained to the aesthetic quality of the human environment and more specifically to the enhanced role of nature in an urbanized society. Another pertained to health and the reduction of levels of pollution that impaired human health and the resources of nature. Still a third pertained to the larger question of the sustainability of quality of life and whether or not higher levels of population and consumption jeopardized that quality of life in the long run. For the most part these values played quite a limited role in earlier rural societies. Their gradual evolution can be traced with the growth of urbanization and their fuller expression can be traced especially with the rapid pace of urbanization in the twentieth century.

One environmental objective was to bring more of the natural world into the modern urbanized society. There were many such attempts, ranging from those which sought to bring the natural into the highly developed parts of cities, to those that sought to establish and protect natural beachheads within the urban region and the countryside, to those that sought to protect from development parts of the nation's wildlands. Many specific programs were involved such as the Conservation Commissions and open space programs of the 1960s; wilderness, wild and scenic rivers and hiking trails of the 1970s; state natural area programs, strategies to enhance nongame wildlife and endangered species; rails to trails programs; land conservancies, now numbering over 1100; environmental education and natural history programs; the growth of interest in biodiversity; urban gardening and urban forestry; the great number of state and county referenda to approve spending for open space and natural areas.[50]

The examples are legion and they all add up to the notion that urban people wish to incorporate into urban society a larger amount of nature. The role of such activities in the modern world is subject to considerable differences of interpretation by the environmental intellectuals and the environmental practitioners. Environmental intellectuals have wrestled philosophically with the historical relationship between people and nature and some environmental philosophy is cast in terms of a benign nature disrupted by rapacious humans, with the argument that such activities involve a desire to return to that earlier nature. But people engaged in expanding the role of nature in modern society and hence their own quality of life, aim not to "return" to an earlier nature but to "advance" to an enhanced role for nature in an urban society. While the intellectuals ask "Is there a role for humans amid nature?" the practitioners ask "Is there a role for nature amid humans?" Such practitioners do not reject urbanized society in favor of nature but seek to supplement one aspect of their lives with another that is more natural.[51]

The values involved in this approach to nature are quite different from the values involved in the role of nature in a more rural society. Rural peoples stressed the extraction of resources as commodities for material use; urban peoples add to this the preservation of resources for appreciative use to enhance the quality of life. The two types of uses involve quite different values and in a number of cases the transition in values over the years is quite sharply defined. At one time, forested areas were thought of in negative terms and "wilderness" indicated a place of danger; now wilderness and forested areas are thought of in positive terms. At one time wetlands were thought of as impediments to beneficial use and should be drained for agriculture; now wetlands are thought of in positive terms and their loss through drainage as harmful. The most extreme case is that of predators, which earlier were only to be exterminated; now some are protected and thought of as valuable in the "wild" despite instances of harm to humans who venture into the wilds.[52]

Alongside the attempt to enhance nature in an urbanizing society was the equal attempt to enhance human health as a major element of quality of life. This also involved major changes in values, a shift from a predominant concern for avoidance of death to growing interest in enhanced levels of physical and mental well-being so as to make life more enjoyable and fulfilling. People sought out ways in which they could enhance their health through their own life styles and sought out medical advisors who could facilitate those goals. Part of that process was a more healthful environment in such matters as air and water pollution that would reduce exposures to potentially harmful chemicals through drinking water and eating, cleaner air, or through reducing exposures generally.

Several changes in demography and health science enhanced this transformation in values. One was the increasing length of life through the decrease in infant mortality and the reduction of adult disease. Interest grew in child development and the effect of pollutant exposures on reducing the human potential, for example, neurological potential, of young children.[53] As the population aged, a growing interest also arose in the quality of life beyond the income-earning years, expressed not only in longer life for the elderly, but in extending the years of creative human activity beyond age 65 or 70. Environmental hazards had long been common in the workplace, but now the adverse effects of pollutants at all ages and for both women and men came to the fore.[54]

Interest in both the beneficial role of nature in an urbanized society and enhanced quality of health to enhance human enjoyment and potential came to the entire nation, but it was spearheaded in the cities and came to less urbanized areas more slowly. Rapid communication such as television facilitated the spread of new values from urban to rural areas, but at the same time more traditional values held on more tenaciously in rural areas, for example, the connection between life style and human health, older and newer foods and diet preferences as well as older and newer attitudes toward the natural world. As environmental values became more widely expressed, therefore, and as the organized environmental movement took shape, it developed a distinctively urban-rural tension and it was quite easy for organizations and political leaders based in the older rural societies to look upon the newer environmental initiatives as threats to their values. The Rocky Mountain West was a particularly distinctive setting for this controversy as it seemed not only to continue to express traditional values, but to attract as newcomers those from elsewhere who expressed such values and sought the western setting as a greater opportunity to do so.[55]

One of the more significant features of the evolution of environmental values, was the degree to which people in cities often found the countryside and the wildlands outside the cities to be a more congenial place in which to realize these newer values. In the nineteenth century the countryside was often sought out as a more healthful place to which those with lung diseases, for example, might go for recovery and rehabilitation. At the same time the countryside was a place where recreation in the natural world could also be beneficial for both mind and body. In those years it was primarily those urbanites of upper incomes who could enjoy the countryside. But in the twentieth century, with the advent of the automobile a much wider sector of society could afford to do so and in the 1920s and therefore an increasing number of city folk found that time spent in the countryside was both pleasing and healthful.

For some urbanites these attempts to enjoy and benefit from the countryside were only occasional visits during weekends and vacations. For many others automobile transportation and cheaper cars, such as the Model T, enabled them to extend the range of their forays into the more natural world and even to acquire a small piece of land there for more regular visits.[56] Some young people from the cities sought to carve out homes in rural areas through homesteading and obtaining a living from the land; this segment of new rural families grew steadily but slowly and at a pace that was less than the growth of urban areas. And an increasing number of retirees sought out the more natural countryside as a place to enjoy their lives. In all of these cases people whose values had been nurtured in the cities now extended them to the countryside.[57]

Environment and Development: The Context of Engagement

The expression of environmental values and the evolution of environmental culture can be understood only in terms of its engagement with opposing values associated with developmental rather than environmental objectives. If one wishes to enhance the role of nature in modern society, one faces the continual process of the substitution of development for the natural world in which the natural world seems to be in retreat in the face of a developmental steam roller. If one wishes to enhance human health and the health of the natural world by restricting exposures to toxic chemicals one faces the continual, and even expansive, diffusion of those chemicals into the atmosphere, waters, and the land. If one is concerned about overdevelopment in the metropolitan suburbs one faces the continued developmental pressures in one's own community.

If one observes only one side of this tension one cannot understand the way in which environmental engagement takes place. It is not a matter of two clear-cut opposing philosophies in contention but more a matter of mixtures which move along a scale in terms of continual interaction between tendencies at times working together but frequently in conflict. It is not the ideologies that define the historical setting which one must examine, but the alternative ways of shaping and using one's environment. And the results are varied. In some cases one notes environmental improvement as a result of engagement; in other cases one notes continued environmental degradation.

The drama of environmental history thus reveals a complex interaction of directions in human values, one in which environmental values and environmental engagement have steadily become more entwined into the nation's culture but which, rather than emerging dominant and triumphant, remain engaged in vigorous tension with opposing values. This tension is a major feature of environmental history first within the world of cities themselves, then through urban and rural conflicts, and then within the countryside as urban values develop there to engage more traditional and non-environmental values. In each case, the world of urbanization and the transition from a more rural to a more urbanized society becomes a central setting of environmental history.

Within cities one could observe from their early history both the desire to enhance the role of modern industrial production for its benefit in terms of jobs and income, and the desire to enhance the role of the city for its benefits as a place to live. In earlier years, cities attracted people for job opportunities and in many a case, tolerated the resulting environmental degradation as a price to pay for the improvement in one's material standard of living. But quite early, people sought to live in more pleasant and healthful surroundings. In those years few could find such surroundings in rural areas, but primarily by living in more attractive places within the city. Hence the beginnings of the process we now call suburbanization.

As environmental culture grew in the last half of the twentieth century its urban manifestation can be seen in the attempt to define cities more fully as attractive places to live rather than just as places to work. Yet, at the same time, there were powerful tendencies within cities to define the urban future in terms of higher levels of production and incomes and those who sought to define the city in terms of quality of life often found themselves with only limited constituencies. Many argued that environmental quality objectives were a constraint to economic development and hence those objectives often took a back seat to increased jobs and production.

Those with environmental objectives might wish to enhance the role of nature in their cities; persistently they sought to but with only limited success because of the continual pressures to develop land rather than to leave it in a more natural state.[58] Or they sought to improve human environmental health within the cities and while they succeeded in reducing the gross and obvious pollution in air, water, and land, they had far more difficulty when it came to the persistent effects of chronic low-level exposures.[59] The consequence of these tensions was that most cities did not generate self-conscious attempts to analyze, report regularly, and develop plans for environmental improvement. Such activities came only through sporadic and limited forays that over the long run added up to some environmental improvement but amid great odds.[60]

Opposition to environmental objectives in the countryside came with greater clarity. In this case people in the countryside found that urban initiatives in the use of the countryside for urban-based objectives were frequently not to their liking and many an issue pitted urban-based and rural-based proposals against each other. The organization of the political impulses involved could be best observed in the state legislatures as representatives of areas of different degrees of urbanization developed different positions over different public policies on issues such as natural values, the disposal of urban pollution and waste, control of sources of pollution, or use of public funds to foster environmental objectives.

As environmental initiatives proceeded to place a value on nature and natural lands, many an issue revealed the differences between the rural preference for natural resource development and the urban preference for natural resource appreciation.[61] Management of public lands and waters led to the same controversies: should they be developed or used for commodity production or should they remain in a more natural condition? Should public resources such as parks be used for the enhancement of jobs in the surrounding rural areas, or for nature appreciation?[62] Should the focus of wildlands management be the production of game for hunting or the appreciation and study of diverse ecological resources?

The vast increase in the production of urban waste raised questions of its disposal and this almost always led to an option attractive to urban areas to dispose of it "out there." This took several forms such as the use of rivers for water-borne waste, or the diffusion of urban air pollution away from cities to fall in the countryside elsewhere, or the transport of solid municipal and industrial waste to landfills in the countryside. Cities as sources of waste sought to dispose of it in the countryside. People in rural areas objected and sought to use zoning powers to prevent such siting; cities, in turn, sought to use state governments to override local zoning decisions. At one time or another all of these entered into legislative debate, and rural legislators either objected to the adverse impact of urban-based waste on their communities, or the application of standards of environmental protection in their areas when they considered the problem to be caused by cities, or the use of tax dollars which they contributed to the cost of clean-up in the state as a whole.[63]

Still a third set of political tensions arose as people from cities and with urban-based values moved into the countryside to express their environmental objectives from within rural areas. At times newcomers came to grips with farmers who sought to dispose of their waste in ways that degraded streams. At other times they objected to the adverse impact of smell and noise from farming operations. Or as newcomers purchased woodlands for their enjoyment they excluded hunters from their lands. They came to the countryside also with ideas about using the natural lands around them for recreation or nature observation. They objected to increases in timber harvest which might compromise aesthetic objectives or lead to the decline in wildlife habitat. As time went on newer rural people sought to emphasize a wider range of appreciative wildlife objectives in contrast with commodity/hunting objectives.[64]

These environmental objectives often were folded into the enhancement of tourism in the countryside by accommodating those environmental values which could be commercialized. Thus, for example, old growth forests might be sources of income from those who sought to view the neotropical songbirds that might be present there; museums and research centers featuring raptors or wolves or bighorn sheep or butterflies and insects might be community economic assets; trails to accommodate bicyclists and hikers could provide business for bikeshops, restaurants, and bed-and-breakfast facilities. Rural people often were reluctant to approve tourism but gradually were drawn into it if and when it led to profitable rural business. At the same time tourism led to other issues such as the way in which natural area designations withdrew land from the local tax rolls, or cleanup of waste left by tourists increased the cost of local government.[65]

III. INTERACTION BETWEEN OLD AND NEW

The most massive historical development of the past two centuries has been the transition from a rural to an urban society. Economy, politics, values, science, law, every facet of life has changed as an integral part of the process of urbanization; rural society, in turn, has declined and become a subordinated but integral part of a resulting urban-rural social and political context. Environmental affairs, the increasing human load on a finite environment, are a major feature of this change and it is within that broader transition from rural to urban society that environmental history must be understood. That context has manifold dimensions.

First, it enables environmental history to move beyond the limited focus on ideologies characteristic of social movement analysis to a much wider range of institutional factors, that is, the way in which people accumulate and organize their collective values, perceptions, ideas, and activities. To trace the environmental history of urbanization pinpoints the way in which urban development was a major instrument of elaborating and increasing the human pressure on the finite environment. This can be done only partially if the subject is limited to the congestion of the environment internal to the city but more fully by tracking the city itself as the major source of the human load on the wider environment of air, water, and land beyond the city.

Second, the focus on the city, where one inevitably emphasizes the people who shaped the city, their values and attitudes, their activities both within the boundaries of the city and in the wider world beyond the city, enables one to move from the rather simplistic notions that arise from environmental movement ideologies and places emphasis on cities and people as institutions, in all their variety and complexity. This involves the complex relationships between old and new values and ideas, as people struggle with developmental and environmental aspirations as interacting and conflicting impulses and institutions.

Third, the urbanization context of environmental history provides environmental historians with an opportunity to integrate their history into the larger context of history. Historians, like those in many fields of knowledge, tend to specialize in terms of topics generated as knowledge evolves, and hence we have economic, political, and social history, and within social history the history of labor, women, and blacks. But while systematic inquiry spins knowledge off in that kind of direction, the real world is an integrative one in which people live in many circumstances at once. The city, the process of urbanization, and the environmental context of that process provides one of the most fruitful integrative contexts for history.

While philosophical debates over environment and development were lively among the environmental intelligentsia who sought clarity from examining broad patterns of ideas, most of those who searched for enhanced environmental quality in their own lives fostered objectives with less overall clear-cut objectives. Every thrust toward environmental improvement might also foster environmental degradation. It was easy for the environmental opposition to identify such inconsistencies and denigrate them. Yet it was rather remarkable that environmental values and environmental culture continued to persist in personal lives, communities and public policies. It was also clear, however, that the direction of change would involve a continual tension between an advancing environmental culture and a competing developmental culture. To examine these tensions most fully one can place them not within contexts of ideas abstracted from circumstance but from the world of people who in grappling with their environment sought to enhance environmental values as incremental improvement. Urbanization is a remarkably instructive context in which to trace this historical development.

THE FUTURE OF ENVIRONMENTAL REGULATION

THE WORLD OF contemporary debate is filled with pronouncements about the sharp turn of events in environmental regulation which we are now amid; the future, so the argument goes, will be vastly different from the past. I am suspicious of such arguments. They have far less to do with accurate descriptions of change and development over time, and far more with the normative arguments of those who advocate rather than observe and analyze change. Such advocates write recent and current history primarily to support their policy prescriptions. I am far more impressed with incrementalism in American environmental institutions. As one reviews the relevant potential subjects for such an analysis—cost-benefit, comparative risk, relationship between private and public, federal separation of powers, federal-state-local relationships, the pattern of political forces—it is not difficult to observe that incrementalism reigns; the direction of regulation in the future will be much like the past, a continuation of the slow and persistent evolution of patterns underway for the past half-century.

From *The Journal of Law and Commerce* 15, no. 2 (Spring 1996): 549–84.

INCREMENTAL ENVIRONMENTAL KNOWLEDGE

The most persistent driving force in environmental affairs is the perception and definition of environmental circumstance—the condition of the environment. Over the years these slowly move from initial to more extensive definition as details accumulate. Both human values and science contribute to this elaboration, on a slow and persistent pace, at times accelerating and at times slowing down. The value side of the equation is on a course that predictably will continue but at its customary demographic pace:[1] the desire for a larger world of nature amid growing urbanization; the interest in probing human well-being as the world of health shifts from mortality to morbidity and physical fitness; the desire for community environmental stability amid a world of fast-paced change. Many of these elements on the value side were stated rather fully in the now-classic comparative risk study by the EPA Environmental Science Board during the tenure of William Reilly.[2] That report is often taken as a major point of change among those that wish to stress comparative risk. But it was less a clear statement of policy alternatives than an extensive elaboration of the values at risk which have driven environmental affairs for several decades.

The slow and incremental expansion of environmental knowledge helps to embed each environmental circumstance and problem just a bit more firmly in the larger political debate. Visibility studies at the Grand Canyon and the Shenandoah Valley, while generating continued controversy, establish just a bit more firmly visibility improvement as an environmental objective.[3] NAPAP underlined the continued importance of atmospheric deposition and while subsequent research has slowed down, in contrast for example with research in Europe,[4] the subject continues to be explored sporadically through the critical load focus of the Adirondack issue,[5] or the problem of nitrogen saturation or the atmospheric transmission of toxic chemicals. New data about environmental hormones expands a wide range of environmental knowledge at a more rapid pace and we are now in the midst of observing its impact on the longer run course of environmental protection.[6] And we slowly go through the persistent, even though painful shift in focus from the acute effects of high-level human and environmental exposures to the chronic effects of low-level exposures. The research often moves slowly, but the desire to explore and understand this environmental world persists, often in subterranean fashion, to continue an affirmation of a wide range of environmental circumstances, benefits, and problems.

To take the evolutionary and developmental view of all this requires that one dispense with the continual context of scientific assessment associated with decision-making, with its sound-bite approach of "good science and bad science," and instead speak of the continuous exploration of the environmental world that has been underway steadily since World War II. In characteristic fashion in the history of science one scientific investigation leads to conclusions which, in turn, lead to other investigations. Along the way new methodologies are applied, such as radio-telemetry in wildlife research or mass spectrometry in identifying toxic chemicals and charting their pathways. Over the long-run knowledge accumulates. The entire process is understood as the exploration of environmental space, a world out there that still often yields more ignorance—knowledge about what is not yet known—than knowledge about what is known. Environmental science is perhaps the most significant development in the history of science in the last half of the twentieth century. It has slow and subtle, but profound effects on how we look at the world; as knowledge grows in range and complexity, it establishes the context of things environmental.

If we take this approach then what we observe is the accumulation of knowledge about environmental circumstance and problems and this, in turn, has major consequences for incremental policy. Air quality issues are now fought out within the context of some fairly reliable data as to both the level of pollution and the sources of emissions. This is why now the ozone issue is defined not so much in terms of the overall problem but the question of who should be required to reduce emissions: automobiles, utilities, or consumers? Autos say they have done their part; now the utilities should be required to do so.[7] Utilities say the opposite. But the issue is fought out within the context of the whole pot of ambient levels and emission sources that embeds the "problem" more firmly as the context of debate. This is the context of the range of approaches such as cap-and-trade in the 1990 Clean Air Act with sulfur dioxide and the more general trading system now advanced by EPA.

Water quality issues are moving incrementally from a focus on individual discharges organized through traditional administrative systems toward a focus on watersheds which are the more ecorealistic context.[8] This is similar to the approach developed in air in that a watershed reflects a total system in which the loading to that system becomes a matter of the data and then the issue becomes transferred from end-of-pipe allowables to Total Maximum Daily Loads for the entire watershed. In this case I see no revolutionary approach underway but only the gradual emergence of a problem-definition that is more firmly embedded in the environmental world as the context of both implementation and debate. The political issue then shifts from debate over the context to debate over the relative responsibility of sources to the total load in the watershed. Scientific and technical knowledge tends to shift the problem from the open-ended realm that characterized environmental affairs early on to the more circumscribed realm that the data gradually brings to the fore. If one wishes to describe environmental history in terms of first wave and second wave, then the shift I have just outlined makes far more sense than most of the reform-driven analyses which use that terminology.

Toxic issues illustrate the problem that arises when the environmental context within which choices are made remains rather uncharted. We know that the environmental world within which toxics move is extensive; two sets of issues help to identify its range, one in the 1960s, the discovery of DDT in the fat of penguins in the Antarctic, and, the other brought into focus several decades later, the ozone hole.[9] The parameters of the toxic world are large primarily because the chemicals at issue persist, are not biodegradable and hence move in wide circles. We are ignorant about most of their intricate pathways so that the argument underlying most of the debate is the more general argument as to whether or not the buildup of persistent chemicals in almost every facet of the environment is a problem. Debate is intensified because we can't pin down what a specific case amounts to in the larger toxic environmental world.

Land-based issues focus on the balance between development and raw material extraction on the one hand and maintenance of a natural environment on the other. They vary often with variation in the firmness of the area within which choices are made. In some cases environmental science has been able to establish more finite parameters, such as wetlands in which we have some fairly good data from which to work, to identify changes over the years and the role of human action in fostering those changes. "No net loss" implies some standard of finiteness from which to proceed. The endangered species program has a similar context in which the world of species environment is identified and in this case the context of thought is "no loss at all." In other cases the fact of public land ownership shapes the debate, because it establishes at least a legal parameter within which policy choices are made; in this case the direction of knowledge is toward elaborating the natural content of the finite amount of land under public jurisdiction and gaining acceptance of the importance of those values as equal in significance to commodity extraction.[10] One of the more focused land contexts, which bears some relationship to the air and water defined environmental limits are those habitat conservation projects which are associated more with the competing values of development and endangered species in specific areas subject to development pressures, such as the Balcones region near Austin, Texas.[11] Such focused "problem areas" obtain considerable resources simply to describe what is there and once those environmental values can be set alongside the developmental values within a given limited land environment, then trade-offs can be made more seriously. But the policy context is more fuzzy when the environmental context is more open-ended and hence appears without finite boundaries, or when most of the technical knowledge about the environmental content is limited.

The attempt to identify environmental values within relatively confined land areas began on a modern scale when northeastern conservation commissions focused on natural environment potential through community surveys.[12] A similar process is now going on with land conservancies generally, which branch out from management of their own land to inventories and action within the wider region of which they are a part.[13] Confined water–based organizations dealing with lakes, bays, and estuaries extend the range of their "environmental system" from the lake to the entire watershed.[14] And within those watersheds lands valued for their environmental qualities are identified as worthy of protection. Another step comes when those inventories are set alongside the lands on which developers have their eye and negotiations begin that are in the direction of a mutual agreement on the location of such valuable areas and their incorporation into plans by being built around and preserved as environmental assets that enhance the residential value of the land. Finite environments in which balances between development and environmental values are worked out slowly but persistently worm their way along to encompass more of the environmental world.[15]

The significant point about all this is that environmental knowledge has a twofold real-world context, one in which the finite parameters of air, land, and water have become more clearly and fully defined and the other in which the environmental elements in those "media" as well as the intricate relationships among those elements has also been more clearly and fully defined. On both these counts there is much more that we do not know and one can argue with some plausibility that our inquiries have increased ignorance much faster than they have increased knowledge. Yet the persistent accumulation of knowledge generates a more elaborate sense of the fact of environmental limits and also an increasingly detailed understanding of the way in which natural processes and human actions work. All this defines the context of environmental circumstance that emerges from a greater understanding of the environmental world and hence the context of policy choices. This has been the course of development in environmental affairs for the past decades and it will continue to be in the future as well.

COST-BENEFIT AND COMPARATIVE RISK

Much of the current discussion about the future of environmental regulation focuses on cost-benefit and comparative risk. Most observers argue that these approaches presage major changes in how regulation takes place. I would argue the contrary, perhaps some changes, but in slow and incremental manner. It is not at all clear how the current debate will turn out, but I think it rather fanciful to think that it will lead to major changes.

Cost-benefit analysis has been with us from the start of environmental regulation and it is quite misleading to argue, at any point of time in the past decades, including now, that we must now apply it with the implication that it has not been applied before.[16] This is simply mythology. The more realistic focus is to observe how it has evolved and developed over the years. And the most significant point is that it has steadily become more elaborate and more detailed. One might take benefit analysis back to the first authorization of the criteria document in the 1963 Clean Air Act and the subsequent debate over the first SO_2 criteria document with which industry was more than unhappy. This then led to a legislative mandate in 1967 that the document be revised under the guidance of an advisory committee with significant industry representation.[17] Or, one might take the cost analysis back to the 1970 Clean Air Act which required a quarterly survey of the impact of the law on jobs which, over the years, concluded that few had been lost and as a result both industry and labor lost interest in the analysis.

In subsequent years the formula has taken several turns. One was the momentary popularity of cost effectiveness during the Carter administration, a formula which assumed that once the objective was agreed on the choice would be over the most economical way of reaching the agreed-on objective.[18] The system fell into some disrepute over the cotton dust (brown-lung) standard which made clear that one could readily make a decision more cost-effective simply by reducing the benefits (personal protection devices rather than technology controls). Another was the intensive analysis of air pollution exposures, the most elaborate of which was undertaken by the California South Coast Air Pollution Management District in which the research design covered several thousand human exposure data-points. Or there was the 500 million dollar attempt to elaborate the effects analysis of acid rain which identified the unknowns as well as the knowns and Congress decided that still "more research before action" called for by the regulated industry, would probably not lead to anything more conclusive.[19] Or, as a final example, there was the cost-benefit analysis in the proposal to eliminate lead in gasoline in which, although the main concern was the adverse effects of lead exposures on the neurological development of children, the analysis ignored most of the up-to-date health knowledge and allocated most of the benefit to improving the function of gasoline motors.[20] Such episodes along the way chart some, but by no means all, of the twists and turns in cost-benefit analysis over the years. The current argument that all this is simply a pro-and-con issue—does one apply cost-benefit analysis or not?— fails to work out a realistic history of the way in which cost-benefit has evolved.

Amid the give-and-take of controversy both sides of the fence, those who wish greater environmental benefits and those who seek to restrain such action, have argued for the need for greater detail through more elaborate studies. That call is now repeated in terms of the current legislation primarily from the environmental opposition. But the record makes clear that more elaborate studies of both costs and benefits don't change the context very much but only add more decision-points in working out cost-benefit so that it takes more time, and through the resulting greater complexity often increases transaction costs of time and money and generates decision-paralysis. In the proposals now being debated I see very little change in that direction. The process will become more detailed, more complex, more cumbersome with a higher level of paralytic potential and more costly.

The issue plaguing cost-benefit analysis over the years is not primarily one of analyzing costs, which are usually more fully done, but benefits, which are poorly done. The major problem which has repeatedly arisen is: how does one work in the benefits? As the give-and-take between costs and benefits evolves the cost side of the analysis has continued to proceed as the dominant side of the formula and benefits as the subordinate side. Amid all the current debate, I do not see that imbalance changing very much. The imbalance is excused often on the grounds of the difficulty in working out benefits, or dismissed on the grounds that benefits are "insignificant" compared with the costs. One might have predicted a more elaborate system for benefit analysis from the SAB report on Comparative Risk when it argued that there are four types of risk—mortality, morbidity, ecological and welfare—and that all of them must be brought into the context of comparative risk.[21] That potential of enhancement of benefit analysis has not emerged save for some rather limited efforts by EPA to elaborate ecological effects, and one cannot predict that this will move forward at more than a snail's pace.[22]

The problems in benefits analysis has been emphasized recently by the experience of the state of Illinois.[23] Cost-benefit analysis was required for all state regulations in a statute approved in 1986. Recently, however, the process has been abandoned. For the most part, the problem has been the difficulty in dealing with the benefit side, which has been bogged down in continual controversy. Hence the regulatory agency has taken up the task of making the trade-offs based on its own personal judgment. The lesson of this experience, which only supplements the lessons of benefit analysis generally, is that if one is serious about trading off costs and benefits the benefit side requires far more development in both analytical strategies and data in order to make it truly commensurate with the cost side in working out a balance. If one takes the debate at the national level as an indicator there is little evidence that this will happen.[24]

The addition of comparative risk to this debate involves similar questions but with the addition of the problem of the common denominator through which trade-offs are made. Seemingly comparing risks is easier and with a more forthright quantitative trade-off than cost-benefits. Risk identification raises the issue of the data base in a manner similar to that of cost-benefit such as the weakness of the morbidity, ecological, and welfare benefit data. But it also adds the issue of a context for tradeoff. How does one find a way of trading off increased childhood exposures that reduce potential nervous system development with extending the life of older people by reducing the incidence of cancer? This has been a favorite way of putting the problem in the course of national debate. The problem of discovering formulae for making such trade-offs is extensive; the SAB categories suggest the range of such problems and many familiar issues can specify them. How to trade off visibility in the Grand Canyon and Shenandoah National Park with weaker lung function or asthma from ozone and particulate exposures?[25]

At issue is the question of the degree of willingness to face the politics of these issues: in cost-benefit the limited scientific data available to calculate benefits; in comparative risk assessment the additional problem of a formula to trade off values. By and large the debate now going on in the Congress ignores these issues by asserting the need for more elaborate studies which conveys an undercurrent of far greater concern for the studies of costs rather than benefits and with only an amateurish approach to the context of trade-offs. Quite a different turn of affairs has been underway in the states in which a number of state-wide committees are at work on comparative risk. Almost all of these have a scientific committee to assess the state of the science required and a general public committee that ranks priorities for state-wide objectives.[26] The general upshot of most of these state processes are two conclusions: first that the science is not available to be systematic about the range of desired environmental objectives; and second, that the value trade-offs are so fundamental and so incapable of being reduced to formulae that wide public participation is required to make sure that the choices can be worked out as broad social choices. These directions in the state sector lead to conclusions that the desired process is not one of expert decision-making alone, but a broad public process that involves the public as well as the experts. After all is said and done it may well be that the customary methods of decision-making that we have seen for several decades will remain.

MARKET FORCES AND PUBLIC REGULATION

An integral part of the plethora of predictions about the future of environmental regulation is that it will involve a major shift toward "market forces" and the private economy. There is no question that there is an ideological overlay in current environmental debate away from government regulation and toward the private market.[27] And this ideological overlay often becomes the center of attention and argument. However, there is another world of practical action that works in the other direction and which, despite the ideological content of debate, has considerable influence in dealing with concrete environmental affairs. All this adds up to a reasonable conclusion that there will be much less emphasis on "market forces" than is predicted and that government will continue to be relied on as a crucial and indispensible instrument of environmental action.

One of the most interesting aspects of this problem is the strategy of public ownership of land as an instrument for enhancing community, regional, and national environmental quality. From the private market theorists we have continued affirmation that the job would be done better through "market forces." As John Baden continually argues, private owners are better watchdogs of environmental quality in land than are public owners; they look out for the interests of others in their use of the land and they look out for the interests of future generations.[28] I see little public agreement with that notion and instead considerable public action toward public land management rather than to shift from public to private. The reason is that there is abundant human experience that private land owners do not manage their land in the interests of other land owners or the public, and do not manage their land in the interests of future generations. This is a case of ideology going one way and practical experience going another way. The persistent experience over the centuries is that private land is often used to the detriment of both other private owners and the public and there are innumerable court cases to try to draw the line between "private rights" and "private wrongs." Through "takings" proposals we now have an effort at legislative override of common law doctrine, and where the issue has been well focused such as in Arizona and Washington, the public clearly rejects the theory. While theory often has popularity when considered in the abstract, its popularity declines sharply when it becomes salient in the context of practical consequences.

An interesting fate of the "private market" ideology is land preservation or "land saving."[29] It is most sharply identified in the recent popularity of land conservancies, which now number over 1100 in the nation and the considerable number of state and local public referenda to provide funds for public land acquisition through either direct taxation or bond issues. The assumption in land saving is that in some way land must be divorced from the private market in order to accomplish environmental objectives. Either it must be purchased to be managed as public land or be acquired in some fashion to be managed by a private land conservancy which combines private ownership and public purposes. Both have been quite popular in recent years. While free market land advocates talk one way, the general public acts another way. I see little change in this in the future since the real world is firmly embedded in human experience: if one wishes to preserve land from development one cannot rely on private, for-profit, institutions which destroy open and natural land through development rather than preserve it.

How does the analysis apply to the role of the private market in environmental protection rather than land saving: air and water pollution, toxic waste, the whole gamut of relevant environmental issues? These issues also involve fundamental conflicts between private and public objectives. Those objectives involve public resources such as air, water, and wildlife, resources that over the years have been firmly embedded in law as involving far wider "public interest" rather than the "pecuniary interests" of profit making private enterprise. Constitutional statements of "environmental rights" which are in a variety of state constitutions state such public values explicitly; water and air quality are protected on the grounds that these are public resources and hence must be maintained in a given level of quality; wildlife has long been a public resource, managed not through private action but through state public regulation. Moreover, publicly owned lands have been a firm part of both federal and state jurisdictions for over a century and the relevant resulting issues have continually defined the problems as a conflict between private management of resources through such soundbites as "exploitation" and public management for broader public objectives.

In thinking more clearly about environmental protection issues beyond the sound bite of "market forces" one must make a distinction between environmental objectives and environmental implementation. Over the past decades the establishment of environmental objectives, such as standards, has come primarily from the public sector because there has been continued dissatisfaction with the level of environmental contamination. While some of these sources are public management agencies most in the debate have involved private management, or "market forces." Cases in which sources of pollution by themselves advocate higher levels of environmental protection, are difficult, if not impossible, to identify. Higher standards come from the public sector and are persistently opposed by the private sector. That opposition continues in such realms as particulates and ozone in air quality, mercury in utility emissions, dioxin in pulp and paper, effluent and ambient water quality. The history of these issues is the constant argument from the regulated industry and some public entities that the proposed additional level of environmental quality is "unnecessary" and "minimal." It would be more than risky to predict that all this will change in any significant degree. In the past "market forces" have persistently enhanced the resistance of the regulated sector to higher levels of environmental quality and will predictably continue to do so with little significant change.

But doesn't the emissions trading scheme in the 1990 Clean Air Act indicate otherwise? Not at all.[30] There is confusion galore about that emissions trading scheme. It had nothing to do with establishing standards, but was confined to implementing them. The standards were set by a legislative decision to reduce SO_2 emissions by 50 percent; they had nothing to do with market forces, but were a traditional type of legislative standard setting, for example, similar to "fishable and swimmable" which came entirely from the public sector. The allowances and emission trading provided a new method of implementation but as additions to customary strategies that had been available for some time. Coal washing, low-sulfur coal, and scrubbing had been such alternatives. The 1990 act did drop the 1977 requirement for mandatory reduction of emissions when using low-sulfur coal but emissions trading only added a fourth implementation strategy to the three long in existence.

And how about that current chestnut, "command and control?" Like "emissions trading" this tends to have a major component of ideology that gets in the way of clear thinking. In environmental administration there are always public choices and private choices, and the task is to identify in a down-to-earth practical manner just what the relative contributions of those choices are. The real world of environmental administration involves choices made by various sectors of the regulated community as well as choices made by the agencies. We could get at all this more fully if we would replace the soundbite "command and control" with the more real world context of regulatory initiative and regulated response.

The closest we have to "command and control" in all this is the use of exemplary cases as technology performance models for the rest of industry to follow: the average of the best, 10 percent in the Clean Water Act and 12 percent in the Clean Air Act.[31] These were legislative decisions to establish standards of technology performance. They were made general in the Clean Water Act as the "average of the best," then defined by EPA as the average of the best 10 percent. This approach then was applied in the 1990 Clean Air Act defined as the average of the top 12 percent for air toxics. These are performance standards. They arise not from agency command and regulated industry control but from the course of technological change in industry itself. The best-performing industries set the pace and EPA then uses those industries as the model.[32] They are technologies in place adopted by the most advanced sectors of the industry which are then used as examples to be taken up by other firms.[33]

The political dynamics of the technology performance standards is not one of EPA versus the regulated industry but is defined by the internal politics of industry which pit the best performers against the rest and involve industry reactions against the attempt to generalize the best technologies already in place. Trade associations object to this way of choosing the model; they are prone to take the median as the "average of the best," as they did in the litigation on the Clean Water Act standard. The political direction of trade associations rarely arises from the "best performers" in the industry because the associations are usually governed through votes by firm rather than volume of production; they respond to the majority of firms and hence to the more numerous conventional rather than the fewer advanced technology firms.[34] In this context the use of "command and control" ideology becomes a political strategy to perpetuate older technologies in place of using the best performers as models for improvement.

In these matters of "market forces" we can expect the continuation of several long-standing directions. First, little of the main thrust of the original "Heinz-Wirth" report on "market forces," that is, the use of pollution taxes, will take place.[35] While such "market forces" have good support in the environmental community, they meet uncompromising resistance in the regulated community. They have been rejected as governmental imposition rather than "market forces" and will undoubtedly continue to be. To include such proposals in a report on "market forces" has always seemed to be incongruous—how does one translate a tax into a market force?—and will continue to be.

Second, the most significant "market force," national environmental standards, will continue to be ignored as a market force. Standards create markets to which potential entrepreneurs can respond in their own way. This role of standards has been and will continue to be the most significant "market force" but also will continue not to be recognized by the "market force" theorists. Pollution standards create markets. While they restrain the emissions of old technologies they establish markets for new ones, and the beauty of such a "market force" is that from the point of the standard on, it is an invitation to investors, scientists, engineers, and entrepreneurs in general to capture that market. Details as to how it works can be followed in the activities of the Institute of Clean Air Companies, and its predecessor organizations, as the standards stimulate new technologies and scrubbers improve in both efficiency and reliability over the years.[36] In this context the 50 percent reduction SO_2 provision in the Clean Air Act of 1990 was a market-building mechanism that has greatly stimulated continued development of this industry. As that industry continually reminds decision makers, the continued role of market forces depends on the continued firmness of standards and their enforcement.

Third, a persistent market force is the continued influence of nation-wide markets in general in working toward continued nation-wide standards. The influence of the national market works in diverse ways. One current case is the agreement between EPA and the manufacturers to lower the lead content of faucets.[37] Another is the negotiation under way between EPA and the manufacturers of truck engines to reduce nitrogen dioxide emissions by 60 percent nation-wide.[38] In both of these the manufacturers have opted for national standards to avoid markets fractured by different standards, state and federal. Amid such forces the ideological context of "command and control" and "market forces" as a tendency to reduce the federal role in establishing standards provides no clear guides to understanding the real world of environmental affairs. I see no reversal of this influence of national markets on national standards.

And fourth, a prediction that is currently reasonable to make follows from the current rationale of the Republican leadership in Congress that what they seek in contrast with "command and control" is "compliance flexibility." Such flexibility has long been the case, such as the activities of "variance boards" in implementing the early days of the Clean Air Act of 1970. And it probably will continue. In such a sound-bite context, "market forces" often seems to be a device for reducing standards rather than more flexible implementation of the standards. This is the case in the greenfield-brownfield issue for hazardous waste standards in which a strategy to redevelop urban sites through relaxed standards has now been applied in several states to provide relaxed standards for greenfield sites as well.[39] In such cases flexibility means relaxed standards rather than adapting compliance to circumstances. If it does mean only the latter then I think we are on an evolutionary course from past decades rather than at some turning point.

SEPARATION OF POWERS AND FEDERALISM

A range of issues which we could collectively call constitutional are an integral part of regulatory analysis. There are two sets of these, one involving the relationship between branches of government in the federal system—legislature, administration, judicial, and the executive branch—and the other involving relationships among levels of government, federal, state, and municipal/local. Can we contemplate major future changes in the environmental relationships among these governing institutions? Here I would continue the general argument that ideology, in which much of this is framed, is one thing, and the world of institutional practice is quite another. While much of the ideological overlay will predictably continue so also will the often opposite direction of institutional practice.

These issues are to be understood within the context of the give and take among the various political forces involved in environmental decisions. So far as the political actors are concerned each governing institution involves an opportunity to use its authority to implement a desired policy or to restrain its opponents. This is not a matter of constitutional theory but of opportunistic action. As one finds one set of institutions useful for one set of objectives and another for another, inconsistencies in theory abound; one can make sense of the jumble only in terms of the continuity of environmental objectives at stake for each party to the environmental drama.

Within that federal context a pattern has emerged: the Congress authorizes administrative agencies to act; objection to agency decisions arises and the issue is taken to the courts; objection arises to the court decisions and then one goes either to the executive branch to get an executive fix or back to the legislature for a legislative fix. From time to time the legislature calls upon some scientific or technical review body such as the National Research Council for a study, but those who lose in this arena at times bypass the science and go directly for a legislative fix, such as in the current issues of pesticide residues in food, wetlands, and endangered species.[40]

This pathway along the institutions in the federal system would be relatively unchanged by the various proposals now before the Congress. Cost-benefit legislation would require EPA to engage in more elaborate analysis than before. The courts will be available to take the next step by those who object to EPA's decisions and under the current proposals that step would increase. One of the most significant constitutional changes now before us is the practice of using the appropriations process for quick and convenient legislative fixes. And inherent in the changes contemplated by current legislation is the possibility that the courts may well take a new tack when confronted with issues that the EPA has either missed its timetables or acted in an "arbitrary and capricious" manner when its ability to carry out legislative mandates is restricted by congressional reduction in resources to do so. This might require the courts to go beyond the context of "arbitrary and capricious" agency behavior, to a judgment about legislative behavior. But this speculation only underlines the limited long-run effect of proposals now in process.

In jockeying for position within the four sets of federal institutions much depends simply on whether or not the executive and the legislature are of the same party. During the Reagan and Bush administrations the environmental opposition sought to enhance the power of the executive and was checked significantly by the Congress.[41] During the Clinton administration we have the opposite, congressional initiatives engineered by the environmental opposition possibly checked by the executive. If in the course of electoral events both the executive and the Congress would be of the same party, then the possibility of major changes would greatly increase. However, even in this case, the problem of changing relative authority among the federal branches so that it would continue beyond the moment would still remain and I would predict that the dynamics I outlined at the start would persist: Congress passes legislation, the agencies carry it out, the losers go to the courts, and then those who still want to carry on the battle go for an executive or a legislative fix.

Institutions involving levels of government, usually described as federal-

ism, are a somewhat different matter.[42] These do not involve federal-state relationships alone. We have still another level of government that while not
provided for in the formal constitutions of both federal and state, plays a significant role in the drama of the vertical interplay of authority and power.
Municipal and local governments are not constitutionally independent, yet as
a practical matter they provide opportunities to exercise authority and power
that are often as crucial as the choices between state and federal. Those who
seek preemption statutes are just as eager to curb the power of local government through state preemption as are those who seek federal preemption of
state. In fact, I would argue that state preemption of local authority is perhaps
the most significant constitutional development in the environmental era.
Many a state legislature has sought to get back the zoning power it gave to
local governments 70 years ago through specific statutes that prohibit local
governments from establishing standards stricter than those established
through state authority. The current debate over drilling in the Antrim gas
field in Michigan is one of the latest of a long-standing set of relevant constitutional issues.[43]

Much of the current debate on this issue is in the context of "returning"
power to the states, a piece of sound-bite mythology rather than a vehicle for
careful analysis. The idea of "returning" federal lands in the West to the states
is a misnomer because those lands have never been owned by the states; the
political context of the issue is two quite different systems of land management with different objectives, one by the states and the other by the federal
government and the issue boils down to whether or not the "new West" really
wants to expand the limited uses of state lands by adding federal land to that
institutional setting.[44] The federal wetlands programs which started with the
waterfowl refuges managed by the U.S. Fish and Wildlife Service never were
state programs, but arose out of federal migratory bird treaties and the program to use proceeds from the federal duck stamp to purchase wetlands along
the major flyways. The states had no significant wetland or endangered species
programs prior to the emergence of these issues.

Or consider the relationship between federal and state in environmental
protection issues which frames much of the federal-state debate. One of the
most obvious is the interstate character of air and water pollution which have
long been defined partly in interstate terms, from the time of the narrowly
stated ones of metropolitan areas or watersheds that cross state boundaries to
the more broadly stated ones of long-distance transport of air pollution.[45]
Over the years, however, an even more powerful influence has come from the
business community which continually seeks interstate uniformity as a pref-

erence to multi-state differences in regulatory programs. This was one of the major reasons for the search for uniform federal standards in the early history of environmental protection programs. Despite the current ideology this industry preference for minimum national standards continues to play a role, for example, in the current negotiations between EPA and the manufacturers of truck engines for a national standard mentioned above.

The search for federal uniformity also comes into play, almost inevitably it would seem, from the issue of interstate equity. The real world of state environmental policy and administration is its enormous variability and at some point along the line the question of fairness arises between people in one state that have higher quality programs and those who have lower quality ones.[46] The current cost-benefit strategies being debated in Congress will certainly bring this question to the fore because of the enormous variability in state scientific and technical capabilities; some can do the job and others cannot. This will involve both questions of the desire for national uniformity deriving from the demands of the national market and the fact that interstate inequities of this kind will become more salient as the scientific and technical requirements are enhanced.

These features of federal-state relationships seem to me to have a powerful and controlling influence on the course of environmental affairs. As I have watched them evolve over the years I have been impressed with the degree to which they persist. Events that come and go may seem to predict major changes, but the long-run tendencies continue to be a driving force. It does not seem possible to reduce the pressures for uniform national standards which derive from the power of national, in contrast with regional and local markets; nor does it seem possible to reduce the variations in the administrative capabilities of the states. Hence if we take a more down-to-earth and realistic view of the situation rather than one that is laced with politically driven mythology it seems relatively safe to predict that the future will not be much different from the past in the relationships among governing institutions that form the context of our constitutional system.

THE STRUCTURE OF POLITICS

Underlying all of these issues is the structure of politics, the various actors and their relationships, the forces that drive and shape the regulatory system. If we predict major changes in the regulatory system in the future, those predictions have to be realistically grounded in changes in the underlying political forces. Will those forces change over the years?[47] I am dubious; patterns of environmental politics have evolved in rather persistent directions for several decades now. Moreover, despite the current display of political power by the regulated community, it is rather far fetched to believe that that pattern is on a new and different course. Moreover, I do not see that middle grounds will be any more prevalent in the future than in the past. For years the great white hope has been that if we just find the right processes we can reduce the controversies and especially avoid litigation. But this hope has not been realized and I cannot observe any significant change in this regard. The current focus is on "reg-neg" or negotiated regulation. While this approach will undoubtedly be tried persistently in the future, the hope that it will play more than a minor role in the process seems illusory. The substantive issues are powerful, and so are the political forces driving them; it is difficult to see that innovation in process alone will mitigate them.

While the political forces in environmental affairs are many and varied, subject to change from issue to issue and time to time, there is a certain consistency which enables one to identify patterns that are simpler in structure and thereby about which one can draw conclusions more effectively. On the one hand is a group of people who are intrigued with the role of the environment as an element in the human standard of living, phrased in terms of quality rather than material goods; they include the general public amid whom these values have arisen in the years after World War II and the professionals, for example, scientists, who seek to understand this newly observed environmental world. Historically all this is quite new. While there are some precedents in earlier years in the cases of prominent environmental writers, common-law nuisance proceedings and municipal sanitation programs, on the whole all this was limited and sporadic and did not become widespread until after World War II. It is mistakenly called a "movement" but it is rather a comprehensive cultural change that involves widely shared values, law and science, the economy and education, the media and governments at all levels as well as something we might call an organized "environmental movement." And it has affected not only policy at all levels, but private initiatives, personal behavior, and community activity. These are the forces pressing for environmental change.[48]

There is, then, a second force, the environmental opposition, that is varied and influential but has not been examined as closely as has the evolving environmental culture. It has been there from the start and continues to be there. It has, in fact, evolved significantly in its political role, as issue has followed issue. But its political position of seeking to restrain and slow down the environmental drive has remained constant over the years. Its tactics have changed as it has increased its political capabilities especially during the Carter and Clinton administrations when new influence of the environmental organizations in those years seemed to be in the offing. And as new communications technology has emerged it has been able to mobilize the public in ways beyond the capability of the environmental organizations. But its strategies have remained rather constant: limit the impact of regulations on its balance sheets, restrict the claims of environmental advocates to natural lands, use the power of public relations to develop the image of "good neighbors," enhance the ability to influence decision-making bodies, denigrate environmental organizations as "self-serving" interest groups rather than instruments of advancing policies of broad public interest, and engage in the continual process of admitting past sins but affirming recent conversions. I see little change in direction in the character of the environmental opposition as well as in the character of the environmental initiatives.

There are two major arenas in which the political choices are carried out, the legislative and the administrative, in which the balance of these forces is somewhat different. The environmental side of affairs has been able to worm its way somewhat into the legislative side. I say somewhat, because I think that the grandiose statements by such writers as Gregg Easterbrook that environmentalists had their own way in the past thirty years is simply more fuzzy mythology.[49] One can point to the many cases in which environmental objectives were watered down in the legislative process and equally many cases in which laws with considerable promise were either ignored or modified in their application, such as the way in which the courts transformed the EIS provision of NEPA into a purely procedural rather than a substantive requirement and the Toxic Substances Control Act, the impact of which has been more than limited. So for the environmental community the legislative arena has been a mixed bag.

In the administrative area, the environmental community has quite limited clout, its strategies being confined primarily to attempts to defend the legislative provisions. For the most part the political arena of administration is the continued face-to-face relationship between the regulators and the regulated and the issues involve their jockeying for position in such matters as the data, broad vs. strict construction of the legislation, the science, the economic impact. For all that we badly need some realistic descriptions of the many facets of this struggle over the application of the statutes, such as the recent New York Times piece on the measurement of VOCs in the wood products industry.[50] But it does seem safe to say that this context of administrative politics will not change in its direction over the years, only its complexity and, because of that complexity, the continuing ability of the regulated industry to restrain action.

Because of the persistence of these political forces I see no significant change in the continued hope for reducing tension through some sort of mediation or negotiation beyond an occasional case. Major comprehensive efforts have had little success, such as the National Coal Policy Project,[51] the Toxic Substances Control Act project which had unrealized hopes of heading off controversies before they emerged,[52] or the TWF, Timber, Wildlife and Fish process in Washington State which was one of the most promising cases because it was fully financed by the legislature, and involved considerable effort to establish an agreed on scientific and field studies base.[53] Moreover, review of mediation efforts make clear that few agencies are willing to finance the basic requirement in mediation that the parties start out from an equal basis of political power before they can succeed at all.

There are a few more hopeful cases at dispute resolution such as habitat conservation projects and development projects that incorporate environmental assets such as wetlands rather than destroy them. These seem to require that both environmental values and developmental values be fully laid out and accepted by both parties, and then arranged on the land in a mutually agreed on zoning pattern. These often arise from initiatives from private land conservancies who reach out to developers with success dependent on the willingness of developers to adjust their projects to environmental values of community significance. But few subjects seem to entail these requirements and hence one cannot generalize extensively from them.

Realistic thinking about these political matters is often muddied by the mythology that the differences in dispute are really matters of the presence or absence of "good will" rather than issues of substance. The regulated community is particularly prone to define the issues this way: the environmental community has ulterior motives other than environmental values and the business community simply wishes to be "a good neighbor." At times the mythology is one of who is an "environmentalist" and who is not. This mythology only inhibits the desire to think very clearly about politics. What we have to accept is that the issues are of major substance and that the give-and-take in politics is not a matter of good will but of the struggle over the substance. Hence clear thinking requires that we formulate analytical ideas based on how the struggle over substance works out rather than to play out the roles involved in the give and take of mythologies.

THE POLITICS OF SCIENCE

The persistence of these features of political controversy is most fully evident in scientific issues which are the most intractable issues of all. The self-image of science is that scientific knowledge fosters agreement out of disagreement and that science, therefore, is far superior to "politics" which fosters disagreement. Yet as one tracks the vast number of scientific disputes in environmental affairs one is impressed with the way in which the world of science itself fosters massive disagreement. Science works not through its own dynamic but through scientists, real live people, and the scientists are highly contentious. Much of that contentiousness comes through specialization; by specializing scientists fracture knowledge, perpetuate division within the world of science and play a major role in perpetuating controversy. That world of controversy is enhanced significantly by the regulated industry that continually challenges science because of the fear that new scientific knowledge will lead to further regulation; hence the regulated industry supports one group of scientists rather than another, and thereby perpetuates scientific disagreement rather than helps to resolve differences.[54]

All of this presents some major difficulties in the attempt to work out analytical formats through which we can assess the course of the politics of science over the years. The most attractive way of thinking is reflected in the sound bite of "good science and bad science" fostered by the scientists themselves, the administrative agencies, and the regulated industry. We need to improve vastly on this mode of analysis, and I suggest two possibilities here.

One is to distinguish the major forces driving environmental science. One such force is exploratory science, the desire to know more about the larger environmental world. Little of that world is known and exploratory science is driven by the age-old scientific desire to find out more of the unknown. This leads to a sequential definition of problems in environmental science that adds up to accumulation of systematic knowledge.[55] The drive tends to bring exploratory science together with environmental values as cooperative tendencies. A second direction is defensive science fostered by the regulated industry. What it wishes to advance is the science that will protect it from environmental regulation. Often the regulated industry will look ahead and see the emerging exploratory science and then take up science which might offset it. A past case is that of the International Lead Zinc Association in its attempt to preempt cadmium regulation through its own sponsored research and a good current case is the announced research program of the Chemical Industry Institute of Technology in the face of the new science of environmental hormones.[56] A third direction in environmental science flows from the regulatory agencies who face disputes over science between the exploratory and defensive strategies and then seek to advance research on specific issues that might resolve differences, underpin a regulatory initiative, and avoid later paralytic dispute and litigation.

The implication of this classification of scientific initiatives as an analytical tool is to reduce a great number of issues to a more manageable framework and to focus on the point that it isn't so much the quality of science, such as the constant plea for "better science," as its direction that helps one to sort out the myriad of disputes. It also enables one to make a judgment about the future in the light of the past. These three directions of science and the involvement of those directions in policy and political dispute over a half century will predictably continue with little change.

A second analytical strategy that flows from the problem of systematically ordering scientific controversy emphasizes "levels of proof." Here the analytical framework is a continuum of dispute from the first identification of the issue through its progress toward greater agreement on the other. On the right end of the spectrum one observes the initial statement of the problem and initial evidence and on the left one approaches the notion of "firm" evidence. Along the way across the continuum evidence accumulates. Research is repeated with similar results; more and varied populations are examined for effects; varied methodologies yield similar results. An important stage in movement along the continuum is when the scientific community first comes to agree that the problem is significant enough to be worth studying, which is about a quarter of the way across the spectrum from right to left. Then the studies increase, knowledge accumulates, sharp differences among some scientists are somewhat muted, and a workable scientific agreement emerges. "Conclusive evidence" and full agreement rarely, if ever, occurs, not even in the case of smoking, but a critical mass of agreement develops in which the dissenters become a smaller, even though vocal, minority and are relegated to the periphery of the debate.[57]

Amid all this the key question for dispute is the level of proof required for agreement—the number of replications that occur, for example in the case of lead exposure and neurological development; or the varied methodologies that are brought to bear, epidemiology and toxicology, field and laboratory research, or the level of disaggregation and variables controlled. Over the years the factors involving "standards of proof" such as the varieties of specialized scientists or the methodologies involved become more elaborate, and the whole process evolves toward complexity. And over the years as the concentration levels at issue become smaller and more difficult to detect, or the causal factors become more elaborate, the context of potential agreement becomes more complex and difficult. Yet the focal point for dispute, the levels of proof, remains and provides an analytical technique for understanding the general course of affairs amid the details of a succession of specific disputes. With this analytical approach in mind, I find it difficult to argue that the future of disputes over environmental science will be much different than the past and that the linear increase in the complexity of science will only make the disputes more intractable.

A major reason for that intractability is the tendency for assessments over science to be closely bound up with the potential consequences of science for regulation. Attempts to separate them have proven to be futile. The early theory of the criteria document was first to develop a scientific assessment and then to apply it in policy; from the start that proved to be impossible because the assessments by the scientists in the Public Health Service were challenged by the affected industries. Tendencies in these questions over the years have been toward a closer and more confusing intermixture of scientific assessment and regulatory implications rather than toward their clear separation. The attempt to sort this out in the context of risk by distinguishing between risk assessment and risk management, one of the most important recent attempts, has failed to change the pattern. Those who conduct the assessments often fall back on the regulatory implications as a basis for drawing their scientific conclusions and those involved in risk management cannot divorce themselves from expressing concern about the implications of the scientific assessments for their management.

These analytical problems most often deal with environmental protection issues, but they are even more volatile in land management where ecological science is now impinging on both public and private land management.[58] In this case several patterns emerge. In matters of endangered species and wetlands the scientists have maintained a rather consistent and firmly scientific position; they have got into hot water because they have not shifted toward policy judgments and, as a result, it is the Congress that has had to say that the issues are policy issues and not scientific ones. In public land management, managers often simply dispense with the science in order to avoid its implications for management. Hence while wildlands biological science has evolved in one direction, forest managers have devised ways and means of warding off its implication for management. The Clinton forest program for the Pacific Northwest has charted out a redirection through its "adaptive management" zones, with the notion that the scientific results in these experiments will lead to revisions of management, first work out the science and then apply it. But this has the potential of becoming just as fuzzy and murky in the relationships between science and management as have past cases. One cannot predict that the future will be much different.

UNDERSTANDING REGULATORY AFFAIRS

The future of environmental regulation, finally, is closely bound up with the ability to bypass the massive overlay of sound-bite terminology which has come to shape the way we think in order to get at the more substantive world of environmental affairs. Will this change much? I think not. Over the years we have developed a series of sound bites that have invaded and come to dominate the world of environmental analysis. Some of these cases I have already introduced. They involve two sets of words and phrases. First are those that evoke only emotions, such as "stringent," "activist," "scare tactics," "rational," "eco-realism," "pristine," "good neighbor," "common sense," or "nature lovers." Second are those which extend the emotive reactions to larger concepts which frame ways of thinking: "use" vs. "nonuse," "cost-benefit," "environment versus the economy," "command and control," "market forces," "special interest," "good science and bad science," "humans versus wildlife," "NIMBY," "first wave and second wave." The groups in the second category shape frames of reference which become the context within which problems are identified, defined, and debated, so that they establish a conceptual framework, even though one that is deeply rooted in emotion.

As one watches the evolution of such soundbites, one becomes interested in their dynamics: from what sectors of the environmental debate do they arise; how do they move from initial presentation to more sustained use; what role do they play in establishing a context of analysis removed from the world of environmental substance; how do they fuse strong emotive content to analytical content? I mention two aspects of this kind of analysis here. First, their use arises from a mixture of professional, technical, administrative sources, and media sources. The media shapes issues into easily understood sound bites; then almost every environmental actor seeks the support of the media and caters to the way in which the media selects and shapes the news. Scientists, economists, and administrators, the major actors in the professional environmental world, take up the same task of formulating and repeating sound bites to express their objectives. Hence my earlier argument that such phrases as "command and control," "cost-benefit," "market forces" and "good science and bad science" are formulated by the experts and sustain concepts in argument more for their emotive appeal than their analytical insight.

Second, the great majority of active sound bites, those that move from initial origin to widespread use come from the environmental opposition rather than from those who advance environmental objectives. It is not that the environmental community does not wish to use sound bites; it does. But it usually finds that its sound bites lose out and hence the simplified context of debate is shaped far more by the environmental opposition rather than those who advance environmental objectives. Few sound bites undergird thinking to sustain those objectives; most undergird the opposition. A few examples might illustrate these points.

One is the term "NIMBY." The general meaning of the term is that in siting issues a community that organizes to oppose siting advocates its own selfish interest in contrast with the larger interest which requires siting. That has established a wide-ranging set of ideas that can readily be called up just by evoking the word "NIMBY." There is a soundbite or two from the environmental side that could shape thinking in quite a different direction; one, for example, places value in a community "sense of place." That phrase "sense of place" is widely used to undergird the values in community common feeling, and is frequently evoked, in other policy circumstances in very positive fashion. By using "sense of place" as a deep-seated human experience shared widely on all sides, this alternative could readily foster some alternative ways of thinking.

This would help to reorient the problem to the real world of differences in political power to shape such issues, and the efforts of those who site to select communities that have less political power to oppose siting in contrast with those who have more. These concepts would start out with the more "real world" recognition that all of us are nimbyites, but while some are "active nimbyites" most of us are "passive nimbyites." That is, we don't have to do much but sit still in order to ward off the intrusion; because of our potential political clout our communities are avoided in siting. Those we call "nimbyites" actually are no different from us, but they have to organize to protect themselves. Unless we can root the term "nimby" in such a real world of environmental politics we simply express emotions with the term "nimby" rather than careful thought and then become part of a political force that has similar emotions that drive the concept.

Consider another example that comes from the field of land and water resources; the terms "use" and "non-use." Resource developers perpetuate an age-old meaning of the term "use" which means material use. Those advocating environmental objectives wish to affirm environmental uses which involve the quality of the environment rather than material uses. A series of terms have arisen to express this set of objectives; some are in the field of wildlife, "non-consumptive use" or, more broadly "appreciative use."[59] Some, such as "land saving" are associated with more natural land use rather than development use, carry the meaning of saving land from the development pressures and would focus more sharply on the inadequacies of the private market. A string of environmental uses, for example, is associated with wetlands: water quality, nature appreciation, science, education. Promoters of resource extraction in forest, range, and mineral issues, disdain such terms and insist on posing the issue as one of use and non-use, while promoters of environmental quality insist on terms that turn "non-uses" into uses and focus on the conflict between older material uses and newer environmental uses. One set of attitude studies about wilderness uses sorted them out into recreation use, existence use, and bequest use. Such terminologies evoke quite different emotions than material use, are not widely adopted and the resource development terminology of older days continues to dominate. It involves a wide range of issues such as contingent evaluation in the assessment of damage to ecological systems as well as a host of land and river protection strategies and now emerges in biodiversity objectives. One might have anticipated that the Comparative Risk Assessment strategy of the EPA Science Advisory Board might have put such issues on a more equal footing by its implied statement that ecological risk was of equal importance to mortality, morbidity, and welfare risk, but to this point I do not see that happening.

A fascinating issue of sound-bite environmental perception is the so-called "alar" issue. All of this started, you will recall, with a report by the Natural Resources Defense Council, called *Intolerable Risk* and ended up in controversy over the report on *60 Minutes*.[60] The report raised a dozen significant environmental issues, each one of which required an analytical framework far beyond the *60 Minutes* sound-bite issue of good science and bad science. They ranged from the debate over neurological development of children versus cancer; how to assess exposures to pesticide residues in food specific to children; how to test the neurological effects of such exposures; the professional composition of the EPA Science Advisory Panel; the relationship between this "alar" episode and a previous one in which Massachusetts and New York abolished its use; the relationship between this issue and the lead issue that involved the same question of the effect of contaminants on the neurological development of children; the interest of the American Society of Pediatrics and the American Psychological Association, representatives of both of which testified at the Senate hearings on the subject on behalf of NRDC; the relationship between *Intolerable Risk* and the NAS report on the same subject; the failure of opponents to discredit the NAS report in contrast with their success in discrediting the NRDC report; or the fate of the ensuing litigation by the apple growers in Washington which the judge dismissed on the grounds that the NRDC study was a perfectly credible study.[61] None of these issues caught the attention of the media which, one is forced to conclude, simply wasn't interested in them or didn't understand them. The same thing, however, can be said of the sources reflecting the views of scientists, economists, policy makers, and administrators; they also jumped on the *60 Minutes* bandwagon. Almost everyone could understand the issue as an attempt to shape a media report on *60 Minutes* and the accompanying framework of "good science" and "bad science"; that episode with its convenient sound bites replaced the wide range of relevant and more complex substantive issues. The entire alar episode on *60 Minutes* has become so firmly embedded in a vast number of articles, books, and reports, that it will be impossible to eradicate it from conventional wisdom and the process of learning about the relevant environmental issues has been lost.

As a fourth example which greatly distorts inquiry into the real environmental world, take the current phrase "humans versus wildlife," popularized by endangered species issues. There is an enormous interest on the part of the American people in wildlife and the natural world. They want more of it amid their urban civilization which they also want, and the real-world context of this debate is over how more of nature can be guaranteed amid the persistent pressures of development to destroy natural environments. Issues involve controversies between humans over the use of land and resources. Instead of issues between "humans and wildlife" they are issues between "humans and humans" over values, and the way in which environmental values about nature can be fostered amid the pressures of development and extractive industries. A more realistic set of sound bites would be "pro wildlife" and "anti-wildlife." Knowledge of human attitudes to foster the natural world is abundant, and much of it has to do with the way in which these values become consumer wants and represent major consumer demands in the economy. It is not difficult to think in this more real-world manner, but the sound bite of "humans versus wildlife" serves as an ideological iron curtain to prevent it.

Looking at a range of such issues over the past three or four decades one might hope for some improvement in the analysis of environmental issues in the decades ahead. But I do not foresee it. The emotions inherent in the intensity of debate and the intensity of desire to reform, evident on all sides, precludes the development of a more detached, informed, and useful analysis.

As a professional observer of environmental affairs with a focus on the contextual meaning of issues rather than their isolated and immediate impact I have little hope that our analytical capabilities will advance in the coming years. Struggle over environmental meaning will continue to be shaped less by more detached and professional observation and will continue to be shaped by struggle over the outcome of issues. This, in turn, will perpetuate the sound-bite as the strategy through which all sides—the professionals, the regulated industry, the environmental community, and the media—shape their environmental perceptions and environmental meaning.

CONCLUSION

To return to the simple context of this presentation, *The Future of Environmental Regulation,* I see environmental regulation in the future as moving ahead in incremental steps from the well-established directions of the decades since World War II. That evolutionary direction is the linear continuation of political forces and strategies within the context of increasing complexity of environmental knowledge. Most of the sound and fury to the contrary is an integral part of the rhetoric of reformers who seek to shape the past and its connection to the future in such a way as to sustain their reforms. To cut through this reformist mythology greater realism is required to understand the vast difference between what one wishes to be and what actually is.

II Forest Debates

THE NEW ENVIRONMENTAL FOREST

I. INTRODUCTION: THE NEW FORESTS AND THE OLD

NATIONAL FORESTS throughout the nation are currently the subject of intense controversy over forest plans being drawn up under the National Forest Management Act of 1976 ("NFMA").[1] Some plans, under severe public criticism, have been withdrawn. Most have been appealed within the agency. A few have become the subject of litigation despite the Forest Service's new-found willingness to negotiate with its opponents. Environmental critics of the Forest Service are increasingly well organized and capable of grappling with today's detailed management issues.[2]

This widespread and intense debate reflects a new public conception of the purpose of forests in America. While the old view emphasized forests as sources of commodities such as timber, water, minerals, and rangeland, the new emphasizes forests as human environments that can be managed for the

From Samuel P. Hays, "The New Environmental Forest," 59 *U. Colo. L. Rev.* 517 (1988). Reprinted with permission of the University of Colorado Law Review.

enjoyment of human life. Although commodities still play an important role in that enjoyment, a new set of values, emphasizing the benefits of natural environments, now play an increasingly important role in defining the American standard of living.[3]

This shift of emphasis has been accompanied by a shift in the form of the forest management disputes now facing the courts. In the 1970s the major type of lawsuit facing the Forest Service involved procedure. In some cases the National Environmental Policy Act ("NEPA") was at issue: did the agency correctly complete the required environmental impact analysis? Other cases involved more general administrative issues: did the agency follow the provisions, as interpreted by the courts, of the Administrative Procedure Act? Still other cases turned on the mandate of the Wilderness Act of 1964 that Congress, not the Forest Service, make important wilderness decisions: did Forest Service policy usurp that legislative authority?[4]

The NFMA and its subsequent forest plans, however, have far more substantive legal implications. NFMA outlines general standards of agency performance. While those standards are not as specific as environmentalists had hoped, they do provide leverage for those who wish to go beyond procedure into substance. Under NEPA, once the agency "does things right" it has considerable freedom to make its own substantive choices. Environmentalists, however, can utilize the NFMA to question whether the agency adopted the correct policy, not just whether it adopted a policy in the correct manner. Thus, the agency now seeks to resolve issues over substantive choices through negotiation rather than litigation.[5]

One can observe and analyze these developments in national forest policy in varied ways. Here I focus on the new values themselves and the impact of those values on substantive conflicts over forest management. Because of the depth and breadth of new conceptions about what a forest is and means to people, the conflicts will not go away. The "standards" contained in the NFMA will hamper efforts by the Forest Service to ignore these new values and their implications for management choices.[6]

The new view of the forest as a human environment rather than as a source of commodities has evolved steadily over the last half of the twentieth century. While there were developments in earlier years, most notably with the establishment of national parks and the beginnings of the wilderness movement, it was not until mass outdoor recreation got into full swing after World War II that a sizable constituency arose to support this new view. Hunting and fishing increased in popularity and the drive for wilderness led in 1964 to the creation of the National Wilderness Preservation System.[7]

The Multiple-Use Sustained-Yield Act of 1960 reflected the new role of the national forests. It specifically identified recreation and fish and wildlife as acceptable uses; in earlier years these had not been high on the Forest Service agenda. And in an oblique fashion that Act recognized the idea of wilderness, not by identifying it as an acceptable use but by stating that it was consistent with the purposes of the Act.[8] Beginning in 1964, wilderness proposals constituted the major substantive departure from traditional national forest policy, resulting in a steady expansion of the Wilderness System. Moreover, this process established a new political climate since the Wilderness Act took the final decisions on wilderness designation out of the hands of the Forest Service and gave them to Congress.[9] This precedent would be followed on many occasions: resistance to new values and new uses by the Forest Service has often produced legislative action that required the agency to adopt new substantive policies.

In the 1970s the citizen-led environmental drive began to move beyond wilderness to a concern for the management of other areas of the forest. The Forest Service had long distinguished between the "general forest" and "special uses," placing new environmental uses like wilderness into the "special" category. Now, however, environmentalists sought to shape management of the "general forest" as well. The effort evolved slowly. In the early part of the decade, it focused on the issue of clearcutting, which led to congressional investigations and some pressure on the Forest Service to reduce the size of clearcuts.[10] The issue became sharper in 1973 when a federal court ruled that the Organic Act of 1897 gave the Forest Service the authority to cut only mature timber (clearcutting led to the harvest of trees of all ages), thereby destroying the theretofore perceived statutory basis of agency harvest policy.[11] This set the stage for the new law, the National Forest Management Act of 1976.

Senator Jennings Randolph of West Virginia worked with environmentalists to shape the new statute toward environmental objectives. They sought to produce a law that would establish substantive standards on such issues as size of cut, streamside strips, harvest on marginal timber lands, and diversity of stand.[12]

The Forest Service, in turn, objected to precise standards in the Act—prescriptive legislation it was called—and insisted that the agency be trusted as a group of "professionals." The Forest Service knew best, so the argument went, and Congress should not get involved in complex, substantive policy issues such as these.[13] Agency discretion, however, was precisely what environmentalists did not want. There was more involved here than merely professionalism: these agency professionals had their own set of values. Their views on what a forest was and should be differed from the views of the environmentalists. The Forest Service could not be trusted to make the right decisions; provisions had to be written into the law to establish substantive constraints on management choices.[14]

The result was a compromise. Standards were stated in general rather than specific terms. Some issues were left to await the recommendations of a "committee of scientists." One could argue that the resulting Act was a major defeat for environmentalists; much of their effort had been deflected. But despite its limitations, the NFMA and the regulations drawn up by the Forest Service after the scientists completed their report provided environmentalists with more substantive leverage on Forest Service policy than had ever been the case.[15]

Much, of course, remained for the future, including a lot of controversy. Planning—each forest was to prepare a plan—was to be the battleground on which the issues were to be resolved. To forest planners, NFMA established a process that gave the agency and its professionals the authority to plan and hence make substantive decisions. But the process also would provide ample opportunities for public involvement in developing the plans and hence would provide a scheme in which all sides—environmentalists, industry, professionals, and foresters—could battle it out. That planning has played this role only testifies to the intensity of the substantive issues at stake.

II. THE NEW POLITICAL CLIMATE

The sharp level of intensity in the current debate on forest management springs largely from the degree to which organized environmental groups have proven their willingness to utilize these new statutory opportunities. During the debate over NFMA it was not at all clear that they would be willing to do this. Criticism of Forest Service policy seemed to come from only a few sources, such as the Sierra Club Legal Defense Fund in the *Monongahela* lawsuit,[16] or the Coalition to Save the National Forests, led by Tom Barlow of the Natural Resources Defense Council. There was only limited popular support.[17]

By the end of the 1970s, however, an environmental constituency had evolved sufficient to support a broad-based challenge to the Forest Service. This came from several sources. First, as the drive to complete the National Forest segment of the wilderness system wound down in several states, energies were transferred to the general forest.[18] Second, a host of organizations became newly involved in forest management issues to find common ground with already active groups, all feeling threatened by the prospect of expanded timber harvests and road construction.[19] Third, the appointment (by President Reagan) of John Crowell, formerly legal counsel for the Louisiana-Pacific Company, as Assistant Secretary of Agriculture in charge of the Forest Service inaugurated a drive for a massive increase in the timber harvest schedules in forest plans, and this in turn greatly stimulated the organization of citizen opposition.[20]

This combination of influences led to the formation of coalitions for almost every national forest to challenge the new plans. The Cascade Holistic Economic Consultants ("CHEC"), led by Randal O'Toole, provided an analytical service that enabled many groups to formulate effective critiques of plans in terms the Forest Service could not readily dismiss.[21] O'Toole enabled citizens to understand specific aspects of the forest service plans (such as suitable timber base, predictions on future productivity, and cost-benefit analysis), thereby allowing them to challenge the agency's own calculations. He reviewed forest plans himself with such effectiveness that the agency, in response, withdrew and reworked some of them, at times even seeking his advice prior to completing a plan so as to avoid after-the-plan challenges. The Wilderness Society formed a Resources Policy and Economics Department with a staff of professional resource economists, ecologists, attorneys, foresters, and land planning specialists. With this expertise at hand, the Society's National Forest Action Center produced citizen guides and handbooks, kept people throughout the country informed about each plan, and provided assistance in the form of economic and legal analysis.[22]

What was particularly striking about all of this was the precise degree to which local and regional groups came to know their own national forests. They were able to challenge forest policies on the ground, transforming general ideas into specific management proposals. A few groups established continuous monitoring systems, not only to chart the implementation of the forest plans, but also to monitor each timber harvest and road construction project. A fund of expertise evolved in the citizen groups that confronted the agency with a depth of detailed knowledge difficult to ignore.

It is also useful to focus on the ideological context of all of this: the idea of multiple use. For many years, the Forest Service had justified its actions in the phraseology of multiple use. The timber and mining industries had taken up the call of multiple use against wilderness, on the ground that wilderness excluded all other uses and thus did not allow for "multiple use." Now the

phrase took on a new meaning. Environmental uses of the forest brought together a wide range of users: backpackers and trail riders, appreciative wildlife
users and big game hunters, naturalists and ecologists.

The combination of road building and accelerated timber harvests came to
be seen as a "single use" that stood in opposition to the "multiple uses" represented by these different groups. Now one heard the phrase "real" or "true"
multiple purpose planning, and the argument was espoused that the Service
had abandoned the concept of multiple use by supporting enhanced timber
harvests and road building. Forest planning provided an opportunity for environmental groups to capture the term multiple use for their own objectives
so as to fulfill the promise of the Multiple-Use Sustained-Yield Act of 1960.[23]

These controversies went to the heart of forest policy: what objectives
should guide the management of the forest? Old and new conceptions of the
forest were at stake. The environmental forest was slowly emerging amid the
backdrop of the commodity forest. When environmentalists confronted Forest Service personnel, the new forest confronted the old. This was not just a
planning process, but an historical process. It had many of the features common to long-term historical change; new and old were in juxtaposition and in
tension. By focusing on this drama of old and new, current controversies can
be better understood.[24]

III. NEW VALUES AND OBJECTIVES

Challenges to forest plans being launched throughout the country provide
many specific instances where new forest values are being expressed and formulated in specific management policy terms. By drawing upon the critiques
prepared by citizen organizations, and appeals within the agency, one can
grasp the specific content of the new demands in a more precise fashion. A
host of articles appearing in the environmental literature—as the critics
sought to gather support for their objectives—provide additional expressions
of opinion upon which to rely.

Soon after the Forest Service formulated its regulations to implement
NFMA, several national environmental groups prepared a document entitled
"National Forest Planning: A Conservationist's Guide," which outlined specific
requirements for the regulations in terms of environmental objectives such as
water quality, wildlife, aesthetics, biological diversity, and wilderness. It also
outlined how commodity objectives, on issues like timber harvest, size of cut,

road construction, oil, gas and mineral extraction, and grazing, could compromise environmental objectives. This guide, first issued in 1981 and reissued in 1983, constitutes a comprehensive statement of the new objectives.[25]

Watershed protection had been one of the major objectives in establishing the national forests in the first place, on the ground that unrestricted timber cutting exposed soils to erosion and created undesirable sedimentation in irrigation and urban water supplies. But over the years this has taken a back seat to the desire of the Forest Service to increase water yield through clearcutting. Lately, however, water quality has obtained new emphasis from sport fishing organizations, Native Americans concerned about fish stocks, and western state fish agencies. All have emphasized the harm to fish from sedimentation caused by logging and road building.[26]

The role of the forest as wildlife habitat has come to be seen as equally important. To many, forests serve as habitats for wild animals, especially predators. This view, in turn, requires that commodity objectives like road building and timber cutting be scaled back. In the East the black bear requires a habitat of considerable size in order to maintain a viable population. In the Northern Rockies elk and grizzly bear are the focal points of interest. In many western states the big game hunters and the pack outfits that cater to them have taken up the cudgels against accelerated harvesting and road construction. They have been joined by the state game agencies.[27]

Habitat for endangered and nongame species calls for a still different kind of objective, one which varies the size and character of habitat according to the needs of smaller as well as larger species. Some endangered species, such as the northern spotted owl in the Pacific Northwest, have sparked major debates in forest planning. The Endangered Species Act[28] and federal and state nongame programs brought into the environmental forest coalitions professional naturalists and the Audubon Society.

Wilderness continues to be a major issue as citizen groups have sought to add to the national wilderness system areas which previously had been rejected or overlooked. It has been difficult for commodity users to accept the idea that some lands should be used for environmental purposes instead of for material production, without roads or logging. To them, such areas are "unused." Environmentalists have sought to affirm that wilderness provides for many uses beyond recreation, including watershed and fisheries protection, wildlife habitat, opportunities for scientific investigation, preservation of ecosystems, scenic beauty, and "existence value." While in most states wilderness activity declined with the passage of bills providing for national forest wilderness, Congress had not agreed on bills for some states (like Colorado, Montana, and Idaho) as of 1988. The wilderness issue remains alive in those states.[29]

Finally, to many users of the forest, outdoor recreation remains uppermost in importance. For some this means hiking, backpacking, camping, and cross-country skiing. For others it means hunting and fishing, with an emphasis on enjoyment rather than on consumption of fish or game. The largest number of users of the forest are the "pleasure drivers." Over time the off-road motorized vehicle, either the motorbike or the snowmobile, the four-wheel drive or the all-terrain vehicle, has become popular. There were intense conflicts between "self-propelled" and motorized recreationists during the wilderness debates, and these conflicts have continued with equal intensity in forest planning.[30]

Three types of substantive issues flowed from these new conceptions of the environmental forest: (1) the enhancement of environmental objectives; (2) the adverse impacts of wood production, including logging and road building; and (3) adjustments in objectives for levels of commodity production, especially timber. We can deal here only with representative examples of each of these and take them up in turn.[31]

The Enhancement of Environmental Objectives

WATER QUALITY

Under authority of the Clean Water Act of 1972,[32] regulatory agencies identify waters of exceptional quality and seek to maintain them in a "non-degraded" state.[33] Many waters in the National Forests fit this description. They are subject primarily to non-point sources of pollution, that is, pollution that comes not from specific sources but from more general practices such as logging. Under the Act, pollution problems caused by non-point sources are dealt with by identifying "best management practices."[34] Theoretically, non-point source pollution problems would be solved if these practices were followed. If a logger was following these practices, it would be presumed that the logger's operations were not causing any water pollution problems. The actual effects of these operations on water quality would not be monitored.

In the case of the National Forests, "best management practices" usually consisted of general policies administered by state forest agencies under state "forest practice acts." States had to certify that their statutes and the then-existing administration of those statutes met the requirements of the Clean Water Act.[35] Few state forest practice programs, however, examined the consequences of their "best management practices" on the ground. Complaints arose that the state forest agencies administering the programs accepted uncritically industry harvest proposals and failed to develop strategies that addressed directly the relationship between a given harvest level and a given level of stream water quality.

In more recent years, however, agencies and organizations with a more direct interest in water quality have become more involved in these matters. The Environmental Protection Agency has reviewed many national forest plans, identified non-point source pollution problems, and questioned the adequacy of state-promulgated "best management practices." State fish agencies and private fishing organizations have argued that in relying on those practices, the state forest agencies and the U.S. Forest Service have failed to measure trends in water quality with in-stream data, and thus effectively ignore the impact of logging on water quality. Litigation in California led to a federal court decision that "best management practices" by themselves were not sufficient to identify acceptable levels of performance by non-point sources with respect to water quality.[36]

These issues focus on state as well as federal agencies. Recently they have arisen, in the context of national forest management, in the states of California, Idaho, and Oregon. In California, the issue is focused on whether state fish and wildlife agency personnel have the authority to review timber harvest proposals.[37] In Idaho, the debate centers on whether regulations governing timber harvesting activity should be set through the use of the old "best management practices" or in-stream water quality levels established by the state Department of Health.[38] The composition of the State Board of Forestry is at issue in Oregon. Considering it to be dominated by timber and logging concerns, environmentalists recently obtained legislation to change the membership of the Board.[39] Activity on these issues has extended to state and private lands in Washington, where protests from Native Americans, fishing organizations, and environmentalists have led to an unusual form of cooperation among those groups, the timber industry, and state agencies.[40]

In order to approach these problems more directly, environmentalists sought to prescribe practices pertaining to the streamside protection mandates of the NFMA. The resulting regulation stipulates that "special attention be given to land and vegetation for approximately 100 feet from the edges of all perennial streams, lakes and other bodies of water."[41] These bodies of water will in most instances be key fish and wildlife habitats. The regulations express an intent to protect streams, stream banks, lakes, shorelines, wetlands, and other bodies of water. Timber harvest is to be allowed in these riparian zones only after examination of soil, vegetation, and other factors.[42] "No management practices causing detrimental changes in water temperature or chemical composition, blockages of water courses, or deposits of sediment shall be permitted within these [zones] which seriously and adversely affect water conditions or fish habitat."[43]

These regulations contain ample substantive standards that must be met by forest plans, and thus provide opportunities for both citizens and courts to evaluate how the plans respond to water quality issues.[44]

WILDLIFE HABITAT

To many Americans the primary role of forests is to serve as a home for wildlife. It is no wonder, therefore, that the role of forests as wildlife habitat is stressed by environmental critics of forest management, ranging from the citizen organizations to the state wildlife agencies. At the same time, the federal Endangered Species Act[45] establishes limits on the implementation of forest policies that endanger particular species. Those who look upon the forest as a source of wood and those who think of it as a habitat for wildlife are engaged in a battle to determine how much further beyond the minimum requirements of the Endangered Species Act the Forest Service should go in attempting to preserve and protect wildlife.[46]

The general mandate of the NFMA and the regulations adopted under it require that the Forest Service monitor selected species, both vertebrate and invertebrate, as indicators of the health of the ecosystem in which they live. The range of species is to include not only those commonly hunted, fished, or trapped, but also threatened, endangered, and nongame species.[47]

Environmentalists have urged that a wide range of indicator species should be selected, representing a variety of habitats: old growth and young growth, cold water and warm water, and undisturbed and disturbed forest. They have argued that the statute requires wildlife diversity and they have imbued the planning process with the idea that wildlife monitoring should identify the impacts of forest development on the indicator species.[48]

A considerable controversy in the forest plans of the East has been generated by the fact that some species of wildlife live at the edge of cut and uncut areas, while others must live in the deeper forest. The Forest Service has argued that roads and openings enhance wildlife opportunities by increasing the "edge effect," which creates a habitat at the edge of plant communities with sunshine and more abundant vegetation. Environmentalists, on the other hand, stress the need for mature trees, citing the use of snags and old trees as nesting and as mast for food. Much of the controversy lies in plans for the mix of species dependent on these varied habitats. On the whole the Forest Service stresses species that can be accommodated to timber harvests and road construction, while environmentalists start with a broader range of wildlife and then accommodate timber harvests and road building to it.[49]

In the West, the argument is over the effects of roads on big game that migrate over longer distances, or which require sizeable areas of habitat for foraging. While environmentalists condemn roadbuilding as interfering with patterns of wildlife movement within a given habitat, thus reducing wildlife population, the Forest Service minimizes the importance of such impacts. Timber cutting and big game, it argues, can co-exist if roads are closed when not being used to harvest timber. Wildlife advocates, on the other hand, belittle the effectiveness of such road closures and develop documented evidence about the failure of such closures to keep out motorized vehicles.[50]

Both the NFMA and its regulations allow for a considerable number of points where the substance of the Forest Service's wildlife policies can be attacked. These range from language on biological diversity or adverse impacts on wildlife, to data-gathering requirements. But the range of issues is rather large and only in a few cases have controversies relating to a plan moved from the general to the specific. One of the most significant of these is the case of the spotted owl in the Pacific Northwest.

In this region, the spotted owl requires a habitat of old growth forest. Measures to protect it, both for its value as a species and for its value as an indicator for assessing the role of old growth in forest management, have produced a controversy: What kind and how much habitat is needed? A group of experts sponsored by the Audubon Society put together one report; the Forest Service put together another. Should spotted owl habitat be distributed among different forest areas, or should it be concentrated in one place? If scattered, how are such fragmented habitats to be connected so as to provide an adequate area within which animals can migrate and forage? Both the Forest Service and the forest industry have sought to limit the areas selected, both in number and size, while environmentalists have sought to expand them.[51]

DIVERSITY

Environmentalists look upon the nation's forests as biological environments within which genetic evolution can proceed according to natural processes. They view the conversion of forests to monocultures of trees selected for their commercial potential as a threat to the diversity of species that stems from these processes. This type of conversion aroused considerable opposition in the southern Appalachians, leading to the inclusion of a provision in the NFMA that regulations provide for steps to be taken to "preserve the diversity of tree species similar to that existing in the region" covered by each plan.[52]

This provision, in contrast with those reflecting wildlife and water quality objectives, involved ideas that were relatively new in forest management. Hence the debates on forest plans have involved a process of slowly specifying and even elaborating this general mandate of the NFMA. In developing its regulations, the Forest Service made the general language of the Act more specific by referring to the need to "maintain viable populations" for each tree species by maintaining "reproductive individuals . . . well distributed in the planning area."[53] Environmentalists elaborated the general idea of "biological diversity" with even greater specificity, although at a slower pace. The forest planning process fostered this elaboration and led to sharp differences between the agency and the environmentalists.

For environmentalists the concept had a strong ecological flavor, was rooted in concepts of the diversity of plants and animals in a given community, and provided an initial context for the environmental mosaic, into which commodity forest activities should fit (instead of the other way around). To forest managers, however, the concept was hardly understandable. It was too far remote from the principles that informed their ideas, a management focus that organized the forest around the primary goal of wood production. Thus their approach toward diversity was altogether different.[54]

The old growth issue in the Pacific Northwest was one of the initial environmental forays into making the diversity provision of the NFMA more specific. In this case research provided evidence of the benefits of old growth forest, 200 years old or more, to the younger forest. The issue also became linked to wildlife habitat as the northern spotted owl was found to require an old growth environment. These factors, coupled with the aesthetic appeal of older trees, produced a fix on the old growth issue as one of the key elements of diversity.[55]

A more ambitious attempt to incorporate diversity into a management plan was attempted by the Wisconsin Conservation Task Force, a group of professional biologists and the Sierra Club. They attempted to apply the theories of island biogeography to their effort to enhance the diversity of the Chequamegon and Nicolet National Forests in Wisconsin. The group suggested that 17 percent of the Chequamegon, and 24 percent of the Nicolet, be managed as "Diversity Maintenance Zones," contiguous blocks of at least 50,000 acres which would be open to hunting, fishing, snowmobiling, skiing, and hiking, but not to timber harvesting or road building.[56] This would provide an area where webs of biological relationships, undisturbed by roads, vehicles, or vegetative manipulation, could be maintained and where diversity arising out of natural ecological processes could be fostered.

The Nicolet planning staff rejected the proposal on the ground that accelerated timber harvesting and road construction objectives required entry into most of the 457,000-acre timber base of the forest within the next ten years. To the Chequamegon foresters, who planned to cut on only 10 percent of their land each decade, the problem was not the amount of cutting but the spatial distribution. They agreed to implement the proposal as an experiment in island biogeography. But the regional forester ordered that it be removed from the plan.

The resulting Chequamegon plan worked out the diversity mandate of NFMA in the agency's own distinctive manner, focusing on the creation of more forest openings, more deer habitat, and the creation of more edge. It did not address the preservation of old growth or other features of a mature forest. The critics of the plan argued that the linear format and constraints of FORPLAN, the computer program used by the agency in its planning analysis, prevented it from dealing with diversity in the planning process.

The Forest Service view of diversity, based less on ecological concepts and more on mechanical management concepts, was exemplified by its thinking on four northern Arizona national forests. Planners there developed a "diversity enhancement" program by dividing the forest into 10,000-acre blocks and representing each age-class within that block through 100-acre units scattered throughout. Each block contained about seventy or eighty individual patches. The proposal was justified as creating an "optimal level of diversity" because it increased the edge effect for wildlife habitat. In ecological terms, however, it only fostered fragmentation and fractured the mosaic of plant-animal relationships in the ecological communities.[57]

The diversity issue provides a sharp example of two conceptions of the forest in conflict, one growing out of the web of biological relationships and the other growing out of the requirements of administrative management, where mechanical rather than biological patterns define the combinations of parts of the whole.[58]

The Adverse Impacts of Wood Production

Environmentalists have long felt that the positive values that can be produced by timber management, values like water quality, enhanced wildlife habitat, and forest diversity, are severely compromised by commodity development.

While a number of commodity-related issues sparked concern (grazing, mineral extraction, oil and gas production, increased water yield), the most sharply debated ones were timber harvesting and new road construction. So far as environmentalists were concerned, both needed to be restricted to protect and enhance environmental values. Instead, plans expanded both timber harvesting and road building. Many of the significant disputes regarding forest plans relate to these two issues.

The initial concern that triggered the contemporary wave of interest in forest management was clearcutting, the practice of cutting a large area (often up to and above 100 acres) cleanly. To the professional forester, clearcutting was the method of harvest required by "even-aged management." Under this method of management, trees are managed in units. The trees within each unit are of the same age; they are planted at the same time, are grown as a unit, and are harvested as a unit. In contrast with single-tree management and harvest, even-age management is simpler and cheaper, permitting measurement, analysis, management, and harvest by area rather than by single trees. This style of management became deeply rooted in professional forestry, not because of its demonstrated benefits to the forest, but because of its ease and its reduced cost of administration.[59]

Many communities, however, argued that the large clearcuts were unsightly and destroyed the aesthetic quality of the forest as an environment. Regeneration would create a new forest environment, but clearcutting deprived the community of that environment's quality for many years to come. To those who had purchased property due to its proximity to the forest, clearcutting diminished the enjoyment of their property and its economic value.

To environmentalists, clearcuts also destroyed habitat for wildlife, led to increased erosion once the forest canopy was destroyed, and disrupted a wide range of biological processes. Not only aesthetic values were at stake. Functioning ecological systems were being transformed by management and harvest methods that sought to eradicate rather than work within the more varied and complex conception of an ecological forest.[60]

Professional foresters reiterated the values that they perceived to flow from clearcutting. It increased water yield by facilitating runoff rather than transpiration. It provided wildlife habitat around the edges of the cut where vegetation was more abundant. It provided more browse for deer during the first decades of regrowth. On the other hand, they argued, the adverse consequences were temporary, lasting only a few years until regeneration began to occur.[61]

Environmentalists, in turn, argued that the increased water yield sacrificed stream water quality by increasing sedimentation and accelerating the loss of forest nutrients. They argued that "wildlife" included more than deer and species that thrived on the edge effect, and that many forest values, including wildlife, required older trees as well as younger ones. They emphasized the need to think of maturity in terms of whole ecological communities rather than in terms of an individual tree.[62]

The environmental alternative to clearcutting was the small opening, the "group selection" cut in which trees in an area of a quarter to a half an acre were harvested as a group, creating smaller openings, permitting the regeneration of shade intolerant species, and providing more diverse habitat and greater watershed protection.[63]

The debate over clearcutting in the early 1970s produced only one major change on the part of the Forest Service—a reduction in the maximum allowable area for clearcutting to forty acres. This change was geared more to the aesthetic impacts of large area cuts and not to arguments concerning effects on ecological communities. The clearcutting issue thus provides continuing fodder for the debate over forest plans.[64]

Closely related to the issue of large harvest openings was the sharp increase in planned road construction. Those who saw the forest primarily as a source of wood also sought to create a denser system of permanent roads to provide continual access. The Forest Service linked new roads with the creation of wildlife habitat and recreational access, arguing that roads increased the edge effect and thus the amount of food available for wild animals. It argued that roads could be managed to reduce interference with wildlife through closings during breeding seasons. The agency plans laid out a desirable road system and then justified it in terms of its benefits for recreation and wildlife, somewhat irrespective of identified recreational and wildlife goals, or of whether these additional "benefits" were needed.

To environmentalists, on the other hand, new roads were detrimental to recreation and wildlife habitat. They emphasized the need for non-motorized recreation, away from roads; they stressed that forest plans underestimated and undervalued this type of recreation. Equally important was the argument that roads disrupted wildlife habitat, blocking migration routes that were a normal part of seasonal wildlife movements and destroying the larger habitats that are essential for big game animals. Moreover, roads facilitated the entry of motorized vehicles, driving the animals deeper into the woodlands. Environmentalists argued against new road construction and against opening up previously closed roads, and urged that many existing open roads be closed.[65]

As environmentalists debated the need for additional roads in the plans, and in some cases succeeded in scaling down the planned increases, they also sought to shape the annual road budgets. But while they interested congressional committees in the matter, budgets were changed only slightly. The specter of an intensely roaded system continues to haunt environmental forest strategy.[66]

The Level of Timber Harvest

Fundamental to the debates on the method of harvest and on road construction was the underlying debate on the level of timber harvest. How much timber would be cut and sold over the next decade or the next fifty years? How would this be translated into the cut for the immediate future?

The timber industry had sought to secure statutory guarantees of a continuous supply in the proposed Timber Supply Act of 1970, but was defeated in a counter-move by national environmental organizations. In the Alaska National Interest Lands and Conservation Act of 1980, however, it obtained a statutory mandate of a minimum annual harvest of 4.5 billion board feet per decade in the Tongass National Forest.[67] It is currently seeking similar guarantees in the Idaho Panhandle.[68]

The Forest Service, on the other hand, sought to withstand this pressure through its formula of "non-declining even flow," which stipulates that for each forest-dependent community there will be an even flow of timber in the future. While the ostensible rationale for this approach was to maintain supplies for local mills, it also seemed to imply a stable rather than increasing future supply. Seeking to foster increased supplies, industry sought modifications to the requirement of "non-declining even flow" (known as "departures") so as to permit increased harvest. New techniques of production, industry argued, would bring about increasing yields of wood in the future, which in turn justified increasing the current harvest to the level of those future predicted yields. Environmentalists became concerned when proposals for such departures appeared in several forest plans.[69]

Not until the Reagan administration took office, however, did the timber industry obtain the political leverage it needed to press the Forest Service into undertaking massive increases in harvest levels. The new Assistant Secretary of Agriculture in charge of the Forest Service, John Crowell, was the former legal counsel to the Louisiana-Pacific Company and was committed to the notion that the national forests should greatly accelerate their harvest schedules. Crowell pressed the planners to adopt schedules that increased cuts far beyond previous levels, and this set the stage for a major battle in forest policy.[70]

The most immediate device that could be used to increase future harvest levels was the overall national forest plan mandated by the 1974 Resources Planning Act. That act required that levels of output for the entire national forest system be set periodically. Such a plan was prepared by the upper level of the Forest Service bureaucracy in conjunction with the regional offices, with only limited grass-root influence that might reflect user demand. The Reagan administration sought to use this strategy to set harvest levels that would then flow downward to each national forest. But in doing so it aroused not only environmental opposition but the opposition of state agencies in the West, who severely criticized the harvest goals as detrimental to fish and wildlife and recreation.[71]

These pressures emanating from the new administration exercised a commanding influence on the debate over the individual forest plans. A host of factors went into calculating the future harvest for each forest, and each of these was analyzed and critiqued in detail by environmentalists. Price and demand forecasts were employed, which if calculated one way justified an increased harvest and if another way justified either a stable or a reduced harvest.[72] Forecasts on the level of future timber production were increased on the basis of concepts like vegetation management, for example, which held in theory that the control of competing vegetation would increase growth in commercial trees.[73] Increases in future production were also to come from regeneration, although the environmentalists argued that regeneration efforts were far less successful than the agency assumed.[74]

There was also the perennial problem of calculating the productive acreage within each forest so as to produce the starting point from which debates on yields and cuts could ensue.[75] On this point, one of the crucial aspects of NFMA was its requirement that marginal lands be eliminated from the timber base. The Act excluded land that, because of physical constraints such as steep slopes, could not be logged without undue damage. But so far as environmentalists were concerned, this exclusion extended as well to lands that were inherently low in productivity. Neither type of land was "suitable" for timber production and hence should not be factored into the calculations.[76]

What were these "marginal lands," "unsuitable" for timber production? The Forest Service defined marginal lands as those that produced less than twenty cubic feet of timber per acre per year. Environmentalists favored the fifty cubic feet minimum, more typically used in private timber management.[77] But the Forest Service went even beyond the specific figure argument and questioned the very meaning of "suitable." It argued that the agency should first determine how much production was needed as a "forest objective," and then classify any land needed to reach that objective as suitable no matter what its inherent productive capacity. To environmentalists, this rendered the entire concept of suitability meaningless.[78]

In analyzing the factors that went into determining harvest levels, environmentalists became increasingly adept at coping with agency methods of resource and economic analysis. Considerable assistance in this regard came from Randal O'Toole of the Cascade Holistic Economic Consultants, whose major emphasis was on effective economic analysis. State fish and wildlife agencies in the West called upon him to help them in analyzing forest plans, as did citizen coalitions in almost every region of the country.[79] While CHEC became a major clearinghouse for forest planning in general, it provided particular assistance in enabling citizen groups to dissect the more complex aspects of agency resource and economic analysis.[80]

IV. INCORPORATING ENVIRONMENTAL OBJECTIVES INTO PLANNING

Statutorily Mandated Protection of Environmental Resources

Special aspects of forest planning provided special opportunities for influence on behalf of environmental objectives. One such aspect is the protection afforded to various environmental resources by statute. This protection will normally require the Forest Service to conduct an impact analysis that emphasizes how agency actions might possibly impact these resources. Some of these protections arise from statutes like the Clean Water Act[81] or the Endangered Species Act.[82] Others, such as maximum clearcut size or protection of riparian zones, arise from the NFMA itself.[83]

The Forest Service describes the limitations on agency action that these protections impose as "minimum management requirements." These requirements reflect the minimum level of management on behalf of environmental resources that is required by statute. The industry and the agency see these requirements as "constraints" on the level of timber harvest. Hence they have become the focal point of attack on the part of those who wish to increase harvest.[84]

In 1986, the timber industry in the Pacific Northwest appealed to the Forest Service to revise the minimum management requirements in the new plans on the ground that they would produce an actual decline in the allowable cut. The appeal was denied by the Chief of the Forest Service, but the issue was reopened when the industry took its case to the Deputy Assistant Secretary of Agriculture, Douglas MacCreery, who ordered a policy review. Environmentalists were disturbed when the resulting policy directed planners to rework their plans to include an alternative that ignored the minimum management requirements as well as one that included them. Plans were also to identify the effects that the latter alternative would have on employment. To the environmentalists, this seemed to undercut the commitment of the agency to legally mandated environmental quality standards. As of yet, however, they have not gone to court to enforce the agency's minimum management requirements since they believe that even those requirements fall far short of what the statutes require.[85]

Alternatives Analysis

Planning under the NFMA also provides opportunities to give more positive focus to the environmental forest through "alternatives" analysis. Draft plans are to display a range of alternatives, from which the agency is to choose one as "preferred."

This has not worked out as well as it might have. Usually the agency would work out a range of choices so that the one it preferred was near the middle of the continuum of possibilities. Environmentalists, in turn, objected that the balance of alternatives was skewed heavily toward timber production and failed to present a comparable range of alternatives on the environmental side.[86]

A review of the plans by the Office of General Counsel of the Department of Agriculture pointed out this deficiency. Not one plan reviewed, the report argued, had selected as its preferred alternative a plan that primarily used the selection cutting method of timber harvesting. Clearcutting remained the dominant method of timber harvesting, despite the fact that criticism of clearcutting was one of the most frequent public objections to forest management.[87] As of this writing the Forest Service has not reacted to this opinion, and environmentalists repeatedly have raised the question of alternatives in proceedings on each forest plan.

Cost/Benefit Analysis

Still another feature of the planning process that has been used to emphasize positive environmental objectives is cost/benefit analysis. Each forest was required to calculate the present net value of its plan, a calculation of long-term benefits over long-term costs, discounted to present values. This put a premium on the method of quantifying environmental benefits and impacts. In particular, debate arose over the value of wildlife, recreation, and wilderness. Environmentalists felt that the agency undervalued environmental benefits and overvalued commodity benefits such as water and timber.[88]

Economic studies that placed quantitative values on environmental benefits were used by citizen groups critiquing the plans. Some of these studies came from work done at forest experiment stations, but others came from economic analyses contracted for by environmental groups. This was especially the case in attempts to put dollar values on wild rivers and wilderness. Such studies enabled environmentalists to advocate their values in the same terms as the commodity values had long been justified, and to enhance the role of environmental values in the total planning process.[89]

One result of these analyses was to demonstrate that in almost every national forest the net present benefit of environmental uses, especially recreation, fish, wildlife, and wilderness, exceeded that for commodity uses such as timber, mineral development, grazing, and oil and gas production. Especially striking was the very low value of timber production. In very few national forests did the value of timber production account for as much as 50 percent of the total value of the forest. In a great majority of cases it did not reach 20 percent of the total; in some cases it fell below 5 percent. Low timber values were particularly prevalent in the Rocky Mountain states, where state recreation planners argued that the net present benefit calculations exposed a sharp gap between the actual value of the forest and the objectives of agency policy.[90]

Below-Cost Timber Sales

This analysis of the relative values of forest uses did not enter the public debate much beyond the regions where the forests were located. A closely related environmental criticism, however, did become a part of the national debate: environmentalists pointed out that few forests produced income from timber sales that exceeded the costs incurred by the Forest Service in making such sales. The case on "below-cost sales" was first made in 1980 by two researchers for the Natural Resources Defense Council, and then was taken up in more extended fashion by the Wilderness Society.[91] While it led to considerable debate in Congress, its most significant result was to prompt the agency to argue that it was not supposed "to make money."

Plans and Appeals

As of February 1, 1988, the Forest Service had released 120 draft plans, all but two of those contemplated in the first round of planning required under the NFMA. Of these, 83 had reached the "final" stage, and 81 of these 83 final plans had been appealed within the agency.[92] In many cases the Forest Service has responded to the appeals with negotiation, and some disputes have been settled in that fashion.[93] Only a few have reached the stage of litigation. In each region environmentalists are working closely with their attorneys and are now prepared to move into the courts if they believe it necessary.

The main effect of the planning process has been to energize the advocates of the environmental forest, providing them with a great number of forums in which they can debate the issues, sharpen their knowledge, and obtain a more detailed view of the forest. They have learned how to use the citizen participation process and, most of all, how to focus on the standards of forest management mandated by NFMA. This has led to a variety of ideas and action throughout the nation, as each region, even each forest, has developed its own peculiar mix of environmental and commodity values.[94]

A MODEL PLAN

The plan for the Green Mountain National Forest in Vermont was notable in that it produced only one appeal from environmentalists seeking to include wild and scenic rivers in the planning process. This appeal was part of an effort to include such rivers in all national forest plans and was agreed to by the Forest Service. From the start, planners at Green Mountain took an environmental view of the forest. The plan states: "We believe that public land in New England is scarce and precious; our management philosophy reflects that belief. The Green Mountain National Forest should be managed to provide benefits that private land does not, and to maintain options and opportunities for the future as well as present generations."[95] The plan emphasizes such forest values as backcountry recreation, wilderness, forest scenery, fish and wildlife habitat, and long rotation sawtimber.[96] It projects no increases in timber production through the next fifty years, construction of only five miles of new roads in the first decade, and management of timber only "where existing roads provide good access and soils are productive." Almost two-thirds of the forest is to be managed as "remote habitat."[97]

REGIONAL ISSUES

To environmental advocates, plans throughout the rest of the country provide a sharp contrast to the Green Mountain plan. In the forests of the Great Lakes states, timber harvest is too dominant; below-cost timber sales prevail, and there is limited attention to wildlife, endangered species, and diversity. In the southern Appalachians, problems include road building, clearcutting, and the conversion of mixed hardwoods to pine monocultures. The northern Rockies confront below-cost sales and timber harvests that are endangering game and water quality. In the southern Rockies, Native American artifacts are threatened by harvesting, and over-grazing is causing damage. In the Pacific Northwest, old growth is jeopardized. Each region has generated its own particular issues. This has led to a variety of ideas and environmental alternatives, some distinctive to a region, others shared throughout the nation.[98]

Some especially distinctive cases have emerged. One involves the six national forests that surround Yellowstone National Park, which environmentalists argue should be considered as an entire ecosystem and managed accordingly. They focus on the migratory patterns of elk and grizzly bears, which cover lands far beyond the park itself. In 1984 several dozen groups in Wyoming, Montana, and Idaho, with support from national environmental organizations, formed the Greater Yellowstone Coalition to highlight regional issues and to shape the six forest plans. Two years later the Wilderness Society produced a report on the region, focusing on environmental objectives. In response, the Forest Service appointed a plan coordinator and in 1987 produced its own report which brought together material from the various plans (but with a limited focus of integrated environmental planning).[99]

The desire to press the issue of diversity in forest planning, in a more specific fashion, is another major focal point of interest. In the Pacific Northwest, this has been done in the context of old growth. To environmentalists, forest diversity includes the presence in the general forest of trees far beyond the age of normal harvest rotation; the region has been a major center of interest on the desirability of old growth from the point of view of ecological diversity. Such views are far more limited in the East, where "old growth" is much younger; as eastern forests become older this view could readily take root in that region as well.[100]

The broader meaning and scope of diversity to environmental forest advocates is only in its early stages of development. Many have drawn upon ideas espoused by ecologists, particularly those in a booklet prepared by the Ecological Society of America titled *Conserving Biologic Diversity in Our National Forests*.[101] The "Diversity Maintenance Zone" concept proposed by Wisconsin environmentalists for the Chequamegon National Forest plan, while not duplicated elsewhere, served as an important first step in providing meaning to the diversity provision of NFMA.[102]

The region of northwestern California and the adjacent area of southwestern Oregon has produced a more traditional alternative to commodity forest management—proposals for the creation of national parks. A combination of issues involving water, wildlife, recreation, and diversity has prompted groups in both states to urge that national forest land be transferred to the management of the National Park Service. One of the legendary stories of public land management in the United States consists of those times, not just a few in number, when environmental advocates turned to the National Park Service when the Forest Service seemed reluctant to even consider their objectives. The establishment of Olympic National Park is an especially well-documented case.[103] Now there are live proposals for creating a park from the entire watershed of the Smith River in northwestern California, and for a Siskiyou National Park in southwestern Oregon.[104]

V. THE DIRECTION OF CHANGE

To this point in time the major effect of environmental involvement in forest planning has been to slow down the increase in the harvest levels and road building programs promoted by the Forest Service in the early years of the Reagan administration. Even where appeals have led to negotiated settlements, few have resulted in more than a reduction in the level of proposed increase for commodity extraction. In the Chugach National Forest in Alaska, for example, the agency and the appellants completed a negotiated settlement in December of 1985 that cut a planned 710 percent increase in timber harvest only in half.[105]

More significant is the long-term potential of a process that has allowed citizen environmental groups to engage the Service more effectively on the management of specific national forests. Planning has produced a range of new ideas and approaches that were not a part of the initial debate in 1976 but that are now an integral part of discussions between the Service and the public. In the new post-Crowell age, these ideas might well obtain some support from within the agency among personnel who were unhappy with the Crowell strategy.[106]

Much of the future course of events depends on the degree to which citizen groups can maintain a high level of interest in, and engagement with, each national forest. If they can do this, the substantive standards are there to be honed more sharply, through direct involvement with the Forest Service backed by the force of law and the threat of litigation.

Some evidence of continuing and sustained interest is the trend toward plan implementation monitoring. Plans for the Chattahoochee-Oconee and Jefferson National Forests in the southern Appalachians provide mechanisms for continued citizen involvement and monitoring.[107] In Colorado, the Colorado Environmental Council has established a computerized data bank on each timber sale conducted on the state's national forests, in order to monitor sales closely so as to identify when intervention would be desirable.[108]

The challenge for environmentalists is whether they can transfer their interest in the environmental forest from the prevention of adverse impacts to the formulation of goals. The Forest Service thinks of environmental concerns as constraints that inhibit desirable commodity-based goals. If the public can persuade or pressure the agency to take steps to shift its emphasis, to establish goals related to water quality, fish and wildlife habitat, diversity, recreation, and wilderness that are to be extended each decade, goals that mandate the adjustment of commodity objectives, then one can be more confident that the environmental forest is emerging from idea to reality.[109]

Two conceptions of this new environmental national forest are at hand. One is fostered by the realization that while some national forest lands are highly productive of timber, most are not. If the agency concentrated its timber production efforts on the highly productive lands, the rest, an ample amount, could be allocated for environmental uses. This view extends the strategy inherent in the Wilderness Act of 1964 to the general forest: environmental values can be provided on lands segregated for that purpose. The nature of the conflict between the two competing uses of the forest, commodity and environmental, requires that areas be allocated to one or the other.[110]

The second conception envisions an integration of uses whereby the mix of environmental objectives, for the most part capable of being dovetailed, become dominant while timber harvest, and its attendant road building, is compromised to these more overarching environmental goals. Such a forest has, in fact, long existed in New England lands managed by private conservation agencies such as the New England Forest Foundation. This view is now reflected as well in the plan of the Green Mountain National Forest, which could well serve as a more forceful model as planning and implementation proceed.[111]

A third scenario, more piecemeal in its approach, seems more likely. In this view the continued attempts by the Forest Service to subvert emerging environmental concepts (such as suitability, diversity, wildlife habitat, and water quality) to the still dominant commodity objective of wood production will arouse further opposition and lead to even more precise and prescriptive legislative pronouncements. A reopening of NFMA for revision would generate far more elaborate proposals for specific standards, and far more extensive grass-roots support, than was the case in 1976. For if anything, citizen involvement in planning has created a more politically influential force behind the concept of environmental forest management.[112] Such action would make clear that the agency's inability to adjust to new values and objectives translates directly into a loss of its discretionary powers.

We are now witnessing a process of typically historical dimensions in which new and old are closely engaged. New values have emerged about what the forest in America is and what role it ought to play in modern society. Planning has provided an opportunity for those values to find expression, and for their advocates to hone and perfect their implementation. Crucial in that effort has been the enactment of statutory standards and the use of litigation to implement them. Both will continue to play a significant role in the further emergence of the new environmental forest.

THE NEW

ENVIRONMENTAL

WEST

OVER THE PAST three decades environmental objectives have emerged in the West with considerable strength and influence to reshape public attitudes. Until World War II agriculture and raw-materials extraction still dominated the region's economic and political views.[1] But in recent years the West has begun to change rapidly. New residents have brought with them new attitudes toward natural resources. Increasingly, those resources are thought of as an environment to enhance individual and regional standards of living rather than as material commodities alone. An indigenous environmental con-stituency has become more vigorous in challenging the previously dominant extractive economy of lumber, grazing, and mining.

This change is most readily observed in the many citizen environmental organizations that have grown up in the past twenty years. They take many forms: statewide groups such as the Colorado Environmental Council,[2] state branches of national organizations such as the Audubon Society and the Sierra Club, specialized state groups such as the Utah Wilderness Association,

From *Journal of Policy History* 3, no. 3 (1991). Reproduced by permission of the Pennsylvania State University.

regional groups such as the Northern Plains Resource Council, and a wide range of local groups such as the Jackson Hole Citizens for Responsible Planning.[3] When the Greater Yellowstone Coalition was formed in 1984 to foster the idea of a Greater Yellowstone Ecosystem, it brought together more than thirty groups in Idaho, Montana, and Wyoming, all of which had been formed since the late 1960s.[4]

Studies of environmental attitudes using a nationwide sample broken down by region enable us to observe the strength of environmental values in the West in comparison with other regions. They indicate a much stronger level of interest there than popular views would suggest. One study used a four-point scale to differentiate the nine census regions with respect to preference for two orientations, one emphasizing resource utilization and the other resource preservation. The greatest preference for the highest level of resource preservation was the Mountain West, at 35 percent, followed by New England with 32 percent and the Pacific Coast with 28 percent. The lowest ranking areas were the West South Central and Middle West regions, with 20 percent each, the South Atlantic with 18 percent, and the Middle South with 17 percent.[5]

Recreation studies indicate that westerners use wilderness areas more frequently than do people in any other region and have a higher awareness of wilderness issues; studies of attitudes toward economic growth indicate that westerners are more interested in restricting it than are those in other regions. The least that one can conclude is that the West is just as strong in its environmental attitudes as are other regions, and in some respects it is stronger.

These new attitudes represent major changes in western demography: the rapid growth of cities and the influx of new inhabitants who have chosen to move there because of higher-quality environments. During the 1970s the population of the Mountain States grew more rapidly than that of any other region. Environmental attitudes have given rise to extensive coverage of environmental issues in regional papers such as the *Deseret News* in Salt Lake City, the *Arizona Star* in Tucson, and the *Missoulian* in Missoula, Montana, and the establishment of regional environmental publications such as *High Country News* first published in Lander, Wyoming, and then in Paonia, Colorado, or *Western Wildlands,* published by the School of Forestry at the University of Montana. Newsletters are published by dozens of environmental groups.[6] Federal and state documents pertaining to western conservation and environmental affairs are, to say the least, abundant. This brief analysis of the "new environmental West" is based on this range of documentary materials.[7]

ISSUES: WILDERNESS AND
FOREST MANAGEMENT

The wilderness issue shaped the West's initial environmental consciousness. In the 1970s groups involved in this issue took up the broader field of forest planning. These have been focal points for activating an indigenous environmental influence that has challenged prevailing forest policy. One can trace the changes within the West through the shift in initiatives on these issues from national to regional organizations.[8]

The older wilderness movement, represented by the formation of the Wilderness Society in 1935, had an important western contingent, but it was dominated by easterners, and its headquarters, then as well as now, was in Washington, D.C. The society lobbied successfully to bring about the primitive area designations by the Forest Service and the Wilderness Act of 1964. But the agenda of the Wilderness Society, limited to designations and reviews of the old primitive-area classifications, was soon challenged in the West as citizens began to argue that major *de facto* wilderness areas had been omitted. The first successful action came from Montana, where citizens persuaded Senator Lee Metcalf to introduce legislation to designate as wilderness the Lincoln-Scapegoat area in that state. This was the beginning of a host of new wilderness reviews and a steadily accelerating drive for more extensive wilderness designations throughout the West and in Alaska.[9]

A shift in the center of gravity of the wilderness movement accompanied these new demands. Beginning with Montana, wilderness organizations grew up in each state amid the general feeling that the vision of the Wilderness Society was too limited. By the end of the 1970s therefore, the national role of the Wilderness Society had ebbed somewhat and a new western umbrella group, the American Wilderness Alliance, was formed, headquartered in Denver and serving as a general networking and inspirational point for western organizations.[10]

The changing focus from nation to region was dramatized by the demand on the part of westerners that the older organizations expand their wilderness horizons to include far more areas than had formerly been on their agenda. In Oregon, for example, the Sierra Club found that its emphasis on the Cascade Mountains as the state's primary region of wilderness potential was challenged by others, who felt that areas in the Coast Range and in central and eastern Oregon should be championed. Others beyond the Sierra Club then formed the Oregon Natural Resources Council, which spearheaded an expanded wilderness vision.[11]

The Wilderness Society faced a similar challenge.[12] Events in Utah dramatized the situation. In 1979 the society, deeply involved with the campaign to protect Alaskan lands, asked its representative in Utah, Dick Carter, to return to Washington to lobby for the Alaska bill. But Carter declined to go, reporting that he was needed in Utah for state issues; he was dismissed as a society representative. He then organized the Utah Wilderness Association, which pressed successfully for the first Utah wilderness program.[13] This initiated an indigenous movement in Utah that led to three state wilderness organizations,[14] with active involvement in wilderness reviews on the lands of both the Forest Service and the Bureau of Land Management and participation in general forest planning.[15]

The revitalization of the Wilderness Society under the direction of William Turnage in the late 1970s led to a different attitude; soon the society developed regional representatives in the West who worked closely with indigenous groups. The West set the direction in wilderness strategy and the national organizations followed and helped.[16]

This shift was reflected in the way in which wilderness bills were formed. No longer were they western or national in scope; now they took the shape of state wilderness bills, as each congressional delegation became the focal point of negotiations within each state between those favoring and those opposing wilderness. Once a bill had been worked out within the context of the state, other members of Congress, deferring to state autonomy in such matters, went along with little question. This strategy led to a spate of laws during the early 1980s that resulted in Ronald Reagan, no advocate of expanded wilderness areas, signing into law more wilderness acreage outside of Alaska than had any previous president.[17]

During the 1970s environmental activity spurred by the wilderness issue expanded into a growing interest in management for a wide range of environmental objectives on national forest lands. The roots lay in community dissatisfaction with timber harvest policies. While the Forest Service was willing to restrict cutting along roads in what were called travel corridors because of the popularity of scenic driving, it was not willing to restrict clearcutting in general. Opposition arose especially on the Monongahela National Forest in West Virginia and the Bitterroot National Forest in Montana, leading to a congressional investigation and a drive by environmentalists to shape a new Forest Management Act. Passed in 1976, the new act specified in greater detail the objectives of forest planning and hence of forest management.[18]

In the subsequent round of planning under the act, the competing values of forest management between the timber industry, which sought to enhance timber harvest, and environmentalists, who sought to reduce it, clashed sharply. Environmentalists brought to bear on planning and management a host of values, such as watershed protection, fish and wildlife habitat, recreation, and aesthetics. Each required lower levels of timber harvest and hence met stiff opposition from the industry as well as the Forest Service. At the local level environmentalists increased their leverage in forest planning and gradually obtained some concessions. The key issues were allowable timber cut and road building. Fearing this opposition, the industry sought to increase its influence at the national level, demanding that timber harvest schedules be established nationally and then be imposed on each forest through individual forest plans.[19]

The Reagan administration's policies sharpened the cleavage. John Crowell, the new assistant secretary of agriculture in charge of the national forests, vigorously sought to impose higher harvest levels on each forest. Environmentalists in turn challenged almost every new plan drawn up under the 1976 act on grounds that it severely harmed a host of environmental values. The issue is still intensely argued,[20] but, while the current round of debate is far from over, environmental objectives in forest management seem slowly to be obtaining greater attention. Crowell's initiatives aroused a revolt among Forest Service employees, threw the service's leadership into disarray, and led to a widely acknowledged crisis in its public credibility.[21]

This controversy has given rise to a battery of new citizen environmental resources in the west. Legal-defense organizations such as the Idaho Natural Resources Fund have been established to finance administrative appeals and court action.[22] State associations formed to advance wilderness have expanded their resources to apply them to forest management as well as to wilderness issues. Forest economist Randall O'Toole of Eugene, Oregon, with a computer capability for analyzing and challenging economic analyses by the Forest Service, has provided numerous critiques of forest plans. His services have been used by citizen environmental groups, Native Americans, and state fish and wildlife agencies in their case against forest plans.[23] Finally, the Wilderness Society developed its own resources to undertake economic analyses of forest plans and has given significant support to the entire venture.[24] The Natural Resources Defense Council and the National Wildlife Federation have provided legal assistance, as have a number of natural resource defense centers within the region.[25]

The technical ability of environmentalists in challenging the computer runs in forest planning has been especially influential. These capabilities seem to be on the point of significant expansion, from planning to monitoring the results of the plans. The Colorado Environmental Council, for example, has organized a project that enables it to track each timber sale on that state's national forests. All this has considerable before-the-fact as well as after-the-fact influence on forest planning and has presented the Forest Service with its most severe challenge in many a decade. While national environmental organizations have helped, the entire effort has deep roots and support in the West, and those influences have set the tone and direction of environmental strategy.[26]

STATE POLICY

The western environmental agenda goes far beyond management of the national forests. Each state environmental council devotes more time and effort to state than to national issues. Each started with a desire to serve as a state legislative environmental lobby, often with volunteer or part-time staff, and many soon developed the resources to hire full-time personnel.[27] Most states now have an organized lobby program, an agenda both to advocate environmental proposals and to ward off opposing ones, a review of legislative performance that includes an analysis of voting on environmental issues, and, in many states, an active electoral campaign organization parallel to but separate from the legislative work.[28]

Some of these state environmental councils were stimulated initially by national organizations. Those in Washington, Oregon, and Idaho were formed through the inspiration of the Northwest office of the Sierra Club. In many states local chapters of national groups such as the Audubon Society, the Sierra Club, and the Izaak Walton League took the initiative to form state and local coalitions to finance legislative activity jointly. These in turn developed an independent ability to exercise influence in state capitals.

To review the entire range of issues that have evolved in all eleven western states would be impossible; a few cases will suffice as illustrations. California, Montana, and Wyoming have established nonconsumptive water uses as legitimate uses for which state agencies, such as in fish and wildlife matters, can reserve or even purchase water rights and establish minimum low flows to protect fish habitat.[29] Oregon and Idaho environmentalists have tackled the effort of timber interests to restrict nonpoint source regulations in federal law by authorizing timber-dominated agencies to determine the "best management practices" to fulfill the law; the environmental option is to establish in stream water-quality standards, monitored regularly as a baseline from which to determine acceptable harvest practices.[30]

Montana and Wyoming developed industrial siting laws and coal severance taxes to finance mitigation of the impacts of coal mining. Almost every state has faced the adverse effects of mining, accumulating over the years, and now considered to be unacceptable community degradation.[31] This may take the form of water pollution in the Clark's Fork in Montana or radioactive emissions from uranium mine tailings in Colorado and New Mexico. In Montana environmentalists successfully warded off for a while industry attempts to relax air-quality standards that were more stringent than the national air standards in preference for a general policy to prohibit air pollution that "interferes with normal daily activities."[32] Citizens in southern Arizona persuaded the state not to renew the sulfur dioxide emissions permit of the Phelps-Dodge smelter at Douglas and in the process gave rise to a new and significant citizen interest in that state's air quality.[33]

The most vigorous environmental agenda is in the Pacific Coast states.[34] California has long been an innovator in environmental policy, ranging from its state park program, which from pre–World War II beginnings moved ahead rapidly after the war, to its state forest practice law and its more recent initiatives in controlling toxic wastes.[35] Oregon is well known for its pioneering ventures in solid-waste management, including the bottle bill and the more recent recycling opportunities act.[36] Washington initiatives include those in water-pollution control, coastal zone management, state environmental-impact analyses, and control of forest practices on state and private land.[37]

The environmental movement in the Mountain States, equally energetic, has met more opposition. Activity in Idaho, Montana, Wyoming, and Colorado came earlier and then later in Utah, Nevada, New Mexico, and Arizona. The drive for a Great Basin National Park in Nevada, the Utah wilderness movement, and the vigorous policies of Governor Bruce Babbitt of Arizona have marked an extension of earlier northern initiatives to the southern part of the region.[38]

These regional differences can be illustrated by variations in the impact of new environmental values on state land management. Some thirty-five million acres of land, obtained from the federal government on statehood, are still owned by western states. They are managed by state land boards, under trust arrangements required by the federal government when the lands were transferred that they be held primarily for permanent income-producing purposes. Hence, the boards argue, the lands cannot be allocated for recreational and environmental uses that do not return revenue to the trust fund. The beneficiaries of the funds, primarily the state educational institutions, strongly agree.[39]

State land boards vary in the degree to which they impose restrictions on recreational and environmental uses, as non-income-producing uses, depending largely on the level of livestock and mining influence in state lands management. Such uses are given some acceptance in the northern states, most notably in Washington, but in the southern states are considered to be acts of trespass and hence subject to legal action.[40] But new ways are being found to cope with such limitations. Governor Babbitt, for example, engineered some complex land exchanges between the state land board and the federal Bureau of Land Management in which state lands with high environmental quality were transferred to the federal agency with the idea that they would be managed by the BLM for environmental objectives.[41]

The most significant role of state land policies, however, came when they figured heavily in the Sagebrush Rebellion of the late 1970s and early 1980s, in which some westerners proposed to transfer federal lands to the states. The effort, publicized as an all-western drive, also aroused considerable opposition within the West. Many began to believe that if federal lands were transferred to the states they would be managed by state land boards that would be heavily influenced by their traditional commodity objectives; recreation and customary environmental uses on federal lands would be jeopardized. Hence, skepticism about the proposed transfer arose in many quarters.[42]

In Idaho, environmentalists sought to tackle this question by proposing a change in the state constitution to require "multiple use" of state lands as the price to be paid for acceptance of the transfer. But the mining, timber, and livestock industries objected to that kind of multiple use and the proposal never got out of legislative committee.[43] In Utah, a similar proposal went further as environmentalists insisted on it as the price they demanded in return for their support of Project Bold, a measure to transfer ownership between state and federal agencies to firm up blocks of land for more efficient management. The bargain, fostered especially by Governor Scott Matheson, was arranged at the state level, but it required approval in Congress, where it became sidetracked. One source of opposition was the Utah mining industry, which objected to the provision of "multiple use" of state lands.[44]

The most extensive impact of environmental objectives on state land management occurred in Washington. Here the Washington Environmental Council teamed up with sportsmen's organizations, Native Americans, and the fish and wildlife agency to object to the dominant role of the timber industry in management of state trust lands. They succeeded in persuading the state's voters to elect a new chair for the state land board and then shaped a rationale for the trustee role of the state in protecting economic values associated with fish, wildlife, and watersheds, as well as grazing and wood production.[45] They were especially effective in promoting the development of detailed studies to establish the adverse role of wood production and timber harvest practices on the environmental quality of state lands.[46]

In all of these wildlands matters, whether state or federal, a major role of the indigenous western environmental movement has been to bolster the political influence of state fish and wildlife agencies. In the late 1960s and early 1970s those agencies had considerable opportunity to advance objectives that had long been thwarted by development-oriented state agencies. By the mid-1970s, however, public reaction forced them to pull back. But the growing effectiveness of environmental groups in state land matters gave fish and wildlife agencies an enhanced degree of influence.[47] Each state agency began to take a more vigorous stand in national forest planning and some have hired Randall O'Toole to make analyses of forest plans in their states. They have been equally active in pressing fish and wildlife interests in the management of both state and private lands.[48]

THE ENVIRONMENTAL OPPOSITION

Environmental issues in the West have sharpened the differences between the older extractive economy and the newer environmental economy. As environmentalists have become more influential, those who represent the region's older economic activities have been strident in their defense of timber, mining, grazing, and irrigation agriculture. Environmentalists have been able to establish a beachhead of influence, but they have not been able to establish a public context for environmental values that can establish an overarching legitimacy for environmental objectives in state affairs. Each legislative session and each state and federal agency is a battleground for continued conflict between environmental and developmental forces, similar to that in other parts of the nation. Here, however, the conflicts are more sharply drawn.[49]

The attempt by the timber industry to use the authority of federal agencies to overcome regional and local demands for environmental forest management has also been made by the coal industry. During the early Reagan ad-ministration arrangements developed under President Carter to determine leasing schedules through joint federal-state committees were cast aside by Secretary of the Interior James Watt in favor of federal supremacy in such de-cisions.[50] The strategy for offshore oil leasing, in which the administration came to loggerheads with the state of California, displayed a similar pattern.[51] Western extractive industries increasingly turned to federal authority to make up for political influence lost in the West.

The series of defeats by the timber industry in wilderness matters led to strategies by the extractive industries simply to oppose additional wilderness. When the Forest Service attempted to work out wilderness issues in Colorado in 1978 through a mediation effort, it failed because, while environmen-talists presented choices among candidate areas, arguing that some deserved wilderness designation while others did not, the industry groups simply op-posed all new areas. As the wilderness issue shifted to BLM lands, the livestock industry added its support to the "no new wilderness" strategy. Utah took the lead. In 1986 Governor Bangartner announced that he opposed any additions to the wilderness system in Utah, and Utah representatives to the Interior Department's Public Lands Council persuaded that group to adopt the same position.[52]

Farmers and ranchers were especially vocal in their environmental opposi-tion. The range of matters on which they took issue was extensive: use of water, use of federal BLM lands for purposes other than livestock grazing, es-tablishment of the Birds of Prey national wildlife refuge in southern Idaho,[53] protection of predators such as wolves and grizzly bears,[54] restrictions on the use of pesticides, and the designation of wild and scenic rivers. Except in the case of the adverse impact of large-scale development, such as strip mining in southeastern Montana and northeastern Wyoming or the development of the MX missile in Nevada, where environmentalists and ranchers cooperated, the two groups were frequently at odds.[55]

Several issues focused more sharply on the clash of the old and the new. One concerned the development of a history of Oregon for use in the public schools. Promoted by a faculty member in the School of Education at Oregon State University in Corvallis, the book was written by teachers and funded by the state's extractive industries with the stated objective of giving their point of view more influence in the state's written history. The book, entitled *Get Oregonized,* was adopted by the State Board of Education after a bitter con-troversy in which representatives of the agricultural and extractive economies expressed deep fears concerning the political influence of Oregon's cities, where environmental political support was strongest.[56]

The environmental opposition had considerable support in the state legislatures. Many legislators came from rural and small-town districts and for the most part reflected the development-oriented interests of their local communities. Those interests found considerable acceptance in the Republican Party, which became the main political vehicle of opposition to state environmental policies. Party differences in environmental voting in each state legislature were similar; the Democrats were skewed toward support of environmental objectives and the Republicans were in opposition. Some toward the middle tended to be small-town or rural Democrats, on the one hand, and urban Republicans, on the other. In most legislatures in the Mountain States, Republicans were dominant, making environmental gains quite difficult.[57]

Governors, on the other hand, were more prone to reflect the changing interests of the state as a whole; as time passed, they were more responsive to growing urban interests than was the legislature. Hence, in the late 1970s and early 1980s many governors in the Mountain States were Democrats, even though the legislatures were Republican. Environmentalists, in turn, found more support from governors than from legislatures.[58]

Members of Congress from the West followed the same divisions: after 1970 Democratic representatives from the West gave stronger support to environmental objectives, while Republicans increased their opposition. To most western Republicans environmental issues had become sharply ideological. All this was in marked contrast with New England, where an overriding context of environmental interest influenced both Republicans and Democrats and resulted in somewhat similar voting patterns in the House of Representatives.[59]

Yet even those western members of Congress who had strong antienvironmental voting records could respond positively when their own constituents were involved. Thus, Wyoming senators and representatives who had low environmental voting records according to the annual surveys of the League of Conservation Voters defended their constituents in Jackson, Wyoming, in opposing oil drilling in nearby Bridger-Teton national forest.[60] And Senator Orrin Hatch, with an equally strong antienvironmental record, responded to his constituents in southwest Utah who were convinced that the high incidence of cancer in their communities had come from fallout from nuclear bomb testing in the 1950s. He fostered a program of compensation and long-range medical surveillance for the victims.[61]

THE LIMITS OF ENVIRONMENTAL ACTION

The environmental opposition has constituted a significant counterweight to the new environmental demands in the West. It has also established firm limitations to action that environmentalists have not been able to overcome. While the timber industry has been challenged with some success, the grazing, agricultural, and mining industries have been able to resist more effectively, and the rising western tourist industry has provided environmentalists with both opportunities and threats to their objectives.

Environmentalists have been singularly unsuccessful in bringing environmental objectives to the Bureau of Land Management. While the BLM Organic Act of 1976 set a new direction, its implementation has come slowly. An opening wedge toward change in the Bureau has been provided by the debate over wilderness designations on BLM lands. And a similar "window of opportunity" can be identified in agency policy to designate Areas of Critical Environmental Concern to protect historic, cultural, scenic, and natural values on its lands. On the whole, however, livestock and mining interests are in firm control at both the district and national level, giving much justification to the environmental quip that BLM means "The Bureau of Livestock and Mining."[62]

The evolution of the political base in the West for environmental policies in the BLM is at least two decades behind that of the Forest Service. Leadership in policy changes under the 1976 act has come primarily from the national organizations, and only slowly has an environmental constituency for BLM lands developed in the region. Several organizations have been formed specifically to deal with BLM policy, most notably in Oregon, Idaho, and southern California, and the Utah Wilderness Association has been distinctive in the degree to which it has become deeply engaged in BLM as well as national forest lands. It seems quite likely that the pattern of organization first for wilderness objectives and later for management policies in general will mark BLM affairs as it has for those on the national forests.[63]

Environmentalists have already laid the groundwork for this larger strategy by investing much time and energy in BLM grazing and mining issues. Through the persistent efforts of attorney Johanna Wald, the Natural Resources Defense Council has painstakingly tried to force the BLM to look at the problem of range deterioration, and during the Carter administration it appeared that some headway could be made. Moreover, then BLM director Frank Gregg was determined to make the agency's wilderness review less controversial than was that of the Forest Service. Finally, the appointments to

BLM advisory committees, at national and state levels, were more diverse in background, representing environmentalists as well as livestock interests.[64]

But with the Reagan administration the environmental tendencies in the agency were reversed. Environmentalists were successful in protecting wilderness areas from oil and gas drilling. But on most counts the new leadership at the Department of the Interior succeeded in countering environmental initiatives.[65] Under Robert Burford, BLM director during the Reagan administration, the livestock industry gained a firmer hold on rangeland management, both by new contractual arrangements with permit holders and by giving them dominant, almost exclusive membership in the advisory committees and councils.[66] The industry successfully resisted any increase in leasing fees and in fact was able to reduce them despite the vast difference between the level of fees on private and public lands that enabled public leaseholders to re-lease their lands at a profit.[67] Jay Hair of the National Wildlife Federation was appointed to the national Public Lands Advisory Council as a token environmentalist, but he later resigned in despair.[68] And environmentalists have been forced to challenge oil and gas drilling on both the national forests and the BLM lands on a case-by-case basis with only limited success.[69]

Closely related to the successful challenge to western environmentalists on rangeland policies is the equally successful challenge from irrigation agriculture. In this case the focal point is the water-conservation district, the organization of farmers that supplies water through federal irrigation works. The lands irrigated are closely tied to public grazing lands in a pattern of seasonal use, linking open rangeland for summer grazing with irrigated hay farming, which provides winter food for cattle. Hence, federal grazing and irrigation programs are intimately bound together in a common set of federal subsidies to the livestock industry. Those ties constitute a formidable force to resist environmental objectives in federal range and water policies.[70]

In this complex of policies environmentalists have been more successful in challenging the long-standing program to bring federally financed water to western agriculture. National environmental organizations in Washington have been able to challenge funding for the Bureau of Reclamation over the years. But this probably is due as much to the fact that there are few, if any, significant irrigation projects remaining to be championed in the West. What is more significant is that environmentalists have not been able to turn back those massive western projects already under way, such as the Central Arizona Project, the Central Utah Project, or the Columbia Basin expansion. In each case, while western political leaders have been willing to compromise on environmental forest issues, they have remained adamant on water issues.[71]

Environmentalists in Colorado have made some headway with the theme of greater efficiency in water use rather than more water-supply reservoirs and are finding allies in that venture with free-market economists at the Political Economy Research Center at the State University of Montana in Bozeman. More significant perhaps is the modification to the Columbia River Basin program that is under way as a result of the joint efforts of environmentalists, fish and wildlife agencies, and Native Americans. Yet these are mere dents in what is a major wall of resistance to environmental objectives by regional water interests.

There have been other limitations to environmental action on public lands as well. Environmentalists have made no headway in their long-sought goal of revising the Mineral Lands Act of 1872, which still over a century later gives the mining industry a privileged position on public lands.[72] The protection of predators such as the grizzly bear and of other wildlife such as the bison generates almost unresolvable conflicts between environmentalists and those who feel that "people are more important than animals."

Equally intractable has been the management of the national parks. Environmentalists have well documented the "threats to the parks" from both intensive use inside and development outside that affects park resources.[73] Some headway has been made in the protection of visibility within the parks, but on the issue of the protection of integral vistas—those seen from within the park but extending beyond its boundaries—environmental objectives were wiped out with a stroke of the pen by Secretary of the Interior Donald Hodel.[74] And the bill to require even an analysis, let alone control, of incompatible development near parks has been met with staunch opposition by the region's political leaders.[75]

Thus, while the western extractive economy has had less success in countering environmentalists within the boundaries of the national forests, parks, and wildlife refuges, it has been able to prevent their attempt to restrict development elsewhere that might impinge on those lands.[76]

On the problem of overuse of the parks that has come with the steady increase in visitors, environmentalists have made some, though limited, gains. They have sought to shift some facilities from inside the parks to lands on their outskirts. But the promise that seemed to come on this score with the Yosemite National Park plan seems to have withered. An even more significant roadblock has been the entrenched position of park concessionaires as a result of the National Park Concession Act of 1965. Environmentalists have had to bite their tongues with the knowledge that one of their heroes, Rep. Morris Udall of Arizona, is the major political protector of those who hold the concessions. In recent years environmentalists have not attempted a significant challenge to the Act of 1965 or the arrangements made under it.[77]

The national parks have long depended for their political support on those who thought they would bring tourist dollars into the region.[78] And environmentalists have long hoped to wean the parks away from the political liabilities created by such policies. But the tourist industry remains highly influential and environmentalists are forced to join hands with them to support such new proposed park ventures as the Great Basin in Nevada. The new environmental West offers environmentalists opportunities but also new liabilities.[79]

THE ENVIRONMENTAL WEST: IMAGE AND ACTION

For most of the nation's media and for many of its specialists in environmental policy, western controversies are thought of as a conflict between those within the region who seek to develop its minerals, timber, water, and grazing lands and those in the East who wish to restrict such activities in favor of environmental objectives. Such a view was fostered by leaders of the Sagebrush Rebellion, by Ronald Reagan during the 1980 campaign, and by his Secretary of the Interior, James Watt. The West symbolized those creative entrepreneurial energies that had been thwarted and that the new administration was pledged to release.

These assessments are incorrect. Vast changes of quite a different sort have been taking place in the West to create a new indigenous environmental movement that has challenged the old commodity economy in a fierce struggle for western turf. To whom does the West belong—the old or the new? The contest over the answer to that question is now the political drama in the West. One observes a slow and persistent incremental advantage for the newer environmental West and a fierce but slowly losing resistance on the part of the older commodity West.

Little of this has been noticed by the eastern political intelligentsia or the media that inform it.[80] Some aspects of the struggle that impinge on easily dramatized federal policies have come to the attention of those in the nation's capital, such as the profitability of national forest management or appropriations for road construction in the national forests. These are major elements of the environmental scene in Washington.

In the West a more extensive and fundamental drama is taking place where the new values and objectives that lie behind it are being played out in a host of arenas of state and national policy. Few of these are ever mentioned in the eastern press, and such magazines as *American Forests* that have a stated interest in such matters provide little information about the events. Even scholars who write about the West often do so by relying on documents produced in the East and bypass almost completely the abundant western sources that give rise to a different understanding of the issues.

Thirty years ago one could hardly have predicted with any degree of conviction the existence of an extensive indigenous environmental movement in the West, one with an ability to meet federal agencies on their own ground, combat the old economy in the context of turf, and mobilize those with new ideas about what the environment of their region might be. This is a vastly new and different place, a region transformed, that can well be described as a "new environmental West."

A CHALLENGE TO

THE PROFESSION

OF FORESTRY

OLD AND NEW: THE CURRENT DEBATE

IT IS NOW MORE than obvious that the management of our forests is undergoing massive debate and controversy. Whether or not that leads to change in management depends on a host of factors. But certainly the role of professional foresters, what they think and propose, what they do in the management agencies, what on-the-ground strategies they foster, will play a major role in the policies that emerge. If we can think of this as a matter of "stewardship" or "ethics" is not at all clear; but whether or not it involves potential major changes in how we think and act is. It is these new circumstances that present the forestry profession with a major challenge.

The roots of the challenge lie in the new attitudes of the American people about the meaning and role of forests. While in earlier years forests were thought of primarily as a source of commodities, with the major emphasis on wood production, they are now thought of increasingly as an environment, a

From James C. Finley and Stephen B. Jones, eds., *Practicing Stewardship and Living a Land Ethic*, Proceedings of the 1991 Penn State Forest Resources Issues Conference, Harrisburg, Pa., Mar. 26–27, 1991 (Pennsylvania State University, 1992).

setting for work, home, and play. Some might like to think of this as a throw-back to something more primitive, but, on the contrary, the environmental view of forests is an integral part of a more modern society, through which people wish to enhance their standard of living. The change was capsuled by Stephen Kellert when he wrote in *American Forests* a few years ago that "the forest is as much a place for growing people as it is for growing trees."[1]

The consequences of this are all around us. They include intense debates over National Forest plans and the subsequent "new directions" of the Forest Service;[2] management of state forests giving rise to debates in Pacific Coast states but now extending to the east, such as with Minnesota's generic environmental impact analysis of enhanced timber harvest;[3] the future of the "northern forest lands" in upper New England and New York;[4] new forest practice acts that are more concerned with environmental uses than were earlier acts;[5] local ordinances prescribing harvest methods that prompt action by industrial and public foresters to enact preemptive state laws;[6] and proposals that wood harvest be ended in a number of smaller national forests on the grounds that those forests constitute unique areas amid a larger acreage of private forests devoted to wood production.[7]

The challenges can be identified by activities within the forest profession as well. There is, for example, the 1984 conference of the Society of American Foresters in Minneapolis, Minn., devoted to the new context of forest affairs.[8] Or there is the new Association of Forest Service Employees for Environmental Ethics that has become a player in national forest policy.[9] Or there is the recent report of the National Academy of Sciences about the state of forest research that framed its recommendations in the context of a shift from commodity forestry to the forest as a human environment.[10] Finally, there is the protest within the Forest Service from forest supervisors and regional foresters against the accelerated timber harvests that in the 1980s they were required to accept.[11]

The most appropriate way of identifying the old and the new in forest management is to distinguish between "commodity forestry" and "environmental forestry." Terminology of this kind has long been suggested but rarely accepted directly. I am reminded of the brief debate that occurred among a few forest professionals in the early 1970s over the issue. A proposal to establish in the Society of American Foresters a working group on "ecological forestry" aroused considerable resistance and was rejected on the grounds that all forestry was already "ecological." Times now have changed. What then could be encompassed as a discussion within the smaller circle of professional foresters is now a wide-ranging public debate. A large segment of the public is distinguishing between "commodity forestry" and "environmental forestry," asserting that a stronger role for environmental forestry be brought into forest management. The issue now influences a wider range of forums and conferences such as this one.

FOREST VALUES AND IDEAS

The first challenge of these developments to the forestry profession is one of values and ideas. To what extent can the profession share with the public the commitment to "environmental forestry" as a set of objectives? It is easy to fuzz all this over and say that what is a presumed distinction is not a distinction at all. But the difference between commodity forestry and environmental forestry is real; it cannot be simply argued away. Can the profession face the distinction and focus on the meaning and implication of environmental forestry fully and squarely?

The debate has sharpened many specifics of environmental forestry.[12] There are issues of water quality—best management practices versus in-stream measurements[13] and biological markers versus chemical markers; the width and management of riparian areas where logging is prohibited or restricted to protect water quality;[14] erosion and sedimentation from road building and logging on steeper slopes; the intensity of recreational development; the impact of harvest methods on soil fertility and logging methods on soil compaction; the allocation of areas to be managed as old growth forests;[15] the restoration and maintenance of native biological diversity;[16] even-aged versus all-aged methods of management with related choices of harvest methods; type conversion that tends toward non-native monocultures; the length of the cutting cycle; the quality and quantity of forest monitoring; allowable cut and harvest levels; road building; the use of marginal lands for wood production.[17]

The 1971 hearings in the U.S. Senate concerning clearcutting on the Bitterroots and the Monongahela seemed quite simple—a debate over even-aged area management.[18] At that time the forestry profession responded with a simple statement by the deans of six schools of forestry as to the benefits of clearcutting as they saw it.[19] That debate led to the formulation of a wider range of issues that became a part of the "prescriptions" of the 1976 Act. Those implications were taken only lightly if the record of proceedings of the ensuing "committee of scientists" is an indication. But as the specifics of the 1976 act came to be worked out in the debate over planning, it appeared that the general idea of "environmental forestry" had wide-ranging implications that emerged steadily. They now have accelerated to major proportions.

It is quite possible to argue that the values of foresters do not differ from the values in the society at large and that we face only differences of means, not of ends. I do not find this plausible. The intensity of debate, the language used, the large role of value-laden terms, the alternative visions advanced of the "desirable forest," all point to something more fundamental than means.[20] If we frame the issue as one of means rather than ends, we will fail to identify the depth or even the meaning of the debates. It will persuade us that the debates are over "interests," as the forest managers like to put it, rather than of much more deeply seated value preferences.

A large body of research about the values of forest users such as recreationists and the owners of private, non-industrial forest lands, underlines the fact that what are often thought of as "special interests" are in fact matters of values. Two recent studies elaborate various elements of values among forest professionals. In one, in the *Journal of Forestry,* Ben Twight and Fremont Lyden examined the values of Forest Service personnel in the context of clientele values and found that the values of Forest Service personnel were closer to the values expressed by commodity groups than those expressed by environmentalists.[21] The second, by James Kennedy and Thomas Quigley in 1989, a study commissioned by the Forest Service, examined the values of various groups of personnel within the agency. It outlined the quite different values of entry level versus senior staff, staff from rural and urban backgrounds, older and newer employees, and those who specialized in commodity-related professions and those who specialized in those that were environmentally related.[22]

One way to focus on values and general ways of thinking is through key words and phrases that we use again and again when we want to convey large ideas in quick and shorthand fashion. The debate over forest management has given rise to a number of these, especially on the part of commodity groups and foresters emphasizing the primacy of wood production who wish to convey that meaning indirectly rather than directly. The phrase "multiple-use" has long been one such phrase, traditionally conveying the meaning that in the mix of forest uses wood production is the "indispensable use." Another was the distinction between "management" and "non-management," a phrase especially used to establish the superiority of commodity values until the U.S. Forest Service published a book on "wilderness management," making clear that management could be for either commodity or environmental objectives.

The search for a terminology that conveys both a larger public meaning and the indispensable importance of commodity production continues. There is, for example, the distinction between economic and non-economic to describe commodity and environmental uses. Environmental uses are as much economic as are commodity uses. The confusion comes from the still powerful association of "economic" with production rather than consumption. Environmental forest services are consumer services, much in the same order as the vast array of aesthetic goods and services that constitute such a large share of our economy and enhance our standard of living. It is not a case of "economic" and "non-economic" as it is two different types of consumption that, in turn, require two different kinds of production, one commodity and the other environmental.

The close relationship between values and words is especially evident in the phrases "use" or "utilization," the notion that commodity uses are uses while environmental uses are not. Closely connected with this is the related argument that forests not used for commodity objectives are wasted. These are merely variants on a concept that is heavily value laden, namely that commodity uses are more important than environmental uses. At times it appears in another form that while commodity consumption represents a "need," environmental consumption reflects only a "want" that is lower in the hierarchy of uses. Such distinctions as these merely reflect the overarching question I started with: disagreements about what forests should be used for.

To understand these controversies in a detached manner rather than to participate actively in the political fray, it is essential to formulate terminology less associated with one set of values or the other. It is for this reason that the terms "commodity forestry" and "environmental forestry" are appropriate; they express directly the value differences at issue.

The entire debate challenges foresters to be willing to accept environmental forest objectives with the same degree of commitment as commodity forest objectives. This means that environmental values be accepted not simply as residuals to be taken into account as impacts of more important commodity objectives, but as objectives in their own right. Environmental users think of environmental objectives as positive goals rather than as negative impacts to be mitigated. And unless one is willing to take the view that environmental consumption is undesirable, that environmental consumers should not want what they want, then language that is less value laden is essential for careful and detached analysis and understanding.

One might think of a simple test as to one's own emotions on this score. Can one be happy in one's role as a professional forester even if one is called upon to manage a forest entirely for environmental objectives, without any provision for commodity timber harvest? My question is not if one should so manage a forest, but whether or not one can be comfortable with such a hypothetical situation. If one is not comfortable with such a possibility, I would suggest that personal value preferences limit one's ability to respond effectively to the new public interest in environmental forestry.

FOREST SCIENCE AND MANAGEMENT SKILLS

Objectives and general ideas in forest management are one thing; implementation of those objectives is quite another. I will deal here with two of these: science and professional skills. The implications of environmental forestry for both present a major challenge to the forest profession.

For many years the main focus of forest research, including that of the U.S. Forest Experiment Stations, has emphasized the forest as a source of wood production. But environmental forestry now requires a much broader range of knowledge. Increasingly the environmental public finds that this new knowledge is being created not in traditional forest institutions but in a wider range of scientific and professional disciplines outside those established arenas. Consider, for example, the scientific sources of the proceedings concerning biodiversity on the Nicolet and Chequamegon National Forest in Wisconsin. Three scientists are spearheading that action. They are not foresters, but botanists—Steven Solheim, William Alverson, and Donald Waller of the University of Wisconsin. Accompanying their appeal within the Forest Service was a series of letters from thirteen scientists almost all of whom come from non-traditional forest research centers: Departments of Biology, at Stanford University, Florida State University, and the University of Pennsylvania; the Missouri Botanical Garden; landscape ecologists in the Harvard Graduate School of Design; the School of Forest Resources and Conservation at the University of Florida; officials of the Society for Conservation Biology; the Center for Conservation Biology at Stanford University; the Museum of Comparative Zoology at Harvard University. Among the thirteen only Larry Harris of the University of Florida comes from a traditional center of forest research.[23] Many of these draw upon the research of Jerry Franklin, whose work has been done from the U.S. Forest Experiment Station at Corvallis; Franklin often appears to be almost alone in such matters as a professional forester.

One can keep in touch with these non-traditional sources not so much through the Society of American Foresters as the Society for Conservation Biology, the Natural Areas Association or the Association of Wetland Managers or through journals such as *Conservation Biology, Restoration Biology, National Wetlands Newsletter, Endangered Species Update,* or a new journal, *Biodiversity and Conservation.*[24] What I conclude from all this is that forest management and the professionals associated with it are not generating from within their own organizations and institutions the science that is now required under the far broader context of environmental forestry.

One effect of the new range of forest knowledge is the way in which professionals with new environmental forest specializations are playing a larger role in forest management. This is a major phase in the recent history of the U.S. Forest Service. The "interdisciplinary in scope" requirement of environmental impact analysis has prompted the Forest Service to add to its staff a considerable number of people in non-traditional disciplines. This new contingent is what lies behind the formation of the Association of American Foresters for Environmental Ethics and the attempt by the Forest Service in its recent study to understand the values that this group has brought to the agency. It remains to be seen how much this change continues within the Forest Service and especially whether it filters down from the national to the regional and the supervisor level. One can establish a "new directions" office in the Washington office, but change in on-the-ground attitudes is far more difficult.

All of this presents a major challenge to forest management agencies. Environmental forestry is driving forest science toward new frontiers of knowledge about how the forest functions in contexts far beyond wood production; over periods of time beyond the time span of commercial maturity of trees; into concepts of ecological rather than single-tree maturity; and over a broader range of biological characteristics into more complex and spatially extended relationships among plants and animals. Old growth, "biodiversity," and landscape ecology issues are signals in these broader perspectives. Amid these new demands, the question is whether or not resources in forest science can meet the demands for new scientific understanding.

As with much environmental science generally, I see the problem as a tension between the enormous expansion of scientific horizons that environmental issues have generated and the limited capability of scientific institutions to respond. One of the more sobering aspects of this realization is that thus far the vast expansion of environmental science has created gaps in knowledge faster than we have been able to fill them. To put it bluntly, one of the main results of the recent increase in public demands on environmental science is that our ignorance has grown faster than our knowledge. Each new piece of research tells us far more about what we don't know than what we do know.

There is a tendency from many in established scientific and professional fields to think about all this in terms of what they describe as their own "rational" approach about science in contrast with the "emotional" understanding on the part of the environmental public or to think of the debate as one of science versus politics. In my view, this way of thinking is quite unproductive. Among the environmental public the commitment to science is strong. This was underlined several years ago by a study of values financed by the business firm the Continental Group, and conducted by some of the most highly recognized figures in values and survey research. Among their conclusions was that people oriented toward management of undisturbed nature had levels of commitment to science greater than did those oriented toward commodity production.[25]

The active environmental community represents a considerable aggregation of scientific training and skills. Among the membership there are a large number of people with scientific and technical training at the BA and MA level; among the leaders of environmental organizations there are many with higher levels of training and some that play a leading role in professional scientific circles. There is among many in the environmental public an intense commitment to self-education in science that is the envy of any university teacher who is perennially concerned with the problem of student motivation. And the policy agendas of citizen environmental organizations have continually included major demands of more scientific research.[26]

The impact of environmental objectives on science has far less to do with the quality of science and far more with its direction. There is a demand that far more be learned about how a forest functions than is now known. Certainly the work of Jerry Franklin about "old growth" forests is of that order; he has fostered new knowledge that brings this aspect of the forest more fully into the realm of scientific knowledge. Environmental forestry is making demands on scientific resources far greater than those resources have the capability of responding. Can we meet that challenge?

The debate over the direction of forest research was highlighted in 1978 when the U.S. Forest Service conducted a review of its research priorities. It asked representatives of five groups—government agencies, professional societies, industry, environmental groups, and consumer organizations—to identify their research priorities for the agency. Environmental representatives preferred for research on pollution, wildlife, recreation, and alternatives uses; in contrast the timber industry placed these subjects low and economics, marketing, harvesting, and biology high. The professionals agreed with the low ranking given by environmentalists to the timber industry priorities but gave only mixed support to the environmental priorities. The Forest Service did not follow any of the preferences and continued to allocate research funds as before.[27]

This tension between commodity and environmental objectives in forest research was again emphasized recently by a panel review of the subject under the auspices of the National Research Council. Headed by Professor John Gordon of Yale University, it was entitled, "Forestry Research: A Mandate for Change," sponsored by the National Research Council. A main thrust of the report was to argue that while a concentration on wood production was probably appropriate during the building boom following World War II, "the number one job today is creating a livable environment." The report stated that "the existing level of knowledge about forests is inadequate to develop sound forest-management policies" and "inadequate to meet society's needs."[28]

MANAGEMENT STRATEGIES

These changes are merely academic unless they are turned into applications in the management of particular forest lands. It is at this level that the debate is actually most intense. It is often easy to agree on general words, but the choice between old and new in forest management comes in on-the-ground applications. Amid the array of such choices that have been live recently in forest matters I will deal here with four very broad categories—description and classification, markers and monitoring, cause-effect analysis, and strategies for advancing forest integration and retarding forest fragmentation.

First is the task of describing forests in ways that reflect environmental meaning. Traditional forests are described in ways that reflect commodity meaning: stands; saplings, poles, and sawtimber; economic maturity; all-aged and even-aged management. These terms arise from the task of defining the forest as a source of commercial wood production. As with any empirical analysis they constitute a system of classifying data around meaningful categories, and in this case the goal that shapes the categories is commodity wood production.

Forests can be described, however, in ways that are more appropriate for environmental management. Some of these descriptive categories are long familiar: wilderness, wild area, natural area, travel corridors, recreational opportunity areas. But now a much larger range of classifications is upon us corresponding with the larger range of environmental forest objectives. Some involve the extension of traditional types of classifications such as wetland habitats, riparian areas, and old growth areas. Others arise from categories of wildlife movement as elaborated by radio collar research. Some follow from the concept of "unique" resources such as the endangered watershed, the endangered ecosystem,[29] the endangered habitat, or the endangered landscape, all arising from the attempt to classify forest environments in terms of relative levels of quality. Others are more extensive such as Michael Scott's species richness analysis.[30] And still others follow the lines of landscape ecology and seek to classify larger areas that might serve to integrate smaller areas of special environmental value.

The rapidly evolving interest in biodiversity calls for classification systems that identify levels and kinds of biodiversity and it appears that one of the most useful is fragment size. The research on that relationship between migratory songbirds and fragment size helps to pinpoint this mode of classification.[31] So does the attempt to identify the size of forest tracts essential for particular species of predators. If forest fragmentation has the impact on biodiversity that conservation biologists maintain then it may well be that forest classification in the future will involve much more than size of commercial timber stand and forest planning will require area analysis in terms of fragment size.

Second is the problem of selecting markers and conducting on-going monitoring on the basis of those markers. There are the familiar markers of threatened and endangered species, identified in terms of population levels, but there are also indicator species, sensitive species, and keystone species in biodiversity management. In each case the question is the particular species that will be selected out of the much larger number for observation, measurement, and assessment.

There are markers of water quality such as total maximum daily loads (TMDLs)[32] to serve as a benchmark against which to measure the effectiveness of best management practices (BMPs); or biological in contrast with chemical markers in assessing water quality so that the impact of pollutants on biological processes can be observed more directly; or markers in visibility, which often can be carried out through simple visual observation and photography;[33] or precipitation/air quality markers such as concentration of chemicals in wet and dry deposition;[34] or soil markers such as the density root hair systems or mycorrhizal fungi through which one might distinguish soil quality in different forests; or markers of fragmentation such as edge/area ratios.

Markers are one thing; comprehensive and continuous monitoring is quite another. Just as one might wish continuous knowledge about volumes of wood production on the full range of managed land, so environmental forest management generates the desire for comprehensive information for environmental resources. The resulting requirements for continuous monitoring and measurement currently far exceed the capacity of managing agencies to supply them.

A third management challenge is the task of being able to draw causal connections in environmental forestry and measuring their direction and magnitude. The task is focused sharply by the environmental impact statement that identifies the need for further cause-and-effect understanding. The call in the EIS requirements for a "full and searching" and "interdisciplinary" analysis of environmental effects drives many new demands for analysis of the consequences of actions on environmental conditions. The environmental strategy in the selection of EIS challenges is often to force inquiry into new facets of environmental forest affairs.

There are, for example, the court cases on best management practices in water quality. It is not enough, said the court, simply to accept the judgement of state forest agencies as to what would protect water quality. One had to demonstrate it with in-stream water quality data to identify cause and effect.[35] Or there is the recent Grider case; national forest environmental analyses must include the effects of clearcuts on the movement of wildlife between forest areas surrounding the cuts.[36] Or there is the effort in the Wisconsin biodiversity cases to push scientific inquiry toward the effect of edge use on interior species, a shift from the traditional emphasis on edge species variety.[37]

Such understanding will be shaped especially by two kinds of cause-effect research: one the wide-ranging effects of fragmenting intrusions in the forest such as roads and power lines and the other the variations in biodiversity that occur in tandem with variations in forest tract size. The first of these is already being called for, with an emphasis on the adverse environmental forest effects of roading on interior species. The second of these is marked by the case of migratory songbirds in which forest tract size is related to neotropical songbird species and populations.[38]

Since environmental forestry has a special focus on long-run objectives, the entire issue of cumulative effects in environmental impact analysis will become increasingly important. In several western court cases the U.S. Forest Service has been required to analyze the cumulative effect of road building over a long period of time. Such cumulative effects are, of course, far more difficult to measure or analyze than are short-term effects, but it seems rather clear that the practice of environmental forestry will shape a persistent tendency in that direction.[39]

Fourth are strategies to foster system integration and limit system fragmentation. The most significant feature of the new biodiversity interest in forest management lies in its emphasis on the integration of diverse elements in the biological system. That system emphasis was always implicit in ecology as a biological discipline, but it has now reappeared more forcefully in biodiversity. Especially significant is the resulting spatial dimension, that the various elements of the forest system located in different places are in some way related in terms of structure and function. This has been quite sharply etched, for example, in new knowledge of animal movements.

All of this brings to focus the need for larger relatively undisturbed areas over which to integrate management for biodiversity. The most dramatic case at the moment is the attempt to bring together the management of Yellowstone National Park and the six surrounding national forests in what is now called the Greater Yellowstone Ecosystem.[40] Similar ideas are brewing in the southern Appalachians. The most immediate focus seems to be the attempt to integrate management across federal agency landholdings that are in proximity. But the same challenge occurs for multiple state land management and the coordination of public and private lands, ranging from backyards for bird habitat to private non-industrial woodlands and larger private holdings.

The reverse of this, the task of retarding the process of fragmentation, is a similar challenge. If land fragmentation is now seen as a major problem that must be solved by strategies of land integration it makes eminent sense to resist land fragmentation. Thus, the call that fragmenting projects such as roads and power lines include in their environmental impact analyses the cumulative impact of physical fragmentation on underlying integrative biological processes.[41]

It may well be that one of the most immediate management strategies on this score will consist of biological corridors. These are in place in several instances such as the series of underpasses along the Tamiami Highway in Florida to facilitate movement of the Florida panther. The Grider case, mentioned previously, carries the same mandate. Or, as a different example, the new Maine Forest Practice Act is concerned primarily with the maintenance of some semblance of biological integration by requiring buffer strips around clearcuts.[42]

I conclude this challenge by focusing on an entirely mundane but vital indicator of forest values: forest terminology.

Any empirical discipline reveals itself most clearly in the terms that it uses to describe itself and to others—terms used to classify and describe the particular piece of the "real world" in which it specializes, justifies research priorities, designs research, educates and trains young people into its profession, and advances claims on the resources of the wider society. Through such terms a profession tells what it values, what it believes, what role it wishes to play in the larger scheme of things.

The relationship between commodity forestry and environmental forestry can be identified most sharply in this realm of forest terminology. A brief examination indicates that the two are quite far apart. I refer as a benchmark to an issue of *Pennsylvania Woodlands,* published by the Cooperative Extension Service of the Pennsylvania State University entitled, "Forest Terminology." It begins with the explanation, "Because forestry is a specialized field of study, it has a vocabulary all its own," and lists some 160 terms with definitions.[43]

In reading over the list I was struck by the degree to which it conveys overwhelmingly the notion that forestry is commodity forestry. I began to construct a list of "environmental forestry" terms and in a rather cursory first cut drew up about 120. When I compared the two I found only a handful that were on both lists. Something rather striking was emerging—two worlds of forestry quite far apart; little of the world of environmental forestry had entered the world of commodity forestry even on this elemental level.

My final and perhaps most important question then, is: can professional foresters construct a list of environmental as well as commodity forest terms so as to create a common body of knowledge into which all foresters will be trained and which they can apply as a common discipline? This is perhaps the most severe test of all.

I will be watching future issues of *Pennsylvania Woodlands.*

FOREWORD TO FREDERICK FRANKENA, *STRATEGIES OF EXPERTISE IN TECHNICAL CONTROVERSIES*

To some, the debate over siting wood-burning power plants, the subject of Fred Frankena's book, might well seem of limited importance. Yet, it focuses sharply on a type of issue that has occurred again and again over the past thirty years and has played a role of considerable significance in environmental politics. Most accounts of such issues have dealt primarily with the drama of the events and have not probed very deeply. Frankena's treatment, however, goes further to focus on the conflict over values and its relationship to population change, science, and technology as they apply to large-scale environmental intrusion in rural areas.

The conventional literature, for the most part, incorporates the political vision of the siting agencies, either private or public. Why, so the question runs, do communities seek to prevent justifiable siting actions that are "necessary" to foster economic objectives? The analytical context then becomes one of a conflict between desirable and undesirable public policies and the

From Frederick Frankena, *Strategies of Expertise in Technical Controversies: A Study of Wood Energy Development* (Bethlehem, Pa.: Lehigh University Press, 1992). 15–27.

exploration of strategies as to how communities can be persuaded to accept what they should rightly agree to accept but do not.

Policy analysts have experienced considerable difficulty extending their vision beyond this limited context, to observe the interplay among factors embedded in the policy choices—factors such as values and value change, the dynamics of the course of scientific inquiry, and debate over the direction of technological innovation. Only if one can back off from the pressures of policy choice to the larger context of historical change in values, science, and technology can the limitations of the policy perspective be overcome. Because Frankena's study brings these factors into a more central role, it provides an opportunity to broaden the context and meaning of policy and policy history.

VALUES AND VALUE CHANGE

The most significant element in Frankena's analysis is the focus on values and value change. Much recent environmental understanding has been concerned with process rather than substance, with how things are carried out rather than with objectives, with details about implementation rather than details about the origin and elaboration of values which underly objectives, with means rather than ends. By emphasizing values Frankena gets much closer to the heart of the historical meaning of environmental issues and environmental debate.

The continuing role of values and value conflict in environmental affairs is often obscured or even denied by environmental analysts and policy makers. Especially those in the regulated industries, administrative circles, and professional institutions argue that there are no fundamental differences in values in environmental affairs. The fact that Congress has enacted much environmental legislation over the years, so the argument goes, reflects national agreement on basic environmental objectives. But the intensity of the continuing debates indicates otherwise. How else explain the innumerable conflicts that seem impossible to resolve? How else explain the language of basic values, "wood production fundamentalism" versus "environmental fundamentalism" that has come into play. How explain the notion often expressed that there are "religions" at odds here?

We must understand the rise of environmental affairs as a broad social development, the emergence of new values associated with a post-manufacturing society that came to the United States after World War II. The lives and values of people changed; what they wanted from public policy to enhance their standard of living now came to be discussed in terms of quality of life and to include a large dose of environmental quality. The change can be charted most precisely through the value changes associated with rising levels of education and which seemed to come largely at the "high school graduate" and "some college" and "BA degree" levels. They seem to be associated with values such as health and smoking, changing size of family, and the changing role of women that are also influenced heavily by education.

These value changes are closely related to changing consumption preferences over the course of time, an evolution from necessities in the nineteenth century to conveniences in the second quarter of the twentieth century to amenities in the post–World War II years. Rising levels of education led to new aspirations and rising levels of income and leisure enabled people to realize those aspirations. The changes have been identified and outlined most elaborately by those who chart consumer attitudes, the market analysts who now have gone beyond the traditional sociological variables to explore the psychological variables that sort out very different clusters of values even within similar socio-economic levels.

It should be noted especially that these value changes did not come uniformly to all Americans at the same time. There are clear differences in the social context in which new values arose, were transmitted and resisted. And that social context often was regional. Some regions of the nation were in the forefront in expressing new environmental values and others were more reluctant to take them up. Suburban areas seemed to lead and as they became the most vigorous location of population growth so also did environmental objectives gain more support. Rural areas often lagged behind, especially as their cultural context remained one of extractive and commodity production. But as rural areas and small towns became attractive places to live their consumption and quality of life features often came to be more important than their commodity production features. It is this social context in which Frankena's wood-burning power plants take on larger significance.

In his descriptions of the organized opponents of the wood-burning power plants, Frankena adds to the evidence about the way in which new values, emerging in a broad demographic way, become transmitted from one place to another. In-migrants to rural areas, so he convincingly argues, brought information and organizational skills with them that they had learned in more urbanized settings and in education. They provided the leadership, knowledge about access to information, and a willingness to confront the more powerful private institutions and public authorities than were traditional rural residents. This pattern Frankena describes is not unusual; it is repeated again and again in such cases of environmental intrusion.

Two aspects of this in-migration are particularly significant. One is its extent and character. Who and how many and over what period of time did they come? Migration to the rural countryside was observed continually during the 1970s and especially after the census of 1980. This was largely a matter of charting rates of population growth and comparing those in urban and rural areas. Hence, by the time of the 1980s, as these comparative rates changed and rural population no longer grew more rapidly than urban, observers argued that the process was over.

But, says Frankena, this may well be in error. First, there is rural out-migration as well as in-migration and the second may well have continued amid the first, thus bringing people with newer values into rural areas even as rural population remained stable or declined. Second, the inflow of new values may not be a product only of population movement and change; cultural values, especially once in motion, are transmitted often by other means as well. Hence the transformation of values in rural communities could well come through more general processes of cultural diffusion rather than solely through migration.

It is also important to observe the relationship between the in-migrants and those already there. Rural reaction to environmental issues has been mixed. Rural people and their elected representatives generally have been skeptical of environmental objectives. Often they have been a major part of the environmental opposition. Hence they view zoning as an attempt by outsiders to control the free disposal and use of land in their communities.

But this reaction is often undermined by intrusions from afar in the form of actions by either private business or government in which local communities feel that they have become the victim of forces set in motion elsewhere that now impinge adversely on their daily affairs. In a wide number of cases, ranging over siting industrial plants and landfills, construction of dams and reservoirs, erection of electrical transmission lines and extraction of coal and other minerals, long-established residents have become environmental activists, working in close tandem with residents more recently arrived. One can rightly describe this as a process in which new environmental values long dormant now are further elaborated and activated by a major community event.

In many rural communities the previously dominant commitment to commodity extraction or primary processing continues to shape community values. In these cases there is intense conflict between new and old usually taking the form of bitter ideological controversy in which old and new values confront each other directly. Frankena's cases are somewhat different. For, as he emphasizes, the use of wood for fuel had long been a community practice and the innovation was the size and scope of that use. In fact, much of the controversy involved a conflict between older and newer fuel uses of wood; the new plants would jeopardize a long-used source of fuel for home heating. Local allies to those from afar who wished to intrude into Frankena's communities were relatively weak because of the degree to which the extractive economy was closely related to the consumer values of those who lived there.

Frankena's cases might well be contrasted with another type of case in which the intrusions and changes are smaller rather than larger in scale and come from within rather than from outside the community. Considerable environmental transformation occurs in less developed areas. Roads are widened and upgraded and so are bridges; farm land is subdivided, not necessarily leading to large condominiums but to large lots; buildings, driveways, and roads lead to a persistent but hardly observable decline in permeable surfaces; farmland is farmed more intensively up to the fence rows, reducing wildlife habitat. In such ways as these transformations that are massive in the long run take place in such a way that they do not appear to be massive intrusions; they make their way with far less if not very little adverse response.

In the cases outlined by Frankena, large-scale, massive intrusions take place that boggle the minds of residents. The size and scale fits neatly with their own perception that the larger world out there, equally massive in size and scale, is an oppressive force against which they must defend themselves. That scale of intrusion, formulated and implemented by external private and public agents, instantaneously shapes a massive conflict in perception and values. From that initial recognition, as Frankena shows, the long-run die is cast. Values and power become entwined as mutually reinforcing causal factors. It is well worth keeping in mind that many environmental issues, not just those in rural areas, involve this close connection between values and power.

One aspect of this type of confrontation needs exploration beyond that emphasized by Frankena, namely the response of those in the industrial, administrative, and professional community to the reactions to their plans by those who live in rural areas. Sociological analysis of such "agents" is rarely undertaken. But they have their own peculiar perspectives, desires, values, and strategies, their own "culture" that needs to be brought into any satisfactory analysis of these environmental debates.

Over the years, experience by siting managers with local resistance has generated a distinctive series of reactions and ideas. Community opposition is, of course, unacceptable to the project proponents, whether private or public. There may be some willingness to modify the process so as to "listen" to the objectors and even to permit them to be participants in a limited sort of way. But the series of controversies, information about which is widely shared among development proponents, has shaped a distinctive point of view, a distinctive culture among those occupied with the task of siting.

One is the language of debate that identifies siting opponents as emotional obstructionists. Managers of development projects have long popularized the notion of NIMBY, "Not in My Backyard," with strongly negative connotations. It is not too much to say that the NIMBY phrase has become a negative symbol that arouses powerful emotions on the part of those who use the term and almost precludes careful and calm discussion. The bottom line is simply the idea that the projects, whether industrial developments or waste sites, "must" be put somewhere, and that those who object to siting them in their own communities are obstructionists. This context of thought and argument is now so firmly embedded that one can speak of an anti-NIMBY culture to be understood not so much in terms of logical argument but of intense and immediate emotional reaction.

A second aspect of the managerial culture is more strategic rather than ideological, the search for ways out in the form of communities that will not or cannot effectively oppose projects. This has taken several forms. One, and perhaps the most successful, is the willingness to provide massive economic benefits to communities to overcome their resistance. This strategy has long been used by private industry to make projects acceptable that would not otherwise be so, usually in the form of major tax contributions to the local community. Such economic benefits have now been fashioned, for example, as a part of the Pennsylvania state program to site a low-level radioactive waste depository. These cases sometimes work out with little fanfare if the community accepts the economic arrangement.

More frequently, however, the strategy has been to sort out communities that are politically vulnerable from those that are not, and to select the former in which to propose siting. Evidence about the location of waste sites in both urban and rural areas supports the argument that such a pattern is implicit in siting decisions. More recently siting consultants have made explicit statements that siting proposals should not be made near middle-class or upper middle-class communities. In a number of cases waste sites have been selected in poor, rural, and black communities, often in "unorganized" townships where resistance would be minimal. Such siting strategies have now been fully described by leaders of the "environmental justice" movement. It would seem plausible that Frankena's cases were among those in which siting managers gradually learned what kinds of communities were politically vulnerable to their objectives and what kinds were not.

VALUES, SCIENCE, AND TECHNOLOGY

A major focus of Frankena's work is the role of science and technology in disputes over siting. It has been customary for many writers to pose this problem in terms of the validity or correctness of the scientific ideas under debate. In recent years, however, a more detached analysis has been taken up that understands technical controversy in terms of the professional and social context of those participating in the debate. Disputes are a result not of degrees of rationality or emotion but of different ways of looking at the world and choices about what in matters of knowledge should be emphasized over alternative approaches. This point of view establishes an analytical relationship between disputes over knowledge and disputes over public policy that is more deeply rooted in the human context and freer of normative choices made by the observer.

For many years matters of science and technology in both history and contemporary affairs have been analyzed much in the terms of how those fields of endeavor view themselves—the search for knowledge, done in an independent and fully objective way, followed by the application of that knowledge. The relationship between knowledge and application is thought of as either direct and unobstructed, carried out by those directly responsive to science and technology as objective forces or often bent and obstructed by popular emotion or by political forces on the part of those who are less knowledgeable.

An increasing body of research and literature, however, poses a far different context for understanding technical knowledge and its relationship to public policy. Conflicts within science and technology are often now understood more in terms of the internal dynamics of those professions, the values and conflicting directions within each discipline, and the differences in perspectives and methods between disciplines. These conflicts within the scientific and technical professions then are examined in their close connection with the larger conflicts in society and politics in fashioning public policy.

Frankena's analysis is in the spirit of this new approach to science and public policy. He emphasizes the connection between scientific controversy and policy controversy in the siting debate.

It might be worthwhile, however, to place the entire matter in a broader context in which the beginning point is not the policy option that one identifies as desirable or undesirable, but the internal historical tendencies within those specialized professions themselves. To understand the relationship between divergent views within science and divergent views within policy one must begin with the internal evolution of science.

The key element in such an analysis is the growing pluralism of scientific expertise since World War II, a development in which environmental issues played a major role. Those issues brought into the scientific world a vast number of new realms of inquiry. Their exploration generated new specializations and along with many other new frontiers of science, helped to expand the range of individuals and groups seeking to shape the discovery and assessment of knowledge. In a considerable number of settings that brought together science and policy, debate shifted from a relatively small to a much larger number of experts and generated a new level of open competition and give-and-take among scientists and scientific ideas.

An early example of such a shift was in the field of atomic energy policy. Here an emphasis on new factors to be taken into account as consequences of siting—such as earthquake-prone sites or the aquatic effects of thermal discharges—led to new technical disciplines being brought into decision-making outside the narrower circle of atomic energy experts who had previously dominated the scene. In the health effects of lead, those emphasizing the potential adverse effect on industrial workers had earlier dominated thought about lead as primarily a problem in ingestion; now the new interest in the effects of lead on child development sharply challenged older views and over the years completely transformed thought about lead science with attendant consequences for lead policy. In our own day the health consequences of toxic chemicals, once confined primarily to cancer, are now being challenged by those who emphasize a wide range of other effects—genetic, reproductive, fetal, pulmonary, and on immune systems.

Cases such as these build up a set of generalizations about the direction of historical development in such matters. Earlier the context was one of scientific and technical expertise within a relatively closed setting of governmental agencies and professional specialists associated with private industry and academic institutions who sought to keep scientific and technical debate relatively free from larger public influence. As time went on, however, the context became more open, in which a wider range of specialists participated and public debate replaced private discussions, often with media participation.

Such was Frankena's case of wood-burning power plants. Several elements in the process deserve a bit more attention

The most fundamental aspect of this shift from a more closed to a more open context of scientific and technical debate was the role of specialization. Within science and technology themselves, specialization leads to varied scientific "publics" that enhance diversity of opinion. Specialists create new institutional worlds often isolated from each other. The ideology of science assumes that the scientific method generates a high level of agreement. But, on the contrary, enhanced scientific specialization enhances disagreement. This discordant tendency arising within the culture of science itself is often obscured by the tendencies of scientific bodies, such as the National Academy of Science, to avoid minority and dissenting views in its reports.

But the divergence of views within science was more powerful than these attempts to impose unanimity on diversity and in the 1970s many dissenting scientific opinions emerged on the public scene. Its roots lay in disciplinary variety. As specialization took place so did the conviction that one's distinctive way of looking at the world should receive greater recognition in the larger context of debate and decision-making. Hence specialization in science and technology carried its own inherent tendency toward centrifugal expression and debate.

This interdisciplinary process was closely intertwined with institutional competition to stimulate variety in opinion and ideas and hence debate and disagreement. One source of this competition came from academic institutional support for science and technology. Academic institutions compete for recognition and in the process often seek to advance one line of inquiry over another. In some countries the centralized organization of research institutions tends to keep these centrifugal tendencies in check, but in the United States the vast number of such institutions, each closely connected with self-images of state and regional prestige, foster assertions of the importance of new research in competition with old, of unconventional ideas amid the conventional. Institutional competition, therefore, becomes a major force for pluralism in scientific and technical debate.

Institutional variety also marked the role of federal agencies in enhancing pluralism in scientific debate. The years after World War II not only witnessed the rise of the overarching scientific branches of the federal governments, such as the National Academy of Sciences and the National Science Foundation, but also a wide range of scientific enterprise in administrative agencies. In matters of health, the Centers for Disease Control and the National Toxicology Program became independent centers of initiative with respect to environmental health effects. The Geological Survey contributed its own on-going water quality measurements and seismological assessments to policy issues arising in the Environmental Protection Agency and the Atomic Energy Agency. The U.S. Fish and Wildlife Service generated its own science about "effects" of a wide range of developments on aquatic life. These tendencies in federal agencies were reflected in and enhanced by the requirement in the National Environmental Policy Act that environmental assessments be "interdisciplinary" and "wide-ranging," a requirement that the federal courts underscored as essential for sound administrative procedure.

State governments have also become important in contributing to the context of scientific pluralism. At one time the federal government was all-powerful in scientific capacity and authority. Especially in environmental affairs, such as environmental health and ecological knowledge, states were heavily dependent on federal agencies for technical knowledge and expertise. With time, however, as states became more affluent their scientific and technical capabilities increased. California, for example, developed environmental capabilities about air pollution and pesticides that could often challenge federal scientists. In the first round of the dispute over the health effects of the pesticide alar both Massachusetts and New York developed their own toxicological analyses that enabled them to challenge the scientific conclusions of federal agencies. In the 1980s a coalition of eight northeastern states pooled their scientific and technical resources, often in cooperation with California, to take up air pollution issues, thus extending the state role in scientific and technical pluralism. Such tendencies often led to scientific conclusions from the state level that were at variance with the federal, thus extending participation in scientific debate in public policy.

Citizen organizations—and this is the focal point of Frankena's argument —played an important role in this tendency toward technical pluralism. From the earliest days of modern environmental affairs in the 1960s citizens concerned with environmental problems reached out to technical specialists. They well understood the role of technical knowledge in policy decision and recognized that if they were to challenge an action they considered to be environmentally detrimental they would have to challenge the technical basis of that action. This was often not difficult to do since many proposals were accompanied by a mere assertion of technical fact rather than an ample demonstration of it and citizens were quite able to bring technical expertise to bear in exposing those limitations. They were especially able to inject into the scientific debate the insight from a disciplinary viewpoint different from those used in a competing analysis.

Thus it was, for example, that when the Pacific Gas and Electric Co. in the 1960s sought to site a nuclear reactor at Bodega Bay, the citizen's group that opposed it found a geological consultant who was able to raise serious questions about the geological safety of the site. The testimony of that expert, in turn, prompted the Secretary of the Interior, Stewart Udall, to bring the U.S. Geological Survey into the fray and because the Atomic Energy Commission had almost no geological expertise at its disposal, the debate over the adequacy of the site soon moved from the close relationship between the utility and the AEC to the larger realm of public discussion. Or, a few years later the U.S. Fish and Wildlife Service was able to bring significant arguments into atomic energy decisions about the detrimental effects of thermal discharges on aquatic life. This case, in fact, played a major role in shaping the requirement that environmental impact analysis be fully interdisciplinary.

In this and many other such cases, the role of citizen organizations reflects a major development in American private and public life—the education of a vast number of individuals who while not technical experts themselves, are knowledgeable about the role of such expertise and where it can be found, and have some keen sense of methods required to ferret out and evaluate knowledge. Common to a wide range of citizen actions is the participation in such groups of people who have had several years of college education, who have undertaken searches as academic projects under the guidance of college and university instructors, and whose investigative skills acquired in such training they now apply to their current environmental circumstances. There are also major cases in which people with only a high school education who because of some incident in their community become self-educated to such an extent that they can challenge the experts associated with public and private agencies. Adult environmental education of this kind has played a major role in modern environmental affairs.

Such ventures, moreover, do not remain simply individual inquiries. For soon the citizen "expert" begins to participate in a world of expertise involving both academic specialists and other citizens who are becoming equally knowledgeable about the subject with which they are concerned. Knowledge becomes shared within networks of amateur and professional specialists. In some cases, a sufficient number of people become interested in the subject so that an organization is formed to become a central clearinghouse for technical information. Here technically trained people are hired to keep in touch with on-going research, follow the journals, establish continuing contacts with professional specialists in universities and government, and serve as major vehicles for scientific and technical transfer not only among themselves but to decision-makers in government. In some cases such activities have given rise to regularly published summaries of research to the extent that they are of distinctive value to specialized researchers in academia, government and private industry.

The enhancement of pluralism in scientific debate and hence in the role of science in public policy has been met with misgivings on the part of many of the most influential leaders in scientific institutions. They are often prone to speak of the resulting controversies in terms of reason versus emotion and good versus bad science. These reactions are understandable as sociological and political responses to innovation in the realm of science and public policy. They are also understandable in terms of the perennial conflicts between old and new in historical change. However, by themselves they are not a useful guide to careful social analysis. New ways of comprehending these disputes are essential in order to assess accurately their role in public affairs.

There are many worlds of scientific and technical environmental networks linking specialists in academic institutions, state and federal governments with those in citizen groups. Frankena's work is a particular case example. It is not by any means the first of such studies and his references can guide the reader to many more. But it provides an excellent account of the way in which scientific and technical information now plays a role in a far more pluralistic universe of expertise than was the case a quarter of a century ago. It is, thus, a case study not only in the history of changing values but also the history of the evolution of science as a public process.

VALUES AND SCIENCE

These two aspects of *Strategies of Expertise in Technical Controversies*—values and science—deserve wide attention. For the heavy policy preference emphasis of most environmental writing has all but ignored both the evolution of environmental values as an historical process and the sociological and political context of expertise.

Value change as a broad-based demographic process seems to fall completely outside the perspective of most environmental analysts. At the same time, they are so absorbed in the task of persuading their publics of the "right" solution to a problem that they instinctively shy away from a more detached observation of choices made by experts.

We who have been professional observers of environmental affairs over the past several decades have often neglected the real world of human values and scientific debate. We have been so preoccupied with following the intricacies of environmental policy formation and implementation that we have neglected the context of historical and sociological understanding. Frankena's study provides an opportunity to set the analysis of environmental public affairs off in quite a different direction and one that would greatly enhance that understanding.

HUMAN CHOICE IN THE GREAT LAKES WILDLANDS

THIS CHAPTER OFFERS historical perspective on the most critical factor in future policy with regard to the Great Lakes forest—the human perceptions, values, and institutions that constitute the major setting in which choices are made. It concerns choices made by people in their daily lives as they have come into direct or vicarious contact with forests, choices made by wood production companies, by forest professionals and managers, by local, state, and national public officials. And it asks how and why these choices changed over the course of time.

Policies regarding the Great Lakes forest stem primarily from this human factor. Alternative policies arise from differences in the perception and meaning of forests to different people and the values they place upon forested areas. Environmental and conservation controversies turn on disputes over such matters. Because the nature and meaning of a forest to people today is vastly different from what it was a century ago, so must the knowledge about the

From Susan Flader, ed., *Environmental Change in the Great Lakes Forest* (Minneapolis: University of Minnesota Press, 1982), 295–318. Reprinted by permission.

forest be different, and also the human interaction with the forest. Our biggest problems lie not so much in our knowledge about the way in which the forest has evolved but in our understanding of the evolution of the human choices that have been made with respect to the forest environment.

Through this perspective, this chapter analyzes changing human choices about the forested wildlands—that area of sparse or no habitation beyond the city and the countryside in the Great Lakes region between about 1840 and the present. This evolution has had three distinct stages: 1850–1910, when wood production predominated; 1910–45, when out-migration took place and real-estate values declined drastically, and when these "lands that nobody wanted" were rescued by public ownership and management; and 1945 to the present, a time of revival of intense interest in the forest. The revolution in forest-related human values that has taken place since 1945 has been so fundamental that a historical approach must inevitably stress change rather than continuity, the degree to which relatively little of the vast stretch of time we have covered thus far is immediately pertinent to the real world of forest choices today. Such an approach emphasizes not so much the impact of the forest on people as the impact of people on the forest. The analysis is organized around three phenomena: changes in the way in which people at large conceived of the Great Lakes forest and their relationship to it; the evolution and development of management perspectives; and the changing role of local communities as the specific context in which choices about the forest are made.

CHANGING PUBLIC ATTITUDES

The most important long-run changes in the Great Lakes forest lay in the way in which people at large valued forested wildlands. How did they perceive them? What role did they wish forests to play in their personal lives, in the life of their community, region, and nation? At the start we can make a simple distinction between the forbidding forest of the nineteenth century and the attractive one of the twentieth, as a source of pleasure, relaxation, and inspiration. Although the word *wilderness* traditionally had a negative connotation, today it has a markedly attractive tone.[1] A dramatic reversal of values has taken place. But this is not peculiar to forests. A similar change has taken place with wetlands, the dry and desert lands of the West, the nation's free-flowing rivers, the pine barrens of the East, the swamps of the South, and the prairies of the plains states.[2] As recently as the early twentieth century, for example, natural wetlands were considered valueless; only by drainage could they be made useful. By the early 1970s the opposite was argued; they were so valuable in their natural state that they should be protected from development (e.g., Virginia Wetlands Act, 1972).[3] A vast change in values has taken place with respect to undeveloped lands and waters. The human meaning of the Great Lakes forest is an integral part of that historical change.

These new values do not represent a desire to return to some primitive, prescientific, pretechnological society. On the contrary, they represent an integral part of the standard of living of an advanced industrial society. There is a reciprocal relationship between the desire to enjoy the material commodities of the world of conveniences and the desire to enjoy intangible experiences in the world of amenities. Consumption in the United States has changed over the years from an emphasis on necessities to one on conveniences and later amenities; each earlier stage has been retained firmly as each later one evolved. Because modern technology has produced a vast array of commodities, one can enjoy and value wildlands more than before; one can live in less-developed areas with modern conveniences, reach them readily, explore them with camera as well as rod and gun, and hike within them with the security created by the gadgetry of modern backpacking.

We know much about these changing values in the years after World War II because they have been examined in detail. There are studies of those who use wildlands for recreation, most of them undertaken as a result of the desire of managers to know who the users are and what they prefer. Those done for the Boundary Waters Canoe Area are typical.[4] We know what fishermen and hunters value, what car campers want in contrast to backpackers, and the values sought by off-road vehicle users. The massive studies of attitudes toward wildlife now under way by Stephen Kellert will enable us to know better the range of human relationships to wildlife as well.[5] These studies point to the way in which forested wildlands mean much more to the vast number of people than simply a source of physical commodities such as wood and minerals.

Even more striking are studies of the values of people who purchase lands in the wildlands for their environmental amenities to enjoy for home, leisure, and recreation. Professional foresters have long been interested in this phenomenon, but from a rather oblique point of view. Why, they have asked, do such owners not wish to produce wood on their properties for commercial sale? In state after state, including the Great Lakes area, it has been found that owners value these lands for their natural setting, their cleaner water, less-cluttered landscape, and cleaner air, their forest and its microclimate. One author[6] examined real estate advertisements in papers in Philadelphia, Harrisburg, and Pittsburgh for properties in Potter County, in the north central highlands of the state. To attract buyers such descriptive phrases as "at the end of a forest road," "by a sparkling stream," "lies along the boundary of a state forest," "in a secluded woodland," were used. To clearcut such areas would destroy the very values for which they were purchased, that is, the environmental quality under the forest canopy; even some form of selection cutting might markedly degrade them.

In the 1970s migration to nonmetropolitan areas has been found to reflect similar values. Professors James D. Williams and Andrew J. Sofranko, of the Department of Agricultural Economics at the University of Illinois, Urbana-Champaign, examined seventy-five nonmetropolitan counties with net immigration rates of 10 percent and higher between 1970 and 1975. Of these, seven were in Minnesota, nine in Wisconsin, and twenty-three in the upper and lower peninsula of Michigan. As reasons for in-migration they found that the quality of living and especially of the natural environment was more important than economic opportunity. Similar quality-of-living objectives were emphasized in a study of residents in Charlevoix and Antrim Counties, Michigan, conducted by Robert Marans and John Wellman for the Survey Research Center at Ann Arbor.[7]

So far, values have been emphasized; similar changes can be observed by focusing on human perception. How do people perceive the forest in general and the Great Lakes forest in particular? Dramatic land forms such as the Great Lakes and their surrounding forests have long been powerful visual images in the minds of the American people, defining for them a visual space far beyond their own immediate neighborhoods, in the region and even the nation at large. The environmental movement, not surprisingly, is strongest in those areas which have such striking land and water forms. We can observe these visual images as they change from the paintings, sketches, and engravings of the nineteenth century, accessible to only a few observers, to the color photography of the twentieth, utilized in mass fashion and extended by television to every nook and cranny of the nation. Contrast, for example, the Inglis guide to northern Michigan published in 1898 for people in Chicago, Detroit, and elsewhere who wished to summer at Mackinac, Charlevoix, or Petoskey with King and Ela's *Faces of the Great Lakes,* full of color and black-and-white visual images published in 1977. From such perceptual images we can draw a number of conclusions about the Great Lakes forest.[8]

The lakes were deeply etched in the minds of urbanites, even in the nineteenth century, in cities such as Detroit, Chicago, Milwaukee and Minneapolis, St. Louis and Cincinnati, and even New Orleans, as dramatic natural features of value in their own right. They were, in the parlance of national parks of the nineteenth century, "natural wonders." When Mackinac Island was established as our second national park, it was its geological and archaeological features rather than its forests that identified it to the wider society to the south. The Boundary Waters Canoe Area has been recognized since the early 1920s as a national and not just a regional resource.[9]

In the post–World War II years, many perceptual features of the forest itself began to emerge. There were the magnificent hardwoods of the Porcupine Mountains, which in the 1950s aroused the attention and concern not only of urbanized areas in the region but also of the Wilderness Society in Washington, D.C. and of other national organizations that identified the area as of unique national value.[10] A similar perceptual identity has evolved in recent years in Michigan in the Pigeon River State Forest, dramatized by the long, drawn-out issue of oil drilling and reflected in the evolution of management plans by the Department of Natural Resources that tend to emphasize natural environment values. In similar fashion, groups far from the lakeshores in areas such as Sleeping Bear Dunes and Pictured Rocks have changed what were initially intended to be intensive-development tourist areas into major battlegrounds for the protection of natural environments.[11] It is no accident that citizen-input meetings on issues such as these are held in Lansing and Ann Arbor as well as in Beulah and Grand Marais.

Sparse evidence for earlier years makes it difficult to chart stages in the evolution of these values and perceptions. The main value of the forest in the nineteenth century lay in its wood and that land which, after cutting, it was hoped could be farmed. Permanent habitation provided little conceptual space for the permanent role of the canopied forest, let alone sustained and continuous wood production. The struggle over tax-delinquent and tax-reverted lands between 1900 and 1930 involved intense controversies over the agricultural possibilities of the formerly forested land; the hope that it could sustain a high level of farming and support farm communities died hard. In Michigan, where the lands reverted to the state, local communities exercised considerable pressure to put them back on the market so that farming could be tried again.[12] Out of this agonizing debate slowly emerged the view that the forest provided the only potential for a sustained economy, that stability in the long-run flow of wood production provided the most sensible relief from the uncertainties of marginal agriculture.

Even in these earlier times one can observe some changing patterns of use that set the direction toward the amenity values of later decades. Local histories tell of old logging camps with large dormitories and cook houses that became hunting and fishing resorts.[13] These were accessible only to the hardy who wished to take a train to the last station some distance from their destination and then by a combination of horseback, walking, and canoeing finally arrive at the refurbished camp. Seclusion by the lake amid the forest was eagerly sought. The visitors came again each summer. The automobile made camps more accessible, and then the great dining hall gave way to the housekeeping cottage. The weekend tourist appeared to add to the seasonal pattern of visits, and still later an increase in permanent migrants. In each of these stages there was a gradual evolution of a new conception of the forest, of wildlands valued early for their amenities, which became even more valuable as the demand for amenities increased while the supply remained constant.

A similar change took place with rivers and lakes. First valued most for their use as transportation for logs, these are now valued primarily for their recreational quality, both in-stream for fishing and canoeing, and streamside for temporary or permanent homesites. One thinks of the massive and now legendary struggle over the boundary water lakes in Minnesota, represented by those two antagonist neighbors, Edward W. Backus and Ernest Oberholzer, as told by R. Newell Searle. But similar struggles involving a similar change in the meaning of lakes and rivers took place throughout the North Woods. Fishing as well as hunting groups were persistent in their support of permanent state ownership of reverted lands in Michigan. At that time these groups were small in membership and composed of the more affluent, but over the years they became mass-membership organizations with an emphasis on public hunting grounds and fishing waters in contrast to private membership clubs. The changing attitudes toward lakes are well charted, since these were prized as locations for summer cottages; lake associations in all three states have arisen not only to protect their natural environment but also to delve into local history. The shift from the commodity to amenity role can be observed in the fate of lakes in two Michigan cities. In Cadillac, what was at one time a large logging pond has now become one of the central visual characteristics of the city, an amenity that enhances the environmental quality of the entire community. In Manistee, on the other hand, the old lumber milling firms remain, with their accompanying salt factories, which prompt the current visitor to view the lake more as an environmental liability than an asset.

It is worth giving special emphasis to the egalitarian character of these changes. The search for environmental quality in home, leisure, and recreation had long been limited to only a few, to those who could afford to travel to the salubrious climate of Petoskey for the summer,[14] or to those who were members of a private hunting or fishing club. The acquisition and increased use of public lands, both state and federal, carried with it a different message, that outdoor amenities were available for use by the masses of the American people. These were public lands for public use, whether they were parks or forests or wildlife refuges. The measure of that equity in use was the low cost of access, for the most part entirely free in the early years, but kept to a low cost even to this day. Environmental amenities have long been sold in the private market in the form of homes in areas of cleaner air and water and less cluttered land, or in the form of private recreation clubs. In contrast, public lands provided amenity opportunities that one could enjoy by the cheapest forms of outdoor recreation—walking, strolling for pleasure, hiking, and back-packing.

In the years after World War II, discovery of the North Country by an increasing number of people has led to an intensity and quality of human involvement in the area's natural environment that was unknown in earlier years. All across the nation people discovered natural lands and came to know them personally by hiking through them, observing them attentively with varied field guides in hand, photographing them so as to sustain memories of their experience and share them with others, and reporting in detail what they observed. Through such personal involvement these areas came to be considered as one's own turf; and involvement with them came to be called "turf building." The pine barrens of New Jersey and the varied physical and biological forms of South Manitou Island came to be valued and protected much as did one's own job or home. The intensity of the politics of turf protection stems directly from the changing value and meaning of the forest and the direct involvement of people with it.

Over the decades there were vast changes in the significance of these wildlands to the people who experienced them. In the nineteenth century they were a raw material for extraction, as people looked beyond the forest to the agricultural lands they hoped would provide permanent homes. In the decades from about 1910 to 1945 they came to be "lands nobody wanted," retained in public ownership, protected, and regenerated by public agencies because of their rapid decline in value to the private economy. But other meanings and uses were being implanted even in these years, to burst forth in the decades after World War II. From the "lands that nobody wanted" emerged the "lands lots of people wanted." Wood production values of the nineteenth century did not stand high. Real estate values told the tale. If land competed both for wood production and for environmental amenities such as a vacation home, the latter brought a far higher price. The contrasting market-price values of the 1920s and 1970s are a measure of the depth of the transformation in perceptions that a century and a half had wrought.

EVOLUTION OF MANAGEMENT PERSPECTIVES

So much for the long-run evolution of public values with respect to wildlands. Let us shift focus from the general public to those who manage the forest, who organize and operate private and public wildlands-management systems. These also involve human choice, the choices made by business entrepreneurs and corporate managers, by administrators in private and public forest agencies. Central to such management are the managers themselves, but surrounding them have arisen an increasing number of technical and professional experts upon whom managers rely for needed skills—scientists, economists, and planners. Forest managerial systems today bring together these skills under single centers of control.

It was not always this way. In the nineteenth century when extraction of raw materials was the dominant story, individual entrepreneurs made their mark in the Great Lakes states. There are numerous examples of enterprising people who saw a good thing, invested, built mills, and shipped lumber; some established manufacturing plants to utilize the raw material.[15] The cost of timber was low and the investment small relative to the size of the operation. All this was short-lived; permanent investment for long-range management was a thing of the future. The authority and control it represented, over both the wood-production enterprise and the dependent communities, did not represent the beginning of a continuous evolution. The entrepreneurs did not want the land, only the timber; they were experts in extraction, not land management. This resulted in temporary institutions and little cumulative acquisition of capital and skills. One can speak of the rise and fall of individual entrepreneurs, but, even more important, of the rise and fall of private exploitation, a passing phase in the long course of Great Lakes forest history.

There are some remnants of this period of time, from 1840 to 1910. Stately houses remain in some towns and cities of the North Country, products of fortunes made from the lumber industry; some of these are now being refurbished amid the current interest in historic restoration. A few state parks stem from land owned by former lumber families, conveyed to states and municipalities—for example, the David H. Day holdings, which are now a part of

Sleeping Bear Dunes National Lakeshore. A few enterprises became the beginnings of later, more intensive and permanent wood-production management systems. But there was little continuity over the years in timber enterprise, unlike iron and copper mining. The private wood-production institutions declined, to create a vacuum into which came other, more permanent, public wildlands management. The private entrepreneurs for the most part abdicated, and when they returned with greater long-run purpose in the mid-twentieth century they had to come on different terms.

Into the institutional void in the first half of the twentieth century came the public forest-management systems—county, state, and federal. We do not need to delineate the many and complex ways that varied public bodies retained or acquired ownership, or the different balances among county, state, and federal holdings in Minnesota, Wisconsin, and Michigan. The important question is the system of management that evolved. Public managers came first as protectors. Here was a resource that had been depleted in dramatic fashion, now left as orphan land, with no permanent care. Unattended, it was giving rise to fire hazards of great magnitude. And so protection against fire and reforestation came to be the major themes of management; slowly but surely a depleted resource was restored. These goals advanced markedly during the New Deal when the Civilian Conservation Corps organized fire crews, built access trails and roads, and planted trees. A breed of caretakers grew up who were distinctive for their time and place, people whose training was in the woods and whose accumulated personal experience in a given wildland gave them an authoritative wisdom about how to protect what they personally knew. They did not exactly welcome the new stage of more highly technical and complex management that was to come.

From the very start, the lakes and rivers of the North Country shaped not only the conceptions of the public forest but also its management. In Minnesota the issue of the future of the lakes was even more important than the future of the forest. The first of the boundary waters laws, the Shipstead-Nolan Act, required that the forested borders of the lakes be protected. In Michigan the decision to retain tax-reverted lands in state ownership was influenced heavily by sportsmen for whom prime objectives were to protect the North Country from fire and bring about regeneration of fish and wildlife habitat. Significant wood production in the Lake States public forest was some years in the future; the use of wildlands for recreation was more current. Michigan provides ample evidence of this legacy. The Michigan United Conservation Clubs, the largest such sportsmen's organization in the lake States, and the *North Woods Call,* published near Charlevoix, reflect the sustained interest in protecting water and wildlife in the Great Lakes forest. In the late 1920s the name of the School of Forestry at the University of Michigan was changed to the School of Natural Resources and a wildlife group was started in the faculty, thus broadening the emphasis beyond the dominant wood-production legacy inspired by Gifford Pinchot and brought to the school initially by its dean, Filibert Roth. Finally, the concern for water and wildlife has long been reflected in the administrative leadership of the Michigan Department of Natural Resources and its Natural Resources Commission.

After World War II came the era of intensive forest management; both the drive for wood production and the public demand for more forest uses grew rapidly. Management shifted from a protective and custodial approach to greater investments of money and skills to achieve ever more intensive outputs. Private timber companies preferred a limited set of objectives dominated almost exclusively by wood production with little room for other uses such as wildlife, recreation, and environmental amenities. Hence they extended their corporate holdings and geared up for continuous and ever more intensive high-yield fiber growth. The management of public lands involved more varied objectives and uses, which increased rapidly over the years from beginnings early in the century through the expansion of access to the countryside which the automobile stimulated in the 1920s, to the flood of users who came with the rising leisure and fast-speed highways after World War II. In response, public forest management undertook a more intensive approach to wildlands resources. They were inventoried and described more precisely; systems of land classification became more intricate with such elaborations as water-influence and travel-influence zones, natural areas, and wilderness; particular uses were confined to particular lands. The U.S. Forest Service took the lead in these changes but the states followed. More intensive use required more precise management.

Amid the growth of intensive forestry one imperative became uppermost —to grow trees and harvest wood.[16] For many years the elementary systems of gathering and classifying information about the forest had been based on that objective. Wildlands were described in terms not of the interaction of species in an ecosystem, but of the standing timber they contained. Site indexes were constructed in terms not of the number of den trees or interacting patterns of layers within the forest from floor to canopy or the aesthetic quality of local forest microclimates, but of the ability of given sites to grow trees to a particular height in a given number of years. Dendrology, the treatment of forest species and their distribution, came to be confined to a study of only a few commercially valuable species so that the trained forester knew only a small portion of the living plant community of the forest.[17] If objectives had been otherwise, systems of description and classification would have differed. Despite the growing demands from other types of forest users, the fundamental way in which the forest was thought of, described, and classified remained heavily influenced by a traditional, dominant concern for wood production.

The management system that evolved after World War II was even-age or area management. This approach grew out of the drive to develop a more simplified method of regulating the flow of products within the forest. How much wood is there on a given area at a given time? How much will there be at a future date? How much can be cut each year in order to achieve the overall objective of renewal and continuous flow? How can the pattern of age classes be reorganized to move from the "middle-age bulge" of the 1960s and 1970s to the smooth lifetime spread of continuous yield? Formerly all this had been dealt with in a somewhat imprecise manner. Skilled woodsmen had eyeballed the various age classes of trees or, at the most, had carefully measured sample plots laid out in regular intervals within the forest. It came to be much easier, however, to organize forestland into areas, corresponding in number to the rotation years and age classes desired. Each area was considered as a single unit, one data point, with a volume figure attached to it, measured to determine growth, cut as a unit, and regenerated as a unit. The product flow from start to finish, and then over again, was vastly simplified for management tasks. Area management could be carried out with simple skills, not requiring the experienced woodsman, but using the lower-skilled forest accountant who could attach numbers to a limited number of areas, computerize the data, and program the resulting manipulations. It could even accommodate inventory description by aerial photography rather than on-the-ground measurement, if one wished to take that shortcut.

These tendencies after World War II defined the world of the forest profession and forest management. At the same time, however, the values of the public as to what a forest meant and should be used for were changing rapidly in a different direction. These changes in values took place in a realm that was, for the most part, beyond the immediate experience of forest managers; as they grew in intensity, managers were taken by surprise. Trained in older ways and accustomed to more traditional objectives and values, managers found it difficult to accept the changing society around them. In the late 1950s and the 1960s forest professionals and managers, private and public, grew apprehensive as aesthetic and recreational demands on the nation's wildlands moved on apace. They opposed an expanded national park system, wilderness designations, and wild and scenic rivers, all of which threatened to make inroads into the uses of forestlands for wood production. Frequently their opposition was symbolic and ideological, emphasizing form more than substance, a threat to their values more than to the real amount of wood production. Hardly a segment of the complex of forest institutions from the Society of American Foresters to the American Forestry Association, from private forest industry to the U.S. Forest Service, from state forest agencies in Maine to those in Georgia, the Lake States, and Oregon, was immune to this response.[18]

The divergence of perspective was expressed no more fully than in the controversy over area age-class management. As people came to appreciate the forest as an environment, they found a preference for diversity rather than uniformity of ages; they recoiled against a large uniform cut in a part of the forest that they had come to enjoy because of its full canopy. Perception of the forest from within gave rise to an image of the full range of its parts, including plants of all sorts and not just commercial trees, and to a structure in terms of vertical layers, spatial arrangements and species variety, all of which differed markedly from the forest structure as imposed by area-wide uniform management. This clash of perceptions reflected a conflict of values and objectives. The Lake States, with their high level of nonmetropolitan growth in the late 1960s and 1970s, and their large downstate population seeking more natural values in the North Woods, have faced this problem only recently, but it differs not at all from similar clashes in perspective all around the nation. The issue can be followed in the *North Woods Call.*

Especially striking was the way in which those who now came to establish personal ties with given pieces of wildland turf came to know the forest in ways similar to the eyeballing field foresters of an earlier day and often, as a result, more intimately than did the official management staffs. These users hiked through and over the wildlands persistently; among them were people with a variety of scientific skills—botanists, zoologists, ornithologists, ecologists, paleontologists, geologists, all of whom provided expert description, often contributing professional skills to the citizen input that were lacking within the forest management team. Looking at the forest with an eye toward aesthetic appreciation and knowledge of ecological communities and processes, they were content to measure and describe the forest in terms of those factors rather than the volume of standing timber.[19] For the systems manager, with an eye to regulating flow of wood production, all this was difficult if not impossible to accept.

Simple problems of terminology reflected this divergence of views. What do we call those lands that city dwellers purchased in the North Country for their amenities? Conventional wisdom, arising from past usage by forest economists, preferred the term "nonindustrial, nonfarm, forest woodlots," a wholly negative phrase, indicating a use of land beyond the ken of the positive values of those using the classification system. To purchasers of such properties they might well be called "environmental forestlands." There was also the practice of referring to lands on which commercial timber harvest would take place as "multiple-use" lands and to those managed for their natural environment values as lands that were "unused." Others might consider natural environment lands, including wilderness, to be used and used heavily —to define the term *multiple-use* as including more than one use that might or might not include commercial wood production. Managers complained that to designate lands as wilderness or to place them in other natural environment categories prevented them from being "managed." Yet management was required for these lands—though for different objectives—as much as for commercial wood production, a fact gradually underlined with the practice of wilderness management and by separate wilderness-management handbooks.[20] The controversy over such terms reflected the cultural lag between the older ideas and values of forest managers and the newer ideas and values of forest users.

These different perspectives, that of the manager and that of the environmental user, one shaped by the efficient manipulation of a resource for wood production and the other shaped by the direct meaning of a wildlands experience, have come into conflict continually since World War II. One result of the conflict has been a slight increase in the variety of skills that have been drawn into public forest management. No longer do professionals come overwhelmingly from wood-production training, even though the majority of them still do. New experts have appeared in the managerial staffs, in such fields as wildlife and fisheries, hydrology and geology, recreation and landscape architecture. Forest planning has stimulated this turn of events as it has required a more comprehensive look at the varied forest resources and their uses. Often the planning-team leader has a degree in landscape architecture or environmental management, a specialization not uncommon in forestry and natural resource schools.[21]

There is also a marked increase in the public contribution of scientific and technical information to forest planning and management. For years the transfer of new forest knowledge into management decisions was often slow, especially if it challenged established policy. From the very start of public involvement in management decisions in the 1950s one of the most significant citizen strategies was to absorb the publications of the experiment stations, the literature in the professional journals, the research of the forest schools, and to bring the ideas in them to bear on management decisions. In numerous hearings, information meetings, and environmental-impact analyses, forest managers were forced to confront new knowledge that heretofore had escaped them. The science information transfer vigorously conducted by citizens was facilitated by the new group of professionals in management itself, who were younger, fresh from forestry school, and more eager than their elders to bring the latest in forest science to their task. All this was especially gratifying to forest scientists who previously felt that their knowledge had not been taken up as fully as it should have been. But it has brought a new dimension to management that has not always been welcomed.[22]

Despite these changes, the professional public forest manager still considers the bottom line to be the periodic removal of mature trees for wood production. This view is not shared by those who view the forest as an environmental amenity and who seek a different mix in forest values. To them regeneration might preferably take place through the decay of mature trees and the constant recreation of smaller openings, leading to a more varied forest. The environmental view gives rise to different systems of measurement and classification of the wildlands resource, to different concepts as to what the flow regulated by management should be, to different management skills and different management plans. Site indexes might be shaped by the ability of given tracts of land to produce varied and diverse biological species, most of which might be plants other than commercial trees. Small area, group-selection type cuts of one-third to one acre might be preferred to forty-acre uniform cuts, and small-scale logging machinery to massive field wood chippers. All this seems incomprehensible in the perspective of large-scale modern management. The difference in view is not a minor one; it goes to the root of how one describes, measures, classifies, and organizes the forest for use, of what one perceives a forest to be.

COMMUNITY CHOICES

There is still a third set of choices we should examine, coming from an altogether different vantage point—the local community. Debates over wildlands policies often involved people far beyond the local community, business corporations whose headquarters and stockholders were far away, public lands managers located at distant state and national capitals, and wildlands users, both direct and vicarious, who lived most often in the major metropolitan centers remote from the forestlands. But ultimately these debates dealt with specific uses of specific lands in specific communities. Located amid the wildlands, these communities had their own perceptions, their own values, their own choices with respect to the forests around them. What were those choices?

In the raw-material extraction phase of the history of the Great Lakes forest, these communities were almost wholly an adjunct to the extractive economy. They provided its labor and they serviced it. They came and went as the entrepreneurs and their timber came and went. Lumber and mill towns were spread throughout the North Country, rising and falling with the march of the economic firms on which they depended. As one reviews this phase of community history, one obtains a sense of fatalism in that era, a realization that the raw material in the woods would not last forever, but, at the same time, an intense preoccupation with the moment of economic glory and without much looking beyond. Perhaps there would be a farming economy after this, but there was not even a clear notion about that. When mills collapsed, it was the natural order of things working itself out. One did not expect permanent and continuous societies and communities to persist in the rush to provide the raw material needs of the burgeoning cities to the south.

The years from 1910 to 1945 were equally insecure for communities throughout the North Country. In these decades there was a constant attempt to build communities on the basis of agriculture. When the poor soils led to failure, there were attempts to try again and again. Whereas in the nineteenth century one could become resigned to the fact that timber would disappear as the foundation for sustained community growth, it was difficult to believe that the soil provided almost as shaky roots. When the agricultural collapse came with a vengeance in the 1920s, the local communities made the ultimate choice to opt for permanent state and federal ownership of tax-reverted land. In northern Minnesota, for example, seven counties that had incurred bonded indebtedness to establish drainage systems conveyed large tracts of tax-reverted land to the state in return for state assumption of the debt; and other counties conveyed their reverted lands to the state with the guarantee that they would receive 50 percent of the income that the state derived from them—the so-called 50-50 lands in the Minnesota state land system.[23]

Our analysis of the community role in both these stages of the history of the Great Lakes wildlands is hampered by the lack of historical inquiry. It is not that the records needed for research are missing, but only that little has been done. Too often we have focused on the widely discussed public events at the national level or at best state affairs and have neglected history from the perspective of the community. Yet what evidence we do have from secondary sources, or from the community histories of the Bicentennial, reflect two eras of rather fragile community life. The lumber economy provided a vigorous but temporary phase; and the limited agrarian economy provided a temporary hope during the prosperous farming years before 1920, but almost complete collapse thereafter. No wonder that the cutover lands of the Great Lakes came to be one of the most severe problem areas of the politics of the 1920s and the New Deal. Suffice it to say that in the long first century of development, from the 1840s to the 1940s, rarely did the forest serve as a basis for building sustained communities.

The years after World War II were vastly different. The forestlands became an integral part of the new economy of the Lakes region. In a few communities, wood production provided an important base; but in many more the main asset of the forest lay in its role as an environment for home, work, and play in the new economy of recreation, leisure, travel, and tourism. Even in a superficial way, one is struck by the degree to which specific forested landmarks such as Hartwick Pines or the jack-pine home of the Kirtland warbler have become distinctive self-identifications of their nearby communities, or the way in which such areas have become vital to agencies that promote travel and tourism. There is a willingness to accept the search for natural areas among such economic boosters for their ability to attract people who wish to "see the sights," the regional "natural wonders." But behind such symbols there is far more afoot in the way in which communities of the Great Lakes look upon themselves and their future, and the role of the forest in that self-image.

Of importance equal with tourism and recreation is the attractiveness of forested areas as a place to live. They are especially welcomed by young people seeking a pleasant environment for home and livelihood and older people seeking similar amenities for retirement. A number of forested regions of the nation took on this significance—Maine, the Ozarks, northwest California, southwest Oregon, the West Virginia Highlands, southern Ohio, Indiana and Illinois, the Ocooch Mountains of southwestern Wisconsin, and the upper parts of Michigan, Wisconsin, and Minnesota. New publications reflect the interests of these new communities: the *Maine Times,* the *Illinois Times, Econews* (Arcata, California), the *Ocooch Mountain News,* the *North Country Anvil,* and *Clearwater Journal.* The environmental quality of these areas, much of them forested, relatively unspoiled, and undeveloped, seems to have been the major reason for their recent settlement. And it has given rise to demands that the forest be managed to enhance those amenities rather than to compromise them.

A number of environmental issues arise repeatedly in these regions. Recently, the most dramatic one has been the reaction to aerial spraying of pesticides to control forest insects and herbicides to control competing vegetation. To contain the drift from spraying and avoid human settlements, their vegetable gardens, and water supplies has been difficult if not impossible. The widespread concern over the use of 2,4,5-T and Silvex is most intense. There is also concern over monoculture and clearcutting, which takes on strength from the desire of people who have chosen to make their permanent home in forested areas to maintain the canopied forest as an environmental asset. Several pockets of new support for wilderness arise from such areas, for example in Trinity County, California, where local environmentalists and businessmen cooperated to work out their own choices in RARE II, which included far more wilderness acreage than the U.S. Forest Service would agree to. In cases such as these, the central factor is the role of the forest in the life of the human settlement that it surrounds. Without such settlements these forest practices would be more remote in their human impact. But with them the adverse effects are direct and immediate.

One piece of conventional wisdom with respect to the role of local communities in the forest is that they are dependencies of state management agencies that draw their political support from faraway urbanites who have little knowledge about or concern for the permanent viability of the communities based upon the forests they use. Among the aspects of this view is the debate over the level of in-lieu tax monies and the constant local demand for more such disbursements, especially as the private demand for environmental forestlands raises local property values and local tax liabilities. There are also the oft-repeated arguments that the issues pit local demands for industry and jobs against well-to-do urbanites who wish to use rural communities as their playgrounds. These familiar arguments are fitting for ideological combat, but they do not provide a sound beginning for an effective social analysis of the role of local communities in the Great Lakes wildlands.

The most striking aspect of all this is the internal controversy over these matters within the wildlands regions. One finds communities in which leadership vigorously pursues population and job growth as well as those which do not. Some seek mass recreation use, others do not. Contrast, for example, Roscommen and Leelanau counties in Michigan, the former containing Houghton Lake, filled with vacation cottages, and the latter a more peaceful place, somewhat off the beaten track of superhighways, which seeks to maintain a more quiet atmosphere. Consider the fact that the major drive for wilderness designations in Sleeping Bear Dunes National Lakeshore has come from the immediate vicinity, supported by planners in Leelanau County and spearheaded by people in Traverse City, with backing from the local chamber of commerce.

There are other twists to this fact of intraregional differences. Throughout the North Woods one comes across many people, long-time residents, who object to the impact on their communities of the load of users—not just the automobile tourists but the fishermen, the canoeists, the off-road vehicle users. Conflicts with hikers and wilderness travelers seem to occur less often because the wildlands they use are more removed from settled areas. Long-time residents are joined by others who have purchased lands and second homes for their environmental amenities and seek to protect those values from the impact of overuse. Lake property owners become an influence for restricting population growth and industrial development as well as maintaining the water quality of their lakes. Farmers join in the drive for farmland preservation. There is a joint concern for population growth and acceptance of zoning as a device for exercising control over that growth. The drama we face increasingly in the North Woods, therefore, is that of political alternatives expressed within the region itself.

These alternatives have internal and external elements. Several studies, for example, have indicated a marked difference within communities between the attitudes of political and economic leaders on the one hand and the general public on the other. The former are more interested in rising levels of population, jobs, real-estate values, and taxes. The latter are far more concerned with environmental quality. Of the few studies that combine in one context attitude surveys of leaders and the general public there is apparently only one for the Great Lakes region, for Niagara County, New York. It indicates that the general public is more concerned about water quality than are leaders, and the leaders are more interested in jobs and population growth. All this helps us to understand the internal dynamics of competing values within the forest region.[24]

There is also competition among external forces, as institutions in the nation at large concerned with economic development vie with those who seek growth in environmental amenities. Some local groups have reached out to establish close ties with the U.S. Economic Development Administration, represented here by the Upper Great Lakes Regional Commission. The commission promoted vigorously the national lakeshores in Michigan and Wisconsin, touting their ability to draw vast numbers of tourists to bolster the local economy. It has promoted industrial parks, vocational training institutions, and a wide range of activities associated far more with economic growth than with growth in environmental amenities. Joining this external involvement with the region are private corporations, some of long standing concerned with mining and wood production, others with more commercial enterprises such as retail franchises, and still others with light industry. All this comprises one set of forces in the wildlands region that originates outside its borders.

External public and private forces also seek to enhance environmental quality and, in doing so, link up with indigenous groups in the region and the community. Many in the southern part of the region seek to influence decisions about the public lands in the North Woods and thus demand that public hearings be held on plans for Sleeping Bear and Pictured Rocks in Ann Arbor and Lansing. Some environmental organizations have downstate and out-state headquarters which aid their local chapters in the Audubon Society and the Sierra Club. All seek aid from state and federal agencies such as the environmental, natural resource, and conservation administrations to enhance their objectives. Nonresidents who have an interest in the North Country but who live elsewhere face the problem that they have no vote there. If they are "turf builders" in the Pigeon River State Forest but live in Lansing, they are disfranchised. Even if they own property in the wildlands but live elsewhere, they find it difficult to represent their point of view. Hence the development of advisory committees that include such viewpoints and the increasing tendency of public land management agencies to hold listening sessions in urban areas.

In the competition between environmental and developmental forces to shape decisions about forested wildlands, there is considerable emphasis on the relative political jurisdiction of community, state, and federal authority. For the most part, local communities seek to protect the quality of their environment by means of local zoning action which they implement in order to ward off the adverse effects of development. This is supplemented by action against specific large-scale projects, usually initiated from outside the community or the state, such as nuclear or coal-fired electric generating plants, waste-disposal sites or incinerators, or projects such as Seafarer and ELF. In previous decades such development went forward with little opposition. Now it is seriously questioned, a reflection of the changed value and meaning of forested areas to the general public. Those advocating large-scale development seek to shift the location of decision making upward to the state and federal levels to override this opposition from local communities and the states that often speak for them. Large-scale private enterprise has steadily advocated more federal power and authority in such matters to overcome objections from communities concerned with their own quality of life.

The relationship between local communities and external groups concerned with environmental quality is more mixed. Environmental groups often seek state and federal authority to protect wildlands from more intensive development such as federal wilderness and wild and scenic rivers programs. Often this leads to local opposition when it appears that it will create a massive influx of recreationists who will interfere with local patterns of life and degrade the environment with litter, noise, and crowds, or when such actions reduce local property-tax revenues. Yet the common interest of both groups in maintaining high levels of environmental quality often leads to effective cooperation after initial suspicions are overcome. Environmentalists from outside the community defend local autonomy in such matters and at the same time urge state and federal authority in the wildlands, depending in pragmatic fashion upon the degree to which environmental quality objectives can be met.

These relationships are a product of the years after World War II. In earlier times less complex demands came from local communities as they simply called upon state governments to aid them in their economic distress, to acquire and manage forestlands, and to put an economic floor under their communities. We are now in a period of history when these lands are highly desired, their use is subject to intense competition, and the competitive pressures represent different values. One can find enormous variations among communities in the North Country on this score. Some seek rapid economic development and population growth; others emphasize community amenities. Within the same community one can find similar divergent tendencies. All this has changed the context from relationships between dominant and dependent regions to a conflict between political forces within the North Woods.

The history of human choices in the Great Lakes forest has gone through several distinct stages. Changes have been especially dramatic since World War II, as an advanced industrial society has taken shape in the United States. New perceptions regarding the role and meaning of forests have arisen that emphasize forests as an environment for home, work, and play rather than as a source of commodities. Yet management systems, with strong and deep roots in the earlier commitments of scientific and professional foresters to wood production, have responded to these changing values slowly and often with strong and bitter resistance. At the same time, the forest community has changed markedly, absorbing many of the new environmental values and expressing in community political choices the desire to protect and enhance environmental quality vis-à-vis many adverse influences from both within and without. These are the current conditions highlighted by historical analysis and upon which future policy must be firmly based if it is to be consistent with present and predictably future human values and choices. If there is historical guidance to our current task of formulating forest policy, it can be found not in the remote past but in the massive changes in human perceptions of the forest that have taken place during the past thirty years.

III *The Politics of Clean Air*

CLEAN AIR

From the 1970 Act to the 1977 Amendments

INTRODUCTION

PASSAGE OF THE 1977 amendments to the Clean Air Act[1] came after seven years of intense experience with the workings of the 1970 law. There was continual litigation, both to restrain and to enhance the application of the former Act, the outcome of which established an evolutionary tone. There was continual evaluation of the process of implementation, and especially of enforcement, creating a changing set of ideas about what would bring results and what would not. Underlying this were both changing public values as to what objectives were desired in a clean air program and an evolving body of information and concepts about the phenomenon of air pollution itself. The significance of this debate was reflected in the intensity of the three-year controversy over the amendments. Our purpose is to provide an historical understanding of the manner by which the program established by the Act of 1970 evolved into the amendments of 1977.[2]

From *Duquesne Law Review* (1978–1979), vol. 17, no.1.

From the point of view of those intimately involved in the workings of the Act of 1970, it established an extremely complex setting, often difficult to grasp due to the sheer weight of detail. There were stationary sources and mobile sources; different programs for the six different criteria pollutants; old sources and new sources; and special provision for hazardous pollutants. There were responsibilities for federal agencies and for state agencies. In addition, there were the more technical details of emission inventories and air modeling, the calculation of credits for tall stacks, the assessment of the state of technology to determine both what innovations might be brought into being and what could not. Amid such details engineers began to live in different worlds from lawyers,[3] the sellers of pollution-control equipment had to negotiate with buyers,[4] and citizens who sought to become involved in decision-making found ways and means of influencing the program despite its complexities.[5]

This world of complex detail, however, can be misleading. In many respects the entire clean air program is extremely simple; and it is important, as a starting point of analysis, to return to those basics. The clean air effort consists of two elements: standards and implementation. The identical issue is how clean the air should be. Any environmental quality program involves a desire either to clean up the air, water, or land, or to prevent its degradation. The problem lies in the degree of cleanness. To be effective, the general concern must be translated into an operating procedure, a performance standard, an acceptable practice on the part of individuals, corporations, or government. Much of the debate has been, and continues to be, over that question. While, to the general public, a standard represents a higher qualitative level of living, to the polluter it represents a cost which reduces both the profits of a private corporation and the budgets of a public enterprise.

Standards constitute only the first step; the second step is implementation. How can the current circumstances be made more desirable? How can a currently desirable condition be prevented from becoming an undesirable one in the future? The effectiveness of implementation reduces or maintains the standards. To hold to the avowed level of quality is a constant challenge. Those whose behavior implementation seeks to change will continually strive to reduce the standards, to claim "overregulation," to argue that implementation goes beyond the intended objectives, to postpone, and thereby to reduce, the impact of regulation. Implementation can become less effective if it is open-ended, with a loose schedule for producing results, or it can become highly controlled with a firm timetable accompanied by the requirement of intervening steps involving specific accomplishments. Despite all these complexities, however, implementation is a simple problem of practical results.

This analysis outlines the major elements of the clean air program in terms of their conceptual content rather than their complexity of detail. We will attempt to avoid the tendency to recount the specifics of the law and its administration and will, instead, provide the reader with some sense of balance and proportion in comprehending the various ingredients of the program.

THE STANDARDS OF THE ACT

The Clean Air Act of 1970 established a dual set of primary and secondary standards.[6] Primary standards were built around the concept of protecting public health; secondary standards were intended to protect a variety of social conditions, collectively known as "public welfare," but more precisely outlined as the effects on materials, agricultural production, ecosystems, and aesthetics such as visibility. Thus the Act intended a wide range of effects to inform the objectives of the air quality program, not confined to health effects, but extending to many other adverse pollution problems. There were to be minimum national standards established by federal authority which, in turn, would be implemented by state agencies.

Administration of the Act, however, resulted in a selective approach to this broad mandate. First, administrative decisions confined the application of the authority of the 1970 Act to six "criteria pollutants";[7] only under legal challenge from citizen groups did the Environmental Protection Agency take steps to include other pollutants, the first of which was lead.[8] The 1977 amendments instruct EPA to consider four specific additional pollutants.[9] The history of the federal clean air program indicates that the regulatory agency was well aware of the desirability of a much broader perspective. Under the preceding Act of 1967,[10] which required the states to set standards and to implement them, the federal National Air Pollution Control Administration commissioned a study by Litton Industries to decide which pollutants it should bring within its purview.[11] The 27-volume report, which covered the health effects of 30 pollutants, was submitted in September, 1969. It is apparent that NAPCA contemplated issuing criteria documents for more than the initial six, since it announced schedules for their appearance during 1969–1970. In establishing a program, however, the successor agency, the EPA, did not take the initiative to expand coverage beyond the six "criteria pollutants."

Also, the secondary standards have not been enforced so strictly as the primary ones, especially in the case of sulfur dioxide. One could argue that the entire clean air program has been influenced overwhelmingly by health effects and, in the process of day-to-day administration, agencies slowly drifted toward a preoccupation with the correction of health problems to justify an action. One of the first major judicial decisions involved a challenge by the smelting industry to the secondary sulfur dioxide annual average standards. The case was remanded by the court to the EPA for further consideration, and it has never reemerged.[12] Visibility as a specific element of an aesthetic air quality standard was not taken seriously by EPA. It did appear in a number of state programs, and the 1977 amendments explicitly incorporated visibility into the federal program for most national parks and wilderness areas.[13] Thus, the 1977 amendments attempted to capture a broader spectrum of objectives in standard setting, as originally outlined in the 1970 Act.

Third, some states established standards of maximum allowable pollution levels which were lower than the federal standards. The 1970 Act permitted this for stationary sources, clearly indicating that the federal levels were to be a minimum effort and that states were not prohibited from setting them lower. Some states have done so,[14] and challenges by industry to such state discretion have been rejected by the courts on a number of occasions.[15] Few states, however, have utilized this option. The Act of 1970 witnessed an intense controversy concerning state discretion with respect to mobile sources. Despite massive opposition from the automobile industry, California waged a long and successful battle to secure authority to establish allowable automobile emission levels lower than federal levels.[16] No other state has secured that option. The 1977 amendments extended the alternative to other states as well.[17]

State discretion in standard setting for the evolution of the clean air program permits some experimentation beyond the federal minimal requirements. It would be easy for the federal program to become frozen into established patterns, thereby creating a barrier to innovation. In fact, regulated industries tend to promote such rigidity. The clean air program, however, contains a dynamic element of new experience, new knowledge, and new public values. It is important to observe the degree to which administrative agencies either resist or incorporate these evolving circumstances external to administration itself. There appears to be a natural tendency to do things the old way and to resist the implications of innovations in perspective. State freedom to innovate provides some countertendencies to this conservatism. Flexibility does not guarantee innovation, since states also need resources, such as a firm research base to bolster legal argument to act independently. The California experience, however, is instructive. While the federal 24-hour particulate standard is 260 μg/m3,[18] the California standard is 100 μg/m3. While the federal 24-hour sulfur dioxide standard is .14 ppm,[19] the California standard is .05 ppm when both oxidant and particulate levels are at the maximum 24-hour allowable.[20] The regulated industries may not appreciate such increasingly stringent standards since these serve as examples which other states might be tempted to follow.

A fourth aspect of the standards is whether or not they should go beyond primary and secondary levels to the entire range of air quality in every area of the nation. This issue, in the form of the "prevention of significant deterioration" (PSD) program, became one of the most heated controversies in the years between 1970 and 1977. Environmental groups, led by the Sierra Club, argued that the Act of 1970 required a program to prevent the deterioration of air cleaner than the secondary standards.[21] The issue was debated intensely during administrative rule-making in 1971 and, when no instructions were provided to the states to establish a PSD program in the guidelines, litigation ensued. The resulting court decision upheld the environmentalists' argument and led to EPA regulations and an explicit program spelled out in the 1977 amendments.[22] The most significant effect of all this was to extend the clean air program from the cities to the entire countryside and to establish maximum allowable levels of pollution in every area of the nation. While the Act of 1970 limited the explicit standards to certain areas of the country, the 1977 amendments extended them to all areas.

Standard setting under the 1970 Act required a rationale and a data base to provide support for the chosen level. Thus, the health standard must be based on information about health effects, to determine the precise level of pollution beyond which adverse effects on human health occur. Similar information is required for "welfare" effects, such as data about the effects on materials, crops, and visibility. The 1970 Act, following innovations in the former Clean Air Act of 1963 and the Air Quality Act of 1967, provided for the compilation of "criteria documents"—summaries of the available scientific information on air pollution effects. These were to establish the basis upon which standards would be set, by first determining the level of observable adverse effects and then reducing that level further by a "margin of safety" factor. For "welfare effects," no such margin of safety was provided in calculating the standard.[23]

The initial point of controversy in standard setting arose from the conclusions about environmental effects in the criteria documents. If one wishes to protect health and can establish that adverse effects cannot be observed lower than 360 micrograms per cubic meter of particulates, then far less cleanup will be required than if those adverse effects can be observed at 120 micro-grams per cubic meter. Debate over the summaries of research for health effects mounted during the late 1960s. When the National Air Pollution Control Administration developed the initial criteria document for sulfur oxides early in 1967, the coal industry raised such intense protest that in the 1967 law Congress directed the Administration to reexamine the evidence.[24] During the debate over the 1970 Act and the ensuing standard setting for both old and new sources in 1971, many industries testified concerning their conclusions about the scientific data on health effects. The conclusions varied greatly, depending, for the most part, on the degree to which clean-up would be required in that particular industry.[25]

For a number of years, the original criteria documents remained unmodified. At the same time, the Act of 1970 had stimulated an extensive amount of scientific information far beyond that available in the late 1960s, when the documents were formulated. As a result, in 1976 the Air Quality Criteria Advisory Committee of the EPA recommended that the documents be revised. A schedule was established for all six "criteria pollutants," which initially involved completion of revision by the end of 1979. Later, the date was extended to 1980.[26] The amendments of 1977 establish a periodic schedule for revision, and explicitly require that a nitrogen dioxide criteria document for short-term exposure be issued not later than six months after enactment. In authorizing this revision, Congress was explicit about the range of effects to be considered: "nitric and nitrous acids, nitrites, nitrates, nitrosamines, and other carcinogenic and potentially carcinogenic derivatives of oxides of nitrogen."[27]

Controversy over the criteria documents and their conclusions is not over. Perhaps it is just beginning. Revision now underway will provide a major opportunity for all sides to the controversies, especially those wanting higher allowable contaminant levels and those wanting lower, to reopen the issues fully. This controversy will be even more intense precisely because all parties are far more aware now of the critical importance of the summaries of the scientific data and particularly because environmentalists are far better prepared to bring their case to bear on the evaluations of the scientific evidence. The stakes are high for both improved environmental quality, on the one hand, and costs to polluters, on the other. The outcome of the wider debate over air quality programs rests, more than anything else, on the outcome of the debates over the state of scientific knowledge about environmental effects.

Some of the more generic controversies are significant. First is the question of the admissible types of evidence. Are toxicological studies of effects of pollutants on animals acceptable grounds for drawing conclusions about effects on human life? Medical experts are divided on this issue. Do epidemiological studies, complex statistical analyses of the relationship between the incidence of environmental pollutants and environmental effects, provide sufficient basis for making judgments about the causal relationship between the two? Some medical experts argue that the relationships are so complex and impossibly confused that no sound conclusions can be drawn; others argue that, in spite of this, the weight of the evidence does establish an acceptable basis for action. Also, there are arguments over what populations should be taken into account in describing health effects: the healthiest segment of mature adults or the more susceptible groups, such as the very young, the very old, and the chronically ill. Finally, there are arguments regarding the actual quantitative relationships, such as that between the level of lead in blood and the level in the ambient air.[28]

In such matters as these, medical experts' opinions range along a spectrum. On one end are the "hard liners" who argue that conclusive proof of harm should be established before action justifiable; on the other are those "health protectionists" who argue that "substantial risk" can be established when "conclusive proof of harm" cannot, and that the purpose of environmental protection is to reduce such risk. This range of opinion about the degree of proof required before conclusions can be drawn is a rather common phenomenon among scientists and is not peculiar to environmental effects analysis.[29] It can be expected, therefore, that the controversies will continue. As long as the public has differences of opinion about the degree of environmental quality which is desirable, and scientists disagree concerning the "degree of required proof" to justify different levels of regulation and control, the controversies will persist.

Deep debate over interpretation of health effects continues. Recently the steel industry, through the American Iron and Steel Institute, petitioned the federal courts to require EPA to revise the criteria document for particulates more rapidly than scheduled.[30] Underlying this action is the steel industry's own "criteria document" about the environmental effects of particulates. It was drawn up by eight British medical experts under the lead authorship of Dr. W. W. Holland, Professor of Clinical Epidemiology and Social Medicine at St. Thomas Hospital Medical School of London.[31] The Holland document discounts the reliability of both toxicological studies on animals and epidemiological analyses of chronic health effects as a basis for drawing conclusions about human health effects and standards. It argues that the current particulate annual average standard of 75 µg/m3 can safely be doubled to 150 µg/m3. Such arguments do not go unchallenged in the environmental health and regulatory fields. For example, California's own criteria documents, supported by medical opinion in that state, take a very different tack. The American Petroleum Institute has made a similar challenge of the current oxidant standard.[32] Challenges such as these will constitute a major, and critical, focal point of debate over the clean air program in this phase of criteria document revision for a half-dozen years to come and perhaps perennially thereafter.

IMPLEMENTATION OF THE ACT

Action to implement the standards has provided equally intense debate. In concept the implementation or control system anticipated by the 1970 Act was quite simple. First, there was the ambient air standard,[33] a bench mark which established outer limits of air contamination. Behind this was a source that emitted pollutants which had to be controlled in order to improve air quality. Some system had to be devised to relate emissions from the source to the level of ambient air quality. That system turned out to be a process of mathematical modeling which served as a predicting device. Given a pattern of sources, with given levels of emissions, located in given terrain and amid given wind speeds and direction, the ambient air quality would be predictable. One could work backwards from ambient air quality to allowable emissions at the source.

Needless to say, this was very complex and provided opportunities for considerable choice, personal judgment, and error in establishing an effective causal relationship. Because of this extensive "grey area" for choice, in the 1970 Act some environmentalists had preferred a direct emission limitation with prescribed technological controls rather than the cumbersome attempt to relate emissions to ambient levels; but their views were rejected.[34] The initial calculations were based on limited knowledge of source emissions. As control plans evolved in the mid and late 1970s, more elaborate data were developed. Many calculations distinguished between "point sources"—the larger emissions sources, and "area sources"—the small and the more generalized such as wind-blown dust.[35] Even after agreeing upon this data, much choice remained. For example, what model should be utilized to establish the relationships? There were a number of options, often varying with the weights given to various factors such as unmeasureable sources, wind direction, and terrain. Even if all could agree about the model itself, there was the question of changes in the emission sources which might occur after the initial inventory, including increases and decreases in the number of sources and in the kind and mix of fuels used which generated varying emission levels.

Options also arose concerning the location in which ambient air was to be measured. Traditionally such measurements were taken in the vicinity of the source. In the Bay Area Pollution Control District in California, for example, the relevant monitor was located at the property line of the source at ground level; no more distant measurements applied. In such circumstances sources were tempted to develop techniques to diffuse pollution into the wider atmosphere and to reduce its local impact, such as with a tall smokestack which carried the air upward into the atmosphere, as much as 1000 feet, to "disperse" it. "Dispersion enhancement" techniques were adopted by electric utilities as a preferred "control system." This led to vast discrepancies between the ambient standard and the emission. In the case of the Bay Area Pollution Control District, the Exxon oil refinery at Benecia emitted sulfur dioxide at a rate of 6000 ppm (24-hour average) when measurements at the property line at ground level were 0.04 ppm; this placed the source in compliance. The actual emissions were dispersed into the San Joaquin Valley to the east, contributing two-thirds of the total sulfur dioxide load there.[36]

Such practical difficulties as these, encountered in establishing a firm control system for relating emissions to ambient air, with persistent opportunities for escaping control, increased the popularity of a direct, technological standard which would prescribe the precise technology to be required. This development was shaped heavily by the debate over intermittent controls for power plants, involving the use of tall stacks. The EPA argued that the law permitted it to require new technologies, such as flue gas scrubbers, to remove sulfur oxides, while the industry maintained that the law permitted dispersion by means of tall stacks. Court decisions persistently favored the EPA interpretation,[37] and in the 1977 amendments the language was changed to prevent ambiguity. It required all new sources to establish the "best technological system of continuous emission reduction," thereby defining control systems in terms of technology rather than of "meeting the standard."[38]

The gradual specification of controls in terms of technology was much akin to the same tendency which had occurred in water pollution control. Over a decade of experience emphasizing ambient water quality had brought out the vast difficulties in relating specific water discharges to general water quality. Consequently, the Clean Water Act of 1972 had specified technological standards: the first stage was described as the "best practicable technology" and the second as the "best available technology." Such an approach in air quality gave rise to a number of terms, such as "best available control technology," or "lowest achievable emission rate," each of which represented an attempt to spell out technological controls more precisely. The precision was not always achieved, as one set of terms became confused with another; but the general drift toward technology standards as the most effective means of source controls persisted.

To be effective, the conceptual control system just described had to be translated into an administrative control system. Some administrative strategies had to be devised in order to establish a regulatory process. In the first instance, this had two elements. First, each state had to develop a "state implementation plan" (SIP) which established the administrative rationale by which the federal standards, or more stringent state standards, would be achieved. The federal EPA would approve or disapprove the SIP on the grounds of whether or not it would enable the standards to be met. The specific control system involved a mixture of orders, reviews and permits, varying with each state. Usually a variance system was established whereby a source could secure permission not to meet the emission level in the prescribed time in exchange for an agreement to meet a given set of conditions in a more extended timetable.

Such a regulatory scheme set in motion a vast amount of legal action which brought enforcement squarely into the courts. If a polluter did not comply with the conditions of the permit, or with the terms of a variance, enforcement action could be brought. Often the initial stage of enforcement action led to an impasse in the courts; polluters argued that the needed technology was not "available" while the agencies argued that it was. Left in the middle of such controversies, courts frequently supervised an agreement between the contending parties which emerged in the form of a consent decree or a court order. Such action, however, did not guarantee compliance. Often, especially in the case of industries in which cleanup was more difficult, it only set off another round of lack of compliance, enforcement action, and litigation.

By the mid-1970s many from the enforcement agencies and the active environmental public began to argue that the courts were used merely to stall pollution abatement, that litigation was, in fact, less expensive than the cost of implementing controls and that some device should be developed in order to make the regulatory process more direct and effective. Economists had long argued that the major focus of regulation should be a tax, such as an emissions fee, to internalize the social costs of pollution.[39] Such a proposal was made by President Nixon at one point and was quickly withdrawn. An economic penalty of a different sort, the noncompliance penalty, was incorporated into the 1977 amendments. The theory behind it was that if polluters did not clean up by the specified compliance date, they would be permitted to continue, without legal action taken against them, but with a fine, imposed daily, equal to the cost advantage for not complying. This, it was argued, would substitute a direct economic penalty for lengthy litigation; but such arguments did not clarify how the details of such a fee, its specific level and rationale, could themselves escape prolonged court action.[40]

Despite all these mechanisms for implementation of the desired levels of air quality, the primary focus of the program was to stimulate a more socially desirable technology. Existing technology had social impacts which were considered to be socially undesirable. Shifts to more acceptable technologies did not seem to come through private market action alone; therefore, some sort of public action was deemed essential. In the midst of the details of enforcement, participants often lost sight of the fact that the major thrust of the 1970 Act was "technology forcing."[41] It was easy to argue that technology was "available" or that it was not, and to focus on some stage of technological development as the critical point in whether or not it was. The legal questions surrounding such debates often obscured the most important point: how can public action be taken to stimulate the development of technology which was not yet in place?

The public sector has available a considerable number of options to achieve that objective. Such techniques have been used for decades, even centuries; and they should be brought alongside each other for comparative analysis, in order to focus on the major technological thrust of the Clean Air Act. The nuclear power industry, for example, was promoted by direct public investment; it would be equally possible for the federal government to build and operate a prototype coke oven or electric utility for the precise purpose of developing and demonstrating new technologies. The role of the Tennessee Valley Authority innovation in electrical transmission to rural areas is a classic case. Many environmentalists wondered why the TVA, as a publicly owned utility, could not play a similar role in creating a cleaner coal-burning technology. By the time of the Carter administration and the appointment of S. David Freeman to the TVA Board, it appeared that such an opportunity was at hand.

The major means utilized by the Clean Air Act of 1970 to stimulate new technology was the guaranteed market. Firm compliance dates for installation of pollution-control equipment—flue gas scrubbers, for example, established a firm market for potential manufacture of that technology. With such a guarantee, capital risks would be undertaken by enterprising engineering firms. The economic incentive in such an arrangement lay not with either the regulator or the regulated, but with the third party, the manufacturers of the control equipment. The success of the technology-forcing mechanism of the guaranteed market would lie in the degree to which it stimulated innovation. If one followed the course of the history of member firms of the Industrial Gas Cleaning Institute, which represented industrial air-cleaning industries, one could readily conclude that the market-stimulating mechanisms of the Act had worked.[42] EPA developed close relationships with such firms in order actively to stimulate the new technologies.

Technological innovation depended upon the commitment of installing firms to meet compliance schedules and to work cooperatively with equipment manufacturers to perfect it. Some did and some did not. Some utilities, for example, established unusual contractual terms for the purchase of equipment, requiring guarantees for unusually long trouble-free performance, and relatively high levels of consequential damages.[43] Installation of flue gas scrubbers by utilities often depended upon their willingness to employ chemical engineers who could deal with the attendant chemical problems in an industry long dominated by other technical expertise. Once commitments had been made to investment in one form of environmental control technique, considerable additional incentive arose for alternative suppliers to develop new techniques to lower the cost. The initial step of willingness to comply developed quickly into an even more powerful incentive—cost reduction—once commitment to control had been made. Problems such as these emphasized the degree to which a direct approach to technological innovation became more important as the air-quality program evolved.

The focus on new technology took on even sharper emphasis as the timetable for urban cleanup was not met and the question arose regarding whether or not new sources would be allowed in such areas which had not yet attained the primary air quality standards. By 1976 this was known as the "nonattainment" problem, and considerable debate ensued over the options. The issue was forced by the application for permits from new large sources in several cities such as Pittsburgh, Houston, and Los Angeles. In each case, failure of old sources to clean up made it difficult to justify the creation of new sources which would create backsliding in air quality by raising allowable pollution levels. Lack of attainment of desired emission levels by old sources restricted the growth of new industry. This implication of the Clean Air Act of 1970 was sharpened as the federal EPA devised a policy both to permit such new sources and, at the same time, to guarantee progress toward meeting the standards. By 1977 the nonattainment problem became one of the major elements of debate over amendments to the Act. It placed sharp focus on the need for technological innovation from both old and new sources if economic growth in "dirty air areas" was to proceed.

INNOVATIONS

Although the Clean Air Act amendments of 1977 covered a wide range of subjects, it is generally recognized that three constituted the most extensive innovations from the 1970 Act: provisions for prevention of significant deterioration, nonattainment, and delayed compliance penalties.[44] Since the evolving circumstances which gave rise to these provisions have been discussed above, we will turn to their implications.

While in 1970 the prevention of significant deterioration occupied a peripheral role in the Act, by 1977 it had come to play a central part; this was one of the more dramatic changes in the context of air-quality politics. During the 1960s federal officials responsible for the air-quality program had committed themselves publicly to a "nondegradation" policy. Such commitments had been repeated in legislative committee reports during debate on the 1970 law; however, few members of the public or of active environmental organizations had taken up the issue. In pressing the nondegradation implications of the 1970 Act, and in carrying on the ensuing debate which arose from this, the Sierra Club generated an active constituency that was much larger than before. Although some concern for protecting clean air areas had existed previously, it certainly had remained latent and was not activated until the issue was pressed. By 1977 a significant political base for a "prevention of significant deterioration" policy had developed.

As the issue evolved from a set of EPA regulations to explicit legislation, the latter moved beyond even the former. EPA regulations had established a series of air quality classes—I, II, and III. Each would have permitted some deterioration of air quality—Class I permitting the least and Class III the most—up to the level of secondary standards. Eventually, therefore, there would have been two levels of air quality standards in addition to the primary and secondary levels already in existence.[45] EPA regulations, moreover, established machinery in which all areas of the nation outside the "nonattainment" areas would automatically be designated Class II; each state had to set in motion machinery whereby, after extensive procedural requirements, Class II areas could be redesignated either Class I or Class III.

In three important respects environmentalists considered this scheme to be flawed. First, no areas were declared to be mandatory Class I areas, a limitation which, in the absence of state action, could have excluded any area from being subject to the least amount of deterioration. Second, Class III areas could deteriorate to the level of secondary standards when, it was contended, they should be required to fall short of that level, thus establishing a five-tiered system instead of the EPA four-level plan. Third, the EPA regulations applied only to particulates and sulfur dioxide, not to the remaining four criteria pollutants.[46] The ensuing debate in Congress resulted in approval of all three of these principles, thus reflecting the enhanced degree of interest in PSD beyond the EPA action as well as the 1970 Act.[47]

Closely connected with the legislatively mandated PSD program was the equally innovative explicit protection of visibility in certain park and wilderness areas. The amendments provided that the Secretary of the Interior designate the precise areas where visibility was an important value and that states incorporate those designations into their implementation plans.[48] As discussed above, visibility had been among the "welfare effects" covered by the secondary standards, but had received little subsequent attention. Concern increased, however, about visibility in the scenic areas of the west, with special attention to the impact of coal-burning electric generating plants on both the Grand Canyon and the parks of southern Utah. The National Park Service had taken up the issue of the resulting destruction of scenic resources, and the drive for explicit protection in the 1977 amendments was successful.[49]

One important aspect of the PSD provisions was to limit an escape hatch which had permitted polluting sources to move from more polluted to cleaner air areas. Heretofore there were few restrictions on such a move; air quality professionals had previously stated that such action was desirable in order to enable polluting facilities to move beyond the urban areas.[50] The PSD provisions now placed restrictions on this option. Especially significant was the procedure adopted by EPA that implementation would require new sources, even in nonattainment areas, to undergo review for their potential impact on adjacent cleaner air areas.[51] The long-distance transmission of air pollution made it impossible to consider such sources in isolation, within their own air quality region, and required impact analyses on cleaner air areas at some distance. This type of analysis was destined to bring a new perspective to air quality measurement, control, and evaluation throughout many areas not hitherto subject to intensive air quality management.

The nonattainment provisions of the 1977 amendments had equally significant implications. Most important was their implication that one had to think in terms of total pollution loads and not just percentage reductions from given historic levels. Previously it had been customary to think in terms of reductions from 1970 base lines. There was general recognition that such reductions could be more than offset by increases in the number of polluting sources and that, at some future date, the more severe problem of constraints in terms of total loads would have to be confronted. Initially, however, this was postponed. During the early years of implementation of the 1970 Act, successful litigation by environmentalists resulted in the requirement that EPA plan not only for reaching air quality levels but also for maintaining them in the face of economic growth.[52] The program was implemented by a number of less urbanized governmental units facing potential air deterioration from future growth, but it was generally ignored in the larger cities where standards had not yet been reached and there were no primary levels yet to maintain.

In these areas the issue of the impact of new sources was faced by proposals for new industries amid nonattainment of the primary standards. As the issue became more sharply etched, it defined the air quality problem as one of finite air resources pressed by increasing quantities of pollution associated with economic growth. This classic definition of ecological problems became clearer as the clean air program evolved and especially as the nonattainment problem became prominent.

The critical role of technological innovation in such nonattainment areas also became more sharply etched. If growth were to be permitted, the level of cleanup from each source would have to be greater than heretofore envisaged. Earlier the "best" technology had been thought of as the "best available control technology" or BACT; now the nonattainment policy defined "best" as the "lowest achievable emission rate." The latter brought a wider range of comparisons into focus, enabling the administering agency to draw upon technological examples from anywhere in the world to demonstrate what was achievable. The model to be followed was not just what could be "demonstrated" but what could be "achieved." Such a test was not above controversy, but it constituted greater pressure for technological improvement in order to forestall the need to limit growth in the face of heavy pollution loads pressing against finite air resources.

The nonattainment policy provided some innovative mechanisms which could have rather extensive ramifications. A new source would be permitted in a nonattainment area if the total combined pollution from that and old sources were reduced over previous levels. Such allowable action envisaged the practice of new sources, which would increase pollution, working out "trade-offs" with old sources to reduce pollution even more, thereby permitting the new source to be constructed. Actions taken to reach the requirements of the state implementation plan would not be allowed as part of the "credit" in such a trade-off, but reductions beyond that point would. Hence, incentive would be built into the construction of new sources which would encourage those who wanted to build new plants to take private action to reduce pollution levels. One could well envisage the purchase and sale of pollution "credits" and perhaps even the process of "banking" them to be used in the future.

This trade-off policy placed the entire burden of facilitating new growth in a nonattainment area on those promoting that growth when, in fact, the responsibility for restricting growth lay in the failure of old sources to clean up. Should not the burden of action fall on the old rather than the new source? Debate over this issue during action on the 1977 amendments led to another approach which would place more burden for creating allowable air quality increments on old sources. It emphasized revision of the state implementation plans to provide for a "growth factor." Merely to meet the standards, maximum air contamination levels would have to be modified to include a margin for new growth in addition to the standards. Responsibility for creating this cushion would fall on old sources for whom cleanup would now have to be greater in order to accommodate new growth.[53] The approach was very similar to the "growth factor" required in allocating water pollution waste loads on water quality limited streams.

The delayed compliance penalty, the third of the major innovations of the 1977 amendments, arose out of the general concern for program effectiveness. How could a regulatory scheme produce better results more rapidly? The focus on results generated a variety of opinions as to what the problem was and what innovations should be made. To many environmentalists and regulators, the main problem was the way in which litigation provided an opportunity to stall because it was cheaper than compliance. Their aim was to reverse the advantage and to make litigation more costly than compliance. To economists, the problem was one of general rules applied to varied circumstances, resulting in wide variations in the costs incurred by polluters as compared with the benefits. To them, the source should first be confronted with a cost, such as a fee for the "right" to pollute, and then be free to determine what action should be taken to clean up in order to avoid the cost. To legislators and regulators, one of the most severe problems in implementation was equity. How to develop a program which would apply fairly and equitably to all and would avoid the claim, with resulting litigation, that one community or state, or one firm in an industrial category, had an advantage over another? Finally, if one emphasized the larger problem of forcing a more desirable technology, then direct technology requirements made sense irrespective of issues of litigation escape hatches, variable cost-benefit ratios, or equity in application.

When the private market seemed too slow in generating and diffusing desirable technology, did it not make sense to establish public technology forcing programs across the board?

The 1977 amendments dealt with this problem in only a limited way; in fact, debate over the amendments did not focus sharply on these issues. For the most part, they emphasized the immediate litigation problems of enforcement: how to end the interminable round of agreements, failure to meet agreements, litigation, consent orders, and further stalling, all apparently because such action was less expensive than compliance? The answer was the noncompliance penalty which permitted sources to go beyond the prescribed compliance data by paying a penalty equivalent to the economic advantage of noncompliance. This, it was hoped, would prod the more recalcitrant sources into action. For the most part, this scheme would give regulators more leverage in negotiating with polluters to persuade them to install less polluting technology without delay. By this scheme existing enforcement could produce the prescribed results more rapidly.

The focus on enforcement often obscured the major goal of technological innovation. The fundamental controversy over air quality was one of developing new technologies. Private industry had failed to bring about more socially desirable methods of production, thus giving rise to public action to stimulate change. The most dramatic expression of this concern lay in the continual emphasis, even though relatively obscured from public view, on the development of a pollution-free automobile, and the constant exasperation on all sides about the slow pace with which private industry moved in this direction. Public funding was provided for some innovations, but it often appeared that efforts toward more pollution-free technologies moved far too slowly. The air quality program did drive change somewhat in this direction, such as fluid bed combustion which, could make possible a much cleaner method of burning coal. Even more important was the hope that on-site solar energy systems, and especially design of passive systems, solar collectors, and photovoltaic cells would generate a more "benign" process of energy conversion and application.

While the 1977 amendments addressed themselves to more effective enforcement through the noncompliance penalty, they did not focus more precisely on the problem of technological innovation. In this all-important aspect of air quality, one could detect only a limited evolution of focused thought between the 1970 and 1977 acts.

DEVELOPMENTAL PERSPECTIVES

Thus far we have emphasized the legislative and administrative evolution of the Clean Air acts. Underlying these more formal aspects of change, however, lay some significant developments in perspective. Some of these arose from the realities encountered in implementation, but others came from scientific inquiries which took place in the 1970s. What was known in 1977 about air pollution, its creation, movement, and effects, was vastly greater than what was known in 1970. The impact of this new knowledge was more a matter of redefinition of the problem than acquisition of firm answers. One could well argue that by 1977 the conception of air pollution as a problem had changed markedly since 1970 and that such a change in perception had a profound influence on the course of the politics of air quality. New realities and new perceptions of problems exercised, in a subtle way, a controlling influence on the evolution of programs and policies.

First was the emergence of cancer to take a more central role in the health effects problem.[54] Most of the discussion about air pollution in the 1960s, which provided the background of perspective in which the 1970 Act was formulated, concerned the acute effects of high-level episodes. "Disasters" were cited such as those in Donora, London, and in the Meuse Valley in France. The health effects of these episodes usually emphasized deaths due to pulmonary or cardiovascular diseases, or the worsening of such problems in susceptible populations. It was not surprising that one of the major groups to become involved in the drive for clean air was the American Lung Association. It was around such problems that much of the meaning of the term "environmental health" developed.

By the mid-1970s, however, the environmental causes of cancer began to define the health effects of air pollution. It became accepted that 60–90 percent of all cancers were environmentally caused. The term "environment" in this case covered a wide range of circumstances, of which the most important was smoking, and probably 15 percent consisted of ambient air pollutants. The emphasis provided a new focus for air pollution concerns. The "criteria" pollutants, as well as additional hazardous airborne materials, might contribute significantly to the growing incidence of cancer. One aspect involved the components of particulates which heretofore had been subjected to gross measurement. Analysis of particulates emphasized the importance of sulfates and nitrates as derivative pollutants. It also stressed the much larger number of additional harmful chemicals inherent in fossil fuel combustion, such as coal tars in general, benzoapyrene, and trace metals. When isolated in experimental situations, these could be identified as having distinctive adverse health effects.

Environmental cancer effects first became prominent in the regulation of pesticides. The DDT issue, in the initial administrative proceedings in Wisconsin, emphasized adverse effects on bird reproduction.[55] As pesticide regulation evolved, however, the potential cancer effects on humans moved into the spotlight. A new emphasis on similar effects of chemicals in the workplace also emerged by the mid-1970s to generalize the cancer problem still further. Epidemiological work by Dr. Irving Selikoff in asbestos exposure played an especially important role in extending this perspective. By 1977 the Occupational Health and Safety Administration had evolved a generic policy on carcinogens through which it hoped to deal with a broad range of potential carcinogenic substances in the workplace.[56] Late in 1977 the Environmental Defense Fund petitioned the EPA to apply the same approach to hazardous air pollutants. Although the Act of 1970 had contemplated action on this front, the EPA sought to regulate few such ambient air pollutants.[57] The EDF petition brought cancer effects back to a significant role in air pollution policy.

An equally important new perspective began to emerge as the combined effects of two or more pollutants—their "synergistic effects"—were investigated.[58] The 1970 Act program envisaged separate controls for six separate criteria pollutants;[59] but as new knowledge accumulated, it became clear that this did not accurately reflect the way in which effects occurred. The combined impact of two pollutants acting together was often greater than either one singly. Adverse effects of one in conjunction with another could be observed at levels lower than with the one by itself. Such synergistic effects could be observed most clearly in laboratory situations where exposures to plants and animals could be controlled. They were more difficult to determine in the case of human life not subject to experiments. Yet it was generally accepted that air pollution involved exposure to many substances in combination. This recognition led some to hope that epidemiological studies could be advanced to measure the total impact of exposure to varied human populations.[60]

If one were inclined to accept the importance of "welfare effects" on crop production or the validity of experimentation on laboratory animals as a basis for drawing conclusions about human life, then the experimental data would become increasingly impressive. Ozone was found to enhance the effects of sulfur dioxide in crops and food plants; some triple combinations, such as ozone, sulfur dioxide, and particulates, were found to be operative. It was difficult to know how to specify such effects precisely, yet increasing knowledge about them convinced many that the effects analysis of the initial criteria documents might not be sufficiently stringent rather than the reverse. In California it gave rise to standards more stringent than the federal.[61] Knowledge about synergistic relationships would profoundly affect the way in which air pollution impacts were viewed and, even in the absence of precise information, would tend to make judgments about allowable levels more conservative.

Even more profound was the increasing knowledge about long-distance transmission of pollutants and their transformation into chemical forms that might be even more harmful.[62] Scientific data emphasized the creation of derivatives of the criteria pollutants in the atmosphere. This included transformation of sulfur dioxide and nitrogen oxide into sulfates, sulfuric acid, nitrates, nitrites, and nitric acid, and a range of results, especially ozone, derived from photochemical reaction with hydrocarbons and nitrogen oxides. These brought into focus new types of health effects. Sulfur dioxide, for example, was recognized as harmful to human life not in itself, but from its transformation into sulfates and sulfuric acid mists. Similar effects occur with nitrogen compounds. The first of these to receive explicit attention was sulfates. By the end of 1977 California had adopted a sulfate standard and the EPA, prodded by environmentalist litigation, had such action under consideration.[63]

The problem of transformation generated a new, regional, dimension to the definition of air pollution as a problem. Chemical derivatives, which formed during transmission in the air, produced effects at great distances from the sources where their parent precursors were generated. Whereas formerly air pollution was viewed as a local problem, with primary emphasis on local fallout, new knowledge began to define it as a regional problem, often cutting far across state lines and requiring coordinated regional control. Data on the creation of ozone as wind currents moved from New York City northeast across New England gave rise to a demand from Massachusetts that some control be exercised on the source of the problem in New York. By early 1978, litigation on this issue to force New York City to control its oxidant precursors had been initiated. An increasing amount of data defined the movement of wind currents from coal combustion sources in the Midwest, such as Illinois, Ohio, and Indiana, to the Middle Atlantic States and New England.[64] Resulting acid precipitation had significant adverse impacts on aquatic life in areas such as the Adirondacks. The phenomenon of "acid rain" created a new problem perspective in air pollution matters.[65]

These new perspectives—the definition of health effects in chronic, rather than acute, terms with emphasis on long-term accumulated impacts and especially cancer; the observation of the greater effects from synergistic reactions; and the long-distance transmission and transformation of pollution—had their complex and their simple elements. One could argue that such new knowledge added complexity and confusion to an already confused situation and that little sound knowledge for action was available. Cutting through these details, however, were perspectives which defined a set of problems, each relatively simple in conception, which exercised considerable power in how air quality problems were approached. Caution increased in allowing a higher level of pollution as did a willingness to argue that standards might not be stringent enough. Also, there arose a strong sense of the need to control pollution at the source rather than to permit it to disperse, thereby incurring the risks which expanding knowledge seemed to emphasize.[66]

These new perspectives gave rise gradually to a growing conception of clean air as a source and limited resource. In 1970 clean air had been thought of as a goal to be achieved. Pollution was the problem, and a program was devised to reduce it. During the decade, however, a gradual shift in awareness took place; clean air was viewed as something both valuable and finite. The constant pressures of pollution, in spite of efforts to clean up, gave rise to a more protective stance, one which focused more on the air as a resource to be defended against persistent intrusion. The fund of clean air could not be expanded alongside the expansive potential of pollution. As that fact became more deeply etched into human consciousness, clean air as a finite resource became the starting point in problem definition.

Thus, urban areas realized that if limited available clean air were used for one purpose, it could not be used for another. If one source polluted air, this preempted the available air and prevented use by another. The finiteness of clean air itself constituted a limit on new economic growth which depended on limited allowable levels of pollution. As pollution spread across the nation, even into nonurban areas, a growing sense of the limited number of cleaner air areas in the nation arose. Measurements by the mid-1970s indicated that while sulfur dioxide levels had been reduced in the cities, they had remained more stable in areas beyond. Moreover, in the nonurban areas, sulfate levels remained high. Ozone, the most ubiquitous pollutant of all, pervaded the entire eastern part of the nation which was declared, in its entirety, a nonattainment area for that pollutant. Such facts as these added incremental weight to the implicit definition of air quality problems as the protection of a finite resource against invasion by pollution.

STRUGGLES IN THE EVOLUTION
OF THE AMENDMENTS

The most surprising aspect of the debate over the 1977 amendments was the strength of the environmental side of the controversy. Witnesses to three years of intense struggle over the amendments frequently attested to the heavy political resources brought to bear by various economic groups to weaken the 1970 law. Yet at each stage of the legislative process, firm counterforces were at work to protect, and even strengthen, the Act. When it finally emerged from the tortuous process, few serious inroads had been made in it; and in some respects it had become stronger. In spite of the persistent claims that environmental strength was at an ebb and had declined since the 1970 Act, such was not the case. Although we cannot hope to identify and explain this strength fully, it calls for some analysis within the evolving political context.

As the drive for national air quality standards accelerated in the late 1960s, industrial opposition to them, spearheaded by such groups as the American Mining Congress, the National Coal Association, the American Petroleum Institute, and the American Iron and Steel Institute did so as well.[67] The 1970 Act was changed considerably in the final stages of legislation in the direction of a stronger national program; this caught industrial opposition somewhat by surprise. This, in turn, generated a major counterattack during 1971 as three rule-making processes under the Act took place: ambient air quality standards, guidelines for states under which they were to draw up implementation plans, and new source performance standards. Input into these rule-making processes by industry was heavy. Industry took an especially strong stand on the implementation guidelines and utilized successfully its informal relationships with the Department of Commerce, the Federal Power Commission, and the Office of Management and Budget in order to thwart stronger federal leadership. It was especially successful in weakening severely the guidelines to the states, one of which pertained to an anti-degradation program. Environmentalists were able to defend both the ambient and the new source performance standards more effectively.

A major instrument of industrial influence in these early years of the Act was the National Industrial Pollution Control Council, established by President Nixon and composed of representatives of corporate firms and housed in the U.S. Department of Commerce.[68] While the Council (NIPCC) ostensibly served to provide useful information to the administration, in doing so it constituted a strategic political influence on policy. Often it and the Department of Commerce, through which it spoke, were instruments of action at the Office of Management and Budget and in interagency deliberations. Meetings of the Council were closed to the public, but its work was financed by public funds. These two factors proved to be its undoing. Environmental criticism of its work focused on the facts of secrecy and finance. Finally, Representative John Dingell of Michigan took the lead in a successful move to cut off funding and eliminate it as a focal point of influence.

The attack on the 1970 Act from the industrial community continued at a persistent pace. It sought to influence public opinion by emphasizing such themes as "overregulation" or "overkill," as the term was widely used for a few years, and the loss of jobs, an argument which came to be prominent as industry sought active support from labor. When it became clear that environmental regulations led to the loss of few jobs and in fact created more than they eliminated, the arguments shifted to capital costs and inflation. In a considerable number of court cases, industry took up a legal attack on the Act which persisted throughout the decade, but with only mixed results; up through the 1977 amendments the courts had upheld the major elements of the 1970 law. The effort to discredit the scientific basis for air quality regulations, begun in the late 1960s, continued through such actions as the attempt to undermine the credibility of reports from the National Academy of Sciences[69] and the widely debated CHESS report drawn up by EPA.[70] Utilities and the coal industry focused especially on the sulfur dioxide standard and the analysis of its health effects; they were increasingly concerned with the new role of sulfates and long-distance transmission on regulatory programs.

Despite these attacks, the environmental side, though greatly outweighed in financial and technical resources, was able to organize sufficient strength to mobilize latent public support effectively in the political debate. One crucial organization in this was the Natural Resources Defense Council which emphasized litigation and brought many of the environmental clean air cases.[71] These were carefully selected to affect general problems of rule making and administrative policy. The NRDC was the front line of environmental defense of the air quality program. Especially valuable to environmentalists was the expertise which evolved within NRDC with respect to the complexities of administrative action and the scientific and technical aspects of air quality. By drawing experts into the orbit of litigation, the environmental movement was able to exercise significant leverage. By mobilizing such skills, litigation organizations became centers of political strength which EPA and other participants in air quality politics had to take into account in their daily decisions.

Equally important was the effort to mobilize political strength for legislative revision. This came in the form of the Clean Air Coalition, which brought together representatives of many environmental organizations interested in clean air. Some of these were national groups, such as Friends of the Earth, the American Lung Association, and the Sierra Club; others were state and local groups, such as New Mexico Citizens for Clean Air and Water or the Los Angeles Coalition for Clean Air. The Coalition organized the legislative defense of the Clean Air Act. It monitored the legislative process in Washington, kept its member organizations informed regarding the details of action, and mobilized citizens for input into each stage of legislation. Equally important, in the battle for information, it was able to ferret out technical data to influence the course of legislative thought and action.

Especially valuable to the defense of the 1970 Act was the support of groups which, although not integral parts of the Clean Air Coalition, worked in cooperation with it. While the Oil, Chemical and Atomic Workers Union was a Coalition member, having formed close ties with environmentalists on the common ground of protecting workers from pollutants in industry, other unions were not. Yet during the debate over the Clean Air Act, organized labor threw its weight in defense of the Act and against weakening it,[72] save for the major exception of postponing the automobile standards. This role reflected a failure by industry to win over labor fully to its side except in a few selected issues. By 1977 many segments of organized labor realized the adverse health impacts of polluted air at work and attempted to maintain a balance in the twin drives for jobs and clean air. On the jobs issue, they were drawn toward industrial management; on the clean air issue, toward environmentalists. Amid the intensity of the debate, they continued to maintain a middle ground, but refused to budge on the basic principles of the Clean Air Act. Even more surprising was the degree to which labor supported the principle of prevention of significant deterioration, not in itself a workplace issue. While organized labor was quite willing to work out agreements for a cleanup timetable which might extend beyond the previous requirements, it also insisted on progress toward that end and was not willing to compromise the needed regulatory systems.[73]

A critical aspect of the give-and-take of political struggle in the evolution of the 1977 amendments was the role of the steel industry. This was one of the major industrial groups which remained to comply with the 1970 Act. Its slow progress was emphasized by a rather dramatic session which took place at hearings conducted on revision of the 1970 Act by the House Subcommittee on Health and the Environment, chaired by Rep. Paul Rogers of Florida.[74] At the meeting were representatives of the American Iron and Steel Institute, in the person of corporate leaders of the largest steel firms in the nation. Rep.

Rogers asked each one, in turn, about the progress made by his firm in meeting clean air requirements. Were any sources in compliance? Each replied that, in fact, none were. The expression of shock from Rep. Rogers was repeated on later occasions; the episode was described in the Report of the House Committee and continued to play an important role in the somewhat negative attitudes toward the steel industry which persisted in Congress during enactment of the amendments.[75]

The United Steelworkers of America did not support industry in its attempt to weaken the Clean Air Act. While it persistently spoke of the need to protect jobs, it also refused to succumb to industry's claims that, if the law were implemented, a massive loss in jobs would result. Both labor and environmentalists referred to such threats as "blackmail," and described them as management tactics not in the interest of labor. On a variety of occasions, union representatives continued to maintain that environmental controls had not been responsible for job losses and that reduction of steelworker employment was due far more to new technology and increased labor productivity.[76] After the amendments were passed in 1977 labor's own analysis of the Act's strengths and weaknesses was surprisingly similar to those made by environmentalists.[77] While the steelworkers were interested primarily in more healthful working conditions, they maintained a broader view of the importance of the clean air program in general.

The political struggle over the clean air program, as it evolved between 1970 and 1977, demonstrated the critical importance of scientific and technical capability as a key element of political strength. Increasingly, many issues turned on the ability to bring the decision a convincing array of facts and arguments about the effects of cleaner air. On this score industry had resources, such as technical and legal staffs, which far outweighed those of environmentalists. The latter had to rely on studies conducted elsewhere, in government and the universities, and on experts beyond their own personnel who could be persuaded to join in the effort to protect and extend air quality programs. Legal defense organizations at times had a few "in-house" experts, but for the most part, few resources to employ such skills were available. Staff members could identify and utilize studies conducted elsewhere.

An emerging problem of extraordinary significance—the long distance transmission and transformation of air pollutants—came into prominence during the debate over the amendments and pinpointed the political significance of research resources. This issue constituted a major example of the attempt to influence the direction of scientific inquiry. The problem was simple. Evidence was accumulating that a number of pollutants were transported for long distances, that in the process they were transformed into derivatives more harmful than their precursors, and that they "fell out" in areas far distant from their place of origin. Neither EPA nor industry was oblivious to the significance of this, and both rushed to undertake studies of it. The electric utilities especially took up the challenge, since one of the major problems was sulfates. The issue was joined in one instance in the Ohio River Basin Energy Study, authorized by EPA, which focused research on the long-range effects of sources in the Ohio Valley. The utility industry objected to identification of the problem as a major factor to be taken into account in analyzing the impact of the Valley's energy growth.[78] It seems apparent that the "facts" about long-range transport and transformation of air pollution would become the center of one of the most critical political air quality struggles in the ensuing years.

It was equally apparent that the struggle over the "facts" about health effects would be critical. The most immediate pending focus for that controversy was the revision of both the criteria documents and the standards. To industry it appeared that revision would discredit the earlier standards; they were convinced that health effects would be found to be far less severe than the earlier documents had concluded. To environmentalists, on the other hand, new data with respect to almost every pollutant fully justified the standards and perhaps even lower maximum contaminant levels. A major aspect of the anticipated struggle would be the balance in the range of scientific expertise which would be called upon to approve the criteria documents and the range of values which they expressed in their judgments. To a large extent, the crux of the political struggle lay in that choice.

CONCLUSION

As one reviews the historical development of air quality policies between the Acts of 1970 and the 1977 amendments, he is struck by the rapid evolution of the context of policy-making. First there was the persistent development of public values as reflected in the "prevention of significant deterioration" program, the successful litigation by environmentalists to supervise administration of the Act, and the equally successful defense and extension of the Act in the 1977 amendments. Those amendments were convincing evidence that the environmental movement, as it pertained to air quality, would not go away; they also helped to persuade environmentalists that they did reflect persistent public values and that they could mount effective political programs.

Second, there was the remarkable evolution of ideas and perspective which came with the extension of knowledge about air pollution. By 1977 this could still be described as rudimentary in comparison with what was desired to be known; yet it was far more extensive than what was known in 1970, and it established the contours of perception and thought which would shape air quality politics for the future. It was this perspective, arising from a far different "cognitive map" about the nature of air quality, which made the political setting of 1977 so vastly different from that of 1970. Much of the success of the environmental thrust lay in the evolution of this knowledge and its dissemination to the environmental public. The continuing inquiries which were connected with this expansion of knowledge set the stage for much of the politics of knowledge acquisition which constituted the focal point of struggles in the late 1970s.

Far less clear was the degree to which the debate over mechanisms of air quality control had led to significant changes. The move to bolster regulation with a noncompliance fee and a stiffer civil penalty authority was clear enough in the 1977 amendments. These were experimental, though, and gave rise to no strong confidence that they would lead to a new long-range context for air quality policy. During the 1975–1977 debates over revision of the Act, one might well have looked for innovations in the technical context of air quality control. How could more socially desirable technologies be achieved more rapidly? There were a number of technical initiatives underway that appeared to be promising, and there were constant demands that private industry make greater progress toward cleaner technology. Little of this came to constitute a focus for national debate and vigorous policy initiatives.

The evolution of public debate over clean air from 1970 to 1977 reflected significant changes in public values and scientific perception, but technological perspectives lagged considerably. Perhaps it gave rise to a fundamental question: while public policy can reflect changes in public values to a considerable degree and can generate new scientific knowledge though public funds, can it also create in the private sector new and more socially desirable technologies?

CLEAN AIR

From 1977 to 1990

IN OCTOBER 1990 Congress passed and in November President George Bush signed the new Clean Air Act (CAA). It had been thirteen years since the passage of the previous act in 1977, supposedly to be renewed again in five years.[1] But efforts by Congress to complete revision in the early 1980s failed because of disagreement within the Congress and between the Congress and President Reagan. President Bush, in contrast, desired to foster a revision and his persistence was crucial in the eventual passage in 1990.

The resulting statute is complex beyond belief, accurately reflecting a policy arena that is also complex beyond belief and it is an immense challenge to make sense out of either the process or the resulting law.[2] It would be safest simply to recount the provisions of its main titles, such as acid rain, urban smog, and toxics in the customary manner of "legislative history." But here I will attempt a more perilous task, that of outlining the meaning of the law in terms of the forces that work themselves out in the give-and-take of political struggle and place the act in a developmental context.

CHANGE AND CONTINUITY

The CAA of 1990 constitutes one stage in the evolution of a national clean air program that has been underway for about 30 years and will continue to evolve in one way or another for decades to come. To argue that because of this Act we will have some end point such as "clean air" in a date certain, the year 2000 for example, is more than utopian. The debate will continue far beyond that; to think otherwise only obscures the persistent change within which the Act must be understood.

Amid the details of the CAA one can observe a wide range of problems understood to exist but not yet dealt with. Some were self-consciously postponed through the strategy of "research." Others were left for the Environmental Protection Agency (EPA) to work out under previous authority, but predictably subject to continuing dispute and more-than-likely future legislative amendment. Still others constituted either treading water or backsliding. And Congress simply left some to another day.

More important is the way in which, as with statutes generally, many provisions remain subject to interpretation, leading to persistent dispute over implementation and resulting litigation. Past experience would predict that this act will not "settle down" in the arena of disputes for at least a decade, and that substantial implementation will not take place until then. Neither lawyers nor political analysts need fear that the Act will diminish their opportunities, for the contending parties will make sure that both are fully employed.

This continuity of struggle over the evolution of policy provides the continuity in the history of air quality politics. It has two features. One is the persistence of the constitutional patterns of relationships between the Congress and the administrative agencies. For some three decades that pattern has been one of legislative directives amid administrative strict construction of statutory authority. Legislative oversight has arisen to try to keep the nose of the agencies to the grindstone and when that has not been sufficient, statutory amendments have been more prescriptive and detailed.

Experience with the CAA of 1990 already indicates that this tussle will continue as EPA seeks to satisfy demands from the Executive Office of the President to reduce the impact of the new law on the regulated industries. The continuing struggle underlines how difficult it is for EPA to take substantial initiatives when it has legislative discretion and prompts one to pay close attention to those discretionary elements of the new Act. The drama of legislative-executive interaction does not display signs of ebbing.

Equally continuous is the lineup of parties in contention and the substance of the debate, both of which have changed but little over the past thirty years. The same political antagonists of the 1960s continued into the debates of a quarter century later. And the issues remain the same: (1) What are the standards of acceptable air quality? (2) How should the scientific data about the health and environmental effects of air pollution be assessed? (3) How can more socially acceptable technologies be put into place more rapidly? It seems safe to predict that as the politics of implementation proceed the parties in dispute will remain little changed.

THE POLITICAL CONTEXT OF CLEAN AIR POLICY

First, a brief review of the political dynamics. The broad policy objectives, such as improved health, water quality, or visibility, are set in general public debate. These public objectives are then translated into specifics by organized citizen groups and legislative bodies and, in turn, are countered by the environmental opposition who seek to influence both legislation and implementation. Administrative agencies play the "middle ground" in which they not only implement the law on the regulated community but also seek to restrain demands from the public and therefore become involved in continual tension with both.

In this political setting four issues emerge; each was a major focal point of debate in the CAA of 1990: standards, technology, science, and costs.

Standards

The traditional approach to establishing "how clean is clean" in air quality matters has been through the "criteria document" leading to standard setting. An assessment is made of the effects of specific air pollutants and an acceptable "threshold" of pollution established. Provisions of the 1990 CAA constitute significant changes in these traditional procedures and are the law's most "revolutionary" features.

The most obvious is a reduction in sulfur dioxide emissions by 50 percent to a level of 8.9 million tons annually and maintenance of that figure as a permanent ceiling or "cap." That strategy was determined not through the formal procedures of applied science, the model of the criteria document process, but through broad public debate and broad public choice, ratified finally when President Bush decided to accept both the reduction and the cap.[3]

A similar revision in standard setting took place with air toxic emissions. In this case EPA had regulated only eight chemicals since it obtained the authority to do so in 1970. The agency had not been able to make clean scientific determinations about the effects of toxics because the complexity of the "real world" of toxics made it almost impossible for any assessment to withstand the challenge of those who wished to prevent regulation.[4] Following a similar approach to water toxics in the 1977 Clean Water Act, the 1990 CAA simply identified 189 such chemicals as air pollutants that EPA would control.[5]

Air toxics were now subject to "technology standards" rather than a scientific assessment and threshold determination. Copying the Clean Water Act, the initial standard required of all sources will be the best technology in place, called the Maximum Available Control Technology or MACT. That "best" was specified in the Act to be the best 12 percent of technologies in any one type of industrial production. A further "residual standard"—also a feature of the Clean Water Act—would apply after MACT was in place if EPA determined that the technology standards did not reach a prescribed level of health protection.

Both the sulfur dioxide and air toxics provisions constituted legislative rather than administrative standard setting. In both cases EPA had had statutory authority as early as the 1970 Clean Air Act to set standards in those areas on its own initiative but did not. EPA had repeatedly been brought to task for not taking up the acid rain issue, but the courts had upheld agency inaction and agency action on air toxics had been minimal. Almost twenty years of EPA inaction, therefore, lay behind the decision of Congress to take standard setting in these cases out of the hands of the agency and to make the decision itself.

In the case of lead EPA had taken a different route; after many years of similar reluctance to act and under prodding from federal health agencies as well as legislative committees and its own Science Advisory Board, the EPA greatly reduced lead in gasoline as a source of air pollution.[6] But in the cases of acid rain and air toxics agency action had not been forthcoming. Significant standard setting for other pollutants, especially ozone and particulates, are in the offing. It seems safe to say that agency temporizing on these will once again likely lead to future legislative intervention.

Technology and Markets

The CAA of 1990 relies heavily on technology requirements. Technical performance is substituted for effects numbers because the Congress was convinced that the latter had proved to be a weak reed for action.

All four substantive parts of the law involve attempts to stimulate technological innovation directly. Some call this "technology forcing" but it is, in fact, a series of "market creating opportunities."[7] As Lyman Clark, president of Environmental Economics Associates of Traverse City, Michigan, wrote shortly after the CAA was passed, "$25 billion spent by one group of people is revenue for another.... It does not vanish into thin air."[8] Or as Joel Hirschhorn wrote in the environmental business magazine, *In Business,* "Government actually creates market niches every time a major regulation is promulgated. Some will see the costs. Others will see the opportunities and help make new ones."[9]

By establishing legally enforceable emission limits to be met at a date certain the law creates a market. Investors, inventors, engineers, marketing specialists, and entrepreneurs now are alerted that if they use their ingenuity and talents a market beckons them to profitable business. The regulatory system creates a "hidden hand" that radiates throughout the producer side of the economy. The firmer the control the greater assurance of a market and hence of technological innovation. Over the years an environmental market has created expanding economic opportunities and played a major role in generating an ever expanding "environmental economy."

The Act fosters a range of more environmentally acceptable technologies: new stationary source emissions control technology, to new fuels and new tailpipe emission controls, to new technologies to reduce toxic emissions. While earlier laws tackled technological innovation only by bits and pieces, the central feature of the 1990 Act was a wide-ranging attempt to foster technological innovation more directly.[10]

Science and Economics

In contrast, science and economics played a problematic role in the legislative debate; they were not unimportant, but their role was limited. They set general and often vague boundaries of choice rather than applied firm knowledge to problems. Both were a fringe rather than a central element in the proceedings.

As early as 1980 the acid rain issue had reached such a prominent level in public affairs that it was dealt with through a massive 10-year federal research program of $500 million, the National Acid Precipitation Assessment Program (NAPAP). By the time of the 1989–1990 CAA debate the final report from this assessment was imminent. Yet that report was not completed until after the Act was passed and it figured in the debate only as a background factor. The utility industry argued that action prior to the report was premature But while this argument had been successful in postponing action during the previous ten years, it now was laid aside as almost irrelevant. When President Bush advocated sulfur dioxide reductions of 50 percent now and a permanent cap, the scientific debate was over.[11]

The role of this decision was underscored by the fact that the administration's budget proposals for fiscal year 1992 included no funds to continue acid rain research. The policy decision had been made and hence no more science was needed. Congress, however, took a different tack and authorized continued monitoring to chart the long-term consequences of emission reductions. Congress, in other words, did not simply wish to cut through the science and act, but also to establish a strategy so that it could revisit the program in future years.

Economics played a similar indirect role. The costs of the 1990 Act to the regulated community were variously estimated ranging from the administration's $23 billion[12] to the environmentalists $10 billion[13] to industry's $91 billion.[14] This spread of estimates only underlined the political role of cost analyses. Most economic analyses tended to convey a sense of disaster by emphasizing the costs and downplaying the benefits as "minor." The course of the debate made clear that these views were not taken too precisely or too seriously.

Environmentalists were as frustrated in focusing on benefits as were the economists in focusing on costs. The American Lung Association sponsored an analysis of eight major benefit studies that outlined a far higher level of benefits than had previously been estimated and these were known to the Congress.[15] Benefit data received far less media attention because of the continual emphasis on costs by industry, the Executive Office of the President, and professional economists. Hence benefits figured in the debate, as did costs, in more background fashion rather than as the direct application of advanced knowledge.[16]

Congress rather than economists or environmentalists made the cost-benefit trade-offs in the broader political arena. The regulated industry's cry of disaster if the Act were passed seemed extreme to legislators. To environmentalists analyses of benefits hardly surfaced at all in the debate. Both costs and benefits, however, served as quantitative expressions of the trade-offs being made in the legislative arena. They played their role in setting the outer perimeters of the debate and gave some weight to one side or another, but that role was one of political give-and-take rather than firmly applied knowledge.[17]

The Context of Contending Political Forces

THE PRESIDENT AND THE CONGRESS

The CAA of 1990 has been described as an initiative from President Bush and a response from Congress. A more accurate description would be the reverse. For almost a decade Congress had debated the various elements of a revision and by 1988 had formulated clear legislative packages that were reintroduced in the early days of the 101st Congress. These packages presented the new president with a legislative agenda to which he then reacted.[18]

The appropriate presidential response to these congressional initiatives was debated extensively in the Domestic Policy Council. Some wished Bush to take the same tack as had Reagan, that is, ignore the initiatives and let Congress proceed. But others argued for a more active role on the grounds that congressional action alone would lead to an unacceptable measure that the president would feel obliged to veto. If he entered the fray from the start he could exercise more control over the legislation and shape a bill more scaled down and less offensive to industry and to the president.[19]

The second strategy prevailed.[20] It involved first a decision to give rather strong support to the environmental proposals on acid rain including the phase-down and cap on sulfur dioxide emissions but at the same time to favor the industry side on urban smog and toxic air emissions. Second was the decision to play an active role in restraining the environmental contingent in Congress and to bolster the political clout of the environmental opposition. This was done by working with that opposition among the the Republicans, especially in the Senate, and by joining a presidential veto threat with a threat of a Senate filibuster. This led to a strategy of caution among Senate Democratic leaders, persuaded them to enter closed-door negotiating sessions with the White House, and moved the bill significantly toward the president's position.[21]

The White House had less influence in the House. Here events were shaped by the competing roles of Rep. John Dingell, chair of the House Committee on Commerce, and Rep. Henry Waxman, chair of its Sub-Committee on Health and the Environment.[22] Their long-standing rivalry as leaders of two environmental factions in the House constituted high drama for the media.

The two House rivals bargained through much of the proceedings in that chamber, often away from the public eye in a closed forum similar to that in the Senate. But here the environmental strength on the House floor often shifted the balance away from rather than toward the president.[23] A final effort by the White House to influence the conference committee proceedings was more than inept and only backfired.[24]

THE ORGANIZED GROUPS

Beyond the closer relationship between the Congress and the Executive Office of the president were the organized groups that represent political forces in the wider society. These reflected little change over the previous three decades.

Some represented the organized environmental constituency. In the debates over revision of the Act in 1975–76, several of these had come together in the Clean Air Coalition under the leadership of Rafe Pomerance of Friends of the Earth.[25] Among environmental health groups, the American Lung Association and the American Public Health Association were the most notable.[26] Another were the various community groups that had been energized by air toxic events and had begun to organize around the annual reports of toxic emissions mandated by Congress in 1984. Still another was the interest in air pollution by the National Wildlife Federation and the Sierra Club.[27] Involved in the Clean Air Coalition previously, they put more than casual effort into clean air issues in the late 1980s.[28]

The environmental opposition that developed in the 1960s to oppose both mobile and stationary source emissions remained relatively unchanged over the years: coal and coal-using industries, electric utilities, oil and automobiles, and the chemical industries. In previous years each sector had tended to carve out its own advantage with the complex clean air legislative package. Now greater interindustry cooperation prevailed in the form of the Clean Air Working Group that enabled industry to restrain more effectively the clean air drive.[29]

After such a long legislative debate, each side was relieved that at least this phase of the continuing struggle was over. While some environmental leaders, for example, the Sierra Club, put a strongly positive cast on the results, others such as David Hawkins of the Clean Air Coalition emphasized the compromises made by the environmental side. This, he argued, was because Congress did not feel an urgency about the issue that, in turn, came from weak interest in the nation at large.[30]

Those who spoke for the largest industry coalition felt that the debate had unfairly gone in favor of the environmental side, that the cost to industry and the nation had never been taken seriously, and that the environmental benefits were negligible. Yet they also argued that much worse had been avoided— risk analysis, for example, replaced by a technological standard for toxic air emissions.[31]

Suffice it to say that environmental advocates and environmental opponents continued their roles in this never-ending debate, both with greater activity than in the past, the one working through the Congress and the other through the Executive Office of the President. This pattern of political forces would be as important in the ensuing contest over implementation of the new act. One might predict, in fact, that because the act extended the clean air regulations to a wider range of sources and tightened enforcement mechanisms, it would increase clean air opposition in the business community.

THE POLITICAL PARTIES

As with the organized groups, so with the political parties. The sharp differences between the Democrats and Republicans over environmental issues generally were reflected rather precisely in the clean air debate. Senate roll call votes on eight major amendments divided the parties in roughly the same manner as had a larger cluster of votes on varied issues in the 1989 session as a whole. The data is in Table 1.

Table 1
1990 Clean Air Act Votes Compared with 1989
Environmental Votes, U.S. Senate, by Party

Clean Air Act Score	Democrats (%)	Republicans (%)
75% to 100%	43.6	8.9
50% to 74%	25.4	11.1
25% to 49%	18.2	24.4
0% to 24%	12.8	55.6
1989 Environmental Issues Score		
75% to 100%	50.9	6.7
50% to 74%	27.2	20.0
25% to 49%	16.4	33.3
0% to 24%	5.5	40.0

Over the years from 1970 to 1990, while legislative support for environmental policies had grown steadily, the Democratic Party had been forging a

national consensus on environmental issues, while the Republican party had
been developing a marked regional divergence.[32] The CAA debate furthered
those tendencies. CAA votes produced greater agreement among Democrats
than was the case with environmental issues generally. Table 1 indicates that
the difference among Democrats was 30.8 points on the CAA and 45.4 points
for environmental issues generally while the difference among Republicans
was 46.7 points and 33.3 points respectively.[33]

As a voting bloc, Republicans in the regions of low environmental support
played a significant role in the environmental opposition in the CAA.[34] Ten
Republican senators from the eight Rocky Mountain states presented the
clearest case; constituting almost one-fourth of the Republican Senate total,
they had considerable leverage on the outcome. Some of the most vigorous
and influential Republican opponents, Symms and McClure of Idaho, Wallop
and Simpson of Wyoming, and Garn of Utah, were from that region. It was
they with whom the Senate Democratic leaders had to contend in shaping a
majority for the legislation and with whom the White House could work to
weaken the Act.[35]

THE STATES

The most significant new influence in the politics of clean air were the state
and local air pollution control administrators organized in the State and Ter-
ritorial Air Pollution Control Association (STAPPA) and the Association of
Local Air Pollution Control Officials (ALAPCO). They were far more active in
the 1990 debates than in previous years.[36]

STAPPA/ALAPCO served to bring state influence into most features of the
clean air debate. William Becker, Washington representative of both groups,
took a keen interest in the entire bill and enabled state and local administrators to be significant players in the CAA legislation. Local and state air quality
administrators fought for a strengthened federal program to enhance their
work.

Stateside contributions to the CAA debate were focused by the leading role
of California in clean air policy. From the very early days of federal air quality
legislation the State of California had maintained authority to establish its
own program for mobile sources.[37] Changes in the Clean Air Act in 1977 gave
other states an opening to adopt the California "standards," and over the 1980s
this opportunity was taken up by the eight northeastern states organized as
the Northeastern States for Coordinated Air Use Management (NESCAUM).
This group began to explore and adopt the "California program."[38]

In June of 1990 during debate over the CAA those states announced that they would adopt the "California standards" which were more stringent than the then-existing federal standards. This softened considerably opposition to adopting those standards in the new CAA.[39] But it also established a pattern of future action. As California moved ahead further so might the northeastern states and still others might follow.

ACID RAIN

The CAA of 1990 had four main substantive elements: acid rain, urban smog, toxic emissions, and stratospheric ozone. Each played a distinctive role in the debate.

The "acid rain" provisions were the least controversial because they evoked the president's firmest commitment, a stance that precluded significant controversy. That commitment was firmed especially by his alliance with the Environmental Defense Fund that took up the cudgels for emissions trading and further enabled Bush to associate himself ideologically with "market forces."[40]

The acid rain provisions—reduce sulfur dioxide emissions by 50 percent from the 1980 baseline to 8.9 million tons per year and "cap" that emission level permanently—were truly innovative. At the same time they simply carried out long-standing air quality objectives never implemented. The acidifying consequences of sulfur emissions had long been known. A two-tracked approach to air pollution that developed in the 1960s distinguished between two sets of air pollution effects—primary and secondary, or "health" and "welfare" (including ecological, aesthetic, and material damage). By the time the Clean Air Act of 1970 was passed and EPA came upon the scene interest in both "ecological effects" and "welfare effects" of air pollution had waned.

A resurgence of interest in secondary effects of air pollution arose in the 1970s through popular interest in acid rain that gave new support to long-standing scientific interest in the subject. Existing data demonstrated close patterns in the geographical distribution of acid measurements (pH) from rainfall and upwind sources. In the mid-1970s two new sets of measurements added to the evidence. One identified the photochemical transformation of sulfur dioxide into sulfates as it was transported over long distances through the atmosphere, from upwind sources to downwind effects. The other used visibility data—sulfates were acknowledged to be the largest single source of visibility impairment—gathered at airports for many decades to chart overall changes in visibility over the years.[41]

By 1990 scientists had identified a "critical load" of maximum sulfate deposition of 18 kilograms per hectare per year and this was the basis for a proposed reduction of 50 percent in sulfur dioxide emissions. By the end of the Carter administration a joint Canadian-U.S. scientific body had agreed on this figure as a target for public policy.

The Canadian-U.S. joint committee fell apart as the new Reagan administration pulled out the U.S. contingent, and each country went its own way in assessing acid rain. In the United States the science was tossed back and forth between the administration and the scientists and was caught up in the assessment of the 10-year research program that Congress inaugurated in 1980. The Canadians, on the other hand, worked with scientists in Europe who took the entire problem more seriously and developed critical loads for nitrates as well. The decision of the Bush administration in 1990 to accept the 50 percent reduction target and the cap returned the issue to where it had stood in 1980.[42]

Much had happened in the meantime. One was the constant tussle between environmentalists and the EPA over whether or not the EPA should take action. The agency had wide authority to do so, but it continually argued that there were no grounds for action. A second was the research arising from the National Acid Precipitation Assessment Program that provided evidence on both sides of the issue and kept the acid rain policy debate boiling.[43] By 1990 it appeared that more research would only provide more fuel for debate. Minnesota and Massachusetts, moreover, had taken steps to scale back their own emissions in accord with what they felt was their share of the problem. Senator Kerry from Massachusetts and Representative Sikorski from Minnesota transferred those initiatives to the Congress.[44]

The decisions to reduce emissions by 50 percent and to establish a permanent cap created a "zero sum game" for sulfur dioxide emissions. Only so much was allowed—the amounts were called allowances—and if some regions got more others would get less. Some senators sought special provisions for their own electric utility plants that would "break" the total level of allowances. But others brought the issue back to the "zero sum game" by forcing members to recognize that more for some would mean less for others. Intense bargaining ensued that at least in theory and on paper kept the total within the limit of 8.9 million tons per year.[45]

All this was accompanied by a variety of cross-currents. One was the political role of midwestern coal states whose emissions had remained high despite the requirements of the Clean Air Act. To bring emissions down now would be quite a wrench and they formed their own bloc of votes for self-protection. But much of the rest of the country did not sympathize with the midwest, for if the midwest were to be allowed to continue its emissions level, the "cleaner" states to the south and west would be prevented from expanding their coal-fired power production. Hence major bargains took place between the "dirty" and the "clean" states within the context of the cap and the allowances that enabled the clean states to expand production in the future.

An equally extensive controversy took place between high-sulfur and low-sulfur regions. Would sulfur dioxide emissions be reduced by using high-sulfur coal cleaned by flue-gas scrubbers or by using low-sulfur coal? The 1977 act had benefited eastern coal by requiring that no coal, even low-sulfur coal, could be used alone on new power plants and would be "scrubbed." The northern Rocky Mountain/Plains states had long chafed under this restriction and their main objective in revising the Clean Air Act was to eliminate it. The Act repealed the 1977 requirements, thereby satisfying western states; but it also provided benefits to high-sulfur states.[46]

A new strategy was added, "emissions trading," that would, so the westerners thought, greatly facilitate the use of low-sulfur coal. Each source, if it reduced emissions below the required amount, would obtain a permit that gave it the "right to emit" for the amount reduced. This, then, could be sold to other sources that needed an allowance to increase their emissions. The provision was intended to encourage utilities to use the cheapest alternative to reduce emissions and it was widely felt that this would be western low-sulfur coal.

Many implications of the cap/allowance system emerged during the debate in Congress and still others arose after the act was passed. One was the belief that utilities might keep rather than sell emission rights to provide for their future expansion or to prevent a competitor from expanding. To counteract this possibility EPA was to hold back a significant number of allowances to sell and to auction to utilities. Another was the the availability of firm emissions data through "continuous monitoring"; was this sufficiently available to enable everyone to be confident as to what precisely was being traded and that trading in the "right to emit" would have a clearly defined benefit for air quality? How the trading system would, in fact, work, remained to be seen.[47]

Urban Smog

While some progress had been made over the years in reducing sulfur dioxide and particulate levels and much progress with lead, relatively little had occurred with urban smog. The main problem was ozone and the main source of the problem was the automobile. Considerable advances had been made in reducing automobile emissions by using the catalytic converter, but a doubling of auto mileage between 1970 and 1990 offset those gains.

The continuing problem had generated many new ideas about how to cope with it that were ready for the legislative hopper as revision of the 1977 act proceeded; the CAA incorporated a number of these. The urban smog section of the law is its most complex precisely because of pressure for effective action that lay behind it and the range of strategies that it took up. Yet there remained the nagging realization that even the most heroic efforts would surely once again be offset by increased motor vehicle mileage.

The CAA urban smog provisions involved a new scheme of classifying cities in terms of the severity of emission problems, degree of nonattainment of previous objectives, and different levels of action required for each class. There were five classes: marginal, moderate, serious, severe, and extreme. Controls were to be increasingly stringent as the severity of the problem increased. If areas in a less severe category do not meet their deadlines they can be "bumped" up into a more severe one. While this scheme seems to involve a more systematic approach than in the past, it remains to be seen whether or not the "sanctions," withholding federal highway funds or requiring more extensive reductions, will work any better than in the past.[48]

The 1970 act had placed primary emphasis on nitrogen dioxide and hydrocarbon emissions. But during the 1970s it was concluded that the pollutant of most serious concern was ozone for which nitrogen dioxide and hydrocarbons were precursors. This brought volatile organic compounds (VOCs) as a general category of precursors more sharply into the picture. Thirty percent of the VOCs came from industries, 20 percent from smaller sources, such as repair shops, drycleaners, or consumer products, and 50 percent from automobiles. In the 1990 CAA Congress sought to tackle all three.

The most obvious approach was to tighten automobile exhaust standards. California had already done so in what was referred to as a Phase I strategy; the state was on the point of advancing to Phase II, a still tighter level of emissions to go into effect in 1996. For those seeking a more effective urban smog strategy, therefore, the first objective was to extend the California program to the entire country. The 1990 Act did so for the Phase I standards but left Phase II to EPA's future discretion.

Adoption of the Phase I standards was relatively easy because the automobile industry had already made considerable progress toward the new California standards. More important, the eight northeastern NESCAUM states announced that they would soon adopt the California standards.[49] This meant that about a quarter of the nation's automobile market would be limited to the "California car." Tighter Phase I tailpipe controls merely ratified and extended these innovations already underway in the states.[50] But the

Bush administration firmly opposed adding to the CAA the California "Phase II" auto standards and its views prevailed.[51]

As an alternative to the Phase II auto standards the administration offered a "clean fuels" and a "clean car" strategy. The first emphasized new fuels such as reformulated gasoline, methanol, ethanol, and natural gas, and the second the introduction of new "clean cars" in municipal and private fleets. Both were to be required for those cities that had the worst ozone problem. The petroleum and automobile industries were adamantly opposed to both, but the EPA and several members of the White House staff strongly supported them as pilot programs and the Senate Environment Committee included both Phase II standards and a clean fuels/clean car program in its proposals. To avoid Phase II standards, the industry, therefore, accepted a sharply scaled-down version of the initial clean fuels/clean car proposal. CAA provisions on this score were shaped heavily by action in California which was moving rapidly in this direction and it appeared that the northeastern states would follow.[52]

Other mobile source controls were added: control of fuel evaporation during refueling and engine operation; fuel volatility and "running losses" that came from heating up the fuel tank during vehicle operation; gasoline spillage and vapors escaping during refueling. EPA had already taken steps to deal with some of these but had been thwarted by industry opposition. Now these controls would move ahead more rapidly.

New provisions extended the effectiveness of emission controls. One increased their required life from five years or 50,000 miles to 10 years or 100,000 miles. Manufacturers would now guarantee catalytic converter parts for seven years or 70,000 miles. The inspection and maintenance (I/M) program was tightened to make it more effective. Required electronic onboard diagnostic systems would enable both the car owner and the repair shop to diagnose readily the performance of emission control equipment.[53]

Other provisions of the act adopted new strategies to tackle urban smog. One pertained to smaller sources of VOCs, called area sources, the small repair shops, drycleaners, or print shops, and another to consumer products such as household paints, oil, charcoal lighter fluid, hairspray, and deodorants. Few attempts had been made to bring these sources under control; the new CAA seeks to do so through requiring permits and compliance plans for smaller sources and strategies to introduce substitute consumer products.

Trucks were a major source of smog-producing emissions not yet seriously controlled and the new act made some headway on this score. Light-duty trucks were placed on a rule-making schedule to control hydrocartons, carbon monoxide, nitrogen oxides, and particulates. Standards for light-duty trucks of less than 6,000 pounds were to be phased in beginning with 1994 model years and those of more than 6,000 pounds beginning with the 1996 model years. Further reductions were contemplated only after EPA study. For heavy-duty trucks, however, EPA was given far more discretion; it could issue standards based on health effects. Whether or not this discretionary provision would lead to EPA action remained to be seen.

Much ozone comes from industry and environmentalists had argued for a reduction in its precursor nitrogen dioxide of 4 million tons a year from those sources to go along with the 50 percent reduction in sulfur dioxide, but Congress approved only 2 million tons.[54] The strategy of reduction and cap applied to sulfur dioxide was not applied to stationary nitrogen dioxide sources. The South Coast Air Quality Management District had already applied a cap to these emissions and was on the point of reducing it further, but such a reduction/cap strategy for nitrogen dioxide was not included in the new CAA.[55]

Toxic Emissions

Public concern with air toxics had grown steadily during the 1970s and 1980s. While the CAA of 1970 had granted EPA authority to regulate toxic air emissions it had done so only in eight cases.

Congress in 1984 had brought a new element into the air toxics issue that expanded political support for action. It required each source to report its toxic emissions annually and that the data be made available to the public. Each community could know the specific chemicals to which it was exposed and the amount and the specific firms from which the chemicals were emitted.[56] This provided a community-based focus to toxics exposures, somewhat akin to the way in which hazardous waste sites did, and generated considerable organizing on behalf of policies to reduce toxic emissions.[57]

Here was a classic "market force" in operation—consumer knowledge. It focused consumer preferences for reduced toxic exposures. Two general provisions of the CAA resulted: (1) a goal of reducing cancer risks from toxic chemicals by 75 percent in five years and (2) implementation through a direct application of new technologies, rather than through the former chemical-by-chemical assessment of health effects.

The best performing technologies in terms of emissions would set the standard by which all other sources in a given line of production would be required to improve. Copying the strategy of the Clean Water Act of 1972, tech-

nologies used by the "exemplary" firms were required of others. The plan
would not dictate new technologies but constituted a technology generalizing
strategy in which the best in place would be required of all. How would one
define the "best performing" technologies? For water EPA had opted for the
top 10 percent of all firms. A similar approach was now applied to air, but with
a slightly different level of "best"—the top 12 percent.[58]

This strategy focused on the central problem: how can public policy bring
about more socially desirable technologies? One way is to foster research
through public funding, a strategy that seems often to move rather slowly.
Another is to activate consumer demand as was the case in the air toxics provision. Still another is to require a certain level of emissions to be reached by
a certain date which then creates a market that enterprising firms can meet by
creating new technologies. And still another, implicit in the technology standards, is to establish the "best" as a required public benchmark. One of the intriguing elements of this approach is that some firms will adopt technologies
even beyond the "best" and hence by improving the benchmark exercise a
continual pressure on technology improvement.

In the debates on the CAA of 1990 the technology standards approach to
reducing air toxic emissions competed heavily with the more conventional
"risk assessment" approach. In this case one identifies the adverse health
effect and then formulates a "threshold" standard of acceptable exposure or
harm which requires controls to meet that standard. The "effects" so identified increasingly had been thought about in terms of reducing risk of death.
Hence basic to every regulatory action was an assessment of that risk.[59]

Many were more than skeptical about risk analysis because it seemed to be
so limited in the effects it could "take into account." Most data pertained to
cancer and yet it seemed clear that there was a vast range of health effects beyond cancer for which the data was more than limited.[60] Some industry
groups, especially in iron and steel, were equally skeptical about risk analysis.
EPA had identified coke batteries as posing especially high risks to the communities around them and the iron and steel industry had registered their objections by attempting to undermine the credibility of risk assessments.

The debate over technology versus risk assessment in the CAA was resolved by applying a technology strategy as the first stage of action and postponing risk analysis as a "residual strategy" which EPA could apply as a "second
round" of action in the future if it thought desirable. The CAA also provided
that the National Academy of Sciences undertake a study of the usefulness of
risk analysis.[61]

An overriding issue postponed to the future was the level of risk to serve as the standard. There were several aspects of this. One was the acceptable level of risk: what "chance" of additional premature cancer deaths would trigger action? Environmentalists sought throughout the debate to apply a one-in-a-million standard; policy should seek to reduce risks from cancer to that level. A second was how risk should be calculated. No step in the method was minimally clear and most often they were expressed in terms of ranges of probability. In such cases would one steer the analysis in the direction of estimating higher risks or lower risks? The third was use of an "adequate margin of safety," a factor intended to account for future new knowledge that would predictably identify adverse effects of pollution exposures at lower levels than currently known.

The CAA of 1990 left all of these issues for future debate. EPA was left to decide for itself what residual risk strategy should be applied after technology standards had been put into practice. The report requested of the National Academy of Sciences seemed to presage not so much a firm conclusion that EPA could use as a guideline, but another ingredient in an ongoing controversy. Thus, while the CAA provided an opportunity to focus sharply on a first round of technology standards action, it only postponed these risk issues to the future.[62]

Several other aspects of air toxics were postponed to the future. One was toxic emissions from mobile sources. This was left for further study and possible rule making.[63] A second involved special concessions to two major industry sources: the long-term exemption for the iron and steel industry from the toxics provisions of the act,[64] and the postponement of utility toxics emissions for further study before action.[65]

Still a third was the atmospheric deposition of toxic chemicals, a problem that focused especially on the Great Lakes where significant scientific data had been developed about the problem. Representatives from the Great Lakes region attempted to obtain an action program for Great Lakes toxics in the 1990 Act but had to settle for further research.[66]

CFCs—INDOOR AIR—GLOBAL WARMING

Most of the debate on the CAA revolved around issues that the Congress had been considering for a decade. Several newer issues, however, kept intruding, such as the stratospheric ozone problem, indoor air, and global warming. Some of these became important aspects of the revised law; others were dropped from consideration.

The stratospheric ozone issue was the most successful in making its way into the new CAA as a separate Title VI, "Protecting Stratospheric Ozone."[67] In the Senate it was pressed by Senator John Chaffee of Rhode Island and in the House by Representative Jim Bates of California. Senator Mitchell, the Senate Majority Leader, sought to sidetrack Chaffee's effort, but failed, and when Chaffee tested the waters with the first Senate floor vote on the bill, a proposal to ban methyl chloroform after 2000, it passed by a 98–2 vote. In the House the Bates measure had the support of Rep. Henry Waxman but equally strong opposition from Rep. John Dingell. A stratospheric ozone measure easily passed the House. In conference committee it was the first issue to be resolved successfully.[68]

Two features of the CFC action stand out. One is the degree to which there was little effective political opposition. The science seemed to be clear and as the debate proceeded more scientific data emerged to indicate both the continuation and expansion of the ozone hole over the Antarctic and the appearance of similar holes in the Arctic and elsewhere. Hence the issue was not delayed by endless scientific controversy. By the same token the issue was singularly devoid of cost/benefit arguments, even though there were some objections from industry about the rapidity with which substitutes for CFCs and other ozone depleting chemicals could be found.

The same high degree of consensus—unusual for an environmental issue —shaped the details of a far-reaching system of control. The offending chemicals are to be phased out; emissions from most refrigeration sectors are to be reduced; motor vehicle air conditioner CFCs are to be recycled; warning labels are to be placed on consumer products; EPA must approve of all substitutes for ozone-depleting substances. All this is added to the Agency's existing system of marketable production permits for ozone-depleting chemicals that involves production limits and allowances in a system quite similar to that established for sulfur dioxide by the CAA.[69]

In sharp contrast were two issues that did not play a role in the CAA but could well have been thought of as integral parts of a satisfactory clean air program: indoor air quality and global warming. In both cases only the barest and most tangential moves were made to include them in the act and the legislative managers explicitly sought to keep them as separate issues so as not to "weigh down" the bill.

Indoor air quality was of special interest to EPA. Its administrators had long argued that indoor toxics entailed far more of a risk than did outdoor toxics. Hence when the agency was asked to comment on the air toxics bills emerging in both the Senate and the House it argued with considerable force that neither measure was justifiable or worth the cost.[70] Yet the momentum for controlling toxic chemicals from industrial sources was high and there seemed to be no way that EPA could divert it. More important, however, was the fact that while EPA had sought for a decade to develop a major strategy for controlling indoor air pollution, adamant opposition from the Reagan and Bush administrations had thwarted its efforts.[71]

The desire to attach some elements of a global warming program to the CAA was taken a bit more seriously. But once again the "go slow" strategy of the administration diverted efforts to extend the minimum mileage requirement for new cars[72] and gave short shrift to proposals for a carbon tax.[73] A proposal to require utilities to monitor their CO_2 emissions and report them to the EPA was approved after it was found that it did not involve continuous monitoring, that it could be met by estimating emissions from the content of coal and that customary utility reports to the Department of Energy would suffice.[74]

IMPLEMENTATION

The CAA of 1990 was dominated by policies to stimulate technological innovation to foster cleaner air; equal in importance were administrative innovations to implement these strategies. Administrative arrangements in place since 1970 were massively updated to make implementation more effective.

PERMITS

The central feature of these innovations was a far-reaching permit system. Now all sources will be required to obtain emission permits from the states with residual enforcement by both the EPA and citizen litigants. The permit program is modeled after that for water quality established in 1972 in the National Pollution Discharge Elimination System known as NPDES permits.[75]

This innovation was not an integral part of the package of revisions contemplated in the early stages of congressional debate. They came from the EPA, were submitted to the White House, and were an integral part of the president's initial proposal. They appeared on the political scene rather quietly, and it took some time for their implications to be understood by the regulated or the environmental community. Once so understood, however, the permit provisions aroused intense opposition from industry as the most feared part of the new law.[76] Alerted to this opposition, the administration tried to undo its own handiwork but the damage had been done and both EPA and environmentalists dug in to protect the permit provisions.[77] Some of the most bitterly fought issues on the Senate floor involved unsuccessful attempts to water down the proposal.[78]

Each stationary source, no matter what it emits, will be required to secure a permit that includes (1) a consolidation of all regulatory requirements for that source, (2) a compliance schedule for meeting those requirements, (3) periodic reporting of emissions, and (4) a periodic six-month report as to progress in meeting the compliance schedule.

Under the 1970 Clean Air Act the main regulatory device had been the State Implementation Plan (SIP) with which sources had to comply. To implement that program some 18 states had developed some form of a permit. But most of these were operating permits that did not provide a context for continuous enforcement based on compliance with specific mandates.[79]

The new air quality permits will require periodic monitoring reports so that both the agency and citizens can observe the degree to which permit requirements are being met. For citizen organizations this provides a new opportunity. Water quality permits have long enabled citizens to take up legal action against dischargers because they include both state-allowable discharge levels and periodic reporting of actual levels. Because no such record was available for air emissions, similar legal action was precluded in that quarter. The CAA of 1990 now opens up this possibility.[80] The response of the regulated industry to the permit program, including its attempt on the Senate floor to modify citizen enforcement provisions, makes clear that anticipated citizen suits are a major source of its opposition.

ENFORCEMENT

The 1990 amendments add, as one authority from the regulated community noted, "a full panoply of tough new enforcement authorities" including both civil and criminal sanctions which brings the air program into line with other major environmental statutes. Administrative penalties of up to $25,000 per day can be issued by the EPA without securing approval from the Department of Justice or initiating court proceedings; field citations for minor violations can be imposed by investigating officials up to $5,000 a day for each violation; administrative compliance orders can be issued where compliance can be achieved within a year, greatly extending the reach from the "within one month" provision of the previous act. Added to these civil penalties are new criminal penalties; the amendments convert the knowing violation of almost every requirement into a felony.[81]

EMISSIONS TRADING

In some quarters the "marketable permits" section of the CAA was emphasized as a major, even revolutionary innovation in implementation strategies. Frequently described as a "market force," it was touted as an alternative to the customary regulatory system and far less costly.[82] Yet the enormous attractiveness of "marketable permits" as a theory obscured its dubious role as an implementation strategy.

In the larger dimensions of the acid rain section of the law, the emissions trading system played a secondary role, exclusively as an implementing device. The major objectives, reduction in total emissions to 8.9 million tons per year and the cap on those emissions were legislative decisions alone; moreover the allocation of allowances to states and sources was a matter of political bargaining among legislators. The basic scheme, therefore, was dominated by a traditional regulatory style in which "market forces" played no role at all.

Emissions training was not so much a "market force" as a strategy to enhance managerial choice. It provided the firm with a subsidy in the form of a property right that could be bought and sold and its value to the firm was as an "economic commodity."[83] The "emissions credit" system, therefore, took its place among the panoply of traditional subsidies to production enterprise such as railroad land grants, farm price supports, low-interest loans for pollution control equipment, or tax abatements to new industry.

For utility managers the emissions trading system provided a new option among a variety of long-existing options: coal washing, low-sulfur coal, and stack-gas scrubbers. In the 1977 act, use of low-sulfur coal on new power plants was restricted by requiring that it undergo scrubbing. This requirement was now dropped and the option of "marketable permits" was added. Yet for the utility manager the marketable permit might well not enter into the firm's calculations as the theorists had presumed. It all depended upon whether or not this alternative was attractive as a new option.[84]

It seems more than likely that the market for emission credits will diminish in the face of greater scrubber efficiency and lower costs and the rising price of emission credits amid their fixed supply and increasing demand for them.[85] The main result of the program may well be to reinforce the traditional role of the regulatory system to build markets for pollution control and pollution reduction technologies.[86]

State Initiatives and Preemption

In the past three decades the states have increasingly taken initiative in environmental affairs, much to the consternation of the regulated industries, and as a consequence the issue of preemption—whether or not federal law and regulations preempt state authority—has grown. During debate on the CAA, a number of such issues emerged.

In the Act of 1970, California, alone among the states, obtained the right to establish standards stricter than the federal for mobile sources. Amendments in the 1977 CAA made it possible for other states to opt into the California program and require a "California car" and in the intervening years the eight northeastern states had taken steps to do so. It was their actions, in fact, that forced the issue on the new Phase I auto standards in the 1990 act. But there was more yet to come, such as California's "clean car," and other states looked to California for leadership.

During the debate on the CAA this issue was revisited.[87] Could a state, even if it opted for the California car, develop its own mobile source enforcement strategy, for example, require its own system of auto recall for defective emission control equipment? Would this require a "third car"? This possibility deeply troubled the automobile industry and their champion in the Congress, Rep. John Dingell, wished to require EPA supervision to make it nationally uniform. In a compromise, states were allowed to enforce the provision but they were required to rely on designated accredited test labs. The issue clearly was not fully resolved. Shortly after passage of the 1990 Act, New York instituted a California program and was immediately sued by the automobile industry for requiring a "third car." It would remain for the courts to define more precisely where the federal-state line would be drawn in this issue.

Another CAA provision established a national standard that preempted the states and led to the first breach in California's freedom to establish its own air quality standards. The subject was off-road engines, such as tractors and construction equipment; they contributed up to 15 percent of California's inventory of ozone-causing emissions, and the California Air Resources Board was developing nine rules to control them.[88]

In making political trade-offs with Rep. Dingell on passenger vehicle tailpipe emission standards Rep. Waxman agreed that the control of off-road vehicle emissions would be by EPA regulation alone. Waxman apparently did not know the significance of the issue to California and he was immediately taken to task for it by California Republicans, including Senator Pete Wilson, then running for governor. But the deal was made and since the entire House proceeding tended to be a matter of firm agreements firmly held to by Waxman and Dingell it stuck.

The debate over federal preemption with respect to fuel volatility turned out to the advantage of the states. Fuel volatility was an important factor in creating ozone-forming hydrocarbon precursors.[89] In this case EPA had promulgated a standard of 10.5 pounds per square inch (psi), Reid Vapor Pressure. But the northeastern states opted for a 9.0 psi standard. Their right to do so was uncertain until EPA, over the objections of the petroleum industry, upheld a Massachusetts standard of 9.0 psi level. Massachusetts estimated that this action would reduce its VOCs for the year by 9,000 tons. Early in 1990 EPA announced that it was gearing up for a revision of its gasoline volatility regulation to go into effect in the summer of 1992 and that it would be a 9.0 RVP standard.

During debate over the CAA in 1990 the paint industry, under the leadership of the National Paint and Coatings Association, proposed that national regulations be adopted to reduce ozone-forming emissions from paints with federal preemption of state standards.[90] The industry faced a familiar context: a variety of differing state regulations pertaining to emission limits, labeling, and distribution requirements, and it preferred to deal with one federal regulatory agency rather than fifty state ones. At the same time, arguing that some state regulations were too strict, by shifting to the national level it hoped to develop lower standards.

The industry secured EPA backing and asked the administration to make its proposal a part of the conference proceedings. It aroused strong opposition from the states where a "control technique guideline" rather than a preemptive federal standard was favored. State officials were more than surprised that EPA endorsed the proposal without consulting them, arguing that many products already met the proposed standards and hence the plan would not force technology as much as it should. The paint proposal did not become a part of the CAA.

Regulation of CFCs also became involved in preemption issues when EPA floated a CFC recycling plan that some feared might preempt tougher local laws.[91] The industry group, The Alliance for Responsible CFC Policy, petitioned EPA to make uniform its federal standards for CFC conservation and recycling but state, local, and environmental groups argued that states should have the right to establish stricter standards, to "move ahead" where EPA "lagged behind." The Act provided a limited two-year preemption for the design of appliances only but not for servicing products.

In the 1977 Clean Air Act states and localities had been given the authority to establish their own air quality standards for radionuclides and several communities had done so. But now the atomic industry sought to overcome this local authority with federal preemption and Senator Alan Simpson of Wyoming was its champion.[92] Several Senators, however, defended local autonomy, among them Senator John Heinz of Pennsylvania and Senator John Glenn of Ohio among whose constituents were communities faced with atomic facilities which they sought to restrict. Through a floor vote on a CAA amendment they were able to derail the attempt to establish federal preemption.

The 1990 CAA established new source performance standards to control air emissions from solid waste incinerators burning municipal, hospital and medical, and other commercial and industrial waste. The standards are similar to Maximum Available Control Technology (MACT) standards for toxic air emissions generally and EPA must issue residual risk standards for incineration units if required under the residual risk provisions pertaining to toxic emissions generally. States were given the authority to adopt more stringent requirements.[93]

Several features of the CAA involving federal-state relations went beyond matters of preemption to deference to state and regional leadership in which federal action would follow state initiatives stronger than federal regulations.

This was the case in the clean fuels program which included requirements for fleet standards, such as taxis and delivery vans, to be introduced in 25 ozone or carbon monoxide non-attainment areas. These must meet California standards for low-emission vehicles starting in 1998, if such vehicles are available in California. If California establishes state standards for a vehicle category that are in the aggregate more stringent than the federal clean-fuel vehicle standards, the California standards will become the federal standards for that vehicle.[94]

New provisions for regional ozone transport commissions provide for co-operative state initiatives. These commissions are to develop regulations that span several states. These are intended to create more consistency between adjacent states but in addition have the authority to establish tighter standards for air quality programs than the federal. The EPA administrator can reject the proposed regulations but if so he must propose an equally effective strategy. Once established by the commission the reduction goal cannot be changed either by the commission or by the EPA.[95]

Postponing New Standards and Objectives

In earlier years emerging values and knowledge combined to shape new clean air policy directions, for example, the Prevention of Significant Deterioration and visibility provisions of the CAA of 1977.[96] But the CAA of 1990 did not play a similar role. New objectives and new knowledge were in play but their implications for legislative policy were postponed to a later day. To consider them in this round of debate, so Congress and most of the clean air political actors apparently felt, would jeopardize the more important task of improving implementation of established objectives.

The range of further possibilities were outlined rather fully in a report issued by the Science Advisory Board of the EPA in the summer of 1990 through its committee on Relative Risk Reduction.[97] While the avowed purpose of that committee was to formulate a common context to consider all environmental "risk" to subject it to relative risk analysis, the more striking aspect of the venture was the range of environmental conditions that it sought to encompass: mortality and morbidity in human health and ecological and welfare effects in the broader environment. These objectives and their related science could well have defined new public policy thrusts.[98]

The 1977 Act requires that National Ambient Air Quality Standards (NAAQS) be reissued every five years. Yet few revisions had occurred. The ozone standard was last set in 1979 and the sulfur dioxide standard in 1971. The CAA of 1990 was silent on this question. Morton Lippman, chair of the EPA Clean Air Scientific Advisory Committee from 1983 to 1987, wrote, "I have long been concerned about the ability of successive EPA Administrators to ignore the Act's clear mandate for timely promulgation of the NAAQS, and am disturbed by the lack of any provision to correct this in the new Act Amendments."[99] While Congress insisted on new prescriptive legislation to establish mandatory technologies because it was dissatisfied with EPA's past performance, it did not take up similar action with respect to standards.[100]

One of Lippman's primary concerns was the adverse effects of ozone on the pulmonary development of young children. He has done research on that issue, was a champion of a growing body of opinion that the relaxation of the ozone standard from .08 to .12 ppm in 1979 was a mistake, and urged that the standard be restored to the earlier level.[101] The Clean Air Scientific Advisory Committee has been somewhat divided on the question and EPA announced that it would take no action until the scientific community was in greater agreement; the result was stalemate.[102] California, exercising its conventional leading sector role in air quality matters moved ahead toward the .08 standard.[103]

Studies linking particulates lower than the federal standard with early mortality were also leading to demands for revision of that standard. The current. PM_{10} standard (particulates of 10 microns or less) was 150 $\mu g/m^3$ over a 24-hour activity period. But mortality effects were measured at 50 $\mu g/m^3$. The PM_{10} standard was set in 1987 but in the latter part of 1990 as the CAA was coming to a close, some in EPA were advocating a revision.

In deciding to use technology standards as the main approach to airborne toxics Congress also decided to postpone the analysis of health effects to a later round of action after the technology standards had been applied and to leave that analysis up to EPA. At the same time the National Academy of Sciences was given the task of making another study of risk analysis as an acceptable method of determining those residual health effects. The strategy only postponed the intense debate over the health effects of toxic chemicals, the use of risk analysis, and the acceptable level of risk.

Congress was equally reluctant to pursue frontier arenas of ecological effects. The acid rain issue featured the environmental effects of sulfates, a problem identified first in the early 1970s and ratified, as it were, by the massive National Atmospheric Pollution Assessment Program. But the emerging focus of atmospheric deposition lay not so much with sulfates as with nitrates.[104]

New scientific work was taking the "acid rain" issue in that direction, calling for a focus on nitrogen dioxide emissions from stationary sources. Throughout the debate on the Act, however, this issue hardly surfaced. The environmental community called for at least a 4-million-ton reduction in nitrogen dioxide emissions, but made little headway and the Act provided for reduction of only 2 million tons.

Equally set aside was the long-distance transport and fate of toxic chemicals. The entire issue of airborne toxics seemed to be thought of exclusively in terms of their effects on the communities surrounding emission sources and the risk to the "maximum exposed person" in those communities.[105] But research into long-distance transport of air pollutants had extended knowledge beyond sulfates and nitrates to toxic chemicals as well. The data had been most fully developed for the Great Lakes and a program to control toxic deposition there had become a part of the proposed CAA. But the conference committee replaced a regulatory program with "further study."[106]

This shift from the immediate vicinity of the source to the diffusion of toxic chemicals into the global environment entailed major implications for policy objectives. This included the measurement of toxic levels and their effects on plants and animals as indicators of potential human effects, as well as their in-cidence in air, water, and soil. Congress chose not to carve out new frontiers of environmental policy but to implement old frontiers more effectively.[107]

BACKSLIDING: ROCKY MOUNTAIN WEST

In one region of the country, the Rocky Mountain West, the CAA predictably would lead to environmental deterioration rather than improvement. The background for such a policy was the political influence of a bloc of ten Re-publican Senators from that region, interested primarily in the acid rain title of the Act.

One of the main objectives of this group was to abolish the "percentage re-duction" scheme of the 1977 Act that required all low-sulfur coal used in new power plants to be partially scrubbed. This protection for eastern higher sul-fur coal was galling to the western senators and they were especially gratified that the bill explicitly repealed it. But for this they paid a price; the repeal was combined with the cap and the CAA explicitly provided that the repeal would stand only so long as the cap stood.[108] Only Senator Symms of Idaho refused to remain silent about the implications of that trade; he publicly denounced the cap as setting a lid on coal production both in the west and elsewhere.[109]

It was widely acknowledged that the CAA as approved would increase sul-fur dioxide pollution levels in the Mountain States by at least 25 percent. Thus, while the East would enjoy a marked improvement in acidification and visibility the Mountain West could look forward to the opposite.[110]

Two issues bore on this question: the prevention of significant deteriora-tion (PSD) and visibility impairment. These involved two different features of the 1977 law that Mountain States lawmakers had bitterly resisted then and still did. Their intransigence on both issues made clear that the CAA would have a rocky road ahead if it did not satisfy their demands.

In February 1990 the General Accounting Office reported that sources near national parks were, for all practical purposes, exempt from regulation and thereby caused as much as 90 percent of pollution related to visibility impair-ment to go uncontrolled. Representative Mike Synar of Oklahoma sought to take up the issue, but the effort gathered no steam.[111]

Visiblity protection obtained some support because it was a case in which the EPA had failed in thirteen years to produce regulations mandated in two years by Congress in 1977 to reduce "regional haze." Representative Wyden of

Oregon sought to take up this lack of agency action through a more precise amendment in the CAA. A watered-down version of his original regulatory proposal passed the House, but the Senate rejected a similar attempt by Senator Brock Williams of Washington and reduced it to a research-only program.[112]

Even before it came to the floor of the House the northern Rocky Mountain Senators made clear that if it proceeded to conference Senator Garn would filibuster the bill and that Senators Simpson, Symms, McClure, and Hatch would join in.[113] Garn's filibuster of the Clean Air Act in 1976 on the same issues of PSD and visibility had prevented action in that year. The Conference dropped the House visibility proposal. It was left for Wyden to make clear on the House floor during final action on the conference report that EPA still faced the mandate of 1977 to develop regulations to control "regional haze," that its obligations under that law were not repealed or lessened by the conference bill, and that "I encourage EPA to implement that law fully as soon as possible."[114]

The Rocky Mountain West also flexed its muscles on the control of radionuclides, an issue that had been active for two decades and of great importance to active uranium mining areas in the West as well as to western communities plagued with uranium mine tailings.[115] Senator Simpson once again took up the issue. The EPA and the Nuclear Regulatory Commission had long been at odds over the allowable level of human exposure to radionuclides from sources such as nuclear power plants, nuclear facilities, and uranium mine tailings. Currently the EPA would set an exposure dose limit of 10 millirem/year to the person living nearest a facility licensed by NRC while NRC would limit it to 100 millirem.

The setting for the dispute goes back to 1970 when President Nixon transferred authority to establish exposure limits from the old Atomic Energy Commission to the newly established EPA in order to resolve a contentious dispute: should the agency that promoted nuclear energy also regulate its health effects? But the transfer did not end the problem; the AEC and its successor NRC have long opposed EPA's standards and the issue has been perennially in the courts. The issue remains one of the acceptable levels of exposure and disagreement over the interpretation of health effects data.

In order to break the log jam in a direction favorable to the industry Simpson succeeded in including in the CAA a provision that put the burden on EPA by allowing it not to regulate rationuclides if the agency found NRC's regulations sufficient to protect public health. After the 1990 amendments were adopted Simpson took this discretionary statutory language as grounds for insisting that EPA rescind its regulations for certain radioactive air emissions, arguing that EPA regulations for NRC licensees and uranium mill tailing facilities are "neither necessary nor appropriate" and that EPA's regulations would not achieve "any additional health benefit."

In both these provisions of the 1990 CAA, policy underwent not slower advances both actual backsliding. In both the key factor was the opposition of Republican senators from the Rocky Mountain West who constituted a major bloc in the Republican contingent in Congress and hence exercised significant leverage on Senate action.

Steps Along the Historical Way

The CAA of 1990 did not carve out new objectives but sought to implement old ones more effectively. The Congress was unhappy with the EPA; the EPA wanted to strengthen implementation; the public was unhappy about past results. From all quarters came a host of ideas about better implementation; the CAA came in response.

Technology standards and a permit system long central in water pollution control, now were applied to air. These features of a regulatory program had, on the whole, worked well.

The marketable permit program in the acid rain section of the law was a relatively minor part of the CAA. During debate over the CAA it was more a matter of theory than of practice, so fuzzy in its implications that Congress hemmed it in with statutory mandates. The "hidden hand" of the market played a small role amid the "overt hand" of legislative bargaining. And it remained to be seen how the "hidden hand" portion of the strategy would work.

Amid this overwhelming emphasis on strategies and techniques of implementation evolving environmental objectives were set aside for another place and time. A few of these merited a research rather than an action agenda. But Congress did not want to work into the act the implications of emerging scientific knowledge about the health effects of particulates and ozone, the environmental effect of ozone on forests and vegetation, or the environmental dispersion and incidence of toxic chemicals.

The debate over the CAA was also a case study in the role of science and economic analysis in environmental affairs. Both are essential to give debate legitimacy; one side can render the other politically helpless just by demonstrating weakness in either set of knowledge. But there is much more to the role of each than simply to sustain the arguments of advocates. A $500 million acid rain research program led not to solutions but more intense arguments shaped by the complexities of knowledge. This, in turn, raised two questions: will not more research simply lead to more complexity and more debate; and is the cost of the research worth it? Hence the science played a background role in the debate rather than provided applicable knowledge as a basis for action or served to resolve disagreement.

In debate on the CAA the economists were equally upstaged, unable to specify environmental benefits they continued to dismiss as "minor." In the 1989–90 CAA debate, therefore, benefits entered policy not by precise assessment but by general public support for a higher level of achievement. Those opposed to further environmental improvement continued to minimize benefits in their cost/benefit equations and maintain that they were "inconsequential." But public debate led to the conclusion that they were sufficiently important and consequential that they merited further action.

Every environmental issue provides a building block in the ongoing relationships among governing bodies. They tease out the ingredients of the "living constitution," the relationships of authority and power among the institutions of government.

Two of these we have emphasized. The first is the relationship between Congress and the Executive Branch. The customary political role of environmental administration is to exercise restraint in environmental affairs and to move slowly along the lines of "strict construction" of statutory authority. Hence the CAA is an expression of impatience with the EPA and an attempt to restrain that discretion.

Equally significant in the CAA was the relationship between federal and state authority. Environmental issues have a way of multiplying issues of federal preemption. States have taken considerable lead in such matters and both industry and the Executive Office of the President finds this to be pernicious. The CAA of 1990 constituted a small but still significant step in this constitutional development.

The debate over the CAA of 1990 is over and we are well into the implementation phase. This new round of action already reinforces the now-conventional wisdom that politics really begins after a law is passed.[116]

One might follow this phase with several questions: Will compliance levels and dates be sufficiently clear and tight so as to create effective markets for new pollution control technologies? Will emission permits be effective in reducing pollution? Can sulfur dioxide emissions be monitored with sufficient precision to make trading as "economic commodities" effective? Can cities really meet the ozone objectives or will these provisions go the way of earlier efforts? Can toxic emission data reliably indicate progress in toxics reduction, or will it become a political football in the argument over how much improvement has occurred?

Equally important, the very complexity of implementation shifts the context of political choice from a Congress that has some responsiveness to general public attitudes to an EPA more divorced from the public and more responsive to immediate pressures from the White House and the regulated industry. As the Clean Air program becomes more complex the regulated industry can bring to bear the weight of its superior knowledge of the complexities of production and reduce the influence of both Congress and citizen environmental organizations.

As the CAA of 1990 is being implemented amid the drama of administrative politics the issues postponed by the CAA of 1990 will continue to evolve: the long-distance transport of pollutants beyond sulfur oxides to nitrates and ozone; the way in which gains in mobile source emissions will continue to be offset with increases in passenger miles as was the case between 1970 and 1990; and the pervasive infusion of toxic chemicals throughout the globe to build an ever-growing level of toxic "background" in both humans and their environment.

The CAA of 1990 is a milestone in environmental history. But there is much more to come.

EMISSIONS

TRADING

MYTHOLOGY

PUBLIC DEBATE OVER environmental affairs has its share of mythologizing, but perhaps none is more striking than that about emissions trading under the acid rain provision of the Clean Air Act Amendments of 1990. Discussion surrounding that provision has been remarkable for its panoply of symbols and slogans, so much so that little of the reality of emissions trading—its importance, usefulness, and effect—has got through the fog.

Emissions trading is a relatively minor provision of the act. It pales into insignificance in the face of the massive, overriding decision to reduce sulfur dioxide emissions from utilities by 50 percent, to 8.95 million tons per year, and to cap it at that figure. While "emissions trading" and the "market forces" it was to unleash got the headlines, the reduction and the cap were the real news. Emissions trading is only a secondary feature, a means to the end, and only one of a variety of means at that. It is worth pointing out, moreover, that both the reduction and the cap are in no sense a product of "market forces," but, in fact, reflect market failure. They were established not by the market but by legislative decision. The implication? The market cannot establish

Originally published in *Environmental Forum* (January/February 1995): 15–20.

standards as goals, but might be useful, once goals are established, to help reach the goal. To establish firm emissions standards or limits, legislation is the wave of the past, present, and future.

Another important change in the 1990 amendments, as reflected in both the reduction and the cap, is a major shift in how standards are measured—from concentrations to quantities. Heretofore air quality standards were set in terms of parts per million or micrograms per cubic meter. But increases in production, even with progressively lower emission concentrations, led to increased quantitative emissions. The automobile is a dramatic case in point: significant reductions in emissions per mile led to no significant total reductions because of the rapid increase in miles traveled. This shift from concentrations to quantities in the 1990 act seems to be so obvious that few have even mentioned it in the face of all the talk about emissions trading.

Some careful observers will remember that when the Senate first mentioned quantitative limits for sulfur dioxide emissions in the early 1980s, EPA Administrator Anne Gorsuch waxed eloquent about the proposal as "revolutionary." She was right. They have been adopted for CFCs, lead in gasoline, and now sulfur dioxide. Without quantitative limits, emissions trading is relatively meaningless. Many of the trading schemes now being considered recognize that total emissions limits are an integral element of any successful scheme. But many blithely assume that trading without a cap makes sense when in fact a cap is essential to the trading system. We should be up front with this feature of the program and be explicit that quantitative reduction in limits is the first requirement of any future air pollution control program.

But go a bit deeper. Behind the quantitative limits in the sulfur dioxide emissions program is something far more fundamental and almost totally obscured in American clean air policy: standards measured in terms of critical loads. Critical loads are calculations of how much deposition an ecosystem can stand without long-run damage. Curious that amid the mythology of emissions trading I have not seen one treatment of just why a 50-percent reduction figure. Why not 40 or 60? In fact, the figure came from the early stages in the application of the concept of critical load to aquatic ecosystem protection. The concept, first applied in the joint Canadian-U.S. scientific commission that President Carter established to determine just how much reduction was needed, seems to have originated with University of Minnesota ecologist Eville Gorham. When Ronald Reagan became president, the commission was abolished and its functions transferred to the Office of the President. But the 50-percent figure stuck and was carried over into the Senate bill and then retained in the provisions enacted in 1990.

More interesting, however, U.S. policy makers forgot and abandoned the concept of critical load, and hence the ensuing debate included no rationale for the 50-percent reduction figure. The Canadians, on the other hand, began to discuss critical loads with Europeans and through the Economic Commission for Europe. The ECE carried out scientific consultations and research over the years to work out the scientific basis for critical loads for both sulfur and nitrogen, research that is now shaping their standards for these two pollutants. All this, however, almost passed the United States by.

One American who participated in the European discussions tried to bring the critical load concept back to the United States, in a 1989 conference in Washington, but failed to make much of a dent. There is a provision in the Clean Air Act that the National Acid Precipitation Assessment Program must develop this same strategy by determining the deposition reductions needed to prevent adverse ecological effects and examining deposition standards to "protect sensitive and critically sensitive aquatic and terrestrial resources in the United States and Canada." NAPAP acknowledges its responsibilities along this line, but progress seems limited, and it appears that it will be many years before the United States catches up with Europe. Hence observers do not seem prepared for the day when the scientific basis for critical loads worked out in Europe makes its dent on American thinking to call for marked quantitative reductions in nitrogen emissions and further reductions in sulfur emissions. If measured in terms of effects on the order of the European calculations of the benchmarks of critical loads, 8.9 million tons in sulfur emissions will not be enough.

So we go from reductions and caps to quantitative rather than concentration standards to critical loads. These are the crucial elements of the acid rain provisions of the Clean Air Act. In the face of these factors, emission trading pales into insignificance and the fact that emissions trading has taken much of the spotlight has only obscured what the act really is all about.

Then there are allowances. Most treatments of the act go from the 50-percent reduction to the allowances without much pause even to consider how the allowances got there or what they mean. The systems of allowances and their allocation seems to be so logical and orderly that one only has to mention it and then pass on to a description of how it is supposed to work. But just what are the allowances all about?

The allowances do not merely represent how large the allocated emissions will be for each source. More important to the utility, they are a piece of paper that can be bought and sold. They are worth money. They represent a gift to the utilities to which they are allocated, and in that sense they are a subsidy.

True, they are not an outright contribution from the government to the utility. But they are an act of creating property out of whole cloth—out of the emission reduction—and while they do not represent a cost to government, they represent income to the utility. This is a rather remarkable event in the history of property. The federal government waves a wand and creates a piece of property and gives it to the utility. The utility then can sell the property and earn income, and soon the emission allowance is bought and sold in the market—or at least that is the theory.

Now it could be argued that the allowance is not an integral part of the emission control system—after all Congress could simply have mandated that reductions be achieved utility by utility in the same degree as the allowances were allocated. But it was crucial in the way in which Congress got acceptance from the utilities of the entire emissions reduction system. It was, of course, a brilliant move, since without it the crucial part of the system—the 50-percent reduction—would more than likely have met such fierce resistance that it would not even have been ventured. And certainly President Bush would not have advocated it. So what the allowance system turned out to be was an old fashioned subsidy program, very much like one might foster in emission controls by providing low-interest loans to industries. One thinks back to the nineteenth century, when the Congress stimulated railroad construction by land grants. In this case Congress gave real property as a subsidy but it was almost as painless as giving away the right to emit.

There is more monetary implication to the allowances than merely the ability of the utility to sell them and to earn income. The recent flap with the Internal Revenue Service over taxation of allowance income underlines the central fact of allowances as property. When the allowance is issued, so the IRS argues, it has zero tax value, and hence the sale represents a 100-percent capital gain. Of course the utilities say that this is unfair, but one might also argue that among all the participants in the debate the IRS is uniquely able to call a capital gain a capital gain.

There is also the issue of what the utility does with the income that it earns; does it go to stockholders as increased earnings, or does it go to consumers as lower rates? The issue came up with the very first trade announced, between the Wisconsin Power and Light Company on the one hand and Duquesne Light Company and the Tennessee Valley Authority on the other. In this case Wisconsin Power had been required to reduce its emissions by a 1986 state law and obtained a rate increase to cover the cost. All this was quite independent of the requirements of the federal act. But in the rush to apply the program Wisconsin Power was given "allowances" for the emissions reduction it had already carried out under the Wisconsin law. So when the trade was completed there was an even more tense argument over whether or not the stockholders or the customers should get the benefit. After all, the customers had already paid once; should they not then get the benefit of the proceeds from the sale? The Wisconsin Public Service Commission resolved the issue by passing the benefit of the income on to consumers in its rate making calculations.

No need to go into more ramifications of the fact that to the utilities the allowances are primarily income that sweetened their reluctant acceptance of the sulfur dioxide emission reduction. Clearly the state public utility commissions are deeply involved in these implications, and there is much likelihood that EPA, in exercising some supervision, not yet clear just how much, will become somewhat of a market regulating agency as well. And, as the Long Island Lighting Company effort to keep secret its 1993 trade with Amax Coal Industries makes clear, one unanticipated issue is whether or not the facts of trades are to be publicized. When buying and selling become the heart of the trading system, so also does the debate over openness or secrecy intensify.

How were the allowances allocated? That needs also to be examined in the glare of the real world. During the debate on the 1990 act, when the Senate became convinced by some of its bolder leaders that it could not just continue to add allowance to allowance, but had to stay within the cap, an intense round of horse trading started. The horse trading had little to do with the geographic location of the effects that the emissions might cause, but more the geographical location of senators who were speaking for their utilities. That was when we first heard of "clean states" and "dirty states."

But wait, there were some effects implied by all of this, and soon they raised their ugly heads. Defenders of the Adirondacks pointed out, and a court case resulted, that emissions trading might well lead to sources upwind from the Adirondacks buying emissions rights rather than reducing emissions, thereby producing adverse effects on the forests and waters in upstate New York. This type of issue has arisen in other cases and will continue to arise, primarily because the United States abandoned the critical load concept and went simply for a nationwide 50-percent reduction. As the critical load concept developed further in Europe, it came to be applied with considerable geographical selectivity. Some soils were more vulnerable than others; some ecosystems were more sensitive than others. Hence in Europe a close connection arose between the specifics of the ecosystem to be protected and the amount of deposition to be allowed. No such connection between causes and effects came about in the United States, yet allocations of the right to emit clearly could result not from senatorial infighting but from environmental effects.

In the recent settlement of the lawsuit brought by the Adirondack Council in New York, which argued that the allowance system endangered New York lakes, the EPA recognized this "environmental effects" problem. It agreed to examine studies of New York lakes to determine if the pollution reduction that will result from the program is sufficient for the lakes to recover. While recovery from harm is not the same as determining harm in the form of a critical load, it at least moves lightly in that direction.

It seems agreed on all sides that a successful trading system depends on accurate monitoring. After all, what is the point of trading unless one knows precisely what is being traded? This is one aspect of the market which could well discipline trading and make it work. As long as trades were within firms in the form of netting or between sources balanced through administrative choices rather than the price-and-market system, they could be fuzzed over. It was relatively easy to say that so much presumed fugitive emissions was equal to so much point source emissions. But it seems rather unlikely that buyers and sellers with a stake in the market would want their property to be described in so hazy a manner. After all, who would want to buy a piece of land if the survey described the property in such loose terms?

No wonder, therefore, that as the trading system was set in motion, it focused on a system to monitor emissions continually rather than sporadically. This procedure, called continuous emissions monitoring, or CEM, is considered to be the most crucial technical feature of the trading system. And no wonder that it was highly contentious. It was found that CEM is not as precise as had been anticipated during the legislative debate, and that the lack of data requires extrapolations that have led to disputes. Accounts of the emissions trading program and the futures market that developed around it have not always been forthright and up-front about the crucial role of CEM.

Advances in the technology of continuous emissions monitoring, in fact, are the major innovations in this whole system that can be attributed distinctively to "market forces." The situation is well laid out by Robert W. McIlvaine of the McIlvaine Company of Northbrook, Illinois, who keeps track of the technology and manufacturing results of the act and whose reports in the authoritative journal *Air and Waste* are worth keeping an eye on. McIlvaine points out that since imprecise emission measurements now mean dollars to utilities who buy and sell allowances, those utilities want CEM equipment that is precise. Measurement variations of 5 percent or more might be acceptable in a regulatory system, but in a market system they are not. Hence the trading system has prompted utilities to demand higher levels of monitoring precision from the manufacturers, and that market force in turn is enabling American manufacturers of monitoring equipment to forge ahead of their competitors abroad.

One could take some simple lessons on this score from the history of commodities futures trading. In his recent book *Nature's Metropolis,* William Cronon traces the development of the market for grain, beef, and lumber in Chicago, and works out in intricate detail the way in which precise quantitative measurements of all three were essential before a successful market could develop. He is especially instructive as to the way in which firm predictability was essential for futures trading. Trading in emission credits is no exception. And it seems safe to say that any emission trading system will stand or fall on the ability to know precisely what is being traded.

So while old-fashioned regulation sets the tone of the whole system, the perfection of CEM equipment is the most currently observable result from these "market forces."

The demonizing of command and control is an integral part of the emissions trading mythology. For the advocates of market forces had to have something undesirable against which to pit their something desirable. In the sulfur dioxide program, command and control usually means that in the dark ages before the 1990 act, the regulatory agencies gave the utilities no choices; they had to accept the method of control dictated by EPA. But take another look. From the beginning of federal and state programs to control utility sulfur emissions, three choices were open to the power companies: fuel switching to low sulfur coal, coal washing, and scrubbers. This was the case with the federal program for new sources and also for some states, such as Pennsylvania, where the sulfur-in-coal standards were applied to old power plants as well. The agencies made clear that they were determining the standard and its sulfur-in-coal counterparts, not the method used to reach the standard. The utilities could make a choice.

The three choices were quite alive and continued to be so until the 1977 amendments, in which the percentage reduction clause required that utilities could not use low sulfur coal by itself, but were required to reduce the sulfur-in-coal content of that coal as well. It was this mandatory requirement that served as the backdrop to define command and control in the 1977 Clean Air Act, and it was this one requirement that led the western senators to drive hard for allowances and the trading system in 1990, since they were convinced that it would put western low-sulfur coal back into demand. Emission allowances did add a choice in the new package of options, but it was merely a fourth to the three that had always existed.

Command and control, of course, is not a precise term at all, but simply a generalized term that the market economists use to shorthand their general theories for public consumption. The most unusual part of the entire exercise is the fact that within the umbrella of this market force strategy that supposedly replaces command and control, the regulatory system for the clean air program has been sharpened into an even tighter system of regulation. That system has two elements, one the absolute limit on emissions and the other the automatic tax for excess emissions.

That tax is rarely mentioned. How will the sulfur emissions reduction scheme be enforced once it is in place? Answer: a pollution tax. Excess emissions simply will be subject to a tax of $2,000 for each ton over the allowance. No civil fine disputed in the courts but an automatic tax. And, in addition, the next year the offending source must reduce its emissions by the same amount as the excess it enjoyed in the present year. Looks like a good, healthy dose of command and control.

The mythology of emissions trading has obscured much of the real world of the acid rain provision of the Clean Air Act: reductions in total amount, the cap, the critical load, the allowance allocations, the cause-effect relationships in deposition, the distribution of income by utilities, the secrecy in trades, all of which involve the need to think realistically about the program. Beyond all this, however, it is the increasingly stark realization that the enthusiasm for the program as myth will prevent us from ever evaluating whether or not the program really works.

As Michael Boskin, then head of the Council of Economic Advisers, is reported to have remarked soon after the act was passed, "Thus far it's been theory; now we will see if it works." Fair enough. But the problem clearly has been that the commitment to the theory, and the mythology that accompanies it, has been so intense that it is doubtful that we can ever cut through the wishful thinking to examine with any degree of realism just how, and how well, the program works.

Over the last two and a half years, we have been subject to a series of events that more than suggests that the program doesn't have the zip that it was supposed to. Expectations have been scaled back again and again. The purchase prices of the allowances have continued to decline steadily, for instance, from the $1,600 anticipated during the congressional debate on the 1990 amendments (EPA still can sell allowances for $1,600 but there have been no takers) to the $131 paid by Carolina Power and Light, the largest purchaser of the allowances at the first EPA auction at the Chicago Board of Trade, in 1993. The very weak demand for allowances was more than underscored by the fact that when the private utilities offered allowances at the 1993 auction, only 10 were purchased. We have been assured almost monthly that the trading system will soon take off. First we were told to wait until EPA had the system set up; then until the 1993 auction; and now we are told that we must wait until EPA has completed the tracking system. Mary Nichols, head of EPA's Air Office, reported recently to Congress that the system is still not in operation. Some are beginning to shift from "just wait" to assigning blame for failure, such as the slow pace of state public utility commissions to rule on rate making implications of the trades or the provisions of the 1990 act that encourage states to protect their high sulfur coal industry. An article in *Clean Air Monitor* finally called a spade a spade and referred to the market as "sluggish," and another one in the *Wall Street Journal* trumpeted, "Trading in pollution allowances fizzles."

Almost every analysis of what utilities are expected to do to meet the reductions required by the act makes one skeptical about the assumption that most will do so by purchasing emission allowances. It seems probable that the old standbys—coal washing, fuel switching, and scrubbers—will dominate, and that the presumably large-scale cost savings from using low sulfur coal will not materialize. It seems more than likely that the entire program will establish a framework around which decisions will turn out quite differently than anticipated. In such a case it is vitally important to be able to free one's mind of the clutter of mythology so that one can see the world straight. After its 1994 auction, its second, EPA finally postponed the day of nirvana by announcing that it never expected much trading under Phase I, beginning in 1995; trading will begin seriously only under Phase II, beginning in the year 2000.

The choice of technical applications is worth looking at through the eyes of the technical specializations that are the subjects of choice. There are three of these: economists, biologists-geologists, and engineers. Each of these professions has made a claim to shape the outcome of the debate, with varying degrees of success.

Most of the thinking has been dominated by the economists. They have waxed heavily about the horrors of command and control and the splendid benefits of the market. Much has been written about the vast cost savings that will come if only the emissions trading system were finally applied. Economists have established dominance over how all this is thought about. But in doing so they have obscured much of the real world of the 1990 act. They, of course, would call it theory, general ideas that can be applied in practice. But when that practice from the real world is so contrary to the theory, and seems to rely on simply repeating the theory rather than working with that real world, the statement and restatement of the theory takes on the role of mythology.

Then there are the biologists and geologists, who focus on the effects of acidification. Two streams of evolution in biological and geological science seem to have arisen from the interest in the problem over the past two decades. One in the United States took the form of a detailed examination of "effects" in the National Acid Precipitation Assessment Program that provided little guidance as to critical loads that might demarcate the assimilative capacity of underlying geological and biological circumstances. The other in Europe through the Economic Council for Europe led to an examination of the variations in underlying geology and biology to determine variations in critical loads for both sulfur and nitrogen. In the development of the Clean Air Act in the United States, the economists dominated. Aside from helping to shape the 50-percent reduction, the biologists and geologists have played little role since.

And finally there are the engineers who build the emission control equipment, and might well win out as the utilities position themselves amid the uncertainties of just how the 1990 act will work out. The economics of buying and selling emission credits might well enter into the calculations of utilities in the short run. But an engineering response that would reduce emissions now and for several decades to come seems to involve a firmer, more predictable, and more long-run response. Firm controls are more attractive than chancy market values attached to emission credits influenced by many market uncertainties.

From all this it would seem that the biologists and geologists have far more in common with the engineers than with the economists. The biologists and geologists are looking for real reductions in emissions and the engineers are offering ways to bring them about. The economists offer cost and income choices that bear only an indirect and often fuzzy relationship with the real world of ecological circumstance. Might not one conclude, therefore, that it is the combination of engineer and biologist-geologist that provides the opportunity to cut through the mythology about emissions trading that, after all, was fostered by the economist?

The acid rain program, with its emission reductions and caps, its allowances allocated by political horse trading, and its failure to develop a reasoned program to relate emissions to effects is, of course, complex. More important is the way in which the enthusiasm for the emissions trading system has given rise to a mythology in which there has been more repetition of slogans rather than examination of substantive content.

It would seem especially unwise to extend the emissions trading program to other more grandiose schemes until one has a clear grasp of its basic elements, to understand more fully its substance. There is already much wishful thinking. To veer off into further flights of fancy entails far more risk in the misallocation of energy, resources, and money than does the most ardent command and control system for which it is supposedly a corrective.

The new acid rain program consists of two conventional legislative decisions, one to reduce total emissions and the other to tax those who exceed allowances. They bear little relationship to so-called market forces. This mythology played an important role in obtaining acceptance of the program. But to continue to believe that it reflects the real world of pollution control prevents clear thinking about both the results of emissions trading and its potential wider role.

THE ROLE OF VALUES IN SCIENCE AND POLICY

The Case of Lead

I. INTRODUCTION

The human health effects of lead are a subject of ancient interest and of great contemporary concern. Its science and its public policy have been debated with both light and heat. This chapter will concentrate on both lead science and lead policy in their close relationship as society seeks to define an acceptable level of exposure. That acceptable level involves not just policy choices, but values expressed by scientists, citizens, and policy makers. A closer examination of the lead issue promises greater insight as to the role of values in both science and public policy.[1-4]

II. THE CONTEXT OF VALUE CHOICE

The focus of analysis is the level of lead in humans thought to be acceptable. Different terms have arisen in different fields of specialization to identify such

From *Human Lead Exposure*, ed. Herbert L. Needleman (Boca Raton, Fla.: CRC Press, 1992). Reprinted by permission.

a level—in public health, a threshold; in environmental science, a critical load; in public regulation, a standard. They refer to the goal to be achieved in regulation. Each chemical or metal in question, therefore, becomes the subject of scientific investigation and the results play a significant role in the public policy debate. What to investigate, the research design, and the assessment of results are so intimately bound with policy choices that each, in turn, becomes as controversial as those choices themselves.

These debates clarify scientific research and assessment as far more than a simple process of the discovery and application of truth. Objections to the contemplated policies give rise to challenges to the underlying science, especially if policy requires changes in human behavior—either through the practices of business firms or in the daily lives of individuals. Scientific inquiry as a result becomes controversial at every step because of its continued implications for public policy.[5-6]

Disagreement and debate are also inherent in the scientific enterprise. Scientists differ in their experience and training, their commitment to profession and methodology, and their personal values. As they become involved in research and its implications they choose one side or the other of scientific dispute. The interaction between specialized knowledge and personal values creates commitments which lead to persistent differences, often shaped into personal antagonisms. Scientific choices become policy choices partly because of the values which scientists bring to those choices.

Lead is a convenient case for analysis of this problem for two reasons: (1) it is far simpler than many other pollutants and (2) it has been a focus of public policy debate for so many years that its numerous episodes of dispute provide an opportunity for systematic longitudinal analysis.[7-10]

The debate over the health effects of lead over the past several decades has taken place around a progressive reduction in the acceptable level of lead in blood. Until the 1960s it was thought that the line between the acceptable and unacceptable was 80 µg/dl of blood. These standards had been formulated largely from observation of the effects of lead on able-bodied workers. With time, however, concern shifted to young children, the threshold level went down to 60, then 40, then 30 and finally 25 µg/dl. The declining concentration brought into play new problems, new measurement techniques, new methodological alternatives, new assessments of effect, and new standards of acceptability.

This downward trend in the threshold level for blood lead provides a convenient format from which to analyze the scientific debate. At each point in the debate some scientists argued that the current level provided ample protection and others argued that new knowledge required that the issue be reopened. For the most part scientists who pressed one side of the argument at one blood lead level did so also at the next level. One suspects, therefore, that it is not the data itself that is the controlling factor in the debate, but the values that scientists bring to it.

Throughout these years a major shift began in environmental science and policy from concern about the acute effects of high-level exposures to pollutants to concern about the chronic effects of persistent low-level exposures. While the former are readily observable, the latter are more difficult to detect and require more sensitive measurements. Chronic low-level effects involve much smaller observed differences and give rise to greater controversy. Often the methods of analysis in acute and high-level exposure cases are not appropriate to the investigation of chronic and low-level effects.

Environmental science and policy now face major challenges shaped by this new context of low-level exposures and subtle effects. To the scientist they present opportunities to expand the frontiers of knowledge to new realms of understanding. To the general public the opportunities lie in the expansion of benefits beyond those few acutely affected to the many who have experienced lower levels of harm. To the regulated they present the need to defend themselves against the controls established by public policies. To the policy maker they present the need to find ways to foster effective policy when difficult-to-resolve controversies can well immobilize action.

III. THE CONTEXT OF POLICY CHOICE

The public dispute over the health effects of lead was shaped by selected stages in the lead biogeochemical cycle that became focal points of concern.[11]

One of the first foci in the twentieth century was lead in paint. This came about because of the discovery by Australian physicians of the connection between blood lead levels in children and paint.[12-14] For decades this information lay unused. In the 1960s community groups in poorer sections of cities demanded that action be taken to reduce the threat.[15,16] This led to legislation in the United States in 1971 and 1977 that lowered the level of allowable lead in paint and to proposals to remove old paint from houses.[17,18] The lead-in-paint issue long remained because of the slow pace of removal of leaded paint in housing.[19-20]

By the late 1960s the focal point of policy was shifting to lead in gasoline. Administrative responsibility for action on this issue was in the Environmental Protection Agency (EPA), created in 1970. For 4 years the issue was hotly debated and by 1974 EPA decided to take action to require unleaded gasoline in new cars and to phase down the allowable levels of lead in gasoline over the next decade.[21] That schedule proceeded as planned until action was initiated by the Reagan administration in 1981 to reverse the phasedown schedule and to permit an increase in lead in gasoline. Faced with intense debate over the issue, the agency reversed itself and even accelerated the phasedown.

Lead in the ambient air became another point of debate. After implementing regulations for six pollutants in the ambient air as required by the Clean Air Act of 1970, EPA did not take up others for action. Under court order as a result of litigation brought by the Natural Resources Defense Council, EPA developed an assessment of the health effects of lead—a criteria document—which would serve as a basis for regulation. After considerable debate the agency established an ambient air level of 1.5 $\mu g/m^3$. This survived a court challenge from the lead industry and by the early 1980s the new standard was in process of implementation.[22]

Still a fourth focal point of dispute was the "lead advisory" drawn up by the Centers for Disease Control (CDC) in the U.S. Department of Health and Human Services, intended for circulation to physicians and public health officials. Such a document had no legal standing by itself, but served as medical advice to health specialists as to the blood lead levels at which they should take action. The CDC advisory became authoritative, however, far beyond the audience of clinicians. It was taken as a highly significant scientific judgment by regulatory agencies and the courts. Hence CDC's judgment, and the way it was drawn up, become an issue in the lead debate.[23]

Closely interwoven with official policy making were debates in varied private and public settings. Two reports from the National Academy of Sciences (NAS) were among the most influential. The first, drawn up in 1971, was commissioned by the EPA and the second, issued in 1977, was underwritten by the Department of Housing and Urban Development. The first became a major center of controversy over the balance of views represented by the people selected for the review committee.[24,25]

Equally significant debate took place in scientific meetings or journals. Some of the more revealing involved questions, in one fashion or another, of bias resulting from the sources of funding, of selection of scientists to present papers and provision for rebuttal, and of the balance represented by the conference reports. Debate within scientific journals was lively, as key pieces of research became highly controversial and failure of writers to identify the sources of their funding (especially in the case of research funded by the lead industry) was challenged by opponents.[26-35]

Especially significant was the scientific assessment process carried out by EPA as the basis for establishing standards. This was done informally in preparation for the lead-in-gasoline standard, but much more formally through preparation of a criteria document for the ambient air standard. The criteria document process originated in 1963 when Congress directed the U.S. Public Health Service to draw them up at its discretion. The first attempt, with sulfur oxides prepared initially in March 1967, was criticized heavily by the coal and utility industries. Henceforth the criteria document and the personnel chosen to prepare it became the most important focal point of scientific, and hence political, choice in the regulation of air pollution.[36,37]

Litigation was another forum in which the lead issue was debated. Lawsuits received considerable media publicity in the regions in which they occurred, such as Toronto, Canada, Kellogg, ID, and El Paso, TX. The importance of these trials extended beyond the litigants; they became significant opportunities for the contending parties to marshall their scientific and technical expertise. The same expert witnesses appeared for each side in these cases, rotating from one locality to another and controversy in litigation was closely interwoven with debates in other forums.[38]

These scientific disputes all took place within the context of the appropriate environmental standard. What level of ambient concentration, or emissions, lead in gasoline or paint, should be applied in order to achieve what level of health? The issue of standards, which involved matters of costs to sources of lead in the environment and health levels to those affected, could not be dealt with independently of the personal values and views of the scientists as well as of the decision makers. Ultimately the issue came to be whether or not one placed greater value on industrial production or on improved personal and public health.

The gap between existing knowledge and a desired standard focused on debate over two questions. The first, evolving quite early and continuing through the 1970s, involved the "margin of safety." Acknowledging the fact that emerging knowledge seemed to indicate adverse health effects at lower levels of concentration, should one set the standard at a level lower than the agreed-on scientific knowledge indicated? Health protection required a preventive strategy in which one would err on the side of health benefits rather than economic protection for the emission sources. Specialists on either side of the scientific issues took predictable positions on either side of the issue of the margin of safety.[39-41]

By the late 1970s and early 1980s as newer knowledge emerged, the margin of safety issue often became absorbed into the issue of an "adverse health effect." Those seeking to restrict further regulation of lead often accepted the new knowledge and argued that the health effect it identified was not significant enough to justify regulation of lead at lower levels. Especially important was the issue of whether or not indicators such as minor malformations or changes in blood chemistry in young children had larger health meaning. What one thought about this question was as much a subject of personal values as how one thought about the margin of safety.[42]

IV. HISTORICAL EVOLUTION OF THE DEBATE: 1923 TO 1971

The debate over the environmental effects of lead went through several distinct historical stages, shaped by the state of scientific knowledge, the openness of debate, the relative influence of the lead industry and public health advocates, and the freedom and willingness of government agencies to transfer new scientific knowledge into policy. Over the years the advance of scientific knowledge, and the openness of debate enabled public health advocates to overcome the resistance of the lead industry and some public agencies and thereby permitted other public agencies to take a stronger stance.

The initial debate over lead arose in the 1920s when it appeared that workers in the new factories which produced tetraethyl lead for gasoline suffered from lead poisoning. Several cities, notably New York, passed ordinances that prohibited the use of lead in gasoline. Both the U.S. Bureau of Mines and the U.S. Public Health Service, called upon to assess the health effects of lead, decided that it presented no problem for the public. The city ordinances were declared unconstitutional and lead continued to be used in gasoline.[43,44]

This first flurry of debate outlined the basic viewpoints that were to continue to the present day: industry defended the use of lead as beneficial; the public was concerned about the health effects; industry attempted to secure verdicts from health authorities that lead was not harmful; government agencies with an interest in promoting the use of lead were on one side of the issue and those with an interest in promoting public health were potential advocates of the other.

The issue did not arise again until the 1960s when the industry sought to increase the level of lead in gasoline and approached the U.S. Public Health Service for an opinion about its safety. This led to cooperative action between industry and the service through the Lead Liaison Committee. This committee, with representatives from each side, fostered research concerning the relation between air lead and blood lead concentrations. The research was carried out under the auspices of the Public Health Service, with funding from the industry and under the direction of Lloyd Tepper who was considered friendly to the industry point of view. This "Seven-Cities Study" examined the relationship between lead in the air and blood lead levels in seven U.S. cities. It was conducted under the express provision that the results would not be made public without the permission of the industry.[37]

During these years and up until the late 1960s, research on lead was dominated by the Kettering Laboratory at the University of Cincinnati, directed by Robert Kehoe. Kehoe was also chief medical adviser to the Ethyl Corporation, the primary manufacturer of tetraethyl lead. By the 1960s Kehoe was the nation's leading expert on lead; his ideas constituted the dominant wisdom until challenged in the late 1960s.

Kehoe argued that most lead in the human body came from weathering in the soil which found its way into food and water. Since the source was widespread, human uptake of lead was commonplace, whether in industrial or nonindustrial societies, urban or nonurban settings. Lead uptake, moreover, was relatively harmless, since most lead was rapidly excreted and little remained permanently in the body. Most cases of lead poisoning, Kehoe argued, arose from improper nutrition which fostered lead uptake and hampered excretion. The appropriate approach to lead problems was to assure that those unduly exposed had proper nutrition.[45]

Occupational lead exposure was a somewhat different matter, since in this case the source did not come from ingestion but from inhalation. But, it was felt, this was only a temporary problem since it was possible to treat seriously exposed workers by chelation therapy. Once treated, it was argued, there was no permanent effect and, in fact, workers, once having undergone therapy, could return to their jobs. Chelation therapy became a standard operating procedure for workers exposed in battery plants, lead smelters, and other major industrial sources of lead.

This mode of reasoning was also applied to children. They, too, it was argued, could be treated with chelation therapy as were adults, and once the obvious clinical symptoms had disappeared then the patient was pronounced cured. Such conclusions about the long-run effects of lead came not from direct research about the health effects of lead on children, but from reasoning from research on able-bodied workers.

In 1943, Byers and Lord[46, 47] argued that cases of lead poisoning, thought to be cured, later displayed significant effects on mental development. While there already had been concern about lead poisoning in children, this report emphasized its effect on the early development of the nervous system. The immediate evidence came from a follow-up study of 20 children with lead poisoning who had been discharged as "cured" yet all but one were doing poorly in school. The effect of these observations was not immediate, for it took another 30 years before controlled investigations documented the fact. But they reflected a potentially new departure in lead research that focused on children rather than adults, low-level rather than high-level exposures, and long-term rather than short-term effects.

This new departure was facilitated by research already undertaken in Australia which linked childhood lead poisoning with ingested paint. As early as 1897 Turner[13,14] of Queensland observed that many children became ill after changing residence and those who apparently recovered in hospitals suffered a recurrence of symptoms a few months after discharge. By 1904 his colleague, Gibson,[12] identified the hand-to-mouth ingestion of lead paint as the source of the problem. But these observations lay dormant and were rediscovered only in the late 1960s as the new focus on childhood chronic lead poisoning came to the fore.[12-14]

V. THE TRANSFORMATION OF LEAD POLITICS: 1971–1981

During the decade after 1971 a veritable revolution took place in the politics of lead in which a range of factors came to bear on the debate that had been relatively neglected before. New researchers contributed a host of discoveries about the health effects of lead especially on children; new methods of measuring blood lead were developed which greatly reduced the cost and time of gathering data about lead levels; the debate shifted from the private realm of Industry-Public Health Service relationships to an open and public forum; the role of lead inhalation came to assume an importance far greater than ingestion; and frontier knowledge came to play a more immediate and significant effect in the assessment of lead science and hence in public policy.[48]

The role of new scientists and new science was rather crucial. Patterson[49] of the California Institute of Technology argued that the blood-lead levels of humans in urban-industrial societies were not at all natural, but were far higher than the levels in people in nonindustrial societies. Patterson showed that most lead measurements by researchers in the past had been contaminated by lead from all sorts of sources: the air in the laboratory, the hands of the experimental staff, and the materials used in research. He developed a laboratory that was far freer from lead contamination and thus was able to make much more accurate measurements.

Patterson and others[50,51] compared lead levels in humans in the United States with those in Nepal, away from urban-industrial air, and measured the lead in bones of "ancients" from Peru. They calculated lead levels in water in rivers upstream and in their lower estuaries, in top, middle, and lower strata of the ocean, in raw and canned tuna, in sediment cores in lakes and ice cores in Greenland. The data refuted the conventional wisdom that natural and industrial society lead levels were similar. It generated extensive descriptions of many phases of the lead biogeochemical cycle and enabled observers to place each instance of lead in a broader context of both contemporary and historical patterns of lead distribution.

Patterson's work was first presented to a public audience in 1965 before the Senate Environment Sub-Committee headed by Senator Edmund Muskie.[52] His views were sharply challenged by researchers in occupational medicine and representatives of the lead industry.[52,53] The debate fostered a considerable amount of new research, and while some continued to challenge Patterson, he convinced an increasing number of people that his data was accurate, his methodological argument sound, and his results reliable.[54,55]

Other new researchers contributed to the lead debate. Lin-Fu issued her first article on lead poisoning in children in 1967 as a publication of the Department of Health, Education and Welfare and contributed a series of articles on the subject throughout the 1970s. Needleman devised a method of measuring long-term body burdens of lead, in contrast with the more short-lived blood-lead levels, by calculating the lead deposited in children's teeth, and related that level with both their IQ scores and their behavioral patterns in school. Silbergeld investigated experimentally the biochemical effects of lead on laboratory animals.[48]

Especially significant was the development by Piomelli[56] of New York University Medical School of a new technique for measuring blood-lead levels. Piomelli discovered a test not directly of lead in blood but of a biochemical derivative, ethyrocyte protoporphyrin, which served as a reliable marker of blood-lead concentration. This greatly reduced the time and cost of monitoring and greatly expanded the range of subjects.

The initial impact of these new developments came with the first lead report by the NAS, because the report did not take them up fully. The NAS report came under considerable criticism because it was dominated by researchers knowledgeable about ingestion rather than inhalation of lead, came under the influence of Gordon Stopps of the Haskell Laboratory at Dupont,[24] and viewed the lead issue much in the same way as in the past.

The proceedings of this committee came to be widely known through articles published in *Science* by Gillette.[57] Gillette reported that concern about the committee's work led it to select outside reviewers. One of them, Harriet Hardy of the Boston General Hospital, was highly critical of the report. Especially significant was Gillette's argument that the committee was composed primarily of those with more traditional interests in lead ingestion, drew upon experts from animal nutrition, and included none who were specialists in the newer work on inhalation and the health effects on children.

Even more sensational was a later report of the entire case by Boffey,[58] another reporter, in a general analysis of the work of the NAS. Boffey reported that scientists who had "sounded the alarm about alleged dangers of atmospheric lead concentrations" had been excluded from the panel: this group included John Goldsmith, head of the California Health Department's epidemiology unit; Henry A. Schroeder, head of Dartmouth College's Trace Metal Laboratory; Clair Patterson, geochemist at the California Institute of Technology; Paul P. Craig, a physicist who headed the Environmental Defense Fund's lead committee; and T. J. Chow, a geochemist at Scripps Institute of Oceanography.

Goldsmith,[59] a pioneer in focusing on air-pollution science and standards, pressed for a California ambient air standard for lead of 1.5 mg/m³. The lead industry took an active role in opposing the contemplated standard. Even though industry and the Public Health Service had previously agreed not to report the results until the work was completed, the industry now sought to inject into the proceedings selective parts of the Seven Cities Study. But due to the initiative of Goldsmith the entire study came to light.[37]

A new arena of debate arose within the EPA. The earlier Lead Liaison Committee, formed in the late 1950s, had been a major forum of internal EPA proceedings. But in the early 1970s environmental issues were shaping a more public setting for debate. In 1972 the EPA, inheriting the Lead Liaison Committee from the Public Health Service, opened its proceedings and its minutes to scrutiny from the public. From that time on, new scientific information was brought into debate more quickly than before and with greater effect.[37]

In considering the regulation of lead in gasoline, EPA had confined its science evaluations to personnel within the agency. This often led to stalemate. The logjam with EPA was broken by litigation brought by the Natural Resources Defense Council in which the court set a deadline for EPA action and knocked the issue loose from internal agency paralysis.[60]

The assessment leading up to the ambient air standard in 1978 was carried out through a more open process in which the agency's Science Advisory Committee (SAC) composed of external experts played a crucial role. Internal agency personnel, still convinced that an ambient air standard of 2 µg/m³ (the industry argued for a 5 µg standard) was sufficient to protect health, drew up the first draft, but it was severely criticized by members of the SAC on the grounds that it did not incorporate into its findings the most recent data on lead. A second draft fared little better and only after a third draft from the staff did the SAC find it acceptable.[61]

Each draft of the document was available to the public and each session was publicized. The Natural Resources Defense Council persuaded Needleman and Piomelli[62] to write a summary document presenting the latest lead research. This strategy worked in tandem with the fact that the SAC had a balance of members that included several scientists who were vigorous in pressing the case for reduced exposures, for example, Dr. Samuel Epstein of the University of Illinois Medical School and Dr. Eula Bingham of the University of Cincinnati Kettering Laboratory. Through their efforts the Committee revised the criteria document to require an ambient standard of 1.5 µg/m³ and EPA adopted that standard.

Closely related in time with the development of the ambient lead standard was the belief within the CDC that new scientific data required a downward revision of the acceptable blood-lead threshold to 30 µg/dl. That position followed an earlier decision by the American Academy of Pediatrics to accept 30 µg/dl as well. EPA drew on views of both the Centers and the Academy to justify its policies.[23]

Even more definitive was the decision of the federal court to accept these actions as scientifically valid. The lead industry appealed both EPA's lead-in-gasoline decision and its ambient air standard. The scientific conclusions, it argued, were highly controversial and therefore, EPA was "arbitrary and capricious" in adopting the 30 µg threshold. But, replied the court, to require "conclusive proof of harm" on which all would agree prior to a decision, was unrealistic. Rarely did such agreement exist in scientific matters; to wait until it did prevail would foster inaction. It was sufficient that a significant body of medical opinion supported the judgment and since both the American Academy of Pediatrics and the CDC did so, as well as a goodly body of scientists, then EPA's judgment should prevail. Such a judgment, even though still controversial, had a sound basis.[21,63-65]

One small but significant indicator of the new and wider context of debate and action was the second lead study completed by NAS in 1978. This time Patterson[66] was included on the review committee. He prepared a minority statement, unconventional in Academy reports, which called for even more stringent regulation of lead than that advocated by the full committee report.

VI. THE LEAD-IN-GASOLINE PHASEDOWN

The first Reagan administration constituted a new period in the politics of lead. New policy leaders identified the scheduled phasedown of lead in gasoline as one of many regulations that should be lifted from industry. But the attempt backfired and the proceedings led to the opposite result—an accelerated phasedown. This turn of events came from a combination of circumstances: the impact of new science, the desire of the administration to enhance its environmental credibility in the 1984 presidential campaign, and vigorous action by some policy makers in EPA to take advantage of openings for action.[67,68]

Early in the first Reagan term, the EPA administrator, Anne Gorsuch, let it be known that the agency did not intend to enforce the phasedown regulations against small refiners and, in fact, would soon move to increase the allowable concentrations of lead in gasoline. Under the direction of a White House regulatory review committee headed by Vice President George Bush, the administration worked closely with industry behind closed doors to undermine the existing phasedown program.[69,70]

But while Gorsuch could convey assurances quietly and informally to the industry, new regulatory policy required a more open procedure. At the outset EPA apparently thought that the proceedings would go smoothly in its favor. However, they provided an opportunity for evidence accumulating during the 1970s to influence public debate. This evidence included data on low-level effects on the neurological development of children and on animals; statistical studies which demonstrated correlations between declining levels of lead in gasoline, in the ambient air, and in blood leads during the years of the phasedown; and the second report on lead from NAS.

At the hearings these reports were featured so effectively by pediatric lead scientists and citizen groups that EPA found little support for its venture to reverse the phasedown. Initiative shifted to those who wished to take the new data seriously.[71,72] EPA abandoned its effort to increase lead levels in gasoline. A year later the agency announced that it would accelerate the phasedown and, in fact, would move to eliminate lead from gasoline entirely.

There were two stages in this process, the first during 1981 and 1982 and the second during 1983 and 1984. As a result of the first proceeding, EPA announced that it would continue the phase down and change the method of determining acceptable gasoline lead levels from an average for all gasoline, leaded and unleaded combined, to an average for leaded gasoline only. This tightened considerably the allowable level of lead.[73,74]

The second action, more extensive and dramatic, lowered the allowable level of lead in leaded gasoline from 1.1 g per leaded gallon on January 1, 1985, to 0.1 g per leaded gallon on January 1, 1986. The proposal was made public first in April 1983 and debated until the early part of 1984. It came from within the administration rather than from additional external initiatives, took participants in the lead debate by surprise, and was finally implemented with limited change.[75-77]

The controlling factor in the EPA action was the upcoming presidential campaign and the need by the administration to establish a new environmental credibility. EPA administrator Anne Gorsuch had resigned and her replacement, William Ruckelshaus, now took up the task of restoring the agency's image. This led to new strategies on the part of several relevant government agencies.[78]

The most immediate took place in the EPA Criteria Assessment Office (ECAO) which, under the direction of Lester Grant, was revising the 1977 Lead Criteria Document. In doing so, two types of recent lead research became a major point of dispute. One was the work on the neurological effects of low-level lead exposures and another was the data developed at CDC indicating a correlation between declining levels of lead in gasoline and blood leads. On both these types of evidence the ECAO seemed to be mesmerized by its decision to take industry's objections seriously and to subject them to extended review.[79-87]

The work of EPA staff in drawing up the revised criteria document, however, was now influenced heavily by the Clean Air Science Advisory Committee (CASAC), a subdivision of the EPA Science Advisory Board. That Board was just emerging from a cloud of suspicion which had arisen in the early Reagan years when appointments to scientific advisory positions in the government seemed to be influenced heavily by administrative preference for those scientists who leaned toward industry views. Ruckelshaus now brought into the Board a wider range of scientific opinion that was more open to newer environmental health studies. The CASAC took up both of the subjects at issue within the ECAO and rejected industry arguments. This cleared the way for the new studies to play a major role in the new criteria document as well as regulatory policy.[88]

Even more important was an action within the CDC to revise the lead advisory last drawn up in 1978. The CDC constituted quite a different forum for assessment and action than did the EPA. Its role was advisory rather than regulatory. Its immediate audience was the pediatric clinicians across the country who observed and treated patients and its role was to help them improve the health of their patients. It had already played an important, even crucial role, in better treatment of lead cases by establishing reduced threshold levels of 35 µg/dl and then 30 µg/dl. In each case it had responded directly to the new scientific knowledge and it was prepared to do so now.

In 1983 it appeared to Dr. Vernon Houk of the CDC, that it was time once again to review the new research and consider the possibility of lowering the threshold. This standard was an even more crucial point of debate than was the criteria document.[89, 90] The lead industry continued to argue that the lowest acceptable level that could be scientifically supported was 40 µg/dl. But CDC's lower lead level persuaded the court in litigation over the 1977 ambient air standards to reject the industry challenge to the ambient lead standard. The lead industry feared a lower CDC "standard" and tried to prevent CDC action but failed, and in April 1984 CDC announced a new effect level of 25 µg/dl.[91-93]

The administration's political needs and the advancing scientific knowledge as reflected in the criteria document and the CDC lead advisory provided an opportunity for EPA staff in the Office of Policy Analysis and Evaluation (OPAE) to press for a phasedown in lead in gasoline. This represented a marked change from the inability of EPA to act on lead in gasoline in 1973 and even in the ambient air quality standard in 1977. In both previous cases action was forced by external legal pressure from the Natural Resources Defense Council. But in 1983 to 1984 the OPAE and the CASAC took advantage of the opening provided by the administration's political needs to take the initiative and overcome the long standing lethargy of the ECAO.

On February 3, 1984, 18 months after the EPA announced its policy reversal of 1982 which put lead phasedown back on track, the agency reported a draft cost/benefit study of an accelerated phasedown, and even a total ban, which reflected staff acceptance of the new lead data. In late March it released an internal OPAE cost-benefit study showing that 1988 phasedown benefits outweighed costs by some $700 million. The analysis was approved by the Office of Management and Budget which described OPAE's work as "conservative."[94] In August, Ruckelshaus approved reduction of lead in gasoline from 1.1 g/Pb gal (grams per leaded gallon) on January 1, 1985, to 0.1 g/Pb gal on January 1, 1986. Because of White House opposition the complete ban on leaded gasoline was rejected.[95, 96]

The work of the OPAE was spearheaded by Joel Schwartz who became impressed with the new health effects data and worked out the cost/benefit analysis. At the same time OPAE took the initiative to undertake statistical studies of the data in the Second National Health and Nutritional Examination Survey (NHANES II) to demonstrate a correlation between blood leads and anemia in children at low levels, which highlighted and confirmed earlier studies. And in August the OPAE reported a similar relationship between blood lead and hypertension, also based upon the NHANES II data. In 1987, after the phasedown regulations were well in place staff statisticians reported a relationship between blood-lead levels and hearing loss which held statistically down to a level of 5 µg/dl of blood lead.[97-98]

The health effects data brought to bear on the lead phasedown issue by the criteria document, the CDC action, and the statistical analysis by the OPAE played more of a background rather than a direct role in the regulatory action. The cost/benefit analysis itself placed far more emphasis on the costs saved on automobile maintenance than on the health benefits from reduced lead levels. Moreover, only health benefits based upon protecting children with blood levels over 30 µg/dl were included and only those benefits from reduced costs of health examinations and remedial education were brought into the analysis as benefits.[99]

The supporting documents leading up to the regulatory action had provided also some useful suggestions about additional benefit implications of lower blood-lead levels. One was the higher lifetime earnings that would come from higher IQ levels. EPA staff analysis had referred to a well-established relationship between the two.[100] Such calculations had, in fact, been used as the basis of court awards in lead liability cases. But this benefit was not used for the analysis.

It was quite apparent that EPA was willing to draw upon the new health effects data in a background manner to provide indirect support for its action, but did not desire to work it directly into regulatory action for fear that it would draw challenges from industry and jeopardize the phasedown effort.

VII. THE RESPONSE OF
THE LEAD INDUSTRY

The lead and lead-using industries, traditional opponents of lead regulation, sought to hold back this sequence of actions, but were powerless to do so. While in earlier years it had been able to work quietly within governmental and professional bodies to exercise influence, the more open political realm placed it at a major disadvantage.[101]

Fundamental to lead industry opposition was the continuing conviction that there were no adverse health effects from blood leads lower than 40 µg/dl. Lead industry representatives continually expressed their disagreement with the direction of the assessments of the health effects of lead.[102,103]

In his report on behalf of the Lead Industries Association in 1984, Jim Tozzi wrote "that cognitive and behavioral deficits occur at blood lead levels just above 30 µg/d/ . . ." is an "erroneous assumption." In testimony before the Senate of Environment and Public Works Committee, Dr. Jerome Cole of the International Lead-Zinc Research Organization argued that the main source of lead poisoning in children was lead-based paint and that lead in the ambient air was "only a minor contributor" to the problem. And, according to Lawrence Blanchard, Vice Chairman of Ethyl Corporation, in spite of "overwhelming information to the contrary, EPA continues to allege adverse effects of low-level lead exposure on neurobehavior." Earlier he was more pointed: EPA has "followed the same process of deliberately distorting the facts as they have for the past 12 years. As usual, they have studiously overruled every piece of evidence presented by industry and have accepted every claim by the environmentalists."[104,105]

The lead industry looked to two important forums for potential influence, the CDC advisory proceedings and the EPA criteria document. The first of these provided the industry with only temporary leverage. Dr. Vernon Houk of the CDC had initially hoped to appoint an informal committee to proceed rapidly with the revision instead of the more lengthy process required by law for formal advisory committees. The industry threatened to sue on the grounds that the procedure was irregular. Houk, however, backed off, took up the more formal procedure, and despite further legal threats from the industry, revised the document.[106-108]

The EPA proceeding on the criteria document provided the industry with a more amenable and far-reaching forum in which to press its case. The issues were the studies on neurological effects of lead and the relationship between the downward trends in lead in gasoline, ambient air lead, and blood leads.

The EPA staff writing the criteria document took these industry contentions and subjected each one to review. This brought to the criteria document proceedings friendly-to-industry experts' arguments, some of whom had been peripheral to the lead debate. Few were pediatric clinicians; a number from England had opposed efforts to reduce lead exposure in that country. Some were biostatisticians and social psychologists who while they brought their expertise to bear on the statistical analysis often did so in a manner uninformed about either the clinical problem or the meaning of the issues in dispute.[79-81]

It took the CASAC, composed of scientists rather than EPA staff, to reject these initiatives from industry and to break the logjam within the ECAO. Its meeting of April 26 to 27, 1984, crucial to the entire lead phasedown proceeding, was, in large part, a review of these arguments. One reporter described the results: the CASAC "both blessed the controversial IQ studies and overwhelmingly 'trashed' studies by Ethyl Corporation and Dupont down-playing the linkage between lead in gas and blood lead levels. . . ." While the Office of Criteria Assessment in EPA had earlier recommended that the neurological studies be disregarded in agency action on ambient lead, now it took the cue from CASAC and incorporated them fully into its report.[109]

Having failed to dislodge the health scientists in either the CDC or the CASAC, the industry now chose to tackle the OPAE by developing a critique of its cost/benefit study. It hired as its principal analyst the former director of information and regulatory affairs in the Office of Management and Budget (OMB), Jim Tozzi. Tozzi had a reputation with environmental managers as fairminded and hence was usually taken more seriously than were direct representatives of industry. He had been involved in earlier lead analyses in OMB and after he left government in early 1984 he established his own consulting service and was hired by the Lead Industries Association to press its case.[110,111]

Tozzi proceeded to do so with a report that the EPA's cost/benefit analysis was seriously flawed and that a more proper study would indicate that "benefits represent only a fraction of the costs"—benefits of $559 million and costs of $9,922 million, much the reverse of the EPA figures. Embedded in this analysis was major objection both to the EPA conclusions about the health effects of lead and the damage from lead to automobile engines. A comment from one EPA staffer reflected the agency's reaction: "It just goes to show that for the right amount of money you can make the numbers say anything." Tozzi continued to press the industry's cost/benefit case, but it had no substantial effect on the outcome of the proposed phasedown.[112-114]

While the lead industry could not hold back the drive to phase down the level of lead in gasoline to 0.1 g/Pb gal by January 1, 1986, its strategies did have an important retarding effect on lead regulation with EPA. For while the agency did take up much of the new health effects data as background argument to its regulatory proposal, it did not bring that data directly into the regulatory rationale. It believed that such action would prompt a severe legal challenge from the industry which it did not want to risk. By its actions, therefore, the industry made the EPA quite cautious and prevented it from giving more substantial and formal support to the new health effects research and assessments. It could not prevent a certain amount of action on lead in the lead-in-gasoline phasedown, but it could and did create a climate which helped to retard future further lead action on a variety of fronts.[115]

The phasedown of lead in gasoline, completed by 1987, brought a pause to policy action on lead. The announced intention to completely eliminate lead from gasoline was not followed up,[116-119] the revision of the ambient air standard for lead proceeded slowly,[120-122] and an attempt to focus on lead in drinking water was only partially successful.[123-125] At the same time, however, knowledge about adverse effects of lead at even lower levels of exposure set in motion action to establish lower threshold levels in the range of 12 to 15 mg/dl of blood and prompted public officials to call for further action. But new policy emerged slowly.

VIII. PATTERNS OF DISPUTES: SCIENCE AND VALUES

The debate over lead involved a close connection between disputes over the meaning of science and disputes over desirable public policy. Hardly an event in the series of lead controversies failed to reflect the intense differences of opinion in the two realms. There are a sufficient number of cases of dispute and of individuals participating in the disputes to establish some historical patterns and to analyze systematically their meaning. I take three forays into this problem.

The first is to array the scientists in terms of their positions in the debates over both science and policy. This leads to the conclusion that some consistently were on one side of the issue and others consistently on the other. Some argued that newly emerging scientific data should be taken seriously and incorporated rapidly into public policy—Vernon Houk, Philip Landrigan, Herbert Needleman, and Sergio Piomelli. Others expressed skepticism about the significance of new data, stressed causal factors other than lead in human health problems, and cautioned against taking new data too seriously— Robert Bornshein, Jerome Cole, Paul Hammond, Robert Kehoe, and Gordon Stopps.[126]

These scientists were on opposite sides of the issues in a variety of public proceedings: regulatory policy, litigation, federal legislation and city ordinances, scientific assessments, and public health advisories. They were arrayed similarly in scientific symposia and technical workshops. To observe these patterns in a wide range of settings over 25 years provides ample support for the notion that patterns in scientific dispute are closely linked with patterns of advocacy in public policy.

A second mode of analysis is to relate these patterns with institutional affiliations. The first group were associated more with hospitals and medical schools, obtained their research funds more from public sources such as the National Institutes of Health or the EPA, gathered around the CDC and the CASAC as their main hope for action and worked closely with public health and environmental organizations such as the American Academy of Pediatrics, the Natural Resource Defense Council, or the Environmental Defense Fund.

The second group associated more closely with industry and its major funding agencies, the International Lead-Zinc Research Organization (ILZRO) or the Lead Industries Association. They tended to speak for those organizations in public proceedings, and they were active participants in symposia which those organizations sponsored and financed. In 1978, for example, the Department of Environmental Health at the University of Cincinnati sponsored a "Second International Symposium on Environmental Lead Research," which provided an opportunity for attenders to "hear ILZRO lead research grantees speak on all major facets of the ILZRO lead environmental health program." Among the participants were those closely associated with the lead industry's policy positions—Robert Bornshein, Paul Hammond, Donald Lynam, and Henrietta Sachs.[127]

Still a third foray into the systematic analysis of the relationship between the values of scientists and policy choices involves patterns of consistency or change in view as the acceptable level of blood lead declined over the years and the focal point of dispute shifted. Did scientists on either side of the dispute at one level change their minds in the debate when it shifted to another level? The evidence suggests rather strongly that little such change took place. At each threshold level, one group of scientists rather consistently argued that it was not low enough and that emerging research required that it be lowered further, while another argued that the level had been reduced far enough, if not too far, and that it was quite satisfactory for health protection. At present this pattern of scientific dispute, which occurred at levels of 30 µg/dl and then 25 µg/dl, is being replayed for levels below 25 µg/dl.

How does one identify the origin of these patterns? It seems quite plausible to argue that institutional affiliation plays a significant role in scientific judgments on lead, as Frances Lynn demonstrated with survey data about disputes over cancer.[128] It seems also plausible to argue that this relationship has a twofold origin. On the one hand, individuals with particular values seek out institutions with which they feel compatible and institutions, in turn, seek out scientists who have made known views acceptable to them. On the other, it is also plausible to argue that personal values associated with distinctive scientific judgments change as one becomes affiliated with a given type of institution.

Still other factors are relevant. One is the role of professional specialization. It is conventional wisdom in science that because it applies objective methods it serves as a unifying force and brings together divergent views in the context of objective knowledge. Yet the general course of science is quite the opposite—increasingly specialized knowledge fractures science and fosters intense dispute. Individual scientists display considerable loyalty to particular bodies of data, methods of research, and analytical emphases. The lead issue involves differences between those who specialize in nutrition or inhalation, occupational health or biogeochemical cycles, and those who are clinical pediatricians or laboratory researchers.

Another causal element is more personal and less institutional, arising from the particular psychological orientation of the scientist. Some do not feel personally secure unless they have in hand an extensive level of detailed description and a very high level of proof. Others are more willing to take a risk in their role in the scientific community by advocating a more rapid application of frontier knowledge about environmental health; they feel challenged by the possibilities that taking risks in advocating new approaches might well have great human benefit. These personal differences might well underlie both the distinctions in professional commitments and institutional affiliations; at the least they reinforce each other.

In the analysis of environmental politics it has been especially difficult to systematically and dispassionately, focus on these differences in scientific views, often even to obtain acceptance of the problem as worthy of research and debate.

Yet a review of the close relationship between scientific dispute and policy dispute in the case of lead makes clear the need to conduct research on the role of values in science and their relationship to public policy. To fully bring such matters to light might lead participants in these debates to contribute to decision-making in a more informed manner.

IV   *Environmental Politics*

Since World War II

THE STRUCTURE
OF ENVIRONMENTAL
POLITICS SINCE
WORLD WAR II

ON A NUMBER OF occasions during the past twenty years I have attempted to
formulate a general interpretation of American political structure based upon
persistent tensions between centralizing and decentralizing tendencies in
American society and politics.[1] The analysis of environmental affairs since
World War II presented here constitutes an extension of that argument to a
more recent time period. The political tendencies within environmental objectives and the controversies which they generated seem to make most sense
when brought together within a centralizing-decentralizing conceptual context. The relevant ideas involve distinctions among local, state, and national
levels of political life, ever-increasing scales of human experience, networks,
and institutions, and persistent tensions between larger and smaller modes of
organizing and expressing political impulses. But first let me elaborate the
general line of larger argument.

One of the most serious problems of historical conceptualization is the
need to find one context of thought that will encompass human affairs which

From *Journal of Social History* 14 (1981): 719–38. Reprinted by permission.

take place at different levels of social organization: the grass roots, the region, and the nation. These comprise a hierarchy of human involvement, each of which is a distinctive source of perception and experience, institutional organization, and action. At times historians are preoccupied with national affairs and define historical problems as understood by those engaged in organizing action and ideas at a large, national level. In recent years social history has stressed the opposite end of this spectrum, the family, the community, the networks of primary group relationships often best observed in matters of education and religion, ethnicity and race, work, recreation, and leisure. The outpouring of research in social history over the past two decades has riveted our attention on levels of human life far removed from the more traditional emphases on national politics.

An adequate set of historical concepts requires that we weave together these two levels of society and politics. Some years ago I suggested a three-tiered approach by adding a middle level to these divergent grass-roots and national sectors.[2] One could visualize a set of human relationships and activities larger than the community, yet smaller than the nation, which could be encompassed by the concept of a region, and perhaps be got at most readily by an analysis of affairs which came together in state government. The appropriate social analysis of politics, then, could come from the identification of political impulses arising from each of these three levels and their interaction. An historical perspective limited to any one of them would be far too narrow. Each one must be examined separately and then fitted into a pattern which draws together all three. Environmental politics since World War II provide an excellent opportunity to undertake this approach.

The events, people, and issues in environmental affairs over the past three decades reflect each of these different levels of society and politics. The environmental thrust took its shape largely from the concerns of people in their daily lives: home, work, and leisure in one's community of residence and recreation.[3] These involved a preoccupation with a given place and the environmental quality of that place. Hence a host of issues concerning cleaner air and water, toxic chemicals in food and drink, noise and congestion, open space in suburb and countryside, wilderness and wetlands, seashore and desert, all arose from that focus. As human preoccupation shifted from work to family and leisure in the years after World War II, the concern for the environmental quality of personal activities grew and fed persistent demands that it be enhanced and protected.[4] Much of the environmental movement arose from those experiences: people sought to improve their standard of living by adding amenities and well-being to earlier emphases on consumption of necessities and conveniences.[5]

Intimately bound up with environmental affairs is another world of political life remote from these concerns, a world of system and organization, emphasizing the development of large-scale private and public institutions which direct, manage, and manipulate large-scale affairs.[6] Some are developmental institutions, both private corporate and public systems; others are public lands and environmental management agencies. They represent an institutional order which gives rise to experiences and activities associated with the management, perpetuation, and advancement of large-scale systems. Over the course of a century or more smaller-scale institutions in an industrializing society have evolved into larger ones, comprising increasing numbers of people and resources, bringing together in one context of management ever more complex affairs, and gathering extensive amounts of empirical data as a basis for exercising more effective control over their institutional surroundings.[7]

Over the years the substance of the relationships between local and larger institutions changed significantly. Prior to World War II the community related to the larger world primarily as a specific site for the location of the nation's productive economy organized by regional and national institutions. It was dependent on that larger system, with meager technical, professional, and organizational resources to cope with the growing power of institutions beyond it but with which it was intimately involved. With increasing standards of living, however, the environmental quality of the residential community loomed much larger and development projects formerly seen as undergirding the local economy were now often looked upon as threats to a "way of life." At the same time places of outdoor recreation to which increasing numbers of people took particular fancy came to be thought of as additional vital pieces of "turf" to be protected from intrusion. Amid these changing personal and community values rising living standards brought to the community a wider range of resources, many of them professional, technical, and organizational, which were utilized effectively as political leverage. Stress on environmental enhancement of the community now came to constitute a major political force which often competed successfully with the larger institutional world of production systems.

These two worlds, that of the ultimate user of environmental resources in daily living, in home, community, and leisure, and of the manager of resource systems who directed and manipulated larger-scale institutions through which resource delivery was organized, constituted two separate and conflicting realms. While one was involved in decentralizing tendencies which defined problems in terms of ultimate human consumption at the grass-roots level, the other entailed centralizing activities which defined problems in terms of centralized and coordinated management. These worlds were far apart, rarely met, and often came into conflict. In between them, however, was a set of institutions organized at a middle level of state governmental affairs. Because they lay at the middle, these institutions became one of the most significant focal points of environmental politics. Both sets of forces, from the grass roots and from national systems, converged upon state government to pull it first one way and then another. The interplay of the two outer levels can often be examined most effectively in the context of state environmental politics.

THE GRASS-ROOTS SEARCH

In its initiative and its direction the environmental impulse in America after World War II came from the grass roots. People were stirred to action in the context of their personal lives, as a result of happenings in family and community, in place of work, residence, and recreation. It is relatively easy, if one is confined to the evidence of national debate, administration, or managerial and professional literature, to miss all this. But if one takes the time to focus on the massive amount of action and ideas, of organization and written record in the city and the countryside, then the impression of intensely personal reactions to environmental quality and environmental degradation is unmistakable. The emotion, the drive, the persistence of what is often called environmental activism stems from the meaning of environmental values at this primary group context of life.[8]

Several types of environmental activities reflect this thrust. The first, in point of time, and the most continuous was the wilderness movement.[9] At the roots of wilderness politics were people who found specific areas in the nation's forests and mountains, east and west, enjoyable for recreation and relaxation. An intensely personal relationship arose between particular groups of people and particular "special places." Individuals hiked through such areas, photographed them to convey their experiences to others, looked at them with an eye to scientific observation and wrote guide books which were combinations of where to go and what to appreciate for those who had not yet been there.[10] And when such areas came to be threatened by logging or off-road vehicles or mineral development, this combination of appreciative and scientific personal encounters aroused many to action: "To explore, enjoy and protect."[11] It was this personal involvement with nature which gave rise to the wilderness movement.

In the same manner one can observe personal involvement with a host of different types of natural areas which had the same consequences. Particular areas of open space in one's community became objects of attachment. Local private groups and public agencies such as the conservation committees of New England and the Middle Atlantic States served to focus attention on open lands, to enhance their identification to the community as a unique asset worth protecting.[12] Few conflicts over these community assets, and there were many of them, reached national notice, and hence rarely became a part of the larger, national environmental debate. One particular feature, however, did become more prominent—wetlands protection. In the mid-1960s interest in coastal wetlands began to accelerate as places of aesthetic interest, recreational activity such as bird watching, and environmental functions such as natural flood reservoirs, pollution treatment systems, and barriers against the larger elements of wind and wave.[13] From Massachusetts to Maryland and in Florida states passed laws to protect wetlands in the late 1960s and early 1970s. Interest then turned inland where New York, Michigan, and Wisconsin, among a number of states, developed programs to protect inland wetlands as a result of wide public interest which defined them as a community asset. Disappearing wetlands were a loss to the community as a whole. Local towns organized a variety of activities to protect and manage wetlands, including handbooks of land and water use; and citizen groups grew up to promote private and public action to acquire them for permanent protection, as well as to regulate the location, type, and manner of intrusions.[14]

A host of natural systems became objects of environmental action: lakes and free-flowing rivers,[15] southern swamps, prairies in the western midwest, areas of unique plants and animals,[16] the pine barrens of New Jersey and Long Island,[17] and deserts. The last is one of the most intriguing.[18] Over the years the desert, as most of these areas did, changed dramatically in the imagination of Americans from a place forbidding to one of wonder and beauty— all because of personal encounters with the desert, the attraction of desert photography, and the growing vicarious identification of people with wild places. When the Bureau of Land Management in 1976 sponsored a survey among Americans about their attitudes toward the western dry lands, well over half felt that they knew enough about them that they wished to express an opinion as to how they should be managed. Most wanted them to remain undeveloped and without intrusions of roads or off-road vehicles.[19] They, too, had become a natural asset identified with personal values and national and community well-being.[20]

The positive attraction to specific places, of either residence or recreation, or even vicariously experienced at a distance, gave rise to many environmental activities that were more negative, that is, aimed at protecting against threats and degradation. Many an environmental struggle took on the character of recreational and community protection. The threats were often conceived of and spoken of as intrusions from the "outside," as the impact of some alien large-scale activity by industry or government initiated elsewhere, even from afar, but impacting the quality of life in the community. Especially significant were the very large-scale, massive intrusions which modern technology engendered. Sometimes these were dams proposed by federal agencies, whether on the Colorado River near the Grand Canyon or Hells Canyon on the Snake,[21] or on Wildcat Creek near West Lafayette, Indiana. Some new and unexpected threats, such as synthetic fuel plans or the MX missile in Utah and Nevada even made believers out of people who previously had thought of themselves as confirmed anti-environmentalists.[22]

The cases of intrusion were legion: coal-fired and atomic electric generating plants, oil refineries on the coast of Maine and near San Francisco Bay; 765-kilovolt electric power lines in New York and Minnesota; channelization projects in Florida and the Afatchalaya Swamp in Louisiana. There were massive surface mines in Ohio and the Upper Plains; energy park proposals in Pennsylvania each one comprising 10,000 megawatts of electric generating capacity; interstate highways which threatened favorite wetlands, scenic views, urban communities, or parks; and uranium mining which threatened miners and with its tailings posed a long-run problem for the community. In every such case the dynamic force was the individual's and the community's own sense of self-defense. Larger environmental organizations often supported protective action and thereby drew people into their orbit. But the sustaining drive of those organizations was not their national agenda, but their accumulation of local grievances and thwarted hopes.[23]

These protective environmental actions involved not only land, but also air and water quality. The most important single source of public involvement in these pollution issues was their impact on the community. The initial drive against air pollution emphasized smoke as aesthetically degrading, or foul odors and smells. And the initial protest against water pollution came from a similar repugnance at the way in which floating sewage and industrial waste simply repelled the human senses in one's personal experience. The office in the U.S. Public Health Service which first dealt with air pollution was called the office of "Community Programs." In matters of water quality fishermen became aroused when their fishing grounds were polluted, the fish destroyed or made uneatable by toxic chemicals.[24] Waste in the ambient air and water threatened the entire community. And the initial solutions were simply to divert it elsewhere, to direct sewage downstream, untreated, so that others would have to bear the brunt, or to build tall smokestacks and divert air pollution into the atmosphere to blow it away from surrounding homes and offices.

In the latter part of the 1970s a new turn of affairs which emphasized toxic chemicals and radioactive waste gave an even more intensive twist to the effort of localities to protect themselves. Proposals to locate hazardous and radioactive waste disposal aroused community after community until decision-makers became convinced that only "remote" sites would do. But they also found that few sites were, in fact, "remote," because somebody had a personal interest in almost every area of the nation. Community reaction against waste disposal became even more dramatic with the discovery of many an old toxic waste dump which threatened community health. Love Canal was only among the most dramatic of these. As information about the location of these "inactive" sites became more widespread, many a newspaper reporter delved into the details of their origin and present condition with an aura of defending the community. These were only the more dramatic versions of equally contested disposal sites which involved landfills for the burial of urban garbage and solid waste.[25]

Still a third personal and grass-roots tendency in environmental affairs stressed self-reliance in matters of health protection. This dovetails with the protection of place. Reduction in the threat of bacterial disease, with World War II as an historical dividing line, brought a new perspective in matters of human health. On the one hand people looked forward to a longer and less hazardous life and adopted a greater concern for long-term chronic health problems such as cancer rather than momentary infectious diseases. On the other, they thought of health not in terms of sickness but of wellness, the persistent capacity to keep physically and mentally fit so as to perform daily tasks in work and play at a high level of activity. But amid such a change in perspective they often found that medical authorities, including their own physicians, could not offer much help. Increasingly they took their health, their physical fitness, into their own hands, in a posture of self-responsibility. Physical exercise and nutrition became key elements in this new focus on self-reliant wellness.[26]

The environmental phase of this change in human attitudes came from the long-term, low-level chronic effects of pollutants on human health. These subtle effects were not well charted by medical authorities; yet both popular and scientific knowledge emphasized the hazards. Cancer, birth defects, fetal disorders, genetic changes all seemed to be real possibilities; so also did environmental effects on male and female reproductive capacity, immune systems, and aging.[27] The traditional emphasis on mortality from environmental causes came to shift to a concern for morbidity.[28] Confrontation with the vast number of new chemicals released into the environment gave rise to enormous human frustration. On the one hand the hazard seemed clear, but on the other those who spoke for the chemical industry and almost as often for public regulatory agencies, de-emphasized the danger. Suspecting citizens who lived near toxic waste dumps were told that the levels of chemicals found in their drinking water were too low to be harmful. Yet there seemed to be a continual, if not a growing, gap between these assurances on the one hand and what seemed to be confirmed by personal experience on the other. Citizens, in fact, often conducted their own epidemiological investigations as a device to jar public authorities into action.[29]

This frustration fed a stance of self-reliance in matters of health. One of its most significant consequences was the natural foods movement, the search for food which because it was not produced with synthetic fertilizers or pesticides was thought to be less hazardous. It was no wonder that attitude studies indicated a co-existence of concern about the health effects of chemicals and preference for organic gardening or natural foods. Water supplies were a more serious problem. As toxic chemicals leaked into ground water, and as an increasing number of such sources of drinking water were found to be contaminated with synthetic organics and other chemicals, concern for safe drinking water rose. If one depended upon well water the threat was impossible to combat directly. Bottled water drawn from supposedly safer sources became more popular. Such efforts as these constituted major attempts to exercise control over one's environment from degrading influences as fully as did the effort to keep disposal sites away from one's community.[30]

Each of these environmental concerns—the protection of scarce and valuable natural areas, the attempt to ward off threats to community environmental degradation, and the search for protection of one's health—constituted sources of grass-roots social and political drives which came to be the environmental movement. What is especially important is to observe this development as a new turn of affairs in the American community. For over a century the driving force in economic, political, and social development had rested with those who were organizing American life on an ever-larger scale, in business, government, and social institutions. Amid these drives the local community was both bypassed and subverted, often destroyed. Institutions formed on a far grander scale moved on apace and the local community remained in the backwater. Environmental politics is one case of a reversal of this trend which appeared in a number of forms to reassert the role of the grass-roots community in public affairs. Its tone is one of enhancing the quality of life of the community and individuals within it. Environmentalists from this vantage point viewed large-scale institutions of modern life as intrusions as much as aids, and often as threats to local affairs. A key factor in the ability to fight back was that with rising standards of living those who sought to protect residential and recreational sites began to acquire the technical resources, the knowledge and expertise to confront those in the wider world on their own terms. Many an environmental activist reached out to acquire scientific and technical knowledge, to forge alliances with trained professionals in order to fight their battles effectively. This new source of political strength marked a change in the capacity of small-scale institutions to ward off intrusions from institutions far above and beyond them.

MANAGERIAL SYSTEMS AND THE ENVIRONMENTAL IMPULSE

Environmental affairs involved another realm of life quite remote from daily personal and community concerns, a world of system and organization, in which the emphasis lay on the development of private and public institutions to direct, manage, and manipulate large-scale affairs. The size and scale of these systems grew rapidly after World War II, at a pace similar to the growth of environmental values themselves. Both were integral aspects of the advanced industrial society. The range of their effects on air, land, and water increased in scope. On the one hand the machines which came to be utilized —the earth-moving equipment in highway building, the shovels and drag lines in strip mining, the 1000-megawatt power plants and their intense output of waste heat, the wood harvesting equipment—all dwarfed human scale and created what appeared to be massive modifications in the human environment. On the other hand, the expanding chemical economy created a new chemical environment in air, land, and water that seemed to encompass daily life with threats that were persistent, pervasive, mysterious, and often out of control. This realm of scale seemed to come from sources "out there" which were beyond the comprehension, let alone the influence, of the average individual and community.

These systems, ever-larger in scale, impacted environmental impulses in a number of ways. The great majority of large-scale institutions in both private and public affairs, and often in their symbiotic relationships, were concerned with developmental rather than environmental goals. Especially in the realm of material, commodity production these institutions found themselves at odds with environmental objectives. For environmental objectives emphasized qualitative factors. Amenities required that high-quality areas of air, water, and land be identified and protected as community, regional, and national assets, which precluded development, and that development be modified to make it less destructive to newly defined environmental standards of living. At the same time commodity development often generated polluting by-products, which affected a wide range of people in their daily lives, their health, their aesthetic enjoyment, and the biological world which enhanced their communities and their recreation and leisure affairs. To developmental leaders these concerns were secondary. Amenity values in living standards should give way to more overriding commodity social needs; at the same time, so they argued, the social harm from developmental activities was greatly overemphasized. Hence they tended to consider environmental objections to their activities as more contrived than real, more an irritating and unwelcomed hindrance rather than a reflection of substantive social goals involving new values in an advanced industrial society.

Similar large-scale systems evolved in the management of environmental resources—air, water, and land—and these, too, became a focal point of controversy: public land management in national and state forests, parks, wildlife refuges, and the western public domain; the management of water development, of water quality, air quality, and solid waste; coastal zone management and the management of surface mining and its reclamation; power plant siting and the management of land use. In almost every realm of environmental affairs management systems arose in which a resource with a combination of commodity and amenity ingredients was maintained by a central group of managers whose actions affected large numbers of people. The environmental objectives with which these managers were concerned did not necessarily make them responsive to environmental objectives expressed by the public. On the contrary, it frequently was the case that managers of environmental systems often found their perspectives to be more compatible with the managers of developmental systems, sharing common views on the meaning and role of large-scale, centrally directed affairs and often drawing upon similar technical disciplines in science, engineering, economics, and planning where developmental values seemed to predominate.[31]

Large-scale systems had a special impact on the management of biological resources in which environmentalists took great interest. Management seemed to thrive on organizational patterns which stressed uniformity in the units to be managed so that they could be subject to a single system of administrative control. Yet biological systems often were more intricate than this, and especially in the course of natural succession gave rise to diversity and complexity rather than uniformity.[32] Intensive agriculture was a model of managerial impulses in biological management. Applied to wood production in the forest, it gave rise to even-aged management in which large areas were treated uniformly, clear-cut all at one time, planted at the same time, and dealt with a single-aged system of trees.[33] At the same time monoculture replaced diversity of species in intensive tree farming. Or, to take another example, the uniform application of pesticides to a field destroyed all insects, both those that were damaging to crops and their predators as well, and actually gave rise to an increase in pest populations.[34] The environmental alternatives to these approaches was to dovetail management to small contexts—individual tree or group selection in tree harvest on the one hand, and integrated pest management which adapted treatments to specific target pests on the other.[35] Both sets of issues became classic controversies in the tension between large-scale management and environmental objectives.

Over the course of the 1960s and 1970s those who elaborated large-scale systems in American society—the managers and their attendant scientists, economists, planners, and engineers—became increasingly irritated and hostile to what they considered to be environmental roadblocks to their goals and objectives. There were, for example, the successful efforts of environmentalists to require that the environmental effects of projects be analyzed prior to approval and that less damaging environmental alternatives be selected. Or there were the requirements for "public participation" first worked out in the review of wilderness proposals under the 1964 Wilderness Act, and then extended to a wide range of administrative, planning, and litigation actions. All these were objected to strenuously by developmental leaders who sought to turn back "citizen involvement" practices. While they did not succeed in formal changes in that direction, they were often able to reduce citizen influence significantly and to turn environmental impact statements to their own advantage. Such statements were, according to one study, applied to only 1 percent of all developmental projects, and of these only 20 percent, 1 in 500 of the total, produced delay litigation, abandonment, or other complications.[36] The

EIS, however, became a highly significant political radar device, an "early warning signal," whereby developers were able to identify potential public opposition ahead of time and devise strategies to overcome it.[37]

Equally significant was the way in which scientists and engineers associated with large-scale management came to be increasingly hostile to objectives formulated by the environmental public. In matters of pollution control, for example, air and water professionals in the 1960s were delighted at the growing public concern for such matters because it provided federal funds for the research they had long advocated. But this positive response soon changed as the objectives of pollution control programs went far beyond what the professionals thought desirable, such as requiring secondary treatment of municipal sewage, or the protection of cleaner air and water against degradation.[38] In wildlands management, professional foresters in both private and public management systems objected to new environmental forest objectives, retarded rather than took leadership in the wilderness movement[39] and, after each stage of environmental forest controversy came back to concepts most familiar to them: that large-scale management for wood production was their "bottom line" objective.[40] In river development the issue was more sharply drawn, since there were far fewer opportunities to fuzz over differences; a host of technical and professional people associated with water development staunchly opposed the protection of free-flowing rivers for their natural values.[41] In all these cases managerial opposition to environmental objectives seemed to involve a series of rear-guard actions to contain them, and throughout the 1970s hardened steadily.

The controversy over "alternate technologies," and especially decentralized energy systems, became a highly significant focus for this reaction. While environmentalists were enthusiastic about the possibilities of decentralized solar energy systems, large-scale, "high-technology" system managers were equally skeptical and even hostile. The political struggle over choices of federal funds for energy research and development dramatized the differences. Those who organized large-scale energy systems in private affairs, and whose views were shared by the dominant energy policy makers in government, espoused intensively capitalized, large-scale, centrally managed systems.[42] But decentralists emphasized on-site technologies, and especially solar, not only because they provided an alternative source of energy but also because they were more consistent with their decentralist social and political tendencies.[43] From the winter of 1973–74 on these options came to be delineated with increasing sharpness so as to shape alternative political forces. A study of the attitudes of leaders in the two camps done in 1979 brought out their vastly divergent views about the social and economic as well as the political order. They constituted two visions of society in collision.[44]

This focus on divergent attitudes was reflected in a number of studies conducted in the last few years of the 1970s which compared, in one research design, the attitudes of the general public with those of what were called "thought leaders." The American Forest Institute sponsored one which dealt with American attitudes toward forest management. While 62 percent of the American people in general thought that the U.S. Forest Service should "continue to preserve . . . trees in their natural state" rather than "try to increase the yield and sales of timber from our National Forests" only 38 percent of the "thought leaders" agreed.[45] Two years later the AFI sponsored a second study which reflected about the same differences of opinion over the role of forests in American society: the general public viewed them primarily as habitat for wildlife and the leaders as a source of wood production.[46] A similar difference in values was found with respect to chemical risk. This study was conducted in 1979 by the insurance broker Marsh and McLennan.[47] According to the general public risks in society had increased over the years and would become greater in the future; but according to "thought leaders" they had and would continue to decline. While leaders felt that there was little risk and that the public's views were exaggerated, the public generally mistrusted the views of business and government about such matters, felt that all available information about hazards should be made readily available, and that they, not leaders, should make the choices.

Such observations as these define differences in political tendencies over the last two environmental decades between those who organized and directed large-scale systems on the one hand, and those who expressed environmental objectives in smaller contexts of daily life on the other. These were two separate worlds in political contention. Much of the struggle focused on scientific and technical information, not on just what was the "accurate" information, but on control of the resources by which information was generated, disseminated, gathered, and applied in decision-making. Large-scale systems were marked by massive information resources and capabilities, and control over the production and flow of information came to be one of their major political strategies. A host of issues arose over the problems on which research should be conducted,[48] how it should be designed, how the results should be assessed, and who should have the right of access to the findings. No wonder that some of the most bitterly fought environmental issues involved assessment of the health and ecological effects of development.[49] And it is no wonder that strategies of citizen environmental institutions were heavily directed toward acquiring resources to enhance their capabilities in the political struggle over information. It is not too much to argue that the "new political inequality" of the advanced industrial society was one of unequal access to scientific and technical information.

THE MIDDLE LEVELS: STATE ENVIRONMENTAL POLITICS

The clash between these two sets of forces, personal and community environmental values and large-scale systems of organized production, occurred in a host of specific environmental issues across the nation. The most useful context within which to observe them, however, is at the level of state government.[50] This is often an overlooked facet of environmental politics. Yet it would seem logical that forces organized at a national level which sought to occupy specific sites for development, and people who used those sites for environmental objectives, would end up confronting each other through state political institutions. I am especially intrigued with the role of such clashes in that broad expanse of land, water, and air between the city and the nation's wildlands, a countryside of working farmlands, farm woodlots and small forests, coal mines, of a "rural non-farm" population which has grown steadily over the course of the twentieth century.

Since World War II this countryside has been up for grabs. On the one hand it has been rediscovered by the American people. After decades of economic and population decline, of abandoned "marginal lands," and declining communities, these lands have been newly occupied by a host of urbanites who have sought them out for occasional visits or permanent residences, and largely for reasons of environmental quality. While before World War II they were "lands which nobody wanted" as one recent study describes them,[51] they have become lands which lots of people wanted—a fact testified to by the remarkable reversal in trends in real estate values since the 1930s. But these lands have also been searched out by a host of industrial entrepreneurs as sites for their activities, for mineral extraction such as strip mining, for rights-of-way for oil, gas, and coal slurry pipelines, electrical transmission lines, industrial "greenfield" factories, oil refineries, liquified natural gas installations and petrochemical plants. They have also come to be looked on by cities as convenient places in which to move their unwanted industry, such as electric power plants, their air pollution which is shunted elsewhere via tall stacks, their solid waste and sewage sludge in landfills in the land "out there," and their radioactive waste.

These two sets of forces have repeatedly clashed over the past three decades for control of the countryside. The intensity of the clash is heightened by the fact that the land in question is truly yet to be "occupied." Its use has not been finalized, as has been the case for the most part with land in the city. Hence use could go one way or the other. Many segments of the countryside contain areas of high environmental quality which environmentalists seek out to identify and protect as enclaves amid the rush to development: scenic rivers, wetlands, pine barrens, natural areas, sand dunes, and barrier islands. At the same time development forces seek to appropriate much of this land for their use and to protect it against the intrusion of those who want it for homes and for recreation and leisure-time activities. The countryside is the most intense battleground of all in the environmental-developmental contest, and it is at the state level—in the legislatures, the administrative agencies, and the hearing boards and courts—that these controversies can be best identified.

One of the most convenient ways to observe all this is through the voting patterns of the state legislatures. In some 20 states environmental organizations have compiled voting records of legislators over the past decade, and attributed scores to those records.[52] The methods of compilation vary from state to state, but they serve as a readily available source of data which can be ordered to observe geographical variations in voting support. I have worked out these votes for several states such as Michigan and Oregon, and have found that the most readily observable pattern involves a rural-urban dimension.[53] The strongest environmental support came from the cities and the weakest from the rural areas. This is true of the full range of environmental-developmental issues involving pollution control and protection of natural systems. Rural communities anticipating development of all kinds—farming, industry, population growth—all objected to what they consider to be constraints upon them arising from the cities. On the other hand, a host of large-scale development proposals were of such massive consequence and implications that they gave rise to intense negative reactions from the countryside itself: large-scale industry siting, utility rights-of-way, waste disposal facilities (especially for hazardous and radioactive waste), all of which rural communities felt were about to be imposed upon them by the larger urban-industrial society.[54] On these issues rural legislators were on the point of becoming avid environmentalists, and voted accordingly.

An even more significant focal point for the tension between centralizing and decentralizing tendencies was the level of the authority within the hierarchy of government which would have jurisdiction over such matters as environmental standards and siting decisions. This is generally known as the "pre-emption" problem. Shall states have the authority to establish environmental standards higher than those enforced by federal agencies? In many cases, such as automobile air pollution or noise, they did not. The attempt by Minnesota to require lower levels of radioactive releases from nuclear power plants than that required by the Atomic Energy Commission became a classic issue of federal-state relations.[55] This question of levels of authority, however, was shaped even more by changing authority as between local and state government. And here the pre-emption of local by state authority was widespread. In many a state, counties, townships, and cities could not enact standards higher than those provided in state strip mining, air pollution, pesticide, forest practice, and hazardous waste controls, and could not exercise final control over siting large-scale development, either by popular referendum or vote of local officials.[56] In this case the constant pressure from higher levels of economic and political organization was able to reduce dramatically the influence of local government. Power shifted upward to the state level. This enhancement of state power and authority over local government was a major legacy of the environmental controversies of the 1960s and 1970s.

On issues such as these the states became complex battlegrounds. Environmentalists, for example, fought to keep open the option for states to establish higher environmental standards than those required by the federal programs; while they were able to provide this in some cases, they failed in others. They had equal difficulty in securing positive state action to create higher standards. At the same time they sought to enhance state authority to prevent federal pre-emption of industrial and waste disposal siting, and in doing so often traded off state pre-emption of local authority to achieve that objective. On the question of protection of high-quality environmental areas, however, in land, air, and water, they actively sought an enhanced federal role in order to prod the states to take action which was often thwarted by developmental influences in state affairs. Hence they supported federal endangered species, wilderness, wild and scenic rivers, natural area, wetlands, barrier islands, and air and water non-degradation programs which involved federal initiative in identification and designation, as well as in providing funds for purchase of lands and waters.

Developmentalists, on the other hand, promoted an enhanced role for the federal government in precisely the realms that environmentalists advocated state and local action. They sought to use federal authority to prevent higher environmental standards from the states, and when outright pre-emption could not be obtained, they tried, usually successfully, to secure state laws which prohibited state standards from being higher than federal.[57] At the same time they actively worked for federal pre-emption of state influence in large-scale siting proposals, such as oil refineries in the coastal zone, and energy facilities in general;[58] the proposal in the late 1970s to establish a federal Energy Mobilization Board that had power to waive state environmental laws was such an instance. And they advocated state control over land use in natural environment designation in order to prevent an enhanced federal role in protecting areas of high environmental quality.

These divergent lines of interest in governmental authority became sharply defined in the controversy over the proposed federal land-use legislation in the early 1970s. In the course of that controversy environmentalists came to the conclusion that large-scale industry favored a federal land-use program in order to be able to pre-empt sites for industrial development. Hence they backed off, and when the proposal went down to defeat, did not display much disappointment. Controversies over the more limited land-use program in the Coastal Zone Management Act of 1972 made clear what the stakes were. For in that case federal authority was advocated by large-scale industry to facilitate its plans. Environmentalists joined with states in opposing that drive, and successfully blunted the initiative of energy companies who sought to turn the Act into support for a federal override of state authority. Environmentalists, in turn, came out of the earlier land-use controversy quite willing to struggle through a host of separate land-use programs rather than to devise a single, overall approach. When they gathered to formulate an environmental strategy for the new Carter Administration in late 1976 they found little support for including the larger land-use scheme on their agenda.[59]

There is still another dimension of these levels of scale and authority which became a subtle but significant element of environmental politics. Developmentalists had often been able to exercise disproportionate influence over local government because of their superior technical resources. When issues involved the health effects of air pollution, for example, few local governments could command the scientific resources to question industry experts. It was precisely for this reason that local governments often sought authoritative assessments of scientific data from federal agencies, such as the so-called "criteria documents," assessments of health and ecological effects which were first authorized in 1963.[60] This identifies the significance of scientific and technical capability in environmental politics, and the emerging roles played in that struggle by the two sets of institutions, the federal government and industry, which had the resources to carry out independent scientific and technical work.

In this technical setting of environmental politics the states were especially limited. While they often had authority to act they did not have the resources to do so. Only California consistently was able to draw on its own experts, make its own assessments of health and ecological effects, and support, in such a way that courts would accept, its own standards in the face of the counter-expertise of industry personnel.[61] Some other states did take up independent assessments, most recently Montana, but this happened in few cases.[62] Even larger states such as Michigan and Pennsylvania did not have the resources to act independently.[63] This fostered a two-fold strategy by developmentalists, first to seek to overwhelm states and even municipalities with expertise so as to dominate their scientific and technical analyses[64] and then to concentrate public technical and scientific resources at the federal level so as to exercise influence over its deployment. The weakness of the states enhanced the maneuverability of industry. By the end of the 1970s one of the most critical environmental issues came to be the selection of experts who would make the scientific assessments upon which standards were based.[65] This politics of environmental science was carried out primarily at the federal level; it constituted part of the superstructure of large-scale technical system action in national political affairs.

THE PARTS AND THE WHOLE

There is a tendency for environmental historians to write about the historical antecedents of the various pieces of environmental policy—air and water pollution, wilderness and wild rivers, energy, pesticides, and occupational health—as logically distinct subjects. While this often is productive, it does not advance the integration of the separate pieces into a larger framework. Hence, like so much historical research, it cannot readily be fit intelligibly into the whole. It takes its place, alongside innumerable isolated pieces, to be added up mechanically into a single, larger work. But conceptually the parts remain isolated and distinct, and the way in which environmental history fits into the larger context of historical evolution remains undefined. In the minds of future historians the only justification for including it might well be because the subject was argued about by contemporaries and written about by observers. Unless we inform our research in environmental history more broadly its meaning for the larger frame of historical writing will remain obscure.

To rectify this limitation we should be sensitive to the problem of the relationship of the part to the whole as we go along: it should be built directly into the way in which we think about the part, the way in which we define problems for research and the conceptual context through which we put it together. All this, of course, is not peculiar to environmental history, and hence the task of integration of pieces into the larger picture is generic rather than special to the subject of this paper. Throughout this effort to put together environmental politics since World War II, I have sought to work out that larger perspective. And as I have fiddled with the pieces of the jigsaw puzzle and its larger outline implicit in the shapes and colors of the border, the framework of levels of hierarchy in scale of human perception and understanding, of networks of human relationships and of institutions seems to provide the most meaningful overall pattern.

If such a conceptual context is valid, then it provides not only an opportunity to make sense out of this particular segment of recent American history, but also an equal possibility to make it fit into larger modes of thinking about history. The levels-of-scale pattern, with its varied formulations such as a three-tiered hierarchy of institutions seems to put together a host of historical happenings and to provide a way of integrating a wide range of human circumstance. It enables one to hold in a single framework of thought the larger realms of national politics and the smaller contexts of personal and community life; and it provides a working formula for bringing together processes of change as well as patterns of structure. This way of looking at environmental affairs helps to confirm larger historical theory as well as to understand ourselves as part of the drama of contemporary historical evolution.

THREE DECADES OF ENVIRONMENTAL POLITICS

The Historical Context

THE NATION'S POLITICAL INTELLIGENTSIA—those institutional leaders who think about, write about, and try to explain contemporary public life— have been more than puzzled about the rise of environmental affairs to a rank of national importance over the past thirty years. Although they have come to accept the reality of the political drive the rise entails, they have been persistently skeptical about the wisdom of its objectives. Rarely have they taken the role of leading the nation into new environmental frontiers. Their mixed emotions have led to a curious mixture of ideas about what this rise means. Many are tempted to accept the rather crude analyses of William Tucker and Ron Arnold that it is a plot of the "privileged classes" to lure the nation into untrustworthy paths and that the instruments of that plot are the environmental organizations whose leaders delight in manipulating an unwary public.[1] Those who cannot accept such polemical writings have taken more seriously a version of the same argument by Mary Douglas and Aaron Wildavsky, two scholars of high repute. They also argue that there is something

From *Government and Environmental Politics: Essays on Historical Developments Since World War Two*, ed. Michael J. Lacey (Lanham, Md.: The Woodrow Wilson Center Press, 1989).

here that is divorced from reality and must be explained away by the cultural peculiarities that make people subject to irrational fear and manipulation by others. "Primitive ways of thought," they have called it.[2]

It is a formidable task to challenge all this sophistry, which is so attractive to those who express skepticism about the wisdom and justification of environmental objectives. But that is precisely the purpose of this essay. From the vantage point of historical analysis, these efforts to explain away a social and political phenomenon that has been with us for three decades are the "ways of thought" that seem strange, remote from the real world, subject themselves to being explained through sociological and cultural analyses as "curious twists of mind." For environmental affairs are deeply rooted in the forces of history, in changes in society and demography, in the new world that emerged after World War II. They are but one aspect of massive social changes that include television and the computer, new realms of production beyond manufacturing, new attitudes about the relationships between men and women, new levels of income and education, and new intensities of information acquisition and exchange. Our task is not to be tempted constantly with the hope that it will all go away because it is an aberration of some sort, but to understand— seriously—what it is all about as a deeply rooted historical phenomenon. It is time we quit looking superficially at the environmental movement and instead looked at it straight. It is here and it is here to stay. What is it all about?

It may be of some help to provide an idea of the particular part of the beast I will be examining—the sources and the evidence. There is the vast product of media reporting that brings into focus the large issues of political controversy. But soon one finds that all that is superficial and is, in fact, a source of much of the confusion among our political intelligentsia. To go beyond the media requires an examination of the record of political give-and-take embedded in the documents created by administrative agencies, the courts, and the legislatures. Also a part of the recorded history are the newsletters dealing with air and water, land and the coastal zone, chemicals and occupational health, wetlands and wildlife, and even periscopic views into the inside of the Environmental Protection Agency (EPA).[3] There are also publications of the actors, the chemical, coal, and nuclear industries on the one hand, and the environmental organizations on the other: *Chemical Week, Coal Age, Nucleonics Week, Not Man Apart, National News Report* of the Sierra Club, *Exposure*, and *Nutrition Action.* And innumerable books have appeared in recent years.

In my review of this literature and in my personal inquiries, I have been especially interested in analysis at the deeper levels of social demography and values. I believe along with John Naisbett that one cannot really understand this country in the midst of vast social change if one's attention is limited to the media level of national politics.[4] I have been particularly interested in those studies, many commissioned by industry, that describe geographical variations in environmental attitudes.[5] I have also sought to construct regional patterns from legislative votes compiled by the League of Conservation Voters and a number of state environmental organizations. I have attempted to keep an eye on live environmental matters in more than a dozen states, from Maine and New Hampshire to Pennsylvania and Michigan, to Florida and Tennessee, and on to the Rocky Mountains, the Pacific Coast, and Alaska. I have consulted a wide range of materials, from state documents to newspapers to the publications of state and local environmental organizations, that provide clues as to the meaning of environmental values and actions.[6] I have sought out evidence concerning the environmental thrust from the bottom up as well as from the top down.

Let me also provide, at the outset, a warning: my analysis is in the style of a historian and not that of a policy analyst. My question is not one of which policy has been desirable or undesirable, has worked or not; I do not identify a problem and describe the resulting governmental action and outcomes of policy.[7] Rather, my concern is with historical evolution, with change and response to change. I am interested in problems, but at the level of analyzing how problems came to be defined in the particular way they were; I am interested in science and technology, but primarily in terms of why one path rather than another was taken; I am interested in management and its associated technical expertise, but primarily in terms of why managers and experts took up their own peculiar ways of thinking and acting. Above all, I am interested in the relationship between society and politics, between social change and political change. What are the roots of the environmental impulse, and how was it translated into public objectives? What interplay took place between these new public objectives and the older institutions with older values, which accepted the new objectives only with such difficulty? The drama unfolds the give-and-take in the political order.

FROM CONSERVATION TO ENVIRONMENT

The new interest in environmental objectives grew out of the vast social and economic changes that took place in the United States after World War II. Although some beginnings could be seen in earlier years, in the rising interest in outdoor recreation in the 1930s, for example, or in the few cases of concern for urban air and water pollution in the late nineteenth century, these trends are little more than precedents. It was the advanced consumer economy that came into existence following World War II that gave rise to a wide range of new public needs and wants. Incomes and standards of living rose; values changed amid rising levels of education; demands persisted that government supplement the private market to advance the new aims of the expanding and changing middle class. The roots of environmental interest lay in social demography, which was undergoing a fundamental historical transformation. The American people of the 1950s and 1960s differed markedly from those of a half-century before, and one among many of those differences lay in the new aspirations of personal, community, regional, and national life that were embodied in environmental affairs.[8]

It is customary for historians to link the environmental movement with the earlier conservation movement, yet they were quite dissimilar. While the conservation movement was concerned with efficiency in the use and development of material resources, the environmental movement was concerned with amenities and quality of life. The first was a part of the history of production; the second, of the history of consumption. The conservation movement arose not from public demand but from the strivings of professionals, scientists, and administrators to turn the wasteful use of resources into more efficient production. Efforts by these leaders to fashion a sustained political base in the form of organized activity failed miserably; for example, they continually rejected the policy initiatives of the most extensive conservation public of the time—the women's clubs.[9] The environmental movement, on the other hand, arose from the wider public to set new goals and demands about which the nation's administrative, technical, and professional leadership was usually skeptical. Environmental impulses, fueled from the public at large, constantly pressed the nation's leaders to go further than they felt desirable. Many of these reluctant participants in environmental affairs were, in fact, direct professional and institutional descendants of the early conservation leaders.

The conservation movement arose amid the concern for waste in the use of waters and forests.[10] Its classic elements were the use of engineering works to manage rivers and sustained-yield forest management to establish systems of continuous cropping. Water conservation originated in western irrigation, which reached a milestone with the Reclamation Act of 1902 and spread to the construction of reservoirs to enhance electric power production, navigation, and flood control, that panoply of multiple uses which reached its highest expression in the Tennessee Valley Authority.[11] The spiritual leader of forest conservation was Gifford Pinchot, who emphasized the primacy of wood production in forest management, expressed disdain for amenity values in woodlands, and spawned a host of public lands activities and professionalizing measures to establish himself firmly as the founding father of the entire forestry movement.[12] All these ideas moved forward rapidly during the administrations of Theodore Roosevelt. Conservation entered a later phase during the 1930s with the establishment of a soil conservation program that emphasized the efficient use and management of the nation's soil resources to undergird a sustainable agriculture.[13] This spirit was reflected even more in the many and varied resource development activities of the New Deal in public works projects and the Civilian Conservation Corps.[14] The New Deal fostered a massive drive for development in the nation's rivers and wildlands.[15]

The environmental movement turned the nation from this historical stage to a new direction that was not at all to the liking of conservation leaders. Environmentalists began to redefine "natural resources" according to not their physical, but their environmental, character. They emphasized not just the material resource itself but the human relationship to it. Rivers could be sources of water as a commodity to be used for agriculture, human consumption, electric power production, or navigation, but they could also be environments for human enjoyment. Forests could be sources of wood, but they could also be settings for home, work, and play that enhanced the quality of human life. The new environmental interest set off a widespread and fundamental debate over just what natural resources were in terms of their relationships with people. That meaning had been assumed in the earlier conservation movement; now it was subject to explicit interpretation and disagreement. While environmentalists affirmed the value of rivers as free-flowing waters and hence set off a series of controversies from Echo Park and Hells Canyon down to a host of smaller streams throughout the nation, those interested in more traditional conservation objectives affirmed the vital importance of rivers as sources of water as a developed commodity.[16] There was an equally vast gulf between those who affirmed the importance of wilderness and those who wanted to produce lumber from the nation's forests. The meaning and purpose of forests in human life was being redefined, and the older conservationists of the Pinchot vintage simply could not accept the change.[17] In the 1950s and the 1960s, the older conservationists and the newer environmentalists clashed repeatedly over the use of land and water resources.

Two conservation innovations of the 1930s played very different roles in this transition. The soil conservation movement, closely akin to the earlier water and forest conservation activities, was concerned with production, not environmental, resources. Hence, it was relatively easy in the 1950s for the Soil

Conservation Service to take on the new task of land and water development by building upstream reservoirs and draining wetlands. Both of these tasks ran headlong into the newly developing environmental interests, which looked on both tributaries and wetlands as valuable natural environments.[18] The wildlife movement, in contrast, bridged the transition between the old and the new. Interest in sustainable game populations had brought the game management movement into the orbit of "natural resources" activities in the spirit of conservation; the task of sustained-yield game management did not differ markedly from that of sustained-yield forest management. To the wildlife community, however, water, land, and forests were important not in their own right but as habitat for animals. As the perception of wildlife as game broadened into the larger interest in appreciating wildlife for its own sake, that context was strengthened. Concern over habitat emphasized the environment surrounding animals, on which they depend for propagation and survival. Hence, while the water, forest, and soils components of the conservation movement clashed persistently with the emerging environmental interests, the wildlife component found common ground with it and served as a bridge between old attitudes and new ones.

The new interest in pollution also served to distinguish environment from conservation. In this case, the precedents one might be tempted to use to establish firm historical roots are tenuous. There was, of course, the successful public health drive to reduce infectious disease, with triumphs such as the purification of drinking water and the use of antibiotics. There were fitful efforts to deal with urban environmental problems such as air pollution and noise, sewage disposal and industrial wastewater,[19] but it was not until the 1960s that these efforts gained widespread support and led to equally widespread action. One need not go into detail to establish the point that all these efforts, including the later interest in toxic chemicals, were associated with postwar change and had no significant roots in the early twentieth century. It is a history of change, not continuity, that unfolds as we examine U.S. environmental issues in the twentieth century.

While the public interest in natural environments rested on aesthetic objectives, the concern for pollution had its roots in new attitudes toward the biological environment and human health. The emerging interest in biology and the environment was expressed in terms of "ecology," the functioning of biological systems and how pollution interfered with it. The developing water quality program acquired an ecological focus that appeared explicitly in the statement of purpose of the 1972 Clean Water Act: to "restore and maintain the integrity of the nation's waters." This viewpoint came to be articulated in the early years particularly by the U.S. Fish and Wildlife Service.[20] Ideas about environmental threats to health, conversely, arose from new health aspirations that came after the control of infectious disease and were expressed in words such as "preventive medicine" and "wellness." Increasingly, control of air and water pollution came to be thought of as an aspect of advance in human health protection.

In both these expressions of concern about pollution, one could detect a sense of heightened goals and aspirations associated with a desire for a higher standard of living and "quality of life." While one could easily focus on the crisis aspect of pollution problems (and this usually was the tone of media coverage), on a more fundamental level the notion of pollution as a problem arose far more from new attitudes that valued both smoothly functioning ecosystems and higher levels of human health.

The roots of these new environmental interests lay in the changing demography and social values of the post–World War II years. Many studies describe those changes: of public attitudes and membership in environmental organizations;[21] of the values of outdoor recreationists individually and in groups;[22] of values sought by purchasers of woodlands, the "non-farm, non-industrial woodlot owners."[23] To these can be added more qualitative evidence in the form of expressions of environmental interest and values in environmental publications. These sources identify values associated with leading rather than lagging sectors of demographic change, those that emerge in greater scope and intensity over time, rather than diminish. They are associated with younger people and the more educated, and the changing values that they express. With age, environmental interest tends to decline, and with education it tends to rise. Environmental values do not seem to be distinctively associated with rising occupational or income levels and do not seem to increase markedly after the attainment of a college degree. They are associated with value changes at work primarily between elementary school and the fourth year of college.[24]

Environmental interest is a feature of the rise of the new mass middle class, which has come to play an increasing role in American society and politics. From the production side, that new middle class is associated with the new information economy; it is also associated with the new consumer economy, a fact that defines its direction of values and interest more precisely. One can formulate a sequence of historical change in patterns of consumption. In the late nineteenth century, necessities dominated consumption; in the 1920s a new interest in conveniences emerged, with a major focus on consumer durables. After World War II, the growing emphasis on consumption lay in amenities, both as new items of consumption and as integral parts of both necessities and conveniences. Now consumers had considerable discretionary income, which could be spent in many ways to make life more enjoyable. Environmental consumption was an integral part of this new direction of the economy.

Some of these environmental goods and services could be purchased in the private market. One could buy property in areas of cleaner air and water and amid more natural surroundings, either on the urban fringe or in the wider countryside, and one could enhance the environmental quality of one's own home. Many environmental amenities, in contrast, involved collective goods, such as air, water, or public lands, in which the private market did not determine the allocation of use. These amenities hence became the subject of public action and of public controversy and debate. Although environmental amenities had long been sought out by the more affluent, in the twentieth century that desire became a mass movement. The very rich could still escape to distant islands and retreats,[25] but within the United States, the environmental movement emphasized environmental equity, a broader sharing of environmental amenities than the private market could provide.[26] Public land management stressed such equity, and the process by which nineteenth-century private estates were transferred to public ownership and management symbolized the thrust of action.[27] Public management of air and water involved similar objectives of broad public benefit. What at one time in history had been thought of as a luxury available only to a few—one had to be able to travel to the "north woods" to enjoy more salubrious air—came to be thought of as an integral aspect of the mass consumption economy.

Several twists in the social analysis of environmental values help to indicate more clearly their roots. One was the examination of population shifts undertaken by geographer Ronald Briggs for the decade of the 1970s.[28] Briggs went beyond the customary analysis of state population trends and examined county-level data. Population shifts, he argued, were not confined to flows from the North to the South and West, but took place also within each region. Analysis revealed a dominant pattern of movement from amenity-poor to amenity-rich areas. The presence or absence of natural amenities was the major factor in people's choices to leave one area and to go to another. The second analytical twist distinguishes regional variations in environmental values.[29] Change did not come uniformly to the entire nation, and a few analyses went beyond the nationwide samples to disaggregate by region. There were regions of great strength in environmental values: New England, Florida, the Upper Great Lakes, the Pacific Coast, and the Mountain West. There were also regions that lagged markedly, such as the mid-South and the

Gulf states, and the midsection of the nation from the Dakotas down through Texas. The old factory belt from Pennsylvania through Illinois lay in between. These variations seemed to be consistent with variations in the spread of demographic change—and especially values associated with education—throughout the nation.

Some further insight comes from recent attempts to associate environmental values with psychological factors beyond the more traditional demography. The 1982 Continental Group study of environmental attitudes is especially useful in extending the analysis in this way.[30] That study ranged attitude expressions in a spectrum from resource development on one end to resource preservation on the other and sought to associate that range of opinion with other values. Two such relationships are of interest. In one, environmental values were associated with drives for higher levels of personal and occupational achievement, and developmental values with job security and more modest levels of aspiration. In the other, values were associated with the question of whether in the midst of difficult problems one turned to religion or to science. Those associated with developmental values tended to turn to religion; and those with environmental values, to science. These tendencies prompt one even more to associate evolving environmental values with the leading edge of change, rather than with older and more traditional ways of thought.

From the point of view of historical analysis, environmental politics displays a fairly typical case of change and response to change. At many times in history, major innovations occur that transform the economy, society, and politics, and these in turn create tensions between the new and the old, as the new challenges more accustomed patterns of thinking and acting. Such was the case in the transformation of an agricultural society in the nineteenth century to an industrial and manufacturing one. Such is also the case in the latter half of the twentieth century, as a manufacturing economy is transformed into an information and service one. A wide range of ways of thinking, of attitudes and values, of private and public institutions rooted in the manufacturing economy now are challenged by new modes of production and new modes of consumption. More strikingly, the role of consumption in the economy, subordinated in both economic thought and public policy in earlier eras, has come to assume a more formative influence in shaping personal choice and institutional patterns. From the broadest point of view, environmental controversy arises from the impact of new environmental consumer impulses on older institutions of material production rooted in earlier manufacturing and agricultural eras.

THE ENVIRONMENTAL IMPULSES

The environmental impulses that stemmed from these changes in values can be sorted out into different strands, each of which arose at a different point in time to take its place alongside those that had evolved earlier. The first to appear, dominating the years from 1958 to 1965, was the drive to manage resources as natural environments for human enjoyment. This drive arose out of the expansion of outdoor recreation, which had grown steadily between the two world wars and then expanded even more rapidly after 1945. First the National Park Service and then the U.S. Forest Service extended their outdoor recreation programs, and then the national Outdoor Recreation Resources Review Commission laid out a massive national plan to promote outdoor recreation. A host of proposals arose to identify areas of value as natural environments so as to manage them permanently in a natural state. The most widely debated feature of this thrust was wilderness, which led to the Wilderness Act of 1964; but the Wild and Scenic Rivers Act and the National Trails Act, both in 1968, reflected similar objectives.[31]

These more dramatic cases of interest in natural environments should not obscure its many and varied forms. In the urban environment, there were attempts to carve out beachheads in the midst of overwhelming pressures for development: the open space acquisition program of the Department of Housing and Urban Development, the interest in urban forestry and urban wildlife, the slow and persistent efforts to recapture the urban waterfront for low-density use and open space.[32] Far more was done in the countryside between the nation's cities and its wildlands, where the use of land, air, and water was in the balance, "up for grabs," so to speak, and where the contest between natural and developed environments was intensely keen. Here, a host of resources were identified as valuable: wetlands, natural rivers, barrier islands, pine barrens, tall-grass prairies, swamps, and those remnants of endangered flora and fauna called natural areas. All came to be the subject of identification, description, allocation, and management as natural environments.[33]

The drive also came to include the protection and management of high-quality air and water. Environmentalists obtained statutory authority that would protect air and water from degradation in programs centering on non-degradation and Prevention of Significant Deterioration (PSD).[34] The implementation of both went slowly. They were most effective in areas where the land was publicly owned and had already been classified as park or wilderness. Although the legal machinery led to little immediate action, a slowly rising trend in public interest in such matters could be followed, for example, through the growing prominence of visibility as a problem. Visibility standards were first applied in the Clean Air Act of 1977 to the national parks, but soon the standards came to be thought of as having wider relevance and were given special focus in the debate over acid deposition.[35]

Especially significant in extending an interest in natural environments was the growing appreciative interest in wildlife. What in earlier years had been thought of as "game" now came to be extended to include "nongame" animals under the more general rubric of wildlife. In 1973, the American Game Policy published in 1930 was revised under the new title of the North American Wildlife Policy.[36] The appreciative use of wildlife for observation came to exceed that of hunting; the majority of those who used even public game lands sought to shoot with a camera rather than a gun.[37] Out of all this interest came new nongame or appreciative wildlife programs, such as those for endangered species and ocean mammals, and new forms of financing, such as the state income-tax checkoffs. The U.S. Fish and Wildlife Service responded to these new interests with its programmatic environmental impact analysis, published in 1976, and its extensive studies of the attitudes of Americans toward wildlife, conducted by Stephen Kellert of the Yale Forestry School.[38] Appreciative wildlife attitudes undergirded almost every program to establish an aesthetic interest in natural environments.

All these actions represented not a throwback to some preindustrial longing, as detractors were inclined to argue, but a desire for an advanced standard of living that included a far larger share of natural environment amid developed environment than had been thought appropriate in years past. Such natural environments formerly had been looked upon as "useless," waiting only to be developed. Now they were thought of as "useful" for filling human wants and needs. They played a role as significant in the advanced consumer society as such material goods as hi-fi sets or indoor gardens. Architects and corporate business sought to express such values by incorporating nature into the design of hotels, office buildings, convention centers, and shopping malls in the built-up environment. This drive for natural environments was the most extensive and enduring feature of the organized environmental movement. For the largest environmental organizations, that interest was uppermost, and over the years its political base expanded from Washington, D.C., to almost every nook and cranny of the nation.[39] By 1984 the wilderness movement, which in the 1950s had been dominated by the Wilderness Society in Washington, had come to be organized in every western state, with local constituencies fashioning logrolling coalitions to put together state packages of proposals for wilderness designation, each unit of which was looked upon as someone's backyard. Reflecting this continuing public interest in natural environments, two organizations with such concerns, the Wilderness Society and the Nature Conservancy, each with very different political strategies, grew rapidly in the late 1970s and early 1980s.[40]

Between 1965 and 1972, air and water pollution came to exercise a formative influence in environmental affairs alongside the search for natural environments. The legislative landmarks were the Clean Air Acts of 1963, 1967, and 1970, the Clean Water Acts of 1965, 1970, and 1972, and the new pesticide law of 1972. All this activity had a twist, distinctive for the times, which emphasized ecological change and which later events tended to obscure. The concern for ecology or the "integrity of biological systems" seemed to structure ideas about pollution in this first stage of public policy toward it. The concern for ecology was closely related to the earlier concern for the aesthetic natural environment out of which it evolved. The new concern for pollution was not primarily focused on human health. Instead, it emphasized the role of pollution in the functioning of ecological systems, a degraded ecology as an undesirable human context, and a concern for protection of natural ecological processes. One heard of an overload in carrying capacity, the way in which animal populations outran food supplies, biological simplification under stress, disturbances in aquatic ecosystems under acidification, and reduced forest growth due to air pollution.[41]

The initial concern in this vein seemed to come from those who protested the destruction of wildlife habitat by development. During the 1960s there were many objections to the construction of dams and roads, the release of waste heat from power plants into rivers and lakes, and the destruction of wetland habitat by residential construction.[42] The U.S. Fish and Wildlife Service came to be the major source of objection to these threats and, within the inner realms of the federal government, a defender of ecological systems and values. It was that concern from which arose the initial concept of "adverse environmental impacts," and it was from the House Subcommittee on Fish and Wildlife that many new initiatives along this line came, including both the National Environmental Policy Act (NEPA) and the Council on Environmental Quality (CEQ).[43] The fact that the appropriation for staff activities of the CEQ rests with the Fish and Wildlife Subcommittee is no historical accident, and the initial context that shaped the NEPA, namely interagency review rather than public review, was influenced heavily by attempts by the Fish and Wildlife Service and the Water Pollution Control Administration (WPCA) to protect fish and wildlife habitat.

Several other features of these years reflect this ecological context. The new interest in water pollution emphasized streams and lakes as ecological systems; it was this new drive that led to the removal of the water pollution control program from the Public Health Service (PHS), first to an independent agency within the Department of Health, Education and Welfare (HEW) and then to the Department of the Interior. Fishing interests argued that the PHS cared little for water pollution beyond chlorination. The initial concern over atomic energy in the late 1960s emphasized thermal pollution rather than radioactive release or reactor accidents.[44] And the new interest in pesticides emphasized heavily, as did *Silent Spring,* their detrimental effects on wildlife.[45] By the 1970s much of this emphasis on pollution matters had changed to focus more exclusively on human health, but between 1965 and 1972, ecology provided a transitional context of the new interest in pollution.

Several observations mark the decline of the ecological focus. One was the shift in the interests of the Conservation Foundation, which in its origins and its role in environmental leadership in the 1960s thought and acted from an ecological point of view.[46] By the end of the 1970s, it was difficult to detect much of that past in the work of the foundation. Equally remarkable was the way in which the formulation of ideas about an extensive federal "ecological service" was soon forgotten. Amid debates about heightened federal environmental action in the late 1960s, the proposal for a major ecological research program to undergird environmental policy, coming in no small part from the Subcommittee on Fish and Wildlife, was cast aside in favor of impact analysis.[47] The idea survived with some success in the form of the Office of Biological Services in the Fish and Wildlife Service until the arrival of the Reagan administration, but not with the formative influence anticipated in the 1960s.[48] Amid the growing attention to human health in environmental matters in the 1970s, ecology took a backseat.

The ecological focus reappeared late in the 1970s from the entirely different quarter of the new interest in acid deposition. The main significance of that new debate lay in the renewal of interest in welfare effects of air pollution. In the 1960s, these forces played as important a role in air pollution matters as health concerns. The first version of the sulfur oxides criteria document issued in the spring of 1967 contained a major section on visibility as well as material on agricultural crops, reflecting the technical background of John Middleton, first director of the National Air Pollution Control Administration.[49] But implementation of the Clean Air Act veered strongly toward a dominant focus on health. In the early 1970s, the EPA lost the court case concerning secondary annual standards for sulfur dioxide, and it did not pursue the matter further. The issue of acid rain, however, along with increased scientific knowledge about transport, deposition, and effects, revived the concern with welfare impacts, and by extension, ecological disturbances. The major significance of the acid precipitation issue concerned the role of these secondary effects in public regulation. This perception of the matter tended to restore the broad context in which air pollution had been considered in the 1960s.[50]

New Environmental Impulses

During the 1970s, three new environmental impulses emerged to take their place alongside previous ones. One of these, emphasizing resource shortages and the "limits to growth," seemed to arouse little public interest. The rise in energy prices after 1973 led to public action to reduce the burden of increases in the cost of living. Environmentalists carried the concern further, discussing energy efficiency, least-cost supplies, and alternative sources.[51] But even this concern generated little analysis of the inflation that seemed to be a result of rising real energy costs, the decline in lower real-cost supplies, and the movement toward higher real-cost levels. Real-cost inflation was merely the way in which resource limits made themselves felt in the economy. By the beginning of the 1980s, the declining pressure on energy prices reduced even this limited public interest in the large problem.

Interest in resource shortages and limits to growth was expressed not so much by the public as by technical and professional leaders. It was in these circles that studies were made, articles written, warnings of the future announced, and influence applied to public policy. These were debates among the nation's political intelligentsia without significant public action. In the late 1960s, there had been some interest in the "population problem,"[52] but even here it seemed that public interest was shaped far more by family size and the "limits to growth" within the family context than by any broader global concern.[53] The report of the Commission on Population and the Nation's Future was shelved as quickly by the public as by President Nixon, and despite continued action on the part of environmental leaders, the matter was not revived as a broad public issue outside the context of immigration.[54] The low public interest in such matters was reflected in the very limited public attention displayed for both the Global 2000 Report and the World Conservation Strategy.[55] Similar relative indifference was expressed concerning farmland conversion and soil erosion, which the American Land Forum sought to foster as issues in the early 1980s.[56]

Far more extensive in terms of popular involvement was a second new twist to environmental affairs in the 1970s, the practice and ideology of personal and community autonomy and decentralization. Limits-to-growth issues stirred public debate without stirring the public; the decentralist movement stirred public interest in the form of personal and community action without stirring much public debate. Evidence concerning wide public involvement in such matters was abundant. *Mother Earth News* and *Organic Garden* were extremely popular magazines; ideas concerning the wisdom of "human scale" provided one of the few ventures into well-formulated ideology in the environmental movement.[57] There seemed to be a major demographic trend associated with self-help and self-reliance in which people in the city, the suburbs, and the countryside sought to pursue life with more independence.[58] Modern technology furthered the trend by making self-reliance less burdensome in time and human energy. The community focus on the enhancement of natural environment values and protection against threats from large-scale development and pollution helped to enhance this tendency. So did efforts to make personal choices about lifestyle that might protect one against chemical hazards.

There was the great popularity of new habits of eating, with an emphasis on organically grown foods. Natural food stores witnessed a major growth in the 1970s, and general food markets began to take on some of their products.[59] Many people sought to grow their own vegetables so that potential chemical threats could be lessened; by the 1980s it was estimated that more than 35 million American families had some sort of vegetable garden. The concern for toxic chemicals in the 1970s often took the form of efforts to protect supplies of drinking water by insulating sources from potential groundwater contamination, or by seeking to declare one's home and grounds off limits to pesticide spray drift.[60] All these trends underlined both changes in personal lifestyles and a new interest in political autonomy and decentralization. One of its most striking expressions was the community energy movement and the promise of solar energy, which seemed to make possible a higher level of freedom from larger energy systems.[61]

Although both the limits-to-growth impulse and the personal-and-community-autonomy impulse, each in its own way, constituted new elements in environmental affairs in the 1970s, both were overshadowed in policy debate and action by new concerns for human health. These reflected a persistent transformation in human attitudes marked by the triumph over infectious disease and by the emergence of new health concerns, expressed by such words as "wellness" and embracing concepts such as physical fitness and optimum health. Most people were no longer worried about imminent death or uncontrolled infectious diseases. Major chemical threat episodes, such as the Donora smog, kepone in the James River, and PPBs in Michigan and Love Canal, all dramatized the concern.[62] Underlying it was a change in attitudes and values. Increasingly Americans expressed their interest in health in terms of a capacity to engage in daily affairs at an optimum level of physical and mental health. They began to change their personal habits of eating, smoking, drinking, and exercise. They came to look on chemical agents in the environment as having an adverse effect on their aspirations.

This new interest in human health seemed to be at variance with the dominant trends and capabilities of American science and medicine. Leaders in those fields tended to identify advances in health in terms of mortality. Periodic reports from the surgeon general marked progress with data about reduced death rates in various age categories.[63] Medical practitioners, moreover, tended to be concerned more with curing sickness than preventing it, and hence Americans experienced a limited ability by physicians to cope with knotty problems of optimum health.[64] While preventive medicine had made impressive accomplishments in vaccination against infectious diseases, it now seemed to be less interested in the limitations on optimum health that might come from environmental causes. Pollution issues seemed to be wrapped up in these contradictory tendencies—the high level of aspiration by the public for greater wellness on the one hand, and the relatively limited capacity of science and medicine to respond on the other. Hence, a major aspect of the public's concern for chemical pollution was either to take matters into their own hands and avoid contaminants by means of new personal lifestyles, or to demand public action to prevent exposure.[65] In such affairs the medical profession often followed rather than led public attitudes.

The range of health effects at issue seemed to expand steadily. Most attention was given to cancer, but soon a wider range emerged: genetic and reproductive disorders, fetal and infant malformations, neurological deficits and modified enzyme systems, lowered immunity and premature aging.[66] Interest in chemical pollution as a possible cause of such health effects seemed to widen. Attempts to prevent exposure to carcinogens led to many battles over specific chemicals and to unsuccessful efforts to establish generic cancer regulation, first by the EPA in its formulation of "cancer principles" in the mid-1970s, and then by the Occupational Safety and Health Administration (OSHA) in its abortive "generic cancer" policy a few years later.[67] Cancer took up most of the debate, but expanding scientific knowledge tended to expand the range of concerns that were being taken more seriously with each passing year. There were massive implications. If it could be demonstrated, for example, that blood-lead levels common to most Americans as "normal" reduced IQ scores by three points, the cost when widely shared by large numbers of Americans could be extensive—it was estimated that for each point of IQ deficit one's lifetime earnings were reduced by 1 percent.[68] Potentially more dramatic was the research linking toxic chemicals to reduced male and female fertility. In February 1984, *Chemical Week* reported soberly on the implications for the industry of the fact that three and a half million American families were not able to have children.[69]

Occupational health provided an especially sharp focus for these concerns.[70] In earlier years, occupational hazards had been thought of primarily in terms of physical injury, but after World War II, occupational illness received increasing attention.The use of antibiotics made other problems such as cancer and reproductive defects more visible. Workers were reluctant to take up such issues, often because it might well mean removal from the job and hence financial loss. Nevertheless, several labor unions pressed forward, lobbied for the Occupational Health and Safety Act, hired their own industrial hygiene professionals to tackle the issues, and pressed OSHA to move toward stricter regulation. The format of the resulting controversies was typical: the affected workers expanded the frontiers of scientific knowledge and sought to reduce exposures in the workplace; the industries demanded higher levels of proof, resisted emission controls, and opted for protective devices worn by workers. Change often came most readily as a result of liability suits. In the case of asbestos, for example, the courts, rather than the administrative agencies, pinpointed responsibility and assessed damages for injury. Such action often caused controls to be tightened voluntarily so that industries could avoid such costs in the future.

Here was the crux of the political interplay: the public was demanding that frontiers of knowledge and action with respect to health be expanded more rapidly than was possible, given the limited capabilities of science and medicine. Public controversy revealed how little was known about the presence of chemicals of potential harm, either in the environment or in humans.[71] The first comprehensive measurements of blood-lead levels for the entire population were made only after 1975, and such monitoring was rare.[72] Occupational health experts continually stressed the degree to which the lack of exposure records as a part of medical case histories inhibited diagnosis. The problem was one of data. The collection of mortality data had long been standard operating procedure, and information was readily available about the "reportable" infectious diseases. Modern medicine now focused on a much different type of statistic; even cancer incidence, in contrast with mortality, proved difficult to determine. On a wide range of subjects, public demand for knowledge and action outran capability.

The historic change that all this implied for health science and medicine was the task of retooling from concern with acute effects of high-level exposures to the more subtle chronic effects of persistent low-level ones. Scientific method and analysis appropriate for the first were found to be far less able to identify the second. Thus, epidemiological studies that traditionally relied on the 5 percent confidence level used by biostatisticians might not be appropriate for smaller effects, because these were almost invariably, by their very size, beyond such limits. Such was the relationship found between lead and child behavior.[73] Environmental demands had contributed in no small part to the extension of chemical measurement capabilities from parts per million to parts per trillion in concentration. But the cost of such measurement made it all but impossible to chart the presence of chemicals, such as dioxin, in more than a few cases. A new test for blood lead developed in the late 1970s greatly lowered the cost of surveillance, but for most of the new health effects, diagnostic cost greatly limited the public demand for knowledge. The public desire to know was thwarted by the increasing "real cost" of knowing.

Underlying the new concern for chemical harm was the public perception of a chemical world out of control. In a series of episodes, from the early experience with atomic testing and pesticides to later cases of toxic chemicals in air and water and on land, the public gradually formulated fairly clear notions about the chemical universe: chemicals were persistent, not biodegradable, lasting in the environment for long periods of time; they were ubiquitous, transported through air and water to places far distant from their source; they "biomagnified" in the food chain so as to become more highly concentrated in the higher orders of mammals; and they were mysterious in that they could suddenly appear in ways not previously known or suspected. Chemicals dispersed into the environment affected biological life, and humans in particular, in such a way that their effects could be even partially controlled only with the greatest difficulty. The nuclear reactor episode at Three Mile Island conveyed the image of a technology that was out of control; the sudden realization that hazardous waste had been permitted to pervade the environment and now seemed impossible to contain reinforced that perception. How could an individual person bring under control a potential harm which the nation's prevailing institutions could not?

THE IMPACT ON PUBLIC AFFAIRS

Environmental impulses had varied effects on public affairs and shaped varied debates. One of the first of these involved the question of "how much," the level of public benefit that should be sought. What was the balance that should be struck between natural and developed environment? How much wilderness; how many miles of free-flowing rivers; how much in the way of wetlands, estuaries, barrier islands, and natural areas; how much open space and parkland within the metropolitan region? Each case involved conflict between those who wanted to develop land and water and those who wanted to manage them as a natural environment. No formula seemed to be available or offered as to "how much" in some ultimate sense; the issues were fought over case by case, as environmentalists pressed their claims as to the social desirability of more natural environments. These competing claims constituted some of the most celebrated cases in the politics of the environmental era.

National goals with respect to environmental pollution were far more focused. Early in the 1960s, the notion that social objectives should be thought of in terms of standards of environmental quality was agreed on. The debate over the precise level of ambient air or water or biological burden was another matter; the establishment and reestablishment of standards continued year after year as the contending forces debated the issue of "how much." Those responsible for emissions persistently sought to increase the allowable levels, and those who felt harmed equally sought to reduce them. These debates over standards took many forms. One was the threshold margin-of-safety formula, which in standard setting sought to add a cushion that took into account the plausible unknowns on top of known scientific evidence about harm. Another was cost-benefit analysis which sought to establish a common denominator for the value of adverse effects, which, through control, could become a social benefit and hence could be compared with costs.[74] Still a third approach, which became more popular with industries responsible for pollution and with environmental managers toward the end of the 1970s, was risk analysis. Analysts were heavily influenced by the concern with cancer, which sought to establish some mathematical statement about risk of premature mortality. This strategy was limited to firmly known effects and did not incorporate the plausible unknowns; and it seemed to focus heavily on mortality rather than morbidity.[75]

Although the policymaking strategy of setting standards and implementing them seemed to give a degree of precise discipline to the issue of social goals, it did so only by excluding the more debatable frontiers of knowledge.

Were secondary welfare standards to be given as much consideration as human health? Environmentalists sought to bring a wide range of effects into standard setting, but those responsible for emissions sought to narrow the range so as to limit their responsibility. Industry vigorously opposed the expansion of the visibility standard to integral vistas in the national parks, for example, and ridiculed the gradual extension of visibility as a policy objective throughout the East, all because it would justify tighter controls over sulfur dioxide emissions. While environmentalists sought to extend health protection from premature mortality to temporary and reversible morbidity, such as the Montana objective of preventing air pollution that would interfere with normal daily activities, industries sought to contain that drive.[76]

One is struck also by the limited degree to which developmental agencies in government incorporated environmental objectives into their daily way of thinking and acting. What little transformation they underwent was associated with the mitigation of environmental impact rather than the enhancement of environmental objectives. To conform to requirements of the law, the environmental impact statement (EIS) became widely used, although its role in the work of developmental agencies would seem to be more one of providing an early warning signal as to potential opposition to the agency than of enhancing environmental goals. An approach that focused more directly on objectives was the dual-stream planning process of the Principles and Standards of the Water Resources Council.[77] This process called for as much attention to planning for environmental objectives as for developmental ones. Similar attention was given to environmental goals through the various "futures" strategies used by several state governments.[78] Nevertheless, agencies such as the U.S. Army Corps of Engineers, the U.S. Forest Service, the Bureau of Land Management, and the U.S. Department of Agriculture continued to conceive of their missions as developmental, to look upon environmental objectives as requirements to which they would adjust minimally in the face of legal and political necessity. One can detect little significant change in the values they sought to advance, little leadership to innovate and enhance environmental objectives.[79]

A second effect of the environmental impulse on public policy was its influence in expanding frontiers in science and technology. Contrary to much of the political debate, environmentalists did not reject science and technology, but instead sought to extend them. Controversies over such issues involved disputes over the use of scarce resources. In matters scientific, environmentalists sought to allocate resources to extend the frontiers of scientific knowledge about the functioning of the biological world and human health and the environmental effects on them. In matters technological, they sought to pro-mote innovation to reduce emissions at the source, rather than rely on either treatment or dispersion. In both cases, the political significance lay in the fact that environmentalists placed such great demands on existing scientific and technical resources and institutions that they could not respond effectively.

Environmentalists pressed for more monitoring and research on the one hand and the incorporation of new knowledge more quickly into the scien-tific consensus on the other. Environmental monitoring was very limited. Air quality monitoring was confined to the areas of high pollution or the isolated "hot spots," rather than extended into a comprehensive system; there was lit-tle information about changing levels of air quality in the cleaner areas, those that Pennsylvania, for example, called its "non-air basins." Hence there was the intense controversy over measurements, which would chart degradation under the PSD program. Water quality monitoring was a bit better because of the wide interest in a fuller range of quality measurements desired by fishing interests, but even here the extension of parameters outran resources.[80] The weakness of baseline ecological measurement was underlined by the acid pre-cipitation controversy, which focused on the Hubbard Brook experiment station as the only case with twenty years of significant monitoring. As ground-water increased as an issue, the limited data only underlined the weakness of knowledge about biogeochemical cycles. Perhaps the most extensive data in-volved lead, largely because of the persistent effort by Clair Patterson of the California Institute of Technology to chart lead in a wide range of environ-mental media throughout the world.[81] And a major result of the acid precip-itation issue was to enhance a wide range of environmental monitoring.[82]

Environmental demands also stimulated experimental research. Knowl-edge about the effects of lower levels of human exposure was pursued. The draft lead criteria document issued in 1983 relied heavily on new research re-ported since the earlier 1977 version to detail an increasing range of health effects at lower levels of exposure.[83] Research on the effects of acidification on lakes, building materials, visibility, forests, and agricultural crops came about largely because of the intensity with which environmentalists pursued the acid rain issue. There was an explosion of environmental research after the 1960s, with a large number of new scientific journals appearing to accommo-date publication of results. Much of this activity took on a regional focus, as reflected in a new journal, *Northeastern Environmental Science,* which began publication in 1982.[84] But in some realms of research, environmental influences were limited. The regional experiment stations of the U.S. Forest Service un-dertook research on environmental uses of the forests primarily in response to recreational and landscape demands expressed by users and not from its own internal initiatives. The composition of its research advisory committees and the choices they made in research strategies reflected limited environmental interest.[85] The same was true of the new sea grant institutions, where research seemed to be shaped by developmental rather than environmental objectives.

The series of controversies that emerged after the mid-1960s over the assessment of scientific studies about environmental effects identifies more precisely the role of the environmental impulse in matters scientific. These controversies followed a general pattern. At one end were those who required high levels of direct proof of harm before they would believe that action was justified; at the other were those who sought to bring frontier knowledge about adverse effects into assessments as a ground for action more quickly. Many views ranged in between. As new scientific data appeared, no matter what the total fund of knowledge, there was continual disagreement between those who hesitated to draw conclusions because not enough was known and those who sought to act on the basis of newly discovered frontier knowledge.[86] There were disagreements over levels of proof. Environmentalists associated themselves with frontier scientists who sought the more rapid use of new knowledge because it would speed up action. Sources of pollution associated themselves with high-proof scientists so as to retard such action.[87] Although some in the scientific world were prone to describe these debates as being between "good science" and "bad science," such a scheme does not seem to be workable in identifying the nature of the controversy. Far more significant were the predispositions of scientists in the face of expanding knowledge: their institutional attachments; their commitments to particular methods such as epidemiology and experimental biochemistry; their psychological values, which predisposed them in personal choices to play it safe or to be innovative. In these matters, environmentalists played an important role in advancing the frontiers of knowledge, in giving support to scientists so engaged, and in bringing that knowledge more quickly into the workable consensus building that provided political support for public decisions.[88]

The environmental impulse also stimulated innovation in technology. In pollution matters, environmentalists stressed source reduction rather than treatment or dispersion. The weight of their influence on such matters at any one time seemed minimal, but over the years the direction was clear. Once dispersion in the form of either dilution (in water pollution) or the use of tall stacks (in air pollution) had come to be rejected, then treatment technology was stimulated. Once the cost of treatment came to be accepted, third-party innovators were prompted to become inventive with respect to alternative and lower-cost treatment technologies. Higher treatment costs promoted source reduction technologies. This gave rise in some quarters to the view that "pollution prevention pays," because it both increased conventional productivity and reduced pollution.[89] Joseph Ling of the 3M Corporation sought to popularize this point of view, but it was not widely accepted in the United States. In Europe, Ling's views were more popular.[90]

The debates had to do with the pace of technological innovation.[91] Environmentalists pressed for it to proceed more rapidly; for example, to coal washing, fluid bed combustion, and limestone injection in controlling sulfur dioxide. But existing technologies carried with them a built-in conservatism, a demand that they be continued through their economic life rather than be discarded because of technological obsolescence. Within each line of industry there was a range of technical modernization, from old plants to newer ones. In the normal course of events the old would gradually give way to the new. Environmentalists believed, however, that the pace was too slow; it should be accelerated. They sought to focus on the presence of obsolescence in the face of rapid technological change. Hence came the idea of technology standards in water pollution treatment and the view that all plants should conform to the "average of the best" technology in the industry. The dispute focused on which "average" and which "best." When industry sought to define it as the median among all plants, the EPA argued that the law justified the average of the "best 10 percent." The courts agreed. All this identified the resistance to new technological innovation as a form of diseconomy arising from previous investment commitments.

Environmentalists sought to press on with a number of frontier technologies: photovoltaic solar cells, the electronically controlled internal combustion engine, biological farming, integrated pest management, decentralized source-stream recycling of materials, closed-loop water process recycling, least-cost energy efficiencies.[92] Many of these innovations assumed a point of view that stressed decentralization rather than support the historical preference for large-scale technologies. In that new emphasis on light rather than heavy technologies, environmental ideas about such matters seemed to be more than slightly in tune with the flexibility and versatility of the electronic age. The innovations were viewed with scorn by those associated with older and heavier technologies.

An understanding of the historical role that environmental action played requires a focus on the rapid changes in both science and technology in the latter half of the twentieth century throughout American society, and not on the less-than-adequate analytical context of pro- and antiscience or pro- and antitechnology. If one sorts out the old and the new in such matters, the environmental impulse was strongly associated with the frontiers of discovery and innovation.

THE ENVIRONMENTAL OPPOSITION

The environmental impulses and their impact on public life gave rise to formidable and persistent opposition. While those engaged in the daily round of environmental politics well recognized that resistance, the forces arrayed in opposition to the environmental movement have received little systematic treatment as a major element of environmental history. They deserve analysis as careful and complete as the environmental drive itself. The historical drama is one of thrust and counterthrust, of new values and old, of new impulses seeking to turn public policy toward new goals in the face of the reluctance of the old order to modify customary ways of thought and action. The prevailing pattern of politics in the years before World War II involved contests among diverse segments of development—business, labor, and agriculture—each seeking to gain a larger share of public benefits. Now those groups faced a significant challenge from the consumer side. The environmental drive was a forceful part of that challenge. It is no surprise that developmentalists fought back.[93]

Much of the strength of the opposition lay in its own reinvigoration in post–World War II society. Developmental institutions advanced in their role in tandem with environmental objectives. The drama of the political scene lay in the intensity of debate over rival claimants for public policy: those who wanted to expand material production rapidly and those who wanted to expand the environmental benefits of the advanced consumer society. A striking case of that drama lay in the Rocky Mountain West, where the old and the new competed vigorously for a claim to turf.[94] The traditional developmental institutions there, such as stockraising, lumbering, and hard rock mining, were now augmented by a range of new energy activities. But that region now expressed some of the strongest environmental objectives in the nation.[95] The new order made claims of its own for wilderness, wildlife, environmental forestry, outdoor recreation, cleaner water and air, and in-stream water flows; it contributed much to the defeat from within the region of both the Sagebrush Rebellion and the Reagan administration's asset management program. The old order fought back with its own claims, seeking to use the power of the federal government to restrain the environmental forces from within the West.

One can chart the environmental opposition through confrontations in state and federal legislatures, administrative agencies, and the courts. The fight was intense and persistent. Many have sought to argue that the passage of federal environmental legislation reflected fundamental agreement on public environmental values and objectives and that disagreement was secondary and concerned with differences over implementation of goals rather than of goals themselves. This view is more of an argumentative contrivance than a faithful recording of the facts. Many decisions by administrative agencies and courts expressed fundamental disagreements over objectives. Often it was the debate within the agencies and the courts that revealed most fully the intensity of the controversy. The opposition to environmental objectives in each arena of politics was more than relentless; it constituted a strategy of maximum feasible resistance and minimum feasible retreat.

So many cases of opposition are on record that it would be foolhardy to do more than categorize some generic types. There was, for example, the attempt to shape the course of scientific assessment. This appeared with the first criteria document, the draft sulfur oxides report in the spring of 1967, which led to a storm of protest from the coal and utility industries over the scientific conclusions. The intensity of this opposition gave rise to concern by some state public health authorities; if the National Air Pollution Control Administration (NAPCA) buckled under to demands that the conclusions be altered, no state could withstand the ensuing pressure.[96] The answer came with an instruction from Congress through the work of Senator Jennings Randolph that the criteria document be revised under the guidance of an advisory committee that included representatives from the affected industries.[97] From that time forward, no scientific assessment, whether a criteria document or otherwise, remained independent of the real world of very high stakes involved in scientific assessment.[98] The vast importance of all this to the environmental opposition was reflected in the Reagan administration's strategy of replacing one group of scientific advisers with another more receptive to the views of the opposition. The resulting furor revealed environmental politics at its most basic level. That politics could be observed in the care, or lack thereof, with which EPA administrators chose members of their science advisory boards.[99]

A major strategy of containment by the environmental opposition was to restrict both in numbers and in geographical territory the identification of natural resources that were valuable environmental assets subject to potential management for environmental objectives. Mere listing of specific areas of high environmental value, such as wilderness, wetlands, barrier islands, estuaries, parks, and wildlife species, became crucial, because such listing could well be the first step toward action. Hence, classification of wilderness under the three wilderness inventory programs, or state inventories of "areas of critical environmental concern" in the coastal zone, became targets of contention. By the same token, pollution sources sought to restrict the identification of sources of harm, such as toxic waste dumps or chemical carcinogens, in order to minimize the range of environmental controls to which they might be subject. As was the case with standards, identification of environmental assets or environmental problems involved fundamental debates over goals. They were not simply issues of implementation of agreed-on policies; on the contrary, they constituted a continual set of cases, one by one displaying a repeated drama: different groups in American society differing over the wisdom of pursuing specific environmental goals.

It is important to emphasize the high degrees of success enjoyed by the environmental opposition. The main theme of recent environmental history has emphasized the environmental triumphs. A careful assessment calls for a mixed review. There were significant, though less publicized, failures, which in the customary legislative record are forgotten. Significant attempts to add to the range of publicly owned and managed natural environment areas were turned back: a program of national estuarine areas as extensive as the lakeshore and seashore program was transformed into a small set of research areas;[100] the drive to protect barrier islands in a similar manner, proposed by Congressman Philip Burton, was restricted to control of federal activities on such islands;[101] the marine sanctuary program advanced at a snail's pace; purchase of inholdings within the national parks moved equally slowly; the drive for urban national parks met little success beyond the initial choices in the early 1970s.

Equally noticeable was the modest, even slow, pace of pollution control activity. The Clean Air Act had anticipated a program extending far beyond the original six criteria pollutants, and NAPCA announced in 1968 that several dozen criteria documents were in the offing.[102] But lead alone has been added to the list, and this only by a series of citizen actions and court orders.[103] A research program in behavioral toxicology, which in the late 1960s seemed more than promising, could have greatly expanded air pollution problems to include temporary disability that led to lost time at work and in personal affairs.[104] This program did not go beyond the beginning stage. An initial effort in 1965 by Senator Abraham Ribicoff to control pesticide discharges into streams by direct inspection and supervision of manufacturing processes was turned back without difficulty, and the pesticide control program throughout its history has had to struggle for effectiveness. The control of toxic chemicals has been marked more by lack of action than by vigor; few chemicals have been tested for low-level chronic effects of low-level exposures; the promise of strategies to move beyond the acute effects of acute exposures has not yet been realized.

Two subtle but vastly important realms of success for the environmental opposition have been little noticed. One was the degree to which it was able to shape the terms of environmental debate. There was hardly a realm of public thought in which those who feared and struggled against environmental action did not take the initiative to dominate the definition of environmental issues. In so doing they described environmental affairs in terms of what they were not rather than what they were: antitechnology, bad science, single-issue politics, adversarial strategy, the environment versus the economy, no-risk philosophy, hostility to cost-benefit and cost-effective analyses, housewives' data, pollutant of the week, elitism, and populism. These words and phrases and the ideas they implied often structured the way in which the public media and the professional media defined the discussion. Most of the intellectual efforts of environmentalists, therefore, were channeled into acts of self-defense defined by their opponents rather than into positive initiatives they themselves had shaped. This gave the opposition considerable leverage with the nation's political intelligentsia.

The opposition's second success was a marked shift in the drift of scientific opinion and assessment toward an acceptance of the demand for higher levels of proof of harm. In the 1960s, scientific experts were more likely to talk approvingly about the need to act in the absence of full knowledge, to work in terms of "reasonable anticipation of harm," to bring frontier knowledge more quickly into the realm of public policy. Much of the early pollution control program in air and water was worked out under the assumption of a forceful role for this kind of scientific inference.[105] But over the years, pollution sources demanded higher levels of proof and singled out frontier scientists for special—and often massive—attack. Scientists have seen the professional careers of a number of their colleagues severely damaged, including John Gofman, Ernest Sternglass, Samuel Epstein, James Allen, Thomas Mancuso, Beverly Paigen, Dante Piciano, and Melvin Reuber. Although they have admired those few who have been able to remain strong professionally in the face of these attacks, such as Irving Selikoff, Clair Patterson, Edward Radford, Karl Morgan, and Herbert Needleman, most scientists have not been willing to take such professional risks.[106] In the face of such criticism, often sharpened by attempts from the environmental opposition to define all such issues in terms of "good science versus bad science," the self-images of scientists have worked a powerful influence on those less self-confident. A special focus of this growing influence of the demand for higher levels of proof of harm was the weakened role of the "margin of safety," that nebulous area of plausible inference that is the heart of every decision about standards.[107] While the "margin of safety" still remained by 1984, over the years it had become severely bruised and battered.

The response of traditional production sectors to the environmental impulse was not uniform. Agriculture, for example, had played a major role in the earlier conservation movement; when the issue now could be defined either as soil erosion or as the loss of productive cropland, some of the older players reached a common ground with environmentalists. Nevertheless, a host of issues about farming methods, from pesticides to commercial fertilizers, from the destruction of fence rows to the use of no-till agriculture,[108] from non-point water pollution to field burning, as well as land use planning and the use of the countryside for recreation—all served to divide farmers from environmentalists. Within the states, rural legislators provided the strongest environmental opposition, objecting both to carving out natural environment lands and programs within the countryside and to imposing on rural areas pollution controls really meant, they argued, for the cities.[109] Only when it came to siting large-scale industrial and waste facilities in rural areas, or the massive impacts of raw materials extraction, did farmers and environmentalists reach common ground. The various "resource councils" of the Dakotas, Montana, and Wyoming reflected that kind of cooperation.[110]

Cooperation between environmental groups and organized labor was more frequent. In this case, one must distinguish between the construction unions and the industrial unions.[111] The former were often at odds with environmentalists over siting and federal funding for large-scale projects. With industrial unions it was different; they had joined with environmentalists in the early 1950s in opposing the construction of the Echo Park dam in western Colorado. The United Steelworkers of America held the first nationwide citizen conference on air pollution in Washington, D.C., in 1969.[112] As the 1970s wore on, environmental ties with the Industrial Union Department of the AFL-CIO grew on such joint interests as occupational health, community air pollution, toxic chemicals, and the "right to know." There were major controversies between environmentalists and the steel workers over such issues as the bottle bill, and though coal miners joined the antinuclear drive, they still sided with the coal companies on sulfur dioxide control and (especially) acid

rain. The relationships were mixed, but in general they provided more opportunities for cooperation than for conflict.

With industry, in contrast, such opportunities for cooperation were limited; industry provided most of the leadership and the resources for the environmental opposition. There was nothing mysterious about this; the two
groups had mutually exclusive interests. Lands managed as wilderness were
not available for mining and lumbering. Waste treatment added new production costs. Chemical companies wanted to increase the use of pesticides, and
environmentalists wanted to reduce them. These normal conflicts between
those who produce and those who consume, those who adversely affect others
and those adversely affected by them, ran through much of the economy. Many
such conflicts could be resolved by adjusting prices in the private market, but
others inevitably led to public action. This was especially the case where the
resource itself was widely shared or publicly owned, such as the public lands,
water in streams or lakes, or air. Perhaps the most curious aspect of these relationships between industry and environmentalists was the failure to find
common ground on the basis of a shared interest in technical process innovations which, as Joseph Ling pointed out, would kill several birds with one
stone. While efforts to establish such a middle ground took place in Britain,
they did not occur in the United States.[113]

All the actors in the environmental opposition came together on one objective: to slow down the pace of environmental advance. Attempts to enhance natural environment management should be restricted; there was
already too much wilderness, there were too many parks, there were too many
protected wetlands; those that existed were too restricted as to use. "Multiple
use" became the battle cry of those who sought to enhance development on
environmental lands.[114] The drive for pollution control had gone too far;
more time should be spent on accepting the existing levels of pollution—they
were not harmful at all—and on protecting human and biological life from
the impact rather than on preventing emissions in the first place.[115] Light
technologies should not be allowed to impede the growth of more important
heavy ones. Notions about limits to physical resources were simply either a result of misinformation or a result of preoccupation with the future.[116] There
was a distrust of the expanded influence of the public on environmental decision making, and especially on scientific and technical questions about
which only the better-informed were capable of making sound judgments. As
the environmental opposition grew in numbers and political strength throughout the 1970s and into the 1980s, it attacked on a wide front. Its influence rose
in the latter years of the Carter administration, and with the Reagan presi-

dency it succeeded beyond its wildest hopes.[117] The alacrity with which it took advantage of the new opening backfired, but even with the adjustments that the administration made in response to political protests from environmentalists, the opposition still scored high. Despite its growth in numbers and resources, by 1984 the environmental movement could maintain little more than a holding action against its opposition.[118]

THE POLITICS OF ENVIRONMENTAL MANAGEMENT

As environmental politics evolved, its context shifted from broader public debate to management. Increasingly one spoke of air quality management, water quality management, forest management, range management, the Bureau of Land Management, Coastal Zone Management, risk management, river management, and wilderness management. Hardly an environmental problem could be dealt with outside the terminology and conceptual focus of management, and, in turn, management played a powerful role in shaping the world of environmental choice. The influence of management grew because of its power and its authority to coordinate discordant elements in the "system" on its own terms, and even more because it constituted the persistent institution of government, with ongoing day-to-day capabilities for communication and action. Institutional power was the stuff of political power; it arose from a continuous presence requiring that others reckon with it day in and day out; it set the bounds of choice if not the actual agenda. While the larger ideological debates in environmental affairs came and went, management shaped the world of day-to-day political affairs.[119]

Frequently it is argued that administrators simply implement policies made elsewhere in the legislature. Hence, administrative choices are secondary and derivative. This distinction between lawmaking and law-implementing institutions makes sense in terms of the formal structure of government, but when one explores political controversy through the various governmental functions, the argument breaks down. It is in management that the fundamental choices are made. The legislature and the court establish some of the outer limits of possibility, but the choices that make a difference to those concerned with the outcome are made by the managers. As soon as a law is passed by Congress, the parties rush to the agency to influence the way it decides to carry out the law. That outcome can range all the way from closely following the legislative objectives to virtually nullifying them. Administrative choice is more final; hence, it is more critical. Management and administration, and the politics of management and administration, are at the heart of the American political system.

When environmental political choice shifted from the wider public arena to the realm of administration and management, it was transformed into a vast array of technical issues: allowable cut and non-declining even flow; visual corridors and residual pricing; animal unit months; discount rates; mixing zones and lethal concentration 50s; acentric chromosome fragments and erythrocyte protoporphyrin; case control epidemiology and levels of significance; benign and malignant tumors; minimum low flows; integral vistas; oxygen depletion; buffering capacity and aluminum mobilization; Class I, II, and III PSD areas and testing protocols. Such issues did not reduce the intensity of debate; they only specified it and structured it more precisely. Far more important, debate was shifted from options that both the public and the media understood to seemingly esoteric issues that neither sought to comprehend. Hence, decisions became more obscured from the public view, more private and less public. Management and administration shaped an arena of politics in which the range of actors diminished in number, and only the initiated could follow and participate. That changed neither the significance of the debate nor its stakes.

It is within this realm of technical politics, therefore, that one can observe and follow most precisely the course of give-and-take in environmental affairs. Movement forward or backward with respect to environmental objectives, success or defeat for one side or the other, or just stalemate, can be identified in this arena with great precision. Here the main competing pressures and options were worked out, such as the clash between high proof of harm and frontier science about adverse environmental effects, or the balance between developed and natural environments, or the degree to which government sought to influence the direction of technical innovation. Whether the arena of choice was extended to include the legislature or the courts on the one hand, or the wider public on the other, depended on managerial action. The extent to which management sought to be innovative or conservative with respect to the cutting edge of questions about values, science, and technology was the main point of the drama. The major structural achievement of the environmental era was the erection of this managerial and administrative apparatus of political action. The major historical problem is to observe the degree to which it succeeded in disciplining contending environmental and developmental forces in the wider society so as to facilitate action.

To develop an ability to engage in environmental politics in the arena of managerial choice was the major achievement of citizen environmental organizations. Although their success in mobilizing members and the public, and their accomplishments in legislative action and litigation, were more noticeable, the test of what they could accomplish lay in their ability to work within the managerial and administrative orbit. Long-standing tendencies in administrative politics emphasized the face-to-face relationships between the regulators and the regulated as each sought to modify choices amid the anticipatory power and influence of the other. Those relationships had hinged on technical matters of administrative arrangements, on science and technology. Because they shared a common perspective about efficiency in matters of production, they found it relatively easy to come to terms. The injection of sustained institutional influence from the consumer side, however, into this traditional pattern upset the balance and brought to the relationships between regulators and regulated an intrusion that led to far greater uncertainty. Environmentalists sought to shape the direction of values, science, and technology; their demands and their strategies were less than welcome.

Thus there was a constant debate over the "opening up" of administrative decisions so that the new directions could be given more weight. In this effort, environmentalists benefited from the judicial commitment to supervising the Administrative Procedures Act of 1946 within the doctrine of "fairness." Freedom of information strategies had come from sources far beyond the environmental impulse,[120] but the court's supervision of the National Environmental Policy Act was shaped by much the same concerns.[121] While the act had been conceived in its earliest days as concerned primarily with interagency review, it was the court that modified it into a procedure for public review.[122] Similarly, the court required full participation in, and "on the record" bases for, administrative choices.[123] It balked only at the thought that the Executive Office of the President should be bound by the same open procedures.[124] Nevertheless, environmentalists were faced with constant efforts by both the regulated and the administrators to limit openness, to manage it for their own ends, and to restrict the new influences.[125]

Three focal points of administrative environmental politics were science, economic analysis, and planning. In all three, environmental organizations sought to increase their abilities to meet their opponents effectively. This was difficult, for the technical resources essential to each were readily available to both administrators and developmentalists in the business community and relatively unavailable to environmentalists. In the early years of the environmental era, citizen organizations often relied on volunteer contributions from technical and professional experts, such as analysis of the costs and benefits of the Cross-Florida Barge Canal, the environmental effects of pesticides, the effects of clearcutting, or the ecological role of wetlands. Such volunteer contributions continued, but over the years, environmental organizations began to develop their own in-house skills. Much of this came with environmental litigation at the Environmental Defense Fund (EDF) or the Natural Resources Defense Council (NRDC).[126] The Wilderness Society developed its own capacity for economic analysis.[127] The National Clean Air Coalition (NCAC) was able to finance outside technical studies. Environmental citizen involvement in forest planning was assisted greatly by the technical expertise of Randy O'Toole and the Cascade Holistic Economic Consultants of Eugene, Oregon.[128]

The most extensive capabilities in such matters came with the review and analysis of existing literature so that the latest in scientific and technical knowledge could be brought to bear on nuclear energy, forest management, environmental and health effects of pollution, atmospheric transmission, and wetlands protection. Environmentalists applied the investigative skills they had learned in higher education to the environmental scene and contributed their own bit to the opening up of scientific and technical choice. The expansion of knowledge often went far beyond the capability of individuals or institutions to absorb and apply it. Often those who made assessments about such matters did so on the basis of selective analyses made by others rather than through a review of original literature.[129] On more than one occasion, environmentalists unclogged avenues of communication and transfer that were either sluggish or choked. The NRDC, for example, brought two frontier researchers, Sergio Piomelli and Herbert Needleman, into the scientific assessment proceedings on the first lead criteria document, and thereby worked their new findings more rapidly into decision making on lead.[130] But this was only an especially dramatic case. Among citizen environmentalists generally, there occurred an extensive search for the latest scientific data so that it could be used to bolster their case.[131] In so doing they considerably increased the level and speed at which information was transferred.

Administrative environmental politics involved a still broader realm beyond the immediate interface of management, the regulated, and environmentalists; the relationships between administrators and the general public. Over the years, these two sectors became estranged. On the one hand, there was persistent public pessimism about the degree of commitment of management to environmental progress; on the other, there was persistent management distrust of the ability of the public to comprehend wisely and act

reasonably on environmental issues. To the public, environmental administrators moved slowly, temporized continually, followed the wishes of the regulated too frequently, and were generally characterized by lethargy and
inaction. To administrators, the public became too emotional and excited
about environmental concerns and was incapable of participating effectively
in decisions about technical matters. Much of the blame, they argued, fell on
the news media, which simply fanned the flames of public fear.[132] This mutual distrust reached new heights amid the toxic chemical issues of the late
1970s and the early 1980s.[133]

Much of the distrust arose from the persistent pressure on administrators
by the environmental public. Resource agencies retained their older primary
developmental missions, which were sustained not only by administrative
loyalties but also by personal and professional commitments to commodity
management; they found themselves constrained by these loyalties from playing a lead role in advancing values expressed by the environmental public.[134]
By the 1970s, agencies managing land and water resources seemed to be trapped
in persistent tension with public environmental demands. There was similar
mutual distrust with respect to health and ecological objectives. As the public
demanded that health frontiers be advanced to include new problems of
genetic defects, reproductive effects, immune capabilities, and physiological
and neurological disorders, as well as cancer, managerial agencies felt pressed
beyond their capabilities and defended more limited action. Frequently they
were tempted to affirm with confidence that a supposed threat presented little
harm when the public was convinced that the unknowns and even the plausible unknowns could not justify such statements.[135] The public remained suspicious of talk and action that tended to diminish the importance or wisdom
of higher health and environmental aspiration.

By the beginning of the 1980s, attitude studies had begun to reveal this vast
difference in attitude between managerial leaders and the environmental
public. Research was designed to compare public attitudes about environmental affairs with the attitudes of public leaders. One study conducted by
the American Forest Institute found that the public was far more inclined to
believe that trees in the national forests should be preserved rather than cut,
in contrast to the views of "thought leaders" in Washington. The survey firm
urged its clients to direct their public relations campaigns to those leaders, because they, so the firm argued, perceived the issue "more rationally and with
greater expertise."[136] The EPA began to define its relationship to the public as
one of public relations, rather than substance. The public was emotional,

tended to accept "bad science," and was subject to erratic media influence. The agency's main task was to restore public confidence by persuading the public to change its views rather than by greater managerial effectiveness in response to public definition of problems. The EPA strategy did not satisfy the public. The image evolved and persisted: a public that sought more environmental progress and an agency that held back.

Environmental management came to exercise an influence that was restraining, more than formative, in the advance of environmental objectives. Those objectives, rooted in changing public values, had a role in public affairs largely because the public mobilized to influence the apparatus of government. On occasion, leading sector initiatives came from management, but these were few. The prevailing pattern was one of public thrust and managerial reaction, of public impulses pushing managers further and faster than they thought wise. Hence, agencies acted and reacted somewhat reluctantly, defensively, seeking to parry and hold off rather than to serve as vigorous agents of environmental change. The Forest Service, for example, did not seek out ways to establish a lead role in innovation in wilderness expansion; the National Park Service did not follow up on early efforts to reduce the pressures on parks of growing numbers of visitors; the EPA did not extend pollution control readily into new realms of toxic air contaminants and acid deposition. The incorporation of environmental impulses into management constituted a system of decision making and control that disciplined and retarded as much as it implemented, that held back public demands as much as it carried them out.

For environmentalists, management provided both luring opportunities and significant risks. If one established a system of environmental planning that relied heavily on managerial strategy, it could be used for either environmental or developmental purposes. Federal air quality standards could be used as a weapon either to prevent further action or to force advances.[137] Forest planning could be used to increase allowable cuts and endanger environmental forest values as well as to enhance them.[138] Coastal zone management could enhance identification of areas of critical environmental concern or focus on commodity development under the rubric of multiple use.[139] The requirement that criteria documents be updated regularly could support either action or inaction, depending upon whether the agency felt sufficiently strong politically in its relationship with the regulated industry.[140] Despite the fact that management could be used against environmental objectives, there seemed to be little way out; hence, environmentalists felt just as constrained as their opponents to accept the administrative machinery and to seek to influence it for their own ends.[141] The vast importance of administrative choice in the national drama of environmental affairs was therefore solidified.

During the later years of the 1970s, several environmental institutions sought to serve as a middle ground in the debate between environmentalists and developmentalists. These organizations did not directly represent citizens but were rooted in professional and technical institutions somewhat separate from the process of mobilizing and expressing public values. Foremost among them were the Conservation Foundation and the Environmental Law Institute. They devoted considerable time and effort to negotiating amid the conflicting sectors of administrative decision making. The Conservation Foundation stressed what came to be called environmental mediation, the intervention of third parties into disputes to seek out a middle ground of compromise.[142] The Environmental Law Institute veered more toward a context of legal action, in which all parties to disputes would be dealt with evenhandedly.[143] In these strategies, both organizations deliberately sought not to identify themselves with the cutting edge of environmental impulses, but to occupy a middle ground and hence to urge that environmental objectives be restrained sufficiently to meet similar initiatives for restraint on the developmental side. Their actions took them out of the mainstream of environmental action and identified them as brokers among competing interests. In their emphasis on independence and professionalism, they sought—not always successfully—to rise above the fray. They found common ground with still another "middle ground" force, the technical experts with a self-image of independence rather than advocacy. By 1980, this group of experts had formed the National Association of Environmental Professionals.[144]

The middle ground that these groups sought to establish was distinctive. Rather than expressing agreement with frontier actions to advance natural values, the frontiers of science about health and environmental effects, or advances in process technology, they tended to convey skepticism about pushing too fast and too far. They sought to work within the managerial context in which considerable skepticism was expressed about too-rapid environmental progress. They tended to share the views of environmental managers that such progress was either limited in potential, too costly, or unnecessary. The middle ground that these efforts sought to capture drew them away from citizen environmental action and into the orbit of managerial thinking. Hence, their strategies were often discounted by those seeking to advance environmental progress in leading-edge fashion as too closely associated with efforts to constrain environmental impulses.[145]

THE RESPONSE OF GOVERNING INSTITUTIONS

The environmental drive inevitably became intertwined with two sets of governing institutions. One can be described by the term "separation of powers" and the other by the term "federalism." We should extend each of these terms beyond its usual meaning. The varied "powers" that were separated involved not just the legislative, administrative, and judicial branches, but also a differentiation within the administrative branch between the agencies and the Executive Office of the President. In effect, there were four branches of the federal government. "Federalism" involved not just relationships between state and nation but the entire hierarchy of local, state, and national institutions. Here was a varied lot of independent and autonomous institutions of public decision making that provided diverse opportunities for political expression.

Those seeking to influence government find one institution more responsive to their demands and another less so; hence, they pick and choose where to call for action, and patterns relating particular impulses and particular institutions evolve. At the federal level, environmentalists found Congress and the courts more willing to reflect their views, and the agencies and the Executive Office of the President more reluctant. The initial step in environmental action was to work through Congress to establish policies that administrative agencies by themselves resisted. The drive for wilderness set this pattern, and it was repeated on many an occasion. Congress provided the arena in which public demands were expressed. Here environmentalists found leverage as legislators responded to their constituents, and a host of environmental laws resulted.

The courts were equally responsive, not in terms of offering policy choices but in establishing the legitimacy of the new public interest in environmental affairs. Courts approved of standing to defend an environmental interest as being of equal importance as the defense of person and property. They accepted environmental demands as a legitimate part of administrative choice, and in that spirit, readily took up the environmental impact statement. The courts emphasized procedure rather than substance. Their role was to decide whether environmental impulses were legitimate demands on government, not that they should win out in competition with other demands. In much the same manner, courts accepted environmental objectives as a legitimate use of the state's police powers, though a balance had to be struck with other objectives.

The administrative agencies and the Executive Office of the President sought to exercise restraint on environmental demands. The flow of ideas and actions that came to public life through these branches of government tended to arise not from broadly based public values but from the more limited concerns of technical, professional, and administrative cultures. That leadership remained skeptical about the wisdom of the environmental impulse. When environmentalists found the agencies to be open procedurally to them, their opposition began to view the Executive Office of the President as a more useful source of environmental restraint. The opposition obtained significant leverage at that level during the last two years of the Carter administration, and far more with the advent of the presidency of Ronald Reagan. The Reagan strategy was to bring the agencies under firmer control; and those who advocated a more powerful executive came to their views, in part, in opposition to the influence of environmental values in public affairs. No matter that to the "middle ground" environmental professionals the Reaganites went much too far and invited backlash; such discomfort did not entice them to embrace the innovative role of either Congress or the courts, but only to reform the executive strategy of restraint.[146]

Federalism provided opportunities either to enhance or to restrain authority at one level when action at another was not favorable. Many issues involved a choice to use either state or national action in cases that concerned the preemption of state powers by federal authority. There were also options as to state or local action, described by the word "override." Many state statutes provided that local governments could not establish legal conditions more stringent than those of the state.[147] The constitutional setting in this case was somewhat different. Whereas the division between state and federal authority required a sorting out of constitutional powers, the division between state and local authority did not. Local governments were created by state governments, and the two did not hold ultimate authority concurrently. For all practical purposes, however, this contest for authority was as intense as that between state and national levels. Many land use questions were framed by the question of whether the state should "recapture" powers it had given to municipalities through zoning legislation.

Environmental action often consisted of a defense of one's home and community against some developmental intrusion. Hence, that action often appealed to the right of localities to make decisions about their environmental quality. Perhaps it was a matter of siting an unwanted industrial plant or a waste disposal facility. A variety of strategies, from zoning to local referenda, were devised. To circumvent such local opposition, developers in turn sought an "override" from state government in which state agencies could make decisions that localities would be required to accept. Amid local protest, however, state agencies were reluctant to act. As the environmental era proceeded, an accumulation of such cases led to hesitation by state governments to force undesired siting into communities against their wishes. Disposal of hazardous and radioactive wastes sharply fixed the issue. Even though most legislatures had provided that in hazardous waste siting decisions, communities could advise but not veto, state agencies still hesitated to force decisions against overwhelming opposition.

In response to such state lethargy, developers sought out the power of the federal government to preempt the power of the states. Environmental impulses arising from the grass roots had gone too far and corrupted state policy. Only strong federal preemption would work. Such authority had arisen in certain cases, such as the federal noise control program in which railroads and airlines had sought federal regulations to prohibit communities from establishing noise control levels that they felt were too strict.[148] There were many other cases: local and state pesticide regulations stricter than federal ones;[149] action by communities to restrict the transport of radioactive waste through their jurisdictions;[150] actions to prevent states and communities from passing "right-to-know" laws stricter than federal ones;[151] federal action to prevent states from restricting siting of energy facilities on the coastal zone.[152] This repeated drive by industry to use federal power to override that of the states and localities was greatly aided by the new Reagan administration.

The public lands presented a different case. Federal lands inevitably created a contest over the use of federal power. Over the years, conservationists and environmentalists sought to enhance federal authority as friendly to their public land interest. Commodity users, on the other hand, had always relied on state authority, on occasion had fostered strategies to transfer federal lands to the states, and had upheld land management in the western states as an appropriate model. Such political positions underwent some modification in the environmental era. Throughout the West, environmental impulses steadily grew to exercise influence in public land management at the local and state levels. Support for environmental public land uses increased among state recreational and fish and wildlife agencies and in executive departments of state governments. There were indigenous demands for wilderness, against clearcutting, for visual corridors, for protection of streams against sedimentation, and for restrictions in the use of herbicides and pesticides.[153] As these demands began to restrain wood production in first one and then another national forest, sentiment began to emerge among those on both the private and public sides of wood production objectives for an upward flow of authority within the U.S. Forest Service. This appeared in the demand during the Reagan administration for marked increases in the allowable cut through Washington-based decisions. This, in turn, generated a vigorous opposition within the West and fostered a state environmental stance against national authority.[154]

There were many variations on these themes. Environmentalists usually sought federal action to further natural-environment objectives for managing air, water, and land, but at the same time they developed extensive pragmatic strategies when they found that federal planning could be used against them and that local and state action could be used in their behalf. Developmentalists continued to rely on local and state action when it could be associated with issues of jobs and economic development that had local support. That strategy, however, now had to compete in many places with local interest in environmental quality, and this fact tended to push developmentalists toward higher levels of authority. Hence, amid the complexities of federalism, one could discern a tendency for the consumer-oriented stance of environmental expression to emphasize local choice and the producer-oriented stance of large-scale production to emphasize national choice.

These alternatives in the use of governmental institutions were closely associated with the politics of technical information. The context of environmental decision making was heavily laden with the detail of science and technology, of future prediction and past record, of economic analysis, of finely tuned administrative mechanisms. Political give-and-take involved the ability to command, communicate, and apply detail to decisions. Hence, the ability to carry out effective information strategy played a critical role in political success or failure. Much of this depended on the resources available to environmentalists or developmentalists to command technical detail through their own experts. Much of it also depended on the ability to command government resources, either to turn technical knowledge to one's advantage or to prevent critical information from becoming available to one's opponents. It was their capability in these matters that often gave the environmental opposition a considerable edge. That opposition often sought government as an ally in restricting the flow of information to the environmental public. Hence, the politics of information became closely intertwined with the varied roles of governmental institutions.

Several cases illustrate the problem. In the 1960s, the U.S. Public Health Service (PHS) sought to obtain an inventory of industrial waste water as complete as the inventory already available for municipal sewage. During various river basin water quality conferences, industries had declined to provide this information. State public health authorities defended their secrecy, since what information they had obtained had been secured on the condition of confidentiality.[155] The PHS drew up a survey form and sought to submit it to industrial sources to acquire the information. The survey had to be cleared by the Bureau of the Budget (BOB) on the grounds that it involved public expenditures. But the BOB committee that had to approve the survey included several industry representatives, so it refused to approve the action. It took a congressional subcommittee report to bring the issue to a head, and by the time of the debate over revision of water quality legislation in 1972, a mechanism for requiring such information had been worked out.[156] In this case federal action was used to open up information that had been closed off at the state level.

There was also the case of the Lead Liaison Committee established by the Public Health Service in the late 1950s to provide continuing discussion with industry over the health effects of lead. The mechanism served as an opportunity for scientific and technical experts from both industry and government to share their views and work out conclusions about such matters among themselves. The meetings were not open to the public. By the early 1970s, however, in a new era of openness in government, the EPA decided that the committee's proceedings would be made public. In return the lead industry withdrew from the committee, explaining in later years that the publicity reduced the committee's effectiveness.[157] The regulation of lead involved intensely debated scientific and technical issues. The shift from private to public debate over these issues constituted a major change in the relationship between government, on the one hand, and environmentalists and industry, on the other. From that point on the inability to control the flow and assessment of information was the lead industry's most crucial weakness.[158]

The courts constituted an equally significant arena in the politics of information. The judiciary valued a "full record," both for its own decisions and in supervising decision making by federal agencies. The judicial record could be enhanced by the process of discovery, in which one litigant could obtain evidence from the files of its opponent, or by the court proceeding itself, in which information from documents and witnesses could be placed on the record. Many a proceeding hinged on the issue of whether the parties wanted to risk creating a record that in future actions as well as the one in question might be detrimental to their interests. Discovery greatly fostered the claims of injury by persons exposed to asbestos, for example, for it brought to light that industry had known about carcinogenic effects much earlier than had been thought before.[159] To forestall such a record of environmental harm was a prime consideration in environmental litigation, and led to many an out-of-court settlement in which the defendant refused to accept liability and prevented "record building" by agreeing to make payments to those who claimed injury.[160]

The courts insisted on openness in administrative proceedings as well. Decisions had to be made on the record that would be open to all interested parties, including legislators, other administrators, and the public, and no decision could be made on the basis of information obtained after the record had been formally closed. What of the tendency, however, for administrative decisions to be made not in the agency but in the Executive Office of the President, and especially the Office of Management and Budget? It was at this point that the court hesitated. Did the president have the authority to make decisions privately or not? The shift invited the use of the Executive Office of the President as a context of influence by the environmental opposition that did not have to be publicly exposed.[161] When the Reagan administration sought to reduce openness at the agency level through private meetings between the regulators and the regulated, the strategy backfired, and the most manifest procedural norms the courts had evolved were restored.[162] But this only enhanced the role of the Executive Office of the President as the agency of unpublicized political choice.

Within the realm of federalism, the most striking fact was the enormous variation in technical and information capabilities between the various levels of government. The air pollution program in the 1960s focused squarely on the problem. Given the superior resources that enabled industry to bring experts to bear on decision making, local governments seeking increased control of air pollution had little clout. They tried to enhance the technical role of the Public Health Service to increase their leverage. Congress provided funds for community air quality programs to build up local and state management capabilities, and fostered the criteria document assessment strategy to provide authoritative statements about environmental effects that localities and states could use. Environmentalists used the first draft criteria document on sulfur oxides in a number of local and state proceedings in the late 1960s; this action led to stricter standards than industry wanted. Industry, in turn, looked on the use of federal expertise as an "interference" in local affairs. Nevertheless, the use of nationally mobilized scientific and technical opinion remained highly influential in state and local action. Only a few states, such as California, developed a scientific and technical capability that sustained even stronger pollution control strategies than those maintained by the federal government. Most states simply followed the national lead.

Environmental implementation was a different matter. In this area the technical ability of industry often far outweighed that of state and local agencies. In issues of air quality emissions and water quality discharges, both involving the impacts of individual sources on ambient quality, modeling became the basis of regulatory choice. The industry would make its case with supporting technical detail and then the regulatory agency would not have sufficient time or resources to counter it.[163] Often such resources hinged on federal grants to the states, and when such funds declined, so did the states' ability to compete on a technical basis. During the 1960s and 1970s, federal funds considerably strengthened the capabilities of state governments, but the Reagan administration's strategy of transferring costs to the states set in motion an opposite tendency that weakened the role of state government. At times, states sought to shift the cost of environmental management to the regulated industries, but this strategy had little success. In a host of managerial actions ranging from monitoring to modeling, technical limitations of state and local environmental authorities reduced their effectiveness in the face of the far superior resources of the regulated industries.

One of the more significant features of the politics of information concerned the issue of the right of the public or public authorities to information about the practices of those responsible for harm. Public action depended on information, but private sources argued that the information demanded was confidential, proprietary, a trade secret. Such a political strategy stymied many an environmental action. Claims ranged from the identity of chemicals subject to toxic substances regulation,[164] to packaging (subject to scrutiny to determine whether resulting waste could be reduced), to the potential toxic properties of strip mine overburden. The stakes were focused especially by information about exposures and health effects in the workplace. The Occupational Safety and Health Administration promulgated regulations requiring that health and exposure records of workers be available for epidemiological study, but industry countered that such information was privileged and defended the "right" of workers to confidentiality. Then there was the similar protest by industry against the spate of right-to-know proposals concerning workers and communities exposed to chemicals.[165] Every case involved control of information that might be used either to protect industry against legal action or to aid those affected who sought protection. Workers initially looked for help at the federal level when they tried to exercise their "right to know," but industry blocked their efforts. When protective action shifted to states and localities, with some success, industry sought a federal override from a sympathetic Reagan administration. Although this case has had more than its share of political drama, it should not obscure the fact that a host of choices about disclosure of information became closely intertwined with choices about the level of government at which information control strategies were worked out.

VALUES AND LIMITS

Throughout these twists and turns of environmental politics one can observe two broad forces at work. One is the new set of values that emerged in the years after World War II, deeply rooted in changing demography, standards of health and living, and enhanced levels of human aspiration. Environmental politics has involved the working out of these historic changes in what people sought to think, be, and do. The other force has involved the private and public apparatus that constitutes the organizational society, the way in which some people fashion managerial institutions to shape the social and political order according to their views of desired arrangements. From the public came demands for environmental improvement and progress. From the managerial world of science, technology, economic analysis, and planning came the message that that aspiration was on the point of outrunning resources. It was ironic that in creating such doubts about environmental demands, the nation's institutional leaders were giving stark testimony to the "limits of growth" that many of them often denied. The world, they argued, simply could not be made as healthful or clean or safe or filled with natural beauty as the environmental public seemed to want. One would have to settle for less.

It was a curious twist that environmentalists were the conveyors of optimism about the possibilities of human achievement, while the administrative and technical leadership were consistently the bearers of bad news. In the media the roles were reversed: environmentalists warned of impending catastrophe, while the technical leadership exuded optimism. Such language was used even by the parties to the debate. To remain, however, on this level of media understanding seems not to fit the wide range of evidence about what people did and the values implicit in their actions. The driving public force behind environmental affairs was rooted in hope and confidence about possibilities for a better life; there was a constant search for the very latest in science and technology to harness to such aspiration. The opposition, which in the grand debates over "limits" radiated confidence about the future, was constantly warning environmentalists that their demands were extravagant and beyond the capability of existing resources.[166]

Such discrepancies between what people do and how they explain what they do are not unique; they are the stock-in-trade of sensitive historical analysis concerned with self-images as well as actions. So we need not pause to unravel inconsistencies inherent in daily human life. What is particularly interesting is the way in which the new mass middle class sought to shape a newer world revolving around its values and conceptions about the good life, and in so doing gave expression to precisely the rising standard of living that the managerial and technological leaders professed to extol. Like Karl Marx's proletariat, the successful middle class turned out to be different from what its creators sought, and began to demand that the production system generate environmental goods and services for themselves and their children. One could go even a step further and point out that it was Adam Smith who said that the main purpose of production was consumption, and that when consumer wants were no longer filled by the existing mode of production, it was time for a change. Such was the challenge of the environmental impulse to America's prevailing managerial institutions.[167]

A HISTORICAL
PERSPECTIVE ON
CONTEMPORARY
ENVIRONMENTALISM

WE HAVE NOW WITNESSED three decades of vigorous environmental activity in the United States. Since the late 1950s environmental issues have played a significant role on the national agenda; environmental objectives have been increasingly advanced by organized citizen groups and the political resistance to those objectives has been equally elaborated.

As time passes we can understand all this from an historical perspective: what long-term patterns of continuity or change does it represent? The intensity of contemporary environmental debate tends to generate a momentary perspective. But larger meaning can be grasped if one backs away from the event to focus on the longer span of time. Moreover, a contemporary focus emphasizes problems and problem solving, while an evolutionary approach highlights the process of continuity and change over time. Here I emphasize environmentalism highlighted by an historical approach.

I focus on the last three decades, from the late 1950s to 1990 and this raises a major point of interpretation: the turning point in environmental history came not with Earth Day 1970, but in the late 1950s as deep-seated changes in American society began to shape environmental objectives. The benchmark of Earth Day 1970 has distorted the meaning of environmental affairs; it reflects the personal experience of those who at that time became aware of environmental matters rather than a significant shift in history. We have three rather than two environmental decades to consider and within which to identify patterns of change and continuity.

FROM CONSERVATION TO ENVIRONMENT

It is conventional to draw lines of continuity between the earlier conservation movement and the later environmental movement. But the two were markedly different. The conservation movement was associated with efforts of managerial and technical leaders to use physical resources more efficiently;[1] the environmental movement sought to improve the quality of the air, water, and land as a human environment.[2] Conservation arose out of the production or supply side of the economy, the environment out of the consumer or demand side.

Equally significant is a marked difference in sources of support. The conservation movement was not deeply rooted; attempts in the early twentieth century to organize the public behind conservation objectives failed miserably. In contrast, a half-century later there was an outpouring of public environmental support. Environmentalism was a broadly popular affair arising from the American mass middle class.

One can also pinpoint a contrast in policy. The conservation movement, for example, emphasized multiple-purpose river development; the environmental movement, on the other hand, advocated that rivers be used as free-flowing streams devoid of engineering obstructions. Two quite different conceptions of the meaning and purpose of rivers were at stake; what was central in the conservation movement was unacceptable in the environmental movement.

In forest management, to take another case, conservation emphasized sustained-yield wood production; later the concept of the forest as an environment competed with that notion. The two views clashed in the debate over the use of the forest as wilderness, and then in planning under the Forest Management Act of 1976.[3] Earlier wood production commitments gave way to newer environmental forest objectives only slowly. In this debate two very different conceptions of the meaning of forests were at stake. One harkens back to the conservation movement, the other arises from the environmental movement.

A different but subordinated strand in earlier conservation affairs emphasized "great geologic wonders" for their historic and aesthetic value. The main focus was the national park movement, beginning with Yellowstone, then shaping the National Park established in 1916 and continuing with additions to the national park system and the growing popularity of tourism.[4] Yet resource development continued to dominate federal policy as witnessed by the massive river development and road building programs undertaken by the New Deal.

The soil conservation movement continued this contrast between conservation and environment. The New Deal soil conservation program emphasized sustainable production; it had no significant environmental content. Production objectives became clearer in the 1950s when a new program authorized the Soil Conservation Service to build dams and channelize streams. Environmentalists challenged the projects as destructive to fish and wildlife habitat. Soil conservation came to be as much a target of environmental attack as did river development and wood production.

When in time does one pinpoint this transition from conservation to environment? This is a matter of the evolution of new social objectives which challenge old ones. That point had been reached by the late 1950s as outdoor recreation sustained a new emphasis on natural resources as environments rather than commodities. A transition took place from Presidents Eisenhower and Kennedy on the one hand to Johnson on the other. Historic marking points are the report of the National Outdoor Recreation Resource Review Commission, established during the Eisenhower administration and a spate of laws in the 1960s, most notably the Wilderness Act of 1964.

How does one fit pollution concerns into this analysis? While interest in air and water pollution was considerably greater in the 1960s than in earlier years, the direction of interest had significant roots in the past. There was more historical continuity here than with natural resource issues. As cities grew in the nineteenth century a host of environmental conditions arose that were dealt with in the courts as nuisances. There were water supply and waste disposal problems;[5] there were population shifts within cities much akin to twentieth century suburbanization in which people sought quieter and pleasanter places to live in less congested places away from factories.

By the late nineteenth century much of this was known as the sanitary movement and the term "environmental health" arose to describe it; there is direct continuity with current "environmental health" issues. The toxic problem was new in the Environmental Era, but the direction of its concern extended earlier patterns. What was new was the extent of organized citizen demand for environmental improvement. Only sporadic prior to World War II, by the 1960s that organized effort came to play a major role in public affairs.

EVOLUTION OF THE ENVIRONMENTAL MOVEMENT

One could trace environmental change during the three decades after the late 1950s through the sequence of policy issues: from outdoor recreation to pollution, from a focus on ecology to a focus on human health, from conventional air and water pollution to toxic pollution, from national to state and international issues. To trace these would merely repeat what is well known. Instead I prefer to highlight some less obvious roles for environmentalism since the late 1950s.

Most significant is the evolution of the institutional strength of the citizen environmental movement. Despite a decade of action prior to 1970, by that date the environmental movement was relatively fragile. Organizational membership had increased during the previous decade but Earth Day 1970 was marked more by a momentary outburst of public sentiment that prompted some legislation victories; it generated only limited institutional capability or political staying power.

The environmental victories around Earth Day 1970 are often mentioned; significant defeats deserve equal emphasis. The proposal to establish a national estuarine system under the administration of the National Park Service was sidetracked into a small system of research areas. Substantive administrative environmental review of development projects gave way to more limited procedural review under NEPA. Congress failed to approve both a national citizen environmental suit statute and an affirmation of environmental rights which had been an original part of the Senate version of NEPA. Proposals to develop federal source permits and technology guidelines for air pollution failed and the secondary annual air quality standards for sulfur dioxide fell into disuse after they were struck down by the courts. The industry challenge to the sulfur oxides criteria document in 1967 instituted a process of continual industry influence in scientific assessments and undermined agency desires to carry through with air quality standard setting beyond the six criteria pollutants. Interest in solid waste recycling, with which much of the Earth Day environmental youth movement was associated, soon evaporated. Ecological and wildlife objectives that had shaped much of the thinking of the

1960s soon gave way to a far more predominant interest in human health. The new FIFRA Act in 1972, while factoring in health effects of pesticides for the first time was notably weak in contrast with other pollution laws. The once strong interest in population problems collapsed almost as soon as the report of the President's Commission appeared.

In the ensuing years, however, the institutional capability of environmentalism increased steadily, not sudden or dramatic in its effect, but persisting in ways often not readily apparent. Membership in national organizations grew steadily; a host of specialized organizations arose to focus on specific issues, often eclipsing the larger organizations in effectiveness; community action evolved persistently in such forms as conservation commissions, land trusts and the environmental justice movement; political strategies expanded from lobbying to legal action to electoral involvement; state legislative and administrative action grew steadily as well as electoral action on all fronts; international environmental networks expanded in the 1980s.

At the same time, major institutional weaknesses abound. Citizen involvement in administrative decision-making, a crucial arena for political choice, is minimal. Environmental organizations have limited ability to inform the public, beyond their own members, about environmental affairs. Even more striking is the inability of environmentalists to shape the course of science and technology, save to keep up with innovations sparked by others and to bring them into public policy.

Less obvious but even more significant, little of the environmental agenda has worked itself into the wider institutions of American public affairs. It is important to analyze this process with more than casual attention. Evidence from public opinion polls is one thing, but also needed is evidence about a variety of institutions: the public media, institutional leaders, local and state governments, federal administrators. A rather massive gap persists between the environmental movement as it has evolved from its own resources and institutions and the environmental objectives fostered by the dominant institutions of American society.

Only on rare occasions, for example, have presidents taken up firm environmental leadership. President Johnson did so for a few years in the 1960s; President Nixon advanced environmental objectives momentarily; and Jimmy Carter identified himself with environmentalism in the first two years of his administration and in the Alaska lands issue. These chief executives exercised leadership through environmental messages,[6] an active Council on Environmental Quality, and appointment of administrators from citizen environmental organizations.

Environmental advances in the 1980s—there were more of them than usually acknowledged—came in spite of presidential opposition: revision of Superfund, the clean water act, and the safe drinking water act. President Reagan accepted one of the most significant actions of those years, the phasedown of lead in gasoline, as a result of his electoral needs in 1984. Finally, while declining to go on the offensive against emerging environmental policies, President Bush has yet to identify himself with them. Numerous pieces of major environmental legislation are now wending their way through Congress. Thus far Bush has commented on only a few, more frequently to weaken rather than to strengthen them. The pattern established during the 1970s, congressional initiative and presidential response, still prevails.

More significant is the limited emergence of environmental issues in the nation's wider institutional structure. Almost no national public figures have emerged as environmental statesmen, attempting to articulate national and long-term objectives that the public seeks as its own aspirations. It is not too difficult to associate environmental aspirations with the long-term social good, higher standards of living, expanding scientific knowledge, technological innovation for public benefit, or advancing stages of the economy. Instead, national leadership focuses more on the liabilities of environmental aspiration and seeks to check it as excessive. Only when such centers of environmental statesmanship appear can one argue that environmental objectives are part of the mainstream of American society.

The media constitutes still another indicator. Thus far there have been two levels of public environmental information, publications of membership organizations and the mass media. Both tend to identify environmental matters as peripheral to the nation's information system. Publications of environmental organizations focus on the limited issues in which they are interested to rally their members to action. The mass media, on the other hand, prefer only the dramatic and the sensational and hence miss more mundane news that is often far more important. One can obtain much information from a variety of specialized publications such as scientific and technical journals, trade association magazines, and newsletters. But environmental affairs will arrive in the mainstream of American society only when environmental information becomes more central in the mainstream media.

Another indicator is the degree to which environmental organizations are accepted by institutional leaders as the primary sources of ideas for national policy. Environmentalists have not yet reached this level of legitimacy. In contrast with the Reagan years, they are now accepted as one of the acceptable players, but their formulation of the nation's environmental aspirations does not rank high with the nation's leaders. Consider, for example, the publication, *Blueprint for the Environment,*[7] drawn up by 17 environmental organizations as an agenda for the 1990s and presented to president-elect Bush in December 1988. That publication reflects a citizen agenda that evolved incrementally over 30 years, codifying the objectives of the entire movement. It has been met by the president, national leaders, and the mass media with remarkable silence.

The environmental community, moreover, is not yet a source of administrative appointments. Jimmy Carter drew on them but this has not been the case subsequently. The appointment of William Reilly as EPA administrator is a gesture toward the environmental community, but the Conservation Foundation, from which he came, separated itself from the mainstream environmental constituency in the early 1970s and has not joined in such formulations of common environmental objectives as represented by Project Blueprint.

ENVIRONMENTAL OBJECTIVES

Environmentalism has played an important role in the larger context of public affairs and that role helps to identify its more long-term historical significance. Here I discuss several of these new social objectives: advances in science and technology; and the environmental economy.

Foremost among these changes is the role of environmentalism in shaping new social objectives, described often as quality of life objectives, a new stage in the continual drive for a higher standard of living. Many of the deepest environmental controversies involve debate over these goals. Those with primary commitments to commodity and developmental objectives find the stress on environmental objectives unacceptable and many in public management agencies, while accepting them to some extent, often seek to restrain them. From an historical perspective, the significance of environmentalism is the significance of these new values and objectives in American life.

Citizen environmental organizations advocate, for example, expansion of the nation's permanent wildlands. Much of their energy and political capability over the past three decades has been devoted to that goal. Expansion of the National Wilderness Preservation System established in 1964, now over 90 million acres in extent, is one of the environmental movement's successes.[8] The Wild and Scenic Rivers program has been less spectacular but in recent years more successful. Each piece of wildlands and water turf is fought over intensely, with environmentalists on one side and commodity groups on the other.

In the drive for wildlands environmental objectives, the administrative-technical community as a whole has been less than enthusiastic. The land management agencies, both federal and state, have accepted each new stage of wilderness designation only reluctantly in the face of political forces they cannot overcome. Professional resource managers have either taken up similar opposition or have remained on the sidelines, while the burden of political action has been borne by citizen groups. When technical-managerial groups rank order environmental "problems" protection of wildland areas comes near the bottom.

Wildlife objectives have enjoyed less success. Appreciative wildlife use has reached very high levels. But public policy achievements have been meager. The rare and endangered species program has had only limited success; listing has proceeded slowly, and habitat and recovery strategies even more so. The Fish and Wildlife Conservation Act of 1980, the most comprehensive federal wildlife statute, has never been funded. Attempts to apply new concepts in wildlife management such as wildlife corridors remain dormant and the federal land agencies have resisted biodiversity as a major objective in public lands management.[9] Most significant, the enhanced position that the Fish and Wildlife Service seemed destined to play in environmental affairs in the late 1960s soon evaporated; it has continually faced constraint rather than enjoyed a leading role.

Pollution control has involved a series of settings for the goal of a cleaner environment to be played out. The issue in each has been "how clean is clean?" although only in the hazardous waste realm has it been put precisely in those words. The lines were clearly drawn in the 1960s and have continued since. Environmental organizations press for a higher level of cleanup; industry rejects that drive on the grounds that the existing level of pollution is not harmful; and administrative agencies, often seeking a middle course, bring some increased pressure on sources of pollution, but accept some permanent environmental contamination on the grounds that it is "negligible" and "acceptable."

There are a host of implementation questions in matters of pollution control, but the debate over these issues throughout the last thirty years has been shaped by the issues of objectives in the first place. If one is serious about the "no discharge" of effluent into streams as an objective, then it seems logical to argue that mixing zones compromise that objective; that any reduction in discharge through advanced technology should lower the overall allowable on the stream rather than be reallocated to other sources; that total loads should replace concentrations as the standard for permissible discharge; that the reissuance of NPDES permits should carry with them some progress toward the "no discharge" goal; and that the entire water quality system should be organized in terms of bodies of water rather than state administrative units. Each of these administrative issues is significant primarily in terms of basic objectives in water quality management. Environmentalists seek to lower emissions progressively; sources of pollution scoff at the potential harm either to humans or the environment and resist such pressures. In the midst of the crunch of alternative objectives, administrators often interpret their authority narrowly so as to avoid having to press for further pollution cleanup and develop justifications for emissions described as "insignificant."

The lead in gasoline issue pinpoints the continuing controversy over objectives. On the one hand a group of pediatric scientists and practitioners sought to reduce lead exposure to young children and with the help of the Natural Resources Defense Council brought emerging science about the childhood neurological effects of lead to the debate. Industry on the other hand sought to discredit their conclusions about health effects. At each stage of the debate pediatric health scientists emphasized new research that identified effects at lower levels of exposure. Administrators at first resisted stricter standards but modified their views under the pressure of court order and the new scientific data that was brought into the debate by pediatric scientists working through the Centers for Disease Control. Even in its final rationale for the phasedown of lead in gasoline in 1984 EPA continued to place less emphasis on health effects and more on engine maintenance.[10]

On a third set of issues involving the balance between population and resources, the so-called "limits to growth" issue, the evolution of environmental objectives has taken a different turn. While that issue achieved a considerable amount of visibility in the late 1960s and was pinpointed by the report of the President's Commission on Population and the Nation's Future (1972), it aroused only limited interest thereafter. Americans have accepted the rapid increase in the nation's population over the last two decades with hardly a murmur. A few groups, such as Zero Population Growth, Population-Environmental Balance, and the Population Committee of the Sierra Club have remained in the fray but with limited impact on the environmental agenda.

This is a rather remarkable fact. Extensive growth in population and consumption over the past several decades placed persistently increasing pressures on the environment. But neither citizen environmental organizations nor environmental administrators have given much attention to its implications.

There are several exceptions to this. The most important involves local rather than national activity, arising from community concern about the costs of growth due to more population, jobs, and construction. In the early 1970s there was some interest expressed about the effects of community growth; an initial round of state land-use planning laws expressed this concern, but the interest soon dissipated.

This interest, however, recently has revived. Growth issues appeared in a number of local elections in 1988. Since the early 1970s environmentalists have argued that growth not only brings more taxes to public coffers, but also requires more public expenditure to deal with its costs. Now a number of growth control actions, for example in Florida, stress the need to have in place the services which growth engenders before new construction is approved.

The most vigorous growth related strategies have been actions to "save" land from development. Land conservancies now number some 700, according to the network association, the Land Trust Exchange (1989). The strategies of the Nature Conservancy, geared primarily to permanent protection of land for endangered plants and animals as well as biological diversity has had similar results with marked membership and financial support.

ISSUE PATTERNS: ENVIRONMENTAL SCIENCE

Environmental science has been one of the most significant aspects of the drive to implement environmental objectives. Environmentalists, according to many observers, have been hostile to science but a closer look makes clear that they have played an important role in its advance.

They have been especially influential in identifying and transferring frontier environmental science into policy-making. With limited resources to conduct original research confined primarily to monitoring, they provide moral support and back funding for scientists in government and the universities. They follow ongoing research closely, establish ties with research scientists, evaluate scientific work as it emerges and bring it into policy making. They have fostered knowledge about chemical and biological cycles in the environment at large, the environmental effect of development, and the effect of chemicals at lower concentrations on both humans and the environment.

The lead case provides an example of these varied activities. Knowledge about lead in the 1960s and 1970s proceeded on two fronts, the lead biogeochemical cycle and the impact of lead on humans. The work of Clair Patterson gave rise to a wide-ranging set of measurements that generated a rather comprehensive picture of the levels of lead in many media and at many historical points of time.[11] The work of Sergio Piomelli and Herbert Needleman sparked investigations into the effect of low-level lead exposure on humans. Citizen groups helped to transfer this knowledge into public policy through the work of community organizations, the Natural Resources Defense Council and the Environmental Defense Fund; they brought lead scientists into regulatory proceedings and employed lead researchers on their staffs.[12]

They played a similar role in knowledge about atmospheric chemical transport, transformation, and deposition. Acid rain research came about through both citizen environmental demands and the desire of the affected industries to postpone regulatory action. It built up a detailed understanding about sulfur and nitrogen cycles and their effects in both humans and the environment. The entire research effort led to an outpouring of knowledge; the current debate rests upon a far more extensive base of knowledge than was the case a decade ago.

Knowledge about the ecological environment, however, has proceeded more slowly than knowledge about human health. In the 1960s environmental impacts were thought of primarily as the effect of developments such as highways, power plants, pesticides, or dredging on the ecological environment and especially wildlife. The Fish and Wildlife Service was the major federal agency to express concern about these environmental effects and the policy problem was one of providing a more significant role for that agency. An Ecological Research Service similar to the National Science Foundation was proposed to create the scientific contest for effective environmental policy. But that proposal gave way to the National Environmental Policy Act. The resulting procedural, rather than substantive approach in NEPA led to only limited efforts to advance ecological knowledge.

Ever since then ecological science has limped along through piecemeal rather than comprehensive efforts. The acid rain research is the main exception. System-oriented data collection in the form of monitoring, such as that carried out by the U.S. Geological Survey or the National Oceanic and Atmospheric Administration has been limited to a few projects.[13] No wonder that the *Blueprint for the Environment* once again called for the establishment of an Ecological Research Service much like the proposal of the 1960s.[14]

Dispute over the direction of science usually remained in the background of public debate. Far more visible controversy arose over the meaning of the research. Scientific assessments played a direct role in administrative rulemaking but they were ever present in a wide range of actions resting on key questions of cause-effect relationships. Debate over the meaning of the science shaped any policy choices

Assessments of the effects of low-level pollution exposures dominated these controversies. Environmental science arose from a concern for the acute effects of episodic high-level exposures but gradually became involved with the chronic effects of persistent low-level exposures. These new inquiries were more controversial because they involved far lower chemical concentrations, shifting from parts per million in the late 1960s to parts per trillion currently, in which it is increasingly difficult to bring about agreement on cause-and-effect relationships. At the same time a host of human health effects—genetic, reproductive, fetal, neurological, immunological, and pulmonary—have emerged to shape environmental health analysis beyond traditional preoccupation with cancer.

An instructive context for these disputes was the criteria document, instituted by the Clean Air Act of 1963, that assessed the state of scientific knowledge for a given air pollutant. As these documents were shaped, a patterned spectrum of opinion arose ranging from frontier scientists on the one end who urged that new research findings be brought into assessments and policy more quickly to those on the other end who with equal vigor argued that higher levels of proof be required before conclusions were drawn and action taken. The variations in opinion were shaped into "either-or" alternatives by the requirements of action, and scientists ranged themselves on one side or the other. Persistence of these viewpoints suggests that personal values were often the crucial element in scientific controversy.

Scientific assessments in land and water management have taken a somewhat different turn. In this case the major result of environmental influence has been to "take into account" the environmental effects of development rather than to expand frontiers of scientific knowledge. Here the crucial document was the environmental impact statement. But its procedural rather than substantive emphasis contributed less to substantive knowledge and more to bringing more diverse specializations into the review process. Within the Forest Service, for example, new professional skills have been added to each forest staff. In contrast, however, few environmental effects analyses have been shaped by the debate over acceptable limits described in terms of "critical loads," the environmental counterpart of the "threshold" in human effects which has been central in environmental health debates.

At the same time, the well-established research resources of the Forest Experiment Stations, while devoted primarily to commodity production issues, has provided some room for emerging environmental forest science. The main examples are the Hubbard Brook Experiment Station in New Hampshire which has generated the longest time-series of data about environmental acidification as a part of its mass-balance watershed studies; and the Corvallis station work under the direction of Jerry Franklin that has given rise to a new fund of knowledge about old growth forests. In both cases the scientific research has played an important role in the debates over forest policy. But, given the enormous research capability of the experiment stations, one is struck with the very limited resources devoted to environmental forest research.

Environmental issues have played a more mixed role in scientific research in other federal land and water agencies. National Park Service science has taken a slow but steady upward turn, especially from the emerging concern about the resource impacts of human use within the parks and developments outside them. The journal, *Park Science,* reports these developments regularly.[15] For the Bureau of Land Management, however, the emergence of science on behalf of environmental objectives has been extremely limited. The Bureau does not have the research facilities enjoyed by the Forest Service and has not developed the extensive agency-university type arrangements used by the Park Service.

Extensive research facilities and vast health knowledge have focused environmental health science on debates over the assessment of health effects. In environmental-ecological matters, however, a significant research infrastructure remains to be established and a critical mass of activity from which new ideas and research can be formulated remains limited. The model of desired activity might well be taken from the large-scale acid rain research program of the past decade; one waits for research of similar extent to be developed for other aspects of the ecological environment.

ISSUE PATTERNS: FOSTERING NEW TECHNOLOGIES

The environmental agenda has also included more environmentally acceptable technologies. In environmental science, knowledge skills, readily acquired, enable one to keep in touch with frontier knowledge and generate credible assessments. With environmental technology, on the other hand, innovation requires extensive funds over which environmentalists have little control. They can foster technology transfer by way of ideas, but the opportunities for application are far less than in the case of environmental science.

One such strategy has been technology forcing in clean air and clean water programs, but their application, while successful, has been limited, in air quality to automobiles more than stationary sources and in water quality more to end-of-pipe technology rather than process changes and source reduction.

In these cases two points should be stressed. First, the key element in technology forcing is not so much to require the regulated source to apply a new technology as it is to foster a "third party" pollution control industry separate from either the regulator or the regulated. Second, the aim of technology forcing is to create a market for pollution control equipment by requiring technological achievement by a specific date. Firm compliance deadlines are crucial in order to create predictability and hence to bring into the market engineering skills and capital investment.

The most successful example of this process is automotive emission controls. The regular postponement of emission deadlines retarded the growth of the emission control industry, but when the deadlines became more firm the industry proceeded rapidly and by the late 1980s had positioned itself to move even beyond the existing standards. One records here a commitment of skills and resources to foster continual technological innovation that creates persistent environmental progress.

Environmental debate highlighted a number of innovative technologies such as efficiency in energy end-use, low-input farming, direct steel making, coal washing and fluid bed combustion in coal-fired utility boilers, and process change in manufacturing to limit waste production. These strategies shifted technologies from older to newer forms, some more successful than others, some benefiting from market forces in which increasing costs fostered new techniques of production and use.

In these ventures environmentalists have long preferred source reduction to dispersion or waste treatment but the course of environmental change has moved slowly across that spectrum. Only limited action has been taken to close off dispersion alternatives that are more popular among those who create and manage pollution. Environmentalists have not been able to mount a comprehensive initiative emphasizing source reduction largely because of industry resistance to innovation as long as older technologies are profitable.

A bellwether in this effort in the years between about 1975 and 1985 was

Joseph Ling, 3M Corporation vice president for environmental affairs.[16] Ling argued that "pollution prevention pays" and within the 3M Corporation encouraged the inventiveness of each employee to foster lower resource input and waste output. The reduced costs of disposal, Ling argued, were far greater than the costs of pollution prevention. Ling was rather lionized by environmentalists—he was on the board of directors of Earth Day 1980—but he was far more well known in Europe than in the U.S. where he was not popular among industrial leaders.

In more recent years pollution prevention has been given much more emphasis because the economic feasibility of both waste disposal and waste treatment has been sharply reduced. EPA has established a pollution prevention program. But it is not yet clear how much this means, only volume reduction through waste management or source reduction of waste in the first place. Nevertheless through current tendencies toward reducing both the dispersion option and the treatment option, source reduction is obtaining more visibility than earlier.

Over the years there has been a persistent tendency toward working relationships between those in the private economy fostering technological innovation in pollution control and environmental organizations. The Industrial Gas Cleaning Institute has testified persistently in Congress in favor of stricter controls and firm deadlines as an incentive to advance its industry and the Association of Emission Control Manufacturers has supported more advanced auto emission controls.

ISSUE PATTERNS: ENVIRONMENT AS ECONOMY

Environmental politics has often featured debate over relationships between the environment and the economy. In the more limited context this involves arguments by industry that environmental requirements are too costly for them; in the larger context, economists stress adverse effects on the economy as a whole.

In these arguments mainstream economists have demanded cost-benefit analyses on the grounds that the economy could absorb the costs of only a limited amount of environmental progress. Cost-benefit analyses became progressively more elaborate and influential over the years. They tended to steer thought about the relationship between environmental objectives and the economy into channels of costs to the supply side of economic affairs and to obscure the demand and benefit side.

Cost analysis has gone through several stages of evolution from a focus on jobs and inflation to the migration of industries abroad. Each has led to contrary studies by environmental sectors that environmental programs increase rather than reduce employment, often reduce pressures on prices, and do not foster migration to countries with lower environmental standards. These studies have come from a variety of research sources: quarterly job reports from EPA required by Congress; inflation studies by the Council on Environmental Quality; analysis of transfer of industry abroad by the Conservation Foundation.

Somewhat more persistent in economic debate, however, has been the sequence of approaches known as cost/benefit, cost/effective, and risk analysis. The initiative in using each was taken by those who sought to restrain environmental objectives, either industry, the administrative agencies or professional economists. Cost/benefit analyses tended to expand the range of cost factors and to limit analysis of benefit factors that were more difficult to identify and measure. Cost/effective analyses presumed to take benefits as given and then to assess the least costly means of reaching them, but they often had a way of basing "least cost" on reductions in benefit and hence were politically vulnerable. By the 1980s risk analysis had become more central, especially in human health matters. Yet risk analyses also came under fire because of the limited data on which they were based.[17]

Environmentalists often lacked resources to construct their counter economic analyses. But through several devices they were able to express their own views. The Forest Service, for example, was required to identify the management output of each national forest in terms of comparative net present benefits. Environmentalists were able to play a major role in the critique of this process because of the technical resources provided by citizen environmental organizations.[18] These analyses focused more sharply on benefits and underscored the conclusion that environmental benefits in forest management far outpaced wood production benefits.[19]

In 1989 two risk analyses constructed by environmental organizations entered the public debate, one involving the effect of pesticides on the development of preschool children and the other the effect of chemicals in Lake Michigan on the use of fish as food.[20] In each case the risk analyses advanced the debate considerably. They demonstrated that the vast number of unknowns in risk analysis could be assessed in quite different ways, depending on one's values and frame of reference. Their major significance was to establish citizen environmental organizations as serious participants in the politics of risk analysis.

The lead-in-gasoline controversy illustrated the potential role of cost-benefit analysis. In this case EPA's analyses generated support for the phasedown by both the Office of Management and Budget and the Executive Office of the President. But the overwhelming focus of the EPA analysis was on lower engine maintenance costs rather than improved health. Both the lead advisory of the Centers for Disease Control and the lead criteria document approved by the EPA Science Advisory Board concluded that lead damage to children was occurring at still lower levels of exposure than assumed by the EPA.[21] But EPA made no effort to incorporate that frontier knowledge into its analysis.[22] It especially declined to shift analysis to the benefits of increased human neurological potential, such as the greater human earning capacity with higher levels of IQ.[23]

The possibility of a more thorough cost/benefit analysis from the environmental side was underlined with a study completed for the California South Coast Air Quality Management District in 1989 that brought into the cost-avoided benefits a wider range of factors such as increased life spans, decreased episodes of respiratory infections and other illnesses, decreased number of days of discomfort, increased days of work and of school, and decreased uses of medication to relieve irritation, headaches, nausea, and wheezing. Even this analysis dealt with only two of the nine principal air pollutants and did not include savings from higher crop yields and reduced damage to buildings. Such studies underlined the degree to which the political role of economic analysis depended heavily upon the extent to which environmental benefits could be taken into account.

From a broader vantage point the relationship between the environment and the economy has been debated through the question: can the environment and the economy co-exist? The political context of this question is the adverse rather than positive effect of the environment on the economy. From a more comprehensive perspective, however, environmental activity is, in fact, part of the economy, not something separate from it and represents innovations in both demand and supply, constituting a significant aspect of enhanced economic activity.

Environmental affairs are new consumer demands that can be understood as part of the history of consumption. A three-part sequence in that history identifies shifts from an emphasis on necessities to conveniences to amenities.

Since World War II an increasing share of consumer demand as well as of supply has involved the use of higher levels of income to enhance the qualitative dimension of the nation's standard of living. Even traditional necessities—food, clothing, and shelter—involve major elements of qualitative value. Environmental wants and needs create new markets and lead to entrepreneurial activity to generate new sources of supply.[24]

Environmental action is consumer-based: the demand for natural environments, such as wilderness and open space; appreciative wildlife use now sought by a large majority of the population; higher levels of health and well-being, in contrast with the former emphasis on reducing premature mortality; food that does not contain toxic chemicals; residential areas that are free from large-scale industrial facilities. Much contemporary production and consumption involves such goods and services that provide quality of life needs; they are an integral part of new stages of economic development.

Several aspects of the environmental economy illustrate its role as part of the new post-industrial economy. One is the elaboration of environmental consumer demand itself. Some of this is filled through the private market. Homes are bought and sold because of the higher levels of surrounding environmental amenities; products and travel are purchased to facilitate environmental enjoyment as leisure and recreation; environmental information is bought and sold; 80 percent of all Americans expend funds on appreciative wildlife activities.

In the newly touted "green consumerism," producers seek to meet environmental consumer demand. More widely developed in Germany, Britain, Canada, and Japan, this movement is now appearing in the United States.[25] Especially marked is consumer preference for foods without toxic chemical residues.[26] The environmental consumer movement stresses product labeling, such as on electrical appliances and food. California's proposition 65 extends this market strategy to choice in a wide range of consumer products that involve toxic exposures.

New environmental consumer demand has brought about innovations in supply. The environmental leisure and recreation industries are the most obvious cases. A less noted component are the industries that produce technologies to clean up pollution or reduce its emission in the first place. A recent study of pollution control industries concludes that in 1985 it represented over $100 billion in Gross National Product and 162,000 jobs.[27]

POLITICAL FORCES IN THE EVOLUTION OF ENVIRONMENTALISM

As we stand at the beginning of what some predict will be the "decade of the environment" it might be useful to assess the results of the past and the forces shaping those results.

Most such assessments have been rather unsystematic. For the most part we hear arguments that such and such has worked in the past but can no longer do so; hence the affirmation of "market forces" to replace "command and control" strategies. Such a approach may be useful as a rationale for changes in policy but is not particularly helpful for systematic analysis of results.

I prefer an approach that begins with classifying types of policies and strategies in terms of the degree to which they have worked or not. One can establish a four-stage rank order of best, good, fair, and poor for policies on the one hand and strategies on the other. I then proceed to a series of comparative observations to relate policy results to causal factors.

In the "best" category are the expansion of the national wilderness system, private land protection through land trusts and the Nature Conservancy, the reduction of lead in gasoline, energy efficiency, the control of sulfur dioxide emissions from new power plants, and reduced rates of auto emission. Among poor policy results are population stabilization, restrained consumption levels, control of air toxic emissions, indoor air pollution strategies, nonpoint water pollution controls, wetlands protection, domestic biodiversity objectives, national billboard removal, nongame wildlife programs, and environmental objectives in BLM land management.

The "best" environmental strategies include governmental regulation via emission limits and compliance dates; emission trading within clear regulatory limits such as in the lead phasedown; technology forcing such as with auto emissions; public and private land acquisition that insulates land use from the commercial market; NPDES permit enforcement through citizen litigation; frontier scientific knowledge applied to policy as in the case of lead and acid rain. Among the "poor" strategies, on the other hand, are industry self-monitoring, institutionalized secrecy such as in industrial "trade secrets" or court orders to close information to public scrutiny; OMB autonomy from public and legislative influence; state override of local decision-making and federal preemption of state; advisory body membership that excludes parity for environmental representatives.

What sorts out the best, the good, the fair, and the poor? Through the maze of issues run common patterns of political forces involving relative political strength between those fostering environmental objectives and those seeking to restrain them. These patterns are well recognized by the participants and described explicitly and rather fully in their own media; they can also be reconstructed readily by taking each issue into its political context. In wilderness and lead issues, for example, environmentalists were able to muster political strength to win out over their industry opposition. In wetlands protection and BLM management they were not. Each case often has a unique combination of elements but contributes to a general pattern of continuing historical conflict between environmental and developmental political forces.

A second strategy for analysis of past results rests on environmental voting patterns in the U.S. House of Representatives. I have done this for each session since 1971, using the records published by the League of Conservation Voters. The distributions lead to an emphasis on both spatial and party factors.

Voting patterns vary by region and persist in rather stable fashion over the years. The highest voting scores are in New England, New York and New Jersey, the Upper North Central states, and the Pacific Coast. The lowest scores are in the South, the Plains, and the Mountain West. The "factory belt" from Pennsylvania through Illinois scores in the middle. These patterns are also reflected in the qualitative analysis of the relative state strength of the organized environmental movement and of environmental policies.

This disaggregated mode of analysis reflects the crucial importance of leading and lagging geographical sectors. Some states and regions sustain a more and others a less favorable environmental political context. Whether or not environmental objectives succeed both within the regions and within the nation depends heavily on this underlying climate of public values and interest.

Legislative voting identifies party as a factor of similar importance. From the early 1970s onward Democratic legislators persistently scored much higher than did Republicans in almost every region even amid regional variations. While the Democratic party forged innovations in environmental policy the Republican party held back. There were some notable Republican environmental leaders in the Congress, but as a whole that party constituted a major restraining force on environmental policy. That distinction between the parties did not change in the 1989 session. As with the regional distributions the party patterns are quite stable.

But the two parties also differed in their temporal patterns. Regional Democratic Party differences in the early 1970s between the South, the Plains States, and the Mountain West on the one hand and the rest of the nation on the other declined markedly by the late 1980s. In the Republican Party, on the other hand, regional variations not only persisted but widened. The highest Republican scores continued in the Northeast, the next in the Midwest, and the lowest in the South and West. But while in the Northeast and Midwest the scores tended to become slightly more environmental, in the South and the Pacific Coast they remained stable and in the Mountain West actually declined.

From this analysis, two factors are closely associated with the environmental policies: the underlying social setting and party environmental leadership. Environmental successes over the past two decades have stemmed from distinctive constituency support and Democratic Party initiatives, while resistance has come from distinctive constituency opposition and the Republican Party.

A LOOK TO THE 1990S

One can summarize this analysis of contemporary environmentalism with several observations. First, its evolution rests heavily on changing values that create a widespread desire for higher environmental standards of living and become more extensive and more deeply rooted over the years. These values, second, have driven wide-ranging innovations in public policy at all levels of government and have helped to shape new directions in science, technology, and the economy with resulting tensions between the old and the new. Third, persistent differences have arisen between leading and lagging environmental forces involving different geographical regions, interest groups, and political parties. Finally, a division has arisen between the environmental public and environmental organizations on the one hand and the nation's institutional leaders on the other over the desirability of allocating increasing amounts of national resources to expanding environmental objectives.

All of these factors, evolving over the years, are currently active and will predictably persist in the coming decade.

ENVIRONMENTAL POLITICAL CULTURE AND ENVIRONMENTAL POLITICAL DEVELOPMENT

An Analysis of Legislative Voting, 1971–1989

ON A NUMBER OF recent occasions I have argued that environmental affairs since World War II arose from widespread changes in values associated with the evolution of the American society and economy. The change was slow and persistent, demographic in character, as people became more educated and more affluent. Older types of production and consumption gave way to newer and among the newer was "environmental quality," a new component in the persistent desire for a higher "standard of living." Such new values were held more strongly among younger people and became diffused throughout society more fully with each new generation.[1]

Much of that argument rested on qualitative evidence, drawn from the publications of environmental organizations, new developments in environmental science, public policy at state and federal levels, the debates in legislative bodies, regulatory agencies, and executive offices, and the contests implicit in litigation. At the same time, some of it was quantitative, especially that provided by public opinion polls and attitude studies and data about the rising membership of main-line environmental organizations.[2]

From *Environmental History Review* (Summer 1992): 1–22.

As I developed this argument, the qualitative evidence made clear that there were major centers of both environmental strength and environmental weakness. Why the difference? At the same time there appeared to be a steady increase in the political strength of environmental affairs from the mid-1950s onward. Why the increase and why was it incremental rather than sudden? As these concerns were sharpened I struck upon the use of votes in the U.S. House of Representatives as a source of evidence that was uniform in format over 435 units of analysis—the congressional districts—and over a relatively long period of time—each session of each Congress, now running for 19 years from 1971 through 1989.

Here I work from legislative voting data in the form of voting scores constructed by the League of Conservation Voters from 1971 through 1989 for over 400 congressional votes. These are organized into states and regions and also by time periods, so as to analyze both sets of variations. I have also sorted the data by political parties, Republican and Democrat, and in turn analyzed these in terms of regional variations and variations over time. Some observations here refer to "career scores," the average of scores for an individual member of the House over an entire House career. The analysis both confirms and extends the earlier arguments. It makes more firm and more extensive the regional patterns, charts the changes over time more discretely and systematically, and takes the analysis more fully into the varied responses of political parties to environmental initiatives.[3]

One can summarize the argument in terms of three observations. First there are wide variations in what might be called regional environmental cultures. I use the term "environmental culture" to describe a complex of environmental values and institutions that make up degrees of strength in the expression of environmental objectives. That strength of expression varies from one region to another and gives rise to variations in political support for environmental policies.

Second, there is the notion of stages in the evolution of environmental culture that distinguishes between older and newer patterns of economy and society, between leading and lagging regions, and those in transition between the two. Initially distinctively strong in some regions, environmental values penetrate still other regions, in some cases more rapidly and in others more slowly.

Third, these patterns and changes in environmental culture are reflected in varying support of environmental objectives by the political parties. The Democrats expressed the new values more fully, the Republicans far more weakly. While the Democratic Party developed a stronger national environmental consensus over the years, the Republican Party became deeply divided as in some regions its environmental support increased and in other regions it declined. From such observations one can mark stages in the response of the parties to changes in environmental culture and hence formulate a concept of stages in environmental political development.

REGIONAL VARIATION

The League of Conservation Voters (LCV) voting scores display considerable variation between regions—organized into nine here—but considerable consistency in that variation over time.[4] The data is arrayed in Table I and broken down by states in a further table in the notes.[5] Geographical areas in which legislators score highest are New England, New York and New Jersey, the upper North Central states of Michigan, Wisconsin and Minnesota, Florida, and the Pacific Coast states. Those in the low category are in the southern Plains, the Mountain states, and the Gulf South. In the middling category are the South Atlantic and Central Plateau states and the old factory belt ranging from Pennsylvania on the east to Illinois on the West.[6]

Table I
Environmental Voting Scores, House of Representatives, 1971 and 1989, by Region

Region	1971	1989
New England	68.4	89.2
Mid Atlantic	55.8	64.5
South Atlantic	23.8	55.8
Gulf	15.4	32.8
Central Plateau	30.4	47.0
North Central	46.8	59.0
Plains	31.6	53.1
Mountain	33.3	40.0
Pacific	44.5	63.6

The meaning of this data is immediately obvious: environmental affairs varied in their strength from region to region. Thus, the question: Why is it the case that environmental strength marked New England and environmental weakness the Gulf regions in 1971 and that these opposites in levels of environmental support continued to 1989? We will explore this question more fully later.[7]

REGIONAL CHANGE

Changes in voting patterns over the years from 1971 to 1989 provide further insight into recent environmental political history. One can readily compare and contrast regional voting scores in 1971 and 1989 and identify variations in those changes. The data is provided in Table II.

Table II
Changes in Regional Environmental Voting Scores, 1971 to 1989, by Rank Order

South Atlantic	32.0
Plains	21.5
New England	20.8
Pacific	19.1
Gulf	17.4
Central Plateau	16.6
North Central	12.2
Mid Atlantic	8.7
Mountain	7.7

In every region of the country environmental scores increased between 1971 and 1989. However, that increase ranged from 32.0 in the South Atlantic States to 7.7 in the Mountain States. Some areas that were high in 1971 increased their strength markedly; New England ranking first in 1971 also ranked first in 1989. The Mountain region, ranking second lowest in 1971, increased its environmental support the least of all regions and now ranked lowest. The changes, however, were mixed and require analysis of each region to sort out differences.

Most instructive of all these changes were those in the South Atlantic region. Ranking ninth in 1971, those states ranked fifth in 1989 almost reaching the level of the North Central States. While the five states of the region all posted marked gains, they were strongest in North and South Carolina, Georgia, and Florida. Scores for these states are in Table III.

Table III
Changes in Voting Scores, South Atlantic States, 1971–1989

State	1971	1989	Change
S. Carolina	7.5	63.3	55.8
Georgia	10.5	54.0	43.5
N. Carolina	27.1	62.8	35.7
Florida	41.3	61.9	20.6
Virginia	22.2	34.0	11.8

These South Atlantic changes are persistent over the years, displaying few dramatic increases from session to session but slow and incremental changes, at times declining but over the two decades rising steadily. The data is in Table IV. This seems to reflect rather fundamental changes in society, economy, and politics between 1971 and 1989.

Table IV
Incremental Changes in Voting Scores, South Atlantic States, 1971–1989

State	1971	1973	1975	1977	1979	1981	1983	1985	1987	1989
S. Carolina	7.5	9.3	33.8	40.2	34.2	33.0	47.0	43.8	60.5	63.3
Georgia	10.5	24.0	25.9	31.4	30.4	37.0	50.8	46.8	48.2	54.0
N. Carolina	27.1	21.1	36.5	36.0	30.0	39.5	48.9	35.2	52.4	62.8
Florida	41.3	44.9	46.5	45.1	39.1	33.5	47.6	49.0	49.4	61.9
Virginia	22.2	9.3	30.4	31.1	24.5	22.9	30.6	32.1	42.0	34.0

PARTY DIFFERENCES

Party was as significant as region in variations in environmental support. On the whole by 1989 the Democratic Party scored about twice as high as did the Republican Party. This difference held, for the most part across the regions. The exceptions were New England where the two parties scored at about the same level in 1971 and 1989 and in New Jersey where party environmental differences by 1989 had all but disappeared. In the South Atlantic and Gulf regions the two parties were also fairly close in 1971, with Republican scores being somewhat higher than Democratic, but by 1989 this had changed markedly and here also Democrats far outscored Republicans. The data is in Table V.

Party changes in regional environmental support between 1971 and 1979 differed. They are displayed in Table VI. For the Democrats, environmental scores increased in all of the regions, even though by amounts ranging from 12.4 points to 47.2 points. For the Republicans, however, some regions increased 4.7 points to 18.2 points while other regions remained relatively stable at .4 to .8 points increase and still others decreased their support from 4 to 13.4 points. Thus, while the Democratic party was responding in the same direction to environmental objectives in every region, the Republicans were moving in two directions at once.

Table V

Party Differences, Regional Environmental Voting Scores, 1971 and 1989

Region	1971 Dem.	1971 Rep.	1989 Dem.	1989 Rep.
New England	68.3	68.8	90.7	87.0
Mid Atlantic	62.2	45.5	76.7	46.3
South Atlantic	21.3	28.9	68.5	36.2
Gulf	14.7	19.1	44.3	5.7
Central Plateaus	33.7	19.8	64.8	15.8
North Central	63.8	34.4	76.2	34.8
Plains	35.1	28.8	77.8	21.4
Mountain	38.8	28.4	75.6	18.7
Pacific Coast	62.5	29.7	87.3	34.4

Table VI

Changes in Regional Environmental Voting Scores Between 1971 and 1989, by Party

Democrats		Republicans	
South Atlantic	47.2	New England	18.2
Plains	41.2	South Atlantic	7.3
Mountain	36.8	Pacific Coast	4.7
Central Plateaus	31.1	Mid Atlantic	.8
Gulf	29.6	North Central	.4
Pacific	24.8	Central Plateaus	-4.0
New England	22.4	Plains	-7.4
Mid Atlantic	14.5	Mountain	-9.7
North Central	12.4	Gulf	-13.4

Within both parties regional differences were quite similar, with strongest and weakest regions being roughly the same. But those differences were at quite different levels of environmental support. In the Democratic Party in 1971 only four of the nine regions had scored 50 points or more, but by 1989 eight out of nine scored over 50 points and the lowest, the Gulf states, scored 44.3. The Democratic Party was forging agreement among regional sectors that were responding positively, though in different degrees, to a broadly shared environmental opinion.

The Republican Party, on the other hand, was increasingly more divided. New England Republicans participated as fully in the new environmental culture as did the Democrats, and significant gains had been made in environmental scores between 1971 and 1989 in the South Atlantic and Pacific Coast states. The Mid Atlantic and North Central regions, however, remained almost unchanged, with slight increases under one percentage point. But the regions that had been lowest in Republican support in 1971 were now in 1989 even lower; their environmental scores had declined. For the Republicans as a national party, therefore, the task of forging an environmental consensus was a problem of bringing together representatives from regions who were moving in quite opposite directions.

These patterns of party support and especially the changes over the years sharpen the relationship between social and political change. The parties are mediators in that relationship, working within the context of social change that varies from region to region, and responding to it in different ways. Differential regional patterns identify regional differences in the degree to which environmental social change works itself into legislative policy.

ENVIRONMENTAL POLITICAL DEVELOPMENT

These party differences in environmental scores chart several stages in the way in which changing environmental values affected political parties. There were three such stages: first, a time period in which both parties responded only weakly to environmental objectives; second, one in which the Democratic party responded well and the Republican party poorly; and third, a stage in which both parties gave relatively high levels of support.

In 1971 five regions of the country displayed very low environmental scores in both parties; the South Atlantic, Gulf, Central Plateau, Plains, and Mountain regions. In these regions environmental values had not yet emerged to play a positive role in the strategies of either party. Democrats posted scores almost as low as did Republicans and, in fact, in the South Atlantic and Gulf regions, although both were quite low in environmental support, Republicans scored higher than did Democrats. Hence these regions represent the earliest stage in the historical process of environmental political development.

Three regions, the Mid Atlantic, North Central, and Pacific Coast regions, by 1971 had evolved to a second stage in which the Democratic Party had begun to incorporate those values into their political programs as reflected in their respective congressional scores of 62.2, 63.8, and 62.5. In those same states Republican scores remained considerably lower, indicating a reluctance of that party to embrace environmental objectives to the same extent as did the Democrats. There was some variation in this reluctance; Pacific Coast Republicans posted a 29.7 score, the North Central party 34.8, and the Middle Atlantic contingent 45.5.

Only in New England had the third stage of environmental development appeared by 1971. Here the two parties displayed a relatively high and relatively similar environmental voting support, 68.8 for the Republicans and 68.3 for the Democrats. One might speculate that in immediately previous years the New England political scene might well have been characterized by the second stage, of strong party differences. This is suggested by the two seats in New Hampshire and the one in Connecticut in which Republican scores were 24.4, 36.3, and 43.5 respectively in 1971 but by 1989 had risen to 64.8. 60.0, and 57.0 respectively. Perhaps still earlier both parties in New England might have been relatively uninfluenced by environmental issues, reflecting the first stage posted by the five regions in 1971.[8]

By 1989 no region remained in the first stage of environmental development in which both parties posted low environmental scores. Four of the regions in that category in 1971 had changed to a stage of sharp party competition in which the Democrats had taken up environmental objectives while Republicans had not, a clear evolution from stage one to stage two. These were the Plains, Mountain, Central Plateaus, and Gulf regions. In 1971 these had the lowest environmental scores of all the regions and in 1989 remained in that rank. But while Democratic scores in these regions rose over those years by 42.7, 36.8, 31.1, and 29.6 points respectively, Republican party scores had in fact declined. Here one could find no district that displayed a trend toward increasing Republican environmental support.

The three regions that were in the stage two development in 1971—the Middle Atlantic, North Central, and Pacific Coast—remained there in 1989. Each of these cases were marked by increasing Democratic environmental support, registering gains in scores since 1971 of 14.5, 12.4, and 24.8 points respectively, thereby reinforcing the strong ties that the Democratic Party had established with environmental objectives in earlier years. Republican scores in these regions, however, had increased only .8, .4, and 4.7 points respectively indicating a widening gap between the two parties in these regions. In that gap these three regions were very much like the four regions that had changed from stage one to stage two in environmental party development between 1971 and 1989. But while those four regions had moved from stage one to stage two, the three now considered had remained in stage two, and as a whole, had not moved further toward a stage three level.

As in 1971, only New England in 1989 displayed the third stage of environmental political development. Here both parties had increased their environmental strength considerably over those years, 22.4 points for the Democrats and 18.2 for the Republicans. While now the Democratic strength was slightly higher than the Republican, both continued to score higher, within their own respective parties, than any other region. At the same time, however, several regions, most notably the South Atlantic region, indicated trends toward, although not yet reaching, this third state.

EMERGING REPUBLICAN ENVIRONMENTAL STRENGTH

By 1989 the development of environmental strength in the Democratic Party had become a familiar story of increasing levels throughout the nation. Support within the Republican party was more limited and the trends were in quite varied directions. Hence the Republican party is of special interest and deserves more detailed analysis. Here we emphasize especially the states and regions where Republican environmental strength was growing and individual Republicans scoring higher in order to pinpoint the distinctive source of increasing environmental support in that party.

In New England the Republicans competed vigorously with Democrats in a context of shared environmental objectives. That had been evident in 1971; it was even more so in 1989 since by that time several districts of weak Republican support in 1971 had changed to strong Republican support 19 years later. The region is distinctive in the degree to which it displays a relatively shared environmental context within which debate over policy is carried out. Here Republicans compete vigorously with Democrats within the same culture of environmental meaning and objectives and citizen environmental organizations support Republican as well as Democratic candidates.

Second to New England, the South Atlantic states displayed the highest Republican gains over these two decades, a regional increase of 7.3 points. Here there was a semi-concentration of individual member Republican gains. Especially marked by 1989 were Arthur Ravenel of South Carolina's first district (1987–89 career score of 68.0) and newly elected members Craig James (1989 score of 80) and Ileana Ros Lentinen (1989 score of 86) of Florida's fourth and eighteenth districts. All these Republicans had replaced Democratic incumbents and in 1989 scored higher than did their Democratic predecessors. Such factors might presage region-wide Republican environmental gains and movement of the region into a stage three of environmental political development.

By 1989 a similar stage three pattern had developed in New Jersey. Here a

Democratic-Republican difference in 1971 (D-65.7 and R-43.2) had evolved into virtual similarity in support in 1989 (D-70.0 and R-71.7). Table VII includes several additional years so as to follow changes in this pattern over the two decades.

Table VII

Party Environmental Scores, New Jersey, Selected Years

Party	1971	1975	1980	1985	1989
Democratic	65.7	72.6	72.7	72.3	70.0
Republican	43.2	68.7	69.8	65.3	71.7

This transition in New Jersey involved all four types of party-to-party change: Republican to Democrat, Democrat to Democrat, Republican to Republican, and Democrat to Republican.[9] Throughout the 1970s and 1980s an environmental political culture had arisen in New Jersey very similar to that in New England. While both New York and Pennsylvania remained in a stage two environmental political development, New Jersey had evolved into stage three.

Washington and Florida were also in transition between stage two and stage three, displaying higher Republican scores and a more competitive context for party debate. The data is in Tables VIII and IX.

Table VIII

Party Environmental Scores, Washington, Selected Years

Party	1971	1975	1980	1985	1989
Democratic	46.5	53.3	59.0	60.1	85.0
Republican	41.0	28.0	62.0	50.0	70.0

Table IX

Party Environmental Scores, Florida, Selected Years

Party	1971	1975	1980	1985	1989
Democratic	39.9	49.1	37.8	59.5	75.0
Republican	45.6	41.4	29.3	31.0	52.4

In Washington Republican scores rose from 41.0 in 1971 to 70.0 in 1989 and Democratic from 46.5 to 85.0. Changes occurred both in districts that continued to be Republican and districts that continued to be Democratic.[10] The changes in Florida were marked by different patterns in which a few high scoring Republicans replaced lower scoring Democrats and, at the same time, the entire Republican delegation scored over 40, relatively high for Republicans.[11] These suggest movement in Florida toward a higher level of environmental political development.

Beyond identifying states where Republican environmental strength has emerged, one can also note individuals elsewhere with relatively strong environmental scores. Table X indicates the location of individual Republicans who scored more than 50 in 1971 and 1989. The number grew from 40 in 1971 to 54 in 1989; their location holds some clues as to the nature of increasing Republican environmental strength.

Table X
Republicans Scoring 50 Points or More, 1971 and 1989, by Region

	Total	*Number*
New England	7	9
Mid Atlantic	12	13
South Atlantic	2	7
North Central	14	11
Plains	1	1
Pacific Coast	3	9
Gulf	1	1
Mountain	0	2
Central Plateaus	0	1
Total	40	54

Most of these are in the regions and states already described as in transition toward a third stage of environmental political development. But others are in other states such as New York, Wisconsin, Michigan, and California. They reflect "outposts" of Republican environmental strength in states that have not yet been marked as having a significant Republican environmental contingent.

In a few cases in the western regions, strong Republican scores provide some insight about party environmental change. Three stand out: the third district of Kansas in which Republican Janet Meyers succeeded Republican Larry Winn in 1984 to raise the career environmental score from 17.5 to 67.0; the first district in Washington in which a succession of three Republicans from 1971 to 1989 raised the scores from 47.0 to 51.5 to 79.3; and the eleventh district in California represented by four Republicans since 1971 with scores of 69.98, 54.3 44.0, and 100.0. In all three of these cases Republicans represented urban/metropolitan districts; they might well indicate a direction in which the party in that region is slowly moving.

Sub-regional analysis in the Plains, Mountain, and Pacific regions is also suggestive. In Kansas and Nebraska, for example, environmental scores in the eastern more urban congressional districts are much higher than in the western; in Colorado the higher environmental scores are in the Denver area and the lower in the less urbanized parts of the state; in California, Oregon, and Washington, the urban-rural differences are especially marked.

IMPLICATIONS: REGIONAL DIFFERENCES

Patterns of environmental legislative voting outlined here have three major analytical implications. They arise from the three main sets of observations presented here: variations among regions, changes over time, and both spatial and temporal observations of political party response.

First, differences between regions of stronger and weaker environmental support point to contrasting social contexts that identify the distinctive historical roots of environmental impulses. The legislative voting data confirms the qualitative data and leads one to formulate a notion of contrasting environmental cultures. The phrase "environmental culture" is used as a term of convenience that brings together a range of factors that go to make up the relationship between environmental society and environmental politics.

Fundamental to environmental culture is the set of values that prompt people to emphasize environmental quality as a major element in their standard of living. These, in turn, become public, i.e., political, as well as personal values. The regional strength of such values can be identified in the variety, number, and size of citizen environmental organizations. It is also reflected in media coverage of environmental affairs; the strength or weakness of environmental research and curricula in academic institutions; the degree to which the business community as an environmental opposition deems it wise to make adjustments to the environmental presence or to confront, combat, or manipulate it directly; the initiative that governmental leaders take in advancing environmental objectives; and the degree to which citizen environmental leaders are incorporated into governing structures.

Both quantitative and qualitative data provide fairly firm evidence as to the differences between regions of strong and weak environmental support. Most important is the degree to which the region's society and economy is rooted in raw material/commodity production and manufacturing closely associated with related processing, or to which it is removed from those activities in a newer economy that is based more on service/information production. The same difference is manifest in the types of consumption distinctive to those regions. Areas of high environmental quality attract people as a place to live, and draw especially younger people seeking a higher "quality of life" and retirees seeking attractive environmental surroundings for their permanent residence.

Areas of environmental weakness are closely associated with raw material/commodity production. In legislative voting they tend, for example, to be more rural than urban. At the same time, centers of livestock grazing, wood production, oil and gas production, coal and hardrock mining all display, in the votes of their representatives, weak environmental support. The Mountain region displays major elements of both, raw material/extractive activities that have long underpinned its economy and newer major centers that have built communities and new economic activities based on the region's environmental assets: rivers, mountains, and deserts. In this case the two cultures, one environmental, the other commodity, are locked more fully in vigorous combat than in any other region of the nation.[12]

Other evidence tends to confirm these observations. One deals with state variations in environmental policy. Reviews of policy conducted by Renew America and by the Center for Southern Studies indicate that the regions identified here as high in environmental scores, for example New England and the Pacific Coast, rank high in state environmental performance, while those that rank low here also rank low in environmental performance.[13]

Cases of sub-regional analysis, based on the legislative voting scores used here, point in the same direction. One is the distinctively low scores of Pennsylvania and Ohio, with values and institutions still heavily rooted in an older coal and iron/steel economy, as compared with other states in the Middle Atlantic and the North Central regions. Another is the lower scores in Louisiana and Texas compared with Mississippi and Alabama which one might well attribute to the greater dominance of the oil and gas economy in the western in contrast with the eastern Gulf.

These commodity/service, older and newer consumer values and rural/urban differences are suggested especially sharply in state level legislative votes on which I have carried out a limited foray. About half the states have created data similar to the LCV reports and about a dozen have done so for almost two decades. They reflect far smaller units of representation and hence involve far more precise identifications of the social roots of environmental voting. For two states, Oregon and Michigan, relationships have been explored between state legislative voting and degrees of urbanization. The fit is quite consistent. This line of research remains to be carried out fully but that already done leads to conclusions similar to conclusions drawn from data about the U.S. House of Representatives.[14]

IMPLICATIONS: POLITICAL CHANGE

Changes in legislative voting support provide additional insight as to the social roots of environmental objectives. As the years pass, the time series extends over more years and enhances the quality of the quantitative analysis. By observing change in regional and party support over almost two decades one obtains a sense of the spread of environmental culture and through the distinctive patterns of dissemination of that culture the analytical base for understanding environmental affairs is enhanced.

Several types of observations come to mind. One is that changes took place gradually over the years, were persistent rather than sudden, and point to social, economic, and political forces that were incremental rather than episodic. This observation has considerable import for an understanding of environmental change. Most literature on the subject has emphasized the episodes, Earth Day 1970 and 1990, environmental "disasters" such as the Santa Barbara oil spill in 1969 or the Chernobyl and Bhophal events. At the same time it stresses the contribution of individual writers such as Rachel Carson or the role of legislative events such as passage of the National Environmental Policy Act.

More significant, however, is the incremental rather than the episodic nature of environmental affairs, with the argument that the key is not to identify the episodes but to explain the receptivity in the society at large to those episodes. Without identifying the slow and persistent changes in how people think about and what they value in their environment, one cannot explain why it is that such reactions occurred at this particular time of history.

The legislative data, when arrayed in terms of time series over almost two decades, underlines and supports this view of environmental affairs as incremental, slow and gradual. While the changes took place at times in fits and starts, never precisely smooth from year to year, they added up to distinctive "secular" trends over almost two decades. The data prompts one to associate that development with similar types of incremental phenomenon, such as changes in values about the role of women or those associated generally with rising levels of education and to root them in demographic-type phenomena.

Incremental environmental change points to regions in transition between older and newer environmental circumstances. The region of greatest environmental change, the South Atlantic states, readily fits this analysis. These states became urbanized more rapidly after World War II and that urbanization rested not on the strength of an older commodity/raw material economy but a far more service/information one. New migrants into the region brought new values, either in the case of young people looking for job opportunities or retirees looking for an attractive place to live. It is not difficult to work out this relationship between new demography, new consumer wants, new types of production, and new public policies.

The role of the South in environmental change can be identified more precisely by contrasting it with the quite different trends in Pennsylvania and Ohio, the states of the Middle Atlantic and North Central regions that display especially modest environmental scores in contrast with their level of urbanization. While Pennsylvania and Ohio gained in environmental scores between 1971 and 1989, that gain was quite limited in contrast with the South Atlantic states and, while the South Atlantic states gained markedly in rank in environmental legislative voting over those years, Pennsylvania and Ohio dropped equally markedly. In 1971 Pennsylvania and Ohio had both scored higher than North Carolina, South Carolina, Georgia, and Florida and in 1989 they scored below those states—and Alabama as well. The scores are in Table XI.

Table XI
Environmental Voting Scores, House of Representatives, 1971 and 1989, Selected States

State	1971	1989
Pennsylvania	45.7	52.6
Ohio	43.6	51.4
North Carolina	27.1	62.8
South Carolina	7.5	63.3
Georgia	10.5	54.0
Florida	41.3	61.9
Alabama	15.7	54.3

One might well argue, as a working hypothesis, that the extractive/manufacturing legacy of Pennsylvania and Ohio as major elements of the "old factory belt" retarded the evolution of an environmental culture in those states and left an influential inheritance of both values and institutions from the heavy industry sector of the economy and the society. In the South Atlantic states quite a different historical sequence held sway in which the transition from an agricultural and extractive economy was more direct with less of the heavy industry/manufacturing interval that played such a dominant influence in the old factory belt. Florida is the prime example of such an historical process; it led the environmental scores of the South Atlantic states in 1971 and almost kept pace with the Carolinas by 1989.

The process of incremental change can also be examined through the careers of individual members of Congress in their "career scores." These changes occurred incrementally over the years, in some cases as Democrats succeeded Democrats, in others as Republicans succeeded Republicans, most often as Democrats succeeded Republicans but even in some cases as Republicans succeeded Democrats.

One distinction in this process is indicative. Changes in voting scores came most readily in the transition from one member to another and less readily within the careers of individual members. One could interpret this as the differential process by which social change becomes reflected in political leadership. Members elected in earlier times continued to think in older ways rather than to respond directly and immediately to changes among their constituents, while newer members were freer in terms of their own personal values to respond to the new interests of their districts.

IMPLICATIONS: POLITICAL PARTIES

The analysis of party differences adds still further to the historical understanding of environmental affairs by observing the differential response of the parties and the gradual incorporation of environmental impulses into party strategies. One can examine this in terms of both the strength of environmental culture as an influence on parties and the decisions of party leaders, as individuals or as parties, to respond to the electorate.

It seems rather clear that the Democratic party as a whole has chosen to foster agendas of public environmental objectives, while the Republican party as a whole has not. One could undoubtedly conclude as much from details of party platforms. But the legislative voting record demonstrates this decisively. The overall party environmental support by the Democrats is rather consistently about twice that of the Republicans. Even more telling is the spread of Democratic support from only some regions in 1971 to almost every one by 1989. By 1989 only the Gulf region remained below a score of 50 for the Democrats. This data outlines stages by which the Democratic party incorporated these newly evolving public objectives into its national agenda.

Especially striking is the way in which this took place in regions of the country which are considered to be relatively weak supporters of emerging "liberal" or "progressive" political agendas. Environmental strength in all three southern regions and in the Mountain states, for example, has grown steadily through these two decades to establish a context for relatively unified nation-wide action. One does not detect a "southern strategy" by segments of the Democratic party on environmental issues markedly different from that of the rest of the nation. In terms of our schema of stages of environmental political development, the Democratic party has moved rather quickly from the first, through the second, and considerably far toward the third stage.

The Republican party has taken quite a different course in which the response to environmental objectives has been mixed. That differential response has considerable bearing on the idea of varied levels of "environmental culture." Republicans in New England live within a high level of environmental culture and respond accordingly. Those in the southern and Mountain regions live within regions that have only recently developed such a perspective on environmental affairs and provide an opportunity for the Republican party to find meaning in responding more fully to developmental rather than environmental values.

Especially significant is the difference in style and tone of political competition in such contrasting areas. In New England both parties compete for environmental values. As a result, the political debate is posed largely in terms of which party can do the best job in environmental policy and results are evaluated in terms of environmental consequences.[15]

In the Mountain region, by way of contrast, the debate is far more ideological, with sharply contrasting views in which value conflicts come to the fore and accusations are rife that environmentalists seek to destroy what is at the heart of the region's history and culture. While environmental supporters pose their policies in terms of quality of life, often approached in terms of pragmatic politics, their opponents are prone to speak in terms of defending a "way of life" against those who would destroy it. At times they suggest or explicitly state that their opponents are "un-American" or even subversive.[16]

This analysis demonstrates that legislative voting has great usefulness in probing the historical meaning of environmental affairs. By these three analytical formats of contrasting regional strength in "environmental culture," incremental change over time, and the differential response of parties, much is added to conclusions drawn from qualitative data.

It helps especially to forge links and connections between environmental history and American history in general. By focusing on values, it associates environmental affairs with a wide range of value changes in American society since World War II. By emphasizing incremental change it helps to define the relationships between dramatic events and demographic change in those same years. And by examining the differential response of the political parties to environmental objectives, it provides evidence about the way in which parties responded to massive social change since World War II. In such ways as these, recent environmental history stands not just by itself, but as an integral part of recent American history.

THE POLITICS OF ENVIRONMENTAL ADMINISTRATION

THE EVOLUTION OF federal administration since the New Deal years, and especially since World War II, has loomed large in recent American history. Since the mid-1960s, moreover, environmental affairs have become an increasingly important element of that development. They have also played more than an equal role in the debate over the "federal bureaucracy" and the issue of "big government." In this analysis I hope to go beyond the limited scope of that debate to the larger historical question of the role environmental administration has played in recent American politics—especially as an example of institutional development. This constitutes a somewhat limited case study, but I hope it is one that sheds light on the larger growth of recent federal administration as a whole.

Administration is the centerpiece of our modern political system in the United States. It is in administration that the major sustained political choices are now made. For many years it was customary to divide administration from legislation by distinguishing the making of laws from their implementation. Congress decides policy, and the agencies carry it out. But as administrative decision making has been brought under closer scrutiny, its political role has become clearer. As soon as a law is passed the parties at interest shift their attention from Congress to the agency and continue their combat with even greater intensity. The setting is different, but the controversies are the same. Administration is a political context of technical detail, bureaucratic jungles, and professional experts, but it is no less one in which political demands are massive and the adjustment of conflicting interests is central. In the technical apparatus of administration, scientific research and assessment, economic analysis, planning, and management are all devices not for implementing politics in a disinterested manner but for bringing workable agreement out of disagreement. Administration is the main arena of political combat where environmental political choices of enormous consequence are made.[1]

As a second introductory observation, I shall take with a massive amount of skepticism notions about the centrality of a continuing struggle between government and private enterprise. This is the ideology of political debate. But historians have long understood that government is not something alien to the institutions of corporate enterprise, that large-scale management is quite similar whether conducted under private or public auspices, and that business firms have continually sought an active government to help them achieve ends they could not accomplish by themselves.[2] Not the least example of this was the National Recovery Administration of the New Deal, in which trade association majorities, long frustrated by recalcitrants within their ranks, sought the legal power of government to force trade association minorities to accept their decisions.[3] The issue has been not whether there should be an activist federal government, but who should control it and for what ends. Upon reflection it seems preposterous to believe the ever-larger scales of organization that private corporate institutions have fashioned would not also arise in government. It seems equally clear that organizational development in the private economy not only constituted a model for government to follow[4] but in fact was a major influence in the evolution of large-scale organization in the public economy. As we examine federal administration as an institution rather than an ideology, we become peculiarly aware of the integrative and even symbiotic relationships it embodies between itself and private corporate America.[5]

Finally, I will also be concerned with the significance this common drive for scale has for the larger vertical hierarchy of American economic and political institutions, ranging from the community to the city, the town and township to the county, the county and city to the state, and on to the federal government. We argue, often I fear with little reflection, that the big issues of the day are those of "returning" government power and authority to local levels. So runs the ideological debate. But we can be misled if we do not keep an eagle eye on the more crucial element of institutional development. Often the ideology of a devolution of authority only obscures the practice of its concentration. Today this appears, for example, in the form of federal "preemption" of state authority or state "override" of local action. Environmental politics and administration are shot through with such choices as to the level in the hierarchy of government where decisions are to be made. I shall explore these in some detail.[6]

I shall stress government administration, then, as a set of institutions and their evolution as a case of institution building. My question will be the way environmental administration has evolved as a system of control, and the political options represented by the peculiar substantive choices that have been made. I do not wish to denigrate political ideology, the ideology of administration as a nonpolitical process of implementing choices made elsewhere, the ideology of continuing combat between government and private enterprise, or the ideology of struggle between centralization and decentralization of power and authority. All these play an overarching role in shaping how people understand and explain their political world. But in this effort I wish to concentrate more precisely on the institutions and how they have evolved, on government administration as a phenomenon that has come to play the central role in environmental politics.

Environmental politics reflect major changes in American society and values. People want new services from government stemming from new desires associated with the advanced consumer economy that came into being after World War II. Some of these services pertain to outdoor recreation and the allocation of air, land, and water to natural environment management and use; others pertain to new objectives concerning health and well-being and to the adverse effects of pollution on both biological life and human beings; still others deal with matters such as "least cost" technologies in energy, smaller-scale production, and population-resource balance. Most of these objectives are described by advocates of environmental policies as quality-of-life concerns. All of them reflect new types of demands upon government that leaders in older public institutions have often found strange and difficult to comprehend.[7]

It would be worthwhile to emphasize several aspects of these changes that help one to understand their significance. First, they constitute not temporary but permanent changes in social values; they represent an evolutionary tendency associated with rising standards of living and human expectations. One cannot consider them momentary aberrations any more than one can consider the general desire for new household durables an aberration. Moreover, they reflect desires and values that are widely held, perhaps expressed by only a small segment of society a century ago, but now reflecting a mass phenomenon. Environmental values are perhaps weaker in the top tenth of the social order and the bottom third. But they have a broad middle base that is reflected in a host of attitude studies carried out by both independent agencies and business corporations.[8]

Second, environmental values can be understood historically as a facet in the evolution of consumer desires, as a part of the history of consumption. A century ago necessities such as food, clothing, and shelter were the main items of consumption. By the 1920s a new phase had come onto the scene emphasizing conveniences, taking the form of consumer durables such as the automobile, household appliances, and the radio. This phase continued into the 1930s, reflecting changes in consumer preferences that evolved even during the depression decade.[9] After World War II a third stage of consumption had been reached, that of amenities—goods and services that made life more enjoyable, not just livable and convenient. It encompassed new material goods, new amenity elements of both necessities and conveniences, and a host of new products reflecting purchasing power that came to be called discretionary income. Environmental values and services were a part of this new stage of consumption, not less rooted or firm in the demand side of the economy than were hi-fi sets or the creative art of photography.

Third, the kinds of demands these new consumer wants placed upon politics and government were new. In previous years public economic policy was concerned primarily with matters of production. It grew out of conflicts among producers. Much of what is known as economic regulation by government resulted from the internal politics of the business community in which one sector sought to limit action by another through the coercive power of public law. Conflicts among agriculture, labor, and business emphasized the relative shares each would receive from the surplus of production. The entry of new consumer values into this interplay of political forces represented something quite different. Consumers had played only a minor, extremely weak, and even insignificant role in economic policy during the Progressive Era and the New Deal years. In the 1960s they became more influential, and environmentalists were among them. Hence we should expect tensions between older government arrangements heavily shaped by interaction among producers and the newer demands of environmental consumers.[10]

The transition from the old to the new can be observed in the shift in government regulation. One can distinguish between the older regulatory agencies such as the Interstate Commerce Commission or the Securities and Exchange Commission, which as their major function policed relationships among producers, and the newer regulatory agencies in which consumer objectives were more central. In the older types of regulation a common perspective seemed to arise between the regulator and the regulated that led to persistent cooperation between them.[11] In this consumers had little influence. In the new regulatory system consumers began to develop a capacity to inject a new force into the relationships between the regulators and the regulated. They argued in favor of relaxing older-style regulation on the grounds that the freer market would benefit consumers; at the same time they argued for more regulation of the newer type to benefit consumers.[12]

Environmental administration is part of a new stage in the evolution of government agencies. New values, widely shared, reflecting a significant challenge to an older order of government policy now are on the scene. I will have occasion at several points to contrast the new and the old in order to refer back to the historical context. It is well to keep that sense of evolution, that marked difference between the old and new and the tension between them, clearly in mind in order to comprehend the evolution of environmental administration over the past several decades.

The various sectors of environmental administration can be distinguished in terms of their relation to these new values and political demands. First of all there are those agencies concerned with land resources that long had maintained a mission for commodity development. These include the U.S. Forest Service in the Department of Agriculture, in charge of the national forests;[13] the Soil Conservation Service, which since the early New Deal had been preoccupied with preventing soil erosion but which in the 1950s became more involved in land development;[14] and the Bureau of Land Management, which had arisen out of the decision in the Taylor Grazing Act of 1934 to stabilize grazing on the western public lands and reverse a persistent decline in forage capacity.[15]

Each of these agencies sought to promote the development of material resources: wood, farm products, and forage. Each had taken a stance, described as "conservation," that stressed applied science in order to increase production efficiency.[16] Scientific, technical, and professional leaders in those fields fashioned a common approach to their tasks of resource management. And each in turn found that the new environmental thrust was quite different from its traditional mission. Upon each of them now there were demands to take up new management objectives, called environmental, which in each case involved lower levels of development and more management of lands as natural environment areas. The Forest Service faced demands for wilderness areas where no future development, such as roads or wood harvest, would occur.[17] The Soil Conservation Service was roundly condemned for destroying valuable natural wildlife habitat with its channelization and drainage projects.[18] The Bureau of Land Management found itself faced with competitors for grazing land from among those interested in enhancing wildlife on the western range and those who found western drylands to have amenity and aesthetic value.[19]

The Bureau of Reclamation and the Federal Power Commission were deeply involved with water development. For many years their objective had been to harness rivers that flowed unused, as the argument went, to the sea. The U.S. Army Corps of Engineers was engaged in a similar task. Together they shared the view that engineered rivers could provide varied commodity benefits such as irrigation, navigation, hydroelectric power, and flood control. The culmination of these ambitions came with the Tennessee Valley Authority. But as the environmental movement advanced, an increasing number of people asserted that rivers were more valuable in their natural free-flowing state.[20] The issue was dramatically sharpened by a Supreme Court decision in 1968 concerning a dispute over who should build a dam on the Snake River in Hell's Canyon, Idaho. In reviewing a Federal Power Commission decision, the Court argued that the agency had failed to consider one alternative—no dam at all—remanded the case for further consideration, and set off a series of steps that led to congressional action over a decade later to manage that part of the Snake as a natural river.[21]

All these were straightforward cases. Agencies with older missions now were faced with new environmental demands that had widespread public support. The conflicts were intense. Each agency was administered by technical professionals who were committed to commodity development, had been trained in disciplines with that orientation, and shared deeply the similar values of those in private institutions—forestry, agriculture, livestock raising, navigation, electric power, manufacturing industry—that the primary objective of public policy should be material development. They could hardly understand, let alone accept, the new environmental thrust that emphasized intangible values in the surroundings of one's home and places of recreation.

There was little if any common ground, and what concessions were made by the old to the new were made grudgingly as a result of political constraints from Congress and the courts. Change did not come internally through modified attitudes and values in line with those of the wider public.[22]

This, then, is one context in which to examine the larger role of environmental administration. A second consists of those agencies that accepted environmental values more readily as part of their agency mission. Several of these had been established in the past but received new impetus in the environmental era: the National Park Service, formed in 1916 both to protect scenic resources and to encourage visits to them,[23] and the U.S. Fish and Wildlife Service, which first took shape in 1936. Others came later in the 1960s and 1970s. There was the Bureau of Outdoor Recreation, established in 1964 to promote outdoor recreational activities, but especially important in supervising the distribution of federal moneys from the Land and Water Conservation Fund and in planning a system of national hiking trails and wild and scenic rivers. These agencies served as spearheads of newer environmental values, often clashed with commodity agencies, and became involved in a series of controversies among the administrative bodies of each presidency. While they tended to advance environmental objectives in their own missions, to the commodity agencies they also tended to constitute a subversive influence.

The environmental era also spawned a number of new agencies with environmental missions, reflecting especially the new concern for pollution from chemical residuals of industrial and agricultural production. These included air and water pollution agencies that were established in the Department of Health, Education, and Welfare and via different routes ended up with the Environmental Protection Agency when it came into being in 1970.[24] Among them also were the two bodies responsible for industrial health, closely related to community air problems—the National Institute for Occupational Safety and Health, which made scientific assessments and was located in HEW, and the Occupational Safety and Health Administration, which set standards and carried out enforcement in the Department of Labor.[25] Finally, they included the Consumer Product Safety Commission, which had its own legislative mandate to protect consumers from dangers from manufactured products. All these shared a common perspective, the use of scientific and technical assessments to gauge the adverse effect of products and residuals on human health and biological life and then to set standards of acceptable exposure and effects and enforce them. Hence they had a common set of relationships with varied clientele groups, producers of harm on the one hand and victims on the other, which generated a pattern of political interplay somewhat different from that of those who managed land and water resources. There arose the distinction between "resource management" and "environmental protection" as the two arms of environmental administration.

Two specialized problems of land use gave rise to two new laws and hence two new federal agencies. One concerned the coastal zone. After a seven-year debate, in 1972 Congress adopted a Coastal Zone Management Act to try to iron out competing uses. These involved a range of conflicts between development on the one hand, such as energy facility siting, and environmental uses on the other, such as aesthetic and amenity use and ecological protection. The Office of Coastal Zone Management, established to administer the act, began with a brave mission to enhance environmental values, but save for a few states it soon became heavily burdened by the political weight of developmental concerns.[26]

Even less successful in establishing an environmental mission was the Office of Surface Mining, growing out of the Surface Mining Act of 1977. A product of an equally lengthy debate, that act sought to establish firm control of surface mining, to restore the contour of land through reclamation, to reduce water pollution and restore premining levels of water quality, and to prohibit mining in places of particular environmental concern. Passage of the act reflected a persistent and apparently irreconcilable conflict between coal producers and environmentalists. Immediately after passage those opposing forces transferred their battleground to the new agency. Slowly but steadily the environmental objectives that had been crafted into the law lost ground in the process of administration, as the mining industry was able to influence heavily the policies of the new office.[27]

Environmental factors played a significant role in a variety of other agencies. The Department of Energy dealt with alternative energy programs, especially solar energy; this became a special interest of environmentalists.[28] The Department of Agriculture made a few efforts to foster organic farming during the Carter administration under agriculture secretary Robert Berglund.[29] The State Department maintained some activity in international environmental affairs, such as the export of toxic materials,[30] and the Natural Resources Division of the Department of Justice could well play a crucial role in advancing or retarding environmental goals through litigation strategies. Finally, the most explicitly environmental agency of all, the Council on Environmental Quality, identified the advancement of environmental objectives as its major mission. This was reflected most widely in its annual reports on the state of the environment, which became standard reference material.[31]

This brief review of agencies with environmental components underlines the wide range of government administration that arose from the new values and attitudes. They represent the remarkable pervasiveness of those changes. One can often trace the nation's preoccupations through the evolution of government agencies: the concern in the late eighteenth century with foreign affairs as reflected in the Departments of War, Navy, State, and Treasury; to concerns with internal economic development in the nineteenth and early twentieth centuries with Interior, Agriculture, Commerce, and Labor; to the post–World War II years in which the Departments of Health, Education, and Welfare, Transportation, and Housing and Urban Development stressed national problems that had first emerged in the 1930s; and then the new consumer and environmental bodies such as the Environmental Protection Agency and the Council on Environmental Quality, which reflected still newer concerns. Thus, the pervasiveness of the new objectives in many agencies is just as striking as the far more long-standing pervasiveness of producer objectives.

The range and extent of these innovations provide an especially useful opportunity to examine some major features of government administration. I will explore four of these: the relationships between agencies and the public reflecting both environmental and developmental interests; the relationships of agency to agency and, as a whole, to the Congress, the courts, and the Executive Office; the relationships of federal to state and local administration; and running through them all, the new scientific and technical context of public decision making as a whole. Each of these provides an opportunity to observe distinctive features of the role of environmental administration in American society and politics.

Administrative agencies live and work amid constant interest in their affairs by many groups that have a stake in the outcome of decisions.[32] Hence one beginning point of analysis is the relationship of an agency to the active public. When bureaucracies become controversial this often stems from the dissatisfaction of someone with the impact of action upon them. If we are to understand what that is all about we should go far beyond the general notion of a "meddlesome bureaucracy" to this larger setting of the relationship between agency and public.

In the environmental case the initial impact lay in the strategy of environmentalists to establish new federal agencies and shape existing ones to implement their objectives. We have already identified those agencies and the impact of environmental values on them. But several attempts to shape decisions cut across specific agencies and had a more general import. There was, for example, the environmental impact statement, which sought to bring environmental objectives more fully into decision making by requiring agencies to identify them and to assess effects upon them.[33] There were the new approaches to planning that it was hoped would bring environmental values into agency actions as objectives on a par with developmental goals.[34] There were changes in administrative procedures that required agency decisions to be open and on the record so that they would be subject to greater influence by those with environmental purposes.[35] There was the Freedom of Information Act, which enabled environmentalists, among others, to obtain information to press their cause when otherwise it would not be available.[36] And there were the courts, which permitted environmentalists to mount legal challenges to administrative decisions.[37]

All of these provided agencies with a new and continuous environmental presence that established limits to their actions if they had a developmental mission and facilitated those actions if their missions were environmental. Environmental political action became transformed from a sporadic social movement into a persistent and permanent political force that the agencies continually had to take into account. Environmentalists transformed their political strength from "after the fact" actions external to the agency to "before the fact" anticipations to which the agency constantly had to be attuned. In shaping this influence environmentalists were developing the same kind of anticipatory power that producer groups had long been able to forge. When agencies made choices they now had to take into account the possible consequences from the side of environmentalists as well as developmentalists. They no longer were confronted by claims from producer groups alone but now found that almost all those groups were being challenged by a new environmental consumer force.

The developmental agencies were none too happy with this state of affairs and resisted it mightily. They objected to the environmental impact statement, adopted it slowly, and continually sought to restrict its role. Over the years they succeeded in transforming the EIS to their advantage, both by using it to focus on economic as well as environmental impact and emphasizing trade-offs between them and by making it a political radar device that helped identify opposition to their proposals.[38] They sought, but with less success, to modify the Freedom of Information provisions by limiting the information that could be obtained; perhaps their failure to get far on this score stemmed from the fact that FOI was as useful to the business community in securing information about competitors as it was to environmental and consumer groups. And for much the same reason, administrators were not able to modify demands placed upon them by the courts for open procedures on the record; to the business community that was as vital for exercising their influence as it was to environmentalists.[39]

For environmental agencies the response was more mixed. On the one hand they welcomed public support that environmentalists gave to their missions and hence reached out with public awareness or citizen participation strategies.[40] These ranged from the more traditional public relations ventures to those that gave environmentalists opportunities to influence decisions. They made documents far more readily available to citizens than had been the case in the past.[41] Yet they found that public involvement could work both ways; it could raise up constraints on agency policy as well as provide support. Hence even agencies such as the Environmental Protection Agency did not take the initiative to advance such procedures but instead worked to keep them—for example, citizen suits—under control.[42] A significant bit of nomenclature indicated, however, that they differed from development agencies in their relationship to the environmental public. Whereas they described environmentalists as "citizen groups," the developmental agencies described them as "special interests."

The political history of these varied forms of administration seemed to follow a common pattern. Each one was established by legislation that private developers had opposed. They had been able to neutralize some laws in the process of passage, but with others they had been less successful. Hence they faced new agencies and new branches of old ones that displayed missions they objected to. In the face of clean air and clean water legislation, private industry responded with disbelief that it had come onto the statute books. Environmental impact statements and citizen suits seemed to give all the edge to the opposition. And they were shocked at the environmentally oriented appointments that came with the Carter administration and the choices of technical advisers who gave the benefit of the doubt to victims instead of to sources of pollution.[43]

Yet the regulated industries regrouped rather quickly and fought back through new strategies. They sought especially to control the procedures by which administrative choices were made. In earlier years their main device for doing this was the Administrative Procedures Act of 1946, which enabled them to avoid surprise in regulatory action and to check decisions early in the process by injecting their own expertise into the action. But these "fair" administrative procedures, supervised by the courts, had come to be used also by consumers and environmentalists. Hence they were far less useful to the regulated industries than they had been earlier. A new strategy developed. The court-mandated requirement that regulations had to be based on the written record could be avoided by shifting action to the Executive Office of the President and especially the Office of Management and Budget. Here presidential authority instead of agency authority gave scope to communication and influence that were personal rather than "on the record." The industries perfected this strategy during the Carter years, and by the time of the Reagan administration it was firmly in place.[44]

Other strategies came into being as devices to bring the environmental agencies more toward the developmental side. One was to restrict the range of scientific and technical expertise the agency relied on to those more friendly to a high level of direct evidence as a standard of proof in making judgments.[45] Another was to demand that the agency make increasingly elaborate cost-benefit analyses; this became as important an instrument for slowing up environmental action as environmental impact statements were for slowing up developmental action.[46] Another strategy was to restrict steps to identify positive environmental objectives such as high-quality land and water[47] or health objectives beyond death and irreversible disease so as to weaken the positive benchmarks for environmental action.[48] Still another technique was to restrict the environmental information base by limiting research and monitoring so that the absence of information would open more options for leaving environmental problems relatively unattended.[49] Finally, a significant strategy was to transfer general standards of environmental objectives into specific application so detailed as to render agency action burdensome.[50] One variant of this was the pervasive issue of "burden of proof." Would it fall on the regulating agency or the regulated? When in the pesticide program EPA succeeded in shifting the burden of proof to the chemical companies, they responded by submitting such masses of evidence that the regulatory proceedings almost came to a standstill.[51]

By the mid-1970s, therefore, environmental agencies faced both environmental mandates and an increasingly capable set of political groups that sought to implement them, and also developmental groups that had long since learned to use new procedural devices in their own behalf. Environmental agencies found themselves checked and double checked. Their momentum on behalf of environmental goals slowed down. They began to accept demands from industry to be "neutral" rather than to serve as "advocates."[52] Hence agencies that were mandated by legislation to carry out one set of objectives were mesmerized into temporizing and inaction. Many now could not act at all, even within the requirements of legislation, without clear and recurring political crises that might again highlight the urgency of an environmental problem.[53]

Often it was argued that federal environmental agencies exceeded their authority as defined by statute; they took unwarranted initiative beyond the meaning of the law. I am far more impressed by the opposite—by administrative lethargy and inaction, by the degree to which agencies' freedom and will to act on behalf of environmental objectives was limited and restrained. An example might illustrate the point. Under the Clean Air Act of 1967 the National Air Pollution Control Administration was mandated to develop standards for six air pollutants and, in addition, for others for which its investigations might indicate this was desirable. In 1968 the agency announced that standards were in process for some two dozen pollutants beyond the six and that assessments of their harm and guidelines for regulation would appear in the future.[54] But none did appear. The initial assessment of sulfur oxides issued early in 1967 had aroused such intense opposition from the coal industry that the agency became extremely wary of taking on too many political opponents from the industry side.[55] Thereafter only one additional pollutant, lead, came under regulation, and that was a result of continual litigation from citizen environmental groups and a series of court orders—all over strenuous opposition from EPA.[56]

This was a characteristic case. Environmental bureaucracies are cautious and conservative, tend toward inertia, and must continually be prodded into action by external influences. After the lead issue had been resolved, the deputy administrator of EPA made it clear that without the litigation hanging over its head the agency could not have acted.[57] Administrative action generates forces and counterforces galore. The problem is not to keep environmental bureaucracies from excesses but to find some way to enable them to act in behalf of environmental goals.

The new administration of Ronald Reagan in 1981 resolved this deadlock, at least temporarily, by insulating agencies from environmental political influences and thereby enabling administrators to act more forthrightly on behalf of the regulated industries. This was done primarily through the power of appointment, in which environmental agencies were led by new administrators committed to reducing the level of regulation upon industry and giving it a freer hand. They proceeded to shift agency decisions in a marked antienvironmental direction and to reverse environmental policies of two decades, whether of Republican or Democratic vintage. This was facilitated by the administration's conviction that public environmental values were held only lightly—that there was little popular support for organizations active on the political environmental scene and hence that they could be ignored. It took few pains to hide its hostility, even contempt, for the "environmental establishment" creating a climate that closed off communication, let alone influence, from that quarter and left agency leaders free to work out their day-to-day decisions directly with those on the developmental and regulated side of environmental affairs.[58]

The resulting political repercussions indicated both the pervasiveness of public sentiment favorable to environmental objectives and the political liabilities the administration's assault entailed. The Reagan challenge strengthened environmental political support, which under the Carter administration had become somewhat lethargic. Membership increased; financial resources grew; technical capabilities advanced; and cooperation among the various groups in the nation's capital strengthened.[59] Moreover, environmental organizations worked closely with Congress to provide a counterweight to industry influence and served, in some cases, to blunt the force of the administration's mission to turn back environmental gains.[60] The entire exercise was a laboratory experiment in the depth and strength of public environmental values. The short-run effect was to produce considerable chaos in some agencies and some severe political liabilities for the Reagan administration.[61] How far it would work, in the long run, to turn an activist antienvironmental administration back to one more on center remained to be seen.[62]

Environmental agencies also lived within the context of a host of government bodies. There were other administrative agencies with which objectives could conflict; there was Congress, which increasingly kept a watch on agency affairs through its appropriations and oversight functions; and there were the courts, which were prone to consider themselves a special watchdog for preventing agencies from taking arbitrary action not authorized by law or not consistent with the courts' view of "fair procedure." On all sides agencies with environmental responsibilities had to cope with either initiatives or resistance from other branches of government.

Conflicts among agencies over environmental matters constituted one of the initial battlegrounds between environmental and developmental objectives. Citizen concerns as expressed in the 1960s over the adverse effects of development often came to be injected into the political arena most forcefully through action by agencies who felt those effects on their own missions. The most notable of these was the Fish and Wildlife Service.[63] Initial objections to projects by the Army Corps of Engineers, the Atomic Energy Commission, the Tennessee Valley Authority, the Federal Power Commission, and the Bureau of Reclamation were expressed most forcefully within the counsels of government by the Service. Such projects, it argued, destroyed fish and wildlife habitat. The agency, of course, had its own environmental constituents; it served as an important instrument of their action because it shared their views.[64]

The federal highway department was building highways through wildlife refuges that had been purchased with federal funds, much of which had been contributed by citizens through the duck hunting stamp.[65] The Atomic Energy Commission was planning multiple-steam-generating plants on Biscayne Bay in Florida that would cause considerable thermal pollution and threaten aquatic life.[66] The Tennessee Valley Authority was planning to build the Tellico Dam on the Little Tennessee River, thereby destroying one of the main cold-water trout streams in eastern Tennessee.[67] The Corps of Engineers was inundating acres of wildlife habitat by building reservoirs. Despite a Fish and Wildlife Coordination Act passed years earlier, the Corps refused to consider, let alone implement, proposals to purchase equivalent lands, called mitigation lands, to replace them. And the Corps was also destroying valuable coastal wetlands in places like Florida by approving dredge-and-fill operations for housing.[68] The Fish and Wildlife Service had many an environmental grievance against other federal agencies.[69]

From this context arose the environmental impact statement.[70] It is often forgotten that the EIS, in its original form, was a device not for citizen review of developmental projects, but for interagency review. It was a procedure for dealing not with citizen objections but with agency objections, meant to facilitate a process by which the Executive Office of the President could resolve differences among its own agencies. When the first EIS documents were in the offing in 1970 officials of the Council on Environmental Quality, which supervised the EIS program, were asked what would be done with them. Would they be shown to the public? The answer was no. They would be circulated within the government and used to assemble the views of other agencies, and only after interagency disputes had been resolved and a decision made would they be released to the public. The device was an instrument to facilitate executive decision making, not to organize public involvement. That came only later.[71]

It is important to identify what the EIS did not do as well as what it did do in interagency relationships. It was confined wholly to agency comment. But some, especially the Fish and Wildlife Service, wanted the procedure also to give its objectives substantive support. An earlier episode had indicated both the possibilities and the pitfalls. In the case of opposition to dredge-and-fill permits issued by the Corps in coastal wetlands, Congressman John Dingell prepared legislation that would have given the Service authority to approve each Corps permit. Perhaps the strategy was only a political weapon to force the Corps to change its policies. At any rate it worked. The Corps agreed to a more effective "consultation" procedure with the Fish and Wildlife Service, and the legislation was withdrawn.[72] In the early days of the EIS the Water Pollution Control Administration, still in the Department of the Interior, tried a similar strategy, this time in the case of thermal pollution from steam generating plants. It asked the Council on Environmental Quality to go beyond supervising the EIS process to the point of throwing its influence behind substantive water quality goals. CEQ declined to become involved in such interagency disputes; it had its hands full merely supervising the new procedure.

Still another way of dealing with interagency conflict was to restructure government. If environmentalists objected to pesticide policy administered by the Department of Agriculture on the grounds that it favored agriculture and the agricultural chemical industry rather than those harmed by pesticides, it could advocate that administration of the law be moved to an agency that had a protective rather than a developmental mission. And so when the Environmental Protection Agency was created in 1970 pesticide regulation was moved to it. The industry complained that the Department of Agriculture had not made sufficient effort to retain jurisdiction.[73] Or if it was argued that the Atomic Energy Commission was not sufficiently concerned about standards of radiation protection, the task of setting them could be transferred to another agency that had those concerns as a primary mission; that too happened when EPA was established. The formation of the EPA itself involved the transfer of air, water, and other environmental protection programs from Health, Education, and Welfare and Interior, to give more primary mission focus to those objectives. Those were not so clearly moves to defuse immediate interagency conflict as they were to provide a more visible presence for new environmental goals. A host of other environmental-developmental controversies remained as such agencies as EPA, the Park Service, and the Fish and Wildlife Service continued to do battle with Agriculture, Energy, Commerce, and a variety of subdepartmental agencies.[74]

Environmental agencies had to cope with Congress as well. This could cut two ways. On the one hand, congressional committees with developmental missions could thwart environmental action; the appropriations subcommittee in charge of the Department of Agriculture budget was a focal point for the defense of pesticides and could threaten the entire EPA budget, over which it had jurisdiction. The actions of Congressman Jamie Whitten of Mississippi were well known in this regard. More friendly subcommittees, on the other hand, could defend agencies against attack, as was the case with the appropriations subcommittee in charge of the Department of the Interior budget when its chair, Congressman Sidney Yates, successfully challenged attempts by the Reagan administration to reduce and even abolish the Land and Water Conservation Fund in 1981 and 1982.

Quite a different kind of congressional limitation came from the way environmentalists sought to use legislative strategy to force reluctant agencies to act. On a number of occasions the agency lethargy described earlier had arisen as a result of developmental opposition that prompted the agency to temporize. While industry argued that agencies exceeded their powers, environmentalists argued that they avoided using authority that Congress had already given them. To counteract agency inaction, environmentalists demanded more prescriptive legislation, making agency responsibility far more precise and far less avoidable. In place of the general requirement that the agency regulate toxic pollutants it found to be harmful, for example, amendments to the Clean Water Act of 1977 set forth specific chemicals and families of chemicals on which it was mandated to act. In other legislation, polychlorinated biphenyls were specifically identified for action, and in debate over revision of the Clean Air Act in the early 1980s environmentalists sought similar specific mandates for toxic air pollutants.[75] It was relatively easy to argue, and many did so, that to be so prescriptive tied the hands of administrators too tightly. But this depended upon one's views about the substantive wisdom of the action.[76]

Industry equally sought such prescriptive amendments on its behalf. Strategy on this score depended primarily on whether the agency was following one's wishes and hence whether one saw the need for external pressure from Congress to force it to act. On the whole, however, since the major administrative political reality was the ability of industry to frighten agencies with environmental missions into inaction, the most significant use of prescriptive legislation was to force administrators to act on behalf of environmental goals.

An equally significant role of Congress in setting limits on administrative discretion was its investigative powers, which were exercised primarily in oversight functions. Congressional subcommittees could well serve as instruments through which information from within the agency could be leaked both to Congress and to the public. Or more formal investigations could bring information and issues into the open. In the 1960s the industrial water pollution control program was frustrated simply because of the inability of the federal government to collect information about the extent of the problem. Industries refused to divulge that information, and for almost a decade they held up a system of voluntary reporting by blocking agreement on the details of a proposed reporting form. They had considerable influence over this as a result of membership on the relevant committee in the Office of Management and Budget that had to approve the form. Congressman Henry Reuss publicized this recalcitrance through the work of a congressional subcommittee he chaired, and some change resulted in the Water Pollution Control Act of 1972.[77] A decade later a congressional oversight committee publicized private meetings between the EPA and the Formaldehyde Institute, an industry trade association, which led to joint agreement that experiments indicating that formaldehyde caused throat cancer in laboratory animals were not sufficient evidence for curtailing the chemical's use.[78] A variety of settings for controversy over that issue within the Reagan administration is now on the record because of congressional oversight inquiries.

Agencies tended to take refuge in Executive Office devices to shield their activities from legislative attack, and environmentalists tended to use Congress as a device to expose limitations in agency action. The general tightening of executive authority and power that came with the Reagan administration, therefore, was a rather consistent extension of tendencies established earlier. Potential conflict between agencies and the Executive Office of the President that earlier had been in the offing now were reduced as the new Reagan appointees and new authority exercised by the Office of Management and Budget, which sought to change substantive policy through the budget process, subordinated the agencies more fully to the White House.[79] This only enhanced the countervailing tendency of environmentalists to work with Congress to expose, to defend, and on a few occasions to take the initiative against a more unified and disciplined executive branch. Environmental concerns had far more support in Congress than in the Reagan administration. In earlier years the relationships between Congress and the environmental agencies had been more complex, involving both friendly and hostile interaction. The Reagan administration simplified these into a sharper set of patterns more akin to persistent confrontation.

The courts, so far as the agencies were concerned, were quite another matter. They were not so reachable; their mandates were less avoidable; access to them by environmentalists was less controllable. The courts were far more willing than were the agencies to view environmental concerns as reflecting permanent changes in American society and hence as a new and continuing "interest" that should be represented before them. Standing before the courts was now often accorded to those who could demonstrate a clear "environmental interest," as fully as was the case for one who had an interest in property or personal health and safety. At the same time the courts held that environmental matters were as legitimate a part of the "public welfare" and hence as subject to the exercise of the state's police powers as was the case with more traditional realms of public policy. In supervising administrative procedure, as in the Administrative Procedures Act or environmental impact statements, the courts made clear that they recognized substantive environmental values as of considerable merit, fully balanceable in competition with other values.

The major effect of court decisions on agencies was to police procedures of decision making. Although that constituted a burden because of the costs, it only occasionally led to serious modifications of agency action.[80] Whether or not substantive environmental goals obtained any further strength in administrative decisions depended entirely upon the degree to which environmentalists could organize their demands in competition with their opponents. The courts, then, opened the door wider to environmentalists but in no sense guaranteed their influence. Once again such leverage as environmentalists could exercise in this way came more through "anticipatory power," the fear potential litigation might strike in the hearts of administrators, and their need to formulate actions in a way that would make them acceptable to the courts. Agencies were eager to avoid litigation because of the burden of time and cost; and preemptive action was more economical than legal action after the fact. The courts, then, under the influence of new environmental concerns, set limits on agencies' actions and left them to their own devices to find ways and means of protecting themselves against even greater limits.

It should not be thought that environmentalists were the only or even the main users of the courts.[81] A great number of environmental lawsuits were filed by industry. One study found that even those filed under citizen suit provisions, let alone general equity actions, were often instigated by sources other than environmentalists, such as industry and state and local governments.[82] At the same time, it should not be thought that environmental litigation was extensive; on the contrary, it was minimal, a very small fraction of lawsuits, and miniscule compared with the large amount of private contract litigation.[83] Ideological debate and media strategies on the part of antienvironmentalists made the role of litigation appear far larger than it actually was and obscured the degree to which agency action was frustrated by industry as much as by environmentalist litigation.[84] Court decisions were important in some crucial cases and hence did constitute a limitation to action on one side of the agency, as did Congress on the other. In both types of cases, moreover, one must emphasize that the center of day-to-day decisions of consequence was the administrative agency. Despite limitations by Congress and courts, administration played the central role in government decisions; to the actors, influence over those decisions became a crucial element of strategy.[85]

Two conclusions emerge from this examination of the relationships between agencies and the other two branches of the federal government. The first is that the old-fashioned notion that these branches differ according to function—making, executing, and interpreting laws—is more than inadequate in describing their varied roles. Each is a focus of political controversy and hence of political choice. Political initiatives and interests gather around each, and often the political battles are simply transferred from one to the other. When legislation is passed the contestants shift to the administrative agency, and when that goes the wrong way then to the courts. And then back to the agency or Congress. We thus must understand administration as one variant of three sets of political processes in each of the three branches of government. We can distinguish them by their procedures and rules of the game rather than by their contending participants. Administration is the persistent focus of political struggle, and Congress and the courts are more peripheral, entering and leaving the drama at various times and only setting some limits to administrative choice.

Workable public choices, moreover, require that a dispute wend its way through all three sets of institutions and that some degree of compatibility be fashioned in the way each disposes of it. For Congress to approve legislation does not end the matter. Each party to the dispute assumes that the entire issue can be reopened in the process of administration. Hence the history of environmental administration is a case of developmentalists exercising considerable influence in implementing laws that environmentalists have persuaded Congress to enact. Amid all this the administrative process is the ultimate denominator in disputes. If agreement can be fashioned there in the day-to-day relationships among contending parties, it will be far more lasting than with either Congress or the courts. For it means it is an agreement that objectors have accepted or have become resigned to or believe they cannot change. In environmental affairs innovative impulses have come through Congress and the courts. Reaction to these innovations by developmentalists has come largely through administration. Hence administration plays the role of slowing down initiatives from other segments of government and sets the minimal basis for longer-run workable agreements among the contending parties.

I have examined environmental administration in relation to political groups in the wider society and to other branches of government. One should focus also on the hierarchy of government institutions. Traditionally this is thought of as "federalism," with stress on the relative powers of federal and state governments. But there are also important relationships between local governments and the states. With respect to environmental affairs, two sets of controversies arise. There are clashes between federal and state authority in issues of preemption. Shall federal authority be allowed to preempt that of the state? But the same kinds of issues arise as between states and their subdivisions, often described as a problem of "override." Can states "override" decisions of local governments and prevent them from taking action? Preemption is the better-known case; state override is far more obscure but in environmental affairs often more pervasive.

Behind these "constitutional" issues are several substantive realities. One is the politically decentralizing tendency that is inherent in much environmental action. Environmental objectives have a strong grass-roots character. People seek to defend their homes and their places of recreation and leisure from intrusion and degradation. Hence they use local government to avert environmental threats. A typical case might involve a proposal to construct a large-scale facility such as an electric power plant, a synthetic oil plant, an oil tanker terminal, or a chemical plant in the vicinity of one's home. These initiatives seem to come from "out there." Can the local government take action to deflect them? Strategies involve zoning against undesired land use, local referenda to express opposition, or local ordinances that establish higher environmental standards than those provided by state and federal governments.[86]

In response, developers seek action at the state level to override decisions by local government. In some states local air pollution control authorities are prohibited from establishing air quality standards more stringent than those of the state.[87] Most state strip-mining reclamation laws prohibit local municipalities from adopting standards of either land reclamation or water quality that go beyond those of the state.[88] Many a state has enacted laws on hazardous waste facility siting that provide for eventual state action even against the objections of communities.[89] In Wisconsin, state wetland regulations prohibit counties from establishing standards stricter than those of the state.[90] The history of air pollution control in the 1960s is instructive. Many cities and urban counties enacted ordinances to restrict emissions. Objecting industries, in turn, sought to establish state air pollution control commissions that would shift authority from the locality to the state and, they hoped, provide for greater industry influence.[91] For a few years they had considerable success.

This kind of state override did not always work. As environmental interest increased, the accumulation of many local grievances led to a sufficiently large political force that state governments began to take up environmental concerns in ways industry disapproved; in response those industries sought federal laws to override action by the states. An instructive case came in the debate over the 1970 Clean Air Act. Under the previous 1967 law each state had been instructed to adopt air pollution standards, and many had done so. But public enthusiasm, so far as industry was concerned, went much too far; standards were too stringent.[92] In Pennsylvania, for example, the state Air Pollution Control Commission, whose chair was an official of Bethlehem Steel Corporation, recommended a state sulfur dioxide standard of 100 µg/m³. Well-attended citizen meetings in Pittsburgh and Philadelphia, however, indicated public support for a much stricter standard. The United Steelworkers of America and the congressman from the Pittsburgh steel area, Joseph Gaydos, took the same view and persuaded the governor to join them. The standard was lowered to 60 µg/m³.[93] Faced with similar action in a number of states, the steel industry testified in Congress that it would not be averse to federal air standards that would keep the states in check.[94]

As the 1970s wore on a host of environmental issues involved industry attempts to use federal authority to preempt state environmental action. One of the sharpest had to do with the Coastal Zone Management Act of 1972, in which a "consistency clause" applied.[95] Federal actions such as permits to construct, the statute read, must be "consistent" with coastal zone management plans drawn up by the states. But who should determine whether such actions were "consistent"—the federal agencies alone, who might interpret in favor of development, or a cooperative state-federal action, which would give the states more power to object? Regulatory action during the Carter administration had gone in favor of the states. The oil companies had taken up legal proceedings in the federal courts and in two cases had lost.[96] After the 1980 election they urged the new administration to change the regulations in their favor and provide for a federal preemption. It began to do so. But opposition in Congress made it clear that the contemplated change would meet with congressional disapproval, and the action was dropped.[97]

Actions by the Reagan administration are especially instructive on this score. That administration's ideology was one of transferring power from the federal level to the state; yet it was aligned with corporate business groups who sought to use federal power to override state action.[98] In some cases the administration responded as the business community wished. There was, for example, the case of action by a number of cities to prohibit transport of radioactive materials through their jurisdictions, proposals that prompted the atomic energy industry to push for federal regulations to override such actions. They succeeded during the Carter administration. Final rules were promulgated in the late hours of its tenure, and this was one of the few Carter "midnight regulations" that the Reaganites did not hold up for review.[99] Or there was the case of federal noise regulations that Reagan administrators, on ideological grounds, thought could readily be abolished. Little did they know that those federal standards were in place so that railroads, trucks, and airplanes could use federal authority to override persistent efforts by local governments to establish noise control regulations to which they objected. Soon educated about the issue, the administration reversed field.[100]

On several such proposals the Reagan administration declined to act. One concerned the long-standing desire of the agricultural chemical industry to require that states not issue pesticide regulations more stringent than the federal ones.[101] The immediate issue concerned the insistence of the California government that it have the right to require more technical information about proposed pesticides than was required by the federal government. During debate on the federal act in 1982 the administration declined to back the industry's demand to include a federal preemption provision because it feared compromising its states' rights ideology on an issue on which federal action would be difficult to conceal. In subsequent action on the matter, however, the administration shifted ground.[102]

These relationships between political forces and the levels of government at which action takes place do not follow a neat pattern. One overriding factor is federal ownership of public lands, which leads to federal political action and well-mobilized environmental interest in the four national land systems. Federal agencies are often more responsive to environmental objectives, and developmental interests are allied with local and state governments. Over the years, old-style conservationists and new-style environmentalists fought efforts to transfer federal lands to the states.[103] But in recent years a subtle change has been taking place. As the West has become more densely populated, a considerable number of urban people there have taken up environmental values in public land management. This in turn has led to support within the West for an effective federal presence. Natural environment values are strong in the Rocky Mountain West, often stronger than in most other sections of the nation.[104] This became sharply etched during the first two years of the Reagan administration in controversies over mining and oil drilling in western wilderness areas. It was the West itself that protested these developmental proposals by the Reagan administration and prompted both the president and Secretary James Watt to change political direction.[105]

Another episode, the Sagebrush Rebellion, is equally instructive. This movement, from the West, sought to raise support for transfer of federal lands to the states. But once the western public understood the options, the drive collapsed. The eleven western states manage 35 million acres of state lands, almost all for income-producing purposes in which hunting and fishing and environmental land uses are greatly restricted, often prohibited. Once Rocky Mountain citizens interested in those uses realized that the same restrictive policies would hold for lands acquired from the federal government, they exercised considerable opposition to the proposal.[106] The Sagebrush Rebellion arose out of conflicts within the Rocky Mountain region, in which developmentalists sought to restrain a rising indigenous environmental sentiment by defining the region as developmental, constrained in its ambitions by the environmental East. The effort failed primarily because those with environmental objectives within the West itself were fashioning their own political clout in regional politics.[107]

Environmental air and water quality standards involve a more complex set of circumstances. In the late 1960s and early 1970s environmentalists were convinced that local and state governments were unreliable on that score. Hence they chose to use the federal government for leverage against the states. They worked on behalf of federal standard setting and viewed their actions as devices to force recalcitrant states to act.[108] Industry, on the other hand, sought to shift standard setting to the states, or maintain it there, for precisely the same reason—their belief that now, after federal standards were in place, the states might be more lenient. In some cases federal standards ran headlong into opposition from the general public and state governments on such issues as mandatory inspection and maintenance of motorized vehicles, transport controls, and controls over indirect sources such as shopping centers. All of these backfired on the EPA owing to the protests of automobile owners and organized automobile associations.[109]

In the protection of the highest quality air and water through what were known as the "prevention of significant deterioration" and "antidegradation" programs, environmentalists also sought a federal lead.[110] In both cases the objective was not to clean up dirty areas but to prevent cleaner ones from becoming degraded. Most state governments were reluctant to take up such initiatives because of their implications for land use. But citizen support emerged in some quarters such as Wyoming, where the state took action under the air quality provisions, and Pennsylvania, where the protection of high-quality waters was upgraded because of federal and citizen prodding. Grass-roots support for federal air quality programs seemed to increase steadily in the 1970s and often took on an aura of local protection against larger private and public institutions similar to the case of hazardous wastes. But these were only glimmers of change rather than clearly identifiable trends.

Environmentalists especially sought an increasing level of federal action in the scientific and technical aspects of environmental affairs. Few states, aside from the financially stronger ones such as California and New York, could provide the resources necessary to undergird environmental action with scientific and technical data. Research into the health effects of pollutants, alternative energy conversion, or the environmental effects of development all required massive funding, which only the federal government seemed to be able to provide. Program implementation required technical skills (for example in air quality management at state and local levels) and equipment (for example, for monitoring) that most states found they could not afford save at relatively limited levels. Federal agencies alone seemed to be capable of financing the needed science and technology.[111]

Developmentalists, in contrast, sought to reduce such expenditures for the opposite reason, to limit the capabilities of management agencies to act and hence to limit the level of environmental protection. Often it was a contest between research financed by industry to argue against action and research financed by government to bolster it.[112] Industry well understood the political leverage of its own technical capabilities and knew that controversies often turned on the relative ability of the contending parties to apply scientific and technical data to the issue.[113] Hence it sought to scale down federal activities on behalf of environmental aims, such as research concerning indoor air pollution or the monitoring of radiation releases from atomic power plants.

An episode early in the air quality program illustrated the problem. In the early 1960s many communities had sought to restrict pollution emissions and passed ordinances to that effect. When industries challenged them in court on the grounds that existing pollution levels were not harmful, local governments had few if any resources to counter those claims. In contrast to industry's ability to present its case about health effects, the municipalities were woefully weak. Hence in the 1963 Clean Air Act they successfully established a program whereby the U.S. Public Health Service would expand its technical air quality capabilities and use that expertise to assist local government. As this aid developed and was so used, industry objected that this was unwarranted interference by the Public Health Service in local air quality matters. The implications of this episode continued to structure environmental politics. Those who sought environmental protection reached out for technical assistance from many quarters. But on the whole the resources of municipal and state governments were extremely limited and only those of federal agencies seemed equal to the task. Environmentalists sought to advance these technical capabilities, and that drive continued with some success until it was severely blunted by the Reagan administration.[114]

Administrative environmental decision making was heavily influenced by technical considerations. Hardly an environmental question failed to require ever-increasing amounts of empirical data and analysis. This was the case with the full range of environmental effects issues, problems of the balance between natural and developed resources, and larger questions of the balance between population and resources. Cutting across all such issues were questions of economic analysis and planning that seemed to involve the application of empirical detail in ever greater quantity and refinement. Environmental administration became heavily infused with technical experts—scientists and engineers, economists and planners.

Most of these technical activities conveyed the aura of being value free, of constituting what were called rational processes, of seeking "objective" solutions to contentious political disputes. None, so the self-perceptions went, were steered by personal value judgment; instead all constituted modes of action that submerged such values in the face of facts and analyses derived from more objective circumstances. And so it was that as administration brought together these technical disciplines to apply knowledge in the service of public policy, it too thought of itself and described itself to others as being above day-to-day political battles. The U.S. Forest Service argued that its decisions carried out an impartial spirit of "wise use," while the U.S. Army Corps of Engineers maintained that it simply carried out the law rather than expressed its own preferences. All sought to give their actions validity at the highest level of discourse by identifying their objectives with the "national interest."

But the details of controversy often revealed that even objective technical questions involved personal judgments and provided an opportunity for particular rather than universal values to prevail. Arguments over the meaning of scientific and technical experiments on the effects of lead on human health turned not so much on the "facts" per se as on the way they were assessed. The patterns of debate over two decades reflected consistently held opinions on the part of individual scientists and individual institutions depending on personal values and agency missions. Scientists in industries that sought to continue the use of lead in gasoline persistently found that lead was not harmful at low levels of exposure, while those who sought to protect the health of children came to the opposite conclusion. Those competing viewpoints continued even though over the same span of years the exposure levels around which the argument raged declined from 10 to 5 and then to 1.5 μg/m³ of ambient air and from 80 to 60 to 25 μg/dl of blood. Something more than the facts alone shaped the persistent disagreement.[115]

One could make the same observation about economic analysis. The effects of this or that regulation on the "economy" fueled debate from the earliest days of environmental regulation, and in each case exponents of diverse views could develop diversely favorable analyses.[116] Much depended on one's ability to command the computer resources that provided a more "sophisticated" model—that is, with more variables accounted for—than one's opponent's.[117] Often the legislative as well as the administrative debate took the form of last minute injections into the argument of the "latest" study, which demonstrated conclusively the wisdom of one's previously declared position. Given time the opposition could usually marshal contrary evidence or interpretation, but it was especially convenient, once the hearing record with the agency had closed, to persuade the Executive Office that one's latest economic impact analysis rendered the regulatory effort indefensible.

All this is merely to underline the extensive scientific and technical context of decisions and to serve as the starting point for investigating the "politics of science," "the politics of economic analysis," the "politics of planning," and, running through all of them, the "politics of information," which lay at the root of many a political choice in environmental affairs. The parties to disputes recognized that the new scientific and technical context of administrative choice was all pervasive, that the most fundamental of all political stakes lay in the ability to shape the information on which decisions were based. This rarely involved overt strategies of control; rather, more subtle ones were used—seeking to discredit the validity of an opponent's information, to protect information as privileged and hence not subject to disclosure, and to overload the decision process with quantities of information that would bog it down or increase its cost. It also involved the political legitimacy of experts, since part of the political game lay in attempts to raise or lower the credibility of individual scientists or economists.[118]

From the developmental side a variety of strategies emerged. One involved devices to prevent information from entering arenas where it could be used by the public. Many a regulatory program was stymied by the argument that such and such information was a "trade secret" and could not be divulged. That claim was made by the chemical companies from the first moves to regulate pesticides; it reached its highest use when the EPA attempted to implement the Toxic Substances Control Act of 1976 and found that companies applying to register chemicals demanded that information about their names, the names of the chemicals in question, and the quantities produced not be released. Environmentalists complained that this made it impossible for them to make their own evaluations of chemical safety.[119]

A variant on this issue was the "right to know," the argument by workers that they should be allowed to know what chemicals they were exposed to. They wanted this for their own purposes, either in order to press claims for liability in the future or to enable their own industrial health scientists to investigate the effects of exposure to chemicals. As the movement for public disclosure grew in the early 1980s, supported by municipal fire departments, which found that lack of knowledge often led to critical dangers for their personnel in chemical fires, several cities and states passed "right to know" ordinances. The companies struck back with a proposal that they would provide for some disclosure, limit it at their own discretion, and so reduce the usefulness of the information to those exposed.[120]

A somewhat different strategy of information control lay in efforts to command the technical resources that generated information. In some cases this involved computerized data. The "allowable cut" in public forest management, for example, that is, the amount of wood that could be cut each year, depended on complex calculations based on annual growth rates over the life of a forest and even over several generations. It also hinged upon the results of "inputs," such as herbicides, fertilizers, or improved seed, that might increase yield in any one generation.[121] All the relevant information was fed into the computer to determine the appropriate level of cut. But if one wished to question such decisions one had to be able to question the assumptions involved in either the data input or the analytical bases of computer programs. Environmentalists who might be critical of Forest Service choices had little opportunity to develop competing computer analyses and hence little basis for challenging Forest Service allowable cut policies.[122]

Still a third focus for the politics of information lay in controversies over the methods to be used in analyzing the effects of pollutants. Was information from experiments on laboratory animals sufficient proof of potential harm to humans to warrant regulation? Was epidemiological evidence essential before regulation could be adopted? And if epidemiological evidence was required, was it sufficient to compare a study group with a norm, or would a matched case control method be mandatory? In the earlier years of environmental protection controversy probable anticipated harm was an acceptable standard of proof, and for this reasoning from animal data, for example, seemed to be widely accepted. But the political stakes involved in the issues led to persistent demands from the regulated industries for higher levels of proof: more direct evidence on human effects, more specific case control methods, and far more extensive procedures for ruling out "confounding variables." Their demands had considerable impact on scientists, who in turn insisted on higher levels of proof and more direct evidence before conclusions were drawn.[123] One can debate the issue as to whether or not changes in scientific approach came through the internal evolution of science alone or as a result of constant exposure to the demands from industry, which in turn gradually sharpened latent tendencies within science. The two seemed to work in tandem. Whatever the cause, it provided a constantly changing context for administrative action; industry and scientists demanding ever higher levels of proof sought to shape the strategies of decision makers concerning the choice of scientist and scientific assessments on which action or inaction concerning environmental harm would be based.[124]

For environmentalists this mobilization of resources to shape and control information constituted one of their most difficult political problems. Their own technical resources were limited. Hence they had to be far more selective in their approach, emphasizing not massive mobilization of expertise, but more critical points of action and analysis. Litigation seemed to be adapted to their limited resources, for in this arena it was not massive overkill that carried the day but crucial and telling argument. Several well-constructed pieces of scientific investigation that were to the point might well outweigh a hundred pieces of technical data that were not directly relevant. Hence environmental strategies lay more in the search, through literature reviews and discussion with scientists, for critical research.[125] Litigation organizations such as the Environmental Defense Fund and the Natural Resources Defense Council brought onto their staffs technical experts who were sufficiently knowledgeable to be able to keep abreast of ongoing work.[126] Most important, they brought frontier as well as more conventional studies into decision making.[127] Hence they played a vital role in science and technology transfer from the world of research to the world of administrative action.

Environmentalists also found that the media were of considerable help. Many a controversial issue, ranging from radiation to lead to pesticides to asbestos, involved a series of controversies in which industry and the agencies carried out a parallel effort to control the flow of technical information to the public and to disparage the significance of information about adverse effects. A sequence of issues generated a pattern in the public mind and the media: information was subject to persistent "management" by private and public authorities so as to minimize public concern. This only led the media to believe there was more to environmental effects than met the eye and to engage in vigorous detective work to get at the bottom of affairs. Often potential victims of pollution, such as toxic waste dumps, found that the media were valuable allies to force action when government agencies held back.[128] The ensuing struggle over publicity about environmental harm came to be one of the major battlegrounds in the politics of information.[129]

In this struggle to control information administrative agencies seemed to be increasingly skeptical about the public's ability to understand or accept the scientific facts and to be convinced that the media greatly exaggerated harm in order to arouse public concern. Hence they sought to establish their own ability as far greater than that of the media or the public to determine the extent of potential harm. Scientific and technical determinations were best made by the "experts." Out of these circumstances grew much mutual distrust. The public readily believed that the agencies were deliberately underestimating harm and were willing to subject the public to higher levels of risk, while the technical experts of the agencies believed that the public was simply misinformed and a victim of manipulation. Agencies spoke of "perceived harm" with the clear meaning that beliefs about harm were not justified, and when they took action to restrict harm they increasingly did so on the grounds that their purpose was to restore "public confidence" rather than solve a "real" problem.

During the Reagan administration the public came to believe that technical decisions were being made behind closed doors and to its detriment. In the 1960s pollution control agencies had often established "liaison committees" between government and industry to take up relevant scientific and technical questions. These inevitably involved the assessment of harm and hence the degree of pollution abatement desired. Early in the 1970s, however, the proceedings of such committees came to be more open and subject to public scrutiny. Hence industry found them to be no longer useful, and often the ventures came to an end. But the assessment of harm as reflected in the criteria documents continued, and over the years the EPA developed a strategy for a rather extensive and far more open process for coming to conclusions about the meaning of the evidence. Under these arrangements industry chafed considerably. At the advent of the Reagan administration it was able to persuade administrators to make such decisions in more "closed door" sessions much akin to the practices of over a decade before. This only encouraged Congress and the media to undertake campaigns to "expose" undue industry influence and served as the major twist in Reagan administration policy to undermine confidence in the EPA and bring about a change in agency leadership.[130]

To the relatively disinterested observer it as tempting to dismiss such disputes as matters of mere "politics," to argue that scientific and technical questions should be above such maneuvering. Such issues were a matter of what was accurate and what was not, of "good" and "bad" science, of facts about a world "out there" that could be discovered and applied by impartial experts. If one's own conception of expertise was heavily laden with self-images of "rationality," it was relatively easy to project that view onto the larger scene of public affairs and imagine that "politics" was the culprit that restricted one's freedom to act. But the details of such disputes make it clear that considerations of personal values, professional commitment, and institutional interest had the capacity to manufacture disagreement out of many an accumulation of objective facts.[131] In the world of technical politics those who had superior resources sought to obscure value choices with a burden of technical overlay, and those who had fewer equally sought to ferret out and expose the value choices as best they could. The problem in political analysis was to identify the value choices embedded in the technical detail. At the least this could provide an understanding of many important issues in environmental administration. At the most it identified variations in the ability to control information as one of the most significant elements of modern political inequality.

We might, at the end of this analysis, focus especially on several general conclusions. First of all, people want government. They want environmental programs and environmental administration because they produce desired benefits. California voters approved Proposition 13, but in the same election they approved a statewide bond issue for water quality programs and a local bond issue in San Diego for purchase of open-spaced land. A recent Harris poll indicates that people want less regulation in general but more regulation on behalf of consumers. There are always mixed reactions to government action, for what benefits one can easily work hardship on another. And this gives rise to hostility to government. But we must not lose sight of the institutional changes beneath the overlay of ideology. The mixture adds up to the fact that government environmental programs rest heavily on the public's desire for them.

There are also implications for the ties between the wider society and government. Usually, it is argued, all this involves a "welfare state" that benefits the lowest third of the socioeconomic order. But social service policies provide more benefits to the middle class and serve to attach that broad stratum of society to government. Since the New Deal, government social programs have created strong bonds between the middle layers of society and an activist federal government. Social security and the financial underpinning of private housing constituted such beginnings in the 1930s. Health and education services added to that. And the more recent social service programs involving consumers, women, environmentalists, and the arts only cemented further the attachment of the middle class to the state.

Environmental administration also involves a major element of equity. Benefits are provided for the middle class that formerly were available only to the very top levels of society, such as enjoyment of wildland natural environments. The starting point for equity in this case was the public lands, where outdoor recreation was available at a low cost. In Europe, where much outdoor recreation could be enjoyed only on suffrance from the landed aristocracy, equity in the form of "access" was and still is a constant political battle.[132] Cleaning up pollution where masses of people lived made available to them what others had earlier enjoyed by being able to travel to cleaner environments or by purchasing urban housing upwind from pollution sources.[133] With limited resources, as was the case with high-quality land, air, and water, the private market of increasing demand amid fixed supply tended toward inequalities of benefits;[134] the public environmental economy provided equalizing influences.

Finally, while the public is positive about government benefits, it often becomes hostile when administrators compromise environmental objectives in the face of opposition. It is not government per se that generates cynicism, but the processes by which public objectives realized through legislation become markedly changed through administration. The environmental movement has sought to expand greatly the use of science and technology for environmental benefits. But the public readily becomes cynical when the development, assessment, and use of information are controlled by antienvironmentalists. According to a recent survey of attitudes toward chemical risk, the public believes that knowledge of effects should be widely disseminated and that the public, not the experts or administrators, should decide the use to which it should be put.[135]

The realm of environmental affairs, and especially environmental administration, can serve as a useful device through which to examine many aspects of the new consumer-information society. It gives special focus to the personal, family, and community context within which values are generated. It also highlights the technical and managerial processes by which resources are organized through private and government administrative systems. Even more, it emphasizes the modes of interaction between these two large sets of social processes. By and large Americans have accepted large-scale organization in the delivery of goods and services, including large corporations and big government, if the resulting benefits respond to their changing values, needs, and wants. In neither realm have they rejected bigness, but they have insisted that delivery systems of all kinds, both private and public, continually justify themselves by performance. Acceptable environmental administration rests upon the realization of environmental benefits as part of Americans' continuing desire for a higher standard of living. These are the grounds on which Americans test the environmental sector of the social service state.

NOTES

Foreword

1. Michael H. Ebner, Stuart M. Blumin, Lynn Hollen Lees, Bruce M. Stave, Samuel P. Hays, "Samuel P. Hays and the Social Analysis of the City," *Journal of Urban History* 19 (Aug. 1993): 86.

2. Samuel P. Hays in collaboration with Barbara D. Hays, *Beauty, Health, and Permanence: Environmental Politics in the United States. 1955–1985* (New York: Cambridge University Press, 1987).

3. In 1975, in an interview for the *Journal of Urban History,* Hays noted that his experience with the Oregon and California Revested Lands Administration was critical: "All these things connected with forestry. That was really where I got my first interest in conservation." See Bruce M. Stave, "A Conversation with Samuel P. Hays," *Journal of Urban History* 2 (Nov. 1975): 91. Stave had written his Ph.D. dissertation under Hays's direction.

4. Samuel P. Hays, *Conservation and the Gospel of Efficiency: The Progressive Conservation Movement, 1890–1920* (Cambridge, Mass.: Harvard University Press, 1959; 2nd ed., 1968).

5. Stave, "A Conversation with Samuel P. Hays," 98; Samuel P. Hays, *American Political History as Social Analysis: Essays by Samuel P. Hays* (Knoxville: University of Tennessee Press, 1980), 20.

6. It should be acknowledged that Hays has always been generous in reading and commenting on the work of others regardless of area.

7. Samuel P. Hays to Joel A. Tarr, July 25, 1997.

8. In writing about his studies of environmental politics, Hays has emphasized the continuity of the environmental publications with his earlier work, rather than the differences. In the preface to *Beauty, Health, and Permanence,* for instance, he notes that "the contribution of the following pages lies far more in an attempt to understand the broader relationship between society and politics than in environmental history as such. . . . It is about social change and governance in America as analyzed through the role of these emerging public values and objectives" (p. x).

9. Hays to Tarr, July 25, 1997.

10. Ibid.; Hays, *Beauty, Health, and Permanence,* pp. xxii–xv.

11. Hays, *American Political History as Social Analysis,* p. 6.

12. Hays, *Beauty, Health, and Permanence,* 528; Samuel P. Hays, "Comment: The Trouble with Bill Cronon's Wilderness," *Environmental History* 1 (Jan. 1996): 29–32.

13. Ibid., 50.

Introduction

1. Samuel P. Hays, *Conservation and the Gospel of Efficiency: the Progressive Conservation Movement* (Cambridge: Harvard University Press, 1958).

2. Samuel P. Hays, *American Political History as Social Analysis* (Knoxville: University of Tennessee Press, 1980).

3. Samuel P. Hays, "History as Human Behavior," *Iowa Journal of History* 58 (1960): 193–206.

4. Samuel P. Hays, "Modernizing Values in the History of the United States," *Peasant Studies* 6 (1977) 68–79; see also Hays, *The Response to Industrialism*, 2nd ed. (Chicago: University of Chicago Press, 1995), chap. 2.

5. Samuel P. Hays, in collaboration with Barbara D. Hays, *Beauty, Health and Permanence: Environmental Politics in the United States, 1955–1985.* (Cambridge: Cambridge University Press, 1987). *Beauty, Health and Permanence* drew together a wide range of topics in environmental history which few have dealt with elsewhere and which constituted the most focused statements about them; many are dealt with in this article. They include the evolution of environmental values, the environmental opposition, environmental science, the political middleground of management, comparative regional and state analysis, and the constitutional features of environmental politics.

6. This activity led to a considerable number of written testimonies about river development, wilderness, clean air and forestry and a newsletter, "Conservation News" produced from 1973 through 1977, copies of which are in the author's file.

7. Roderick Nash, *Wilderness and the American Mind* (New Haven: Yale University Press, 1961) is one of the most widely known attempts to define history in terms of "historical roots." My own approach is not to examine the intellectual forerunners of developments such as the wilderness movement or earlier efforts to cope with urban waste but to understand the more widely shared popular values that arise less from reading what these prominent authors have said and more from direct human experience, much of which is personal, visual, and perceptual rather than intellectual. See Hays, *Beauty, Health, and Permanence,* 21–39.

8. The two past presidents of the American Society for Environmental History have written in this vein. See William Cronon, "The Trouble with Wilderness, or Getting Back to the Wrong Nature," *Environmental History* 1, (January 1996): 7–28; and Martin Melosi, "Equity, Eco-racism and Environmental History," *Environmental History Review* 19 (fall 1995) 1–16. A larger work that looks at environmental history through the eyes of contemporary "environmental justice" politics is Robert Gottlieb, *Forcing the Spring: the Transformation of the American Environmental Movement* (Washington, D.C.: Island Press, 1993). For quite different approaches more in the context of historical analysis elaborated in this essay, see Samuel P. Hays, "The Trouble With Bill Cronon's Wilderness," in *Environmental History* 1 (January 1996): 29–32; Hays, review of Gottlieb, *Forcing the Spring* in *Environmental History Review* 18 (fall 1994): 75–78; see also "Environmental Equity," in Hays, *Beauty, Health and Permanence,* 265–72.

9. See chapters on these subjects in Hays, *Beauty, Health and Permanence,* 287–362.

10. My interest in the "middle ground" of administration was a theme of my first book on conservation. But it continued in such writing as "The Politics of Environmental Administration," *in Who's Running America? Bureaucracies and Policies in the Years*

Since World War II, ed. Louis Galambos (Baltimore: Johns Hopkins University Press, 1987); see also Hays, *Beauty, Health and Permanence,* 392–426.

11. This includes "The New Environmental West," in this compilation, an article that was turned down by *Forest History* after having been "peer reviewed" by nonhistorians who argued that the subject was well known and thus needed no article; their report, however, made clear that they simply were uncomfortable with a statement that featured environmental objectives in the West.

12. One article, "The Clean Air Act of 1990," is included in this compilation of essays. It involved a commitment by the editor of *Environmental Affairs,* published by the Boston College School of Law, to publish an article on the 1990 Act with an agreement to accept the historical approach in which I would write, a style well known to the editor from my previous law journal articles; when the article was submitted, that style then led to its rejection by a new editorial staff on the grounds that it did not conform to their traditional law journal format.

13. A critic of Dr. Needleman's work objected to a footnote to one of her articles in my article on the politics of lead; I cited the note as one contribution to an ongoing debate on the health effects of lead, and it was taken as a personal attack.

14. My well-known argument about the transition from "conservation" to "environment," with considerable historical discontinuity between them, has received criticism from participants in the environmental movement who wish to give historical firmness to contemporary environmental affairs. I argue that these earlier precedents reflect far less wide and less deeply rooted environmental values than those that evolved in the years after World War II. I have found no way around this controversy, since my critics seem to be more interested in enhancing the contemporary movement through historical accounts, whereas I am more interested in the issue of evolving public environmental attitudes as a feature of environmental history.

15. I was once asked by a television reporter to participate in a discussion following a dramatic oil spill on the Ohio River below Pittsburgh. When I told her that in my contribution I would argue that the daily oil leaks from many sources were more important than this dramatic event, she lost interest. Public relations staffers in environmental organizations often complain that they can't get their desired environmental point across to the news media because of the media's preference for more dramatic and personal affairs. This included, for example, coverage of the Rio Environmental Conference in 1992.

16. Sam Hays, "Demythologizing the Mythology of Emissions Trading," *Environmental Forum,* January 1995.

17. I wrote a brief article for the newsletter of the Society for Environmental Journalists pertaining to the alar case in which I deplored the failure of the media to examine the wide ramification of the issue, a failure that had led to the creation of "conventional wisdom" which would dominate the documentary record and continue to mislead historians for many years to come. It received some initial favorable response but was not published, and I assumed that the leaders of the society did not wish to acknowledge the limitations of their focus on a dramatic episode rather than more extensive, and undoubtedly less exciting, contextual and historical analysis.

18. Ernest Morrison, *J. Horace McFarland: a Thorn for Beauty* (Harrisburg: Pennsylvania Historical and Museum Commission, 1995) see my review *in Environmental History* 1 (April 1996): 103–04 4, which contrasts Muir and McFarland as historical figures.

19. On invitation from the program committee of the American Historical Association, I presented a paper on the appropriate focus of environmental history for the 1994 meeting in San Francisco. Donald Wooster, the main commentator, contended that I did not sufficiently support the ethical objectives of the environmental movement. He took particular exception to my arguments about these three conventional arguments in environmental history. From my point of view, the natural world carries no ethical imperative in itself, but simply provides a series of environmental conditions and processes which human beings seek to include in the developed world around them. While Native Americans in their religious outlook often affirmed environmental cultural values, those values often were contradicted by their actions, and when confronted with the economic opportunities for resource exploitation, such as beaver trapping, had little staying power. There is little basis for a clearly dichotomized gender analysis of the roots of either developmental or environmental impulses, which at the most points to some differences in tendencies depending on time and place. Far more significant are the varied roles of women in environmental affairs, ranging from spearheading opposition to toxic waste dumps, to becoming involved in state and national environmental organizations, to serving in natural resource administrative positions to serving as public relations officers for polluting industries. Considerable evidence is readily available if one is concerned with the behavior of women in relation to environmental affairs rather than with broad gender ideologies.

20. I was asked by sociologist Riley Dunlap to appear on a panel at the 1990 meeting of the American Association for the Advancement of Science, which would result in a book. I was persuaded that I was invited because Dunlap wished to include my broader historical perspective, with which he was well acquainted, but he decided because of"space constrictions" not to publish my paper. When the book was printed, I was surprised to see that well over half of it was devoted to the fringe groups that social movement analysis prefers, whereas my approach was based more on the examination of a broad social context of values and institutions. See Riley E. Dunlap and Angels G. Mertig, *American Environmentalism: The U.S. Environmental Movement, 1970–1990* (Philadelphia: Taylor and Francis, 1992).

21. The list of antienvironmental books, over fifty in my own collection, are too numerous to mention. Two examples are Don Hummel, *Stealing the National Parks: The Destruction of Concessions and Public Access* (Bellevue, Wash.: Free Enterprise Press, 1987); Michel Fumento, *Science Under Siege: Balancing Technology and the Environment* (New York: Morrow, 1993).

22. See Charles T. Rubin, *The Green Crusade: Rethinking the Roots of Environmentalism* New York: Free Press, 1994). Rubin examines the environmental movement through four sets of ideas promoted by environmental writers: Rachel Carson and Barry Commoner; Paul Ehrlich and Garrett Hardin; the Club of Rome; and deep ecology. A social analysis, resting on an examination of the meaning of their activities to those engaged in environmental affairs, would lead in quite a different direction.

23. Focus on the fringe groups, usually identified in terms of writers about "deep ecology," is prevalent in many writings. Two, for example, are Martin V. Lewis, Green Delusions: *An Environmentalist Critique of Radical Environmentalism* (Durham, N.C.: Duke University Press, 1992); and Gregg Easterbrook, *A Moment on the Earth: The Coming Age of Environmental Optimism* (New York: Viking Press, 1995).

24. Samuel P. Hays, "Environmental Political Culture and Environmental Political

Development: An Analysis of Legislative Voting, 1971–1989," *Environmental History Review,* summer 1992, 1–22.

25. For integrated analyses of environmental science, see Sheila Jasanoff, *The Fifth Branch: Science Advisers as Policymakers* (Cambridge, Mass.: Harvard University Press, 1990); see also Hays, *Beauty, Health and Permanence,* 328–62; and Hays, foreword to Fred Frankena, *Strategies of Expertise in Technical Controversies: A Study of Wood Energy Development* (Bethlehem, Pa.: Lehigh University Press, 1992).

26. Todd Wilkinson, "Utah Ushers Its Frogs Toward Oblivion," *High Country News* 28 (27 May 1996): 10–13.)

27. See Hays, *Beauty, Health and Permanence,* 287–328 for one of the few integrated analyses of the environmental opposition.

28. In environmental politics focused on the nation's capital, one can discern a cyclical pattern of environmental thrust and opposition, back and forth over the years. Environmental protection initiatives took place in the early years of the Nixon administration, in the first half of the Carter administration, and the second half of the first Clinton administration, while vigorous and successful responses by opponents took place in the later Nixon and Ford administrations,in the second half of the Carter administration, in the Reagan administration, and in the U.S. Congress during the first Clinton administration. Each environmental thrust gave rise to a vigorous developmental counterthrust.

29. See, for example, "The 1994 Economic Impacts of Fishing, Hunting and Wildlife-Related Recreation on National Forest Lands," prepared by the American Sportfishing Association for the Wildlife, Fish and Rare Plants, U. S. Forest Service (1996).

30. See Paul Ekins, Mayer Hillman, and Robert Hutchinson, *The Gaia Atlas of Green Economics* (New York: Anchor Books, 1992).

31. See, especially, the economic analyses made by Thomas M. Power, chair of the Economic Department at the University of Montana, notably his *Lost Landscapes and Failed Economies: The Search for a Value of Place* (Washington, D.C.: Island Press, 1996); and T. M. Power, ed., "Economic Well-Being and Environmental Protection in the Pacific Northwest: A Consensus Report by Pacific Northwest Economists," manuscript, Economics Department, University of Montana, 1995.

32. The best source for wetlands issues is "National Wetlands Newsletter" published by the Environmental Law Institute, Washington, D.C. (1979–).

33. For "green business ventures, see the magazine, *In Business* (1980–), Emmaus, Pa.

34. In the last half of the 1990s, a major dispute has arisen between the regulated industry that wishes to limit enforcement to monitoring the existence of management systems in place, called Environmental Management Systems (EMS), and the environmental community that insists that industries should provide data about actual emissions they release and that those industries should use that information to certify they are meeting emission limits applicable to them. The debate has focused on EPA's implementation of the reporting requirements authorized for air quality in the 1990 Clean Air Act and the subsequent rule known as the CAM (Compliance Assurance Monitoring) rule. See "Groups Say CAM Rule Undermines Enforcement, Citizens' Right to Know Important Emissions Data," *Environment Reporter* 27 (8 November 1996): 1437–38.

35. Struggles over the catalytic converter to reduce pollution from gasoline motors is a classic example. A more contemporary case is the growth of kenaf to replace wood pulp in paper making.

36. For the role of secrecy in the Office of Management and Budget concerning the asbestos issue, see U. S. House of Representatives, Committee on Energy and Commerce, Subcommittee on Oversight and Investigations, *Report: Case Study on OMB Interference in Agency Rulemaking, Together with Minority Views.* 99th Cong. 1st sess.

37. Coverage of events in the 104th Congress is best followed in the environmental newsletters such as *Environment Reporter and Chemical Regulation Reporter,* published by the Bureau of National Affairs, Inc. in Washington, D.C. and *Clean Air Report* and *Water Policy Report,* both published by Inside Washington, Inc., Washington, D.C. Excellent day-to-day coverage is also provided by more recently established e-mail services, for example, Greenwire, Greenlines, and Sierra-Club Action; printouts for these for 1995 and 1996 are in the author's files.

38. For two books in this vein, see Norman J. Vig and Michael E. Kraft, *Environmental Policy in the 1980s: Reagan's New Agenda* (Washington, D.C.: Congressional Quarterly, 1984); and Vig and Kraft, *Environmental Policy in the 1990s* (Washington, D.C.: Congressional Quarterly, 1990).

39. An excellent recently inaugurated source for science issues is "Risk Policy Report" (Washington, D.C.: Inside Washington Publishers (1994–).

40. For the New Jersey case, see the report, "Early Findings of the Pollution Prevention Program: Part I: On-Site Reviews of Pollution Prevention Plans and Part II: Preliminary Results of Industrial Reporting," Office of Pollution Prevention, Department of Environmental Protection, Trenton, N.J., June 1995.

41. Two of the main focal points of this effort are the Sustainable Forestry Initiative of the American Forest and Paper Association and the international initiative known as ISO 14001, which is the concern primarily of the chemical industry. See "Sustainable Forestry for Tomorrow's World; First Annual Progress Report on the American Forest and Paper Association's Sustainable Forestry Initiative" (American Forest and Paper Association, 1996); see also three articles on ISO 14001 in *Environmental Management,* November 1996, 16–34.

42. For the wise use movement, see John Echeverria and Raymond Booth Eby, eds., *Let the People Judge: Wise Use and the Private Property Rights Movement* (Washington, D.C.: Island Press, 1995). For regional analyses see "Fools' Wisdom; An Analysis of the Anti-Conservation Movement in the Midwest (Madison: Wisconsin's Environmental Decade, 1996); Paul deArmond: "Wise Use in Northern Puget Sound" (Bellingham, Wash.: Whatcom Environmental Council, 1995); William Kevin Burke: "The Scent of Opportunity: A Survey of the Wise Use/Property Rights Movement in New England" (Cambridge, Mass.: Political Research Associates, 1992). See also the newsletter, "New Voices (1992–1996) published by the Wilderness Society in Denver, Colo., and the e-mail service, Clear View.

43. For one of the few integrated statements about the environmental opposition, see Hays, *Beauty, Health and Permanence,* 287–328.

44. For contrasting approaches, see Hays, "The Clean Air Act of 1990," published for the first time in this volume; and Gary C. Bryner, *Blue Skies, Green Politics: the Clean Air Act of 1990* (Washington, D.C.: Congressional Quarterly, 1993).

45. The constitutional implications of environmental affairs are dealt with only, so far as I aware, in Hays, *Beauty, Health and Permanence,* 531–38, in which the U.S. Constitution is defined not as the formal document of 1789 but as the total mix of institutions involving the separation of powers and the vertical layers of government.

46. For occasional forays into its own history, see U.S. Environmental Protection Agency, *EPA Journal* (Washington, D.C., 1975–).

47. Two analyses of the Reagan administration are Jonathan Lash, Katherine Gillman, and David Sheridan, *A Season of Spoils: The Story of the Reagan Administration's Attack on the Environment* (New York, Pantheon, 1984); and Joan Claybook and the staff *of Public Citizen, Retreat from Safety: Reagan's Attack on America's Health* (New York: Pantheon, 1984).

48. In searching for evidence about the historical evolution of wetlands activities, I found discussions with lower-level staff who had been with the agency for several decades far more informative than the statements of higher-level administrators.

49. An incrementalist approach to the analysis of environmental policy is Hays, "The Future of Environmental Regulation," *Journal of Law and Commerce* 15 (spring 1996), 549–84, included in this volume. For another case of my approach to administrative politics see Hays, "The New Environmental Forest," *University of Colorado Law Review* 59 (1988: 517–50).

50. Curiously, political scientists who specialize in policy studies seem to avoid citing the various environmental newsletters published in Washington (and some in the states), which are the best sources for following administrative politics. They seem to concentrate on the Publications of *Congressional Quarterly,* which has a penchant to avoid administrative politics and to ignore these far richer sources. These same policy observers also seem to avoid reading the environmental law journals, which are some of the best sources on the subject. For example, see Walter A. Rosenbaum, *Environmental Politics and Policy* (Washington, D.C.: Congressional Quarterly, 1985), which says little about the central focal points of administrative politics and does not cite these rich sources for such an emphasis. During my year at the Woodrow Wilson International Center for Scholars, when Rosenbaum was also there, we discussed frequently how two specialists from different disciplines could look at the same events and place them in quite different contexts, but came to no conclusion.

51. See Hays, "Value Premises for Planning and Public Policy—The Historical Context" in *Land in America: Commodity or Natural Resource,* ed. Richard N. L. Andrews (Lexington, Mass., 1979), 149–66, also included in this volume.

52. See, as a case study, Hays, "Science and Values: Lead in Historical Perspective" in *Human Lead Exposure,* ed. Herbert L. Needleman (Boca Raton, Fla: CRC Press, 1992), reprinted in this volume. For a summary of significant research in this evolution, see Clair C. Patterson, "Natural Levels of Lead in Humans," *Carolina Environmental Essay Series III,* Institute for Environmental Studies, University of North Carolina, Chapel Hill, 1982.

53. This collection is being transferred to the Archives of Industrial Society, Hillman Library, University of Pittsburgh, as the Samuel P. Hays and Barbara D. Hays Collection of Environmental History; for details, contact Ruth Carter, Director, Archival Service Center, Hillman Library, University of Pittsburgh, Pittsburgh, Pa., 15260. See Samuel P. Hays, "Manuscripts for Recent History: A Proposal for a New Approach," *Journal of American History* 77(June 1990): 208–16.

The Limits-to-Growth Issue

1. The initial statement in the discussion was Donella H. Meadows, Dennis L. Meadows, Jorgen Randers, and William W. Behrens, III, *The Limits to Growth* (New York: Universe Books, 1972).

2. For elaboration of this argument, see Samuel P. Hays, *Conservation and the Gospel*

of Efficiency: The Progressive Conservation Movement. 1890–1920 (Cambridge: Harvard University Press, 1959).

3. Ibid., 189–98.

4. For an account of the establishment and early history of the national parks, see Robert Shankland, *Steve Mather of the National Parks* (New York: Alfred A. Knopf, 1951).

5. State fish and wildlife programs can best be followed in doctoral dissertations—for example, John Henry Reeves, Jr., "The History and Development of Wildlife Conservation in Virginia: A Critical Review" (Virginia Polytechnic Institute, 1960), and Larry Maring Rymon, "A Critical Analysis of Wildlife Conservation in Oregon" (Oregon State University, 1969). Some account of federal wildlife policy in the 1920s is in Donald C. Swain, *Federal Conservation Policy, 1921–1933* (Berkeley and Los Angeles: University of California Press, 1963).

6. The historical development of these activities can best be followed in the publications of such groups as the Potomac Appalachian Trail Club, the Appalachian Trailways Conference, the Appalachian Mountain Club, and the Federation of Western Outdoor Clubs. Some historical material on one well-known aspect of hiking activities is included in Ann and Myron Sutton, *The Appalachian Trail* (Philadelphia: Lippincott, 1967).

7. Two examples of the impact of the amenity focus in forest management are Richard M. Alston, "Forest—Goals and Decision-Making in the Forest Service," United States Department of Agriculture, Forest Service Research Paper Int-128, 1972, and West Virginia Forest Management Practices Commission, "Report on Forest Management Practices on National Forest Lands in West Virginia," mimeo., West Virginia Legislature, August 1970. An excellent blend of the new with the old focus is Leon S. Minckler, *Woodland Ecology: Environmental Forestry for the Small Owner* (Syracuse: Syracuse University Press, 1975).

8. Two books in this vein are Richard L. Berkman and W. Kip Viscusi, *Damming the West (New* York: Crossman Publishers, 1973), and Robert H. Boyle, John Graves, and T. H. Watkins, *The Water Hustlers* (San Francisco, New York: Sierra Club, 1971). The continuing criticism of impoundments can be followed best in the regular publications of the American Rivers Conservation Council in Washington, D.C.

9. A major attack on clear-cutting is Nancy Wood, *Clearcut, the Deforestation of America* (New York: Sierra Club, 1971); a defense is in Eleanor C. J. Horwitz, *Clearcutting:A View from the Top* (Washington, D.C., Acropolis Books Ltd., 1974).

10. For examples of this view, see The Conservation Foundation, *National Parks for the Future* (Washington, D.C.: The Conservation Foundation, 1972), and F. Fraser Darling and Noel D. Eichhorn, *Man and Nature in the National Parks,* 2d ed. (Washington, D.C.: The Conservation Foundation, 1969). Continuing evaluation of the national parks from this point of view can be followed in *National Parks and Conservation Magazine, The Environmental Journal,* published by the National Parks and Conservation Association, Washington, D.C.

11. This conclusion is based on a review of a number of environmental impact statements. See also an elaborate example of this perspective for the U.S. Forest Service in United States Department of Agriculture, Forest Service, General Technical Report NE-2, "The Pinchot Institute System for Environmental Forestry Studies," 1973, which emphasizes exclusively "environmental effects" and excludes consideration of "environmental goals."

12. An excellent publication in the field of pollution control technology that generates

this limited perspective is *Environmental Science and Technology,* published monthly by the American Chemical Society.

13. Some sense of this process can be obtained from a comparison of different nativity groups with respect to children ever born per 1,000 women in 1910, as reported in U.S. Department of Commerce, Bureau of Census, *Current Population Reports,* Series P-20, No. 226 (November 1971), p. 28. The data were: for native whites, 3,251; for foreign born, 4,102; for native blacks and other races, 4,247. For foreign born the data included: England and Wales, 3,269; Ireland, 3,341; Russia, 5,349; Italy, 5,454; and Poland, 5,868. Precise time series to determine these comparative patterns depend upon future accumulation of historical data. By 1960 the data had converged considerably.

14. Ibid., p. 20.

15. The problem of unwanted births and its statistical significance is focused on in Larry Bumpass and Charles F. Westoff, "Unwanted Births and U.S. Population Growth," in Daniel Callahan, ed., *The American Population Debate* (Garden City, N.Y.: Doubleday, 1971), 267–73.

16. See James J. Zuiches and Glenn V. Fugitt, "Residential Preferences: Implications for Population Redistribution in Nonmetropolitan Areas," paper read before the 138th meeting of the American Association for the Advancement of Science," Philadelphia, Pennsylvania, December 1971, in William K. Reilly, ed., *The Use of Land: A Citizens' Policy Guide to Urban Growth* (New York: T. Y. Crowell, 1973), 86.

17. See Elizabeth R. Gilette, *Action for Wilderness* (New York: Sierra Club, 1973), and Michael Frome, *Battle for the Wilderness* (New York: Praeger, 1974).

18. This is a pure estimate visualized by comparing the very small percentage of the American people who in the mid-nineteenth century had access to outdoor amenities such as spas and watering places, as contrasted with the very large number today who have access to state and national parks.

19. The old argument that wilderness hiking and camping was "elitist" now has a hollow ring to it in the face of the increasing numbers of people, well into several millions, who use such areas.

20. For several examples of books in this vein popular among environmentalists, see Wood, *Clearcut;* John F. Stacks, *Stripping: The Surface Mining of America* (San Francisco: Sierra Club, 1972); Helen Leavitt, *Superhighway—Superhoax* (New York Ballantine: 1970).

21. An excellent account of the problems inherent in positive correlations between industrial output and pollution production is Julian McCaull, "The Tide of Industrial Waste," *Environment* 14 (December 1972): 30–39.

22. One recent expression of this is Louise B. Young, *Power Over People* (New York: Oxford University Press, 1973).

23. An analysis of the social costs of this pressure in suburban areas is Council on Environmental Quality, *The Costs of Sprawl, Environmental and Economic Costs of Alternative Residential Development Patterns at the Urban Fringe* (Washington, D.C.: Council on Environmental Quality, 1974).

24. The use of terms to describe state agencies is instructive. New York is distinctive in that its agency is called the Department of Environmental Conservation, reflecting a strong combination of its long-standing involvement in land questions in connection with the Adirondacks and its more recent concern with environmental pollution.

25. The following conclusions are based upon reading a wide range of materials from

national organizations such as the Wilderness Society, the National Wildlife Federation, the Sierra Club, the Environmental Policy Center, and the National Clean Air Coalition; general publications such as *Environmental Science* and *Technology, High Country News,* and *Science;* state general groups such as the Oregon Environmental Council, the Colorado Open Space Council, the Virginia Conservation Council, or the Pennsylvania Environmental Council, and more specialized groups such as the Michigan United Conservation Clubs, California Coastal Alliance, the West Virginia Highlands Conservancy, and the Pittsburgh Group Against Smog and Pollution.

26. A recent example is the effort by Philadelphia to secure disposal sites in northeastern, southwestern, and south central Pennsylvania, each one of which has aroused considerable local opposition.

27. An excellent introduction to the problem of air nondegradation is in *High Country News* 4, no. 20 (September 29, 1972): 1, 4–6.

28. See Laurence I . Moss, "How to Prevent Significant Deterioration of Air Quality in Any Portion of Any State," mimeo., statement before the Environmental Protection Agency, Hearings on Significant Deterioration, Washington, D.C., August 27, 1973; and Moss, "Sierra Club Responds to EPA's Four Clean Air Alternatives," mimeo., statement before the Subcommittee on Air and Water Pollution, Committee on Public Works, U.S. Senate, July 24, 1973.

29. The stream classification system of Pennsylvania is a good example. For a description of it and its application, see Pennsylvania Department of Environmental Resources, Bureau of Water Quality Management, "Final Report of the Pennsylvania Sanitary Water Board, 1923–1971," Publication Number 29, 1971. For an account of the political forces involved and in applying nondegradation concepts, see "Summary of Hearing and Comments" pertaining to stream reclassifications based upon water quality standards, hearings 13–18, January–March 1973, conducted by the Pennsylvania Department of Environmental Resources, available in mimeographed form from the department.

30. The most widely discussed example of a reusable container law is that of Oregon. See Don Waggoner, "Oregon's 'Bottle Bill,'" Oregon Environmental Council, n.d., mimeo.; Waggoner, "Oregon's 'Bottle Bill'—One Year Later," Oregon Environmental Council, 1973, mimeo.; Charles M. Gudger and Jack C. Bailes, "The Economic Impact of Oregon's 'Bottle Bill,'" School of Business and Technology, Oregon State University, 1973.

31. Harvey Molotch, "The City as a Growth Machine," mimeo., University of California, Santa Barbara, July 1973.

32.. There is a wide variety of literature concerning open spaces, which embodies directly and indirectly this sense. Several examples are William K. Reilly, ed., *The Use of Land* (New York: Crowell, 1973); Charles E. Little, *Challenge of the Land: Open Space Preservation at the Local Level* (New York: Pergamon Press, 1968); Richard E. Galantowicz, "The Process of Environmental Assessment," in five parts issued separately, North Jersey Conservation Foundation (Morristown, New Jersey, 1972–1973), and Susan Redlich, ed., *Guiding Growth: A Handbook for New Hampshire Townspeople* (New Hampshire: Society for the Protection of New Hampshire Forests, Concord, 1974).

33. Barry Commoner, *The Closing Circle* (New York: Alfred A. Knopf, 1971); Ian McHarg, *Design with Nature* (Garden City, N.Y.: Doubleday, 1969). For a more recent model in the McHarg mold see the so-called Medford study, Narenda Juneja, "Medford: Performance Requirements for the Maintenance of Social Values Represented by the Natural Environment of Medford Township, New Jersey," Center for Ecological Research

in Planning and Design, Department of Landscape Architecture and Regional Planning, University of Pennsylvania, Philadelphia, Pa., 1974.

34. These conclusions are based on a variety of organizational materials from such groups as the Virginia Conservation Council, the North Carolina Conservation Council, the New York State Environmental Lobby, the Oregon Environmental Council, the Colorado Open Space Council, and the Society for the Protection of New Hampshire Forests.

35. The preferential assessment programs of two states are evaluated in John Kolesar and Jaye Scholl, *Misplaced Hopes, Misspent Millions: Report on Farmland Assessments in New Jersey* (Princeton: The Center for Analysis of Public Issues, 1972), and Jerald W. Hunter, "Preserving Rural Land Resources: The California Westside," *Ecology Law Quarterly* 1, no. 2 (Spring 1971): 330–73.

36. A good statement of the concern for habitat is Nathaniel P. Reed, "Environmental Concern and Wildlife—A Humane Approach," speech given before the American Humane Association, reprinted in *Pennsylvania Game News* 6, no. 44 (June 1973): 15–20.

37. This problem can be followed in the Publications of such groups as the Appalachian Trailway Conference and the Potomac Appalachian Trail Club.

38. The activities of Zero Population Growth can be followed in its monthly, *National Reporter,* and its quarterly, *Equilibrium.*

39. The activities of the Michigan Population Council recounted here are derived from correspondence with it and its releases.

Value Premises for Planning and Public Policy

1. These assumptions have been elaborated in a larger context in Samuel P. Hays, "The New Organizational Society," in *Building the Organizational Society,* ed. Jerry Israel (New York: Free Press, 1972), 1–15.

2. Transformations of scale in urban life are dealt with more fully in Samuel P. Hays, "The Changing Political Structure of the City in Industrial America," *Journal of Urban History,* 1, no. 1 (1974): 6–38. Similar patterns of change are elaborated in a recent work, Social Science Panel, National Academy of Sciences—National Academy of Engineering, *Toward An Understanding of Metropolitan America* (Washington, D.C.: National Academy of Engineering, 1974).

3. For an example of change in police systems see Roger Lane, *Policing the City: Boston, 1822–1885* (Cambridge, Mass.: Harvard University Press, 1967).

4. These changes are dealt with in Susan Kleinberg, "Technology's Stepdaughters: The Impact of Industrialization Upon Workingclass Women, Pittsburgh, 1865–1890" (Ph.D. dissertation, University of Pittsburgh, 1973), see, especially, chap. 5, pp. 125–70.

5. Several recent studies have explored these changes in education. See for example, David B. Tyack, *The One Best System: A History of American Urban Education* (Cambridge, Mass.: Harvard University Press, 1974).

6. For an elaboration of this theme see Samuel P. Hays, "The Politics of Reform in Municipal Government in the Progressive Era," *Pacific Northwest Quarterly* 55, no. 4 (October 1964): 157–69.

7. A good example of this approach is Basil G. Zimmer and Amos H. Hawley, *Metropolitan Area Schools: Resistance to District Reorganization* (Beverly Hills, Calif.: Sage Publications, 1968), which focuses on the "irrational" opposition to school consolidation.

8. This theme, as demonstrated in the early twentieth century resource conservation movement is elaborated in Samuel P. Hays, *Conservation and the Gospel of Efficiency: The Progressive Conservation Movement* (Cambridge, Mass.: Harvard University Press, 1958).

9. This analysis of the environmental movement is elaborated more fully in Samuel P. Hays, "The Limits to Growth Issue: An Historical Perspective," in *Growth in America*, ed. Chester L. Cooper (Westport, Conn.: Greenwood, 1976).

10. Street life and crowdedness were acceptable to many established urban dwellers, but was less so to later generations. For some observations on this see Herbert Gans, *The Urban Villagers* (New York: Free Press, 1962) 19–24.

11. Environmental effects analysis can be followed most effectively in the pages of "102 Monitor," published by the U.S. Government Printing Office, Washington, D.C., for the Council on Environmental Quality.

12. Some states have mandates to develop environmental planning, but these have not progressed very far. See, for example, Department of Environmental Resources, Commonwealth of Pennsylvania, *Environmental Master Plan: Planning Survey Report* (Harrisburg, Pa., 1973).

13. Thus, for example, there is in Pennsylvania the Northwest Pennsylvania Regional Planning and Development Commission as one of a number of regional groupings in the state.

14. See, as one example, "A Preliminary Report" on land use for Crawford County, Pa., prepared by Beckman, Yoder and Seay, Inc., Wexford, Pa., 1972.

15. One such privately financed plan, sponsored by the Western Pennsylvania Conservancy, Pittsburgh, Pa., is William J. Curry III et al., *The Laurel Hill Study* (Pittsburgh, Pa., 1975).

16. See, for example, John J. Roberts, Edward J. Croke, and Samuel Booras, "A Critical Review of the Effect of Air Pollution Control Regulations on Land Use Planning" *Journal of the Air Pollution Control Association*, 25, no. 5 (May 1975) 500–20.

17. Eugene P. Odum, Optimum Population and Environment: A Georgian Microcosm," *Current History* (June 1970): 355–65.

18. For a governmental report in this vein see *Transition, A Report to the Oregon Energy Council Prepared by the Office of Energy Research and Planning*, Office of the Governor, State of Oregon, Eugene, January 1975.

19. See Lee E. Erickson, "A Review of Forecasts for U.S. Energy Consumption in 1980 and 2000," in Barry Commoner, Howard Bokensbaum, and Michael Corr, eds., *Energy and Human Welfare—A Critical Analysis*, vol. 3, *Human Welfare: The End Use for Power* (New York: Macmillan, 1975), 11–16.

20. An example of this approach is Environmental Studies Institute, Carnegie-Mellon University, *Girty's Run: A Study in Urban Watershed Management* (Pittsburgh, 1974).

21. Wayne Davis, "Overpopulated America," *New Republic* 162 (January 20, 1970): 13–15.

22. Eric G. Johnson et al., *Is Population Growth Good for Boulder Citizens?* 2nd ed. (Boulder, Colo.: ZPG, 1971). For another study in a similar vein see Richard C. Bradley, *The Costs of Urban Growth: Observations and Judgments* (Pikes Peak, Colo.: Pikes Peak Area Council of Governments, 1973).

23. Details of this opposition for cases in the Mountain-Plains states can be followed in *High Country News* published in Lander, Wyoming. Data from the recent case of en-

ergy park proposals in Pennsylvania comes from newspaper coverage in the ten candidate site areas, in the author's files.

24. These values are described in Mary Keys Watson, "Behavioral and Environmental Aspects of Recreational Land Sales" (Ph.D. dissertation, The Pennsylvania State University, 1975), 211–60.

25. Harvey Molotch, "The City as a Growth Machine," mimeo, University of California, Santa Barbara, July 1973.

26. Temporary Study Commission on the Future of the Adirondacks, *The Future of the Adirondacks*, 2 vol. (Blue Mountain Lake, N.Y.: The Adirondack Museum, 1971).

Public Values and Management Response

1. Paul Culhane, *Public Lands Politics: Interest Group Influence on the Forest Service and the Bureau of Land Management* (Resources for the Future, Washington, D.C., 1981).

2. See, for example, issues of publications such as *American Forests, The Living Wilderness,* and *Sierra Club Bulletin, 1956–1964,* for articles which reflect the meaning then attached to wilderness.

3. The most extensive of the natural environment photography series is the American Wilderness Series of Time-Life books. They include individual volumes *on The Badlands, Canyons and Mesas, Sagebrush Country,* and *Cactus Country,* combining photographs and texts. See also issues of such collections as the format books published by the Sierra Club and Friends of the Earth.

4. The 1980 edition of the survey of American participation in the arts indicated that the number of Americans engaged in photographic pursuits rose from 19 percent in 1975 to 44 percent in 1980. Westerners tended to be more active (56 percent participation in 1980) than those living in other parts of the country. See American Council for the Arts, *Americans and the Arts* (New York, 1981), 37.

5. See "National Opinions Concerning the California Desert Conservation Area," conducted for the Bureau of Land Management by the Gallup Organization, Princeton, New Jersey, January 1978.

6. One reflection of this circumstance is William E. Shands and Robert G. Healy, *The Lands Nobody Wanted* (The Conservation Foundation, Washington, D.C., 1977).

7. A useful account of this type of transformation for an eastern area is Jane Eblen Keller, *Adirondack Wilderness: A Story of Man and Nature* (Syracuse, N.Y.: Syracuse University Press, 1980).

8. See Ronald Inglehart, *The Silent Revolution: Changing Values and Political Styles Among Western Publics* (Princeton, 1977)

9. See Mary Keys Watson, "Behavioral and Environmental Aspects of Recreational Land Sales," Ph.D. thesis, Pennsylvania State University, 1975.

10. Ronald Briggs, "The Role of Transportation and Environmental Amenity Resources in the Development of Nonmetropolitan America, 1950 to 1980," paper presented at the German-American Seminar on Geography and Regional Policy: Resource Management by Complex Political Systems, Heidelberg, W. Germany, June, 1981.

11. From a summary of the Briggs argument in "Openers," *American Demographics,* August 1981, p. 9.

12. This assessment is drawn from analyses of environmental votes in the U.S. House

of Representatives, 1970–77, made by the author, and from evidence concerning environmental issues and citizen activities in the various states.

13. See "Memorandum," including the full report on the study to the Western Regional Council, from Yankelovich, Skelly and White, Inc., dated Sept. 27, 1978, subject title, "Research on Public Attitudes Toward the Use of Wilderness Lands." See sections on "Outdoor Involvement," 23; "Awareness of the Wilderness Issue," 37; "What People Know About the Wilderness Issue," 38–42; and "Needs Rated as Very Important in Deciding the Use of Wilderness Land," 49.

14. See "The Casper Poll—Wilderness," typescript, 1979, and news story, "Casperites Use Wilderness, and Many Want More," *Casper Star Tribune,* Casper, Wyoming, July 8, 1979. A similar poll for Gallatin County, Montana, conducted by Michael A. Bond, Public Resources Management, Bozeman, Montana, indicated similar attitudes. See Bond, "Public Lands Survey, Gallatin County, Montana, Gallatin and Beaverhead National Forests," May 10, 1981.

15. See Stephen R. Kellert, reports of a study of "American Attitudes, Knowledge and Behaviors Toward Wildlife and Natural Habitats," funded by the U.S. Fish and Wildlife Survey, of which three of four phases were completed as of January 1981. Titles of each of phases I, II and III were: "Public Attitudes Toward Critical Wildlife and Natural Habitat Issues," "Activity of the American Public Relating to Animals," and "Knowledge, Affection and Basic Attitudes Toward Animals in American Society."

16. See, for example, publications and activities of such groups as the Colorado Open Space Council (Denver), the Montana Environmental Information Center (Helena), the Idaho Conservation League and the Idaho Environmental Council, the Utah Wilderness Association (Salt Lake City) and the Wyoming Outdoor Council. Environmental affairs in the entire region can be followed especially in *High Country News* published in Lander, Wyoming.

17. See, for example, the activities of the Northern Plains Resource Council, which can be followed in its publication, *The Plains Truth.* Cooperation on these issues can be followed in Publications of organizations listed in note 16, and fairly good coverage can be found in *Not Man Apart,* monthly newspaper of Friends of the Earth.

18. For a running account of this issue see the pages of the *Missoulian,* of Missoula, Montana, beginning with issue of November 16, 1979, news item, "Company wants to explore for gas, oil inside wilderness." An early statement of Williams' action is in the April 22, 1981 issue, "March dedicated to preservation of Bob Marshall."

19. See "Speech Before the Rocky Mountain Oil and Gas Association, Denver, Colorado, October 8, 1981, release from office of Senator Malcolm Wallop of Wyoming; see also account of Wallop's views in *Jackson Hole News,* October 15, 1981, "Wallop Hits Wilderness Leases."

20. See Publications of these groups for their activities.

21. For a good account of activities in each state, see *Proceedings, 1980 Western Wilderness and Rivers Conference,* November 21 and 22, Denver, Colorado, distributed and apparently published by the American Wilderness Alliance, Denver. See, also issues of *Wild America* (1979–present), published by the Alliance.

22. See fliers and reports published by the Colorado Wilderness Coalition, a branch of the Colorado Open Space Council.

23. See news releases of the Utah Wilderness Association, Salt Lake City, Utah.

24. Ibid., see also "PLI, Others Appeal 29 BLM Wilderness Decisions in Utah," *PLI Newsletter* (October 1981): 2, Publication of the Public Lands Institute.

25. See *El Paisano,* Publication of the Desert Protective Council.

26. The breadth of this planning effort can be gathered from the draft and final plans for the California Desert Conservation Area. See, for example, U.S. Department of the Interior, Bureau of Land Management, "Final Environmental Impact Statement and Proposed Plan, California Desert Conservation Area," Riverside, California, 1980.

27. See, for example, items prepared by the Red Desert Committee, Rock Springs, Wyoming.

28. This development can be followed in *Forest Planning* issued by the Nationwide Forest Planning Clearing house, Eugene, Oregon.

29. A trend in this direction is reflected in an invitation, "Adopt a BLM Wilderness," an issue of the Publication, "BLM Wilderness: A Citizen's Handbook," number 11, October 1981, distributed by the Sierra Club and the Wilderness Society.

30. This perspective can be followed in *High Country News,* note 16.

31. Culhane, *Public Land Politics.*

32. Culhane, esp. 215–26. Culhane deals only with the external pressures on agencies and omits the role of internal agency values on choice; hence he covers only half of the balance of forces, which should include both the agency and the public, both of which are the subject of this session.

33. See for example, Ben W. Twight, "The Tenacity of Value Commitment: The Forest Service and the Olympic National Park" (Ph.D thesis, University of Washington, Seattle, 1971) Pages 1–13 provide a good, general historical account of the problem. By focusing on agency values, Twight provides a useful antidote to Culhane's treatment.

34. For a brief description of canopy closure and vertical layering standards as silviculture objectives see the Rt. Hon. The Earl of Bradford, "An Experiment in Sustainable Forestry," *The Ecologist* (June 1980): 165–66. This is described as a "multi-story continuous-cover system."

35. For varied views on eastern wilderness in "restored" areas see U.S. Senate, Committee on Interior and Insular Affairs, 93rd Congress, 1st Session, *Eastern Wilderness Areas* (3 parts) (Washington, D.C., 1973).

36. See, for example, *PLI Newsletter* (January 1981): 2: "Utah BLM has substituted a concept of confinement for solitude in obvious contrast to inventories elsewhere in the nation."

37. See Mons L. Teigen, Secretary, Montana Public Lands Council to Frank Gregg, Director, BLM, December 12, 1980; Ronald A. Michieli, Director of Government Affairs for Land and Natural Resources, Public Lands Council, to Gregg, December 10, 1980, with enclosure, "Comments of National Cattlemen's Association, Public Lands Council and National Wool Growers Association Regarding Draft Amendments to Grazing Regulations of Bureau of Land Management."

38. See Johanna H. Wald, Natural Resources Defense Council to Gregg, November 17, 1980; Rose Strickland, Great Basin Group of the Toiyabe Chapter of the Sierra Club to Gregg, November 28, 1980; Ginger Merchant, Defenders of Wildlife to Gregg, January 6, 1980.

39. See, for example, Cameron LaFollette, "The New Demands of Diversity," *Forest Planning* (May 1980): 9–10, 20; LaFollette, "A Pilot Plan for Forest Diversity: Bureau of Land Management at Coos Bay, "Cascade Holistic Economic Consultants, Forestry Research Paper Number Nine (n.p. April 1981).

40. In its letter to Frank Gregg concerning BLM grazing policy, fn. 37, the livestock operators argued that "the carrying capacity of a rangeland area is a dynamic reflection

of a large number of biotic and abiotic factors, and is a function of the intensity of management applied to that rangeland area."

41. See Twight, "Tenacity," 15–35, for a treatment of the general problem, and 39–158 for detailed elaboration of a specific case, the Olympic National Park.

42. The U.S. Forest Service described its early "public participation" sessions in forest planning as "listening sessions."

43. A format which reflects this systematic pattern in terms of varieties of desired outdoor recreation experience has been developed by forest planners. See, for example, "Forest Recreation: An Analysis With Special Consideration of the East," Appendix O of *Report of the President's Advisory Panel on Timber and the Environment* (Washington, D.C., 1973), esp. 498.

44. See Arnold Mitchell, "Social Change: Implications of Trends in Values and Lifestyles," VALS Report No. 3, Stanford Research International, Menlo Park, Calif., 1979; and John Naisbitt, "The New Economic and Political Order of the 1980s, speech given to the Foresight Group, Stockholm, Sweden, April 17, 1980, available from the Center for Policy Process, Washington, D.C.

45. See the treatment of this problem in James Gilligan, "The Development of Policy and Administration of Forest Service Primitive and Wilderness Areas in the Western United States, Ph.D. thesis, University of Michigan, 1953 (2v).

46. This interpretation of National Park Service activities comes from personal visits to some twenty-five National Parks over the course of several decades, the observation of values implicit in park displays, literature and programs, and interviews with "summer seasonals" as well as permanent interpretive staff.

47. See, for example, the Publications of the Committee to Preserve Assateague for the continuous debate over the management plan for that park. For Sleeping Bear Dunes see clipping files of the author and in the Traverse City Public Library, Traverse City, Michigan.

48. For the appreciative wildlife interests reflected in these organizations see their Publications, *Audubon, National Wildlife,* and *Defenders.*

49. Laura and William Riley, *Guild to the National Wildlife Refuges* (Anchor Press, Doubleday, 1979).

50. U.S. Fish and Wildlife Service, *Operation of the National Wlldlife Refuge System,* Final Environmental Statement (Washington D.C., 1976).

51. Ibid., ix-12 to ix-188.

52. See citations to Kellert studies in note 15.

53. Twight, "Tenacity," see note 33.

54. Ibid.

55. John C. Hendee, George H. Stankey and Robert C. Lucas, *Wilderness Management,* U.S. Department of Agriculture, Forest Service, Miscellaneous Publication No. 1365 (Washington, D.C., 1977).

56. For several recent statements of the implications of people management, but from sources outside the U.S. Forest Service, see Arnold W. Bolle,"Managing the Wilderness: An Overview," and Ronald G. Strickland, "Wilderness Management Becomes People Management," in *Wild America* (September 1981): 3–9.

57. For the views of foresters, see Gordon L. Bultena and John C. Hendee, "Foresters' Views of Interest Group Positions on Forest Policy," *Journal of Forestry* (June 1972): 337–42. For the attitudes of the Public see Opinion Research Corporation, "The Public's

Participation in Outdoor Activities and Attitudes Toward National Wilderness Areas," prepared for the American Forest Institute (Princeton, 1977).

58. For the BLM polls on desert management see note 5 and "Summary of the Preliminary Desert Market Analysis of the California Desert," n.d., but poll taken November 8–13, 1975; see also Field Research Corporation, "California Public Opinion and Behavior Regarding the California Desert; A Report of the Survey Conducted for the United States Department of the Interior, Bureau of Land Management," October 1977 (San Francisco, 1977).

59. In drawing up its plan for the Jackson-Klamath unit in southern Oregon, the Bureau of Land Management undertook sixty interviews to identify attitudes and social values "which might be affected by BLM actions." The study identified "four groups with diverse social values." "One group is established in farming and logging. Another includes those long-time residents who moved to the valley to work in the mills or light industry; another is composed primarily of young people who were drawn to southern Oregon in the late 1960s and early 1970s to 'return to the land.' The newest groups of arrivals is characterized as financially independent people in search of small town friendliness, good schools, a slower pace of life, cleaner environment, and esthetically pleasing surroundings. The latter two groups generally favor less interference with nature and strongly favor esthetic values over economic values. Alternatively, the established residents who would benefit from economic development (real estate and business interests, logging and light industry) tend to give priority to economic values and favor growth and development." (See BLM, "Final Timber Management Environmental Statement, Jackson-Klamath" (Oregon State Office, Portland, 1979), 2-70.

60. Julia Mewes to Samuel P. Hays, July 10, 1980.

61. Philip C. Hamilton, Chief, Planning and Environmental Coordination Staff to Samuel P. Hays, April 10, 1980.

The Role of Urbanization in Environmental History

1. For the larger setting of urban history within which this article is placed see Samuel P. Hays, "From the History of the City to the History of the Urbanized Society," *Journal of Urban History* 19, no. 4 (August 1993): 3–25.

2. Alan I. Marcus, "The Strange Career of Municipal Health Initiatives: Cincinnati and City Government in the Early Nineteenth Century," *Journal of Urban History* 7, no. 1 (November 1980): 3–29.

3. Dwight Akers: Drivers Up, the Story of American Harness Racing (New York: Putnam, 1947), pp. 27–40.

4. See Joel Tarr with J. McCurley, F. C. McMichael, and T. F. Yosie, "Water and Wastes: A Retrospective Assessment of Wastewater Technology in the U.S., 1800–1932," *Technology and Culture* 25, no. 2 (April 1984): 226–63. For the industrial phase of this process, see Joel Tarr, "Industrial Wastes and Public Health: Some Historical Notes, Part 1, 1816–1932," *American Journal of Public Health* 75, no. 9 (September 1985): 1059–67.)

5. Andrew Hurley, "Creating Ecological Wastelands: Oil Pollution in New York City, 1870–1900," *Journal of Urban History* 20, no. 3 (May 1994): 340–64. Martin Melosi, *Garbage in the Cities: Refuse, Reform, and the Environment, 1880–1980* (Chicago: Dorsey Press, 1981). For the evolution of city streets, see Clay McShane, "Transforming the Use

of Urban Space: A Look at the Revolution in Street Pavements, 1880–1924," *Journal of Urban History*, 5, no. 3 (May 1979): 279–307.

6. A wide range of these urban environmental circumstances are dealt with in a collection of articles by Joel A. Tarr, *The Search for the Ultimate Sink: Urban Pollution in Historical Perspective* (Akron, Ohio: University of Akron Press, 1997).

7. Christine M. Rosen, "Businessmen Against Pollution in Late Nineteenth Century Chicago," *Business History Review* 69 (Autumn 1995) 351–97; Lynne P Snyder, "The fumes of man's ingenuity": Pittsburgh Steel, Public Health, and the Air Pollution Over Donora, Pennsylvania, 1948–1950." Seminar paper, Department of History and Sociology of Science, University of Pennsylvania, n.d.

8. Margaret Byington, *Homestead: the Households of a Mill Town*, 2nd ed (Pittsburgh: University of Pittsburgh Press, 1974).

9. Joseph L Arnold, "The Neighborhood and City Hall: The Origin of Neighborhood Associations in Baltimore, 1880–1911," *Journal of Urban History* 6, no. 1 (November 1979): 3–30.

10. Janet R Daly: "Zoning: Its Historical Context and Importance in the Development of Pittsburgh," *Western Pennsylvania Historical Magazine* 71 (April 1988): 99–125.

11. Janet R Daly-Bednarek, *The Changing Image of the City: Planning for Downtown Omaha 1945–1973* (Lincoln, Neb: University of Nebraska Press, 1992).

12. Joel Tarr with B. Lamperes, "Changing Fuel Use Behavior and Energy Transitions: The Pittsburgh Smoke Control Movement, 1940–1950, A Case Study in Historical Analogy," *Journal of Social History* 14, no. 4 (Summer 1981): 561–88.

13. Pittsburgh is one such example, a city that has long prided itself in its air pollution "clean up" in earlier years that in the 1990s has developed fierce resistance on the part of both industry and government against current improvement programs and has even severely crippled its clean air administrative program—all in the name of needed economic development. See author's clipping file on air pollution in Pittsburgh.

14. See Hays, "From the History of the City to the History of the Urbanized Society," for a more extended argument of this point. *Op cit.*

15. William Cronon's book, *Nature's Metropolis: Chicago and the Great West* (New York, 1991), is devoted to the way in which one city's entrepreneurs organized the extraction, processing and sale of raw materials in the wake of accelerating urban demand.

16. A broad overview of the history of human impacts on water resources is Alice Outwater, *Water: A Natural History* (New York: Harper-Collins, 1996).

17. A flavor of this circumstance is found in James A. Tober, *Who Owns the Wildlife?* (Westport, Conn.: Greenwood Press, 1981), 1–40.

18. For the role of hunting in environmental history, see John F. Reiger *American Sportsmen and the Origins of Conservation* (New York: Winchester Press, 1975).

19. Wildlife values and interests are examined extensively in Stephen R. Kellert, *The Value of Life: Biological Diversity and Human Society* (Washington, D.C.: Island Press, 1996).

20. S. J. Kleinberg, *The Shadow of the Mills: Working-Class Families in Pittsburgh, 1870–1907* (Pittsburgh: University of Pittsburgh Press, 1989).

21. A focused account of changing recreational attitudes and activities over the years is Laura and Guy Waterman, *Forest and Craig: A History of Hiking, Trail Blazing, and Adventure in the Northeast Mountains* (Boston: Appalachian Mountain Club, 1989).

22. An example is the way in which wildlife has been worked into urban planning and

development; see running accounts of this in *Jackson Hole News* published in Jackson, Wyoming.

23. For a succinct summary of attitudes in one region, see David D. Olson, "Realities of Nonindustrial Private Forest Ownership in Northern Michigan: An Extension Forester's Opinion," *Journal of Forestry* (January 1979): 17–18.

24. See the publications of the Land Trust Alliance, Washington, D.C., especially its publication, *The Journal of the Land Trust Alliance*, and its tenth anniversary assessment, "The First Decade and Beyond," published in 1992.

25. A contrast between two historical works that illustrate this problem is William Cronon, *Nature's Metropolis, op. cit.,* which details the way in which Chicago entrepreneurs shaped the extraction, processing of lumber in the North Woods of the Great Lakes States with no attention to the ecological or environmental transformation there, with Samuel P Hays, "Human Choice in the Great Lake Wildlands," in *Environmental Change in the Great Lakes Forest,* ed. Susan Flader (Minneapolis: University of Minnesota Press, 1982).

26. Details about historical monitoring are in Monitoring and Assessment Research Center, *Historical Monitoring,* MARC Report Number 31 (London, 1985).

27. For long-run forest change in the United States, see Michael Williams, *Americans and Their Forests: A Historical Geography* (New York: Cambridge University Press, 1989).

28. See, for example, Vernon Carstensen, *Farms or Forests: Evolution of a State Land Policy for Northern Wisconsin 1850–1932* (Madison, Wis.: University of Wisconsin, College of Agriculture, 1958).

29. Theodore Steinberg, *Nature Incorporated: Industrialization and the Waters of New England* (New York: Cambridge University Press, 1991).

30. William E Shands and Robert G Healy, *The Lands Nobody Wanted: Policy for National Forests in the Eastern United States* (Washington, D.C., The Conservation Foundation, 1977); Barbara McMartin, *The Great Forest of the Adirondacks* (Utica, N.Y.: North Country Books, 1994).

31. The focus on cycles broadened ecology from the community focus of Clements to the larger environment of plant communities and gave rise to the cumbersome but meaningful term "biogeochemical." For this transition in ecology, see Joel B Hagen, *An Entangled Bank: The Origins of Ecosystem Ecology* (New Brunswick, N.J.: Rutgers University Press, 1992).

32. See, for example, E. Atlas and C. S. Giam, "Global Transport of Organic Pollutants: Ambient Concentrations in the Remote Marine Atmosphere," *Science* 211 (9 January 1981): 163–165.

33. European events pertaining to critical loads can be followed best in *Acid News* (Goteborg, Sweden: The Swedish NGO Secretariat on Acid Rain, 1982–); see "Critical Loads: the Limits of Tolerance" *Acid News* (February 1993). For American events, see Douglas G. Fox et al., "A Screening Procedure to Evaluate Air Pollution Effects on Class I Wilderness Areas," U.S. Forest Service, Rocky Mountain Forest and Range Experiment Station, General Technical Report RM-168, known as the Cary Report; see also Forest Service/National Park Service, "Air Resource Management Quarterly Newsletter," published at various places, 1989– .

34. Theo Colborn, Frederick S. vom Saal, and Ana M. Soto, "Developmental Effects of Endocrine-Disrupting Chemicals in Wildlife and Humans, *Environmental Health Perspectives* 101, no. 5 (October 1993): 378–84; Theo Colborn, Dianne Dumanoski, and John

Peterson Myers, *Our Stolen Future: Are We Threatening Our Fertility, Intelligence, and Survival? A Scientific Detective Story* (New York: Dutton, 1996).

35. Thomas M Power, *Lost Landscapes and Failed Economies: The Search for Value of Place* (Washington, D.C.: Island Press, 1996).

36. Mary Keys Watson, "Behavioral and Environmental Aspects of Recreational Home Sales" (Ph.D. dissertation, Pennsylvania State University, 1975).

37. The classic statement of fragmentation is Larry D. Harris, *The Fragmented Forest* (Chicago: University of Chicago Press, 1984).

38. Samuel P. Hays, "From Conservation to Environment: Environmental Politics Since World War II," *Environmental Review* 6 (1982): 14–41.

39. For analysis of one regional context for these tensions, see John B. Wright, *Rocky Mountain Divide: Selling & Saving the West* (Austin, Tex.: University of Texas Press, 1993); Jim Robbins, *Last Refuge: The Environmental Showdown in Yellowstone and the American West* (New York: William Morrow and Co., 1993); Charles F. Wilkinson, *Crossing the Next Meridian: Land, Water, and the Future of the West* (Washington, D.C.: Island Press, 1992).

40. For two contrasting approaches to this problem, see the statement by William Cronon, "The Trouble with Wilderness," and a response from Samuel P. Hays, "The Trouble With Bill Cronon's Wilderness," *Environmental History* 1, no. 1 (January 1996): 7–28, and 29–32.

41. Lester W. Milbraith, *Environmentalists: Vanguard for a New Society* (Albany, N.Y. State University of New York Press, 1984).

42. See Samuel P. Hays, "Restructing Environmental Big Business Revisited: A Critique of an Essay by Christopher Broerner and Jennifer Chilton Kallery of the Center for American Business, privately printed and circulated (Pittsburgh, 1995).

43. See Hays, *Beauty, Health, and Permanence*, 329–62, 392–426, 458–90 for general statements, journals in law such as *Ecology Law Quarterly* (Berkeley: University of California Law School), or science, *Environmental Science and Technology* (Washington, D.C.: American Chemical Society) provided more extensive details in those fields.

44. For a representative example, see Council on Environmental Quality et al., "Public Opinion on Environmental Issues; Results of a National Public Opinion Survey" (Washington, D.C.: Council on Environmental Quality, 1980).

45. Two of the earliest studies based on disaggregated analysis are The Continental Group, *Toward Responsible Growth: Economic and Environmental Concern in the Balance; the Continental Group Report* (Stamford, Conn.: The Continental Group, 1982); American Forest Institute, *The Public's Participation in Outdoor Activities and Attitudes Toward National Wilderness Areas,* prepared by Opinion Research Corporation (Princeton, N.J., 1977). These forays into disaggregation are more than limited and the disaggregated units are organized only in terms of broad regions without definition in terms of environmental circumstance. The disaggregation provided by analysis of votes in the U.S. House of Representatives provide for far more units—435 in all—and enables them to be grouped into more meaningful geographical units; see Samuel P. Hays, "Environmental Political Culture and Environmental Political Development: An Analysis of Legislative Voting, 1971–1989, 29n.

46. James J. Kennedy and Thomas M. Quigley, "How Entry-Level Employees, Forest Supervisors, Regional Foresters and Chiefs View Forest Service Values and the Reward System," a 1989 survey done for the Sunbird Conference, Tucson, Ariz., November 13–16, 1989.

47. Hays, "Environmental Political Culture," 29n.

48. See Wisconsin's Environmental Decade Institute, *Fool's Wisdom: An Analysis of the*

Anti-Conservation Movement in the Midwest (Wisconsin's Environmental Decade Institute, 1996); see page 37 for campaign contributions from various anticonservation sources.

49. Hays, *Beauty, Health and Permanence,* is organized around the emergence of these three values; see 1–70.

50. Ibid., 22–24, 34–39.

51. The dominant intellectual analysis of the relationship between humans and nature emphasizes the human desire to fit modern urban society into a natural setting, but the dominant theme of efforts to protect nature are in terms of fitting nature into an urbanized society. See, for example, the exchange between William Cronon and Samuel P. Hays in *Environmental History Review.*

52. The best account of long-term changes in attitudes toward nature and wildlife is Kellert, *The Values of Life.*

53. For lead see Samuel P Hays, "Science and Values: Lead in Historical Perspective," in Herbert I. Needleman, ed., *Lead in Humans* (Boca Raton, Fla., CRC Press, 1992).

54. For the new health focus of the sixties and thereafter, see Hays, *Beauty, Health and Permanence,* 24–26.

55. Samuel P. Hays, "The New Environmental West" *Journal of Policy History* 3, no. 3 (1991): 223–48. The best general source for events in the West is *High Country News* published in Paonia, Colorado. For its early history see Susan J Harlow, "High Country News: Survival and Change," M.A. thesis, University of Wyoming, Department of Journalism and Telecommunication, 1981.

56. See, as an example, Michael Berger, *The Devil Wagon in God's Country: The Automobile and Social Change in Rural America 1893–1929* (Hamden, 1979).

57. Robert W. Marans and John D. Wellman, *The Quality of Nonmetropolitan Living: Evaluations, Behaviors, and Expectations of Northern Michigan Residents* (Ann Arbor: Survey Research Center, Institute for Social Research, 1978).

58. Urban nature preservation has been fostered especially by the Trust for Public Lands based in San Francisco. See its annual reports for the variety of such projects.

59. Robert W Adler, Jessica C Landman, and Diane M. Cameron, *The Clean Water Act 20 Years Later* (Washington, D.C.: Island Press and Natural Resources Defense Council, 1993).

60. Few analyses of environmental conditions in specific cities have been made. Two are Eric A. Goldstein and Mark A. Izeman, *The New York Environment Book* (Washington, D.C.: Island Press, 1990); and Mary D. Nichols and Stanley Young, *The Amazing LA Environment: A Handbook for Change* (Los Angeles: Living Planet Press, 1991). Both of these were sponsored by a citizen's group, the Natural Resources Defense Council. A more general attempt has been made by the World Resources Institute in his series, *The Information Please Environmental Almanac* published in 1992, 1993, and 1994. The almanac features comparative state assessments from data produced by the states but in order to develop comparative urban assessments it had to collect its own data from individual cities. See "Green Metro Areas," in the 1994 edition, pp. 193–218.

61. For a recent example of the rural/urban divide see a news item concerning the vote on the 1996 New York state bond act, "Bond Act Voting Lets Pataki widen his appeal as a Progressive," *New York Times,* November 7, 1996, B15, which includes a map indicating the county-by-county voting results.

62. See, for example, James M. Ridenour, *The National Parks Compromised: Pork Barrel Politics and America's Treasures* (Merrillville, Ind.: ICS Books, 1994).

63. Hays, *Beauty, Health and Permanence,* 426–57.

64. Hays, "Farmers and Environmental Issues," in ibid., 288–97.

65. J. Christopher Haney and Charles P. Schaadt, "Pennsylvania Ecotourism: A Case Study," final report between the Center for Rural Pennsylvania and the Pennsylvania State University (DuBois, Pa.: Wildlife Technology Program, School of Forest Resources, The Pennsylvania State University, DuBois Campus, 1994) For the rails-to-trails program see "Trailblazer," newsletter of the Rails to Trails Conservancy (Washington, D C , 1986–). For the International Wolf Center, see "International Wolf" (Ely, Minn.: International Wolf Center, 1990–).

The Future of Environmental Regulation

1. For an analysis of value changes underlying environmental affairs, see Samuel P. Hays, *Beauty, Health and Permanence: Environmental Politics in the United States, 1955–1985.* (New York: Cambridge University Press, 1987). See also a disaggregate regional analysis of environmental values, based upon voting patterns in the U.S. House of Representatives, Samuel P. Hays, "Environmental Political Culture and Environmental Political Development: An Analysis of Legislative Voting, 1971–1989," *Environmental History Review* (summer 1992) 1–22.

2. USEPA, Science Advisory Board, "Reducing Risk: Setting Priorities and Strategies for Environmental Protection," SAB-EC 90-021. Washington, D.C., September 1990.

3. For continued coverage of visibility monitoring generally, see *Improve,* a newsletter of Interagency Monitoring of Protected Visual Environments, issued by Air Resource Specialists, Inc., Ft. Collins, Colo., 1992– . For a recent event in these continuing proceedings see "New Air Regs Seen From Effort to Curb Haze in Colorado Plateau," *Clean Air Report* VI, no. 14 (July 13, 1995): 26–27. For the Grand Canyon Issue generally see the reports of the Grand Canyon Visibility Transport Commission, Western Governors' Association, Denver, Colorado.

4. European activity concerning nitrogen deposition is outlined in Michael Freemantle, "The Acid Test for Europe," *Chemical and Engineering News,* (May 1, 1995): 10–17; see also Timothy J. Sullivan, "Whole-System Nitrogen Effects Research in Europe," *Environmental Science and Technology* 27, no. 8 (1993): 1482–86; Plantlife, "The Acid Test for Plants" (London, 1993), a statement of the effect of deposition on British plants. European "acid rain" issues in general can be followed in *Acid News,* published by the Swedish NGO Secretariat on Acid Rain, Goteborg, Sweden.

5. The Clean Air Act of 1990 required EPA to undertake a study to determine if the provisions of the act would be sufficient to protect lakes in the Adirondacks. It also required EPA to make a "critical load" determination as to the level of deposition which would be generally acceptable. When the ensuing EPA study did not do so the Adirondack Council sued and the state's congressional delegation, save for one member, wrote EPA urging that more stringent controls be placed on sources in upwind states. For recent events, see "EPA Admits: Acid Rain Program Won't Save the Adirondacks," *Adirondack Council Newsletter* (Spring 1995): 8; USEPA, "Acid Deposition Standard Feasibility Study Report to Congress; Draft for Public Comment," EPA 430-RE-95-001, Washington, D.C., February 1995; "New York Senate Pushes for Stronger Acid Rain Program," *Clean Air Report* 6, no. 8 (April 20, 1995): 21. "Rep. Solomon Urges Increased Protection for the Adirondacks," *Clean Air Report* 6. no. 14 (July 13, 1995): 20. "EPA Acid Deposition Study Faulted for Lack of Numerical Standard," *Clean Air Report* 6, no. 7 (April 6, 1995):

19. Industry, in turn, called for EPA to back up its draft study with a cost-benefit analysis; see *Clean Air Report* 6. no. 5 (March 9, 1995): 28–29. The toxic deposition program was called the "Great Waters" program. For an item in this ongoing focus on the issue, see "Deposition of Pollutants Into 'Great Waters' Leads EPA to Consider Stricter MACT Standards," *Environment Reporter* (May 29, 1994): 148–50.

6. For early statements of the environmental hormone issue, see Theo Coborn et al., "Developmental Effects of Endocrine-Disrupting Chemicals in Wildlife and Humans," *Environmental Health Perspectives* 101, no. 5 (October 1993): 378–84; Bette Hileman, "Environmental Estrogens Linked to Reproductive Abnormalities, Cancer," *Chemical and Engineering News* (January 31, 1994): 19–23. For recent reports which advance the complexity of the environmental hormone issue, see "Study Suggests Hormone Disruptors Act Via Whole New Mechanism," *Risk Policy Report* 2, no. 6 (June 16, 1995): 3–4; Janet Raloff, "Beyond Estrogens; Why Unmasking Hormone-Mimicking Pollutants Proves So Challenging," *Science News* 148 (July 15, 1995): 44–46. For a specific recent study that indicates the course of the science, see "Study Finds PCBs Harm Great Lakes Birds' Immune Systems," *Water Policy Report* 4, no. 13 (June 21, 1995): 6. A different but corroborating perspective from Great Britain can be found in the publication *Ends Report*. See issue no. 246, July 1995, in a series of articles, "Oestrogenic Chemical Risks," 3–6.

7. Two recent publications state the case in defense of automobiles and utilities: "Clearing the Air: A Report on Emission Trends in Selected Cities," prepared by Energy and Environmental, Analysis, Inc., Arlington, Va., for the American Automobile Association (AAA, Washington, D.C., September 1994); and Public Policy Institute of New York State, Inc., "Coming Clean on the Clean Air Act" (Albany, N.Y., 1994). By September 1995 EPA was tending to focus on reducing NOx emissions from utilities. See "Reducing NOx From Utilities Center of OTAG Discussions," *Clean Air Report* 6, no. 18 (September 7, 1995): 6.

8. For a recent event in this development, see "Funding Pledge Underscores Success of EPA Watershed Program," *Water Policy Report* 4, no. 15 (July 19, 1995): 24–25. Citizen monitoring is playing a significant role in identifying the water quality of many streams, for example, tributaries, which the staffs of water quality agencies have not been able to achieve. See, for example, *The Volunteer Monitor*, the national newsletter of Volunteer Water Quality Monitoring (San Francisco, Calif., 1989–). Such monitoring helps to define these water systems as relatively closed rather than open-ended environmental circumstances. For a specific Pennsylvania case, see *Allarm Bulletin* published by the Alliance for Acid Rain Monitoring, Dickinson College, Carlisle, Pa., 1986– . For the kind of controversy that emerges when relative responsibility within a limited context is fought out, see a case of water very much like that of air: General Motors has argued that it is acid rain rather than its own discharges that are responsible for water pollution and now seems to be generalizing this argument to other locations. See *Water Quality Report* 4, no. 3 (February 1, 1995): 3.

9. The literature on the "ozone hole" is voluminous; one of the more informative secondary works is Sharon L. Roan, *Ozone Crisis: The Fifteen Year Evolution of a Sudden Global Emergency,* 1989.

10. Biodiversity presentations invariably call for more detail about species, communities, and habitats within finite land areas. See, for example, Pennsylvania Biodiversity Technical Committee, "Conserving Pennsylvania's Native Biological Diversity" (Harrisburg, Pa., Pennsylvania Fish and Boat Commission, 1995.

11. For an overview of habitat conservation programs, see Timothy Beatley, *Habitat*

Conservation Planning: Endangered Species and Urban Growth (Austin: University of Texas Press, 1994). For a chronology of the Balcones issue see clippings from the *Austin Statesman-American* in the author's files.

12. A brief account of the early conservation commission is in Hays, *Beauty, Health and Permanence,* 91–92; the activities of these local commissions can be followed best through their statewide coordinating organizations in New Jersey, New York, and most of the New England states.

13. See *Exchange,* the Journal of the Land Trust Alliance (Washington, D.C., 1981–); for a general history of the Alliance, see Land Trust Alliance, *The First Decade and Beyond* (n.p., n.d.).

14. The monthly tabloid of the Alliance for the Chesapeake Bay, *Bay Journal,* provides a running account of that program.

15. The three main land trusts of the northern lower peninsula of Michigan reflect these arrangements; they are the Little Traverse Conservancy at Petosky, Mich.; the Leelanau Conservancy in Leelanau County at Leland; and the four-county Grand Traverse Conservancy at Traverse City. Their newsletters and annual reports (author file) provide the details.

16. For an account of the evolution of cost-benefit analysis from the vantage point of the early 1980s, see Hays, "The Politics of Economic Analysis," *Beauty, Health and Permanence,* 364–78. For a current issue involving cost-benefit analysis of the entire clean air program, required by the 1990 Clean Air Act, see "Preliminary Findings of Study Show Benefits of Air Act Outweigh Its Costs, Official Says," *Environment Reporter* 26, no. 8 (July 14, 1995): 555–56.

17. A brief account of the early years of the criteria document process is in Hays, *Beauty, Health and Permanence,* 73–76. For the dispute over the first sulfur oxides document, see "Air Quality Criteria for Sulfur Oxides Set by HEW," *Environmental Science and Technology* 1 (1967): 282–86; 1 (1967): 400; *Journal of the Air Pollution Control Association* 18 (1968): 443–47; Senate Subcommittee on Air and Water Pollution, *Air Pollution —1967,* 1456–67, 2404–05.

18. The short-lived popularity of cost-effectiveness analysis during the Carter administration can be followed in Hays, *Beauty, Health and Permanence,* 368, with citations to "Economists Jump into Pollution Control Scraps," *CF Letter* (August 1978), The Conservation Foundation, Washington, D.C.; and Richard E. Ayres, "Trading Health for Dollars," *Amicus Journal* 3 (Winter 1980): 5–6.

19. The report of the National Acid Precipitation Assessment Program is voluminous. A more condensed statement of the problem, both the provisions of the statute and the work remaining to be done is in the "1992 Report to Congress" of NAPAP (Washington, D.C., 1992).

20. Samuel P. Hays, "The Role of Values in Science and Policy: The Case of Lead," in Herbert L. Needleman, *Human Lead Exposure* (Boca Raton, Fla.: CRC Press, 1992), 267–83.

21. EPA Science Advisory Board, "Reducing Risk."

22. See USEPA, Office of Research and Development, *Ecological Risk Assessment Issue Papers: Risk Assessment Forum,* EPA/630/R 94/009" (Washington, D.C., 1994). For a recent event in this development, see "Scientists Says Current Ecological Risk Concepts Inadequate," *Risk Policy Report,* 2 (July 21, 1995): 20. This is a statement by James Karr, Institute for Environmental Studies at the University of Washington, Seattle, to the Pres

ident's Commission on Risk Assessment and Risk Management, entitled "Risk Assessment: We Need More Than an Ecological Veneer."

23. For the Illinois case, see "State's Failed Cost-Benefit Law Touted as Lesson for Congress," *Risk Policy Report* 2, no. 6 (June 16, 1995): 32–33. "The benefits analysis always proved 'foggy' . . . because it was difficult to quantify the benefits of a cleaner stream or other environmental conditions a rule might help to achieve." "Moreover, cost-benefit analyses inescapably had to address the question of what value to place on a human life because benefits analysis is, essentially, a question of 'acceptable risk.'" A leader of the U.S. Chamber of Commerce "expresses significant misgivings about trying to calculate costs and benefits because the benefits analysis runs into the insurmountable 'political value' of how much a human life is worth. In Illinois, the cost-benefit requirement created a "quagmire," with rules stagnating because decisions over benefits were not made."

24. See "EPA Issues Long-Awaited Great Lakes Rule, Despite Major Opposition," *Water Policy Report*, special report (March 15, 1995); "Three Industry Groups File First Challenges to EPA Great Lakes Plan," *Water Policy Report* 4, no. 15 (July 19, 1995): 21–22; "Governors' Great Lakes Cost Analysis Bogs Down in Controversy," *Water Policy Report* 4, no. 15 (July 19, 1995): 28; "Industry Report to Show No Net Benefits from Great Lakes Program," *Water Policy Report* 4, no. 18 (August 30, 1995): p. 3: "The industry study may be the only alternative to EPA's cost/benefit study, given that the final draft of the DRI/McGraw Hill analysis commissioned by the Council of Great Lakes Governors (CGLG) does not contain a benefits assessment."

25. It seems rather significant that the publication *Risk Policy Report* devotes considerable space to the controversies over the science, and almost none to the issue of the context of trade-offs. The implication is that the first is a matter of live substance and debate and the second is simply an idea to which little contribution is being made.

26. The state relative risk proceedings can be followed *in The Comparative Risk Bulletin* 1– (January 1991–), The Northeast Center for Comparative Risk, Vermont Law School, South Royalton, Vt. From this source one can access the reports, newsletters, and proceedings from the various states. See, for example, "The ACERP Update" from the Arizona Comparative Environmental Risk Project, May 1995, No. 3, which includes a brief statement of the ranking of Arizona environmental problems drawn up by the project's Public Advisory Committee.

One of the most ambitious—and controversial—of the state relative risk programs was in California, in which the report was attacked by industry and became deeply involved in executive-level political strategies. For the report, see "Toward the Twenty-first Century: Planning for the Protection of California's Environment." Final Report Submitted to California Environmental Protection Agency by California Comparative Risk Project (Sacramento, May 1994). For accounts of the episode, see "Strock Pulls Implementation Memo, Jeopardizing Risk-Ranking Report," *Inside Cal/EPA* 5, no. 24 (June 17, 1994): 1–14; "The Report of the Comparative Risk Project," *California Environmental Insider* (June 30, 1994): 4–8; "CAL/EPA Receives Wave of Appeals to Reject Risk-Ranking Project," *Inside Cal/EPA*, 3–6; "Some Fear California Risk-Ranking Report May Fall By Wayside," *Risk Policy Report* (January 20, 1995) 28–30; "California Report Sets Standard for Comparing Risks," *Science* 266 (October 14, 1994): 214.

27. An ideological approach to environmental issues is taken by the Competitive Enterprise Institute of Washington, D.C. For example, in the "Keystone Dialog on Incentives for Private Landowners to Protect Endangered Species," conducted by the Keystone

Center in Colorado, R. J. Smith, senior environmental scholar at the institute, dropped out of the discussions on the grounds that endangered species action should be voluntary rather than regulatory. See Richard Stone "Incentives Offer Hope for Habitat," *Science* 269 (September 1, 1995): 1212–13.

28. John Baden is a prolific "free enterprise" writer on environmental affairs. A capsule source of his articles is the Publication *Free Perspectives,* issued by the Foundation for Research on Economics and the Environment (1987–), located initially at Bozeman, Montana, and later also in Seattle, Washington.

29. A highly useful source for these "land saving" activities is the newsletter *Common Ground,* published by the Conservation Fund (Arlington, Va., 1990–).

30. Sam Hays, "Emissions Trading Mythology," *The Environmental Forum* (January/February 1995): 15–20.

31. In challenging the EPA selection of the average of the top 10 percent as the "average of the best" requirement in the Clean Water Act of 1972, industry argued that the provision in the statute called for the median; the court rejected the argument.

32. One current issue that seems to be amenable to these influences—technology generalizing—is the EPA initiative toward a multimedia strategy for the pulp and paper industry. The technology seems to have advanced well in Europe and it has been mainly a matter of persuading the America industry to make the investment decisions.

33. Direct consumer based initiatives, e.g., Proposition 65 in California, or pesticide-free food, both reflect the workings of the consumer market on production innovations. The Proposition 65 program in California was considered to be so successful that it became a part of the risk assessment debate in Congress in 1995. "California Toxics Law Draws Strong Commission Interest," *Risk Policy Report* 2, no. 2 (February 21, 1995): 18–19; "Risk Group Urges 'Incentive' System Akin to California's 'Prop 65,'" *Risk Policy Report* 2, no. 2 (February 21, 1995): 22–25.

34. It is more than difficult to analyze the proceedings of trade associations since a documentary record is rarely available. The best historical insight comes from the public record in the some six hundred "codes of fair competition" developed under the National Industrial Recovery Act during the early 1930s when each industry segment developed a decision-making method for its members and worked out voting procedures.

35. *Project 88; Harnessing Market Forces to Protect Our Environment: Initiatives for the New President,* A Public Policy Study sponsored by Senator Timothy E. Wirth, Colorado, and Senator John Heinz, Pennsylvania (Washington, D.C., 1988).

36. The views of the clean air industry can be followed briefly but regularly in a column in the monthly publication of the National Air Pollution Control Association, later the Air and Waste Management Association (Pittsburgh, Pa.).

37. "Seven Faucet Manufacturers to Eliminate Lead in Their Products Over Next Four Years," *Environment Reporter* 26, no. 18 (1995): 865.

38. "U.S. Will Begin Effort to Halve Truck Pollution," *New York Times,* July 11, 1945, Dl, D7; "Regulators, Engine Makers Agree on Plan to Begin Reducing Diesel Emissions in 2004," *Environment Reporter* 26, no. 11 (July 14, 1995): 565–66; "New Limits Planned for Heavy-Duty Engines: Agency Seeks Comments in Developing Proposal," *Environment Reporter* 26, no. 18 (September 1, 1995): 860.

39. For the Pennsylvania issue, see the author's file that follows the media coverage, the legislative reports, and the departmental and citizen environmental publicity.

40. See, for example, *Wetlands: Characteristics and Boundaries* (Washington, D.C.:

National Research Council, 1995); for a brief review, see *Water Policy Report* 4, no. 11 (May 24, 1995), 4.

41. The context of the Reagan administration can be followed in Hays, *Beauty, Health and Permanence*, 491–526.

42. Discussion of federal-state relationships usually fails to recapture two major points: (1) that since World War II, among the three levels of government, state governments have grown the most, local governments the next, and the federal government the least, measured by both expenditures and personnel; and (2) that the major issues of public debate, such as health, education, environment, civil rights, the elderly, have involved an interweaving of programs at all levels of government, each level making a distinctive contribution to the whole. Effective discussion requires the reconstruction of these institutional patterns which turn out to be quite different from the results of the ideological analysis.

43. See the newsletter of the Michigan Land Use Institute (Benzonia, Mich., 1993–), and the author's clipping file.

44. Samuel P. Hays, "The New Environmental West," *Journal of Policy History* 3, no. 3 (1991): 223–48. Transfer of federal lands to the western states inevitably raises the comparison, within the West, between how the states manage their thirty-five million acres of state-owned land and how the transfer would affect those policies. Would the transfer apply the limited uses of state-owned lands to the federally acquired lands, or would the wider range of uses of federal lands be applied to state lands? Eastern observers rarely understand this context because of the intensive overlay of state-federal ideological debate. Within the West, competing political forces go in these alternative directions and form the basis of larger public land debates. This issue thwarted the "transfer to the states" proposals of Secretary James Watt during the Reagan administration, and it is this same issue that lurks behind similar moves in the 104th Congress.

45. A recent expression of this interstate role of air pollution is the litigation initiated by the state of Maine against EPA on the grounds that because EPA does not control sources of emissions upwind of Maine in the Mid-Atlantic and Mid-Western states, Maine cannot meet its ozone standards. See "Maine Request First Warning Shot in Debate Over Regional Controls," *Clean Air Report* 4, no. 17 (August 24, 1995): 8–9.

46. The wide variation in state environmental performance has been the subject of several comparative state studies. See, for example, Bob Hall and Mary Lee Kerr, *1991–1992 Green Index: A State-by-State Guide to the Nation's Environmental Health* (Washington, D.C.: Island Press, 1991).

47. Analysis of the patterns of political forces in environmental politics is still quite primitive. Books about environmental organizations are produced in amateurish fashion, both in the quality of the analysis and the evidence used and hence is quite wanting, while the study of regulated industry politics is all but nonexistent. See the treatment in Hays, *Beauty, Health and Permanence*, 287–328.

48. Few studies sort out the patterns of political environmental impulses over the past several decades. There have been a number of "exposes" of environmental organizations which are cast in the context of advisory prescriptions as to what they do wrong and how they should change, but not in terms of a systematic analysis of their political development. See, for example, Christopher Boerner and Jennifer Chilton Callery, "Restructuring Environmental Big Business" (Center for the Study of American Business, Washington University, St. Louis, 1995), and Samuel P. Hays, "Restructuring Environmental Big Business Revisited" (typescript). At the same time, there have been even

fewer attempts to examine systematically the environmental opposition as a continuing political impulse that changes and develops over the years.

49. For the Easterbrook argument, see Gregg Easterbrook, *A Moment on the Earth* (New York: Viking, 1995), 369–85.

50. "Tall Timber and the E.P.A.: Three Companies and Three Strategies," *New York Times,* May 21, 1995, 1–12.

51. For a general treatment of the National Coal Policy Project, see Hays, *Beauty, Health and Permanence,* 417. For the project report, see Francis X. Murray, ed., *Where We Agree: Report of the National Coal Policy Project,* 2 vols. Published in cooperation with the Center *for Strateg*ies and International Studies, Georgetown University (Boulder, Colo.: Westview Press, 1978).

52. Leadership in this venture was taken by Sam Gusman of the Conservation Foundation. It can be followed, along with related articles, in *Toxic Substances Journal,* vol. 5. 1–5 (New York, 1979–83). See, as a brief statement, Sam Gusman, "TSCA: Hopes and Fears," *Toxic Substances Journal* 1, no. 4 (Spring 1980): 306–15.

53. The TWF process was little known outside the state of Washington. It can be followed most readily in the regular reports of the project through the participation of representatives of the Washington Environmental Council as they reported in the newsletter of the Washington Environmental Council (Seattle, Wash.), and through the Publication *Totem,* of the Washington State Department of Natural Resources.

54. The current controversy over the criteria assessment document for particulates indicates an escalation of the complexity and the disputes in one of the six criteria pollutants. *Risk Policy Report* covered the recent deliberations over a draft of the document (Aug. 18, 1995, vol. 2, no. 8, 161–21). The article posed the issue squarely, "Scientists are squaring off EPA's ongoing review of its federal air quality standard for particulates." See also "Science Committee Expresses Frustration Over PM Document," *Clean Air Report* 6, no. 16 (August 10, 1995): 13–14. For ozone, see "Ozone Standard Debate Heats Up Over Studies, EPA Draft Proposals," *Risk Policy Report* 2, no. 3 (March 17, 1995): 13. For up-to-date treatment of the range of issues involved in the assessments, see "Definition of 'Adverse' Key to Determining Possible Changes to EPA's Ambient Rules," *Environment Reporter,* June 23, 1995, 445–46. The EPA dioxin review involved similar issues but carried the debate further to take on various interpretations of the way in which the EPA Science Advisory Board responded to the discussion. See "SAB Members Concerned over Industry 'Spin' on Panel's Dioxin Review," *Risk Policy Report* 2. no. 6 (June 16, 1995): 20–23.

55. Important sources for exploratory science are *Environmental Science and Technology, Waste Management, Conservation Biology,* and *Natural Areas Journal.*

56. Sources for defensive science in the regulated industry are *EPRI Journal* and *Journal of Forestry.* For reports from the Chemical Industry Institute of Toxicology, see its two publications, *CIIT Activities* and *CIIT Impact,* published from Research Triangle Park, North Carolina.

57. The tobacco issue represents the left-end extreme on the spectrum, with the lead issue close to it. The EMS issue is well along the spectrum from the right toward the middle, about at the 35 percent mark. The global warming issue stands at about the 60 percent mark and the stratospheric ozone issue at 75 percent. These are not precise, but illustrative of the sequence of development across the spectrum.

58. For a statement which identifies the current relationship between ecological science and the forestry profession, see Samuel P. Hays, "A Challenge to the Profession of Forestry," in James C. Finley and Stephen B. Jones, eds., *Practicing Stewardship and Liv-*

ing a Land Ethic, Proceedings of the 1991 Penn State Forest Resources Issues Conference, Harrisburg, Pa., Mar. 26–27, 1991. (School of Forest Resources, The Pennsylvania State University, 1992).

59. For events in natural resource damage regulations, see "NOAA Plan Would Allow Controversial Damage Assessment Method," *Water Policy Report* (January 19, 1994), 3–4; "Ongoing Battle Over Major Resource Valuation Method, Natural Resource Damage Reg Imminent Under Settlement Agreement," *Water Policy Report* 4, no. 15 (July 19, 1995): 29–30. The report stresses the problem of valuing "non-use value" of resources; it states that "non-use value" refers to resources that "lack market value, but whose mere existence is deemed valuable."

60. The 1989 NRDC report was *Intolerable Risk: Pesticides in Our Children's Food* (February 27, 1989).

61. Citations to a few of the missed stories: (1) The scientific and professional context out of which the nine members of the study's peer review, listed in the front of the report, worked; (2) the proceedings in Massachusetts and New York three years before, a proceeding that was well covered in *Chemical Regulation Reporter* as well as in technical studies carried out by those two states; (3) The Senate hearings, U.S. Senate, Committee on Environment and Public Works, Subcommittee on Toxic Substances, Environmental Oversight, Research and Development, "Chemicals and Food Crops," May 15, 1989; (4) The activities of the Science Advisory Panel in the daminozide (alar) case in the subcommittee report, "Government Regulation of Pesticides in Food: The Need for Administrative and Regulatory Reform," 101st Congress, 1st Session, S. Prt. 101–55 (Washington D.C.: GPO, 1989); (5) the outcome of the court case brought by the apple growers which was not reported widely, if at all, and which the judge dismissed with the statement that the NRDC report "is not a polemical tract preying on raw emotions and irrational fears. . . . There are no theatrics, no histrionic expressions of outrage and no visual or auditory hyperbole. . . . As it relates to apples *Risk* is in large measure premised on [Alar manufacturer] Uniroyal's own market-basket and carcinogenicity studies conducted in response to an EPA directive 1984." The foregoing material is in the author's files.

The New Environmental Forest

1. Pub. L. No. 94–588, 90 Stat. 2949 (codified at 16 U..C. §§ 1600–1614 (1982) and other scattered sections of 16 U.S.C.).

2. See generally D. Le Master, *Decade of Change: The Remaking of Statutory Authority During the 1970s* (1985); Wilkinson and Anderson, *Land and Resource Planning in the National Forests,* 64 *Or. L. Rev.* 1 (1985); *The Wilderness Society, Forests of the Future?: An Assessment of the National Forest Planning Process* (1987); Ring, *Taming the Forests,* a series in *The Arizona Star,* February 5–12, 1984; Brewer and Teare, *Our National Forests: A Time of Turmoil,* Gannett News Service special report (1987); *Timber Cutting Replaces Wilderness as Number One Forest Management Issue,* Land Letter, February 1, 1985, a l; *Conflict Looms Over Forest Plans in Northwest States,* Land Letter, July 15, 1986, at 1. This paper relies heavily on *Forest Planning,* later *Forest Watch,* published by Cascade Holistic Economic Consultants from 1981 to the present, for evidence about environmental objectives in forest planning; it is the best and most extensive single source reflecting such views. In sharp contrast, publications such as *Journal of Forestry* (Society of American Foresters) or *American Forestry* (American Forestry Association) provide only scanty in-

formation about either planning issues or environmental objectives; for the analyst of administrative politics they have limited value.

3. For a more extended analysis of the value changes implicit in a wide range of environmental affairs, including forest management, see S. Hays, *Beauty, Health and Permanence: Environmental Politics in the United States, 1955–85* (1987).

4. See National Environmental Policy Act, 42 U.S.C. §§ 4321–47 (1982) [hereinafter NEPA]; Administrative Procedure Act, 5 U.S.C. §§ 551–75 (1982); Wilderness Act of 1964, 16 U.S.C. §§ 1131–36 (1982).

As environmentalists became more deeply involved in substantive issues in forest management they emphasized the limitations of NEPA. "The major shortcoming of NEPA is that its provisions have been held to be procedural in nature." The *Wilderness Society, Issues to Raise in a Forest Plan Appeal: A Citizens Handbook* 67 (1986) [hereinafter *Wilderness Society Handbook*]. An Oregon attorney involved in several forest management cases, Neil Kagan, contrasted the substantive potential of the NFMA of 1976 with NEPA in this fashion: "NEPA is mostly procedural: Did they jump through the right hoops to justify a timber sale? But [under the] NFMA, [the timber companies] have to limit their logging to areas that can be restocked adequately. They have to take actions to preserve habitat. In a sense, there is more of a substantive opportunity for the public to direct the management of the forests than is the case with other agency-managed resources." Schwartz, *Public Interest Attorneys Protecting the Forests, 7:3 Forest Watch* 9, 15 (September 1986) (quoting Neil Kagan).

One of the authors of NEPA, Lynton B. Caldwell, has described the atrophy of the substantive provisions of the statute: "The substantive provisions of NEPA—its declared goals and principles stated in Section 101 and 204-have not been regarded by the court as [amenable] to judicial review and have therefore been discounted as effective law." Caldwell, *NEPA'S Unfulfilled Potential, 3 Envtl. Forum* 38, 38 (1985). This turn of affairs could be contrasted with the Washington State Environmental Policy Act, *Wash. Rev. Code Ann.* §§ 43.21C.010–.914 (1988), patterned closely after the federal act, which the state courts have interpreted substantively. See Settle, "Environmental Assessment: The Washington State Environmental Policy Act," 2 *Northwest Envtl. J.* 35 (Summer 1986).

The Wilderness Society Handbook, however, made clear the continued value of NEPA in bringing issues and information to light and cited how the act's use could be expanded. In January 1985, the Office of General Counsel of the Department of Agriculture pointed out three major deficiencies in forest plan environmental impact statements ("EIS"): (a) they contained an inadequate range of alternatives, (b) the discussion of silviculture techniques gave inadequate treatment to selective or unevenage management, as opposed to clearcutting, and (c) they inadequately analyzed the environmental impacts of proposed timber harvesting on the resources of the forest. See Memorandum from James P. Perry, Offices of General Counsel, to R. Max Peterson, Chief, Forest Service (January 25, 1985), *(rpt. in Wilderness Society Handbook, supra, at E–1 to E–4)*.

5. The substantive provisions of the National Forest Management Act can be contrasted with the lack of such provisions in the Federal Land Policy and Management Act of 1976, 43 U.S.C. §§ 1701–84 (1982 and Supp. III 1986), dealing with the lands administered by the Bureau of Land Management. When environmentalists brought a lawsuit to require BLM to modify grazing permits on the grounds that the agency was overgrazing, Judge James M. Burns wrote: "Plantiffs are understandably upset at what they view to be a lopsided and ecologically insensitive pattern of management of public lands at the hands of the BLM. . . . Congress attempted to remedy this situation . . . but it has done so

with only the broadest sorts of discretionary language, which does not provide helpful standards by which a court can readily adjudicate agency compliance." *National Resources Defense Council, Inc. v. Hodel*, 624 F. Supp. 1045, 1062 (D. Nev. 1985). For reaction by environmentalists, see "Court Rules Against NRDC in Reno Grazing District," *PLI Newsletter* (Public Lands Institute, Natural Resources Defense Council) (January/February 1986), at 3.

6. See Anderson and Wilkinson, "Meeting the Criteria: The Law, Decision-making . . . and the Fate of the Forest Plan," 5:9 *Forest Planning* 14 (December 1984), which deals with resource standards as legal standards that the agency is required to follow.

7. See *Opinion Research Corporation, The Public's Participation in Outdoor Activities and Attitudes Toward National Wilderness Areas* 108 (1977) (to the question, "Do you think the U.S. Forest Service should try to increase the yield and sale of timber from the national forests, or should it continue to preserve these trees in their natural state," 28 percent agreed with the "increase yield" option and 62 percent sided with the "preserve these trees" option). See also S. Kellert, et al., American *Attitudes, Knowledge and Behaviors Toward Wildlife and Natural Habitats,* pts. I–V (1979–1983); Kellert, *Wildlife Values and the Private Landowner,* 90:11 *Am. Forests* 27 (November 1984); Mary Keys Watson, "Behavioral and Environmental Aspects of Recreational Land Sales" (Ph.D. diss., Department of Geography, Pennsylvania State University, 1975); Hamilton and Rader, "Suburban Forest Owners: Goals and Attitudes Toward Forest Practices," *Northern Logger and Timber Processor* (July 1974), at 18–19; Paul V. Ellefson, Sally L. Palm and David C. Lothner, "Disposal of Publicly Owned Tax-Forfeited Land: A Minnesota Case Study," *Station Bulletin* 538–1980, Agricultural Experiment Stations, University of Minnesota (1980).

8. The Multiple-Use Sustained-Yield Act of 1960, 16 U.S.C. §§ 528–31 (1982), recognized five uses of the forest: range, timber, recreation, fish and wildlife, and watershed. A sixth, wilderness, while not listed, was declared consistent with the mix of multiple uses. § 529. By the time of the debate over the National Forest Management Act of 1976, however, wilderness has achieved a more integral status among the mix of multiple uses. Richard M. Alston, in his report, "Forest: Goals and Decision Making in the Forest Service," USDA Forest Service Research Paper INT-128 (Ogden, Utah, 1972), sought to add a sixth use, "aesthetics," to the five in the act.

9. For a general review of wilderness politics, see C. Allin, *The Politics of Wilderness Preservation* (1982).

10. See *"Clear-Cutting" Practices on National Timberlands: Hearings Before the Subcomm. on Public Lands of the Senate Comm. on Interior and Insular Affs.* 92d Cong., 1st Sess., pts. 1–3 (1971); N. Wood, *Clearcut: The Deforestation of America* (1971); E. Horwitz, *Clearcutting: A View From the Top* (1974); J. Shepard, *The Forest Killers: The Destruction of the American Wilderness* (1975).

11. See West Virginia Div. of the Izaak Walton League of Am., Inc. v. Butz, 367 F. Supp. 422 (N.D.W. Va. 1973).

12. See *Forest and Rangeland Management Joint Hearings on S. 2851, S. 2926, and 3091 Before the Subcomm. on Envt., Soil Conservation and Forestry of the Senate Comm. on Agric. and Forestry, and the Subcomm. on Envt. and Land Resources of the Senate Comm. on Interior and Insular Affs.,* 94th Cong., 2nd Sess. (1976); *Forest Management Practices, Hearing on H.R. 10364, H.R. 11894, H.R. 12130 and H.R. 12503 Before the Subcomm. on Forests of the House Comm. on Agric.,* 94th Cong., 2nd Sess. (1976). Events can be followed from an environmental point of view in the *Sierra Club Bulletin. See* Evans, "New

Attack on the National Forests," 61:4 *Sierra Club Bull.* 16 (April 1976); "Last Stand for the National Forests?" 61:5 *Sierra Club Bull.* 36 (May 1976); "Forestry Bill Mark-up Completed in Senate—Floor Fight Next," 61:6 *Sierra Club Bull. 23* (June 1976); Evans, "Washington, D.C.: Last Days of the Forestry Bill," 61:10 *Sierra Club Bull.* 30 (Nov.–Dec. 1976).

13. Professional foresters joined in this argument. For a running account on their attitudes see the issues of the *Journal of Forestry* during the 1976 debate.

14. A number of witnesses speaking for the environmental group Coalition to Save the National Forests testified at the legislative hearings on the need to provide guidelines or standards for the Forest Services. See, e.g., testimony of Brock Evans, Ralph Nader, Thomas J. Barlow, and J. William Futrell, in *Forest and Rangeland Management, supra* note 12, at 522–25, 715–21. Futrell summed up the general view: "[The NFMA] improves on current law by focusing on standards and not on goals." *Id.* at 721. See also Barlow, "NRDC v. NFPA: Two Views on the Monongahela," 74:2 J. *Forestry* 87 (February 1976).

15. See 36 C.F.R. §§ 219.1–.29 (1987) for Forest Service planning regulations. The work of the Committee of Scientists can be followed in the minutes of its meetings, which include much associated material in the form of proposals and papers. (These materials are contained in the author's personal file. Copies may be obtained by writing to Professor Samuel P. Hays, Department of History, University of Pittsburgh, Pittsburgh, Pennsylvania 15260.) At a workshop held by the American Bar Association on the emerging regulations in late 1978, the general consensus was that they were not legally adequate and that "resulting litigation will be profuse." One speaker at the workshop emphasized that the Forest Service had not set up standards and guidelines as required by NFMA, but instead had established a process for setting up such standards and guidelines, and that the regulations thus provided "outstanding material for further litigation." See account of the meeting by Henry H. Carey of the John Muir Institute, in "Notes and Reflections, Meeting of the Committee of Scientists," November 1–2, 1978 (Seattle, Wash., 1978) (contained in author's file, *supra*).

16. *West Virginia Div. of the Izaak Walton league of Am., Inc. v. Butz,* 367 F. Supp. 422 (N.D.W. Va. 1973).

17. See *Forest and Rangeland Management, supra* note 12; literature of the Coalition to Save the National Forests (contained in author's file, *supra* note 15).

18. See, e.g., Mullen, "A Wilderness Group Returns to Planning," 2:1 *Forest Planning* 21 (Apr. 1981) (an account of the role of the Colorado Open Space Council in forest planning in that state). The range of groups involved in protest against the commodity emphasis in the plans varied with each case; their membership can be found in both the proceedings and the literature each group produced to organize support. See, e.g., the four-page tabloid produced by the Gifford Pinchot Task Force for the Gifford Pinchot National Forest in Washington (contained in author's file, *supra* note 15).

19. E.g., The Bighorn Forest Users Coalition, a group concerned with the Bighorn National Forest in Wyoming, brought together thirty-four groups including ranchers, archers, and bowhunters, wildlife organizations, outfitters, water users, a regional professional women's association, a resort owners association, several state organizations such as "Michiganites for the Bighorns," and the Sierra Club.

20. Crowell was widely featured in environmental literature as a target for opposition to national forest timber policies, much as James Watt was at the Department of the Interior. See Cone, "Crowell and the Shadow of Louisiana Pacific," 2:1 *Forest Planning* 13 (April 1981).

21. In addition to publication of Forest Planning (later Forest Watch), Cascade Holistic Economic Consultants ("CHEC") (based in Eugene, Oregon, since April 1980) also

has published the *CHEC Research Bulletin* occasionally since early 1983 as a service to its larger contributors, as well as a wide range of publications to aid citizens in participating in forest planning: *The Citizens' Guide to Forplan* (1983); *The Citizens' Guide to Forest Planning* (1982; rev. 1985); *The Citizens' Guide to Forestry and Economics* (1982). CHEC prepared a list of materials on forest planning for the use of citizen groups that reflects the range of relevant publications; see K. Fletcher, C. Williams and R. O'Toole, Forest Planning Bibliography, CHEC Research Paper No. 15 (February 1985).

22. The Wilderness Society's National Forest Action Center ("NFAC") publishes two newsletters at regular intervals, both beginning on November 1, 1986: *Bi-weekly Update* follows general policy issues and the substantive course of planning on each forest; *Forest Planning Monthly Report* charts the statistics on the issuance of draft and final plans, appeals and litigation. NFAC also published several handbooks: *Issues to Raise in a Forest Plan Appeal: A Citizen Handbook* (1986); *Protecting Water Quality in the National Forest Planning Process: A Citizen Handbook* (1986).

23. See *supra* note 8 and accompanying text. The DeFacto Forest Management Consensus Group, forced to protest the timber harvest and road building schedules on the Upper Green River area of the Bridger-Teton National Forest, argued that while for many years, "the forest land of northern Sublette County were prudently managed under the multiple use concept," this balance was now threatened by "large-scale timber and mineral interests [who] view this forest as a resource the economic potential of which is to be developed as completely and rapidly as possible. They have little or no concern for the long term effects of this program on the other users or on the forest itself." See *Consensus Statement of the Upper Green Forest Users Group* (contained in author's file, *supra* note 15). See also Minckler, "Multiple Use in Eastern Hardwood Forests," 3:9 *Forest Planning* 8 (December–January 1982–83).

24. The intensity of the value differences in forest planning is reflected in Alston, "The Holy War in Forest Planning," 4:7 *Forest Planning* 8 (October 1983). The differences are expressed frequently in environmental literature in contrasting statements of the desirable forest. See, e.g., the following excerpt from a flier disseminated by the Gifford Pinchot Task Force, concerned with planning on the Gifford Pinchot National Forest: "How would you like the Gifford Pinchot National Forest to look ten years from today? How about in 20 years or 50 years? Should the forest be a tree farm where all the trees are identical in size and appearance, evenly spaced, and growing without competition from grass, shrubs, other trees or wildlife? Should the forest be covered with a maze of logging roads and clearcuts that destroy wildlife habitat, obliterate trails, reduce water quality, harm fisheries and ruin breath-taking vistas? Or should the future forest have abundant and diverse fish and wildlife, clean water, majestic old growth forests, many miles of trails and stunning scenery? Should logging occur only in balance with these other resources?" (contained in author's file, *supra* note 15).

25. *National Forest Planning: A Conservationist's Guide* (1981). For a broad view of the environmental objectives in a single state, see "Conservationist's Alternatives" (part 1 & 2), *Idaho Conservation League Newsletter* (October 1981), at 1, and (November 1981), at 5.

26. The Wilderness Society, *Protecting Water Quality in the National Forest Planning Process* (1986); *National Wildlife Federation and Trout Unlimited, Forest Plans and Fisheries; Threat or Promise? A Report to the Regional Forester for the Northern Region on the Fisheries Resource in the Draft Forest Plans* (1985); Thaler, "Timber and Fish, Is It Possible To Manage Both?" 4:7 *Forest Planning* 11 (October 1983).

27. Thomas, "Toward the Managed Forest: Going Places We've Never Been," 7:2 *Forest Watch* 8 (August 1986), describes problems of providing for wildlife habitat in na-

tional forest management. Reid and Behman, "A Common Sense Approach to Grizzly Bear Habitat Evaluation," 8:4 *Forest Watch* 9 (October 1987), contrasts the practice of the Forest Service in describing grizzly bear habitat in terms of types of vegetation, land ownership patterns and policy concerns with that of wildlife biologists in tracing grizzly movements through radio-collar data and other methods developed by the Interagency Grizzly Bear Study Team.

28. 16 U.S.C. §§ 1531–43 (1982).

29. For values in wilderness, see R. Nash, *Wilderness and the American Mind* (1967); L. Graber, *Wilderness As Sacred Space* (1976).

30. For the historical context, see *Resources for the Future, Statistics on Outdoor Recreation*, ed. M. Clawson and C. Van Doren (1984). For a study pertaining to the eastern national forests, see "Forest Recreation: An Analysis With Special Consideration of the East," in *Report of the President's Advisory Commission on Timber and the Environment*, Appendix O (1973). For a recent update, see *The Report of the President's Commission on Americans Outdoors: The Legacy, the Challenge* (1987). Reaction to recent recreation proposals can be followed in the Washington, D.C., newsletter, *Federal Parks and Recreation* (see issues from 1985 to present).

31. Issues not dealt with here include cultural resources, recreation trails, wild and scenic rivers and wilderness. For cultural resources, see "Hearing Held in New Mexico, n 5:2 *Forest Planning* 4 (May 1984), and "Suit Filed in New Mexico," 5:5 *Forest Planning* 4 (August 1984); on hiking trails, see Spring, "National Forest Trails on the Wrong Path: Forest Planning Must Address Loss if Trail Miles and User Conflicts," 6:5 *Forest Planning* 8 (August 1985); on wild and scenic rivers, see Coyle and Dreher, "Protecting Wild and Scenic Rivers on the National Forests: An Overlooked Opportunity in Forest Planning," 7:8 *Forest Watch* 7 (March 1987); on wilderness, see Kerr, "Decision Sets Precedent: Judge Kaltor Points Out Inadequacies of Rare II," 4:10 *Forest Planning* 12 (January–February 1984), and Oregon Natural Resources Council, "Setting Aside Backcounty Areas: Deciding the Fate of National Forest Roadless Areas," 5:6 *Forest Planning* 16 (September 1984).

32. 33 U.S.C. §§ 1251–1376 (1982).

33. 40 C.F.R. § 131.12 (1987). See generally Anderson, "Water Quality Planning for the National Forests," 17 *Envtl. L.* 591 (1987).

34. 33 U.S.C. § 1288 (1982). These are often referred to as "208 Plans."

35. A review of state forest practice laws is Paul V. Ellefson and Frederick W. Cubbage, "State Forest Practice Laws and Regulations; A Review and Case Study for Minnesota," State Bulletin 536–1980, Agricultural Experiment Station, University of Minnesota (St. Paul, 1980). For water quality issues, see "Plans Ignore Fisheries," 6:9 *Forest Watch* 8 (April 1986); Thaler, "Lawyer's Lawdust," 5:6 *Forest Planning* 8 (September 1984); Stahl, "Trout Won't Bite for Beaverhead N. P. Plan," 1:7 *Forest Planning* 17 (October 1980); "Cracking Down on Water Pollution by National Forest Activities," 7:9 *Forest Watch* 4 (April 1987).

36. For a critique of the analysis of landslide potential in the Clearwater National Forest draft plan, see *The Wilderness Society, A Critique of the Clearwater Forest Plan* (1985). Problems with sedimentation from logging helped to sharpen the issue of potential landslides in the Mapleton District of the Siuslaw National Forest. A federal judge halted the sale of timber in the entire Mapleton Ranger District until the Forest Service prepared an adequate EIS. Judge Gus Solomon wrote, "Road building and timber harvesting have dramatically increased the rate of landslide erosion." See *National Wildlife Federation v. United States Forest Serv.*, 592 F. Supp. 931, 934 (D. Or. 1984). See also "Tim-

ber Sales Halted in Mapleton District," 5:1 *Forest Planning* 4 (April 1984): "Mapleton Lawsuit Makes Waves, 5:2 *Forest Planning* 6 (May 1984).

In *Northwest Indian Cemetery Protective Ass'n v. Peterson,* 764 F.2d 581 (th Cir. 1985), *aff'd in part, vacated as moot in part on reh'g,* 795 F.2d 688 (9th Cir. 1986), *rev'd in part on other grounds sub nom. Lyng v. Northwest Indian Cemetery Protective Ass'n,* 56 U.S.L.W. 4292 (U.S. April 16, 1988), the court held that the BMPs were not to supplant state water quality standards, but instead were to act as a means to achieve the appropriate state standards. One commentator noted, "*[Northwest Cemetery]* adds substantive requirements to what has been largely an exercise in procedure." Thaler, "Lawyer's Lawdust," 6:5 *Forest Planning* 6 (August 1985). Shortly after the *Northwest Cemetery* case, Undersecretary of Agriculture Peter Myers asked the EPA to exempt the Forest Service from complying with the decision by ruling that BMPs constitute compliance with the Clean Water Act. Environmentalists, in turn, held a meeting (proceeded by a letter signed by eleven of the nation's largest environmental organizations) with Lee Thomas, EPA administrator, urging him to reject Myers's request. See accounts in The Wilderness Society's *Bi-weekly Update,* October 6 and December 1, 1986 (with copy of the letter to Myers in the December 1 issue).

37. An environmental view of the California Forest Practice Act is contained in The Man Who Walks in the Woods, "The California Forest Practices Act: Is It Tough Enough?," 7:1 *Forest Watch* 7 (July 1986).

38. The Idaho issue can be followed in The Wilderness Society's *Bi-Weekly Update,* June 16 and July 1, 1986; March 16, September 14, October 19, and November 16, 1987. It can also be followed in the newsletters of the Idaho Conservation League and the Idaho Environmental Council and the newspaper *The Idaho Citizen,* published in Boise, Idaho.

39. H.B. 3396, 64th Leg., Reg. Sess. (1987). For coverage of this dispute, see *Earthwatch Oregon,* published monthly by the Oregon Environmental Council, 1986–1988.

40. The Washington state forest issue can be followed in *Alert,* a Publication of the Washington Environmental Council; see also Wells, "Alternative Planning for the Clearwater Basin," 5:3 *Forest Planning* 9 (June 1984); *Washington State Department of Natural Resources, Forest Land Management Plan* (1983); *Washington Environmental Council, Review of Proposed Forest Land Management Plan* (1983).

41. 36 C.F.R. § 219.27(e) (1987).

42. *Id.*

43. *Id.*

44. *National Forest Planning: A Conservationist's Guide, supra* note 25, at 77–78.

45. 16 U.S.C. §§ 1531–43 (1982).

46. LaFollette, "Challenges Facing Wildlife Management: Mitigation Must Be Planned," 1:3 *Forest Management* 7 (June 1980).

47. 36 C.F.R. § 219.19(a) (1) (1987).

48. *National Forest Planning: A Conservationist's Guide, supra* note 25, at 71–74.

49. Harris, Moser, and McKee, "Cutting Out Old Growth Wildlife," 3:6 *Forest Planning* 16 (September 1982); Schoen, Wallmo, and Kirchhoff, "Wildlife Needs Virgin Forests," 2:4 *Forest Planning* 7 (July 1981).

50. "Elk Versus Timber in Wyoming." 2:4 *Forest Planning* 16 (July 1981); Hoops, "Logging vs. Wildlife: A Question of Balance," 2:11 *Forest Planning* 15 (March 1982); Carlton, "The Rare and Elusive Caribou: Mountain Caribou Have Been Forced into Sub-Optimal Habitat," 5:2 *Forest Planning* 11 (May 1984); Mahlein, "Will Forest Plans Enhance Deer and Elk Habitat," 6:9 *Forest Watch* 17 (April 1986); Turbak, "Grizzly on the Ropes," 90:2

Am. Forests 22 (February 1984); Olsen, "The Survival of the Great Bears: Road Construction is Leading Threat to Bear Habitat," 4:11 *Forest Planning* 9 (March 1984).

51. Events in the spotted owl case can be followed in The Wilderness Society's *Biweekly Update*, June 16, October 20, and November 17, 1986; March 16, April 13, May 11, June 1, June 15, August 3 and August 17, 1987; January 18, 1988. See also "The Northern Spotted Owl," 8:3 *Forest Watch* 6 (September 1987).

52. 16 U.S.C. § 1604(g)(3)(B) (1982).

53. 36 C.F.R. § 219.19 (1987).

54. For a general statement of the range of biodiversity issues on the national forests, see E. Norse et al., *Conserving Biological Diversity in Our National Forests* (1986). Environmentalists drew upon a major study of the problem in L. Harris, *The Fragmented Forest: Island Biogeography Theory and the Preservation of Biodiversity* (1984).

55. Lawson, "Economic and Ecological Benefits of a Diverse Forest Stand," 4:2 *Forest Planning* 12 (May 1983); Miller, "Logical Benefits of a Diverse Forest Stand," 4: 2 *Forest Planning* 12 (May 1983); Cameron LaFollette, "Saving All the Pieces: Old Growth Forest in Oregon" (1979) (report prepared for the Oregon State Public Interest Research Group); Jerry Franklin et al., "Ecological Characteristics of Old-Growth Douglas-Fir Forests," USDA Forest Service Research Paper PNW-118 (1981) (summarized in 2:4 *Forest Planning* 12 (July 1981); Cameron LaFollette, "A Pilot Plan for Forest Diversity," CHEC Research Paper No. 9 (1981).

56. Solheim, Alverson, and Waller, "Maintaining Diversity in National Forests: Applying Island Biogeography Concepts in Forest Planning," 7:9 *Forest Watch* 9 (April 1987).

57. Mahlein, "Ecological Diversity Versus the 'Must Manage' Attitude," 7:2 *Forest Watch* 6 (August 1986).

58. In September 1987, the House Subcommittee on Natural Resources, Agricultural Research and Environment considered a bill on biological diversity and asked groups to testify on the advantages and disadvantages of a legislated standard of biological diversity in the United States. Although Forest Service Chief F. Dale Robertson did not supply a national standard or definition, he did support the importance of maintaining biological diversity. Yet in making his general statements specific he defined diversity in the then-current Forest Service terms of varieties of specialized management zones rather than biological diversity within a "mosaic of age classes" as environmentalists were prone to emphasize. See Lawson, "Chief Propounds New Emphasis on Diversity," 8: 5 *Forest Watch* 5 (November 1987).

59. Benjamin A. Roach, "Selection Cutting and Group Selection," State University of New York College of Environmental Science and Forestry, Applied Forestry Research Institute, Miscellaneous Report No. 5 (1974).

60. E. Fritz, *Sterile Forest: The Case Against Clearcutting* (1983); Minckler, "The Problem of Clearcutting and Even-Aged Management." 1:10 *Forest Planning* 18 (January–February 1981).

61. School of Forest Resources, College of Agriculture, The Pennsylvania State University, "Clearcutting In Pennsylvania" (1975); E. Horowitz, *Clearcutting: A View from the Top* (1974) .

62. Robinson, "Which Objections to Clearcutting Are Valid?," 1:4 *Forest Planning* 15 (July 1980); Bytheriver, "How Clearcutting Limits Regeneration," 1:10 *Forest Planning* 125 (January–February 1981). Wildlife biologists in Alaska, concerned about the loss of critical old growth habitat in the Tongass and Chugach National Forests, developed a sharp distinction between the Forest Service's tendency to think of forest maturity in terms of

individual trees and the necessity for wildlife biologists to define maturity in terms of ecological community maturing. See Schoen, Wallmo, and Kirchoff, "Wildlife-Forest Relationships: Is a Reevaluation of Old Growth Necessary?" in Wildlife Management Institute, 46th North American Wildlife and Natural Resource Conference, 1981 531 (1982); Matthews and McKnight, "Renewable Resource Commitments and Conflicts in Southeast Alaska," in Wildlife Management Institute, 47th North American Wildlife and Natural Resource Conference, 1982 573 (1983).

63. Minckler, "Group Selection in Eastern Hardwoods: Long Term Silviculture Should Be Consistent with the Natural Ecosystem," 5:8 *Forest Planning* 8 (November 1984); Minckler, "Group Selection Silviculture in Eastern Mixed Hardwoods," 8:4 *Forest Watch* 22 (October 1987).

64. The original bill proposed by environmentalists called for a limit of twenty-five acres on clearcuts.

65. See Road Construction, in *The Wilderness Society, Forests of the Future?: An Assessment of the National Forest Planning Process* 8, 8 (1987) ("road construction is a primary cause of environmental damage on the national forests").

66. The perennial debate over road construction budgets can be followed in the Wilderness Society's *Bi-Weekly Update;* the *National News Report,* published by the Sierra Club; and *Land Letter.* See also *Hearings before the Subcomm. of the Dep't of Interior, Comm. on Appropriations, House of Representatives,* 100th Cong., 1st Sess. (February 26, 1979) (statement by Barry R. Flamm of the Wilderness Society, on the fiscal year 1988 budget request for the Forest Service).

67. See Southeast Alaska Conservation Council, *The Tongass Timber Problem: The Full Report of the Tongass Accountability Project* (1985); Southeast Alaska Conservation Council, *The Citizens' Guide to the Tongass National Forest: A Handbook for Conservation Activists of Southeast Alaska* (1985): The Wilderness Society, *America's Vanishing Rain Forest: A Report on Federal Timber Management in Southeast Alaska* (1986).

68. The Idaho proposal is described in the *Newsletter of the Idaho Environmental Council,* January 1988, at 3.

69. O'Toole, "Sustained Yield and Even Flow Today," 1:2 *Forest Planning* 6 (May 1980); "Departure from Even Flow Considered for 16 Forests," 1:1 *Forest Planning* 6 (April 1980); O'Toole, "Departure Now Arriving," 4:2 *Forest Planning* 14 (May 1983).

70. O'Toole, "Forest Planning in Crisis," 4:3 *Forest Planning* 16 (June 1983); Lawson, "Looking Ahead to 1985: Crowell's Budget Favors Timber Sales," 4:11 *Forest Planning* 15 (March 1984).

71. "Crowell Ups RPA Timber Target," 4:9 *Forest Planning* 4 (December 1983).

72. O'Toole, "The Trouble With Trends: Use of Price Trends Bias Toward High Future Harvests," 6:4 *Forest Planning* 8 (July 1985); O'Toole, "Forest Service Fights Covert War on Plan Appeals," 8:5 *Forest Watch* 4 (November 1987) (arguing that price trends often led FORPLAN to inflate the suitable timber base).

73. Jan M. Newton, *An Economic Analysis of Herbicide Use for Intensive Forest Management, Part II: Critical Assessment of Arguments and Data Supporting Herbicide Use,* Northwest Coalition for Alternatives to Pesticides, Technical Report No. 2 (1980).

74. Little, "Conducting Your Own Reforestation Survey," 7:8 *Forest Watch* 26 (March 1987); O'Toole, "Are Forest Service Productivity Estimates Accurate?," 1:11 *Forest Planning* 19 (March 1981); Coon, "When Will the Trees Be Free to Grow? Interpretation of the Five-Year Reforestation Standard is Obscured by the Forest Service," 5:7 *Forest Planning* 11 (October 1984); *National Wildlife Federation, Reforestation and Timberland Suitability on*

the Bitterroot National Forest (1985) (analysis of reforestation records in one ranger district).

75. "The Suitable Timber Base, Well-Behaved FORPLAN Models, and Win-Win Situations in National Forest Planning, CHEC Research Paper No. 18 (1988).

76. O'Toole, "An Economic View of Timber Land Suitability," 1:3 *Forest Planning* 4 (June 1980); O'Toole, "Landslide Raises Timber Suitability Question," 2 :10 *Forest Planning* 20 (January–February 1982).

77. R. O'Toole, "The New Reality: Timber Land Suitability in Oregon National Forests," CHEC Research Paper No. 4 (1979); Boulding, "How Productive Can Our Forests Really Be?," 3:7 *Forest Planning* 8 (October 1982) (contains discussion of the views outlined in Criteria for Determining Unsuitable Land, Memo from the Chief of the Forest Service to Regional Foresters for Region Five and Six, July 1983). O'Toole maintains that while the Forest Service traditionally had excluded lands that cannot produce twenty cubic feet per acre per year, the new planning regulations consider them as a potential part of the timber base, requiring planners to do so even if there is no inventory data.

78. Natural Resources Defense Council, *Appeal of Plan and EIS for the Grand Mesa, Uncompahgre and Gunnison National Forests: Statement of Reasons* (1984); "Forest Service Rejects NRDC Appeals," 5:6 *Forest Planning* 5 (September 1984).

79. See comments on the Resources Planning Act program made by state fish and wildlife agencies from Alaska, Arizona, California, Idaho, Montana, Oregon, and Washington in 1984 (contained in author's file, *supra* note 15). The Montana agency, for example, "contracted for a review of the RPA program with a consulting firm from Eugene, Oregon, known as CHEC." Letter, James A. Posewitz, Montana Department of Fish, Wildlife, and Parks to Samuel P. Hays, November 16, 1984 (contained in author's file, *supra* note 15).

80. See, e.g., R. Smythe and J. Pye, A *Review and Critique of the Proposed Land and Resource Management Plan and the Draft Environmental Impact Statement for the Nantahala and Pisgah National Forests* (1986) (containing CHEC review of the plan and draft EIS). Prepared on behalf of the North Carolina Chapter of the Sierra Club and the North Carolina Wildlife Federation. The CHEC reports for environmental organization are reported regularly in this publication, *Forest Planning,* later *Forest Watch.*

81. 33 U.S.C. §§ 1251–1376 (1982).

82. 16 U.S.C. §§ 1531–1543 (1982).

83. 16 U.S.C. §§ 1604(g)(3) (E) and (F) (1982).

84. See generally "New Fight Over Forest Rules Protecting Non-Timber Resources," *Land Letter,* October 1, 1987, at 3.

85. The minimum management requirements issue can be followed in The Wilderness Society's *Bi-Weekly Update,* January 20, February 17, March 2, March 30, June 15, and August 31, 1987. For an environmental view of the outcome of the issue, see "Draft Policy Reduces MMRs' Effectiveness;" 8:4 *Forest Watch* 3 (October 1987).

86. For a brief discussion of the alternatives issue, see *The Wilderness Society, Issues to Raise in a Forest Plan Appeal: A Citizen Handbook* 68–69 (1986).

87. In 1985 the Office of General Counsel of the Department of Agriculture reviewed the "legal sufficiency" of the forest plan environmental impact statements; one of the three defects it emphasized was that "the [final EIS's] contained an inadequate range of alternatives. *Id.* at 67–68.

88. *Valuing Wildlife: Economic and Social Perspectives,* ed. D. Decker and G. Goff

(1987); O'Toole, "How Much Is Recreation Worth?," 6:5 *Forest Planning* 17 (August 1985).

89. Cindy Sorg and John Loomis, "Empirical Estimates of Amenity Forest Values: A Comparative Review," USDA Forest Service Research Paper RM-107 (March 1984).

90. See, e.g., "Comparison of Resource Benefits and Expenditures, Bridger-Teton National Forest, 1986–2035," in *The Wilderness Society, Management Directions for the National Forests of the Greater Yellowstone Ecosystem* 17 (1987), which indicates that timber constituted only 1.2 percent of the benefits in the plan and all commodity resources constituted 26.8 percent.

91. T. Barlow, G. Helfand, T. Orr, and T. Stoel, Jr., *Giving Away the National Forests— An Analysis of U.S. Forest Service Timber Sales Below Cost* (1980); U.S. Gen. Accounting Office, *Congress Needs Better Information on Forest Service's Below Cost Timber Sales (1984);* O'Toole; "Sales Below Cost: The Issue for the 80s; Is The Forest Service Subsidizing the Timber Industries," 5:7 *Forest Planning* 15 (Oct. 1984); E. Javorka, *Public Costs of Idaho Timber Sales,* (1986); Dennis C. Le Master, Barry R. Flamm and John C. Hendee, "Below Cost Timber Sales: Conference Proceedings" (1986) (report on a conference on the economics of national forest timber sales, held February 17–19, 1986 in Spokane, Washington, sponsored by The Wilderness Society, Washington State University Department of Forestry and Range Management and University of Idaho, College of Forestry, Wildlife, and Range Sciences).

92. *Forest Planning Monthly Report,* February 1, 1988 (newsletter issued by The Wilderness Society). Two plans that produced litigation were those for the Rio Grande National Forest and the Texas National Forest. See The Wilderness Society's *Bi-weekly Update,* November 30, 1987, at 3–4.

93. For a running account of one settlement (on the Jefferson National Forest), see The Wilderness Society's *Bi-weekly Update,* July 29, August 25, and December 15, 1986; March 30 and June 15, 1987; and February 1, 1988.

94. A useful analysis of regional variations in environmental objectives in forest planning is contained in "Regional Perspectives," in The Wilderness Society, *Forests of the Future?: An Assessment of the National Forest Planning Process* 27 (1987).

95. U.S. Forest Service, *Land and Resource Management Plan: Green Mountain National Forest* (1986), hereinafter Green Mountain Plan.

96. Long rotation sawtimber involves trees grown for sawlogs rather than wood pulp, and hence grown under long rotation (e.g., hundred years) rather than the short rotation (e.g., forty years).

97. Green Mountain Plan, *supra* note 95.

98. See The Wilderness Society, *Forests of the Future.*

99. Rick Reese, "Greater Yellowstone: The National Park and Adjacent Wildlands," Montana Geographic Series No. 6 (Montana Magazine, Inc. 1984); Greater Yellowstone Coalition, *Threats to Greater Yellowstone, 1984* (1984); Greater Yellowstone Coalition, *Greater Yellowstone Challenges, 1986* (1986); The Greater Yellowstone Coordinating Committee, *The Greater Yellowstone Area; An Aggregation of National Park and National Forest Management Plans* (1987). See also *The Greater Yellowstone Report* (newsletter of the Greater Yellowstone Coalition, published since 1985 in Bozeman, Montana).

100. "Biological Diversity," in The Wilderness Society, *Issues to Raise in a Forest Plan Appeal: A Citizen Handbook* 21 (1986).

101. E. Norse, *supra* note 54.

102. Solheim, Alverson, and Waller, "Maintaining Biological Diversity in National

Forests: Applying Island Biogeography Concepts in Forest Planning," 7:9 *Forest Planning* 8 (April 1987).

103. For an analysis of one celebrated case, see B. Twight, *Organizational Values and Political Power: The Forest Service Versus The Olympic National Park* (1983). A more sketchy but personal view of a number of such issues is contained in H. Albright, *The Birth of the National Park Service: The Founding Years, 1913–33* (as told to R. Cahn, 1985).

104. The Save-the-Redwoods League, which had first proposed a National Park encompassing the Smith River in 1937, proposed in the fall of 1985 that the entire river be incorporated into the national park system. Eighty-five percent of the watershed was managed by the Six Rivers National Forest. In its draft plan, the Forest Service proposed to log almost all of the region's old growth and to increase mining on the North Fork of the Smith River. The agency's intentions were reflected in the approval on September 23, 1987, of a timber sale deep within the remaining old growth forest. The pattern of political forces characteristic of earlier forest-park controversies seemed to be unfolding once again. See "Smith River Update," *Save-the-Redwoods League Fall Bulletin 1987*, at 4.

105. For a brief account of the Chugach case, see The Wilderness Society, Forests of the Future?

106. See *Tongass Accountability Project Interviews* (Eugene, Oreg.; Hot Type Publishers, 1984).

107. As part of the settlement agreement in the conservationist appeal on the Jefferson National Forest plan, the agency agreed to host an annual conference to inform the public of activities on the forest, listen to concerns, and search for solutions to problems. For a brief account of the first meeting, see The Wilderness Society's *Bi-weekly Update* (Feb. 1, 1988), at 5.

108. Smith, "How to Conduct Your Own Timber Sale Monitoring Program," 8:3 *Forest Watch* 24 (September 1987). The Council has published a newsletter on this program, *Timberwatch*, since 1987.

109. "New Forest Management Scheme Proposed by Conservation Advocates," *Land Letter*, August 15, 1985, at 1.

110. This approach is implicit in two critiques of national forest management by forest economists: M. Clawson, *Forests For Whom and For What?* (1975); W. Hyde, *Timber Supply, Land Allocation, and Economic Efficiency* (1980).

111. L. Minckler, *Woodland Ecology: Environmental Forestry For the Small Owner* (1975). See also the annual reports and other descriptive material from The New England Forestry Foundation, 85 Newberry Street, Boston, Mass.

112. Thomas L. Kimball, executive vice president of the National Wildlife Federation, while friendly to the Forest Service in the debate over NFMA in 1976, warned the Society of American Foresters in remarks at its 1976 National Convention that there was more yet to come: "I believe it is inevitable that the Congress will be forced to mandate national forest management by prescription if the forestry profession doesn't take positive measures to preempt such action." 75:1 *Forestry* 5 (January 1977).

The New Environmental West

Note: AF indicates a file in the author's collection.

1. The West in this article includes eleven states: Washington, Oregon, California, Idaho, Montana, Wyoming, Nevada, Utah, Colorado, Arizona, and New Mexico.

2. General statewide groups include the Washington Environmental Council, the Oregon Environmental Council and the Oregon Natural Resources Council, the Idaho Environmental Council and the Idaho Conservation League, the Montana Environmental Information Center, the Wyoming Outdoor Council, the Colorado Environmental Council, the Southwest Environmental Service (Arizona), and the New Mexico Conservation Coordinating Council.

3. Typical regional and local groups, whose publications I have used for this article include the Jackson Hole Alliance for Responsible Planning, Jackson, Wyoming; the North Cascades Conservation Council, Seattle; the Save the Redwoods League, San Francisco; the Silicon Valley Toxics Coalition, San Jose, California; the San Francisco Bay Association; the Siskiyou Mountains Resources Council, Arcata, California; Friends of the Columbia Gorge, Portland, Oregon; the Siuslaw Task Force, Corvallis, Oregon; the Oregon High Desert Study Group, St. Paul; and Preserve Our Poudre, Fort Collins, Colorado.

4. The first western coalition-style environmental group, the Federation of Western Outdoor Clubs, was formed in 1932 as an alliance of hiking and mountaineering clubs; see its publication, *Outdoors West* (Seattle, 1978–). A more recent group, the Utah Wilderness Coalition, was formed in 1986 to protect lands in Utah; it was composed of six Utah groups, nine groups from other western states, and five national organizations. See its newsletter, Utah Wilderness News (Salt Lake City, 1986–).

5. The Continental Group, *Toward Responsible Growth Economic and Environmental Concern in the Balance* (Stamford, Conn., 1982).

6. *High Country News* (Lander, Wyo., and Paonia, Colo., 1970–); Susan J. Harlow, "High Country News: Survival and Change," M.A. thesis, Department of Journalism and Communication, University of Wyoming, Laramie, 1981. See also *Western Wildlands* (Missoula: University of Montana School of Forestry, 1974–). *PLI* [Public Lands Institute] *Newsletter* (Denver and Washington, D.C., 1978); and *Earth First* (Reno and Tucson, 1981–).

7. A representative selection of books relevant to the subject and not cited later are Gregory R. Graves and Sally L. Simon, eds., *A History of Environmental Review in Santa Barbara County, California* (Santa Barbara, 1980); Winston Harrington, *The Regulatory Approach to Air Quality Management: A Case Study of New Mexico* (Washington, D.C., 1981); Carolyn R. Johnson and Eric Hildebrandt, *Still Stripping the Law on Coal* (Denver, 1984); James E. Krier and Edmund Ursin, *Pollution and Policy: A Case Study on California and Federal Experience with Motor Vehicle Air Pollution, 1940-1975* (Berkeley, 1977); Gov. Richard D. Lamm and Michael McCarthy, *The Angry West: A Vulnerable Land and Its Future* (Boston, 1982); League of Women Voters of California, *Protecting the California Environment: A Citizen's Guide* (San Francisco, 1980); Scott M. Matheson, *Out of Balance* (Salt Lake City, 1986); Corry McDonald, Wilderness: *A New Mexico Legacy* (Santa Fe, 1985); Susan Schrepfer, *The Fight to Save The Redwoods* (Madison, Wis., 1983); Ben W. Twight, Organizational Values and *Political Power: The Forest Service Versus the Olympic National Park* (University Park, Pa., 1983).

8. For accounts of the wilderness movement, see Craig Allin, *The Politics of Wilderness Preservation* (Westport, Conn., 1982); James F. Gilligan, "The Development of Policy and Administration of Forest Service Primitive and Wilderness Areas in the Western United States" (Ph.D. diss., University of Michigan, 1953).

9. The first *de facto* wilderness review originated in 1967 when the Forest Service added provisions to the Forest Service Review Manual that required all national forest

lands to be reviewed to determine whether they met specific criteria relating to suitability, availability, and need for allocation as wilderness. The manual required each regional
forester to submit to the chief a list of areas recommended to be classified as New Study
Areas. The agency gave no publicity to this planned review. Under this order little was
done and in 1969 the deadline for recommendations was extended to 30 June, 1972. This
also produced little action and in February 1971 the chief sent another directive to forest
supervisors instructing them to move ahead. In May and June 1971 most of the regional
foresters sent instructions to the supervisors as to how they should proceed; since this
resulted in varied procedures in August 1971, the chief sent out directives to standardize
them. This action also was not published and conservationists first learned of it in mid-
November 1971. See Sierra Club, *National News Report* (San Francisco, 12 June 1972; Dennis M. Roth, *The Wilderness Movement and the National Forests* (College Station, Tex.,
1988).

These moves by the Forest Service were speeded up by the East Meadow Creek, or
Parker, case, in which the court ruled that the agency could not proceed with a timber
sale near the Gore Range-Eagle Nest Primitive Area in East Meadow Creek, Colorado,
until it had been reviewed for wilderness potential. Judge Doyle argued that such a sale
along the border of a primitive area under study would "frustrate the purposes of the
Wilderness Act to vest the ultimate decision as to wilderness classification in the President and the Congress rather than the Forest Service and the Secretary of Agriculture."
See *Parker v. U. S.,* I ER 1163–1170, 27 February 1970.

10. Western state wilderness organizations include the Oregon Natural Resources
Council, the California, Washington, Wyoming, Utah, and Arizona wilderness associations, the Utah Wilderness Coalition, and the New Mexico Wilderness Study Committee. For activities of the American Wilderness Alliance, see its publications, *On the Wild
Side* (Denver, 1979–) and *Wild America* (Denver, 1979–); see also *At The Confluence,* Proceedings, Western Wilderness and Rivers Conference, 21 and 22 November 1980, Denver,
sponsored by the alliance (Denver, 1980). Brock Evans, associate executive director of the
Sierra Club, described the conference: "It really was a historic gathering, I thought, the
first time in memory that the real grassroot leaders from all over the West were brought
together in one place to hear each other"; see Proceedings, introduction. The section of
the report entitled "State Overviews" gives an especially useful description of state
wilderness activities.

11. Interview with Andy Kerr, associate director, Oregon Natural Resources Council,
14 April 1980; for activities of ONRC, see its publication *Wild Oregon* (Eugene, 1972–);
Oregon proposals are included in the Oregon Wilderness Coalition's "The Oregon Alternatives" (draft), n.p., September 1978.

12. The most active western state representative of the Wilderness Society in the 1970s
was Bill Cunningham in Montana. The organization had the strong support of Arnold
Bolle, dean of the School of Forestry at the University of Montana in Missoula and enjoyed a close association with Senator Lee Metcalf. The Wyoming Wilderness Association, independent of the Wilderness Society, was formed in December 1979, following a
meeting of conservation leaders in Laramie (see issues of its newsletter in AF) to revise
the proposed Wyoming wilderness designations known as the RARE II selections and to
prepare a wilderness bill for Wyoming's national forests. The association's interests included national forest management and management of BLM lands, especially the
Wyoming Red Desert; for these items, see the association newsletter, 18 October 1981, and
letter from Dick Randall to the author, 7 February 1981.

13. For information about the organization and activities of the Utah Wilderness Association, see its newsletter and miscellaneous material in AF.

14. See newsletters of the Southern Utah Wilderness Alliance and the Utah Wilderness Coalition, formed to press for more acreage in BLM wilderness than did the Utah Wilderness Association.

15. *On Public Lands* (Salt Lake City, 1986–).

16. For new developments in the Wilderness Society, see its magazine, *Living Wilderness,* and especially articles on the federal public lands.

17. "Wilderness Protection Gets Boost from Congress, Court Injunctions," *Land Letter Special Report* 2 (November 1983); "Agreement on Wilderness Near." *Land Letter* 3 (1 May 1984); "Congress Reaches Wilderness Accord," *Land Letter* 3 (1June 1984). See also U.S. House of Representatives, Subcommittee on Public Lands, *Additions to the National Wilderness Preservation System,* 98th Cong., 2d sess., February 1983–April 1984, parts 1–11 (Washington, D.C., 1984).

18. For a popular account of the issue, see Jack Shepard, *The Forest Killers* (New York, 1975); for an account of the legislative development seen from the viewpoint of an "insider," see Dennis C. LeMaster, *Decade of Change: The Remaking of Forest Service Statutory Authority During the 1970s* (Westport, Conn., 1984). See also U.S. Senate, Committee on Interior and Insular Affairs, Subcommittee on Public Lands, *Clear Cutting Practices on National Timberlands,* 3 parts, 5–6 April 1971, 7 April, 7 May, and 29 June 1971 (Washington, D.C., 1971). This issue led to a proposed Executive Order to restrict clearcutting practices, drawn up by the Executive Office of the President but forestalled by opposition from professional foresters and the timber industry. Especially significant was the defense of clearcutting by a committee of six forestry school deans, intended to counter the criticism of clearcutting by one of their fellow deans, Arnold Bolle of the School of Forestry, University of Montana. An account sympathetic to their views is Eleanor C. J. Horwitz, *Clearcutting: A View from the Top* (Washington, D.C., 1974). For additional items pertaining to events leading up to the 1976 act, see AF. The 1976 act specified that several issues—size of clearcut, riparian strips, marginal lands, and diversity—should be left for the Forest Service to decide, with advice from a "Committee of Experts," rather than to be specified or "prescribed" in the legislation. The Committee of Experts, in turn, gave firm advice on only the first of these and not the last two. See AF for the minutes of its meetings and the documents it prepared for internal use.

19. The most thorough and concise record of the debate over forest policy is in *Forest Planning,* later *Forest Watch* (Eugene, 1980–). For the debate from a Washington, D.C., vantage point, see "Timber Cutting Replaces Wilderness as Number One Forest Management Issue," *Land Letter* 4 (1 February 1985), 1–3; "New Forest Service Management Scheme Proposed by Conservation Advocates," *Land Letter Special Report* 4 (15 August 1985); and "Conflict Looms over Forest Plans in Northwest States: Fish, Wildlife, Economics All Are at Issue," *Land Letter Special Report* 5 (15 July 1986). For western newspaper accounts, see R. H. Ring, "Taming the Forests," *Arizona Star,* 5–12 February 1984, an eight-part series on the impact of western forest planning; Steve Woodruff, "Timber: A Balancing of Values," first of a six-part series in the *Missoulian* (Missoula), 9–24 March 1985; Jim Kadera, "Debate over Forest Economics Heats Up," *The Oregonian* (Portland), 16 December 1984; Keith Ervin, "On a New Front in the Wilderness War," *Seattle Weekly,* 12–18 December 1984; and Russell Sadler, "Public, Private Forest Values Differ," *The Oregonian,* 18 May 1984.

For specifics as to environmental objectives, see "Conservationists' Alternatives," parts 1 and 2 in *Newsletter,* Idaho Conservation League, 8 October and 8 November 1981. Cameron LaFollette, *A Pilot Plan for Forest Diversity: Bureau of Land Management at Coos Bay* (Eugene, 1981); Dieter Mahlein, *The Spotted Owl and Old Growth Forests: A Political Gamble* (Eugene, 1985; Wilma E. Frey, "Scenic and Aesthetic Values in National Forest Planning," *Forest Watch* 7 (September 1986); 25–29. For the entire range of environmental forest objectives as outlined in the National Forest Management Act of 1976, see Sierra Club et al., *A Conservationist's Guide to National Forest Planning* (Washington, D. C., 1981 2d ed., 1983).

20. For detailed accounts of the issues in the case of the Bridger-Teton National Forest in western Wyoming, see *Jackson Hole News,* clippings in AF, and statements from the group Upper Green River Forest Consensus, which brought together a wide range of environmental forest users to protest higher levels of timber cutting (AF). For the Bighorn National Forest in Wyoming, see news clippings from Wyoming newspapers and miscellaneous items from the Bighorn Forest Users Coalition (AF).

21. The environmental opposition in forest planning sought to freeze the planning process until more leverage could be secured for support of increased timber harvest. See Rick Johnson, "Forest Plans Held Up for Timber Study" and "McClure Holds Mock Hearings," *Idaho Conservation League News* 3 (October 1986): 4–5.

22. For a review of forest litigation see Michael Axline and John Bonine, "Watching the Forests Through the Courts," *Forest Watch* 7 (September 1986): 20–24; Lisa Schwartz, "Public Interest Attorneys Protecting the Forests," *Forest Watch* 7 (September 1986): 9–15.

23. For O'Toole's work, all published by the Cascade Holistic Economic Consultants (Eugene), see *Forest Planning* (later *Forest Watch*) (1980–); "CHEC Research Bulletin," (1982–); O'Toole, *An Economic View of Rare II* (1978); O'Toole, *The Citizens' Guide to FORPLAN* (1983); *The Citizens' Guide to Forest Planning* (1982); Ken Fletcher, Cynthia Williams, and Randal O'Toole, *Forest Planning Bibliography* (1985).

24. See publications of the Wilderness Society (Washington, D.C.): *Protecting Roadless Lands in the National Forest Planning Process: A Citizen Handbook* (1985); Elliott A. Norse et al., *Conserving Biological Diversity in Our National Forests* (1986); *Protecting Water Quality in the National Forest Planning Process: A Citizen Handbook* (1986); *How to Appeal a Forest Plan: A Citizen Handbook* (1986); *Issues to Raise in a Forest Plan Appeal* (1986).

25. The earliest interest of the NRDC in forest management came from Tom Barlow, who led the environmental coalition that worked with Senator Jennings Randolph of West Virginia to obtain strict guidelines for forest planning in the 1976 act; for coalition activities, see miscellaneous material in AF. Barlow then took up the analysis of timber sales on national forest land and argued that most sales were unprofitable. See Thomas J. Barlow, Gloria E. Helfand, Trent W. Orr, and Thomas B. Stoehl, Jr., *Giving Away the National Forests: An Analysis of U.S. Forest Service Timber Sales Below Cost* (Washington, D.C., 1980).

26. Disturbed by the public response to its plans in the form of court challenges, the Forest Service tried to analyze what was happening. Most of its response, however, involved strategies for better communications rather than coping with substantive issues. See *Communications/Awareness Discussions* from Regional Foresters and Directors Meeting (Fort Collins, Colo., August 1985).

27. Organizations that tabulated voting records of legislators to distribute to their members and the dates of reports in AF are: Colorado Open Space Council, 1973–78; 1980–82; 1984; Wyoming Outdoor Council, 1974–85; Montana Environmental Informa-

tion Center, 1975, 1977; Idaho Conservation League, 1976–1978, 1981; Idaho Conservation Voters, 1980; Washington Environmental Council, 1980; Oregon Environmental Council, 1971–73; 1975, 1977, 1983, 1985; California League of Conservation Voters, 1979–80.

28. A number of state environmental councils also issued special reports on the progress of legislation during legislative sessions. See, for example, Colorado Open Space Council, Legislative Bulletin, 1981–84 (AF).

29. For Montana, see Hank Fischer, "Montana's Yellowstone River: Who Gets the Water?" *Sierra* 63 (July/August 1978): 13–16; Robin Tawney, "The Yellowstone Will Run Free," *Montana Magazine* 9 (March/April 1979): 32–36.

30. Craig Gehrke, "Timber Industry Sabotages Water Standards," *Idaho Conservation League News* 3 (October 1986): 5; Oregon Environmental Council, *Earthwatch Oregon* (Summer 1985).

31. Susan McDowell O'Connell, "Uranium Mine Tailings . . . Heaps of Trouble," *National Wildlife* 18 (June/July 1980): 24B–24C. Vawter Parker, "Sierra Club Forest Action on Radioactive Tailings," *Sierra* 68 (November/December 1983): 58–59.

32. In 1979 the Montana court ruling that the state air quality plan was unenforceable led to an intense debate over revision of the state's air quality law, in which the older standards, more stringent than the federal ones, were retained. More significant, however, were the new general objectives approved in 1980 to prevent air pollution that "interfere[s]" with normal daily activities" and specifically identified lower lung function in school children as an "adverse effect" that should be prevented. See clippings in the Missoulian (Missoula) in AF; *Down to Earth* (Helena) Mar/April, May/June, and September/October 1980. For the relevant documents, see Department of Health and Environmental Sciences, State of Montana, *Montana Ambient Air Quality Standards Study: Final Environmental Impact Statement* (Helena, 1980).

33. For Arizona air pollution issues, see GASP, newsletter of Groups Against Smelter Pollution (Bisbee, Ariz., 1984–).

34. Regional northwest activities can be covered in *The Northwest Environmental Journal* (Seattle, 1984). For a major northwestern regional environmental initiative, see Daniel Goldrich, "Democracy and Energy Planning: The Pacific Northwest as Prototype," *Environmental Review* 10 (Fall 1986): 199–214.

35. For California parks, see Joseph H. Engbeck, Jr., *State Parks of California from 1864 to the Present* (Portland, 1980); the specific case of toxics in the Silicon Valley can be followed in Silicon Valley Toxics Coalition, *Silicon Valley Toxics News* (San Jose, 1983–). For the California Forest Practice Act, see T. F. Arvola, *Regulation of Logging in California, 1945–1975* (Sacramento, 1976); The Man Who Walks in the Woods, "The California Forest Practices Act; Is It Tough Enough?" *Forest Watch* 7 (July 1986): 7–10. For a more general treatment of state forest practice acts, see John Beuter, "Are State Forest Practice Acts Constitutional?" *Forest Watch* 6 (March 1986): 15–18; Marcy Golde, "Protecting Riparian Zones on Private Lands," *Forest Watch* 6 (March 1986): 19–21; Andy Stahl, "Regulating Harvests on Steep Slopes," *Forest Watch* 6 (March 1986): 22–23.

36. Nancie Fadeley, "Oregon's Bottle Bill Works," *Sierra Club Bulletin* 61 (July/August 1976): 9–10. For Oregon land-use law, see H. Jeffrey Leonard, *Managing Oregon's Growth: The Politics of Development Planning* (Washington, D.C., 1983); *Landmark,* publication of 1000 Friends of Oregon, a citizen group formed in 1975 and devoted primarily to the implementation of the Oregon land-use planning act (Portland, 1984–).

The Northwest Coalition for Alternatives to Pesticides, based in Eugene, was formed in 1977 to restrict the use of pesticides and herbicides in the Northwest, but it soon took on national leadership. See *NCAP News,* later *Journal of Pesticide Reform* (Eugene, 1977–). The group produced a wide range of documents with a high degree of scientific and technical quality. See, for example, Mary H. O'Brien, *On the Trail of a Pesticide: A Guide to Learning About the Chemistry, Effects, and Testing of Pesticides* (Eugene, 1984).

37. For Washington State activities, see *Alert* (1980–), newsletter of the Washington Environmental Council, and *Wildfire* (1980–), newsletter of the Washington Wilderness Association.

38. Idaho sources include newsletters of the Idaho Conservation League and the Idaho Environmental Council and a newspaper, the *Idaho Citizen* (Boise, 1978–). Montana events can be followed in *Down to Earth,* publication of the Montana Environmental Information Center; see also the annual reports of the Montana Council on Environmental Quality as well as the clippings from the *Missoulian* in AF. For Colorado, see the newsletters of the Colorado Open Space Council and its successor, the Colorado Environmental Council. Wyoming events can be followed in the *Jackson Hole News* and publications of the Wyoming Outdoor Association.

39. For the case of Montana, see G. Wesley Burnett, "Montana State Lands; Their Nature and Prospect," *Western Wildlands* (Winter 1978): 15–17.

40. William C. Patric, *Trust Land Administration in the Western States: A Study of the Laws, Policies and Agencies under Which State Lands are Managed in Ten States* (Denver, 1991).

41. For the Arizona exchanges, see Bruce Babbitt, "Saving Habitat in the Desert: Arizona Is Bolstering the Future of Riparian Wildlife with Imaginative Land Trades," *Defenders* (September/October 1986): 20–29, and Charles Bowden, "Miracle on the San Pedro: How Citizens, a Hawk Watcher, a Governor and a Federal Agency Pulled Off a Conservation Coup," *Defenders* (September/October 1986): 31–33.

42. Western opposition to the Sagebrush Rebellion can be followed in issues of *PLI Newsletter* (Public Lands Institute, Denver and Washington, D.C.) and *Outdoor News Bulletin* (Wildlife Management Institute, Washington, D.C.) during 1979–81. See also Bill Gilbert and Robert Sullivan, "Inside Interior: An Abrupt Turn" and "Alone in the Wilderness," *Sports Illustrated* (26 September 1983), 60–70ff. and (3 October 1983), 96–100ff.; see also Russ Shay, "The Sagebrush Rebellion," *Sierra* 65 (January/February 1980): 29–32.

43. Ken Robinson, "Sagebrush Rebellion Could Mean 'This Land Was Your Land,'" *Idaho Citizen* (February 1980), 4.7.

44. For "Project Bold," see Scott M. Matheson, *Out of Balance* (Layton, Utah, 1986), 129–34; "Major State-Federal Land Trade Being Discussed by Utah, BLM," *PLI Newsletter* 4 (September 1981): 3; "Project Bold sponsored by Utah Congressmen," *PLI Newsletter* 6 (April 1983): 4. The draft bill would amend the Enabling Act under which Congress granted Utah lands originally by providing "that lands granted for the support of the common schools shall be managed by the state with multiple-use land management practices, which may include use at less than fair market value for public purposes by agencies of the State and its political subdivisions." See "Utah's Land Exchange About Ready for Congress," *PLI Newsletter* 6 (November 1983): 3.

45. Events in this running debate can be followed in *Alert,* monthly newsletter of The Washington Environmental Council, which covered the work of its Forest Practices Committee; see "Network News: State and Private Forestry," issued by the committee (1986–) in AF. Much of the council's analysis appears in its publication, *Review of Proposed Forest Land Management Program* (Seattle, 1983); see also Washington Environmental Foundation, *Proceedings of the Wild Salmon and Trout Conference,* 11–12 March

1983 (Seattle, 1983). This debate took place around the issue of planning for state forest management. See relevant documents: State of Washington, Department of Natural Resources, *Forest Land Management Program, Draft Environmental Impact Statement* (Olympia, 1979); 2.1 Million Acres of Trees, et al. v. Bert L. Cole, Commissioner of Public Lands of the State of Washington, 17 October 1979, the environmental petition in response to the plan; Washington Department of Natural Resources, *Classic "U" Timber Sale, Final Environmental Impact Statement* (Olympia, 1981), the specific management problem around which innovations in state forest policy were debated.

46. Rollin R. Geppert, Charles W. Lorenz, and Arthur G. Larson, *Cumulative Effects of Forest Practices on the Environment: A State of The Knowledge,* prepared for the Washington Forest Practices Board, Olympia, 1984.

47. For the response of state fish and wildlife agencies to regional forest plans in the West, see comments on those plans by agencies in California, Oregon, Washington, Idaho, Montana, and Arizona in AF. For the case of the Idaho Department of Fish and Game, see Rod Nichols, Carl H. Nellis, and Lonn Kuck, "It's Time to Manage Elk . . . *and* People," and editorial, "Coexistence," in *Idaho Wildlife* 6 (September/October 1986): 4–7, 39.

48. See O'Toole's *Review of the Grand Mesa—Uncompahgre—Gunnison Forests Plan, Prepared for the Colorado Department of Natural Resources* (Eugene; n.d.) and comments of the Colorado Department of Natural Resources concerning the San Juan, Grand Mesa, Uncompahgre, and Gunnison national forests, 30 November 1983, and the settlement agreement between the state and the U.S. Forest Service 17 May 1984 in AF.

49. There were some cases of "direct action" on the part of the commodity resource opposition. At an "emergency meeting" at Moab, Utah, 25 June 1980, the Grand County, Utah, commissioners announced that on Independence Day they would celebrate by bulldozing a road into a wilderness study area proposed by the BLM "to show BLM that our county commissioners are going to take control of the land within our boundaries." See "The Moab Firecracker That Fizzled," *PLI Newsletter* 3 (August 1980): 2. A few months later the County Commissioners of Mineral County, Nevada, authorized the use of county equipment to bulldoze thirteen miles of roads into the Gabbs Valley Range Wilderness Study Area, one hundred miles southeast of Carson City, as a result of pressure from local miners, who demanded that the county provide access to mining claims. *PLI Newsletter* 4 (March 1981): 2.

50. Soon after he became Secretary of the Interior in 1981, James Watt made clear to western governors that he would shift from cooperative strategies with the states on public land development issues to a federal supremacy approach. On 3 April 1981, for example, Governor Schwinden of Montana sent a letter to Watt expressing his desire "to promptly develop, through cooperative agreements a productive partnership between Montana and Interior. With Montana taking an active part in the development of policies, rules and plans, there is no question that state needs will be considered. . . . With Montana sharing approval authority of federal plans, projects, and management decisions, state laws and rights will not be overlooked." In July, three months later, Watt replied with a "non-committal letter," including: "You suggest the use of cooperative agreements, which may be appropriate in some areas to reduce overlap or duplication of responsibilities. However, we must ensure that responsibilities delegated by statute to either the Federal Government or the State are not diluted." Schwinden and his staff interpreted that qualification as a sign that Watt was reluctant to grant Montana the type of partnership it wanted. See David Lambert, "Line of Fire: Montana's Transmission Corridor Controversy," part 2, *Montana Magazine,* December 1981, 31–37.

51. Details of the continuing debate over oil drilling on California offshore lands can be followed in the newsletter *Coastal Zone Management* (Washington, D.C., 1970–). See also Ronald Brownstein and Nina Easton, "Watt and the California Coast: Opening Shots in the OCS War," *Amicus Journal* 3 (Fall 1981): 12–18.

52. In October 1986 a coalition of wilderness opponents was formed in Utah to oppose any more wilderness in that state. It consisted of the Utah Farm Bureau, the cattlemen's and woolgrowers' associations, the mining and petroleum associations, the Utah Forest Industry Council, the Utah Association of Counties, the state Taxpayers Association, and the Utah Manufacturers' Association. The organization supported earlier, similar calls for an end to wilderness designations in Utah by Governor Bangartner, elected in 1985 to succeed Matheson, and by the National Public Lands Advisory Council, which was prompted to take such action by one of its members, San Juan County Commissioner Calvin Black. See Utah Wilderness Association mailing, November 1986.

53. For the Birds of Prey area, see "Birds of Prey Conservation Plan Ready for Congress, *PLI Newsletter* 3 (May 1980): 3; and "Andrus Land Order Protects Enlarged Birds of Prey Area," *PLI Newsletter* 4 (January 1981): 4; Jim Robbins, "Birds of Prey: Raptors and Habitat," *Sierra* 66 (July/August 1981): 44–47, 57.

54. For one account of the perennial conflict over the grizzly bear, see Paul Fritz: "Will the Grizzly Survive?" Newsletter, Idaho Conservation League (October 1986): 1, 8.

55. For the MX missile issue, see Susan Marsh and Russ Shay, "An Enormous Weapon System Comes to the Old West," *Sierra* 65 (July/August 1980): 8–11; on air-quality matters, see Bruce Hamilton, "Northern Great Plains: Indians, Ranchers and Environmentalists Fight for Clean Air," *Sierra Club Bulletin* (November/December 1977): 34–36. In 1978 a joint discussion group of ranchers and environmentalists was formed under the auspices of The Northern Rockies Action Group to seek common ground on such issues as predator control and wilderness. In 1982 it was co-chaired by John Faulkner of Gooding, Wyoming, and Laney Hicks, environmental leader, Dubois, Wyoming.

56. "In Pursuit of Mediocrity," *Earthwatch Oregon* (Spring 1986): 3–5; "Get Oregonized," *Earthwatch Oregon* (Summer 1986): 5; "Get Oregonized Controversy Generates Paper, New Ideas," *Earthwatch Oregon* (Summer 1986: 14–15).

In Wyoming the opposition was led by the Wyoming Heritage Society and its related group, the Wyoming Heritage Foundation, which promoted economic development in the state and took up public lands issues. See miscellaneous material about the two organizations in AF. See also report of a foundation meeting, 6 December 1985, in which speakers attacked environmentalists. Andrew Melnykovych, writer for the *Caspar Star-Tribune,* reported that "the concept of multiple use of federal lands is being threatened by environmentalists who want to drive ranchers, loggers and oilmen off those lands." At the forum Senators Malcolm Wallop and Alan Simpson and Representative Richard Cheney attacked environmentalists in the same manner; said Cheney, "What is really at stake . . . is a desire to drive the livestock producer off the range." *PLI Newsletter* 9 (January/February 1986): 2.

Rural leaders in Utah complained of the urban influence in their areas; hearings on projects there, they argued, were held in the Salt Lake City region, but hearings on relaxing air standards in the Wasatch Front were not held in rural areas. See Joseph Bauman, "Ruralite Goes After Urban Environmentalists," *Deseret News,* 13 March, 1985.

57. Selected state voting on environmental issues, by party, House of Representatives, for Colorado, Wyoming and Oregon:

	Colorado 1984		Wyoming 1983		Oregon 1983	
Proenvironmental voting scores	*R%*	*D%*	*R%*	*D%*	*R%*	*D%*
76–100	19	65	0	16	4	69
51–75	40	22	13	64	25	11
36–50	40	13	71	20	46	17
0–25	1	0	16	0	25	3

58. Western governors sought to take initiatives to soften some of the harsh opposition to environmental objectives by emphasizing multiple use as a broad concept that would permit such uses. They established in the National Governors Association a Range Resource Management Task Force, co-chaired by Governors John V. Evans of Idaho and Ed Herschler of Wyoming. Their focus was a legislative proposal to expand an "experimental stewardship program," authorized under the Public Rangelands Improvement (PRIA) Act of 1978, that had been tried in three places: the Challis area in Idaho, the East Pioneer area in Montana, and the Modoc-Washoe area in northeastern California. The governors looked with favor on the program because it involved the state governments in a more active role in public rangeland management and provided a method of resolving conflicts between livestock grazing, wildlife management, public recreation, and other "multiple-uses" of the public lands. In interpreting the meaning of the venture, one observer suggested that the governors were weary of being caught in the middle without having an effective voice in the resolution of rangeland controversies. See *PLI Newsletter 7* (1984): 1.

59. Regional environmental voting scores of members of the House of Representatives, based on tabulations issued by the League of Conservation Voters:

	Democrats			Republicans		
	1971	*1989*	*Change*	*1971*	*1989*	*Change*
New England	68.3	90.7	22.4	68.8	87.0	18.2
Mid-Atlantic	62.2	76.7	14.5	45.5	46.3	.8
South Atlantic	21.3	68.5	47.2	28.9	36.2	7.3
Gulf	14.7	44.3	29.6	19.1	5.7	-13.4
Central Plateaus	33.7	64.8	31.1	19.8	15.8	-4.0
North Central	63.8	76.2	12.4	34.4	34.8	.4
Plains	35.1	77.8	42.7	28.8	21.4	-7.4
Mountain	38.8	75.6	36.8	28.4	18.7	-9.7
Pacific	62.5	87.3	24.8	29.7	34.4	4.7

60. Because of the pressure from western Wyoming constituents concerning oil drilling, in potential wilderness areas, Senator Malcolm Wallop, who ranked very low in environmental voting on the League of Conservation Voters annual scores, warned the oil and gas industry that it should not apply to drill in such areas. See "Speech Before the Rocky Mountain Oil and Gas Association, Oct. 8, 1981, Denver, Colorado," in news release from the senator's office. Concerning the response of Jackson Hole to proposed drilling in nearby Cache Creek, Wallop reported: "ALL of us—Al Simpson, Dick Cheney, and I—were struck by the unprecedented consensus which the town exhibited in opposing the proposed drilling, especially up Cache Creek. Virtually everyone in that val-

ley from the County, Commissioners . . . to oil industry people with second homes up there . . . to the environmentalists, strongly, and I mean strongly, opposed a well up Cache Creek because of the area's recreational utility, wildlife and scenery."

61. For a popular account of the fallout problem and its effects, see John G. Fuller, *The Day We Bombed Utah: America's Most Lethal Secret* (New York, 1984); Arthur R. Tamplin, "Cancer in Utah: The Aftermath of Nuclear Weapons Testing," *Amicus Journal* 1 (Fall 1979): 13. The issue was covered extensively in the *Deseret-News* (Salt Lake City), clippings in AF; see issues for 1983–84 during the time the court ruled favorably for the victims, which in turn led to action for compensation. For articles dealing specifically with Hatch's interest, see Gordon Eliot White, "Hatch Assures Fallout Victims," 3 December 1983; "House Version of Fallout Bill Is Introduced," 15 June, 1984; Joseph Bauman, "Radiation Risk Study Is Biased, Group Says," 17 September 1984; White, "Scientists Say Charts for Fallout Victims Still Need Some Work," 18 September 1984; "Report Showing the Link of Radiation to Cancer Is Finally Released," 26 February 1985.

62. Convenient sources for following BLM issues are *PLI Newsletter, Public Lands News* (Washington, D.C., 1978–), and *Land Letter* (Washington. D.C., 1982–), all of which cover the NRDC actions concerning public lands.

63. For BLM wilderness reviews, see "Interview: Director Gregg on BLM Wilderness," *Living Wilderness* (April/June 1978): 22–23; John McComb, "The BLM Begins Its Wilderness Review," *Sierra* (January/February 1979): 46; and John Hart, "Deciding the Future of BLM Wilderness," *Sierra* (November/December) 1979: 16–19; for a regional focus, see Ray Wheeler, "Last Stand for the Colorado Plateau," *High Country News* (14 and 28 October 1985).

64. For accounts of the grazing committees, see issues of *PLI Newsletter* in 1985–86 and Charles H. Callison, "Partisan Advice Strictly Preferred," *Amicus Journal* 7 (Fall 1985): 9–11.

65. For oil and gas drilling in wilderness and wilderness candidate areas, see David Sumner, "Oil and Gas Leasing in Wilderness—What the Conflict is About," *Sierra* 67 (May/June 1982): 28–34. For general drilling issues, see "Conservationists Challenge Oil and Gas Leasing by Forest Service, Bureau of Land Management" *Land Letter Special Report* 5 (15May 1986).

66. See "Andrus Names 17 to National Advisory Council for BLM" *PLI Newsletter* 2 (December 1979): 1; "Watt Loads BLM Advisory Council with Ranchers, Miners, Oil People," *PLI Newsletter* 5 (March 1982): 4.

67. For the "modern" stage of the long-time grazing-fee controversy, see "Grazing Fee Controversy Moves Up Front Again," *PLI* Newsletter 9 (January/February 1986): 1–2; "President Orders Grazing Fee Subsidy Extended Indefinitely," *PLI Newsletter* 9 (March 1986): 1.

68. "Dr. Jay Hair Quits Public Lands Advisory Council," *PLI Newsletter* 9 (June 1986): 4; the item describes Hair as "the only member of the 21-member panel qualified or inclined to represent wildlife, recreational and wilderness uses of the public lands," and that in "his letter of resignation to Secretary of the Interior Donald Hodel, Dr. Hair said he considered the Advisory Council useless and a waste of money and recommended it be abolished." As a replacement, Secretary Hodel appointed Gerald J. Creasy of Garibaldi, Oregon, a county commissioner of Tillamook County and president of the Keta Corporation, a salmon aquaculture enterprise. See *PLI Newsletter* 9 (August 1986): 4.

69. Bruce Hamilton, "The Overthrust Belt: Oil and Gas Development in Opposition to Wilderness Once Again," *Sierra* 63 (November/December 1978): 8, 10–11.

70. A useful four-part series on western water is in *High Country News* 18 (29 September, 13 and 27 October, and 10 November 1986).

71. "Is Water Resource Reform in the Cards?" *CF Letter* (Washington, D.C., December 1976).

72. *Interior Should Ensure Against Abuses from Hardrock Mining,* GAO Report RCED-86-48 (Washington, D.C., 1986); "GAO Records BLM's Failure Under Obsolete Mining Law," *PLI Newsletter* 9 (July 1986): 1–2; David Sheridan *Hard Rock Mining on the Public Land* (Washington, D.C., 1978).

73. "Numerous Encroachments Threaten National Parks," *PLI Newsletter* 3 (July 1980): 3.

74. "Governors Can Act to Protect National Monument from Smog," *PLI Newsletter* 2 (October 1979): 1; "Air Quality Study Under Way in Mesa Verde National Park," *PLI Newsletter* 3 (September 1980): 2; "Interior Secretary Won't List Park Vistas for Protection," *PLI Newsletter* 8 (November 1985): 2; "Pollution in Parks: Natural Resources Program, National Park Service," *Park Science* 3 (Summer 1986), includes an extensive description of the National Park Service air-quality research program, a major part of which is visibility research.

75. "Park Protection Bill," *Land Letter* (November 1983): 1–2. When this bill stalled, Senator Chaffee of Rhode Island introduced a similar bill, which was confined to the adverse impacts of adjacent development on park wildlife. See "Chaffee Launches Initiative to Protect Park Wildlife from Federally Financed Activities," *Land Letter Special Report* 3 (15 April 1984). See also "Adjacent Lands Still the Toughest Issue," in "National Parks at a Turning Point: Will Mott Make the Difference?" *Land Letter Special Report* 4 (15 July 1985), which describes the opposition to these measures: "over the past several years, a loose coalition of real estate, energy, mining and forest-industry interests have worked fiercely to block action on the matter—apparently fearing the economic impacts of any extension of NPS influence beyond the park system's physical border."

76. The concepts of the "Greater Yellowstone Ecosystem" covered the most specific application of the idea. See Philip M. Hocker, "Yellowstone: The Region Is Greater Than the Sum of Its Parks," *Sierra* 64 (July/August 1979): 8–12. See also Rick Reese, *Greater Yellowstone: The National Park and Adjacent Wildlands* (Helena, 1984): "The Greater Yellowstone Ecosystem: An Introduction to an Area and Its Issues," *Western Wildlands* 12 (Fall 1986): 2–29. See also publications of the Greater Yellowstone Coalition: *Threats to Greater Yellowstone* (Billings, 1984), *Challengers to Greater Yellowstone,* 1986 (Billings, 1986), and *A Model for Information Integration and Management for the Centennial Ecosystem* (Billings, 1986).

77. Bruce Barnbaum, "Breaking the Stronghold of National Park Concessioners," *Sierra Club Bulletin* 62 (May 1977): 20–22; Michael Frome, "Park Concessions and Concessioners," *National Parks* 55 (June 1981): 16–18. The concessionaires issue played an important role in the dismissal in 1980 of National Parks Service Director William Whalen, who had attempted to tighten the contracts with the concessionaires. "Both press reports and PLI's grapevine suggested that the principal factor behind Whalen's dismissal was political pressure brought to bear by National Park concessionaires, through influential members of Congress." See "Whalen Fired, Russell Dickinson Named Park Service Director," *PLI Newsletter* 3 (June 1980): 3

78. In a specific case in point, the county commissioners of Lewis and Clark County, Montana, favored wilderness designation of the Rocky Mountain Front in 1986 because of its tourist potential; see Douglas H. Chadwick, "Rocky Mountain Front: A Question of Wilderness," *Defenders* 61 (July/August 1986): 20–29.

79. Some environmental organizations have been formed in the West to focus on specific national parks, and the National Parks and Conservation Association has made some (though halfhearted) attempts to bring them together through its National Park Action Project. For a list of groups involved throughout the nation, see "National Park Action Project Members" in AF; for related activities, see the project's newsletter, *Exchange* (Washington, D.C., 1983–); for a newsletter of one group, see *Mount Rainier National Park Associates Newsletter* (Summer 1985). These efforts have been limited and have had only limited success.

80. See, for example, Paul J. Culhane, *Public Lands Politics: Interest Group Influences on the Forest Service and the Bureau of Land Management* (Baltimore, 1981); Robert H. Nelson, "The Subsidized Sagebrush: Why the Privatization Movement Failed," *Regulation* 8 (July/ August 1984): 20–26, 39–43. Although *American Forests*, the monthly magazine of the American Forestry Association, published several focused debates about forest management, it gave little inkling of the objectives and intensity of public criticism of the Forest Service; see issues from 1976 to the present.

A Challenge to the Profession of Forestry

1. Stephen Kellert, "Wildlife Values and the Private Landowner," *American Forests* 90 (November 1984): 27–28, 60–61. Kellert wrote, "The most important product of the forest ecosystem may not be timber or wildlife, but the opportunities for personal growth, a sense of individual place, a feeling of competence, and a degree of peace and meaning in a world increasingly marked by confusion and uncertainty."

2. For a review of the debate over national forest planning see Samuel P. Hays, "The New Environmental Forest," *University of Colorado Law Review* 59, no. 3 (Summer 1988): 517–50.

3. Dave Zumeta, Forest Policy Analyst, Department of Natural Resources, St. Paul, Minnesota, "Work Begins on Timber Harvesting Environmental Impact Study," *Minnesota Forests* 3 (Spring 1990): 2; see also "Generic Environmental Impact Statement on Forest Management and Harvesting in Minnesota," Draft Scoping Document, Minnesota Environmental Quality Board, St. Paul, Minn., July 16, 1990.

4. USDA Forest Service and Governors' Task Force on Northern Forest Lands (April 1990); Sierra Club Northern Forest Campaign, "Sierra Club Response to Draft Northern Forest Lands Study" (Saratoga Springs, N.Y., January 1990); the Wilderness Society, "A Critique of the Draft Northern Forest Lands Study Report" (Boston, Mass., January 1990); miscellaneous clippings in author file.

5. A review of state forest practice laws is Paul V. Ellefson and Frederick W. Cubbage, "State Forest Practice Laws and Regulations: A Review and Case Study for Minnesota" (St. Paul, 1980). The 1989 Maine Forest Practices Act indicates the tendency to include wildlife implications in such laws; for details see miscellaneous material in author file. For an in-depth review of the varied elements in a current process of revision in a major state forest practice in Oregon, see Oregon Department of Forestry, "Executive Summary of the Oregon Board of Forestry's Forest Practice Issues Forum" and "Additional Information Re the December 10, 1990 Forest Practices Issues Forum, December 21, 1990 and January 22, 1991 (Salem, Oreg., 1990, and 1991).

6. For attitudes that underlie local regulations, see Hamilton & Rader, "Suburban

Forest Owners: Goals and Attitudes Toward Forest Practices," *Northern Logger and Timber Processor* (July 1974): 18–19. For industry concern about such regulations, see Hardwood Lumber Manufacturers Association in Pennsylvania, "Facts and Issues: Pennsylvania's Timber and Forest Products Industries," 10: "Pennsylvania is experiencing a widespread proliferation of anti-timber harvesting regulations at the local level. An increasing number of municipalities are using their land-use control authority through zoning ordinances to regulate, and in some cases prohibit, timber harvesting and forest management practices on private land."

7. "New Coalition Calls for Moratorium on Logging in the National Forests of the Midwest," *Forest Watch* (January 1991): 3; see also miscellaneous material from the organization, Heartwood, in author file. This midwestern coalition has brought together separate groups in Missouri, Illinois, Indiana, Kentucky, Ohio, and West Virginia. The group states, "We believe that there is a broad support for an end to logging on our midwestern public forests." See publications of various organizations involved such as Regional Association of Concerned Environmentalists (Illinois) or Protect Our Woods (Indiana) in author file. It should be emphasized that while local branches of national organizations, such as the Audubon Society and the Sierra Club are involved in these activities, the initiative comes from residents in the forested areas themselves rather than those organizations. This new constituency for environmental forest objectives was also characteristic of the recently developing action in Minnesota.

8. James E. Johnson, editor, *Managing North Central Forests for Non-Timber Values*, Proceedings of the Fourth Society of American Foresters Region V Technical Conference, Duluth, Minnesota, November 29–December 1, 1988, SAF Publication 88-04 (Washington, D.C., 1988).

9. See *Inner Voice*, publication of the Association of Forest Service Employees for Environmental Ethics (Eugene, Oregon, 1989–); Anae Boulton, "Foresters Take the 'Moral High Ground,'" *Forest Watch* (November 1989): 6–9.

10. National Research Council, *Forestry Research: A Mandate for Change* (Washington, D.C., 1990).

11 "An Open Letter to the Chief from the Region One Forest Supervisors," U.S. Forest Service, November 1989; "Mutiny on the National Forests," *Reform*, supplement to *Forest Watch* (January 1990): 1–2.

12. The Wilderness Society, National Forest Action Center, *Protecting Water Quality in the National Forest Planning Process: A Citizen Handbook* (Washington, D.C., 1986).

13. An example of controversy over Riparian Area Management areas is described in *Oregon Insider: A Biweekly Digest of Environmental News*, #12, #18, and #26/27.

14. Michael Anderson, "New Directions for National Forest Water Quality Planning," *Forest Watch* (March 1988): 22–28.

15. To follow details in one old growth issue, see Ancient Forest Alliance, "Ancient Forest News" (The Wilderness Society, Washington, D.C., April 1969–).

16. Thomas R. Crow, "Biological Diversity: Why Is It Important to Foresters?" in James E. Johnson, ed., *Managing North Central Forests for Non-Timber Values*.

17. A useful compendium of the issues as they emerged in the very early stages of national forest planning is the Wilderness Society et al., *National Forest Planning: A Conservationist's Guide* (Washington, D.C., 1981). For a more detailed statement applied to one state, see "Conservationists' Alternatives" (parts 1 and 2) *Idaho Conservation League Newsletter* (October 1981): 1, and (November 1981): 5.

18. U.S. Senate, *Clear-Cutting Practices on National Timberlands,* Hearings Before the Subcommittee on Public Lands of the Senate Committee on Interior and Insular Affairs, 92nd Cong., 1st Sess., Pts. 1–3 (1971).

19. Eleanor C. J. Horwitz, *Clearcutting: A View From the Top.* (Washington, D.C.: Acropolis Books Ltd., 1976).

20. The language of dispute reflects deep-seated value judgments; for example, Richard Alston, "The Holy War in Forest Planning," *Forest Planning* (October 1983): 8.

21. Ben W. Twight and Fremont J. Lyden, "Measuring Forest Service Bias; Forestry and the Public Interest: Whose Policies and Values Are Represented by USDA Forest Service Managers?" *Journal of Forestry* 87 (May 1989): 35–41.

22. James J. Kennedy and Thomas M. Quigley, "How Entry-Level Employees, Forest Supervisors, Regional Foresters and Chiefs View Forest Service Values and the Reward System," a 1989 survey done for the Sunbird Conference, second meeting of forest supervisors and chiefs (Tucson, Ariz., November 13–16, 1989).

23. See "Statements by Experts on Biotic Diversity," in "Appendix to Statement of Reasons," In Re Appeal of the Record of Decision, Dated August 11, 1986, Approving the Land and Resource Management Plan and Final Environmental Impact Statement for the Chequamegon National Forest, Sierra Club, John Muir Chapter, and Wisconsin Forest Conservation Task Force, Appellants, Madison, Wis., 1986, pp. 10–34; see also two similar letters from ten Indiana scientists on the subject of biodiversity, Dr. William Buskirk, et al., to Governor Evan Bayh, October 16, 1990 (author file). The ten writers represented biology, life sciences, microbiology and immunology, a professor in a natural resources school and two in a school of public and environmental affairs.

24. *Conservation Biology,* The Journal of the Society for Conservation Biology (1987–) (Cambridge, Mass.: Blackwell Scientific Publications); *Natural Areas Journal,* A Quarterly Publication of the Natural Areas Association (1980–) (Rockford, Ill.: Natural Areas Association); *Endangered Species Update* (1983–) University of Michigan, School of Natural Resources; *Biodiversity and Conservation* "A new quarterly international journal devoted to the publication of articles on all aspects of biological diversity, its description, analysis and conservation, and its controlled rational use by man." (New York: Chapman and Hall).

25. The Continental Group, *Toward Responsible Growth: Economic and Environmental Concern in the Balance* (Stamford, Conn., 1982).

26. T. Allen Comp, ed., *Blueprint for the Environment: A Plan for Federal Action,* outlining fourteen proposals for scientific research at the federal level, to be administered through the Departments of Health and Human Services, the Department of the Interior, the Environmental Protection Agency, the National Oceanic and Atmospheric Administration and the Department of Energy and the U.S. Forest Service.

27. Joseph E. DeSteiguer, "Public Participation in Forestry Research Planning" (Ph.D. thesis, Texas A&M University, 1979).

28. National Research Council, *Forestry Research: A Mandate for Change.*

29. A specific example of ecological classification for inventory purposes, involving biomes, vegetative cover types, and natural communities is George D. Davis, "Biological Diversity: Saving All the Pieces," vol. 1, *Fulfilling the Promise of The Adirondack Park* (Elizabethtown, N.Y.: The Adirondack Council, 1988). For old growth classifications in Pennsylvania, see Thomas L. Smith, "An Overview of Old-Growth Forests in Pennsylvania," *Natural Areas Journal* 9 (1989): 40–44, and for Minnesota, see "Old-Growth Forests in Minnesota, a Preliminary Report," Section on Wildlife—Natural Heritage Program,

Minnesota Department of Natural Resources, Biological Report No. 5 (1989); Minnesota Department of Natural Resources—Division of Forestry, "Old Growth/Old Forest Guidelines: Public Review Draft August 1990" (St. Paul, Minn., 1990). See also Constance E. Hunt, "Creating an Endangered Ecosystems Act," *Endangered Species Update* 6, nos. 3/4: 1–5.

30. J. Michael Scott, Blair Csuti, James D. Jacobi, and John E. Estes, "Species Richness: A Geographic Approach to Protecting Future Biological Diversity," *Bio-Science* 37, no. 11 (December 1987): 782–88.

31. John Terborgh, *Where Have All the Birds Gone? Essays on the Biology and Conservation of Birds That Migrate to the American Tropics* (Princeton University Press, 1989).

32. For one arena of controversy over total maximum daily loads see *Oregon Insider: A Biweekly Digest of Environmental News*, #35.

33. For a statement of visibility values in a forested area, see Agency of Environmental Conservation, Montpelier, Vermont, *Implementation Plan for the Protection of Visibility in the State of Vermont* (Air Pollution Control Section, Environmental Engineering Division, Montpelier, Vt., 1985).

34. For an example of atmospheric deposition monitoring, see James A. Lynch et al., "Atmospheric Deposition: Spatial and Temporal Variations in Pennsylvania" (University Park, Pa.: Environmental Resources Institute, Pennsylvania State University, 1982–).

35. In Northwest Indian Cemetery Protective Association v. Peterson, Court of Appeals, Ninth Circuit, July 22, 1986 (24 ERC 1775) the court held that the BMPs were not to supplant state water quality standards, but instead were to act as means to achieve the appropriate standards. One commentator noted, "[Northwest Cemetery] adds substantive requirements to what has been largely an exercise in procedure." See Thaler, "Lawyer's Lawdust," *Forest Planning* (August 1985): 6.

36. For the Grider case, see "Forest Service Must Consider Impacts on Biological Corridors," *Forest Watch* (September 1990): 4.

37. William S. Alverson, Donald M. Waller, and Stephen L. Sotheim, "Forests Too Deer: Edge Effects in Northern Wisconsin," paper presented at the first annual meeting of the Society for Conservation Biology, Bozeman, Montana, June 25, 1987.

38. Chandler S. Robbins, Deanna K. Dawson, and Barbara A. Dowell, "Habitat Area Requirements of Breeding Forest Birds of the Middle Atlantic States," *Wildlife Monographs*, no. 103 (The Wildlife Society, July 1989). For a project to map forest fragmentation over a fifty-year period, see "The Boundaries of Loss," *Wilderness* (Spring 1991): 12–16.

39. For a forest industry approach to cumulative effects analysis, see "An Industry Proposal to Address Cumulative Effects," in National Council of the Paper Industry for Air and Stream Improvement, Inc. "Comments on Board of Forestry Forest Practices Issues Forum—December 10, 1990" (Oregon Department of Forestry, January 22, 1991).

40. See Greater Yellowstone Coordinating Committee, "Vision for the Future: A Framework for Coordination in the Greater Yellowstone Area," draft (Billings, Mont., August 1990); The Wilderness Society, "Management Directions for the National Forests of the Greater Yellowstone Ecosystem" (Washington, D.C., 1987); see also publications of the Greater Yellowstone Coalition, especially its periodical, "Greater Yellowstone Report" (Bozeman, Mont., 1984–). For a broader application of the concept, see Edward Grumbine, "Protecting Biological Diversity Through the Greater Ecosystem Concept," *Natural Areas Journal* 10, no. 3. (1990): 114–19.

41. For a call for the analysis of the long-term adverse environmental impacts of

roads, see Dr. Reed Noss, "Why We Need to Think Big: Biodiversity and Conservation in Greater Yellowstone," *Greater Yellowstone Report 7*, no. 4 (Fall 1990): 1, 4, 16.

42. For a brief account of the wildlife corridor implications of the Maine Forest Practices Act, see Joe Wiley, "The Forest Practices Act and Wildlife," *Maine Fish and Wildlife* (Winter 1990–91): 28–29.

43. "Forest Terminology," *Pennsylvania Woodlands*, no. 4 (Penn State College of Agriculture, Cooperative Extension).

Human Choice in the Great Lakes Wildlands

1. Opinion Research Corporation, "The Public's Participation in Outdoor Activities and Attitudes Toward National Wilderness Areas," Study commissioned by American Forest Institute, Princeton, N.J.

2. On the wetlands, see Richard J. Angello et al., "Coastal Zone Recreational Activity and Potential Demand of Delaware Residents" (Dover: Delaware Sea Grant College Program, University of Delaware, 1977; on desert lands, see Field Research Corporation, "California Public Opinion and Behavior Regarding the California Desert" (Riverside, Calif.: USDI Bureau of Land Management, 1977).

3. Virginia Office of Environmental Resources, "Preliminary Report on the Virginia Wetlands Act: The First Year" (Richmond, Va.: Division of State Planning and Community Affairs, Commerce and Resources Section, 1973).

4. Robert C. Lucas, *The Recreational Capacity of the Quetico-Superior Area*, USDA Forest Service Research Paper LS-15. (St. Paul: Lakes States For. Exp. Station, 1964).

5. Stephen Kellert, "Public Attitudes Toward Critical Wildlife and Natural Habitat Issues, Phase I" (Washington, D.C.: USDI Fish and Wildlife Service, 1979).

6. Mary Keys Watson, "Behavioral and Environmental Aspects of Recreational Land Sales" (Ph.D. dissertation, Department of Geography, Pennsylvania State University, 1975).

7. James E. Williams and Andrew J. Sofranko, "Motivations for the Immigration Component of Population Turnaround in Non-Metropolitan Areas," *Demography* 16 (1979): 2. Robert W. Marans and John D. Wellman, *The Quality of Non-Metropolitan Living: Evaluations, Behaviors, and Expectations of Northern Michigan Residents* (Ann Arbor: University of Michigan Survey Research Center, 1978).

8. B. A. King and Jonathan Ela, *The Faces of the Great Lakes* (San Francisco: Sierra Club Books, 1977).

9. See Alfred Runte, *National Parks: The American Experience* (Lincoln: University of Nebraska Press, 1979); J. A. Van Fleet, *Summer Resorts of the Mackinac Region and Adjacent Localities* (Detroit, 1882); and R. Newell Searle, *Saving Quetico-Superior: A Land Set Apart* (Minneapolis: Minnesota Historical Society, 1977).

10. Wilderness Society, articles on the Porcupine Mountains in *The Living Wilderness* 10:24–27; 64:28; 65:28–30; 66:29; 67:25 (1944, 1958).

11. The controversy over the Pigeon River State Forest can be followed in Michigan periodicals such as the *North Woods Call.* the newsletter of the West Michigan Environmental Action Council, *Michigan Earth Beat,* and the releases of the Pigeon River Country Association (author file). For the Sleeping Bear Dunes and Pictured Rocks National Lakeshores, see planning documents prepared by the National Park Service and evaluation of them by Friends of Sleeping Bear Dunes and Friends of Pictured Rocks (author

file). Good newspaper clipping files on both issues are in two collections in the Traverse City, Michigan, Public Library, one in the Michigan Room and one in the public affairs room maintained by the League of Women Voters.

12. Norman John Schmaltz, "Cutover Land Crusade: The Michigan Forest Conservation Movement, 1899–1931" (Ph.D. dissertation, University of Michigan, 1972).

13. Roy L. Dodge, *Michigan Ghost Towns* vols. 1–3 (Troy, Mich.: Glenson Publishing, 1970, 1971); Michael Dunn III, *Easy Going: Wisconsin's Northwoods: Vilas and Oneida Counties* (Madison: Tamarack Press, 1978).

14. Keith J. Fennimore, *The Heritage of Bay View* (Grand Rapids, Mich.: Eerdmans, 1975).

15. Rolland H. Maybee, *Michigan's White Pine Era, 1840–1900* (Lansing: Michigan Historical Commission, 1960).

16. Gordon L. Bultena and John C. Hendee, "Foresters' Views of Interest Group Positions on Forest Policy," *Journal of Forestry* 60 (1972): 337–42.

17. The first edition of the initial work on dendrology in the McGraw-Hill American Forestry Series, William M. Harlow and Ellwood S. Harrar, *Textbook of Dendrology Covering the Important Forest Trees of the United States and Canada* (New York: McGraw-Hill, 1937), noted that existing books were unsatisfactory. Sargent's *Silva of North America* was too extensive in species coverage, and other books were too local. In their introduction, Harlow and Harrar advised, "It is felt that students of forestry should first know well the commercial species of North America."

18. See, for example, material in *American Forests* between 1959 and 1964, especially the writings of Kenneth Pomeroy, forester for the American Forestry Association.

19. Descriptions of forests by environmentalists can be found in publications such as *Wild Oregon* (Oregon Wilderness Coalition), but the most detailed and extensive ones are in the hiking and natural history guide books which environmentalists issue in order to acquaint organization members with the natural qualities of specific areas. There are many of these. See, for example, *Oregon Coast Range Wilderness* (Corvallis, Oreg.: Siuslaw Task Force, 1980).

20. John Hendee, George H. Stankey, and Robert C. Lucas, *Wilderness Management*, miscellaneous publication no. 1365 (Washington, D.C.: USDA Forest Service, 1978).

21. One study of the professional backgrounds of U.S. Forest Service personnel was conducted by the Citizens Committee on U.S. Forest Service Management Practices in California; see State of California Resources Agency, "Today, Tomorrow: Report of Citizens Committee on U.S. Forest Service Management Practices in California (Sacramento, 1979), pp. 17–18. It reported that "the professional staff of the Forest Service consists primarily of foresters," and that this category of professional background in California had increased over a five-year period from 698 in 1974 to 843 in 1979, but had declined proportionately from 65 percent to 59 percent of the total. The range of specialists used in forest planning can be observed in the list of those who participated in the first national forest plan under the 1976 Forest Management and Planning Act, in the Lolo National Forest in Montana. See U.S. Forest Service, "The Lolo National Forest Plan: Draft Environmental Impact Statement" (Missoula, Mont., 1980), pp. A-1–A-10.

22. One example is the comment by the Sierra Club, Columbia Group, on the timber management plan prepared by the Gifford Pinchot National Forest; see Final EIS under sections Appendix II, "Ad Hoc Group Input," and Appendix IV, "Public Response to the Draft Environmental Impact Statement." Both contain references to the technical literature. In the second case, a critique of the plan's allowable cut calculations refers to a

1972–1973 series in the *Journal of Forestry* on the allowable cut effect. See also the EIS comments by Randall O'Toole of Cascade Holistic Economic Consultants, Eugene, Oregon, on various Oregon timber management and land use plans. By 1980 environmentalists had begun to issue a quarterly magazine to assist citizens in participating in forest planning throughout the nation; titled *Forest Planning*, it was printed in Eugene, Oregon, and edited by forest economist Randall O'Toole.

23. Samuel T. Dana, "Forest Ownership in Minnesota—Problems and Prospects," *American Forests* 66 (1960): 32–38, 48–60.

24. The gap between leaders and the general public appears in several recent surveys. The Opinion Research Corporation, "The Public's Participation in Outdoor Activities and Attitudes Toward National Wilderness Areas," commissioned by American Forest Institute, Princeton, N.J., 1977, for example, indicated that 62 percent of those questioned felt that the Forest Service should "continue to preserve these trees in their natural state" rather than "try to increase the yield and sales of timber from our National Forests." The ORC also surveyed the attitudes of "thought leaders" in Washington, D.C., which indicated that only 38 percent of these thought that forests should be "preserved in their natural state." The ORC advised the AFI: "We do not find sufficient support among the American people to warrant a mass communications program to increase public support for greater timber harvesting on public lands. Instead, since this issue is perceived more rationally and with greater expertise among Washington thought leaders, we recommend that your persuasive efforts be directed toward this target audience among others" (American Forest Institute, *Research Recap, #10*, Washington, D.C., December 1977). Another survey was conducted for AFI two years later which indicated that although government officials thought timber production was the most important function of the National Forest System, 80 percent of the general public felt that protecting wildlife habitat was the main purpose and that too much timber harvesting was taking place (Sierra Club, *National News Report*, San Francisco, March 7, 1980). In the Niagara County study, Lester W. Milbrath et al., "An Extra Dimension of Representation in Water Quality Planning: A Survey Study of Erie and Niagara Counties, New York, 1976," interim report (Buffalo: SUNY, 1977), which ranked various community factors in terms of "importance," leaders ranked daily work second and job opportunities ninth, and the general public ranked them ninth and thirteenth. The public ranked clean air sixth; the leaders ranked it thirteenth.

Clean Air, 1970–1977

1. Clean Air Act Amendments of 1977, Pub. L. No. 95–96 (codified in scattered sections of 42 U.S.C.A. §§ 7401–7642 (Supp. 1977).

2. For background to the 1970 Act, see, e.g., J. C. Davies, III, *The Politics of Pollution* (1970); J. C. Esposito, *Vanishing Air* (1970); and R. H. K. Vietor, *Environmental Politics of the Coal Industry* 240, doctoral dissertation, University of Pittsburgh, 1975.

3. Compare the technological perspective on air pollution problems which is found generally in *J. Air Pollution Cont. A.* and *Envt'l. Sci. & Tech.* with the legal perspective which is found in *Ecology L.Q., Envt'l. L.* and *Envt'l. Aff.*

4. See G. B. Irwin, "In Defense of the Vendors," 9 *Envt'l. Sci. & Tech.* 534–36 (June 1975).

5. See generally reports of Natural Resources Defense Council and releases of National Clean Air Coalition for information on citizen action in clean air issues.

6. For a review of the Act of 1970 and its early implementation, see 4 *Ecology L.Q.* 441 (1975), the entire issue of which is devoted to the subject. A manual detailing the workings of the Act, from the viewpoint of potential citizen involvement, is J. Cannon, *A Clear View* (1975).

7. The six criteria pollutants are: sulfur oxides, particulates, carbon monoxide, photochemical oxidants, hydrocarbons, and nitrogen oxides. See 40 C.F.R. §§ 50.4–5.11 (1976).

8. Action to force development of a lead standard was brought by the National Resources Defense Council in 1971; on March 31, 1976, EPA listed lead as a criteria pollutant and proceeded to develop a criteria document and standard. The sequence of events and the controversies over formulation of the criteria document may be followed in 7 *Envir. Rep.—Current Dev.* (BNA) 1361 (January 14, 1977), 1486 (February 4, 1977), 1962 (Apr. 22, 1977); 8 *Envir. Rep.—Current Dev.* (BNA) 274 (June 17, 1977), 409 (July 8, 1977), 929 (October 14, 1977). A brief summary of the issues from an environmental viewpoint is contained in H. L. Needleman and S. Piomelli, *The Effects of Low Level Lead Exposure* (1978).

9. 42 U.S.C.A. § 7422(a) (Supp. 1977) The statute lists: "radioactive pollutants (including source material, special nuclear material, and byproduct material), cadmium, arsenic and polycyclic organic matter." *Id.*

10. An excellent account of the climate of change between these two acts is contained in House Comm. of Interstate and Foreign Commerce, Clean Air Act Amendments of 1977, H. R. Rep. No. 294, 95th Cong., 1st Sess., reprinted in [1977] U.S. Code Cong. & Ad. News 1077.

11. See Esposito, *Vanishing Air,* 162, for events surrounding the Litton reports.

12. See *Kennecott Copper Corp. v. EPA,* 462 F.2d 846 (D.C. Cir. 1972).

13. The relevant section is 42 U.S.C.A. § 7491 (Supp. 1977). National Parks Service analysis of visibility in parks in southern Utah, as affected by existing and proposed generating plants, helped to focus the concern for this provision. See U.S. Dept. of the Interior, National Parks Service, Analysis of Kaiparowitz Powerplant Impacts on National Recreation Resources with Interior Review Comments Attached (March 1976).

14. The federal twenty-four-hour standard for sulfur dioxide, for example, is 0.14 ppm. Several states have standards in the range of .10 to 0.13 ppm., and seven states have standards below 0.10 ppm. These include Hawaii with 0.03 ppm., Colorado and California with 0.05 ppm., Vermont with 0.06 ppm., Missouri with 0.07 ppm., and Maine and Georgia with 0.09 ppm.

15. The relevant section is 42 U.S.C.A. § 7411(c) (Supp. 1977). This state authority was contained in the 1967 Act and was upheld in *Houston Compressed Steel Corp. v. State of Texas,* 456 S.W.2d 768 (Tex. Civ. App. 1970).

16. For recent account of the California issue, see J. E. Krier and Ursin, *Pollution and Policy* (1978).

17. See 42 U.S.C.A. § 7422(c)(1) (Supp. 1977).

18. See 42 U.S.C.A. § 7474 (Supp. 1977).

19. *Id.*

20. See note 14 *supra.*

21. For a good account of the early development of the "no significant deterioration" program, as it was initially called, see T. M. Disselhorst, "Sierra Club v. Ruckelshaus," 4 *Ecology L.Q.* 739 (1975).

22. See *Sierra Club v. Ruckelshaus,* 344 F. Supp. 253 (D.D.C. 1972). For the EPA regulations, which were promulgated Dec. 5, 1974, see 40 C.F.R. § 52.21 (1974). For an analysis of the PSD problem, see 1977 U.S. Code Cong. & Ad. News 1181–1257. For an extensive re-

view with bibliographies, see A. C. Stern, "Prevention of Significant Deterioration," 27 *J. of the Air Pollution Cont. A.* 440 (1977).

23. This was a major point at issue in the argument of the plaintiffs in Kennecott Copper Corp. challenge of the secondary sulfur dioxide standard. *Kennecott Copper Corp. v. EPA,* 462 F.2d 849 n.13 (D.C. Cir. 1972).

24. Esposito, *Vanishing Air,* 280.

25. See Vietor, *Environmental Politics.* The American Mining Congress recommended a sulfur dioxide annual average of 130 ug/m3; the American Petroleum Institute, 115 ug/m3; and the American Smelting and Refining Company 2–5 ppm.

26. See 6 *Envir. Rep.—Current Dev.* (BNA) 1393 (December 12, 1975), 1993 (March 26, 1976); 7 *Envir. Rep.—Current Dev.* (BNA) 12 (May 7, 1976), 127 (May 28, 1976), 464 (July 16, 1976), 924 (October 22, 1976).

27. 42 U.S.C.A. § 7408(c) (Supp. 1977).

28. For controversies concerning workplace carcinogens, see 42 Fed. Reg. 54,148 (1977). See also N. Karch, *Explicit Criteria and Principles for Identifying Carcinogens, Decision Making in the Environmental Protection Agency* (NAS, Analytical Studies for the U.S. Environmental Protection Agency, vol. IIa). For the lead relationship dispute, see 7 *Envir. Rep.—Current Dev.* (BNA) 1486 (February 4, 1977).

29. See J. P. Hills, "Legal Decisions and Opinions in Pollution Cases," 10 *Envir'l. Sci. & Tech.* 234 (1976).

30. 8 *Envir. Rep.—Current Dev.* (BNA) 1507 (February 3, 1978).

31. W. W. Holland, *Health Effects of Particulate Pollution: Reappraising the Evidence* (Preliminary) (December 1, 1977) n.p.

32. 7 *Envir. Rep.—Current Dev.* (BNA) 1191 (Dec. 17, 1976), 1919 (April 15, 1977), 1972 (April 22, 1977); 8 *Envir. Rep.— Current Dev.* (BNA) 11 (May 6, 1977).

33. 42 U.S.C.A. § 7409 (Supp. 1977).

34. See Esposito, *Vanishing Air,* 259.

35. For a calculation of sulfur dioxide levels for eight urban air-quality maintenance areas in Pennsylvania, with an emphasis on both point sources and area sources, see "A Study of Existing and Projected Sulfur Dioxide Levels in Pennsylvania"—8 *AQMS's Engineering-Sci*. (1977).

36. "California Air Resources Bd.," 9 *Bull.* 1, 5 (January 1978).

37. *Kennecott Copper Corp. v. Train,* 526 F.2d 1149 (9th Cir. 1975); *Big Rivers Elec. Corp. v. EPA,* 523 F.2d 16 (6th Cir. 1975); *NRDC v. EPA,* 489 F.2d 390 (5th Cir. 1974).

38. See 1977 U.S. Code Cong. & Ad. News 1261–62.

39. A major center for the dissemination of such a view was "Resources for the Future." See, e.g., *Current Issues in U.S. Environmental Policy* (1978).

40. See 1977 U.S. Code Cong. & Ad. News 1150–51. Support for an emissions charge was expressed by a variety of sources such as the National Academy of Sciences, National Academy of Engineering and the Committee for Economic Development. *Id.*

41. See J. E. Bonine, "The Evolution of 'Technology-Forcing' in the Clean Air Act," *Envir. Rep.—Monograph* 21 (July 25, 1975).

42. S. Miller, "The Business of Air Pollution Control," 7 *Envt'l. Sci. & Tech.* 988 (1973).

43. See R. E. Ayers, "Enforcement of Air Pollution Controls on Stationary Sources under the Clean Air Amendments of 1970," 4 *Ecology L.Q.* 445, n.11 (1975) (quoting from EPA, Report of the Hearing Panel, National Public Hearing on the Power Plant Compliance with Sulfur Oxide Air Pollution Regulations, Jan. 1974).

44. For the relevant sections of the statute, see 42 U.S.C.A. §§ 7470–7491, 7501–7508, 7420(d) (Supp. 1977).

45. See 40 C.F.R. § 51.21 (1977).

46. See 1977 U.S. Code Cong. & Ad News 1181–82.

47. See B. I. Raffle, "The New Clean Air Act—Getting Clean and Staying Clean," *Envir. Rep.*—Monograph 47 (May 19, 1978).

48. *Id.* at 17.

49. See note 13 *supra* .

50. See M. W. First, "Process and System Control" in Air Pollution 316 (A. C. Stern ed. 1968).

51. 8 *Envir. Rep.*—*Current Dev.* (BNA) 1109 (Nov. 25, 1977); see also 40 C.F.R. § 52.21(d) (1977).

52. See *NRDC v. EPA,* 475 F.2d 968 (D.C. Cir. 1973). See 38 Fed. Reg. 6279, 9599, 15, 834 (1973); 39 Fed. Reg. 16,343, 25,330, 28,906 (1974); 40 Fed. Reg. 18,726, 23,746 (1975) for the regulations.

53. See "Clean Air Act Amendments of 1977," *Steelworkers Legislative Newsletter,* Sept. 12, 1977, 3–4 (attachment).

54. See 1977 U.S. Code Cong. & Ad. News 1183–84. For current knowledge of low-level pollutants, see H. R. Subcommittee on the Environment and the Atmosphere, Comm. on Science and Technology, *The Costs and Effects of Chronic Exposure to Low-Level Pollutants in the Environment* (1975).

55. See Thomas R. Dunlap, "Publicity, Environmental Law, and DDT" (paper presented at the meeting of the Organization of American Historians, Atlanta, Ga., April 7, 1977).

56. 42 Fed. Reg. 54,148 (1977).

57. Environmental Defense Fund, petition for the Initiation of Rulemaking Proceedings to Establish a Policy Governing the Classification and Regulation of Carcinogenic Air Pollutants Under the Clean Air Act (Nov. 4, 1977). See also EDF, Testimony of the Environmental Defense Fund at a Public Meeting to Solicit Recommendations Useful in Developing a Comprehensive Program for the Regulation of Carcinogenic Air Pollutants (March 23, 1978).

58. See 1977 U.S. Code Cong. & Ad News 1197–98.

59. See note 7 *supra.*

60. See the introductory remarks in EPA, *Health Consequences of Sulfur Oxides: A Report from CHESS, 1970–1971,* No. 650/1-74-004 (May 1974).

61. See California Study, Staff Report, Vegetarian Effects 49 (March 15, 1977).

62. See EPA, Position Paper on Regulation of Atmospheric Sulfates, No. 450/2-75-007 (September 1975); House Subcommittee on the Environment and the Atmosphere, Committee on Science and Technology, Research and Development Related to Sulfates in the Atmosphere (1975); A. P. Altshuler, "Regional Transport and Transformation of Sulfur Dioxide to Sulfates in the U.S.," 26 *J. of the Air Pollution Cont. A.* 318 (1976).

63. See California Air Resources Board, Research Division, *Review of the 24-Hour Sulfate Ambient Air Quality Standard,* Staff Report No. 77-2-3 (September 29, 1977).

64. See EPA, Office of Research and Development, *Research Highlights, 1977,* No. 600/9-77-044 (December 1977); L. F. Smith and B. L. Niemann, "The Ohio River Basin Energy Study: The Future of Air Resources and other Factors Affecting Energy Development," paper presented at the Third International Conference on Environmental Problems of the Extractive Industries in Dayton, Oh., November 29–December 1, 1977.

65. See U.S. Dept. of Agriculture, Forest Service, Proceedings of the First International Symposium on Acid Precipitation and the Forest Ecosystem, General Technical Report NE-23 (1976). For international Canadian–United States implications of acid precipitation in North America, see R. LeBlanc, "Long Range Transport of Air Pollutants," 27 *J. of the Air Pollution Cont.* A. 828 (1977).

66. See note 10 *supra.*

67. See Vietor, *Environmental Politics,* 292.

68. For accounts of the NIPCC, see G. J. C. Smith, *Our Ecological Crisis 167–72* (1974); Vietor, *Vanishing Air,* 292–344.

69. See 5 *Envir. Rep.—Current Dev.* (BNA) 1873 (March 18, 1975) for an account of the NAS report. To counteract the effects of this report, the Federal Energy Administration contracted with Tabershaw/Cooper Associates, Rockville, Maryland, to do a similar evaluation, a draft of which was released almost simultaneously with the NAS report and was entitled "A Critical Evaluation of Current Research Regarding Health Criteria for Sulfur Oxides." According to Frank Zarb, administrator of the FEA, the initial discussions on the contract began in November 1974; it was signed February 5, 1975; the draft was completed February 15, 1975. In discussions on the FEA report before the Senate Public Works Committee, Senator Randolph suggested that it could be called the "tailored report." Zarb argued that both the NAS and the Tabershaw/Cooper reports should be given "equal weight" in assessing health effects. See 5 *Envir. Rep.—Current Dev.* (BNA) 1871 (March 28, 1975).

70. See *Envir. Rep.—Current Dev.* (BNA) 1888 (March 28,1975), 2125 (April 16, 1976); 7 *Envir. Rep.—Current Dev.* (BNA) 32 (May 14, 1976), 285 (June 18, 1976), 496 (July 23, 1976).

71. See generally NRDC's report; for NRDC input into the early 1971 proceedings, see Letter from Richard E. Ayres to William D. Ruckelshaus, March 15, 1971, enclosing comments on the proposed National Primary and Secondary Ambient Air Quality Standards (EPA Record Office, 1971 Air Pollution Standards Comments File).

72. See statement by John J. Sheehan, representative of the United Steelworkers of America, 7 *Envir. Rep.—Current Dev.* (BNA) 240 (June 11, 1976).

73. In the debate over the revision of the Clean Water Act during 1977, Lloyd McBride, president of the United Steelworkers of America, wrote, "Our union does not seek any congressional relaxation of the . . . EPA-OSHA regulations." See letter from McBride to Rep. Charles J. Carney, chairman of the Congressional Steel Caucus, October 19, 1977. During debate over the "environment versus jobs" referendum in Allegheny County, Pennsylvania, in fall 1977, USW representatives testified, "There is no evidence that changing the environmental laws would preserve steel industry jobs." See statement issued on behalf of Joseph Odorcich, vice president of administration, United Steelworkers of America, at a press conference, Pittsburgh, Pa., October 21, 1977.

74. H. R. Subcommittee on Health and the Environment, Committee on Interstate and Foreign Commerce, 94th Cong., Clean Air Act Amendments—1975, at 690.

75. See 1977 U.S. Code Cong. & Ad. News 1289.

76. See note 73 *supra* .

77. See note 53 *supra.*

78. See news release, Ohio River Basin Energy Study (February 15, 1978); see also response, Sy A. Ali, manager, Environmental Programs Public Service Company of Indiana, to Dr. Boyd R. Keenan, Ohio River Basin Energy Study (March 7, 1978).)

Clean Air, 1977–1990

Ephemeral material cited as AF is in the author's personal file.

1. For an account of the 1977 law, to which this review is a sequel, consult Samuel P. Hays, "Clean Air: From the 1970 Act to the 1977 Amendments." *Duquesne Law Review* 17 (1978–79): 33–66.

2. For general reviews of the 1990 act, see "The New Clean Air Act: What It Means to You," *EPA Journal* 17, no. 1 (January–February 1991); John Quarles and William H. Lewis Jr., *The New Clean Air Act: A Guide to the Clean Air Program as Amended in 1990* (Washington, D.C., Morgan, Lewis & Bockius, 1990); Environmental and Energy Study Conference, *1990 Clean Air Act Amendments* (Washington, D.C., Environmental and Energy Study Conference, 1990). For a newspaper overview, see Philip Shabecoff, "In Search of a Better Law to Clean the Air," *New York Times,* May 14, 1989, 4: 1, 5. For the sequence of events in Congress several articles in *Congressional Quarterly* are useful; see "The 'White House Effect' Opens a Long-Locked Political Door," January 20, 1990, 139–44; "For Industry and Opponents, a Showdown Is in the Air," January 20, 1990, 145; "Big Win for Majority Leader Marks His Rite of Passage," April 7, 1990, 1045–47; "Clean Air: War About Over in Both House and Senate," April 7, 1990, 1057–63.

3. "Acid Rain: Federal Report Not Expected to Play Major Role in CAA Debate," *Clean Air Report* (Hereafter CAR) (September 13, 1990): 27–28.

4. Paul Farmer, EPA's outgoing air emissions standards chief, believed that the CAA had "broken through" the old section 112 of the 1970 act under which hazardous pollutants were regulated. Under the old act the agency was mired in the philosophical argument of what constitutes an acceptable risk. See "Air Toxics, Permits Head Agency Work List Under New CAA," CAR (July 5, 1990): 14. But now, said Farmer, "we don't have to deal with the debate" of who should and shouldn't be regulated. See "Outgoing Air Standards Chief: Special Industry Toxics Breaks Will Block Rules," *Inside EPA* (hereafter IN) (December 7, 1990): 12.

5. Henry Waxman, chair of the House Energy and Commerce Subcommittee on Health and the Environment told reporters, "We're not going to leave it to EPA this time to use its discretion to enforce the clean air law. . . . We're spelling out what must be done." "Expansive Clean Air Bill's Toxics Title Sets New Tone for Government Regulation," CRR (November 30, 1990): 1333.

6. Samuel P. Hays, "Science and Values: Lead in Historical Perspective," in Herbert L. Needleman, ed., *Human Lead Exposure* (New York: CRC Press, 1992).

7. For general statements about the business opportunities stimulated by environmental legislation, see Michael Silverstein, *The Environmental Factor: Its Impact on the Future of the World Economy and Your Investments* (Chicago: Longman's Financial Services Publishing, 1990); *In Business: The Magazine for Environmental Entrepreneuring* (Emmaus, Pa., 1978–); Michael E. Porter, "America's Green Strategy," *Scientific American* (April 1991): 168; "Pollution Control Industry Hails Tough Senate Legislation for Creating Jobs," IN (March 30, 1990): 17; Robert W. McIlvaine, "The 1991 Global Air Pollution Control Industry," *Journal of the Air and Waste Management Association* 41 (March 1991): 272–75.

8. The *Wall Street Journal* as cited in *In Business* (November–December 1990): 11. The *Journal* article described, as an example, a service station in Virginia that provided a range of environmental products and services for automobiles.

9. Joel S. Hirschhorn, "Regulations Create New Business Niches," *In Business* (November–December 1990): 40–41.

10. After passage of the CAA such business opportunities were reported regularly. See "CAA Spurs Development of New Cost-Effective Controls for Utilities," CAR (December 6, 1990): 25, stating that "stringent new federal acid rain standards will spur the development of control technologies that are more efficient and cost-effective than existing technologies for cutting emissions of nitrogen oxide and sulfur dioxide." "New Catalyst Puts Off Need for Fuel Switching to Comply," and "Technological Advance in Fuel Efficiency Guts Reformulated Gas Program," CAR (December 6, 1990): 24; "The Greening of Detroit: A Push Is on to Make Cars More Environmentally Friendly," *Business Week* (April 8, 1991): 54–60.

11. "Acid Rain: Federal Report Not Expected to Play Major Role in CAA Debate," CAR (September 13, 1990): 27–28.

12. See "Administration Cites 25-Billion Price Tag, Hopes For Cuts in Conference," CAR (August 16, 1990): 8–10; the text of the Bush letter, "Text—Letter from White House Economic Advisers on Clean Air Act Costs," is in CAR (August 16, 1990): 9–10; "EPA Calls White House Cost Warning the 1st Salvo in Battle for Reductions," CAR (August 30, 1990): 6; "White House Estimates of Senate, House Bills Trigger Bush Veto Threat," CAR (October 11, 1990): 9–10, with detailed analysis of "Administration Cost Estimates," 10–14.

13. See "Lip Service from the Apostles of Cost-Benefit Analysis: The Administration Exaggerates the Costs, Ignores the Benefits of S. 1630," drawn up by the National Clean Air Coalition and attached to letter Richard E. Ayers, chair of the Clean Air Coalition to Senators, February 22, 1990 (AF); "Environmentalists Blast EPS's Senate CAA Cost Estimates as Overblown," IN (March 2, 1990): 17; "Environmentalists Find Extensive Flaws in Industry CAA Cost Estimates," IN (November 8, 1990): 13–14.

14. Building on an earlier report of the Business Roundtable, Robert Hahn and Wilbur Steger prepared an analysis for the Clean Air Working Group that estimated costs from $54 billion up to $90 billion; see "Major Industry Coalition Wages Campaign Against Senate Air Toxics Bill," IN (January 26, 1990): 16–17. Later that year, the Clean Air Working Group argues that the cost of the CAA as it then stood reached $91 billion, more than four times the cost Bush called veto bait. See "Industry Study Puts $91-Billion Price Tag on New Law," CAR (August 16, 1990): 14–15; "Cost of Implementing Air Legislation Could Reach $91 Billion, Industry Group Says," *Environment Reporter* (hereafter ER) (August 3, 1990): 656.

15. The most comprehensive benefit analyses were conducted by the American Lung Association. See "The Health Costs of Air Pollution" (New York: American Lung Association, 1977); James S. Cannon, "The Health Costs of Air Pollution: A Survey of Studies Published 1978–1983" (New York: American Lung Association, 1985), a review of eight comprehensive health cost studies, those actually placing a price tag on human exposure to air pollution; James S. Cannon, "The Health Costs of Air Pollution: A Survey of Studies Published, 1984–1989" (New York: American Lung Association, 1990), a review of twelve studies published during these years. See also Michael P. Walsh, "Pollution on Wheels: The Need for More Stringent Controls on Hydrocarbons and Nitrogen Oxides to Attain Healthy Air Quality Levels Across the United States" (New York: American Lung Association, February 11, 1988); Michael P. Walsh, "Pollution on Wheels II: The Car of the Future" (New York: American Lung Association, January 19, 1990).

16. Realizing that most previous economic analyses had emphasized costs, the Office

of Air and Radiation in EPA wanted to go on record with respect to benefits before legislation was completed. But the agency was divided over what should be included in benefits and the report apparently was not completed. "EPA Staff at Odds Over Benefits Associated With Clean Air Act," CAR (October 11, 1990): 14–15.

17. When the administration submitted a new cost analysis to the Conference Committee in which it argued that changes should be made to reduce the CAA cost, it had little impact. Said one Senate source: "Nobody knows how many jobs will be produced or lost. . . . It's all idle speculation." Said another, "From a parochial standpoint you hear a lot about costs but not from a macroeconomic perspective." And another, "You can always find numbers to back up your argument." "Conferees Question Impact of Administration Cost-Assessment," CAR (August 16, 1990): 19.

18. "In proposing changes to control acid rain, improve urban air quality, and limit toxic chemical emissions, the president became a part of the congressional debate to amend the Clean Air Act during the 101st Congress." "President Proposes to Amend Clean Air Act, New Authority to Regulate Solvent Emissions," *Chemical Regulation Reporter* (hereafter CRR) (June 16, 1989): 386–87. EPA was more deferential to the president; while it prefaced its account of the CAA by describing Bush's proposal as "building on Congressional proposals advanced during the 1980s," it also began its "legislative chronology of events" with Bush's announcement of his proposal, June 12, 1989. See USEPA, "The Clean Air Act Amendments of 1990: Summary materials," November 15, 1990. (AF)

19. Chief support for an administration bill came from Reilly, Sununu and Gray, while opposition came from Richard Darman, head of OMB and Robert Teeter, White House political adviser. See "OMB Chief Darman Said to Raise Concern Over Administration Clean Air Bill," IN (January 27, 1989): 1–8. These differences continued throughout the process of drafting the administration bill. OMB sought the lead to minimize impacts of the bill on industry while EPA felt it should take the lead. See "EPA, OMB, White House Squabble: Who Will Develop Administration CAA Bill?" IN (February 24, 1989): 1–8. See also "Administration Struggles with Merits of Pursuing Least-Cost Acid Rain Bill," IN (April 7, 1989): 1–9; "Administration Reportedly Considers 'Piecemeal' Approach to Clean Air Bill," IN (April 14, 1989): 1–9.

20. For the president's proposal, see "Fact Sheet: President Bush's Clean Air Plan," White House, Office Press Secretary, June 12, 1989.

21. In the Senate, Bush's problem was how to deal with a very strong bloc of Republican senators whose aim was to weaken legislation; he used them both to weaken the bill and prevent them from scuttling the entire process. For administration strategy in the Senate, see "Administration Launches Major, Focused Push to Scale Back Senate CAA," IN (January 26, 1990): 1–2; "Senators Work Quietly to Cull Support for Alternative Clean Air Bill," IN (February 2, 1990): 1–2; "Administration Says Senate CAA Places Own Expertise Above That of EPA, States," IN (February 2, 1990): 13; "EPA: Administration/ House Clean Air Bill Half as Costly as Senate Legislation," IN (February 2, 1990): 13–16.

Administration/Senate leader negotiations can be followed week-by-week: "Core Group of CAA Negotiators Meet in Private to Hash Out Senate Accord," IN (February 9, 1990): 11; "CAA Negotiators Craft Air Toxics Agreement, Easing Industry Restrictions," IN (February 9, 1990): 12; "CAA Negotiators Near Deal to Pare Back Senate Auto Controls," IN (February 9, 1990): 13; "Mitchell/Administration Reach Pact on Major CAA Positions, Next Step: The Floor." IN (March 2, 1990): 1, 7; "Senate/Administration Air Toxics Accord Calls for Industry-Backed Study," IN (March 2, 1990): 12–13.

22. In the House the president's problem was to prevent Republicans wanting a stronger CAA to sign onto Democratic proposals. "Diverse Group of House Republicans Suggests Plan for Administration CAA Bill," IN (March 10, 1989): 6–7, and "Administration Meets with House Republicans; Hopes to Gain Their Support for CAA Bill," IN (March 17, 1989): 1–8. See also "Waxman to Introduce Acid Rain Bill This Week with Strong Republican Support," IN (March 17, 1989); the bill had eighty cosponsors, of whom twenty were Republicans.

23. "Administration Cries That It Is Being Excluded from House CAA Talks," IN (May 4, 1990): 1–7.

24. "Administration Seeks Major Involvement, but Has Few Allies," CAR (July 19, 1990): 11; "Bush Goads CAA Conferees with New Plan," CAR, Special Report (September 28, 1990): 2–5.

25. See publication of the Clean Air Coalition, "Campaign Update," issued periodically during the 1980s debate and superseded for the 1989–90 debate by "Clean Air 101." For its evaluation of the Bush clean air proposal, see "The President's Clean Air Plan: The Words Are Refreshing, but the Substance Must Match" (Washington, 1989) (AF).

26. "Lung Association: Senate Auto Controls Cheap, Effective Way to Cut Pollution," IN (January 26, 1990): 13–14.

27. The national Wildlife Federation was also active in the clean air debate; see its newsletter to "clean air activists" (Washington, D.C., 1987–1990) (AF).

28. The Sierra Club issued fliers and leaflets throughout the debate advocating its positions; see especially its "Clean Air Activist," later "Pollution Activist" (San Francisco, Calif., 1987–1991). Two general publications set forth the policies it advocated: "Darkening Skies: The Mountain Air Pollution Crisis in the United States" (Washington, D.C., 1989); "Clear Choices for Clean Air," a comparison of clean air bills (Washington, D.C., 1990) (AF).

29. The Clean Air Working Group was a coalition of nearly two thousand corporations and trade associations. See interview with William D. Fay, administrator of the group. "Which Provision of the Pending Clean Air Act Will Most Benefit Public Health and Which Provision Will Cost Industry the Most?" CAR (May 10, 1990): 18.

30. The Sierra Club described the act as "a major victory for the environment and public health," and Susan Merrow, president of the club, wrote that "The Clean Air Act of 1990 is like a breath of fresh air after a 10-year smog alert." See Sierra Club, "National News Report" (November 7, 1990): 1–2; (December 3, 1990): 1. For Hawkins's views, see "Public Indifference Yielded Weak CAA, Leading Environmentalist Says," CAR (December 6, 1990): T-15.

31. In an interview with *Clean Air Report*, Ernest Rosenberg, director of legislation and regulation for Occidental Petroleum Corporation's health, environmental, and safety division, said, "We were being cast as the people who were trying to relax controls"; this to a large extent accounted for "the reason why the cost argument never got the hearing it should have." He said the $25 billion price tag "is a joke" and at a minimum it will run upwards of $35 billion. CAR (January 3, 1991): T-16.

32. Samuel P. Hays, "The Republican Party and the Environment," *The Environmental Forum* 7, no. 2 (March/April 1990): 50; Hays, "Environmental Political Culture and Environmental Political Development: An Analysis of Legislative Voting, 1971–1989," paper presented to the conference of the Society for Environmental History (Houston, Tex., March 1, 1991).

33. See Table 1, 1990 Clean Air Act Votes, for data.

34. Cooperation between the administration and the environmental opposition in

the Senate was reflected in the make-up of the Senate/administration negotiating team. It was composed of five Democrats (Mitchell, Baucus, Lautenburg, Byrd, and Breaux) and five Republicans (Chaffee, Simpson, Domenici, McClure, and Dole). Within both parties these representatives stood at the low end of the scale of LCV environmental scores. While those scores generally were seventy for Senate Democrats and thirty-two for Republicans, scores for members of this working group were forty-four for the Democrats and twelve for the Republicans. Three of the five Republicans were from the Mountain West, and all had zero environmental LCV scores. Thus, the negotiating group involved an effort on the part of the Bush administration to work with those at the lower end of the environmental spectrum in the Senate, rather than in the upper end or the middle. The support of the Mountain States Republicans was thought to be crucial.

35. The lead Republican in the Mountain States opposition was Senator Alan Simpson of Wyoming. See "Simpson to Industry: Pull Out All the Stops to Bury Costly CAA Provisions," CAR (August 2, 1990): 12; "Western Senators May Filibuster CAA, Disillusioned with Stringent Deals," CAR (October 11, 1990): 8–9; interview with Senator Alan Simpson, CAR (October 11, 1990): 30.

36. See interview with William Becker, "Clean Air's State Representative Says New Law to Be 'Monumental Task,'" CAR (May 24, 1990): 26; "Colorado Air Director Beckham Calls for Tough Mobile Source Controls," CAR (August 2, 1990): 28; Beckham had been Colorado's chief air quality regulator since 1986 and was president of the board of directors of STAPPA. See also "State Air Officials: Second Tier Tailpipe Standards Should Remain Senate CAA," In (February 23, 1990): 15.

37. James E. Krier and Edmund Ursin, *Pollution & Policy: A Case Essay on California and Federal Experience with Motor Vehicle Air Pollution, 1940–1975.* (Berkeley, Calif.: University of California Press, 1977).

38. The New England Staff for Coordinated Air Use Management was formed in 1967 by the Conference of State Public Health Officials at the recommendation of the New England Governors' Conference. New York joined the group in 1970 and New Jersey in 1979 and the name was changed to Northeast States for Coordinated Air Use Management. NESCAUM began to publish a newsletter about its activities in 1987 and its reports have been widely circulated. See, for example, "Critical Analysis of the Federal Motor Vehicle Control Program" (1988), "An Evaluation of Adopting the California Mobile Source Control Program in the Eight Northeast States" (1989) (AF). For some of its views during the legislative process, see "Northeast States Urge Congressional, Administration Effort to Reduce Acid Rain," IN (February 3, 1989): 14; "Northeast Air Officials Ask for State Opt-in on Visibility Regs, Federal Air Plans," CAR (August 2, 1990): 12.

39. "Report Says Northeast States Could Benefit from Adoption of California Tailpipe Program," ER (May 19, 1989): 153–54; "Northeast States Will Adopt California's Tailpipe Program," CAR (October 25, 1990): 16–17.

40. Peter Passell, "Selling Right to Pollute: Bush Backs Idea in Acid-Rain Fight," *New York Times,* May 17, 1989, A1, A23.

41. National Research Council, *Sulfur Oxides* (Washington, D.C.: National Academy of Sciences, 1978).

42. A ten-million-ton reduction was supported by a wide range of groups; see, for example, the recommendation of the National Governors Association, "Governors Urge 10-Million Ton Reductions, Subsidy in Draft CAA Plan," IN (March 10, 1989): 13.

43. Philip Shabecoff, "Government Acid Rain Report Comes Under Sharp Attack," *New York Times,* September 22, 1988.

44. See statements of Senator John Kerry of Massachusetts, *Congressional Record*

(April 3, 1990): S3812; and Representative Gerry Sikorski, *Congressional Record* (April 21, 1990): H2573; "Dukakis Announces New State Limits on Large Sources of Sulfur Dioxide Emissions," ER (May 5, 1989): 21–22.

45. The cap never figured heavily in congressional debate, was not mentioned in the president's press release on his legislative proposals, was not mentioned in the literature of environmental organizations, and did not appear in press accounts. It was mentioned by the Clean Air Working Group, the industry lobby, as the reason for opposing the Bush bill. See "CAWG Opposes Bush Ceiling On SO-2 Emissions and Hence the Entire Bill," ER (August 4, 1989): 625.

Senator Symms of Idaho was one of the few senators to take up the cudgels against the cap. The cap, he said, is a "virtual death sentence . . . on the future of coal as an energy source"; it was "'lip service' to the concept of allowing the marketplace to determine where to most efficiently achieve acid precursor reductions." See "Symms Blasts Environment Committee Clean Air Bill for Hampering Coal Use," IN (January 5, 1990): 14.

Rep. Bilirakis of Florida sent a "Dear Colleague" letter urging modification of the proposal. The cap, he said, "could have a serious, negative impact on growth in our nations' electric capacity," especially affecting states experiencing population and economic growth. See "Bilirakis Begins Major Assault on Administration's Acid Rain Cap," IN (September 22, 1989): 6.

William Reilly, administrator of EPA, stated before the House Energy and Commerce Committee, Energy and Power Subcommittee, that a bill with no cap would be vetoed, and William Rosenberg, assistant administrator for air, argued in a letter to Representative Bliley on September 8 that the cap is "essential to the goals of the legislation." "EPA Hard Line on Acid Rain Cap Irks Some in White House, Congress," IN (September 22, 1989): 1–10. However, in response to the attacks on the cap, Reilly sought support from environmentalists on the grounds he could not defend the cap alone and the Clean Air Coalition agreed to back the cap but to remain silent on the issue of emissions trading. See "EPA Asks Environmentalists to Support Administration Acid Rain Bill," IN (September 22, 1989): 6; "Environmentalists Agree to Back Bush Cap, but Not Entire Acid Rain Bill," IN (September 29, 1989): 16.

46. To Senator Simpson, "The repeal of percentage reduction is a welcome addition." "Additional Views of Senator Simpson," on the bill reported from the Senate committee, IN (January 5, 1990): 12.

47. "Panel Locked in Debate Over 'Question of Trust,'" CAR, Special Report (February 28, 1991): 2; "Interim Measures, Missing Data Option Thrown in EPA's Lap," CAR (May 9, 1991): 23.

48. See John Seitz, "Urban Air Quality: The Strategy," *EPA Journal* (January/February 1991): 27–29.

49. Harold M. Haskew, David R. Garrett, and James J. Gumbleton, "GM's Results: The EPA/Industry Cooperative Test Program," SAE Technical Paper Series (Warrendale, Pa.: Society of Automotive Engineers, 1988).

50. Soon after the 1990 Act was passed, a number of states took up the "California option" to apply the "second stage" California standards to their state. This involved a wide range of California proposals, including their "low-emission vehicles program." The Northeast States for Coordinated Air Use Management took the lead, and New York was the first, passing authorizing legislation in September 1990; Massachusetts followed suit and by the spring of 1991 action was underway not only in Maine, Rhode Island, Connecticut, and New Jersey—states within the NESCAUM area—but also in Maryland and

Texas. The target of action was the 1995 model year car. There was clear competition here between the federal standards in the 1990 act and the state standards based on the California program. The auto industry took great exception to these new state initiatives, instituting legal action against the New York program by arguing that it contemplated not a "California car" but a "third car" and hence was contrary to the enabling provisions of the federal act. Yet the California-inspired state program moved ahead and it appeared that major innovation in auto standards would come from that quarter rather than from federal action. See "New England Air Director Works with States to Adopt California Auto Standards," CAR (March 28, 1991): T-14; and "Host of States Expected to Adopt California Low-Emission Vehicles Program," "California Report," (April 5, 1991): 2–3.

51. William Rosenberg, EPA Assistant Administrator for Air, said the EPA would not oppose a state that wished to require a second round of tailpipe standards, but would oppose its addition to the CAA. Baucus said several times he would not support use of alternative, clean fuels at "expense of tighter tailpipe standards." "One is not a substitute for the other." See "Conferees Bicker Over Clean Fuel Delay in Clean Air Act Negotiations," *Environmental Reporter* 21, no. 23 (October 5, 1990): 1115–16.

52. "Senate Hears New 'Clean Fuel' Proposals from Chaffee, California and New York Officials," ER (January 19, 1990): 1623–24; "Senate, Administration Agree to Expand Role of Reformulated Gas in Fuels Plan," IN (March 2, 1990): 11–12; "Waxman Likely to Offer CAA Fuels Plan in House Tougher Than Subcommittee's" IN (March 2, 1990): 15; "Senate Environment Would Keep Stiff Tailpipe Standards Plus Clean Fuels Plan," IN (January 19, 1990): 5–6; "Administration, Chaffee CAA Plan Suggests EPA Weakening on Alternative Fuels," IN (February 16, 1990): 1, 7; "Fleet Plan Gains Senate Ground as More Moderate Alternative Fuels Approach," IN (February 16, 1990): 15; "Senators Vote Down Wirth/Wilson Fuels Amendment, Stinging Environmentalists," IN (March 23, 1990): 10.

53. Mobile source provisions are outlined succinctly in Richard D. Wilson, "Motor Vehicles and Fuels: The Strategy," *EPA Journal* 17, no. 1 (January/February 1991): 15.

54. EPA administrator William Reilly argued that additional NOx cuts beyond two-million tons from the projected year 2000 level were so costly that they were not justified. See "Reilly Gives Nod to Senate Repeal of Stringent 'Scrubber' Provisions," IN (September 29, 1989): 14.

55. The cap of 46,120 pounds was adopted in 1989 and in May 1991 more stringent declining limits to 20,490 pounds by the year 2000 were proposed. See "South Coast District Proposes Lower Cap, Tighter Emission Limit for Nitrogen Oxides," ER (May 10, 1991): 117.

56. "Waxman Drafts Prescriptive Air Toxics Bill After Data Show Large Releases," IN (March 31, 1989): 3–4; "House Toxics Control Measure Introduced: Data Tying Emissions to Health Effects Released," CRR (June 16, 1989): 385. The data was required by the Emergency Planning and Community Right-to-Know Act.

57. Community organizing around the Emergency Planning and Community Right-to-Know law can be followed in "Working Notes on Community Right-to-Know" (Washington, D.C.: U.S. Public Interest Research Group Education Fund, 1988–) and *Toxic Times,* newsletter of the National Toxics Campaign (Boston, 1988–).

58. For debate on the toxics provision, see "Senate Air Toxics Provision Becomes Vulnerable as Opposition Mounts," IN (February 2, 1990): 12–13; "Expansive Clean Air Bill's Toxics Title Sets New Tone for Government Regulation," CRR (November 30, 1990): 1333–34.

59. A standard introduction to risk analysis that presumably guides federal agencies

is John J. Cohrssen and Vincent T. Covello, *Risk Analysis: A Guide to Principles and Methods for Analyzing Health and Environmental Risks* (Washington, D.C.: Council on Environmental Quality, 1989). See "Reducing Risk: Setting Priorities and Strategies for Environmental Protection," report of the EPA Relative Risk Reduction Project (Washington, D.C.: Environmental Protection Agency, 1990), and especially its three subcommittee reports, "The Report of the Human Health Subcommittee," "The Report of the Ecology and Welfare Subcommittee," and "The Report of the Strategic Options Subcommittee," EPA SAB-EC 90-021A-C (Washington, D.C., 1989).

60. For an environmental critique of risk assessment, see JoAnn Gutin, "At Our Peril: The False Promise of Risk Assessment," *Greenpeace Magazine* (March/April 1991): 13–18. Judith Shaw of the American Petroleum Institute remarked that distrust of risk assessment was part of the reason Congress bypassed, for the most part, human health as a basis for the new CAA in favor of technology; risk assessment, she said, is more of an art form than a cut-and-dried discipline. See *Environmental Health Letter* (Washington, D.C.: Bureau of National Affairs, March 12, 1991), 54.

61. For legislative proceedings concerning the NAS study, see "Industry Floats CAA Plan Calling for Independent Study of Air Pollution Risks," IN (March 2, 1990): 13; "Air Toxics: Ritter May Offer Industry-Backed Plan for Further Study of Residual Risk," CAR (May 10, 1990): 3–4. General Electric Corporation, author of the proposal, said that it wanted to make the risk assessment process "more realistic and the assumptions less theoretical."

62. The inevitable controversial nature of the NAS report could be predicted by the plans of a broad-based industry group, the American Industrial Health Council, to be "active" in the work of the NAS committee. See "Industry Health Council Seeks Voice in Residual Risk Study," CAR (December 6, 1990): 17.

63. A proposal to amend the Senate/Administration bill to control toxic emissions from mobile sources was defeated on the floor, 65–33; see "Defeat on Air Toxics Amendment Signals Problem for Environmentalists in Senate," IN (March 16, 1990): 1, 7.

64. For coke oven emissions, see "States Urge Conferees to Adopt Swift Regulation of Coke Ovens, Utilities," CAR (October 11, 1990): 18–19; for an analysis of the health effects of coke ovens in one case, see Utah County Clean Air Coalition, "Coke Oven Emissions in Utah County: A Serious Health Threat" (unpublished manuscript, January 1990) (AF).

65. For utilities, see "Utility Industry to Push for Air Toxics Study Over Controls in Senate CAA," IN (January 12, 1990): 13; "Outgoing Air Standards Chief: Special Industry Toxics Breaks Will Block Rules," IN (December 7, 1990): 12; "CAA Negotiators Craft Air Toxics Agreement, Easing Industry Restrictions," IN (February 9, 1990): 12. Mercury emissions from utilities were of special interest to Minnesota and Senator Durenburger; see Edward A. Garvey, "Clean Air Act Passes with Acid Rain Controls," BWCA Wilderness News (Winter 1991): 5. A view of the problem from the vantage point of the utility industry is "New Focus on Air Toxics," *EPRI Journal* 16, no. 2 (March 1991): 4–13.

66. Theodora E. Colburn, Alex Davidson, Sharon N. Green, R.A. (Tony) Hodge, C. Ian Jackson, and Richard A. Liroff, *Great Lakes: Great Legacy?* (Washington, D.C. and Ottawa, Canada: The Conservation Foundation and Institute for Research on Public Policy, 1990); Great Lakes Water Quality Board, "1989 Report on Great Lakes Water Quality" (Windsor, Canada: International Joint Commission, 1989).

67. For an introduction to the problem of stratospheric ozone, see Sharon L. Roan,

Ozone Crisis: The 15 Year Evolution of a Sudden Global Emergency (New York: John Wiley & Sons, 1989).

68. For legislative proceedings, see "Chaffee Calls for Accelerated Ban on CFC Alternatives, Counter to EPA Plan," IN (January 12, 1990): 14. "Chaffee CFC Plan Survives CAA Because Key Substitute Dropped from Ban," IN (March 9, 1990): 15; "Dingell's Opposition to Senate CFC Plan Signals Measure May Not Survive CAA," IN (February 9, 1990): 14–15; "Waxman to Offer CFC Plan with Earlier Phaseout Schedule Than Senate's," IN (May 11, 1990): 12–13; "Clean Air Conferees Agree on Phase-Out of CFCs, Methyl Chloroform, Other Compounds," CRR (August 10, 1990): 771; "Conferees Wrap Up First Round Talks, Agreeing to CFC Cuts," CAR (August 16, 1990): 3–6.

69. See some details of EPA's control program in "EPA Finds CFC Import Violations, Fears for U.S. Montreal Protocol Compliance," IN (April 20, 1990): 5; "New EPA Policy Sets Fine for Even Smallest Violations of CFC Restriction Rules," IN (April 27, 1990): 11–12.

70. "EPA R&D Officials Urge Reilly to Reject Dingell Air Toxics Bill," IN (March 31, 1989): 1–10.

71. "EPA Withholds Endorsement of Indoor Air Bill, Despite Congressional Changes," IN (May 16, 1990): 3; "EPA, DOE Call Indoor Air Rules Premature, in Conflict with Energy Goals," CAR (May 23, 1991): 34–35.

72. The Senate/administration negotiating group agreed to drop fuel efficiency requirements in the Senate bill to combat global warming; see "CAA Negotiators Near Deal to Pare Back Senate Auto Controls," IN (February 9, 1990): 13.

73. "Reilly Takes Aim at Governors' Plan to Abate Global Warming Through CO_2 Cuts," IN (March 2, 1990): 3–4; "Senate Energy's Global Warming Bill Drops Requirement of CO_2 Cuts by Year 2000," IN (April 27, 1990): 5–6. "Senators Urge Bush to Reject Carbon Content Tax in Budget Talks," CAR (July 19, 1990): 22–23.

74. "House-Approved Plan Would Require Utilities to Monitor for CO^2," CAR (May 25, 1990): 16; "Utilities Not Expected to Oppose House Global Warming Monitoring Plan," CAR (July 5, 1990): 24.

75. Stephen E. Roady, "Permitting and Enforcement Under the Clean Air Act Amendments of 1990," *Environmental Law Reporter: News and Analysis* 21, no. 4 (1991): 10178–205. For an analysis of the permit program from an industry point of view as it affects one state, see "Special Report: The Title V Permit Program of the Clean Air Act: Its Effect in California," *California Environmental Insider* 4, no. 23 (May 15, 1991): 3–7.

76. "Air Bills' Industrial Permitting System Hit as Regulatory 'Behemoth' by Trade Group," ER (January 19, 1990): 1620: "New Regime for Permits in Air Act to Touch Almost Every Business," CRR (November 30, 1990): 1334–35; "Industry Meets With Dingell to Flag Bush Bill's Permit Program as Key Concern," IN (October 20, 1989): 15–16. S. William Becker, executive director of t¹ STAPPA/ALAPCO, supported the proposed permitting system. "State officials recognize that the permitting requirements will mean more work, but they support it anyway." See "State Would Get Flexibility in Permitting: Many Questions Remain in EPA Air Act Proposal," *Environmental Reporter* 21, no. 52 (April 26, 1991): 2275.

77. A brief account of the history of the administration's reversal on the permits is in *Congressional Record* (May 26, 1990): S3181–82.

78. The long debate over the permit in the Senate is in *Congressional Record* (March 26, 1990): S3162–89; 3211–18; 3231–40.

79. The toxics section contained some important "hammer" provisions; if EPA does not meet specific deadlines for setting Maximum Achievable Control Technology on various source categories, then the rules take effect whether the rulemaking process is finished or not. See "Outgoing Air Standards Chief: Special Industry Toxics Breaks Will Block Rules." The official remarked that this makes it far more likely that industry will be more cooperative with the agency, "They can't play games with us . . . it's in their interest to get in and be cooperative." IN (December 7, 1990): 12.

80. For the potential of citizen suits under the CAA and their relationship to similar action under the Clean Water Act, see Glenn L. Unterberger, "Citizen Enforcement Suits: Putting Gwaltney to Rest and Setting Sights on the Clean Air Act," ER, "Analysis and Perspective" (January 4, 1991): 1631–36.

81. See Michael S. Alsuhin, "New Enforcement Tools Under the 1990 Amendments," *EPA Journal* (January–February 1991): 40.

82. The classic program statement on behalf of market forces is "Project 88: Harnessing Market Forces to Protect Our Environment: Initiatives for the New President," a public policy study sponsored by Senator Timothy E. Wirth, Colorado and Senator John Heinz, Pennsylvania (Washington, D.C., 1988). See also "Federal Officials Sing Praises of Market-Based Environmental Regulations," IN (April 27, 1990): 9–10; Robert W. Hahn and Robert N. Stavins, "Incentive-Based Environmental Regulation: A New Era from an Old Idea?," *Ecology Law Quarterly* 18, no. 1 (1991): 1–42.

83. The permit was considered to be an "economic commodity" that could be bought and sold and have "durable economic value"; "commercial and other relevant law will apply to allowances and function to protect that value." At the same time, the CAA stipulated that for regulatory actions taken subsequent to the issuance of the allowances that might "revoke or modify" those allowances the "takings clause" of the U.S. Constitution would not apply and "the U.S. government will not be obliged to compensate allowance-holders for loss of the allowances or any loss in their value." See "Senate-Prepared Plan for CAA Implementation," and interpretation of the CAA by the Senate, CAR, special supplement (November 8, 1990): 10–24, at 20.

84. It was widely argued that under previous law, the firm had no choice but was faced with a mandatory technology in meeting emission limits. Yet the options of coal washing, low sulfur coal or flue gas scrubbers had always been available. The Duquesne Light Co., for example, at its Cheswick, Pennsylvania, plant had originally agreed to use scrubbers on its stack, but instead shifted to low sulfur coal and coal washing and obtained an exemption from the county regulatory agency to do so. For a brief account of the options that Duquesne Light had long explored and was continuing to explore, see Elizabeth Corcoran, "Cleaning Up Coal," *Scientific American* (May, 1991): 107–16.

85. One skeptic about the way in which the marketable permits would work was Michael Woo, staffer on the Dingell committee, who prepared a paper, "The President's Acid Rain Plan May Not Work as Intended: Problems, Results, and Solutions"; see "Administration Acid Rain Trading Program Needs Work, Says Dingell Staffer," IN (December 15, 1989): 6. For two other critics, see Kenneth W. Chilton and Anne Sholtz, "Acid Rain and Tradable Permits: How Congress Hobbles the Power of the Marketplace," Center for Study of American Business, Washington University, St. Louis, 1990, as reported in ER (May 25, 1990): 262–63. Estimates of the prices of marketable permits to utilities was not undertaken until after the CAA passed; see "Study Announced to Assess Costs of Credits for Utilities," CAR (March 14, 1991): p.24.

86. Reports as to utility choices under the act varied widely; see, for example, "Ambitious EPA Rule-Making Schedule Has Industry Trying to Get Early Start," ER (March 15, 1991): 2029, describing varied and contradictory opinions. The American Electric Power Company announced that it would opt for low-sulfur coal; "Ohio Utility's Preliminary Call Against Scrubbing Coal Worries Miners," CAR (May 23, 1991): 13–14. The Allegheny Power Systems, in contrast, announced that it was purchasing scrubbers on three 640-megawatt coal-fired units at Harrison, West Virginia; "First Commercial Contracts for Scrubbers Awarded to GE," CAR (March 28, 1991): 34.

87. "Senate Conferees Resist Preempting States' Clean-Fuel Car Rules," CAR (October 11, 1990): 31; "Dingell Accedes to Senate, Allowing States to Enforce Automobile Standards," CAR, special report (October 11, 1990): 2.

88. "Moorhead Plan Would Block U.S. from Preempting State Emission Standards," CAR (March 24, 1990): 17. Dingell's preemption request came, in turn, from Rep. Tom Tauke (R, Iowa) who was responding to a request from a constituent, John Deere & Co., concerned that rulemakings underway in California would harm its business. See "California's Vehicle-Emissions Regulation Seen Threatened by U.S. Clean Air Act," *California Report* (October 22, 1990): 8–9.

89. "NESCAUM Implores EPA to Waive Federal Preemption of Fuel Volatility Rule," IN (January 27, 1989): 10–11. "EPA To Accommodate States' More Stringent Volatility Standard, Equivalent Auto Emissions Nationwide," IN (February 9, 1990).

90. "Some in EPA Say Plan to Cut Paint Pollution Could Be Model for Other Products," IN (January 5, 1990): 16; "EPA Strongly Endorses Industry Plan for National Paint Pollution Standards," IN (April 13, 1990): 14; "Paint Industry Urges National Law for VOC in Paints to Avert Tough State Regs," CAR (July 19, 1990): 4–5. For the dispute within California over its standard, see "BAAQMD Spray-Paint VOC Rule Enforcement Stayed to Jan. 31. Variance Requested," *California Report* (January 11, 1991); (February 22, 1991): 12; "March 7 Deadline for Resolving Spray-Paints Issue in Bay Area" (March 1, 1991): 12; "SCAQMD Advisory Council Working on Coatings Rules' Scientific Basis" (March 15, 1991): 13–14; "Next Stage of Paint-Industry Court Battle Against Air Regulators Soon to Begin."

91. "EPA Floats CFC Recycling Plan That Some Fear May Preempt Tougher Local Laws," IN (May 4, 1990): 10–11; "Waxman to Offer CFC Plan with Earlier Phaseout Schedule Than Senate's," IN (May 11, 1990): 12–13; "Conferees Wrap Up First Round Talks, Agreeing to CFC Cuts," CAR (August 16, 1990): 3–6.

92. For a review of the issue, see Robert M. Hager, "Simpson Amendment Would Weaken Powers of State and Local Government" (Washington, D.C., December 7, 1989) (AF), and for a review of the statutory and legal background, see Hager, "Simpson Amendment of Clean Air Act Would Preempt State and Local Radioactive Pollution Control Laws" (Washington, D.C., December 14, 1989) (AF); National Clean Air Coalition, "NCAC Opposes Simpson Amendments to Weaken Radioactive Air Pollution Controls" (no date, AF). See also Legislative Regulatory Alert from Nuclear Information and Research Service (NIRS), "Senator Glenn Amendments to Remove Simpson Language from and Add Express Nonpreemption Language to the Clean Air Bill," February 1, 1990. Twenty-one state attorneys general wrote to Senators Mitchell and Glenn urging removal of all the Simpson language from the CAA. The National Association of Towns and Townships put out a legislative advisory and sent press releases to help alert members to this threat to local rights. In a nuclear issues update, March 10, 1990, the Sierra

Club, Pennsylvania chapter, reported that Governor Casey, Attorney General Preate, DER Secretary Art Davis, and the Pennsylvania House in a unanimous vote urged defeat of the Simpson amendment (AF).

93. Environment and Energy Study Conference, *1990 Clean Air Act Amendments* (Washington, D.C.; Environmental and Energy Study Conference, 1990), 52.

94. For the lead role of California standards, see "Lead State on CAA Regs to Consider Cars with Zero Emission Capability," CAR (September 13, 1990): 35–36.

95. Regional Commission Action, "New CAA's Ozone Commission Could Force Some States to Enact Tougher Regulations," CAR (December 6, 1990): 4–5.

96. Hays, "Clean Air," *supra*, note 1.

97. The range of effects: USEPA, Science Advisory Board, *Relative Risk Reduction Project,* report and three appendices, "The Report of the Ecology and Welfare Subcommittee," "The Report of the Human Health Subcommittee," and "The Report of the Strategic Options Subcommittee," EPA SAB-EC-90-021A-C (Washington, D.C., September 1990).

98. See U.S. House of Representatives, Committee on Energy and Commerce, *Clean Air Standards,* hearing before the Subcommittee on Health and the Environment, Serial No. 101–6, February 28, 1989 (Washington, D.C., 1989); for a more general review of health effects that appeared at about the same time as action on the CAA, see Robert Read and Cathy Read, "Breathing Can Be Hazardous to Your Health," *New Scientist* (February 23, 1991): 34–37.

99. Morton Lippman, "Implications of the 1990 Clean Air Act Amendments," *Health and Environment Digest* 5, no. 2 (March 1991): 4–5.

100. Lippman wrote, "A potential problem that the framers of the 1990 Act did not consider is that the timetables for reducing ambient O_3 concentrations are based on the assumption that the current National Ambient Air Quality Standards (NAAQS) for O_3 will be retained indefinitely. If the O_3 NAAQS is reduced to reflect the emerging health effects data, however, the mandated O_3 control strategy timetable will be inadequate." Ibid; 5. See also Lippman, "Health Effects of Ozone," *Journal of the Air and Waste Management Association* 39, no. 5 (May 1989); 672–95.

101. "Lung Association Calls for 8-Hour Ozone Standard," CAR (October 11, 1990): 21; "Ozone Nonattainment: EPA Awaits Firmer Science, Seeks Review of Repeat Exposure," CAR (October 25, 1990): 12.

102. Acceptance of new data on O_3 prompted the governing board of the South Coast Air Quality Management District in California to issue health advisories against exercising out of doors at .15 ppm in contrast with earlier advisory levels of .20 ppm. See "Resolution Puts More Pressure on Industries to Cut Ozone-Forming Emissions," California Report (April 12, 1991): 7–8.

103. Joel Schwartz and Allan Marcus, "Mortality and Air Pollution in London: A Time Series Analysis," *American Journal of Epidemiology;* "Studies Linking Particulates with Early Mortality Push Tighter EPA Standard," CAR (December 6, 1990): 3–4; J. Raloff, "Dust to Dust: A Particularly Lethal Legacy," *Science News* 139: 212; Airborne Particulates Greatly Contribute to About 60,000 Deaths Annually Study Says," ER (May 17, 1991): 131–32; "Urban Particulate Pollution May Cause 60,000 Deaths Yearly," *Environmental Health Letter* (May 21, 1991): 102–103. Douglas W. Dockery, Frank E. Speizer, Daniel O. Stram, James H. Ware, John D. Spengler, and Benjamin J. Ferris, Jr., "Effects of Inhalable Particles on Respiratory Health of Children," in S. D. Lee et al., eds., *Aerosols* (Chelsea, Mich.: Lewis Publishers, 1986), 721–30, "positively" associates particulate pollution with chronic cough, bronchitis, and chest illness in school children in six U.S. cities: Portage,

Wisconsin; Topeka, Kansas; Watertown, Massachusetts; Kingston, Tennessee; St. Louis, Missouri; and Steubenville, Ohio.

104. John Flynn, "Forest Without Trees: How Congress Was Duped About Acid Rain's Effects," *The Amicus Journal* (Winter 1991): 28–33; "Crop Losses of 35–45% Estimated from Ozone: Alfalfa, Grapes Cotton Hit Hardest." *California Report* (January 11, 1991): 1–2.

105. For airborne toxics generally, see Curtis C. Travis and Sheri T. Hester, "Global Chemical Pollution," *Environmental Science and Technology* 25, no. 5 (1991): 814–19 for a brief survey of the widespread presence of toxics in the environment, much of which comes from airborne toxics. For wildlife as toxic indicators, see Tony Peterie, *Wildlife Toxicology* (New York: Van Nostrand Reinhold, 1990).

106. For details of the legislative action, see "Sierra Club Great Lakes Washington Report" (July 5, 1989; October 10, 1989; February 14, 1990); "House Strengthens CAA Toxics Bill, Setting Minimum Technology Requirements," IN (October 6, 1989; June 7, 1990; October 5, 1990; November 5, 1990).

107. An EPA report on water pollution caused by air contaminants recommending a research program on the subject was due in Congress in June 1990, but was blocked by the Office of Management and Budget. See "OMB Stalls EPA's Release of Major Research Plan for Air Pollution of Water," IN (March 23, 1990): 3–4.

108. In discussing the Senate Environment Committee bill that had dropped the percentage reduction requirement, EPA Administrator William Reilly said that, given the cap, there was no need to retain the percentage reduction requirement, provided that the cap remained intact and that the administration would not object to this repeal. See "Reilly Gives Nod to Senate Repeal of Stringent 'Scrubber' Provision," IN (September 29, 1989): 14–15.

109. "Symms Blasts Environment Committee Clean Air Bill for Hampering Coal Use," IN (January 5, 1990): 14.

110. Testimony of Robert E. Yuhnke before the Senate Committee on Environment and Public Works, October 6, 1989, "EPA Projects Doubling of SO2 and NOx Emissions in the West by 2010" (MSS AF).

111. "EDF Petitions Court to Overturn EPA Regulations on NOx," IN (February 3, 1989): 15, concerning PSD regulations for nitrogen oxide that EPA issued in October 1988; "House Government OPS Panel to Hold Hearing on Haze Pollution" in national parks on March 9, 1990, IN (February 23, 1990): 7; "GAO: Several Sources Near National Parks Unregulated, Worsening Visibility," IN (March 16, 1990): 17–18; "New CAA Fails to Resolve Permit Problems Cited in Study," GAO report released February 1990, CAR (December 6, 1990): 22.

112. For a brief introduction to the visibility problem in the national parks, see John C. Freemuth, *Islands Under Siege: National Parks and the Politics of External Threats* (Lawrence, Kans.: University Press of Kansas, 1991), 85–130. For the issue as it developed during the debate on the 1990 CAA, see "House Member to Push Tighter Power Plant Regs in CAA To Protect U.S. Parks," IN (January 5, 1990): 4–5; "Two Federal Agencies Find Bush CAA Inadequate on Visibility, Urge EPA Action," IN (March 16, 1990): 1–2; "House Bill Toughens Industry Burden to Show New Sources Won't Pollute Parks," IN (March 16, 1990): 13–14. "Senate Passes Watered Down Visibility CAA Amendment, Requiring Research Only," IN (March 30, 1990): 16. "House Panel Fails to Include Major Visibility Plan, Leaving Issue for Floor," IN (April 13, 1990): 12–13.

113. "Senators Fight Visibility Amendment Slated for House, Threaten Filibuster,"

CAR (May 10, 1990): 2; also IN (May 11, 1990): 11–12, "If this passes, it will be a bill killer," says one Senate source. If it proceeds to conference Garn will filibuster and it is believed that Simpson, Symms, McClure and Hatch will join. "House Members Reach Deal to Scale Back Wyden Visibility Amendment," CAR (May 24, 1990): 12–13; "Visibility: Administration Likely to Vie for Senate Version Over House," CAR (June 7, 1990): 16; "Western Senators Threaten to Veto CAA If House Provisions Remain," CAR (July 19, 1990): 5; interview with Ron Wyden, CAA conferee, CAR (August 2, 1990): 30; "Conferees, Faced with Filibuster, Opt for Senate Visibility Research Plan," (October 23, 1990): 1–2; "EPA and National Park Service Expect Their Share of Yearly $8-Million Research Fund," CAR (November 8, 1990): 14.

114. Statement by Wyden concerning visibility on House floor, October 26, 1990, in CAR (November 22, 1990).

115. "Cancer Risk Study Bolsters EPA Argument for Tough Radiation Standards," IN (January 5, 1990): 3–4; "Air Amendment May Preempt EPA Nuclear Air Emissions Standards," IN (April 13, 1990): 14. "Industry, Environmentalists Suit May Further Stall 7-Year Delay of Rules," CAR (June 21, 1990): 21–22; "Environmental Group Blasts EPA Delays on Petitions, Threatens Lawsuit," CAR (September 27, 1990): 23. "Key Environment Senator Asks EPA to Drop Radiation Air Rules," IN 12, no. 10 (March 8, 1991):13. Simpson said that there was no additional health benefit from EPA rules and that the desire to set radionuclide emission levels below NRC standards was motivated not by health concerns, but "by the inevitable regulatory propensity to ratchet down limits whether or not necessary." See also " A Plan to Suspend Rules Dubbed Unlawful by Key House Member," CAR (March 14, 1991): 17.

116. "Industry, Environmentalists Draw Battle Lines Over Implementation," CAR (November 8, 1990): 1ff.

The Role of Values in Science and Policy

1. M. E. Ames, *Science and the Political Process* (Washington, D.C.: Communications Press, 1978).

2. J. Primack, and F. von Hippel, *Advice and Dissent: Scientists in the Political Arena* (New York: Basic Books, 1974).

3. A. Mazur, *The Dynamics of Technical Controversy* (Washington, D.C.: Communications Press, 1981).

4. Frances M. Lynn, "The Interplay of Science and Values in Assessing and Regulating Environmental Risks," *Science, Technology and Human Values* 11, no. 2 (spring 1986): 40–50.

5. P. Brodeur, *Expendable Americans* (New York: Viking Press, 1973).

6. E. P. Radford, "Risks from Ionizing Radiation," *Technology Review* 84 (1981): 66–78.

7. R. Lansdowne and W. Yule, ed., *Lead Toxicity: History and Environmental Impact* (Baltimore: Johns Hopkins Press, 1986).

8. D. R. Lynam, L. G. Piantanida, and J. F. Cole, *Environmental Lead* (New York: Academic Press, 1981).

9. H. L. Needleman, ed., *Low Level Lead Exposure: The Clinical Implication of Current Research* (New York: Raven Press, 1980).

10. M. Rutter and R. R. Jones, eds., *Lead Versus Health: Sources and Effect of Low Level Exposure* (London: John Wiley & Sons, 1983).

11. J. S. Lin-Fu, "Lead Poisoning and Undue Lead Exposure in Children: History and Current Status," in *Low Level Lead Exposure,* ed. H. L. Needleman (1980): 5.

12. J. L. Gibson, W. Love, D. Hardine, P. Bancroft, and A. J. Turner, Note on Lead Poisoning as Observed Among Children in Brisbane, *Transactions 3rd Intercolonial Medical Congress* 3 (1892): 76–83.

13. A. J. Turner, Lead Poisoning Among Queensland Children, *Australia Medical Gazette* 16 (1897): 475–79.

14. J. L. Gibson, "A Plea for Painted Railings and Painted Walls of Rooms as the Source of Lead Poisoning Among Queensland Children, *Australia Medical Gazette* 23 (1904): 149–53.

15. J. S. Lin-Fu, "Vulnerability of Children to Lead Exposure and Toxicity," *New England Journal of Medicine* 289 (1973): 1229–1233, 1289–1293.

16. J. W. Sayre, E. Charney, and J. Vostal, "House and Hand Dust as a Potential Source of Childhood Lead Exposure," *American Journal of Disabilities of Children* 127 (1974): 167–70.

17. U.S. Senate Committee on Labor and Public Welfare, Subcommittee on Health, Hearing, Lead-based Paint Poisoning, 91st Cong., 2nd Sess., November 23, 1970, Washington, D.C. 1971.

18. U.S. House of Representatives, Banking and Currency Committee, Subcommittee on Housing, hearings, "To Provide Federal Assistance for Eliminating Causes of Lead-Based Paint Poisoning," 91st Cong., 2nd Sess., July 22–23, Washington, D.C., 1970.

19. *Environmental Health Letter,* September 1, 1983, 8; July 1, 1984, 3–4.

20. *Environment Reporter,* April 27, 1979, 2381; September 12, 1980, 683; June 29, 1984, 375; September 7, 1984, 718.

21. D. L. Davis, F. R. Anderson, G. Wetstone, L. S. Ritts, "Judicial Review of Scientific Uncertainty: International Harvester and Ethyl Cases Reconsidered," draft copy, The Environmental Law Institute, Washington, D.C., 1981.

22. Stanton Coerr, EPA's air standard for lead, in *Low Level Lead Exposure,* ed. H. L. Needleman (1980): 153–258.

23. U.S. Department of Health, Education, and Welfare, Public Health Service, Center for Disease Control, "Preventing Lead Poisoning in Young Children," Atlanta, Ga., 1978.

24. National Research Council, *Lead: Airborne Lead in Perspective,* National Academy of Sciences, Washington, D.C., 1972.

25. National Research Council, *Lead in the Human Environment,* National Academy of Sciences, Washington, D.C., 1980.

26. C. B. Ernhart, B. Landa, N. B. Schell, "Subclinical Levels of Lead and Development Deficit—A Multivariate Follow-up Reassessment," *Pediatrics* 67 (1981): 911–19.

27. H. L. Needleman, D. Bellinger, and A. Leviton, "Does Lead at Low Dose Affect Intelligence in Children?," *Pediatrics* 68 (1981): 894–96.

28. C. B. Ernhart, B. Landa, and N. B. Schell, "Lead Levels and Intelligence," letter to the editor, *Pediatrics,* 68 (1981): 903–05.

29. S. Spector and K. E. Brown, "Lead Study Questions," letter to the editor, *Pediatrics* 69 (1982): 134–35.

30. C. B. Ernhart, B. Landa, and N. B. Schell, "Letter to the Editor," *Pediatrics* 69 (1982): 135.

31. Landrigan, "Lead Study Results Questioned," letter to the editor, *Pediatrics* 69 (1982): 248.

32. Ernhart, Landa, and Schell, "Letter to the Editor," 248–49.

33. C. B. Ernhart, B. Landa, and A. W. Wolf, "Subclinical Lead Level and Development Deficits: Reanalyses of Data," *Journal of Learning Disabilities* 18 (1985): 475–79.

34. H. L. Needleman, "Letter to the Editor," *Journal of Learning Disabilities* 19 (1986): 322–23.

35. C. B. Ernhart, "Letter to the Editor," *Journal of Learning Disabilities* 19 (1986): 323.

36. S. P. Hays, *Beauty, Health and Permanence: Environmental Politics in the United States, 1955–1985* (New York: Cambridge University Press, 1987), 73, 74, 75, 184–85, 196–97.

37. G. S. Wetstone and J. Goldman, "Chronology of Events Surrounding the Ethyl Decision," in *Judicial Review of Scientific Uncertainty*, ed. D. L. Davis et al. (draft).

38. *Environment Reporter*, November 30, 1979, 1567–1568; January 29, 1982, 1263; February 26, 1982, 1376; April 15, 1983, 2321.

39. U.S. Senate, Committee on Public Works, *Legislative History of the Clean Air Act Amendments*, vol. I, Serial 98–18.

40. *Environment Reporter*, January 14, 1977, 1361–1362; April 22, 1977, 1962.

41. Environmental Protection Agency, Proposed National Air Quality Standard for Lead, Federal Register, 63076, December 14, 1977.

42. *Environment Reporter*, February 24, 1978, 1651; June 29, 1984, 375.

43. D. Rosner and G. Markowitz, "A Gift of God?: The Public Health Controversy Over Leaded Gasoline During the 1920s," *American Journal of Public Health* 75 (1985): 344–52.

44. *Environmental Health Letter*, April 15, 1985, 5.

45. Committee on Public Works, U.S. Senate, Subcommittee on Air and Water Pollution, 89th Congress, 2nd Sess., Air Pollution, Washington, D.C., 1966, 203–28.

46. R. K. Byers, and E. E. Lord, "Later Effects of Lead Poisoning on Mental Development," *American Journal of Disabled Children* 66 (1943): 471–81.

47. R. K. Byers, "Lead Poisoning: Review of the Literature and Report on 45 Cases," *Pediatrics* 23 (1959): 583–603.

48. U.S. Environmental Protection Agency, Air Quality Criteria for Lead, EPA-600/8-77-017, Research Triangle Park, NC, 1977.

49. C. C. Patterson, "Contaminated and Natural Lead Environments of Man," *Archives of Environmental Health* 11 (1965): 344–60.

50. C. C. Patterson, Natural Levels of Lead in Humans, Carolina Environmental Essay Series, III, The University of North Carolina at Chapel Hill, 1982.

51. T. G. Lovering, ed., Lead in the Environment, U.S. Geological Survey Professional Paper #957, Washington, D.C., 1976.

52. U.S. Senate Committee on Public Works, Subcommittee on Air and Water Pollution, 89th Cong. 2nd Sess., Hearings, Air Pollution, 1966, Washington, D.C., 1966, 311–44.

53. W. Sullivan, "Warning Is Issued on Lead Poisoning," *New York Times*, September 12, 1965, p. 71.

54. S. Budiansky, "Lead: The Debate Goes On, But Not Over Science," *Environmental Science and Technology* 15 (1981): 243–46.

55. Letters, *Environmental Science and Technology* 15 (1981): 722–24.

56. S. Piomelli, "The FEP [free erythrocyte porphyrins] Test: A Screening Micromethod for Lead Poisoning," *Pediatrics* 51 (1973): 254–59.

57. R. Gillette, "Lead in the air: industry weight on academy panel challenged," *Science* 174 (1971): 800–02.

58. P. M. Boffey, *The Brain Bank of America* (New York: McGraw Hill, 1975), 228–44.

59. J. R. Goldsmith and H. L. Needleman, "Lead Exposures of Urban Children: A Handicap in School and Life?" unpublished manuscript, 1984.

60. G. S. Wetstone, ed., Meeting Record from Resolution of Scientific Issues and the Judicial Process: Ethyl Corporation v. EPA, October 21, 1977, (Washington, D.C.: The Environmental Law Institute, 1981), 145.

61. *Environment Reporter,* November 19, 1976, 1043; December 10, 1976, 1253; January 14, 1977, 1361–1362, 1376; February 4, 1977, 1486–1487; March 4, 1977, 1701; March 25, 1977, 1809–1810; April 22, 1977, 1962; June 17, 1977, 274; July 8, 1977, 409–410; September 2, 1977, 686–687; October 14, 1977, 929–930; December 16, 1977, 1235–1236, 1243–1244; January 13, 1978, 1392, 1394; February 24, 1978, 1651; March 31, 1978, 1880.

62. H. L. Needleman and S. Piomelli, *The Effects of Low Level Lead Exposure,* Natural Resources Defense Council in cooperation with American Lung Association, New York, 1978.

63. *Eythl Corporation v. EPA,* 8 Environment Reporter Case, 1785.

64. *Environment Reporter,* August 3, 1979, p. 899.

65. *Lead Industries Association v. EPA,* June 27, 1980, 14 Environment Reporter Cases, 1906, December 8, 1980, 15 Environment Reporter Cases, 2097.

66. C. C. Patterson, "An Alternative Perspective—Lead Pollution in the Human Environment: Origin, Extent, and Significance," in *Lead and the Human Environment* (Washington, D.C.: National Research Council, National Academy of Sciences, 1980).

67. D. Bollier and J. Claybrook, *Freedom from Harm: The Civilizing Influence of Health, Safety, and Environmental Regulation* (Washington, D.C.: Public Citizen, 1986), 105–08, 144, 148.

68. J. Claybrook, *Retreat from Safety: Reagan's Attack on America's Health* (New York: Panthcon Books, 1984), 77, 85–86, 127–28.

69. *Environment Reporter,* August 14, 1981, 483; December 11, 1981, 975–976; February 5, 1982, 1293–1294; April 9, 1982, 1609; April 23, 1982, 1715.

70. *Environmental Health Letter,* August 15, 1981, 1; March 1, 1982, 6.

71. *Environmental Health Letter,* April 15, 1982, 2–3.

72. *Environment Reporter,* April 16, 1982, 1639.

73. *Environment Reporter,* May 21, 1982, 61; June 11, 1982, 165; August 20, 1982, 525–26.

74. *Environmental Health Letter,* August 15, 1982, 4–5.

75. *Inside EPA,* February 3, 1984, 1, 8–9; March 16, 1984, 12–13; March 30, 1984, 13.

76. *Environmental Health Letter,* March 1, 1984, 1–2.

77. *Environment Reporter,* March 2, 1984, 1899; March 16, 1984, 2046; April 6, 1984, 2206–2207.

78. *Inside EPA,* March 30, 1984, 13; July 20, 1984, 3.

79. E. Marshall, "EPA Faults Classic Lead Poisoning Study," *Science* 222 (1983): 906–07.

80. H. L. Needleman, letter, *Science* 223 (1984): 116.

81. P. J. Landrigan and V. N. Houk, letter, *Science* 223 (1984): 116.

82. C. B. Ernhart, letter, *Science* 223 (1984): 116.

83. *Inside EPA,* May 4, 1984, 11.

84. J. L. Annest, J. L. Pirkle, D. Makuc, J. W. Neese, D. D. Bayse, and M. G. Kovar, "Chronological Trend in Blood Lead Levels Between 1976 and 1980," *New England Journal of Medicine* 308 (1983): 1373–1377.

85. J. Schwartz, "The Relationship Between Gasoline Lead Emissions and Blood Poisoning in Americans," unpublished manuscript, n.d.

86. J. Schwartz, "The Link Between Lead in People and Lead in Gas," *EPA Journal* (May 1985): 11, 12.

87. *Environment Reporter,* August 10, 1984, 571; September 7, 1984, 718.

88. *Inside EPA,* May 4, 1984, 14.

89. *Inside EPA,* March 23, 1984, 11.

90. *Environmental Health Letter,* February 15, 1985, 3–4.

91. *Environment Reporter,* June 29, 1984, 380–81.

92. *Inside EPA,* June 29, 1984, 13.

93. U.S. Department of Health and Human Services, Centers for Disease Control, "Preventing Lead Poisoning in Young Children," (Atlanta, Ga., 1985).

94. U.S. Environmental Protection Agency, Office of Policy, Planning and Evaluation, "Costs and Benefits of Reducing Lead in Gasoline," draft final report, EPA-230-03-84-005, Washington, D.C., March 1984, and final report 1985.

95. *Environment Reporter,* August 3, 1984, 532; August 10, 1984, 585ff.

96. *Inside EPA,* August 3, 1984, 8.

97. J. Schwartz and D. Otto, "Blood Lead, Hearing Thresholds, and Neurobehavioral Development in Children and Youth," *Archives of Environmental Health* 42 (1987): 153–60.

98. *Inside EPA,* August 31, 1984, 9; January 23, 1987, 2.

99. B. Goldstein, "Health and the Lead Phasedown: An Interview with Bernard Goldstein, Assistant Administrator for Research and Development," *EPA Journal* 11 (May 1985): 9–12.

100. H. M. Pitcher, Office of Policy, Planning and Evaluation, EPA, "Comments on Issues Raised in the Analysis of the Neuropsychological Effects of Low Level Exposure," n.d.

101. *Environment Reporter,* January 13, 1978, 1392–1393.

102. *Environment Reporter,* August 10, 1984, 571.

103. J. F. Cole, "The Lead in Gasoline Issue and EPA's Lack of Scientific Objectivity," *Environmental Forum* 3 (November 1984): 41.

104. *Environment Reporter,* May 11, 1984, 41; June 29, 1984, 375.

105. *Environmental Health Letter,* September 1, 1982, 4–5.

106. *Environment Reporter,* June 29, 1984, 380–81.

107. *Inside EPA,* June 29, 1984, 13.

108. *Environmental Health Letter,* February 15, 1985, 3–4.

109. *Inside EPA,* May 4, 1984, 11.

110. Anonymous profile, "OMB's Jim Joseph Tozzi," *Environ. Forum* 1 (May 1982): 11–12.

111. *Environmental Health Letter,* August 1, 1984, 3.

112. *Inside EPA,* June 29, 1984, 13; July 10, 1984, 5.

113. *Environmental Health Letter,* July 1, 1984, 3–4.

114. *Environment Reporter,* July 27, 1984, 465.

115. *Environment Reporter,* August 10, 1984, 571.

116. *Environment Reporter,* July 29, 1984, 375.

117. *Inside EPA,* July 20, 1984, 3; July 27, 1984, 1, 11; August 3, 1984, 8; January 4, 1985, 1, 6.

118. *Environmental Health Letter,* March 1, 1985, 1.

119. "U.S. Puts Off Plan to Outlaw Leaded Gasoline," *New York Times,* p. A16, December 15, 1987.

120. *Environment Reporter,* June 1, 1984, 146.

121. Environmental Protection Agency, draft document, "Air Quality Criteria for Lead," EPA 600/8-83-028, Office of Research and Development, Research Triangle Park, 1986.

122. U.S. Environmental Protection Agency, "Review of the National Ambient Air Quality Standards for Lead: Assessment of Scientific and Technical Information," draft staff paper, Office of Air Quality Planning and Standards Research Triangle Park, 1986.

123. *Inside EPA,* May 31, 1985, 12; August 16, 1985, 4; November 14, 1986, 13; November 21, 1986, 1–2, 4; December 5, 1986, 2; December 12, 1986, 3–4; January 23, 1987, 2; April 17, 1987, 15; September 2, 1988, 4.

124. *Environmental Health Letter,* October 1, 1986, 4; November 15, 1986, 7–8; April 1, 1987, 2–3.

125. *Environment Reporter,* May 1, 1987, 9–10; October 9, 1987, 1503; December 18, 1987, 1923–1924; December 18, 1987, 1924–1925.

126. *Environment Reporter,* September 7, 1984, 718.

127. D. R. Lynam, L. G. Piantanida, J. F. and Cole, *Environmental Lead,* Academic Press, London, 1981.

128. Lynn, "The Interplay of Science and Values in Assessing and Regulating Environmental Risks," 40–50.

The Structure of Environmental Politics Since World War II

1. Samuel P. Hays, *Conservation and the Gospel of Efficiency* (Cambridge, Mass., 1958); "The Politics of Reform in Municipal Government in the Progressive Era," *Pacific Northwest Quarterly* 55 (1964); and "The Changing Political Structure of the City in Industrial America," in *Journal of Urban History* I (1974).

2. Samuel P. Hays, "The Social Analysis of American Political History, 1880–1920," *Political Science Quarterly* 80 (1965): 373–94.

3. For examples of citizen action, see Lynton K. Caldwell, Lynton R. Hayes, and Isabel M. MacWhirter, *Citizens and the Environment* (Bloomington, Ind., 1976).

4. These changes in values were common to advanced industrial nations; they are dealt with comprehensively in Ronald Inglehart, *The Silent Revolution: Changing Values and Political Styles Among Western Publics* (Princeton, 1977); see also Lester W. Milbrath, "General Report: U.S. Component of a Comparative Study of Environmental Beliefs and Values," Environmental Studies Center, State University of New York at Buffalo, January 1981.

5. Two comprehensive on-going studies of American values which provide a larger context for environmental attitudes are Arnold Mitchell, Values and Lifestyles Program, at Stanford Research International, and John Naisbitt, *Trend Report,* Center for Policy Process, Washington, D.C. See, for example, Arnold Mitchell, "Social Change: Implications of Trends in Values and Lifestyles," VALS Report No. 3, Stanford Research International, Menlo Park, Calif., 1979; and John Naisbitt, "The New Economic and Political Order of the 1980s," speech given to The Foresight Group, Stockholm, Sweden, April 17, 1980, available from the Center for Policy Process. For continuous contemporary coverage of work on value changes, consult *Leading Edge Bulletin: Frontiers of Social Transformation,* published by Interface Press, Los Angeles, Calif.

6. One of the best brief accounts of this development is Lloyd Warner, Darab B. Unwalla, and John H. Trimm, *Large-Scale Organizations,* vol. 1, *The Emergent American Society* (New Haven, 1967).

7. For further elaboration of this concept, see Samuel P. Hays, "The New Organizational Society," in Jerry Israel, ed., *Building the Organizational Society: Essays on Associational Activities in Modern America* (Glencoe, Ill., 1972).

8. A wide range of materials provides evidence about grass roots activities. Some is produced by local groups and chapters of national organizations such as the Audubon Society and the Sierra Club. Much more comes from a multitude of local groups with no wider organizational attachment, often to deal with only one specific problem. Accounts of local issues are included in newsletters of state environmental organizations such as the Oregon Environmental Council or the Illinois Environmental Council. Newspapers contain many accounts of events pertaining to environmental issues in their territory; see, for example, the *Missoulian* published in Missoula, Montana. Especially useful are some newer weekly "alternative" papers such as the *Maine Times,* the *Illinois Times,* or *Willamette Week* (Portland, Oreg.)

9. The wilderness movement can be charted in its earlier history primarily in the *Living Wilderness* published by the Wilderness Society and the *Sierra Club Bulletin.* Since the 1960s a number of state wilderness organizations have arisen in Oregon, California, Montana, Washington, Colorado, New Mexico, and Utah, each one producing its own activities and publications.

10. Especially significant are the numerous guidebooks to "back country trails," which, along with information about routes, include appreciative descriptions of natural history and accounts of political issues pertinent to those areas. The numerous photographic essays such as the "format books" published by the Sierra Club and Friends of the Earth have played a significant role in the personal association with "wild places."

11. The motto of the Sierra Club.

12. In these states conservation commissions have formed state groups; their newsletters, open space guidebooks, and other publications are excellent sources of information about their activities. For an account of one state in the 1960s, see Andrew J. W. Scheffey, *Conservation Commissions in Massachusetts* (Washington, D.C., 1996).

13. A good introduction to wetlands phenomena is *Our Nation's Wetlands,* an Interagency Task Force Report coordinated by the Council on Environmental Quality (Washington, D.C., 1978). Wetlands matters at the scientific and professional level can be followed in the *National Wetlands Newsletter.* However, citizen action is reflected in few national publications but must be followed in material cited previously. There are a few state wetlands organizations, such as the Wisconsin Wetlands Association, which publish their own newsletters.

14. See, for example, Town of Dunn (Dane County, Wisconsin), *Open Space Preservation Handbook* (n.p., June 1979), and the Catskill Center, *Freshwater Wetlands: A Citizens' Primer* (Hobart, New York, 1978).

15. The wild and scenic rivers movement can be followed in *American Rivers,* newsletter of the American Rivers Conservation Council, Washington, D.C. See also books on specific rivers such as Thomas J. Schoenbaum, *The New River Controversy* (Winston Salem, N.C., 1979) and newsletters from local organizations such as *The Saco River Corridor,* published by the Saco River Corridor Commission, Cornish, Maine.

16. A good perspective on the "natural areas" movement is in the quarterly publication of the Nature Conservancy, *The Nature Conservancy News* (Arlington, Va.).

17. A popular introduction to the pine barrens of New Jersey is John McPhee, *The Pine Barrens* (New York, 1967); current efforts to protect the area are described in State of New Jersey, Pinelands Commission, *New Jersey Pinelands,* Draft Comprehensive Management Plan, 2 vols. (1980).

18. The Desert Protective Council, organized in 1954, has worked to protect the southwest desert. The growing interest of the American people in the western drylands and deserts can be charted in the rising popularity of desert photography, and new western state organizations such as the Oregon High Desert Council.

19. See Field Research Corporation, *Preliminary Desert Market Analysis of the California Desert,* summary produced by the Bureau of Land Management, Riverside, Calif., 1975; Field Research Corporation, *California Public Opinion and Behavior Regarding the California Desert,* Bureau of Land Management, Riverside, Calif., 1977; *National Opinions Concerning the California Desert Conservation Area,* conducted by the Gallup Organization, Inc., for the Bureau of Land Management, U.S. Department of the Interior, 1978.

20. The role of wildlife as a subject of environmental interest and concern has been a subject of comprehensive study by Dr. Stephen R. Kellert of the Yale University School of Forestry and Environmental Studies. Sponsored by the U.S. Fish and Wildlife Service, three of the four phases of this study, *Public Attitudes Toward Critical Wildlife and Natural Habitat Issues,* have now been published. A far more recent but especially intriguing development in the human relationship to the natural environment pertains to the appreciation of the sky; see the organization, For Spacious Skies, headquartered in Boston, Massachusetts, and especially Eric Sloane, *For Spacious Skies* (New York, 1978).

21. See William Ashworth, *Hells Canyon: The Deepest Gorge on Earth* (New York, 1977).

22. Author clipping file, including items from the *New York Times, High Country News* (Lander, Wyo.) and the *Missoulian* (Missoula, Mont.).

23. In some cases these issues have reached treatment in book-length accounts such as Louise B. Young, *Power Over People* (New York, 1973); Jack Doyle and Vic Reinemer, *Lines Across the Land* (Washington, D.C., 1979); and Michael Parfit, *Coal, Power and People* (New York, 1980).

24. In 1962 and 1963 Congressman Robert Jones, chair of the Government Operations Committee of the U.S. House of Representatives, held extensive hearings throughout the nation, soliciting citizen views on water pollution. Many citizen groups responded, but the most consistent and extensive single source of interest was from the commercial and sport fishing organizations. See the Committee hearings, *Water Pollution Control and Abatement* (Washington, D.C., 1963).

25. Several books on these problems are Michael Brown, *Laying Waste* (New York, 1979), Edwin Chen, *PBB: An American Tragedy* (Englewood Cliffs, N.J., 1979); and Joyce Eggington, *The Poisoning of Michigan* (New York, 1980).

26. The earlier years of this interest can be followed in *Prevention Magazine* published by Rodale Press, Emmaus, Pa., and the later years in *Mother Earth News.* There are a number of popular health magazines which also follow the relevant activities; they are often associated with natural foods stores and include *Health Quarterly, Let's Live,* and *Well-Being.*

27. See Environmental Defense Fund and Robert H. Boyle, *Malignant Neglect* (New York, 1979); Samuel S. Epstein, *The Politics of Cancer* (San Francisco, 1978); Christopher Norwood, *At Highest Risk* (New York, 1980).

28. See, for example, Devra Lee Davis, "Multiple Risk Assessment: Preventive Strategy for Public Health," *Toxic Substances Journal* (Winter 1979–80): 205–25.

29. For examples, see Michael Brown and Edwin Chen, note 25. In 1980 the Environmental Defense Fund, a citizen organization, undertook an experiment in monitoring health effects of toxic chemicals with techniques which those affected could readily observe and comprehend; the goal of the project was to enhance citizen confidence in health monitoring. See *EDF Letter,* September/October, 1980 (New York).

30. Efforts at self-protection can be followed in items in note 25.

31. This convergence of views can be followed in publications of professional organizations which bring together private and public managerial and technical specialists, such as the *Journal of the Air Pollution Control Association; Journal, Water Pollution Control Federation;* the *Journal of Forestry,* and *Wildlife Management.*

32. An expression of these divergent points of view is Alaska Board of Game, *Report to the Board of Game on Wildlife and Forest Practices in Southeast Alaska* (Juneau, Alaska, 1980).

33. Two books which reflect opposite sides of the clear-cutting issue are Eleanor C. J. Horwitz, *Clearcutting: A View from the Top* (Washington, D.C., 1974), and Jack Shepherd, *The Forest Killers* (New York, 1975).

34. The pesticide controversy can be followed in four "tracts of the times:" Frank Graham Jr., *Since Silent Spring* (Boston, 1970); Rita Gray Beatty, *The DDT Myth; Triumph of the Amateurs* (New York, 1973); Georg Claus and Karen Bolander, *Ecological Sanity* (New York, 1977); and Robert van den Bosch, *The Pesticide Conspiracy* (New York, 1978).

35. For environmental approaches to forestry, see Leon S. Minckler, *Woodland Ecology: Environmental Forestry for the Small Owner* (Syracuse, 1975), and to pesticide management see the issues of the newsletter *IPM Practitioner* (Berkeley, Calif., 1978–).

36. Stuart L. Hart and Gordon A. Enk, *Green Goals and Greenbacks: A Comparative Study of State-Level Environmental Impact Statement Programs and Their Associated Costs* (Rensselaerville, N.Y.: The Institute on Man and Science, 1978), 46.

37. Agencies have developed considerable capacity to shape the EIS process so as to influence its outcome through such devices as choosing the issues to be considered, assessing the character of public input, and choosing the alternatives to be weighed.

38. Reactions against the evolution of the air and water quality programs can be followed in the professional journals cited in note 31.

39. The reaction of foresters can be traced in the successive stages of the wilderness movement, from the initial phase in the 1920s to the Roadless Area Review and Evaluation (RARE II) of 1979–80. Analysis of the response of both the U.S. Forest Service and professional foresters to each stage indicates persistent efforts to contain rather than to advance the wilderness movement as represented by the leading edge of citizen wilderness action at each stage.

40. In training for and the practice of forestry, fundamental conceptions of what a forest was emphasized trees for their potential wood production rather than other forest values, and hence influenced heavily the response of foresters to new public attitudes toward the forests. The development of dendrology as the study of tree species in the forest, for example, deliberately narrowed those species to ones which were commercially valuable. In the first edition of the initial work on dendrology in the McGraw Hill American Forestry Series, *Textbook of Dendrology Covering the Important Forest Trees of the United States and Canada* (New York, 1937), written by William M. Harlow and Ellwood S. Harrar, the subject was deliberately confined to such species. In their preface they

wrote, "It is felt that students of forestry should first know well the commercial species of North America." A similar narrowing of view is evidenced in the concept of "maturity" in a forest dominant among professionals, which is confined to the "maturity" of individual trees rather than of the entire forest as a system. This distinction became clear in the controversy over "old growth" in the Pacific Northwest and Alaska in the 1970s. To foresters interested primarily in wood production there, maturity meant a "silviculturally mature forest" of trees ready for harvest for wood; to wildlife professionals, however, interested in more diverse forest for wildlife habitat, it meant a "virgin or climax" forest which had reached, over several generations of trees, a relatively stable condition. The two views came into conflict over the issue of retention of "old growth" forest. For a discussion of the two perspectives, see Alaska Fish and Game Commission, *Report to the Board of Game on Wildlife and Forest Practices in Southeast Alaska* (Juneau, 1980).

41. These views can be followed in publications of the two major professional water resource associations, *Water Resources Bulletin* (est. 1965), published by the American Water Resources Association, and *Water Resources Research* (est. 1965), published by the American Geophysical Union.

42. Two analyses of the social context of these controversies are Laura Nader and Norman Milleron, "Dimensions of the 'People Problem' in Energy Research and 'The Factual Basis of Dispersed Energy Futures,'" in *Energy* 4 (1979): 953–67; Laura Nader, "The Search for Alternative Energy Systems and Low Energy Consumption Societies: Dominant Paradigms in Scientific and Methodological Thought and Research and Other Institutional and Ideological Barriers to Change," paper presented at a UNEP-ECE Regional Seminar on Alternative Patterns of Development and Life Style, Ljubljana, Yugoslavia, December 3–8, 1979.

43. See, for example, the publication *Alternative Sources of Energy* (Milaca, Minn., 1974–).

44. Avraham Shama and Ken Jacobs, *Social Values and Solar Energy Policy: The Policy Makers and the Advocates*, Solar Energy Research Institute, October 1979 (SERI-RR-51-329).

45. Opinion Research Corporation, *The Public's Participation in Outdoor Activities and Attitudes Toward National Wilderness Areas* (Princeton, N.J., September 1977); American Forest Institute, *Research Recap #10* (Washington, D.C., December 1977).

46. *National News Report* (Sierra Club), March 7, 1980.

47. Louis Harris and Associates, *Risk in a Complex Society: A Marsh & McLennan Public Opinion Survey* (Marsh and McLennan Companies, Inc., 1980).

48. Few of the contexts of scientific and technical choice outlined here have been elaborated in detail. An exception is an account of research choices made by the U.S. Forest Experiment Stations, which were completed in 1979 for the 1980s and which included a "public participation" process carried out by the U.S. Forest Service. This included representatives from industry, government, the scientific professions, consumers, and environmentalists. This process has been analyzed by Joseph C. deSteiguer, *Public Participation in Forestry Research Planning* (Ph.D. thesis, Texas A&M University, 1979), who makes significant distinctions among the choices as to desired research expressed by each of the five groups. My own review of the relevant documents substantiates deSteiguer's description.

49. The political struggle over "criteria document" assessments can be followed in *Environment Reporter;* see varied issues in 1978–1980 for the question of revision of the documents on sulfur dioxide and particulates. See also two documents pertaining to the

assessment of the effects of particulates: W. W. Holland et al., "Health Effects of Particulate Pollution: Reappraising the Evidence," and Carl M. Shy, "Epidemiologic Evidence and the United States Air Quality Standards," both in *American Journal of Epidemiology* 110 (November and December 1979).

50. Few books have been devoted to general environmental affairs in a given state. One is Luther J. Carter, *The Florida Experience: Land and Water Policy in a Growth State* (Washington, D.C., 1974). Most books on a single state confine themselves to one topic, such as James E. Krier and Edmund Ursin, *Pollution and Policy: A Case Essay on California and Federal Experience with Motor Vehicle Air Pollution, 1940–1975* (Berkeley, Calif., 1977).

51. William E. Shands and Robert G. Healy, *The Lands Nobody Wanted: Policy for National Forests in the Eastern United States* (Washington, D.C., 1977).

52. See, for example, Illinois Environmental Council, *Environmental Voting Record*, 1975, 1976, 1977, 1979, 1980; Colorado Open Space Council, *Legislative Analysis*, 1973–1980; Environmental Planning Lobby, *New York Environmental Voters' Guide*, 1973–1980; Oregon Environmental Council Legislative Poll, 1971, 1972, 1973, 1975, 1977.

53. A capsule summary of voting tabulations for environmental issues in the Michigan House of Representatives is as follows:

	Percent Environmental Vote		
Percent urban district	*1973–74*	*1975–76*	*1977–78*
75–100	57.3 (69)*	62.6 (69)	62.8 (69)
50–75	47.7 (12)	48.7 (12)	41.3 (12)
25–50	33.6 (15)	38.4 (15)	35.1 (15)
1–25	30.7 (10)	38.1 (10)	21.3 (10)
0	19.3 (4)	27.0 (4)	18.3 (4)

*number of legislative districts in each population group

54. One example is the reaction of the upper two-thirds of Michigan and Wisconsin to a series of proposals for radioactive waste disposal. Michigan has passed legislation prohibiting such sites within that state. See author clipping file, various newspapers such as the *Mining Gazette* (Houghton, Mich.); *L'Anse Sentinel* (Baraga, Mich.); the *Mining Journal* (Marquette, Mich.), 1980–1981.

55. This can be followed in greatest detail in the issues of the newsletter *Nucleonics Week* in 1969–1971.

56. Several relevant items are: In Minnesota the air pollution statute provides that "No local government unit shall set standards of air quality which are more stringent than those set by the pollution control agency," *Nucleonics Week* (February 26, 1970); in 1980 Connecticut established a Hazardous Waste Facility Siting Board with power to override local zoning laws, *Environmental Science and Technology* (August 1980): 894; in 1980 the Wisconsin Department of Natural Resources revised its wetlands regulation, NR 115, with legislative approval, which prohibits counties from forming regulations more strict than those of the state, *Our Wetlands*, published by the Wisconsin Wetlands Association, August–September, 1980; in Illinois the mayor of Catlin, near Danville, in Vermillion County, objecting to a proposed 6000-acre strip mine by Amax Coal Company, on prime agricultural land in his township, complained, "The state pre-empted our rights" to regulate coal mining locally, as reported by Harold Henderson, "Caving in on Coal," *Illinois Times* (September 5–11, 1980): 81.

57. Industry actions on this score can be followed in *Environment Reporter,* 1975–1980. The Maryland legislature passed such a provision in 1979; see Maryland Environmental Council, *Newsletter* (March, 1979). Attempts to establish air quality standards higher than federal levels in Montana during 1980 met stiff opposition from industry, but as of April 1981 had failed, one of the few such cases where a state has successfully maintained higher standards in the face of determined industry opposition. See items from the *Missoulian* (Missoula, Mont.), 1980–81 (author clipping file). The classic case of industry support for federal preemption of environmental standards is noise. The issue was well stated by congressional staff early in 1981: "industry generally supports federal noise regulations as preferable to myriad local rules, which would differ from place to place. But local governments . . . want the authority to establish rules that are stricter than the federal regulations. Currently, the noise act pre-empts stricter state and local noise regulations." See Environmental Study Conference, U.S. Congress, *Weekly Bulletin* (February 23, 1981): C7.

58. The struggle over preemption for siting in coastal zone areas was especially bitter, involving interpretation of the "consistency clause" of the Coastal Zone Management Act of 1972. This controversy ended, at least temporarily, when courts upheld the interpretation of the states which gave them equal authority with federal agencies in siting decisions. The issue can be followed in the weekly issues of the newsletter, *Coastal Zone Management,* especially in 1979 and 1980.

59. Author interviews with environmental leaders, Washington, D.C., 1979–80.

60. Mayors and other urban leaders testified before congressional hearings in the 1960s urging such statements from authoritative federal sources in order to increase their ability to counter arguments about health effects from industry. The initial document on sulfur dioxide issue by the Public Health Service in the spring of 1967 was used extensively by citizen air pollution groups and local governments in the first round of state standard setting prior to the Clean Air Act of 1970.

61. The research branch of the California Air Resources Board continually took the initiative in such studies. Its activities are recounted briefly in the board's monthly *Newsletter.* See various research documents produced by the Board (author file).

62. See similar Montana documents (author file) reporting research conducted for the revision of air quality laws in that state in 1980, studies such as the analysis of comparative data about lung function among school children in Great Falls, Butte, and Anaconda.

63. The Michigan Toxic Substances Control Commission is one example of a state which developed, even though in a limited way, an independent capability to assess the effects of toxic pollutants. See various reports of the commission (author file) in 1979–1980. Maine developed a similar specialized capability through its state Pesticides Control Board which utilized expertise from the Poison Control Center at the Maine Medical Center. See items, 1979–1980. in the *Maine Times,* for example, "Maine's Poison Control Center is One of the Best," *Maine Times* (February 6–February 12, 1981): 18–19.

64. An industry consultant in California offered services to overwhelm local governments with statistics about population projections: "Smaller and rural California counties, cities and special districts do not have nor can they afford the necessary technical staff to dispute projects for their area by others, let alone prepare their own. These entities would probably like to challenge (projections produced under the EPA or OMB processes) . . . Providing assistance to such groups will create a technical reliance on the

construction industry and increase their influence over decisions of their elected bodies." This report was prepared under a contact with various building-industry and related organizations. See *Population Report* (Sierra Club), July 1, 1980.

65. This can be followed in the pages of *Environment Reporter*. One dramatic incident was a lawsuit brought by the American Iron and Steel Institute objecting to a closed meeting, excluding scientists preferred by the AISI, planned by EPA to initiate the review of the particulate and sulfur dioxide standards. The Court ruled that the meeting was illegal and that AISI scientific representatives had to be given the opportunity to participate in an open meeting.

Three Decades of Environmental Politics

1. William Tucker, *Progress and Privilege* (New York: Doubleday, 1982); Ron Arnold, *At the Eye of the Storm* (Chicago: Regnery Gateway, 1982).

2. Mary Douglas and Aaron Wildavsky, *Risk and Culture* (Berkeley and Los Angeles: University of California Press, 1982).

3. Newsletters I have found particularly helpful are *Environment Reporter; Chemical Regulation Reporter; National Wetlands Newsletter; Land Letter; Coastal Zone Management; Occupational Health and Safety Letter; Environmental Health Letter; Inside EPA; Land Use Planning Report; Public Land News; Weekly Bulletin of the Environmental Study Institute.*

4. John Naisbitt, *Megatrends* (New York: Warner Books, 1982).

5. Examples of such studies are Stephen R. Kellert, *American Attitudes, Knowledge and Behaviors Toward Wildlife and Natural Habitats* (Washington, D.C.: U.S. Fish and Wildlife Service, 1978–1980); Opinion Research Corporation, *The Public's Participation in Outdoor Activities and Attitudes Toward National Wilderness Areas* (Princeton, N.J., 1977); The Continental Group, *Toward Responsible Growth: Economic and Environmental Concern in the Balance* (Stamford, Conn., 1982).

6. Some state sources are the *Maine Times;* the *New Hampshire Times;* the *Deseret News* (Salt Lake City); the *Missoulian* (Missoula, Mont.); *New York Environmental News;* the *North Woods Call* (Mich.); *Maine Environment; ENFO* (Fla.); the *Plains Truth* (Northern Plains Resource Council); *Newsletter,* Tennessee Citizens for Wilderness Planning; *Our Wetlands* (Wisc.); *Crossroads Monitor* (Wyo.); *Newsletter,* Idaho Environmental Council.

7. A useful, and contrasting, example of a policy approach is Norman J. Vig and Michael E. Kraft, *Environmental Policy in the 1980s: Reagan's New Agenda* (Washington, D.C.: CQ Press, 1984).

8. While the materials of popular debate often cast the environmental movement as negative, with a major focus on opposition to modern values, science, and technology, an approach followed by Tucker, Arnold, and Douglas and Wildavsky, this paper takes a quite different tack to identify the movement as an outgrowth of positive aspiration associated with an advanced industrial society, including advanced applications of science and technology. Douglas and Wildavsky briefly consider, but reject, this approach. See their *Risk and Culture,* 1–15. Their treatment seems to be strikingly devoid of empirical observation about the values of the advanced industrial society and environmental behavior. The values described here were characteristic of advanced industrial societies

throughout the world. See Ronald Inglehart, *The Silent Revolution: Changing Values and Political Styles Among Western Publics* (Princeton, N.J.: Princeton University Press, 1977).

9. Carolyn Merchant, "Women of the Progressive Conservation Movement, 1900–1916," *Environmental Review* 8, no. 1 (Spring 1984): 57–85.

10. For a more extended treatment, see Samuel P. Hays, *Conservation and the Gospel of Efficiency* (Cambridge, Mass.: Harvard University Press, 1958).

11. The classic work on the Tennessee Valley Authority is David Lilienthal, TVA, *Democracy on the March* (New York: Harper, 1944).

12. For Pinchot's own view, see Gifford Pinchot, *Breaking New Ground* (New York: Americana Library, 1947; Seattle: University of Washington Press, 1983).

13. D. Harper Simms, *The Soil Conservation Service* (New York: Praeger, 1970).

14. John A. Salmond, *The Civilian Conservation Corps, 1933–1942* (Durham, N.C.: Duke University Press, 1967).

15. It might well be argued that many aspects of the environmental movement, especially with respect to land and water resources, were a reaction against the extensive developmental projects of the New Deal. The wilderness movement, for example, was fueled by the rapid advance of roads constructed by the Civilian Conservation Corps into wilderness candidate areas.

16. For environmental river values, see *American Rivers,* quarterly publication of the American Rivers Conservation Council (Washington, D.C., 1973–); for river development views, see *Waterways Journal,* published in St. Louis, Missouri, which covers events from the viewpoint of the eastern inland and coastal navigation industry.

17. Publications of the Wilderness Society, *The Living Wilderness,* and the Sierra Club, *Sierra Bulletin* (later *Sierra*), are useful in charting the evolution of environmental wildlands values.

18. The issue came to a dramatic head with channelization. See House Committee on Government Operations, Conservation and Natural Resources Subcommittee, *Stream Channelization* (4 parts), 92d Cong., 1st sess. (Washington. D.C., 1971). Wetlands issues can be followed in the *National Wetlands Newsletter* published by the Environmental Law Institute, Washington, D.C.; a useful, up-to-date report is U.S. Congress, Office of Technology Assessment, *Wetlands: Their Use and Regulation* (Washington, D.C., 1984).

19. The historical context of such issues can be followed in Martin V. Melosi, *Pollution and Reform in American Cities, 1870–1930,* (Austin, Tex.: University of Texas Press, 1980).

20. The Fish and Wildlife Service has received little focused attention from environmentalists or from academic writers. Hence, its role in the 1960s has been greatly underestimated. Some pieces of the puzzle are dealt with in Joseph V. Siry, *Marshes of the Ocean Shore: Development of an Ecological Ethic* (College Station, Tex.: Texas A&M University Press, 1984).

21. See, for example, Robert C. Mitchell, "The Public Speaks Again: A New Environmental Survey," *Resources* (Resources for the Future), no. 60 (September–November 1978); Council on Environmental Quality et al., *Public Opinion on Environmental Issues* (Washington, D.C., 1980); for later data, see Robert C. Mitchell, "Public Opinion and Environmental Politics in the 1970s and 1980s," in Vig and Kraft, *Environmental Policy in the 1980s.* For a review of studies of environmental values, see Kent D. VanLiere and Riley E. Dunlap, "The Social Bases of Environmental Concern: A Review of Hypotheses, Explanations and Empirical Evidence," *Public Opinion Quarterly* 44, no. 2 (Summer 1980): 181–97.

22. For a survey of wilderness users, see John C. Hendee, George H. Stankey, and Robert C. Lucas, "Wilderness Use and Users: Trends and Projections," in their *Wilderness Management,* U.S. Department of Agriculture, Forest Survey Miscellaneous Publication No. 1365 (Washington, D.C., 1978). See also George H. Stankey, "Myths in Wilderness Decision Making," *Journal of Soil and Water Conservation,* September–October 1971.

23. See, for example, Lawrence S. Hamilton and Terry Rader, "Suburban Forest Owners' Goals and Attitudes Toward Forest Practices," *Northern Logger and Timber Processor* (July 1974): 18–19. This is typical of a vast amount of literature.

24. "In general, evidence . . . provides very weak support for the assertion that social class is positively associated with environmental concern. What support there is rests primarily on the moderately strong relationship between environmental concern and education. The evidence for occupational prestige provides very weak support at best, while the overall evidence for income is highly ambiguous." See VanLiere and Dunlap, "The Social Bases of Environmental Concern," 190.

25. See, for example, the magazine *Islands* (1981–) Santa Barbara, Calif.

26. It is relevant to note the very rapid growth of visits to the national forests (from 7,132,000 to 14,332,000) and to the national parks (from 3,248,000 to 15,531,000) during the depression years from 1929 to 1939 to identify the important role of mass, rather than elite, consumption, or to contrast the enormous difficulties of the mass recreation movement in Europe in securing outdoor recreation opportunities amid the traditional exclusionary policies of private estate owners, in contrast with the openness of the American wildlands. For the data, see U.S. Dept. of Commerce, Bureau of the Census, *Historical Statistics of the United States* (Washington, D.C., 1974), Series H808: R104.

27. Significant public land purchases throughout the East, such as those in the Adirondacks, came through acquisition of former private estates or hunting grounds.

28. For a brief summary of Briggs's data, see "Amenity-Rich, Amenity-Poor," *Demographics* 3, no. 7 (July–August 1981).

29. For regional variations in attitude studies, see items in note 5.

30. The Continental Group, *Toward Responsible Growth,* 57, 77.

31. For a general review of wilderness politics, see Craig W. Allin, *The Politics of Wilderness Preservation* (Westport, Conn.: Greenwood Press, 1982).

32. The classic work on urban land use is William K. Reilly, ed., *The Use of Land* (New York: Crowell, 1973). For urban forestry, see Silas Little, ed., *Urban Foresters Notebook* (Northeast Forest Experiment Station, 1978), Forest Service General Technical Report NE-49. For a recent review of waterfront activities, see Patrick Barry, "The Last Urban Frontier," *Environmental Action* 15, no. 9 (May 1984): 14–17; see also Heritage Conservation and Recreation Service, U.S. Department of the Interior, *Urban Waterfront Revitalization; The Role of Recreation and Heritage* (Washington, D.C., 1979). For urban wildlife, see *Urban Wildlife News,* published for several years after 1977 by the Urban Wildlife Research Center, Ellicott City, Maryland.

33. See, for example, *Natural Areas Journal* (1981–), published by the Natural Areas Association. A wide range of these resources are described in various articles in *Nature Conservancy News,* published by the Nature Conservancy.

34. For PSD, see Thomas M. Disselhorst, "Sierra Club v. Ruckelshaus: 'On a Clear Day. . . .'", *Ecology Law Quarterly* 4, no. 3 (1975): 739–80.

35. Rudolph Husar of Washington University, St. Louis, refocused attention sharply on visibility by associating reduced visibility with sulfate particles and by using airport visibility data reaching back to the 1930s to identify trends and patterns in regional vari-

ations. The issue was closely associated with that of acid precipitation. Husar's then-recent work was included in the National Research Council report *Sulfur Oxides,* published by the National Academy of Sciences in 1978; see pp. 29–37.

36. Wildlife Management Institute, "The North American Wildlife Policy, 1973," which includes a copy of the "American Game Policy, 1930" (Washington, D.C., n.d.).

37. In 1975, for example, 21 million Americans participated in hunting and 50 million in wildlife observation.

38. U.S. Fish and Wildlife Service, *Operation of the National Wildlife Refuge System, Final Environmental Impact Statement* (Washington, D.C., 1976); Stephen R. Kellert, *American Attitudes, Knowledge and Behaviors.*

39. The National Wildlife Federation, Sierra Club, Wilderness Society, Friends of the Earth, National Parks and Conservation Association, and Defenders of Wildlife all had firm roots in natural environment issues. By 1984 there were state wilderness organizations throughout the West, and the Nature Conservancy was organized in thirty-five states. By that time wilderness politics had come to focus on separate state bills rather than national bills, reflecting the position of strength within each state from which wilderness advocates were then negotiating.

40. The Wilderness Society increased in membership from 50,000 to 100,000 between 1978 and 1983, the largest rate of growth in its history; the Nature Conservancy had 36,000 members in 1976 and 193,000 in 1983. See the relevant annual reports.

41. For such concepts see, for example, two textbooks, Kenneth E. F. Watt, *Understanding the Environment* (Boston: Allyn and Bacon, 1982); and Penelope ReVelle and Charles ReVelle, *The Environment: Issues and Choices for Society* (Boston: Willard Grant Press, 1981). They indicate the way in which new ecological ideas had come into general thinking.

42. For relevant events, see National Wildlife Federation, Conservation Report, 1966, May 27 (geothermal steam leases); July 28 (pollution of estuaries); September 30 (thermal pollution of waters); and October 7 (highway construction).

43. The first serious proposal in the legislative history of the Environmental Impact Statement (EIS) came from representative John Dingell of the Committee on Merchant Marine and Fisheries on March 23, 1967. The bill reflected the committee's concern for the impact of development on fish and wildlife. This and similar measures frequently took the form of amendments to the Fish and Wildlife Coordination Act.

44. Senate Public Works Committee, *Thermal Pollution,* 90th Cong., 2d sess., 1968, 1969. Hearings on the extent to which environmental factors are considered in selecting power plant sites, with particular emphasis on ecological effects of discharge of waste heat into rivers, lakes, estuaries, and coastal waters.

45. See, for example, Robert L. Rudd, *Pesticides and the Living Landscape* (Madison, Wis.: University of Wisconsin Press, 1964); Thomas R. Dunlap, *DDT: Scientists, Citizens and Public Policy* (Princeton, N.J.: Princeton University Press, 1981).

46. For changes in the approach of the Conservation Foundation, see its annual reports, which chart a transition from its earlier origins in natural history to its later concerns for land use, environmental mediation, and economic limitations to environmental objectives, among others.

47. A number of bills proposed in 1969 anticipated a comprehensive program for "research on natural systems"; see H.R. 952 proposed by Representative Charles Bennett of Florida; H.R. 7923 by Representative James Howard of New Jersey; H.R. 12,900 by Representative John Saylor of Pennsylvania; and S. 1075 by Senators Henry Jackson and Ted

Stevens. These bills spoke of research on "ecological systems, natural resources, and environmental quality."

48. U.S. Department of the Interior, Fish and Wildlife Service, *Biological Services Program* (Fiscal Year 1975–).

49. U.S. Department of Health, Education and Welfare, Public Health Service, *Air Quality Criteria for Sulfur Oxides* (Washington, D.C., 1967), Public Health Service Publication No. 1619.

50. For the broad range of relevant effects see EPA, Office of Research and Development, *The Acidic Deposition Phenomenon and Its Effects: Critical Assessment Review Papers, Public Review Draft* (Washington, D.C., May 1983). For a collection of papers concerning ecological effects, see Frank M. D'Itri, *Acid Precipitation: Effects on Ecological Systems* (Ann Arbor, Mich.: Ann Arbor Science, 1982). An excellent and brief review of effects from a European perspective is Environmental Resources Limited, *Acid Rain: A Review of the Phenomenon in the EEC and Europe* (London, 1983).

51. One of the first major environmental statements on energy appeared in Gerald O. Barney, ed., *The Unfinished Agenda* (New York: Crowell, 1977), 50–68. An even earlier, though brief, statement is The Georgia Conservancy, *The Wolfcreek Statement: Toward a Sustainable Energy Society* (Atlanta, Ga., 1976).

52. One of the two groups to emerge from the organization shaping Earth Day in 1970 was Zero Population Growth, which thereafter worked exclusively on population problems. See its publication, *National Reporter* (1969–).

53. See Samuel P. Hays, "The Limits-to-Growth Issue: An Historical Perspective," in *Growth in America*, ed. Chester L. Cooper (Westport, Conn.: Greenwood Press, 1976).

54. The Commission on Population Growth and the American Future, *Population and the American Future* (Washington, D.C.: U.S. Government Printing Office, 1972).

55. Council on Environmental Quality and U.S. Department of State, *The Global 2000 Report to the President*, 3 vols (Gland, Switzerland: International Union for Conservation of Nature and Natural Resources, 1980); World Wildlife Fund, *World Conservation Strategy* (n.p., 1980). The Year 2000 Committee, established to implement the World Conservation Strategy in the United States, was confined to prominent institutional leaders. The Global Tomorrow Coalition was a coalition of citizen environmental groups; however, its work was not widely publicized, known about, or reflected in grassroots citizen environmental activity. For the work of the coalition, see its publication, *Interaction* (Washington, D.C., 1981–).

56. For the American Land Forum, see its publication, *American Land Forum Magazine* (1980–); also *American Farm Land,* newsletter of the American Farmland Trust (1981–). See also W. Wendell Fletcher and Charles E. Little, *The American Cropland Crisis* (Bethesda, Md.: American Land Forum, 1982).

57. See, for example, Kirkpatrick Sale, *Human Scale* (New York: Coward, McCann, Geoghegan, 1982).

58. Subscribers to *Mother Earth News,* a publication that reflected these views, were about evenly divided among the central city, the suburbs, and the countryside. For self-help ideas, see John Lobell, *The Little Green Book: A Guide to Self-Reliant Living in the 80s* (Boulder, Colo.: Shambhala Publications, 1981).

59. For information about natural food stores, see *Whole Foods,* "the natural foods business journal" (Irvine, Calif., 1977–). This publisher also compiles an annual *Source Directory.* For a convenient collection of articles from its pages, see *Whole Food Natural Foods Guide* (Berkeley, Calif.: And/Or Press, 1979); see especially "First Annual Report on

the Industry" in the *Guide,* 268–74, which concluded that in 1978 there were 6,400 natural food stores in the nation, with sales of $1,152,000,000.

60. The issue of protection against spray drift arose in many forest areas. See, for example, the Oregon case in Carol Van Strum, *A Bitter Fog: Herbicides and Human Rights* (San Francisco: Sierra Club Books, 1983).

61. Alan Okagaki, Albert J. Fritsch, and C. J. Swet, *Solar Energy: One Way to Citizen Control* (Washington, D.C.: Center for Science in the Public Interest, 1976).

62. Relevant sources include Michael Brown, *Laying Waste* (New York: Washington Square Press, 1979); Edwin Chen, *PBB: An American Tragedy* (Englewood Cliffs, N.J.: Prentice-Hall, 1979); Joyce Egginton, *The Poisoning of Michigan* (New York: Norton, 1980); Adeline Gordon Levine, *Love Canal: Science, Politics and People* (Lexington, Mass.: Lexington Books, 1982); Samuel S. Epstein, Lester O. Brown, and Carol Pope, *Hazardous Waste in America* (San Francisco: Sierra Club Books, 1982).

63. See charts in U.S. Department of Health, Education and Welfare, *Healthy People: The Surgeon General's Report on Health Promotion and Disease Prevention,* 1979 (Washington, D.C., 1979), 22–23, 34–35, 44–45, 54–55, 72–73, in which improvements in health for five age groups are charted in terms of reduction in death. The report reflects many concerns for "better health" in each group, which imply notions beyond reduction in deaths, but has difficulty in translating these into clearly defined goals beyond reducing "premature death."

64. This rising public interest is reflected in the growing popularity of *Prevention* magazine. Its circulation rose from 50,000 in 1950 to 270,000 in 1060 to 2,434,017 in 1981, and now stands at over 4,000,000.

65. A persistent, but somewhat subordinated, theme in such matters was the relationship between health and natural environments. Horticultural therapy began to be used in hospitals. A study at Paoli Memorial Hospital near Philadelphia concluded that patients recovered faster if they were in rooms with views of trees and grass than if they saw brick walls, *Pittsburgh Press,* May 22, 1984. Connections were drawn between clearer skies and psychological mood; see Michael R. Cunningham, "Weather, Mood, and Helping Behavior: Quasi Experiments with the Sunshine Samaritan," *Journal of Personality and Social Psychology* 37, no. 11 (1979): 1947–56.

66. For a nontechnical account of infant malformations, see Christopher Norwood, *At Highest Risk: Environmental Hazards to Young and Unborn Children* (New York: McGraw-Hill, 1980). See also Bernard Rimland and Gerald E. Larson, "The Manpower Quality Decline: An Ecological Perspective," *Armed Forces and Society* (Autumn 1981): 21–78.

67. For EPA's "cancer principles," see Nathan J. Karch, "Explicit Criteria and Principles for Identifying Carcinogens: A Focus of the Controversy at the Environmental Protection Agency," *Analytical Studies for the U.S. Environmental Protection Agency:* vol. 2, *Decision Making in the Environmental Protection Agency: Case Studies* (Washington, D.C.: National Research Council, Committee on Environmental Decision Making, 1977). OSHA's attempt can be followed through the pages of *Chemical Regulation Reporter* and *Occupational Health and Safety Reporter.* See also "Industry Raps OSHA's Proposed Cancer Policy," *Chemical and Engineering News* (July 3, 1978): 14–15; "OSHA's War on Cancer: What it Means to Plastics," *Plastics World* (June–September 1978).

68. See Hugh M. Pitcher, "Comments on Issues Raised in the Analysis of the Neuropsychological Effects of Low Level Lead Exposure" (Washington, D.C.: Office of Policy Analysis, U.S. Environmental Protection Agency, 1984). "In reviewing the Draft Lead

Criteria Document we realized that, if substantiated and found to be causal, the cognitive effects of low level lead exposure would generate large social costs. As an indication of the size of this cost, several studies indicate that an IQ difference of one point is associated with a 1% change in lifetime earnings (corrected for education and other socioeconomic characteristics)."

69. "Probing Chemical Causes of Infertility," *Chemical Week* (February 15, 1984): 26, 29.

70. For occupational health issues, see Nicholas A. Ashford, *Crisis in the Workplace: Occupational Disease and Injury* (Cambridge, Mass.: MIT Press, 1976). Events can be followed in *Occupational Health and Safety Letter* (Washington, D.C., 1970–) and *Occupational Health and Safety Reporter* (Washington, D.C., 1970–). See also Daniel M. Berman, *Death on the Job: Occupational Health and Safety Struggles in the United States* (New York: Monthly Review Press, 1979).

71. "Of tens of thousands of commercially important chemicals only a few have been subjected to extensive toxicity testing and most have scarcely been tested at all." So concluded *Toxicity Testing: Strategies to Determine Needs and Priorities* (Washington, D.C.: National Academy of Sciences, 1984).

72. J. L. Annest, J. L. Pirkle, D. Makuc, J. W. Neese, D. D. Bayse, M. G. Kovar, "Chronological Trend in Blood Lead Levels between 1976 and 1980," *New England Journal of Medicine* 308 (1983): 1373–77.

73. The best statements on this problem have been made by British child psychologist Michael Rutter with respect to the neurological effects of lead on children. See his analysis, "Low Level Lead Exposure: Sources, Effects and Implications," in *Lead versus Health: Sources and Effects of Low Level Lead Exposure,* ed. Michael Rutter and Robin Russell Jones (London: Wiley-Interscience, 1983), 333–70. The British debate on this issue was closely followed in the United States, and British lead researchers were brought into the review of the lead criteria document by the EPA Science Advisory Board in 1984. See also Michael Rutter, "The Relationship Between Science and Policy Making: The Case of Lead," *Clean Air* 31, no. 1 (1983): 17–32.

74. A good account of the politics of cost-benefit analysis is Mark Green and Norman Waitzman, *Business War on the Law* (Washington, D.C.: Corporate Accountability Research Group, 1981).

75. For a statement favorable to risk analysis, see the Business Roundtable Air Quality Project, "National Ambient Air Quality Standards," (Cambridge, Mass., 1980).

76. When it revised its air quality regulations in 1980, Montana included the provision that the program's objective was to prevent air pollution that "interfered with normal daily activities," and specifically identified lowered lung function in schoolchildren as an "adverse effect" that should be prevented. See clippings on this issue in the *Missoulian* (Missoula, Mont.) in author file; *Down to Earth* (Helena, Mont.: Montana Environmental Information Center, March–April, May–June, and September–October 1980). For a business-sponsored view, see Benjamin G. Ferris, Jr., and Frank E. Speizer, "Criteria for Establishing Standards for Air Pollutants," *The Business Roundtable Air Quality Project* (Boston, 1980): "We define an adverse effect as medically significant physiologic or pathologic changes generally evidenced by permanent damage or incapacitating illness to the individual."

77. For the issues in the principles and standards problem, see U.S. Water Resources Council, *Summary Analysis of Public Response to the Proposed Principles and Standards for Planning Water and Related Land Resources and Draft Environmental Statement* (Washington, D.C., 1972).

78. See, for example, Commission on Maine's Future, Final Report, December 1, 1977.

79. Two reports that are more sanguine concerning value change in the Corps of Engineers are Daniel A. Mazmanian and Jeanne Nienaber, *Can Organizations Change? Environmental Protection, Citizen Participation and the Corps of Engineers* (Washington, D.C.: Brookings Institution, 1979); Martin Reuss, *Shaping Environmental Awareness: The United States Army Corps of Engineers Environmental Advisory Board, 1970–1980* (Washington, D.C.: Historical Division, Office of Administrative Services, Office of the Chief of Engineers, 1983).

80. For a brief statement of the problem, see Gene E. Likens, "A Priority for Ecological Research," *Bulletin of the Ecological Society of America* 64, no. 4 (December 1983): 234–43; see also James T. Callahan, "Long-Term Ecological Research," *BioScience* 34, no. 6 (June 1984): 363–67.

81. Clair C. Patterson, "Natural Levels of Lead in Humans" (Chapel Hill: Institute for Environmental Studies, University of North Carolina, 1982), Carolina Environmental Essay Series 3. This is a summary of data, much of which was developed by Patterson and his associates.

82. For a brief look at the range of research, including monitoring, stimulated in the private sector, see John D. Kinsman, Joe Wisniewski, and Jimmie Nelson, "Acid Deposition Research in the Private Sector," *Journal of the Air Pollution Control Association* 31, no. 2 (February 1984): 119–23.

83. See U.S. Environmental Protection Agency, *Review Draft Air Quality Criteria for Lead*, vols. 3 and 4 (Research Triangle Park, N.C., 1983). See also Environmental Protection Agency, Office of Policy Analysis, *Costs and Benefits of Reducing Lead in Gasoline, Draft Final Report* (Washington, D.C.: Office of Planning Analysis, Office of Policy, Planning, and Evaluation, EPA, 1984), chaps. 5–6.

84. See *Northeastern Environmental Science* (Troy, N.Y.: Northeastern Science Foundation, 1982–).

85. See Joseph E. DeSteiguer, "Public Participation in Forestry Research Planning" (Ph.D. thesis, Texas A&M University, 1979), which analyzes the public participation process carried out by the U.S. Forest Service in its review of its research program; the author charts significant distinctions among the choices as to desired research expressed by each of five groups. My own review of the relevant documents substantiates DeSteiguer's description and identifies the limited role of research based on enhancing environmental objectives in contrast to that enhancing commodity objectives.

86. The controversy over lead is a useful case for analysis. Covering some three decades of dispute, the debate continued in much the same manner despite a considerable increase in scientific data and a lowering of the consensus view on threshold levels from 80 µg/dl to 30 µg/dl of blood. At each stage of this threshold reduction, the lead industry scientists argued that the accepted level provided ample protection, and public health scientists argued that frontier knowledge indicated the desirability of allowing for effects at lower levels. In air pollution matters generally, sources of pollution argued that more research was needed both in the 1960s when the laws were first being developed and later in the 1980s when the focus was acid deposition.

87. Two major centers of "high-proof" analysis and political action, both heavily supported by industrial sources of pollution, were the Council on Agricultural Science and Technology and the American Council on Science and Health. Their activities can be followed in their publications, *News from CAST* (Ames. Iowa) and *ASCH News and Views* (N.Y.).

88. A useful review of these controversies is contained in Earon S. Davis and Valerie Wilk, *Toxic Chemicals: The Interface Between Law and Science,* published by the Farmworker Justice Fund, Inc., (n.p., 1982). A useful exchange that sharpens some of the issue is "Examining the Role of Science in the Regulatory Process: A Roundtable Discussion About Science at EPA," *Environment* 25, no. 5 (June 1983): 6–14, 33–41. Frontier activities with respect to environmental and occupational health can be followed in an organization that brought such scientists together, the Society for Occupational and Environmental Health. See its publication, *Letter* (Washington, D.C., 1975–).

89. Michael C. Royston, *Pollution Prevention Pays* (Oxford: Pergamon Press, 1979); Donald Huisingh and Vicki Bailey, eds., *Making Pollution Pay: Ecology with Economy as Policy* (New York: Pergamon Press, 1982); Monica E. Campbell and William M. Glenn, *Profit from Pollution Prevention: A Guide to Industrial Waste Reduction and Recycling* (Ontario: Pollution Probe Foundation, 1982).

90. Joseph T. Ling, "Industry's Environmental Challenge: Prevention" (Paper delivered at the International Conference on the Environment, Stockholm, Sweden, April 12–31, 1982). See also "Low- or Non-Pollution Technology Through Pollution Prevention," prepared by 3M Company for the United Nations Environment Programme, Office of Industry and the Environment (n.p., 1982).

91. This issue was referred to as "technology forcing." See John E. Bonine. "The Evolution of 'Technology-Forcing' in the Clean Air Act," *Environment Reporter,* Monograph no. 21, July 25, 1975.

92. For integrated pest management, see the newsletter, *IPM Practitioner* (Berkeley. Calif., 1978–); for biological farming, see the newsletter *Alternative Agriculture News* (Beltsville. Md., 1983–); for recycling, see *BioCycle* (formerly *Compost Science/Land Utilization)* (Emmaus, Pa., 1963–); for solar energy, see *Solar Age* (Harrisville, N.H.. 1975–). No general center in the United States focuses directly on innovative environmental technologies with an emphasis on process change, comparable to Environmental Data Services which does so in England. See its publication, *ENDS Report* (London, 1978–).

93. For a general source of publications by the environmental opposition, see National Council for Environmental Balance, Inc., Louisville, Kentucky.

94. *High Country News* is a good source for these developments. See, for example, Ed Marston, "Fighting for a Land Base," *High Country News* (Paonia, Colo.) (January 23, 1984): 15.

95. See the Continental Group, *Toward Responsible Growth,* 97. The study contrasted attitudes on a four-point scale from resource utilization to resource preservation. It identified the Rocky Mountain West as the strongest region to support its end-point category, "resource preservation." The regional scores on this point were Rocky Mountain, 35 percent; New England, 32 percent; Pacific, 28 percent; Middle Atlantic, 28 percent; North Central, 26 percent; Middle West, 20 percent; West South Central, 25 percent; South Atlantic, 18 percent; and Middle South, 17 percent.

96. Dr. William J. Peeples, Commissioner Department of Health, State of Maryland, to Senator Edmund Muskie, November 15, 1968, in Senate Committee on Public Works, Subcommittee on Air and Water Pollution, *Air Pollution: Hearings on Air Quality Criteria,* 90th Cong., 2d sess., July 1968.

97. For a brief summary of the hearings and the controversy, see *Conservation Foundation Letter,* July 29, 1967. The resulting National Air Quality Criteria Advisory Committee of fifteen members included representatives from the paper, coal, petroleum, and

automobile industries; see *Environmental Science and Technology* 2, no 6 (June 1968): 400.

98. These controversies can be followed most readily in the pages of *Environment Reporter*, especially with respect to lead, sulfur dioxide, particulates, and nitrogen oxide.

99. As the 1970s advanced, appointments to and activities of the EPA Science Advisory Board, which can be followed in *Environmental Reporter* seemed to follow a deliberate policy to make scientific decisions more open and reflect a wider range of opinion. Under the Reagan administration, that policy was reversed. See, for example, the formaldehyde case in House Subcommittee on Investigations and Oversight of the Committee on Science and Technology, *Formaldehyde: Review of Scientific Basis of EPA's Carcinogenic Risk Assessment*, 97th Cong., 2d sess., 1983. A more open policy was established with the appointment of William Ruckelshaus as EPA administrator.

100. The estuarine proposals are included in hearings of the 1960s: House Subcommittee on Fisheries and Wildlife Conservation, *Estuarine and Wetlands Legislation*, 89th Cong., 2d sess., 1966; and *Estuarine Areas*, 90th Cong., 1st sess., 1967.

101. For the larger proposal, see House Subcommittee on National Parks and Insular Affairs, *To Establish a Barrier Islands Protection System: Hearings*, 96th Cong., 2d sess., 1980.

102. See statement by John Middleton, administrator, the National Air Pollution Control Administration, in Senate Committee on Public Works, *Air Pollution: Hearings on Air Quality Criteria*, 90th Cong., 2d sess., 1968.

103. For brief accounts of this issue, see two items, Stanton Coerr, "EPA's Air Standard for Lead," and David Schoenbrod, "Why Regulation of Lead Has Failed," in *Low Level Lead Exposure: The Clinical Implications of Current Research,* ed. Herbert L. Needleman (New York: Raven Press, 1980), 253–57, 258–66. See also Gregory S. Wetstone and Jan Goldman, "Chronology of Events Surrounding the *Ethyl* Decision," (Draft, Washington, D.C.: Environmental Law Institute, 1981).

104. "Behavioral Toxicology Looks at Air Pollutants," *Environmental Science and Technology* 2 no. 10 (October 1968): 731–33, which describes the work of the NAPCA behavioral toxicology unit in Cincinnati under the direction of Dr. Charles Xintaras.

105. These views of the 1960s were reflected in Senate Subcommittee on Air and Water Pollution, *Air Quality Criteria*, 90th Cong., 2d sess., 1968.

106. Few of these cases have received systematic treatment. The attempt by the lead industry to undermine the credibility of Dr. Herbert Needleman, a prominent frontier researcher on the neurological effects of low-level lead exposures on children, is well known. At times their attacks appear on the record. See description of Dr. Needleman as representing "what is at best a minority view that adverse health effects occur at blood-lead levels below 40 mg/dl," in House Subcommittee on Health and the Environment, *Oversight—Clean Air Act Amendments of 1977*, 96th Cong., 1st sess., 1980 (testimony of Jerome Cole of the International Lead Zinc Research Organization), 344. An indirectly related analysis of the roles of dissenting scientists that stresses more the controversial nature of their public role is Rae Goodell, *The Visible Scientists* (Boston: Little, Brown, 1975). For some aspects of the James Allen case, see William J. Broad, "Court Upholds Privacy of Unpublished Data," *Science* 216 (April 2, 1982): 34, 36.

107. See statement concerning the role of the margin of safety in the recent proposed revisions to the particulate standard to control fine particulates in *Environment Reporter* (March 23, 1984): 2121.

108. See, for example, for no-till agriculture, Maureen K. Hinkle, "Problems with Conservation Tillage," *Journal of Soil and Water Conservation* 38, no. 3 (May–June 1983): 201–6.

109. A summary of voting tabulations for environmental issues in the Michigan House of Representatives for several years in the 1970s is as follows:

Percent Urban District	Percent Environmental Vote		
	1973–74	*1975–76*	*1977–78*
75–100	57.3 (69)*	62.6 (69)	62.8 (69)
50–75	47.7 (12)	48.7 (12)	41.3 (12)
25–50	33.6 (15)	38.4 (15)	35.1 (15)
1–25	30.7 (10)	38.1 (10)	21.3 (10)
0	19.3 (4)	27.0 (4)	18.3 (4)

*Number of legislative districts in each population group.

110. See, for example, the activities of the Northern Plains Resource Council, which can be followed in its publication *The Plains Truth.* Cooperation on these issues can be followed in regional publications such as *High Country News* as well as *Not Man Apart,* a monthly publication of Friends of the Earth.

111. For examples of labor-environmental disagreement as well as cooperation see Richard Kazis and Richard L. Grossman, *Fear at Work: Job Blackmail, Labor and the Environment* (New York: Pilgrim Press, 1982). See also activities of the OSHA/Environmental Network (author file).

112. United Steelworkers of America. *Poison in Our Air: Air Pollution Conference* (Washington, D.C., 1969).

113. See *ENDS Report,* note 92.

114. The Oregon Coastal Zone Management Association was formed by development-oriented local governments in western Oregon to counter environmental coastal programs. Its general ideological focus was to stress a policy of "multiple use" on the coast. See its publication *The Oregon Coast,* which was issued first in 1978 and in 1981 was incorporated as a regular feature in a new journal, *Oregon Coast,* which attempted to link aesthetic coastal values with expanded tourist economy activity.

115. The iron and steel industry argued that the particulate standards could be doubled with no adverse health effects. Its attorneys, through the American Iron and Steel Institute, commissioned a study by British scientist W. W. Holland to support its case. See W. W. Holland et al., "Health Effects of Particulate Pollution: Reappraising the Evidence," *American Journal of Epidemiology* 110, no. 5 (November 1979), with subsequent reply by Carl M. Shy, "Epidemiologic Evidence and the United States Air Quality Standards," *ibid.* 110, no. 6 (December 1979): 661–71.

116. Julian Simon, *The Ultimate Resource* (Princeton, N.J.: Princeton University Press, 1981).

117. These activities can be followed in industry publications such as *Chemical Week* and, in a more neutral source, *Environment Reporter,* during the Reagan years. See also an environmental critique, Friends of the Earth et al., *Ronald Reagan and the American Environment* (Andover, Mass.: Brick House Publishing Company, 1982).

118. As of this writing it appears that passage of a large number of state wilderness bills might be the most successful positive action by environmentalists during the Reagan administration.

119. "The bureaucracy and its organized clienteles are surely the most durable com-

ponents of the policy process." See John Edward Chubb, "Interest Groups and the Bureaucracy: The Politics of Energy" (Ph.D. thesis, University of Minnesota, 1979), 21.

120. Andrew C. Gordon and John P. Heinz, eds., *Public Access to Information* (New Brunswick, N.J.: Transaction Books, 1973), esp. 184–222.

121. For NEPA and the courts, see Lettie M. Wenner, *The Environmental Decade in Court* (Bloomington, Ind.: Indiana University Press, 1982); Frederick R. Anderson and Robert H. Daniels, *NEPA in the Courts: A Legal Analysis of the National Environmental Policy Act* (Washington, D.C.: Resources for the Future and Johns Hopkins University Press, 1973).

122. Initially the environmental impact reports were to "accompany the proposal through existing agency review processes." Tim Atkeson, legal officer of the Council on Environmental Quality, said, "As we read the law and the legislative history, the public's involvement comes by disclosure of the thing (report) at the end of the process. The public gets a retrospective look, and their impact comes largely as some comment about the same decision in the future." See *Water Resources Newsletter* 5, no. 6 (December 1970): 4. Court decisions modified this approach considerably.

123. A celebrated "on the record" case concerned regulations proposed by the Office of Surface Mining under the 1977 Surface Mining Act. The President's Council of Economic Advisers (CEA), via its Council on Wage and Price Stability (CWPS), objected to the economic impact of the new regulations. See the CWPS "Report of the Regulatory Analysis Review Group Submitted by the Council on Wage and Price Stability, November 27, 1978, Concerning Proposed Surface Coal Mining and Reclamation" (author file). The Department of the Interior objected to the use of "post record closure" information in the decision making on the regulation which CEA "interference" involved. Its action forced that post-record data into the record to be made available for comment by others, but did not change policy beyond this case. See "Compilation of Conversations and Correspondence on the Permanent Regulatory Program Implementing Section 501(b) of the Surface Mining Control and Reclamation Act of 1977" (author file).

124. For a discussion of this problem with respect to lead, see Gregory S. Wetstone, ed., "Meeting Record from Resolution of Scientific Issues and the Judicial Process: *Ethyl Corporation v. EPA*" (meeting held October 21, 1977, under the auspices of the Environmental Law Institute, Washington, D.C., 1981), discussion on 84ff., and especially between Judges Skelly Wright and Harold Leventhal of the U.S. Court of Appeals, District of Columbia.

125. One recent case indicated that, while the National Oceanic and Atmospheric Administration sought comments on its state program evaluations, it did not feel obligated to respond to them: it rejected a petition by Friends of the Earth to change its policy. See *Environment Reporter,* December 30, 1983, 1497–98. In another case, the Natural Resources Defense Council argued that EPA used negotiation with industry to test chemicals rather than work out agreed-on test rules in order to avoid public participation. See Senate Committee on Environment and Public Works, Subcommittee on Toxic Substances and Environmental Oversight, *Toxic Substances Control Act Oversight: Hearings,* July 29, 30, August 1, 1983 (Washington, D.C., 1984).

126. The works of these two organizations can be followed in their publications, *EDF Letter* and *NRDC Newsletter.* For a specific example of their analytical capabilities, see David G. Hawkins, "A Review of Air Pollution Control Actions Under the Reagan Administration as of July 1982," (Washington, D.C.: NRDC, July 1982).

127. See publications of its Economic Policy Department, such as Peter M. Emerson

and Gloria E. Helfand, *Wilderness and Timber Production in the National Forests of California*, (Washington, D.C., 1983); and Gloria E. Helfand, *Timber Economics and Other Resource Values: The Bighorn-Weitas Roadless Area, Idaho* (Washington, D.C., 1983).

128. See its publication, *Forest Planning* (Eugene, Oreg., 1980–).

129. Members of the EPA Science Advisory Board, in reviewing the draft criteria document for lead, April 26–27, 1984, for example, had available for their evaluation the summaries produced by EPA but not the original literature on which the review was based. The give-and-take of the meeting indicated that only a few members of the board had first-hand knowledge of the research, and these were relied on heavily by other members for that information. (Interview with Dr. Herbert Needleman, who made a presentation at the meeting but was not a member of the board, May 5, 1984.) A similar role was played, for the same reasons, by Gordon J. Stopps of the Haskell Laboratory of Dupont in the proceedings of the first National Academy of Sciences study on lead; committee members deferred to him because of his knowledge of airborne lead and because they were far more familiar with ingested lead. See Philip Boffey, *The Brain Bank of America* (New York: McGraw-Hill, 1973).

130. NRDC, in cooperation with the National Air Conservation Commission of the American Lung Association, persuaded Needleman and Piomelli to publish a summary of frontier findings, "The Effects of Low-Level Lead Exposure," which was incorporated into proceedings on the criteria document. The issue can be followed in *Environment Reporter*, 1977–78; see especially July 7, 1978, 427–28. Needleman later testified at the House Subcommittee on Health and the Environment, *Oversight—Clean Air Act Amendments of 1977*, 96th Cong., 1st sess., 1980, 372–86, concerning the proceedings.

131. The Nuclear Information and Research Service, Washington, D.C., provided offprints of scientific and technical articles; see its publication, *Groundswell* (1979–). The Center for Science in the Public Interest communicated to the readers of *Nutrition Action* (Washington, D.C., 1976–) information concerning food hazards gathered by a staff of professional scientists.

132. For an EPA report highly critical of the role of the media in toxic chemical cases with case studies on kepone, lead (Dallas, Tex.), Love Canal, and dioxin, see *Inside EPA, Weekly Report* (January 13, 1984): 12–14.

133. See, for example the publications of the Citizen's Clearinghouse for Hazardous Wastes, Inc., Arlington, Va., critical of the EPA for its criticism of citizen action with respect to hazardous wastes.

134. A case study of this problem is Ben W. Twight, *Organizational Values and Political Power: The Forest Service Versus the Olympic National Park* (University Park, Pa.: Pennsylvania State University Press, 1983).

135. See the interplay of scientific debate in the Love Canal case as described in Adeline Gordon Levine, *Love Canal: Science, Politics and People* (Lexington, Mass.: Lexington Books, 1982).

136. American Forest Institute, *Research Recap* (November 10, 1977): 3–4.

137. The *Conservation Foundation Letter*, November 1969, reported that citizen successes in setting stricter standards had been so striking that "there are indications that some industries are wondering if they might not fare better under federal standards rather than state standards." For industry reaction to state standards and report on testimony at Senate hearings by Fred E. Tucker, manager of pollution control services for the National Steel Corporation, favoring national air quality standards, see *Environmental Science and Technology* (May 1970): 4–5. Tucker was critical of "the people who appear to

be playing a numbers game with air quality standards by setting lower and lower allowable pollution levels in state standards."

138. The issue can be followed in *Forest Planning* (note 128).

139. See *Conference Proceedings, Coastal Zone Management, Today and Tomorrow, The Necessity for Multiple Use, Economic Considerations of Coastal Zone Management,* sponsored by the Oregon Coastal Zone Management Association, 5 vols. (Newport, Oreg., 1980).

140. A case in point was the EPA action to advance the date for removal of lead in gasoline in 1984. Although revision of the lead criteria document reflected advances in scientific data since the earlier version in 1976, and although that new knowledge was reflected in the cost-benefit analysis produced by the EPA Policy Analysis Division, which took up action on the lead-in-gasoline issue, it declined to use the new health effects data as a basis for its decision on the grounds that the data were too controversial. One can rightly interpret this as a decision in which, in spite of the weight of scientific opinion about the matter, EPA did not feel that it could withstand the political opposition of the lead industry.

141. This mixed potential was implicit in the strong environmental support for planning in both the Forest Management Act of 1976 and the Federal Land Planning and Management Act of 1976.

142. For environmental mediation, see *Resolve,* which was published beginning in 1978 by the Center for Environmental Conflict Resolution in Palo Alto, California. and in early 1982 moved to the Conservation Foundation.

143. The approach of the Environmental Law Institute (ELI) is best reflected in its journal, *Environmental Forum,* which began publication in May 1982; it seemed to be governed by a policy of balancing opinion between various parties in controversy rather than advancing a "leading-edge" environmental position. This could be understood as an attempt by ELI to service its legal professional clientele no matter what side of legal controversy it was on, and to foster an opinion forum of the same political stance.

144. The political position of the National Association of Environmental Professionals can be followed in its journal, *The Environmental Professional* (Elmsford, N.Y.) which began publication in 1979.

145. Citizen environmental organizations considered that both the Conservation Foundation and the Environmental Law Institute were useful within their own limited "middle ground" spheres, but not reliable in advancing environmental objectives in leading-edge fashion. Thus, when the foundation worked with industry in the Clean Sites program in 1984, a joint venture to take private action to clean up hazardous waste sites, most environmental organizations felt that the venture would be used to undermine legislative strategy intended to make the hazardous waste program more effective.

146. This stance is reflected in Vig and Kraft, *Environmental Policy in the 1980s.*

147. In Minnesota, the air pollution statute provides that "no local government unit shall set standards of air quality which are more stringent than those set by the pollution control agency," *Nucleonics Week* (February 26, 1970). In Illinois, the mayor of Catlin, near Danville, objecting to a proposed six-thousand-acre strip mine by the Amax Coal Company on prime agricultural land in his township, complained, "The state pre-empted our rights to regulate coal mining locally," reported by Harold Henderson, "Caving in on Coal," *Illinois Times* (September 5–11, 1980): 81. In 1980, Connecticut established a Hazardous Waste Facility Siting Board with power to override local zoning laws, *Environmental Science and Technology* (August 1980): 894. In 1980, the Wisconsin Department of

Natural Resources revised its wetlands regulation, NR 115, with legislative approval, which prohibits counties from forming regulations more strict than those of the state, *Our Wetlands,* published by the Wisconsin Wetlands Association, August–September 1980.

148. Noise control issues were defined in 1981 by congressional staff: "Industry generally supports federal noise regulations as preferable to myriad local rules which would differ from place to place. But local governments . . . want the authority to establish rules that are stricter than the federal regulations. Currently the noise act pre-empts stricter state and local noise regulations." See Environmental Study Conference, U.S. Congress, *Weekly Bulletin* (February 23, 1981): C7.

149. Industry sought a preemption provision in the 1972 extension of the federal pesticide law, but failed. See *Farm Chemicals* (October 1970): 70; (November 1971): 12; (December 1971): 12. For environmental opposition to preemption, see Senate Subcommittee on Environment, Hearings on the 1972 Pesticide Act, 130–31 (testimony of Cynthia Wilson).

150. Radioactive waste transport was one of a wide range of nuclear issues involving preemption of state authority; see *Groundswell* 4, no. 5 (September–October 1981): 1–3, 5–6, for a listing of state laws subject to potential preemption.

151. Right-to-know controversy can be followed in the publication *Exposure,* issued by the Environmental Action Foundation, Washington, D.C., and in *Chemical Week* (New York), as well as *Chemical Regulation Reporter* (Washington, D.C.).

152. For the main case, from California, see *Coastal Zone Management,* Jan. 2, 1980, 1; subsequent events can be found in later issues, February 25, 1981, 1; May 6, 1981, 1; July 15, 1981, 1; August 5, 1981, 1; August 12, 1981, 2; September 16, 1981, 1–2; September 23, 1981, 4–5; October 7, 1981, 1–2.

153. Evidence from western sources throughout the 1970s and thereafter reflects a wide range of such activity. The best single source is *High Country News,* but it is confined to the Rocky Mountain states. State sources include *Alert,* publication of the Washington Environmental Council; the *Conservator,* the Colorado Open Space Council; *Earthwatch,* Montana Environmental Council; and *Crossroads Monitor,* Wyoming Outdoor Council.

154. A survey of western adverse reaction to the drive to increase allowable cuts during the Reagan administration is in an eight-part series of articles, "Taming the Forests," by R. H. Ring, in the *Arizona Star,* February 5–12, 1984. Especially useful is the last installment, which summarizes responses on the matter from state park and recreation, and fish and game agencies in the West.

155. See, for example. U.S. Department of Health, Education and Welfare, *Proceedings, Conference in the Matter of Pollution of the Interstate Waters of the Mahoning River and its Tributaries,* vol. 1, February 16–17, 1965 (Washington, D.C.: HEW, 1965); 195–213. In this proceeding the state of Ohio maintained that its pollution discharge information could not be divulged without express permission of the discharger.

156. House Committee on Government Operations, Natural Resources and Power Subcommittee, *House Report 1579,* 90th Cong., 2d sess., 1968. This report was given renewed publicity, with extended analysis, by Senator Lee Metcalf in his investigations of advisory committees in 1970.

157. Gregory S. Wetstone and Jan Goldman, "Chronology of Events Surrounding the *Ethyl* Decision" (Washington, D.C.: Environmental Law Institute, 1981), especially 2–3, 13.

158. Frustration of the lead industry with the course of events in the first lead criteria

document is reflected in testimony of Jerome F. Cole, Director of Environmental Health, Lead Industries Association, in Subcommittee on Health and the Environment, *Oversight—Clean Air Act Amendments of 1977 Hearings* 1980, 341–72. In the revision of the lead criteria document in 1983–84, considerable evidence was presented concerning health effects of blood lead levels below 30 µg/dl; this was taken seriously by EPA staff and the EPA Clean Air Science Advisory Committee despite the continued position of the Lead Industries Association (LIA) that there was no evidence of adverse effect below 40 µg/dl. See summary of the health effects evidence in EPA, Office of Policy Analysis, Costs and Benefits of Reducing Lead in Gasoline (Washington, D.C., 1984, draft final report) chaps. 5 and 6. The LIA still disagreed strongly with the conclusion by the Center for Disease Control (CDC), the American Academy of Pediatrics, and EPA that the "threshold point" was 30 µg/dl; hence, when the CDC took action in 1983 to issue an advisory to public health professionals in the nation that the accepted threshold should be lowered, the LIA took up legal action to thwart it.

159. See newspaper clippings following the case in *The New York Times* and *The Washington Post* (author file).

160. The Agent Orange case was only one of the more dramatic instances. See the Tyler, Texas, asbestos suit, which was settled for $20 million "without trial and verdict." *The New York Times,* December 20, 1977.

161. See Council of Economic Advisors, "Compilation of Conversations and Correspondence on the Permanent Regulatory Program Implementing Section 501(b) of the Surface Mining Control and Reclamation Act of 1977" (author file), which indicated considerable reliance by the CEA on the regulated industry for the formulation of its views.

162. The regulation of formaldehyde was the most widely debated case: see note 99. It was not, however, an isolated case; for others, see Robert Nelson, *A World of Preference: Business Access to Reagan's Regulators,* Democracy Project Report—No. 5 (n.p., October 1983).

163. A useful case of the politics of modeling with respect to air pollution is Phyllis Austin, "Keeping the Air Clean: In a New Period of Regulatory Accommodation the Emphasis Is on Granting Licenses Quickly," *Maine Times,* November 1983, 2–5. Another case involved the impact of electric power generation on the Hudson River striped bass population; see L. W. Barnhouse et al., "Population Biology in the Courtroom: The Hudson River Controversy," *BioScience* 34, no. 1 (January 1984): 14–19.

164. A host of issues involved confidentiality. They can be observed, for example, in the first round of premanufacture notices for chemical registration under the 1976 Toxic Substances Control Act and the development of regulations pertaining to Section 5 of that act. See *Chemical Regulation Reporter,* April 27, 1979, 82; May 11, 1979, 147–49; May 18, 1979, 218–19.

165. An excellent source through which to follow this issue is Chemical Week. For its response to the Philadelphia ordnance, see February 4, 1981, 50; see also "Philadelphia Sets Toxic Chemical Rules," *Chemical and Engineering News* (February 2, 1981): 4–5. For California action, see *Chemical Week* (September 28, 1983): 29, 32.

166. See, for example, the speech by EPA administrator William Ruckelshaus before the Detroit Economic Club in April 1984, cited in *Coastal Zone Management* 15, no. 21 (May 24, 1984): 5.

167. "Consumption is the sole end and purpose of all production; and the interest of

the producer ought to be attended to, only so far as it may be necessary for promoting that of the consumer. The maxim is so perfectly self-evident, that it would be absurd to attempt to prove it." See Adam Smith, *An Inquiry Into the Nature and Causes of the Wealth of Nations* (New York: Modern Library Edition, 1937), 625.

A Historical Perspective on Contemporary Environmentalism

1. Samuel P. Hays, *Conservation and the Gospel of Efficiency* (Cambridge, Mass.: Harvard University Press, 1958).

2. Samuel P. Hays, *Beauty, Health and Permanence: Environmental Politics in the United States. 1955–1985* (New York: Cambridge University Press, 1987).

3. Samuel P. Hays, "The New Environmental Forest," *University of Colorado Law Review* 59: 517–50.

4. Alfred E. Runte, *National Parks: The American Experience* (Lincoln: University of Nebraska Press, 1979).

5. Martin Melosi, *Pollution and Reform in American Cities, 1870–1930* (Austin: University of Texas Press, 1980).

6. Council on Environmental Quality, *The President's Environmental Program 1977* (Washington, D.C.: Council on Environmental Quality, 1977).

7. T. Allan Comp, *Blueprint for the Environment: A Plan for Federal Action* (Salt Lake City: Howe Brothers, 1989).

8. Wilderness Society, "Special Report—Wilderness America: A Vision for the Future of the Nation's Wildlands," *Wilderness* 52: 3–64.

9. Defenders of Wildlife, *Preserving Communities and Corridors* (Washington, D.C.: Defenders of Wildlife, 1989); Elliott A. Norse et al., *Conserving Biological Diversity in Our National Forests* (Washington, D.C.: The Wilderness Society, 1986).

10. Samuel P. Hays, "The Role of Values in Science and Policy: The Case of Lead" in *Human Lead Exposure,* ed. Herbert L. Needleman (Boca Raton, Fla.: CRC Press, 1992).

11. Clair C. Patterson, *Natural Levels of Lead in Humans* (Chapel Hill, N.C.: The Institute for Environmental Studies, 1982).

12. Herbert L. Needleman and Sergio Piomelli, "The Effects of Low Level Lead Exposure" (New York: Natural Resources Defense Council, Inc., in cooperation with National Air Conservation Commission, American Lung Association, 1978).

13. National Ocean Service, *A Summary of Selected Data on Chemical Contaminants in Sediments Collected During 1984, 1985, 1986, and 1987* (Rockville, Md.: National Oceanic and Atmospheric Administration, 1988).

14. Comp, *Blueprint for the Environment.*

15. National Park Service, *Park Science* (Corvallis, Oreg.: National Park Service, 1981– .

16. Royston 1979.

17. John J. Cohrssen and Vincent T. Covello, *Risk Analysis: A Guide to Principles and Methods for Analyzing Health and Environmental Risks* (Washington, D.C.: U.S. Council on Environmental Quality, 1989).

18. Randal O'Toole, *The Citizens' Guide to Forplan* (Eugene, Oreg.: Cascade Holistic Economic Consultants, 1983).

19. Wilderness Society, *Management Directions for the National Forests of the Greater Yellowstone Ecosystem* (Washington, D.C.: The Wilderness Society, 1987).

20. Bradford H. Sewell and Robin M. Whyatt, *Intolerable Risk: Pesticides in Our Children's Food* (Washington, D.C.: Natural Resources Defense Council, 1989); Barbara S.

Glenn, *Lake Michigan Sport Fish: Should You Eat Your Catch?* (Ann Arbor: National Wildlife Federation, 1989).

21. Centers for Disease Control 1978, 1985.

22. Bernard Goldstein, "Health and the Lead Phasedown: An Interview with Bernard Goldstein, Assistant Administrator for Research and Development," *EPA Journal* 11, no. 4: 9–12.

23. Hugh M. Pitcher, "Comments on Issues Raised in the Analysis of the Neuropsychological Effects of Low Level Lead Exposure," unpublished paper (Washington, D.C.: Environmental Protection Agency, Office of Policy Planning and Evaluation).

24. Power 1988.

25. Environmental Data Services, *Eco-Labels: Product Management in a Greener Europe* (London: Environmental Data Services, 1989).

26. Keith Schneider, "Food Industry Is Testing for Toxics to Reassure Consumers on Crops," *New York Times,* March 27, 1989, A1, B12; Marilyn Marter, "Testing Service Monitors Pesticide Residues in Foods," *Harrisburg Patriot-News.* December 13, 1989, C5.

27. Roger H. Bezdek, Robert M. Wendling, Jonathan D. Jones, "The Economic and Employment Effects of Investments in Pollution Abatement and Control Technologies," *Ambio* 18: 2/4–/9.

Environmental Political Culture and Environmental Political Development

1. See Samuel P. Hays, "From Conservation to Environment: Environmental Politics in the United States Since World War Two, *Environmental Review* 6 (1982): 14–41; Hays, *Beauty, Health and Permanence: Environmental Politics in the United States, 1955–1985* (New York, 1987), 13–70; Hays, "Three Decades of Environmental Politics," in Michael J. Lacey, ed., *Government and Environmental Politics* (Washington, D.C.: The Wilson Center Press, 1989), 19–79, for a fuller elaboration of this argument.

2. Several studies from political science suggest a similar depth of environmental values and their potential for incremental change in political affairs: Norman J. Vig and Michael E. Kraft, *Environmental Policy in the 1980s; Reagan's New Agenda* (Washington, D.C.: Congressional Quarterly, Inc., 1984); Vig and Kraft, *Environmental Policy in the 1990s* (Washington, D.C.: Congressional Quarterly, Inc., 1990); James P. Lester, ed., *Environmental Politics and Policy: Theories and Evidence* (Durham, N.C.: Duke University Press, 1989).

3. Analyses such as these are inevitably caught up in methodological issues and this one in terms of the reliability of voting scores developed by an interest group as a source of data in contrast with those derived from roll call choices made by the researcher. The latter suffer from the distinctive choices of the researcher that involves both a personal view as to the range of environmental issues to be included and the precise roll calls to be chosen to reflect that issue. Different researchers read their own meaning into votes and make different choices of votes for analysis, leading to different results. Far more reliable as reflecting the substance of the political choices is to let the actors determine what was important to them. LCV ratings used here reflect nineteen different cases in selecting and ranking legislative votes. Over those nineteen different cases the results demonstrate a high degree of consistency in both spatial and temporal patterns. This seems to provide a far more effective "check" on the degree to which one is identifying the real world of politics than the choices of researchers whose similar forays are far

fewer in number and far less consistent in results. In a word, amid this continuing dispute I would argue that the method used here is far more objective than cases in which the researcher makes the roll call choices. A foray into some of these methodological issues is Riley Dunlap and Michael Allen, "Partisan Differences in Environmental Issues: A Congressional Roll-Call Analysis," *Western Political Quarterly* 29 (1976): 384–97.

4. Some previous analyses, also based on League of Conservation Voters data, are: Jerry W. Calvert, "Party Politics and Environmental Policy," in Lester, ed., *Environmental Politics and Policy;* Henry Kenski and Margaret Kenski, "Partisanship, Ideology, and Constituency Differences on Environmental Issues in the U.S. House of Representatives and Senate, 1973–1978," in Dean Mann, ed., *Environmental Policy Formation* (Lexington, Mass.: D.C. Heath, 1981).

5. The state scores for 1971 and 1989 are:

1971				1989			
1. Wyo.	79.0	26. Fla.	41.3	1. Vt.	100.0	26. Colo.	55.0
2. Hii.	73.5	27. Iowa	40.7	2. R.I.	95.0	27. Ala.	54.3
3. Me.	73.5	28. Mont.	40.0	3. Mass.	92.7	28. GA.	54.0
4. Mass.	71.7	29. Mo.	38.5	4. S.D.	90.0	29. Pa.	52.6
5. Del.	71.0	30. Ill.	37.9	5. N.D.	90.0	30. Ohio	51.4
6. Conn.	70.8	31. Kas.	31.8	6. Me.	90.0	31. Iowa	50.0
7. Aka.	64.0	32. W.Va.	31.6	7. Conn.	85.0	32. Del.	50.0
8. R.I.	62.0	33. Neb.	30.3	8. Wa.	78.6	33. N.M.	50.0
9. N.Y.	61.8	34. Ky.	29.0	9. N.J.	70.7	34. Tenn.	48.9
10. Wis.	59.2	35. Colo.	29.0	10. N.H.	70.0	35. Mo.	48.9
11. N.J.	56.7	36. Ark.	27.8	11. Hii.	70.0	36. Miss.	47.2
12. N.D.	56.5	37. N.C.	27.1	12. N.Y.	69.4	37. Okla.	45.0
13. Md.	55.8	38. Tenn.	22.9	13. Md.	68.8	38. Mont.	45.0
14. Mich.	54.6	39. Va.	22.2	14. Ind.	68.0	39. Ky.	141.4
15. Minn.	54.6	40. Utah	18.0	15. Ore.	64.0	40. Id.	40.0
16. S.D.	53.5	41. Tex.	17.6	16. S.C.	63.3	41. Neb.	36.7
17. WA.	47.0	42. Id.	16.5	17. N.C.	62.8	42. Va.	34.0
18. N.H.	46.5	43. Ala.	15.7	18. Mich.	62.8	43. Utah	33.3
19. Ariz.	46.0	44. La.	15.1	19. W.Va.	62.5	44. Ark.	32.5
20. Pa.	45.7	45. Okla.	14.0	20. Fla.	61.9	45. Nev.	30.0
21. Ind.	45.5	46. Ga.	10.5	21. Cal.	61.9	46. Tex.	29.5
22. Ohio	43.6	47. S.C.	7.5	22. Wis.	61.1	47. Ariz.	28.0
23. Cal.	42.5	48. Miss.	5.6	23. Ill.	60.9	48. Aka.	20.0
24. N.M.	42.0	49. Nev.	0.0	24. Minn.	58.8	49. La.	16.3
25. Ore.	42.0	50. Vt. No. Rep.		25. Kas.	58.0	50. Wyo.	10.0

6. The composition of regions is based on patterns found in the congressional voting that indicate similarities and differences among states and qualitative knowledge about state environmental affairs and their relationship to underlying environmental conditions. The states included in each region are as follows:

New England: Connecticut, Maine, Massachusetts, New Hampshire, Rhode Island, and Vermont

Mid-Atlantic: Delaware, Maryland, New Jersey, New York, and Pennsylvania

South Atlantic: Georgia, Florida, North Carolina, South Carolina, and Virginia

Gulf: Alabama, Louisiana, Mississippi, and Texas

Central Plateaus: Arkansas, Kentucky, Missouri, Tennessee, and West Virginia
North Central: Illinois, Indiana, Iowa, Michigan, Minnesota, Ohio, and Wisconsin
Plains: Kansas, Nebraska, North Dakota, Oklahoma, and South Dakota
Mountain: Arizona, Colorado, Idaho, Montana, New Mexico, Nevada, Utah, and
   Wyoming
Pacific: Alaska, California, Hawaii, Oregon, and Washington

7. Several attempts have been made to compare and contrast state environmental affairs in terms of "environmental performance," that is, the outcomes of environmental policy. Those arising from environmental organizations include Renew America, *The State of the States 1987* (Washington, D.C.: Renew America, 1987); idem, *The State of the States 1988;* and idem, *The State of the States 1989;* and Institute for Southern Studies, *1990 Green Index: A State-by-State Report Card on the Nation's Environment* (Durham, N.C.: Institute for Southern Studies, 1990). One conducted by political scientists is Charles E. Davis and James P. Lester, "Federalism and Environmental Policy," in Lester, ed., *Environmental Politics and Policy,* 57–84; see especially 74–79 for their attempt to rank states by policy outcomes. These support generally the fact of variation across the states, but they do not provide an opportunity to conduct systematic analysis of regional patterns in those variations over time and depend heavily upon the personal and idiosyncratic policy outcome choices of the researcher. They also make clear that for meaningful analysis one needs to root quantitative indicators in qualitative description of elements of state and regional environmental culture that cannot be reduced to numerical indexes.

8. An analysis of earlier conservation/environmental voting in the U.S. House of Representatives is Kenneth Charles Martis, "The History of Natural Resource Roll Call Voting in the United States House of Representatives: An Analysis of the Spatial Aspects of Legislative Voting Behavior" (Ph.D. dissertation, University of Michigan, 1976). Its data is not readily incorporated into the format of this analysis.

9. The details of the New Jersey changes are: (1) changes from Republican to Democrat in which Democrat Florio (79.4) replaced Republican Hunt (28.2) in the first district and Democrat Hughes (72.1) replaced Republican Sandman (18.4) in the second district; (2) changes from Democrat to Democrat in which Pallone (90.0) replaced Howard (74.8) in the third district and Torricelli (83.7) replaced Helstoski (81.6) with a high-scoring Republican, Hollenbeck (69.3) in between in the ninth district; and Dwyer (71.0) replaced Patten (58.5) in the fifteenth district; (3) changes from Republican to Republican when Fenwick (79.98) replaced Frelinghuysen (39.4) in the fifth district and Saxton (61.8) replaced Forsythe (43.2) in the sixth district; Republican Roukema (67.4), with a high-scoring Democrat, Maguire (97.8) in between, replaced Republican Widnall (49.6) in the seventh district; Courter (51.2) replaced Maraziti (47.5) with a high-scoring Democrat, Meyner (86.3) in between in the third district; (4) changes from Democrat to Republican in which Republican Smith (71.6) replaced Democrat Thompson (71.6) in the fourth district and Republican Guarini (78.1) replaced Democrat LaFante (74.5) in the fourteenth district.

In three New Jersey seats there was no change in representation from 1971 through 1989. In only one case did any transition involve a decline in environmental scores, in the seventh district where Republican Gallo (67.0) replaced Democrat Minish (83.9).

10. In four of the eight Washington congressional districts Democrats held the seats throughout these years but their scores had generally increased over time. In district two the sequence from Meeds (68.1) to Swift (69.1) had brought only slight change; in district three the sequence from Hansen (37.8) to Bonker (78.1) to Unsoeld (90.0) was more

marked; the fifth district was held by Foley (57.3) throughout the two decades; and the seventh district changed from Adams (72.9) to Lowry (87.8) to McDermott (80) with a sharp decrease when the seat was held by a Republican, Cunningham (19.0) in between Adams and Lowry.

The first district was held by Republicans throughout the years between 1971 and 1989 but had increased in scores from Pelly (47.0) to Pritchard (51.5) to Miller (79.3). The eighth district, organized first in the 1982 election was held by Chandler (47.5) who increased his score steadily over the ensuing years from 39.3 in the first three years of his incumbency to 55.7 in the second three; by 1989 he had scored 70 and the district had taken on a strongly environmental tone. The fourth district, the most agricultural in the state, had been held for a number of years by McCormack whose career score was 38.1; his successor was a Republican, Morrison, whose career score was 31.6 and who scored 50 in 1989. The direction of these successive career scores indicated a marked increase in the environmental context of both parties in Washington.

11. In Florida several high scoring Republicans were accompanied by a state delegation in which every individual but one scored 40 or more and, in a number of cases, Republicans succeeding Democrats had increased their environmental scores. Between 1971 and 1989 the Florida Democratic scores increased from 39.9 to 75.0 and Republican from 45.6 to 52.4. By 1989 there were only two Florida Republicans who scored high, James (80) from the Ft. Augustine area and Ros-Lehtinen (86) from Miami. However, among the other 11 Republicans, two scored at 60, two at 50, and 4 at 40. Only one scored below 40.

12. See Samuel P. Hays, "The New Environmental West," *Journal of Policy History* 3, no. 3 (1991): 223–48.

13. See annual reviews by Renew America and the Institute for Southern Studies and the work of Davis and Lester cited in note 7.

14. Environmental Legislative Votes, Selected Years

	Michigan		
	Percent Environmental Vote		
Percent Urban District	*1973–74*	*1975–76*	*1977–78*
75–100	57.3 (69)*	62.6 (69)	62.8 (69)
50–75	47.7 (12)	48.7 (12)	41.3 (12)
25–50	33.6 (15)	38.4 (15)	35.1 (15)
1–25	30.7 (10)	38.1 (10)	21.3 (10)
0	19.3 (4)	27.0 (4)	18.3 (4)

	Oregon		
	Percent Environmental Vote		
Percent Urban District	*1971*	*1973*	*1975*
75–100	81.8 (17)*	81.8 (23)	76.0 (22)
50–75	77.3 (26)	54.3 (23)	43.9 (23)
25–50	68.8 (12)	25.7 (9)	28.3 (9)
1–25	54.9 (4)	14.7 (4)	6.8 (4)
0	64.0 (1)	4.0 (1)	0 (1)

*Number of legislative districts in each population group.

15. Some may well argue that Republican environmental strength is peculiar to New England and hence related more to the general political culture of that region than to environmental issues in particular. However, the emergence of Republican environmental

voting strength in other states such as New Jersey, Florida, and Washington and also in distinctively urbanized districts in still other states would indicate that something more extensive is at work here related not just to region but to more widely diffused values and objectives.

16. In the face of these regional patterns within the Republican Party two environmental anomalies in the presidential administration of George Bush are of interest. One was the appointment of John Sununu, whose environmental record in New Hampshire has been quite weak in a strong environmental region, as his domestic policy advisor, and the other was the selection of John Turner of Wyoming, whose strong environmental record in the Wyoming legislature was a sharp contrast with the party's weak record in the mountain West, as head of the U.S. Fish and Wildlife Service.

The Politics of Environmental Administration

1. For a more extended version of this argument, see Samuel P. Hays, "Political Choice in Regulatory Administration," in *Regulation in Perspective*, ed. Thomas K. McCraw (Cambridge: Harvard University Press, 1981), 124–54. In the words of a recent analyst, "The bureaucracy and its organized clienteles are surely the most durable components of the policy process." See John Edward Chubb, "Interest Groups and the Bureaucracy: The Politics of Energy" (Ph.D. diss. University of Minnesota, 1979), 21.

2. This argument has been expressed most extensively by the concept of "corporate liberalism" in such works as Gabriel Kolko, *The Triumph of Conservatism: A Reinterpretation of American History, 1900–1916* (New York: Free Press, 1963), and James Weinstein, *The Corporate Ideal in the Liberal State, 1900–1918* (Boston: Beacon Press, 1968).

3. See, for example, Louis Galambos, *Competition and Cooperation: The Emergence of a National Trade Association* (Baltimore: Johns Hopkins University Press, 1966).

4. For an account of the way the corporate model was followed in early twentieth-century municipal government reform, see Samuel P. Hays, "The Politics of Reform in Municipal Government in the Progressive Era," *Pacific Northwest Quarterly* 55 (1964): 157–69.

5. Two studies that elaborate this process in detail are Michael E. Parrish, *Securities Regulation and the New Deal* (New Haven: Yale University Press, 1970), and Stanley P. Caine, *The Myth of a Progressive Reform: Railroad Regulation in Wisconsin, 1903–1910* (Madison: State Historical Society of Wisconsin, 1970).

6. For an extended argument in this vein, see Samuel P. Hays, "The Structure of Environmental Politics Since World War II," *Journal of Social History* 14, no. 4 (1981): 719–38.

7. A more elaborate analysis of value change and environmental affairs is Samuel P. Hays, "From Conservation to Environment: Environmental Politics in the United States since World War Two," *Environmental Review* 6, no. 2 (1982): 14–41.

8. For two specialized studies, see Stephen R. Kellert, *American Attitudes, Knowledge and Behaviors Toward Wildlife and Natural Habitats* (Washington, D.C.: U.S. Fish and Wildlife Service, 1978–80), and Opinion Research Corporation, *The Public's Participation in Outdoor Activities and Attitudes Toward National Wilderness Areas* (Princeton: Opinion Research Corporation, Caravan Surveys, 1977). A more recent study is Continental Group, *Toward Responsible Growth: Economic and Environmental Concern in the Balance* (Stamford, Conn.: Continental Group, 1982).

9. Two items pertaining to evolving consumption patterns in the 1930s are the num-

ber of households with radio sets, which rose between 1929 and 1939 from 10,250,000 to 27,500,000, and the growth of visits to national parks during the same decade, which rose from 3,248,000 to 15,531,000. See U.S. Department of Commerce, Bureau of the Census, *Historical Statistics of the United States* (Washington, D.C.: Government Printing Office, 1975), ser. H 808, R104.

10. For a more extended account see items in notes 1 and 7.

11. Marver H. Bernstein, *Regulating Business by Independent Commission* (Princeton: Princeton University Press, 1955; reprinted Westport, Conn.: Greenwood, 1977).

12. The best-known writings are by the Nader group. See James S. Turner, *The Chemical Feast* (New York: Viking Press, 1970); Edward Finch Cox, *The Nader Report on the Federal Trade Commission* (New York: R. W. Baron, 1969); Ralph Nader, *Unsafe at Any Speed* (New York: Grossman, 1965); Ralph Nader, comp., *The Consumer and Corporate Accountability* (New York: Harcourt, Brace, 1973).

13. Michael Frome, *The Forest Service* (New York: Praeger, 1971); Harold K. Steen, *The U.S. Forest Service* (Seattle: University of Washington Press, 1976).

14. D. Harper Simms, *The Soil Conservation Service* (New York: Praeger, 1970).

15. Marion Clawson, *The Bureau of Land Management* (New York: Praeger, 1971); William Voigt Jr., *Public Grazing Lands: Use and Misuse by Industry and Government* (New Brunswick, N.J.: Rutgers University Press, 1976); Phillip O. Foss, *Politics and Grass: The Administration of Grazing on the Public Domain* (Seattle: University of Washington Press, 1960; reprinted Westport, Conn.: Greenwood, 1975).

16. This theme is developed further in Samuel P. Hays, *Conservation and the Gospel of Efficiency* (Cambridge: Harvard University Press, 1959).

17. A recent account of the wilderness movement is Craig W. Allin, *The Politics of Wilderness Preservation* (Westport, Conn.: Greenwood, 1982).

18. The attack on stream channelization can be followed most fully in U.S. House of Representatives, Committee on Government Operations, *Stream Channelization* (4 parts), 92d Cong., 1st sess. (Washington, D.C.: Government Printing Office, 1971).

19. A running account of land use issues within the Bureau of Land Management from an environmental point of view can be found in *PLI Newsletter*, published by the Public Lands Institute (Denver and Washington, D.C., 1978).

20. For a running account of such issues see *American Rivers*, quarterly publication of the American Rivers Conservation Council (Washington, D.C.,1973–).

21. William Ashworth, *Hells Canyon: The Deepest Gorge on Earth* (New York: Hawthorne Books, 1977).

22. The best account of this "response" involves a study of the U.S. Forest Service; see Ben W. Twight, *Organizational Values and Political Power: The Forest Service Versus the Olympic National Park* (University Park: Pennsylvania State University Press, 1983).

23. See William C. Everhart, *The National Park Service* (New York: Praeger, 1972); Alfred Runte, *National Parks: The American Experience* (Lincoln: University of Nebraska Press, 1979).

24. For accounts of air quality policy, see John C. Esposito, *Vanishing Air* (New York: Center for Responsive Law, 1970), and Richard J. Tobin, *The Social Gamble* (Lexington, Mass.: Lexington Books, 1979). For water quality, see Harvey Lieber, *Federalism and Clean Waters* (Lexington, Mass.: Lexington Books, 1975). A useful introduction to both is Barbara S. Davies and J. Clarence Davies III, *The Politics of Pollution,* 2d ed. (New York: Pegasus, 1975).

25. For a general review of occupation health problems, including administrative agencies, see Nicholas A. Ashford, *Crisis in the Workplace: Occupational Disease and In-*

jury (Cambridge: MIT Press, 1976). The work of the Occupational Safety and Health Administration can be followed best in the two newsletters, *Occupational Health and Safety Letter* (Washington, D.C., 1970–), published by Gerson W. Fishbein, and *Occupational Health and Safety Recorder* (Washington, D.C., 1970–), published by the Bureau of National Affairs.

26. Coastal zone management has spawned an enormous literature, largely because of the extensive funds available for planning. Relevant affairs can be followed in *Coastal Zone Management Journal* (New York, 1974–) and the weekly newsletter, *Coastal Zone Management* (Washington, D.C., 1971–), published by Nautilus Press.

27. A major episode in this process was the dispute between the Office of Surface Mining and the Council of Economic Advisors concerning the economic impact of the new regulations. For CEA concerns, expressed via its Council on Wage and Price Stability, see "Report of the Regulatory Analysis Review Group Submitted by the Council on Wage and Price Stability, November 27, 1978, concerning Proposed Surface Coal Mining and Reclamation" (author file) and the resulting documents submitted for the record by the CEA indicating considerable reliance by the CEA on the regulated industry for the formulation of its views; these documents were submitted under the title "Compilation of Conversations and Correspondence on the Permanent Regulatory Program Implementing Section 501(b) of the Surface Mining Control and Reclamation Act of 1977" (author file). Events in the evolution of the surface mining program can be followed in *Environment Reporter*, May 5, September 1 and 15, 1978: *Washington Post* (September 24, 1978): 6, 7, 13; (January 25, 1979); *New York Times*, December 4, 1978, 7, 8, 14; and January 31, 1979; *Wall Street Journal*, January 2 and 31, 1979. See also author interview with William Eichbaum, former assistant solicitor, Department of the Interior, in charge of surface mining regulations, May 22, 1980. For an account of implementation from an environmental viewpoint, see Carolyn R. Johnson, David S. May, and George W. Pring, *Stripping the Law on Coal: A Study of the Surface Mining Control and Reclamation Act by the U.S. Office of Surface Mining and the State Agencies in Colorado, New Mexico, North Dakota, Utah and Wyoming*, Public Lands Institute Report (Denver: Public Lands Institute, 1980).

28. Solar energy issues can be followed in *Solar Age* (Harrisville, N.H., 1976–), and *Solar Energy Intelligence Report* (Washington, D.C., 1976–).

29. Two convenient sources of information on this issue are *The New Farm* (Emmaus, Pa., 1979–) and *Organic Gardening and Farming* (Emmaus, Pa., 1942–). For the relevant official document, see U.S. Department of Agriculture, "Report and Recommendations on Organic Agriculture," July 1980. Some insight into the political forces involved with reference to research strategies is in Don F. Hadwiger, *The Politics of Agricultural Research* (Lincoln: University of Nebraska Press, 1982).

30. These activities can be followed in several citizen group newsletters; for example, "International Report," published by the Sierra Club (San Francisco, 1973–83).

31. See Council on Environmental Quality, *Environmental Quality*, annual report published in 1971 and annually thereafter.

32. Theory involves influences from without and within the agencies. The former have dominated debate with arguments emphasizing crucial or limited influences of "interest groups." See Paul Culhane, *Public Land Politics* (Baltimore: Johns Hopkins University Press, 1981). The alternative view is well expressed by Twight, *Organizational Values and Political Power* (note 22 above).

33. Richard A. Liroff, *A National Policy for the Environment: NEPA and Its Aftermath* (Bloomington: Indiana University Press, 1976).

34. One, "208" planning under the 1972 Water Quality Act, can be followed in a volume especially prepared for citizens who sought to participate in the process. See Conservation Foundation, *Toward Clean Water: A Guide to Citizen Action* (Washington, D.C.: Conservation Foundation, 1976). Another, the "principles and standards" in national water planning, can be followed in Water Resources Council, "Water and Related Land Resources: Establishment of Principles and Standards for Planning," in *Federal Register* 38, no. 174 (September 10, 1973), part 3.

35. Documents cited in note 27, "Compilation of Conversations and Correspondence," issued by the Council of Economic Advisors, represented a particularly crucial case in that they pertained to decision making in the Executive Office of the President (EOP) after the close of the administrative proceeding record in the Department of the Interior. While the documents in this particular case were made public, legal proceedings intended to extend that practice from the agency to the EOP level did not succeed. For a discussion of this problem, see Gregory S. Wetstone, ed., "Meeting Record from Resolution of Scientific Issues and the Judicial Process: *Ethyl Corporation v. EPA*," October 21, 1977, held under the auspices of the Environmental Law Institute (Washington, D.C., 1981), discussion on 84ff., and especially discussion between Judges Skelly Wright and Harold Leventhal of the U.S. Court of Appeals, District of Columbia.

36. Andrew C. Gordon and John P. Heinz, eds., *Public Access to Information* (New Brunswick, N.J.: Transaction Books, 1973), esp. 184–222.

37. Lettie M. Wenner, *The Environmental Decade in Court* (Bloomington: Indiana University Press, 1982); Frederick R. Anderson and Robert H. Daniels, *NEPA in the Courts: A Legal Analysis of the National Environmental Policy Act* (Baltimore: Johns Hopkins University Press, 1973). For activities of environmental groups, see publications of the Sierra Club, *National News Report,* the Natural Resources Defense Council, *Newsletter,* and Environmental Defense Fund, *EDF Letter.*

38. This is my conclusion, drawn impressionistically rather than systematically, from reading a considerable number of environmental impact analyses, concerning especially forest, range, and national park management, water resources, and coal leasing.

39. See, for example, the dialogue between the parties in the dispute over EPA regulation of lead, in which all affirmed the importance of their own freedom to participate in decision making, in Wetstone, "Meeting Record from Resolution of Scientific Issues" (note 35).

40. For some general remarks on the useful role of the public in environmental administration, see reflections on his tenure as administrator of EPA by Russell Train, in *Conservation Foundation Letter* (Washington, D.C., January 1977). Train remarked, "I think it is clear that the citizen environmental movement has made possible the statutory authorities we now have and it is absolutely essential to keep a fire lit under the administrative agencies at all levels of government" (8).

41. While public participation took place in many instances, one comprehensive example was water planning under section 208 of the 1972 Clean Water Act. In this planning in Pennsylvania, for example, carried out within ten regions of the state, there was a "public participation" coordinator at both state and regional levels, from whom planning documents could be readily secured. Environmental agencies often drew upon League of Women Voters staff for these positions.

42. See opposition of EPA, as well as other agencies to an expanded federal citizen suit bill in 1971; U.S. Senate, Committee on Commerce, *Environmental Protection Act of 1971,* hearings, April 15–16, 1971 (Washington, D.C.: Government Printing Office, 1971).

43. Industry reactions can be obtained from the pages of *Environment Reporter* during the months of late 1976 and early 1977 when the Carter appointments were being made; even more pointed are responses in trade magazines such as *Chemical Week, Coal Age,* and *Waterways Journal.*

44. For the evolution of regulatory politics during the Carter administration, see "Regulatory Controversy: The Case of Health and Safety," conference with proceedings, March 7–8, 1980, Washington, D.C., cosponsored by the Progressive Alliance, the Environmental Law Institute, and the National Center for Policy Alternatives. An account of similar events during the Reagan administration is Robert Nelson, "A World of Preference: Business Access to Reagan's Regulators," Democracy Project Reports, no. 5 (New York: Democracy Project, 1983).

45. Little has been written on the crucial "standards of proof" controversy. Some flavor of the issue within a comparative United Kingdom-United States context is Brendan Gillespie, Dave Eva, and Ron Johnston, "Carcinogenic Risk Assessment in the USA and the UK: The Case of Aldrin/Dieldrin," in *Science in Context,* ed. Barry Barnes and David Edge (Milton Keynes, U.K.,: Open University Press, 1982), 303–35. A telling early case of dispute was the initial version of the sulfur oxides criteria document and the different scientists drawn upon for this and the final version; the second version required far higher levels of proof than did the first. See John C. Esposito, *Vanishing Air* (New York: Center for Responsive Law, 1970), 280–87. For most of the question of shifting and varied scientific assessments one must go to original rather than secondary sources, such as accounts in *Environmental Science and Technology, Journal of the Air Pollution Control Association, Conservation Foundation Letter,* and the hearings held on air quality criteria in 1967 and 1968 by the Senate Committee on Public Works.

46. A good account of the politics of cost-benefit analysis is Mark Green and Normal Waitzman, *Business War on the Law* (Washington, D.C., 1981).

47. A classic case was the controversy over wilderness candidate areas, those that would be selected for study for their potential as wilderness areas. Developmental groups such as timber, mining, and livestock interests continually sought to restrict the selection of candidate areas as well as to restrict the final choices for wilderness designation among candidate areas. Hence the struggle over RARE II, the process by which wilderness candidate areas were decided during the Carter administration. For a general review of wilderness politics see Allin, *Politics of Wilderness Preservation* (note 17).

48. See statement in Benjamin G. Ferris Jr., and Frank E. Speizer, "Criteria for Establishing Standards for Air Pollutants," in *The Business Roundtable Air Quality Project,* vol. 1 (Cambridge: Harvard School of Public Health, Division of Applied Science, Harvard University, 1980): "We define an adverse effect as medically significant physiologic or pathologic changes generally evidenced by permanent damage or incapacitating illness to the individual." The state of Montana, on the other hand, when it revised its air quality regulations in 1980, included the provision that the program's objective was to prevent air pollution that "interfere[s] with normal daily activities" and specifically identified lower lung function in school children as an "adverse effect" that should be prevented. See clippings on this issue in the *Missoulian* (Missoula, Mont.) (author file); *Down to Earth* Montana Environmental Information Center (Helena, Mont.), March/April, May/June, and September/October 1980.

49. Two programs that relied heavily on "baseline" monitoring in order to determine changes from that level that might be due to pollution were the Prevention of Significant Deterioration program, which received statutory provision in the Clean Air Act of 1977,

and the water quality provisions of the Surface Mining Act of 1977. Industry objected strenuously to being required to gather such data, and in both cases the effort to measure environmental change from polluting activities was seriously weakened.

50. In the industrial wastewater treatment program, EPA sought to set up general industrial categories within which the same technology standards would apply; although industry objected strenuously to this approach, the courts upheld EPA's strategy. In chemical regulation, however, efforts by OSHA to establish a generic regulation for determining carcinogenicity were successfully thwarted by industry in preference for a "case-by-case" approach in which carcinogenicity would be determined for each chemical separately and presumably by different methods.

51. The proceeding in the case of the herbicide 2,4,5-T is a case in point. The issue can be followed in *Chemical Regulation Reporter, Chemical Week,* an industry source, and *NCAP News* (Eugene, Ore.), an environmental source, during 1979–81). See especially *Chemical Week* (April 9, 1980): 32–33.

52. A case in point was the Montana Environmental Quality Council, which in its early years in the early 1970s served as a major advocate of environment objectives and produced some rather striking annual reports to that end. By 1981 its appointments had changed so that it had become completely neutralized, was unable to act, and became a "political football." Environmental legislators urged that it be abolished. See, for example, the *Missoulian* (Missoula, Mont.) (February 18, 1981).

53. Relevant examples were the discovery of liver cancer among workers exposed to polyvinyl chloride; discovery of elevated cancer rates in New Orleans as background for the Safe Drinking Water Act of 1974; the kepone incident and others as providing impetus for the Toxic Substances Control Act in 1976; the various hazardous waste incidents such as Love Canal for the 1980 Superfund Act. A similar incident, it is useful to recall, involving the deaths of over one hundred people from an untested sulfanilamide drug, led to passage of the 1938 Pure Food and Drug Act and the requirement that newly marketed drugs be tested for health effects. See Charles O. Jackson, *Food and Drug Legislation in the New Deal* (Princeton: Princeton University Press, 1970).

54. Statement by John Middleton, head of the National Air Pollution Control Administration in U.S. Senate, Committee on Public Works, *Air Pollution, 1968,* 90th Cong., 2d sess., hearings on air quality criteria, July 29–31, 1968 (Washington, D.C.: Government Printing Office, 1968).

55. See items in note 45 pertaining to sulfur oxides criteria document.

56. For a brief account of this issue see two items, Stanton Coerr, "EPA's Air Standard for Lead," and David Schoenbrod, "Why Regulation of Lead Has Failed," in *Low Lead Exposure: The Clinical Implications of Current Research,* ed. Herbert L. Neddleman (New York: Raven, 1980), 253–57 and 258–66. See Gregory S. Wetstone and Jan Goldman, "Chronology of Events Surrounding the *Ethyl* Decision," in *Judicial Review of Scientific Uncertainty,* ed. D. L. Davis et al. (draft). Environmental Law Institute, Washington, D.C., 1981.

57. Wetstone, "Meeting Record," 145 (note 35).

58. Useful summaries of these changes for two agencies are Wilderness Society, *The Watt Record: Bureau of Land Management Lands* (Washington, D.C.: Wilderness Society, 1983), and idem, *The Watt Record: The National Park System* (Washington, D.C.: Wilderness Society, 1983). For a review of direct regulator-regulated contacts during the Reagan administration, see Robert Nelson, A *World of Preference: Business Access to Reagan's Regulators,* Democracy Project Report, no. 5 (New York: Democracy Project, 1983).

59. A useful account of these changes described from the viewpoint of environmental opponents is "The Environmental Activists," *Chemical Week* (October 19, 1983): 48, 50, 52, 54, 56.

60. Relevant events can be followed in the newsletters of environmental groups such as the Sierra Clubs *National News Report,* issued weekly during sessions of Congress, or with less detail in *Environment Reporter,* during the years of the Reagan administration.

61. Details pertaining to the controversies concerning James Watt and the Department of the Interior and Anne Burford and the Environmental Protection Agency can be followed in the *New York Times,* the *Washington Post, Newsweek, Time,* and especially *Environment Reporter,* 1981–83 (author file).

62. By early 1984 a "dead center" policy had been reached in EPA but was not contemplated for the Department of the Interior.

63. Fish and Wildlife Service objections to developmental proposals in the 1960s can be followed in National Wildlife Federation, *Conservation Report,* 1966, May 27 (geothermal steam leases), July 28 (pollution of estuaries), September 30 (thermal pollution of waters), October 7 (highway transportation).

64. Congressman John Dingell, who became chair of the Subcommittee on Fisheries and Wildlife Conservation in the House of Representatives in 1966, spoke out frequently on behalf of the Fish and Wildlife Service. See several hearings on the protection of estuarine areas: U.S. House of Representatives, Subcommittee on Fisheries and Wildlife Conservation, *Estuarine and Wetlands Legislation,* 89th Cong., 1st sess. (Washington, D.C.: Government Printing Office, 1966) and *Estaurine Areas,* 90th Cong., 1st sess. (Washington, D.C.: Government Printing Office, 1967).

65. William G. Wing, "The Concrete Juggernaut," part 2, *Audubon Magazine,* August 1966, for an example of highway construction through the Wheeler National Wildlife Refuge in Alabama.

66. U.S. Senate, Public Works Committee, *Thermal Pollution,* 90th Cong., 2d sess., hearings on the extent to which environmental factors are considered in selecting power-plant sites with particular emphasis on ecological effects of discharge of waste heat into rivers, lakes, estuaries, and coastal waters (Washington, D.C.: Government Printing Office, 1968, 1969).

67. National Wildlife Federation, *Conservation Report* (May 13, 1966; September 23, 1966; September 30, 1966).

68. Subcommittee on Fisheries and Wildlife Conservation, *Estuarine Areas,* 189–207 (note 66).

69. The range of Fish and Wildlife Service concerns can be observed in the scientific research undertaken by its Office of Biological Services to undergird its impact analyses. See U.S. Department of the Interior, Fish and Wildlife Service, *Biological Services Program* (fiscal years 1975ff.).

70. One should recall that the first serious proposal in the legislative history of the EIS was introduced by John Dingell from the Committee on Merchant Marine and Fisheries of the House of Representatives on March 23, 1967. The bill reflected that committee's perennial concern for developmental impacts on fish and wildlife. It is also not without interest that when the House committee reported on a similar measure in the next Congress its legislative form was an amendment to the Fish and Wildlife Coordination Act. The bill written by Senator Jackson was then substituted for the House bill and later passed as the National Environmental Policy Act of 1969. To follow details see National Wildlife Federation, *Conservation Report,* May 2 and 9; June 6; and July 4, 11, and 18, 1969.

71. The environmental impact reports were to "accompany the proposal through existing agency review processes." Tim Atkeson, legal officer of the Council on Environmental Quality, said: "As we read the law and the legislative history, the public's involvement comes by disclosure of the thing [report] at the end of the process. The public gets a retrospective look, and their impact comes largely as some comment about the same decision in the future." See *Water Resources Newsletter* (December 5–6, 1970): 4.

72. National Wildlife Federation, *Conservation Report,* March 10, 1967; October 13, 1967.

73. *Farm Chemicals,* December 1970, 22–23; the article concluded, "Dismayed by USDA's relinquishing of power in pesticide matters and thwarted by the 'closed door' attitude, industry is looking for ways to renew the attitude of partnership that has always characterized its relationship with government."

74. For an analysis of this influence with respect to the Nixon-appointed National Industrial Pollution Control Council, and especially the role of the Department of Commerce, see Richard H. K. Vietor, *Environmental Politics and the Coal Coalition* (College Station: Texas A & M Press, 1980), 168–78.

75. In the 1977 Clean Air Act the EPA was instructed to consider several additional pollutants for regulation: radioactive pollutants, cadmium, arsenic, and polycyclic organic matter; environmentalists chose to specify these because the EPA had been unwilling to take them up on its own initiative.

76. A major statement critical of prescriptive legislation in air pollution is Bruce A. Ackerman and William T. Hassler, *Clean Coal/Dirty Air* (New Haven: Yale University Press, 1981). Ackerman argues in favor of the view that agencies be given considerable leeway to make their own choices; his argument, however, seems to be influenced heavily by his belief that the substantive decision to require mandatory percentage reduction for SO_2 emissions required by the 1977 Clean Air Act was undesirable.

77. U.S. House of Representatives, Committee on Government Operations, Natural Resources and Power Subcommittee, House Report 1579, 90th Cong., 2d sess. (Washington, D.C.: Government Printing Office, 1980). This committee report was given renewed publicity, with more extended analysis, by Senator Metcalf in his investigations of advisory committees in 1970.

78. See, for example, U.S. House of Representatives, Subcommittee on Investigations and Oversight, Committee on Science and Technology, *Formaldehyde: Review of Scientific Basis of EPA's Carcinogenic Risk Assessment,* 97th Cong., 2d sess., May 20, 1982 (Washington, D.C.: Government Printing Office, 1983).

79. See the statement of John E. Daniel, chief of staff of EPA administrator Anne Burford, in testimony to the House Energy and Commerce Committee, as reported in *Environment Reporter* (September 30, 1983): 927-28. See also the dispute over alleged improper influence by the OMB in EPA regulatory action in *Chemical Regulation Reporter* (November 18, 1983): 1252; (November 25, 1983): 1268–69.

80. This is my conclusion drawn from following a considerable number of issues with accompanying EIS statements, especially with respect to the public lands.

81. See data compiled in Wenner, *Environmental Decade in Court* (note 37). Wenner analyzed federal court cases in the 1970s. Out of 1,125 plaintiffs, 636 were environmentalists (p. 41), and in air quality cases out of 233 plaintiffs 81 were environmentalists and 93 came from industry (p. 66).

82. Ross Sandler, "Citizen Suit Litigation," *Environment* (March 1981): 38–39. In a two-year period, January 1979 to January 1981, 19 cases were brought under citizen suit provisions and decided in the federal courts. Of these 12 were brought by environmental groups, 4 by industries, and 3 by state and local governments.

83. Jethro K. Lieberman, *The Litigious Society* (New York: Basic Books, 1981) discusses the varied types of litigation in the federal courts. Of 168,789 civil suits filed between July 1, 1979 and June 30, 1980, 39,810 were initiated by the U.S. government, 49,000 were private contract suits, 22,000 were personal injury claims, 9,000 were social security cases, 23,000 were prisoner petitions, 13,000 were civil rights cases, and 7,755 were product liability cases. There were so few environmental cases that they were not listed.

84. See Wenner, *Environmental Decade in Court*, table, 66 (note 81). The strong emphasis on the high level of environmental litigation was expressed primarily by those promoting environmental mediation who sought to contrast the undesirability of litigation with the desirability of mediation; in so arguing they greatly overemphasized the actual role of litigation. See Center for Environmental Conflict Resolution, *Environmental Mediation: An Effective Alternative?* (Palo Alto, Calif., 1978), esp. v–vi, for the heavy focus on litigation as the main problem.

85. The Reagan environmental revolution was brought about almost exclusively through changes in administrative personnel and policy.

86. See details about local "right to know" ordinances in California in *Chemical Week* (September 28, 1983): 29, 32. In New York, on the other hand, a state appeals court ruled that local governments could not regulate pesticides, which were exclusively the province of state action; *New York Times*, December 28, 1983.

87. In Minnesota the air pollution statute provides that "no local government unit shall set standards of air quality which are more stringent than those set by the pollution control agency." *Nucleonics Week* (February 26, 1970).

88. In Illinois the mayor of Catlin, near Danville, objecting to a proposed 6,000-acre strip mine by Amax Coal Company on prime agricultural land in his township, complained: "The state pre-empted our rights" to regulate coal mining locally. Reported by Harold Henderson, "Caving in on Coal," *Illinois Times* 5, no. 11 (September 1980): 81.

89. In 1980 Connecticut established a Hazardous Waste Facility Siting Board with power to override local zoning laws. *Environmental Science and Technology* (August 1980): 894.

90. In 1980 the Wisconsin Department of Natural Resources revised its wetlands regulation, NR 115, with legislative approval, prohibiting counties from forming regulations stricter than those of the state. *Our Wetlands*, published by the Wisconsin Wetlands Association, August–September 1980.

91. A survey by Gladwin Hill of industry representation on state air and water pollution control commissions was reported in the *New York Times*, December 7, 1970. For concern about this problem see statement by Dr. John T. Middleton of the air pollution division of the EPA, *Environment Reporter* 1, no. 37 (January 8, 1971).

92. In the years after passage of the 1970 federal Clean Air Act, industry representatives attempted to persuade states that previously adopted more stringent standards should be relaxed to the federal level. Usually they were successful. But even by the time of the 1977 amendments seven states still had lower allowable limits of sulfur dioxide than the federal standard.

93. For Pennsylvania standards under the 1967 act see *Journal of the Air Pollution Control Association* 17, no. 7 (July 1967): 474 and 17, no. 11 (November 1967): 762. For citizen group action in forcing modification of the standard, see *Conservation Foundation Letter*, November 1969.

94. The *Conservation Foundation Letter*, November 1969, reported that citizen successes in setting strict standards had been so striking that "there are indications that some industries are wondering if they might not fare better under federal standards

rather than state standards." For the reaction of industry to state standards and a report on testimony at Senate hearings by Fred E. Tucker, manager of pollution control services for National Steel Corporation, favoring national air quality standards, see *Environmental Science and Technology* (May 1970): 4–5. Tucker was critical of "the people who appear to be playing a numbers game with air quality standards, by setting lower and lower allowable pollutant levels in state standards."

95. Coastal zone issues can be followed in greatest detail in the weekly newsletter, *Coastal Zone Management* (Washington, D.C., 1970–).

96. For the California case, see *Coastal Zone Management,* January 2, 1980, 1.

97. Events can be followed in *Coastal Zone Management,* January 2, 1980, 2; February 25, 1981, 1; May 6, 1981, 1; July 15, 1981, 1; August 5, 1981, 1; August 12, 1981, 2; September 16, 1981, 1–2; September 23, 1981, 4–5; and October 7, 1981, 102.

98. For a succinct statement of the conflict inherent in these "two conflicting governance philosophies," see the statement by David Morris before the National Association of Counties County Energy Action Conference, May 1981, as reported in *Energy Information* and *Energy Planning Report,* 5, no. 1 (May 25, 1981): 1, 5.

99. For a general discussion of a wide range of nuclear issues involving federal preemption of state authority, see *Groundswell* 4–5 (September/October 1981): 1–3; a listing of state laws subject to potential preemption is on pages 5–11 of this issue.

100. Early in 1981 congressional staff defined the issue: "Industry generally supports federal noise regulations as preferable to myriad local rules, which would differ from place to place. But local governments . . . want the authority to establish rules that are stricter than the federal regulations. Currently the noise act preempts stricter state and local noise regulations." See Environmental Study Conference, U.S. Congress, *Weekly Bulletin* (February 23, 1981): C7.

101. Industry sought a preemption provision in the 1972 extension of the federal pesticide law but failed. See *Farm Chemicals* (October 1970): 70; (November 1971): 12; (December 1971): 12. For environmental opposition to preemption, see U.S. Senate, Subcommittee on Environment, hearings on the 1972 pesticide act, testimony of Cynthia Wilson, 130–31.

102. This issue can be followed in detail in 1981 and 1982 in Environmental Study Conference, *Weekly Bulletin,* May 25, June 15, September 14 and 21, and November 2, 1981; February 1, March 22 and 29, May 3, June 21, and September 20, 1982, and in the ESC annual report, "Environmental, Energy and Natural Resources Legislation in the 97th Congress," 6.

103. For this campaign in the late 1940s, see Voigt, *Public Grazing Lands* (note 15).

104. The most recent study to distinguish among regions with respect to environmental values sorts out attitudes on a four-point scale from "resource utilization" on one end to "resource preservation" on the other. In terms of the percentage of respondents expressing the strongest "resource preservation" attitudes, the Rocky Mountain states ranked highest with 35 percent, followed by New England 32 percent, the Pacific Coast 28 percent, Middle Atlantic 28 percent, North Central 26 percent, Middle West 20 percent, West South Central 20 percent, South Atlantic 18 percent and Middle South 17 percent. See Continental Group, *Toward Responsible Growth* (note 8). This regional variation is consistent with other environmental attitude studies that provide regional comparisons.

105. Protests against oil drilling in wilderness areas in Montana and Wyoming came from within those states. For a running account of the issue in Montana see the *Missoulian* (Missoula, Mont.), beginning with the November 16, 1979 issue, news item, "Company Wants to Explore for Gas, Oil inside Wilderness." An early statement of reaction to

drilling from Congressman Pat Williams of western Montana is in the *Missoulian,* April 22, 1981 "March Dedicated to Preservation of Bob Marshall." For Wyoming see release from office of Senator Malcolm Wallop of Wyoming, "Speech Before the Rocky Mountain Oil and Gas Association, Denver, Colorado, Oct. 8, 1981." See also account of Wallop's view in *Jackson Hole News,* October 15, 1981, "Wallop Hits Wilderness Leases."

106. Out of this circumstance came drives in several states, especially Idaho and Utah, for changes in state land policies to permit "multiple use."

107. By early October 1983, 50 percent of respondents in a *Deseret News/*KSL poll of residents of Utah approved the view that Secretary James Watt should resign; 33 percent opposed his resignation. See LaVarr Webb, "Half of Utahns Say Watt Should Go," *Deseret News* (October 7, 1983).

108. See items by Esposito, Tobin, Lieber, and Davies (note 24).

109. Joseph T. O'Connor, "The Automobile Controversy—Federal Control of Vehicular Emission," *Ecology Law Quarterly* 4, no. 3 (1975): 661–92, and Luke J. Danielson, "Control of Complex Emission Course—Step Toward Land Use Planning," *Ecology Law Quarterly* 4, no. 3 (1975): 693–737.

110. Thomas M. Disselhorst, "Sierra Club v. Ruckelshaus: 'On a Clear Day . . . ,'" *Ecology Law Quarterly* 4, no. 3 (1975): 739–80.

111. There were some exceptions. California conducted considerable research on its own, thereby enabling it to take a somewhat independent position in many environmental matters. Montana undertook some crucial research, financed by proceeds from its coal severance tax, to undergird its new air quality regulations proposed in 1980. And a number of states took up their own research on the acid rain issue. See, for example, *Proceedings, Acid Precipitation Research Needs Conference* (Syracuse, N.Y.: College of Environmental Science and Forestry, State University of New York, 1982); California Air Resources Board, *California Symposium on Acid Precipitation* (San Francisco: California Air Resources Board, 1981); Wisconsin Department of Natural Resources, *Wisconsin Interpretive Assessment Document on Acid Deposition* (Wisconsin Department of Natural Resources, 1983); Vermont Department of Water Resources and Environmental Engineering, *Vermont Acid Precipitation Program: Long-Term Monitoring, 1981–1982* (Montpelier: Department of Water Resources and Environmental Engineering, 1983).

112. Differences in research strategies by federal, state, and private sponsors on the issue of acid rain can be observed in Keystone Center, *Report on the Acid Precipitation Research Coordination Workshop* (Keystone, Colo.: Keystone Center, 1982).

113. For research undertaken by the electric power industry through the Electric Power Research Institute, see its periodical, *EPRI Journal* (Palo Alto, Calif., 1976–); for work of the Chemical Industry Institute of Toxicology, see its *Annual Report* (Research Triangle Park, N.C., 1978–).

114. One such issue was research in indoor air pollution, which the Reagan administration sought to eliminate. For accounts of the controversy, see *Science* (November 6, 1981): 639; the administration argued that it had no authority to deal with indoor air. See also *Environmental Health Letter* (November 1, 1981).

115. The best account of the history of the lead issue is Wetstone and Goldman, "Chronology of Events" (note 56). However, this account is still quite limited, and the conclusion here is drawn from many items in varied sources such as *Science, Environmental Science and Technology, Journal of the Air Pollution Control Association,* assessments by the National Academy of Sciences, and Herbert L. Needleman, ed., *Low Level Exposure* (New York: Raven, 1980). The issue has yet to receive satisfactory historical analysis.

116. It is often argued that economic effects were never considered in the early history of pollution control. Yet economic analyses were made as the program evolved. The Federal Water Pollution Control Act of 1966, for example, required that the Federal Water Pollution Control Administration assess federal costs. See its report, *Water Pollution Control, 1970–1974: The Federal Costs* (Washington, D.C.: Department of the Interior, Federal Water Pollution Control Administration, 1969).

117. For a case study of a "battle of the models" with reference to the impact of electric power generation on the Hudson River striped bass population, see L. W. Barnhouse et all., "Population Biology in the Courtroom: The Hudson River Controversy," *Bio-Science* 34, no. 1 (January 1984): 14–19.

118. Dr. Herbert Needleman, a prominent frontier researcher on the health effects of lead, was the subject of persistent criticism from the lead industry. See the description of him as representing "what is at best a minority view that adverse health effects occur at blood-lead levels below mg/dl" in U.S. Congress, House of Representatives, Subcommittee on Health and the Environment, *Oversight—Clean Air Act Amendments of 1977*, 96th Cong., 1st sess. (Washington, D.C.: Government Printing Office, 1980), testimony of Jerome Cole of the International Lead Zinc Research Organization, 344.

119. A host of issues involve confidentiality. They can be observed, for example, in the first round of premanufacture notices for chemical registration under the 1976 Toxic Substances Control Act and the development of regulations pertaining to section 5 of that act. See *Chemical Regulation Reporter* (April 27, 1979): 82; (May 11, 1979): 147–49; and (May 18, 1979): 218–19.

120. For a review of state legislation to that time see *Chemical Week* (May 26, 1982): 13–14.

121. See, for example, Jan M. Newton, *An Economic Analysis of Herbicide Use for Intensive Forestry Management* (Eugene, Oreg.: Oregon Public Interest Research Group, 1979).

122. These issues can be followed in *Forest Management* (Eugene, Oreg., 1980–), an environmental journal that seeks to help citizen groups understand the complexities of U.S. Forest Service policy. See its specialized publications such as Randal O'Toole, *The Citizens' Guide to FORPLAN* (Eugene, Oreg.: Cascade Holistic Economic Consultants, 1983).

123. Much of this debate focused ultimately on the alternatives between a "threshold-margin of safety" versus a "risk-assessment" made of establishing an appropriate health objective. For a defense of the latter approach, which came to exercise more influence after the mid-1970s, see *The Business Roundtable Air Quality Project*, vol. 1 (Cambridge: Harvard School of Public Health, Division of Applied Science, Harvard University, 1980).

124. Both business and environmentalists were quite aware of the significance of choices of scientific advisors. The entire issue obtained more concerted focus when in the spring of 1983 a list was uncovered from EPA files concerning acceptable and unacceptable scientists. See *Environmental Health Letter* (March 15, 1983): 3. For changes in Reagan appointments to the Cancer Advisory Board, which involved a similar issue, see letter to the editor by Janet D. Rowley et al., *Science* (January 20, 1984): 236.

125. For examples of technical information services developed by environmentalists, see Nuclear Information and Resource Service, *Groundswell* (Washington, D.C., 1978–); Environmental Law Institute, *National Wetlands Newsletter* (Washington, D.C , 1979–); *Forest Management* (Eugene, Oreg., 1980–); Environmental Action Foundation, *Exposure* (Washington, D.C., 1980–).

126. *Chemical Week,* a persistent chemical industry critic of environmentalists, titled

an article about environmental activity "The Environmental Activists, They've Grown in Competence and They're Working Together," *Chemical Week* (October 19, 1983): 48–50, 52, 54, 56.

127. The EPA criteria document on lead illustrates this process. Through the efforts of David Schoenbrud, attorney for the Natural Resources Defense Council, which brought the legal action to force EPA to adopt an ambient lead standard, lead researchers Herbert Needleman and Sergio Piomelli were brought into the criteria document proceedings. For this purpose NRDC, in cooperation with the National Air Conservation Commission of the American Lung Association, persuaded Needleman and Piomelli to publish a summary of frontier findings, "The Effects of Low-Level Lead Exposure," which was incorporated into proceedings on the criteria document. The issue can be followed in *Environment Reporter*, 1977–78; see especially July 7, 1978, 427–28. Needleman later testified in the House Subcommittee on Health and the Environment, *Oversight—Clean Air Act Amendments of 1977*, 272–86 (note 118).

128. The role of the media in the Love Canal case is reflected extensively in Michael Brown, *Laying Waste: The Poisoning of America by Toxic Chemicals* (New York: Washington Square Press, 1979), 3–96. For a report prepared by EPA highly critical of the role of the media in toxic chemical cases with four case studies of kepone, lead (Dallas), Love Canal, and dioxin, see *Inside EPA, Weekly Report* (January 13, 1984): 12–14.

129. A useful case study in this type of strategy involved the "Seven cities" lead study, carried out under the auspices of the joint industry-government Lead Liaison Committee early in the 1970s. The project was undertaken with the agreement that data would not be made available until the study was completed. But the project director, known to be close to the lead industry, released some data to bolster the industry position in proceedings over the California lead standard. See Wetstone and Goldman, "Chronology of Events" (note 56).

130. Appointments to and activities of the EPA Science Advisory Board, which can be followed in *Environment Reporter*, seemed to be a result of a deliberate policy to make scientific decisions more open. Under the Reagan administration that policy was reversed. See, for example, the formaldehyde case in House of Representatives, Subcommittee on Investigations and Oversight, Committee on Science and Technology, *Formaldehyde: Review of Scientific Basis of EPA's Carcinogenic Risk Assessment*, 97th Cong., 2d sess., 20 May 1982 (Washington, D.C.: Government Printing Office, 1983). A more open policy was established with the appointment of William Ruckelshaus as EPA administrator.

131. For an analysis of water policy in these terms, see Laurence H. Tribe, Corinne S. Schelling, and John Voss, eds., *When Values Conflict: Essays on Environmental Analysis, Discourse and Decision* (Cambridge, Mass.: Ballinger, 1976).

132. For Britain, see Howard Hill, *Freedom to Roam: The Struggle for Access to Britain's Moors and Mountains* (Ashbourne, Derbyshire: Moorland, 1980).

133. For an urban political drive to clean up toxic waste dumps in a working-class neighborhood, see Janice Weiss, "How People Take Power," *Exposure* 34–35 (September–October 1983): 1, 4–6.

134. Fred Hirsch, *Social Limits to Growth* (Cambridge: Harvard University Press, 1976).

135. Louis Harris and Associates, *Risk in a Complex Society: A Marsh and McLennan Public Opinion Survey* (March and McLennan, 1980).

INDEX

Acid rain, 240–41, 251, 354, 389, 472n5, 514n10; and 1990 Clean Air Act, 274, 277; and critical load concept, 284–85; effects of, 346–47; and emissions trading, 269, 280–89; politics around, 254, 258–60; research on, 252–53, 277–78

Administrative Procedures Act of 1946, 365, 428–29

Age, 90–91, 94, 340

Agencies, regulatory, 74, 108, 120, 193–94; development vs. environmental, 431–33; and enforcement of Clean Air Acts, 223–24; and environmental objectives, 353, 358, 386–87; in implementation of Clean Air Acts, 230, 249; in politics of environmental administration, 114–15, 363–69, 418–50, 443, 465n32; relations with government, 435–37; relations with industry, 242–43, 376, 447–48; relations with media, 447; relations with public, 215–16, 366–68, 447, 562n40; science of, 122, 134, 376; state, 164, 459n24; and use of environmental impact statements, 353, 426–27, 432–33, 533n37, 549n122, 565n71; values of, 48–49, 51, 371, 443. *See also specific agencies*

Agriculture, 168, 325, 347, 361; attempts to use timbered land for, 202, 212–13; effects of, 81, 98; and soil conservation, 338–39

Air pollution, 13, 15, 78, 103; analysis of, 106–07, 390; effects of, 346–47, 352–53, 390, 442–43; health effects of, 238–41, 524n100, 524nn102,103, 544n76; opposition to research on, 358; sources of, 228, 235–36, 261–62; state and federal responsibility for, 116, 477n44; state vs. local standards, 438–39, 551n147; state vs. national standards, 567n92, 567n94. *See also* Clean Air Acts; Pollution; Standards

Air quality, 80, 343–44, 354, 392; changing perspectives on, 241; and governmental levels, 375, 441–42; and grass-roots environmental activism, 320–21; indoor, 266–67; standards for, 222, 250–51, 563n48; state planning for, 30, 495n32. *See also* Standards

Air Quality Act of 1967, 225

Alar incident, 126–27

Alaska National Interest Lands and Conservation Act of 1980, 146

Allen, James, 360

Alternatives analysis, in planning under NFMA, 149

Alverson, William, 177

Amenity. *See* Environmental quality

American Forest Institute, 327

American Game Policy, 1930, 344

American Lung Association, 255, 514n15

American Public Health Association, 255

American Wilderness Alliance, 158

Animals, 71. *See also* Wildlife

Army Corps of Engineers, U.S., 7–8, 123, 431–33

Arnold, Ron, 334

Asset management program, 357–58

Association of American Foresters for Environmental Ethics, 178

Atomic Energy Commission, 276-77, 431–32

Atomic energy policy. *See* Nuclear energy

Audubon Society, 61, 141

Automobiles, 11, 441; and air standards, 270; emissions control on, 281, 392; leaded gasoline for, 294–95, 296, 300–05 (*see also* Lead); and smog, 260–61

Autonomy, and decentralization, 315–33, 348

Babbitt, Bruce, 162–63

Backus, Edward W., 203

573